Pro React 16

Adam Freeman

Apress®

Pro React 16

Adam Freeman
London, UK

ISBN-13 (pbk): 978-1-4842-4450-0   ISBN-13 (electronic): 978-1-4842-4451-7
https://doi.org/10.1007/978-1-4842-4451-7

Managing Director, Apress Media LLC: Welmoed Spahr
Acquisitions Editor: Joan Murray
Development Editor: Laura Berendson
Coordinating Editor: Mark Powers

Cover designed by eStudioCalamar
Cover image designed by Freepik (www.freepik.com)

Distributed to the book trade worldwide by Springer Science+Business Media New York, 233 Spring Street, 6th Floor, New York, NY 10013. Phone 1-800-SPRINGER, fax (201) 348-4505, e-mail orders-ny@springer-sbm.com, or visit www.springeronline.com. Apress Media, LLC is a California LLC and the sole member (owner) is Springer Science + Business Media Finance Inc (SSBM Finance Inc). SSBM Finance Inc is a **Delaware** corporation.

For information on translations, please e-mail editorial@apress.com, for reprint, paperback, or audio rights, please email bookpermissions@springernature.com.

Apress titles may be purchased in bulk for academic, corporate, or promotional use. eBook versions and licenses are also available for most titles. For more information, reference our Print and eBook Bulk Sales web page at www.apress.com/bulk-sales.

Any source code or other supplementary material referenced by the author in this book is available to readers on GitHub via the book's product page, located at www.apress.com/9781484244500. For more detailed information, please visit www.apress.com/source-code.

Printed on acid-free paper

Dedicated to my lovely wife, Jacqui Griffyth.
(And also to Peanut.)

Contents

About the Author

Adam Freeman is an experienced IT professional who has held senior positions in a range of companies, most recently serving as chief technology officer and chief operating officer of a global bank. Now retired, he spends his time writing and long-distance running.

About the Technical Reviewer

Fabio Claudio Ferracchiati is a senior consultant and a senior analyst/developer using Microsoft technologies. He works for BluArancio (`www.bluarancio.com`). He is a Microsoft Certified Solution Developer for .NET, a Microsoft Certified Application Developer for .NET, a Microsoft Certified Professional, and a prolific author and technical reviewer. Over the past ten years, he's written articles for Italian and international magazines and coauthored more than ten books on a variety of computer topics.

PART I

Getting Started with React

CHAPTER 1

■ ■ ■

Your First React Application

The best way to get started with React is to dive in. In this chapter, I take you through a simple development process to create an application to keep track of to-do items. In Chapters 5–8, I show you how to create a more complex and realistic application, but, for now, a simple example will be enough to demonstrate how React applications are created and how the basic features work. Don't worry if you don't understand everything in this chapter—the idea is to get an overall sense of how React works. I explain everything in detail in later chapters.

■ **Note** If you want a conventional description of React features, you can jump to Part 2 of this book, where I start the process of describing individual features in depth. Before you go, make sure you install the development tools and packages described in this chapter.

Preparing the Development Environment

There is some preparation required for React development. In the sections that follow, I explain how to get set up and ready to create your first project.

Installing Node.js

The tools used for React development rely on Node.js—also known as Node—which was created in 2009 as a simple and efficient runtime for server-side applications written in JavaScript. Node.js is based on the JavaScript engine used in the Chrome browser and provides an API for executing JavaScript code outside of the browser environment.

Node.js has enjoyed success as an application server, but for this book it is interesting because it has provided the foundation for a new generation of cross-platform development and build tools.

It is important that you download the same version of Node.js that I use throughout this book. Although Node.js is relatively stable, there are still breaking API changes from time to time that may stop the examples I include in the chapters from working. The version I have used is 10.14.1, which is the current Long-Term Support release at the time of writing. There may be a later version available by the time you read this, but you should stick to the 10.14.1 release for the examples in this book. A complete set of 10.14.1 releases, with installers for Windows and macOS and binary packages for other platforms, is available at https://nodejs.org/dist/v10.14.1.

When you install Node.js, make sure you select the option to add the Node.js executables to the path. When the installation is complete, run the command shown in Listing 1-1.

© Adam Freeman 2019
A. Freeman, *Pro React 16*, https://doi.org/10.1007/978-1-4842-4451-7_1

Listing 1-1. Checking the Node Version

```
node -v
```

If the installation has gone as it should, then you will see the following version number displayed:

```
v10.14.1
```

The Node.js installer includes the Node Package Manager (NPM), which is used to manage the packages in a project. Run the command shown in Listing 1-2 to ensure that NPM is working.

Listing 1-2. Checking NPM Works

```
npm -v
```

If everything is working as it should, then you will see the following version number:

```
6.4.1
```

Installing the create-react-app Package

The create-react-app package is the standard way to create and manage complex React packages and provides developers with a complete toolchain. There are other ways to get started with React, but this is the approach that best suits most projects and is the one that I use throughout this book.

To install the package, open a new command prompt and run the command shown in Listing 1-3. If you are using Linux or macOS, you may need to use sudo.

Listing 1-3. Installing the create-react-app Package

```
npm install --global create-react-app@2.1.2
```

Installing Git

The Git revision control tool is required to manage some of the packages required for React development. If you are using Windows or macOS, then download and run the installer from https://git-scm.com/downloads. (On macOS, you may have to change your security settings to open the installer, which has not been signed by the developers.)

Git is already included in most Linux distributions. If you want to install the latest version, then consult the installation instructions for your distribution at https://git-scm.com/download/linux. As an example, for Ubuntu, which is the Linux distribution I use, I used the command shown in Listing 1-4.

Listing 1-4. Installing Git

```
sudo apt-get install git
```

Once you have completed the installation, open a new command prompt and run the command shown in Listing 1-5 to check that Git is installed and available.

Listing 1-5. Checking Git

```
git --version
```

This command prints out the version of the Git package that has been installed. At the time of writing, the latest version of Git for Windows and Linux is 2.20.1, and the latest version of Git for macOS is 2.19.2.

Installing an Editor

React development can be done with any programmer's editor, from which there is an endless number to choose. Some editors have enhanced support for working with React, including highlighting keywords and expressions. If you don't already have a preferred editor for web application development, then you can consider some of the popular options in Table 1-1. I don't rely on any specific editor for this book, and you should use whichever editor you are comfortable working with.

Table 1-1. *Popular Programming Editors*

Name	Description
Sublime Text	Sublime Text is a commercial cross-platform editor that has packages to support most programming languages, frameworks, and platforms. See `www.sublimetext.com` for details.
Atom	Atom is an open-source, cross-platform editor that has a particular emphasis on customization and extensibility. See `atom.io` for details.
Brackets	Brackets is a free open-source editor developed by Adobe. See `brackets.io` for details.
Visual Studio Code	Visual Studio Code is an open-source, cross-platform editor from Microsoft, with an emphasis on extensibility. See `code.visualstudio.com` for details.
Visual Studio	Visual Studio is Microsoft's flagship developer tool. There are free and commercial editions available, and it comes with a wide range of additional tools that integrate into the Microsoft ecosystem.

Installing a Browser

The final choice to make is the browser that you will use to check your work during development. All the current-generation browsers have good developer support and work well with React, but there is a useful extension for Chrome and Firefox called `react-devtools` that provides insights into the state of a React application and that is especially useful in complex projects. See `https://github.com/facebook/react-devtools` for details of installing the extension. I used Google Chrome throughout this book, and this is the browser I recommend you use to follow the examples.

Creating the Project

Projects are created and managed from the command line. Open a new command prompt, navigate to a convenient location, and run the command shown in Listing 1-6 to create the project for this chapter.

■ **Tip** You can download the example project for this chapter—and for all the other chapters in this book—from https://github.com/Apress/pro-react-16.

Listing 1-6. Creating the Project

```
npx create-react-app todo
```

The npx command was installed as part of the Node.js/NPM package in the previous section and is used to run Node.js packages. The create-react-app argument tells npx to run the create-react-app package that is used to create new React projects and was installed in Listing 1-3. The final argument is todo, which is the name of the project to create. When you run this command, the project will be created, and all of the packages required for developing and running a React project will be downloaded and installed. The setup process can take a while because there are a large number of packages to download.

■ **Note** When you create a new project, you may see warnings about security vulnerabilities. React development relies on a large number of packages, each of which has its own dependencies, and security issues will inevitably be discovered. For the examples in this book, it is important to use the package versions specified to ensure you get the expected results. For your own projects, you should review the warnings and update to versions that resolve the problems.

Understanding the Project Structure

Open the todo folder using your preferred editor, and you will see the project structure shown in Figure 1-1. The figure shows the layout in my preferred editor—Visual Studio—and you may see the project content presented slightly differently if you have chosen a different editor.

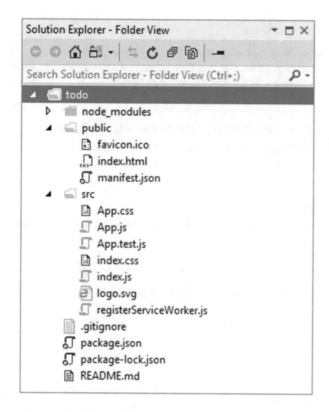

Figure 1-1. *The project structure*

This is the starting point for all projects, and while the purpose of each file may not be obvious at the moment, you will know what each file and folder is for by the end of the book. For the moment, Table 1-2 briefly describes the files that are important for this chapter, and I provide a detailed explanation of React projects in Chapter 9.

Table 1-2. *The Important Files in the Project for This Chapter*

Name	Description
public/index.html	This is the HTML file that is loaded by the browser. It contains an element in which the application is displayed and a script element that loads the application's JavaScript files.
src/index.js	This is the JavaScript file that is responsible for configuring and starting the React application. I use this file to add the Bootstrap CSS framework to the application in the next section.
src/App.js	This is the React component, which contains the HTML content that will be displayed to the user and the JavaScript code required by the HTML. Components are the main building blocks in a React application, and you will see them used throughout this book.

Adding the Bootstrap CSS Framework

I use the excellent Bootstrap CSS framework to style the HTML presented by the examples in this book. I describe the basic use of Bootstrap in Chapter 3, but to get started in this chapter, run the commands shown in Listing 1-7 to navigate to the todo folder and add the Bootstrap package to the project.

■ **Tip**   The command used to manage the packages in a project is npm, which is confusingly similar to npx, which is used only when creating a new project. It is important not to confuse the two commands.

Listing 1-7. Adding the Bootstrap CSS Framework

```
cd todo
npm install bootstrap@4.1.2
```

To include Bootstrap in the application, add the statement shown in Listing 1-8 to the index.js file.

Listing 1-8. Including Bootstrap in the index.js File in the src Folder

```
import React from 'react';
import ReactDOM from 'react-dom';
import './index.css';
import App from './App';
import * as serviceWorker from './serviceWorker';
import 'bootstrap/dist/css/bootstrap.css';

ReactDOM.render(<App />, document.getElementById('root'));

// If you want your app to work offline and load faster, you can change
// unregister() to register() below. Note this comes with some pitfalls.
// Learn more about service workers: http://bit.ly/CRA-PWA
serviceWorker.unregister();
```

As I explain in Chapter 4, the import statement is used to declare a dependency so that it becomes part of the application. The import keyword is most often used to declare dependencies on JavaScript code, but it can also be used for CSS stylesheets.

Starting the Development Tools

When you create a project using the create-react-app package, a complete set of development tools is installed so that the project can be compiled, packaged up, and delivered to the browser. Using the command prompt, run the commands shown in Listing 1-9 in the todo folder to start the development tools.

Listing 1-9. Starting the Development Tools

```
npm start
```

There is an initial preparation process when the development tools start, which can take a moment to complete. Don't be put off by the amount of time the preparation takes because this process is required only when you start a development session. When the startup process is complete, you will see a message like this one, which confirms that the application is running and tells you which HTTP port to connect to:

```
Compiled successfully!
You can now view todo in the browser.
  Local:            http://localhost:3000/
  On Your Network:  http://192.168.0.77:3000/
Note that the development build is not optimized.
To create a production build, use npm run build.
```

The default port used to listen for HTTP requests is 3000, although a different port will be selected if 3000 is in use. Once the initial preparation for the project is complete, a new browser window will open and display the URL http://localhost:3000 and the placeholder content shown in Figure 1-2.

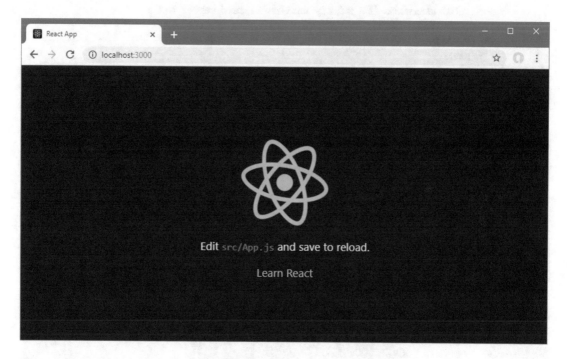

Figure 1-2. *Running the example application*

Replacing the Placeholder Content

The content that is displayed in Figure 1-2 is a placeholder that is used to ensure that the development tools are working. To replace the default content, I changed the App.js file, as shown in Listing 1-10.

Listing 1-10. Removing the Placeholder in the App.js File in the src Folder

```
import React, { Component } from 'react';
//import logo from './logo.svg';
//import './App.css';

export default class App extends Component {

    render() {
        return (
            <div>
                <h4 className="bg-primary text-white text-center p-2">
                    To Do List
                </h4>
            </div>
        )
    };
}
```

The App.js file contains a React *component*, which is named App. Components are the main building block for React applications, and they are written using JSX, which is a superset of JavaScript that allows HTML to be included in code files without requiring any special quoting. I describe JSX in more detail in Chapter 3, but in this listing, the App component defines a render method that React calls to get the content to display to the user.

■ **Tip**   React supports recent additions to the JavaScript language, such as the class keyword, which is used in Listing 1-10. I provide a primer for the most useful JavaScript features in Chapter 4.

When you save the App.js file, the React development tools automatically detect the changes, rebuild the application, and instruct the browser to reload, showing the content in Figure 1-3.

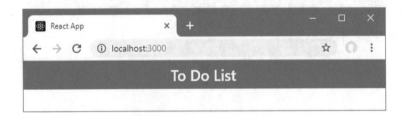

Figure 1-3. *Replacing the placeholder content*

The JSX files used in React development make it easy to mix HTML and JavaScript, but there are some important differences from regular HTML files. You can see a common example in the h4 element in Listing 1-10, shown here:

```
...
<h4 className="bg-primary text-white text-center p-2">
    To Do List
</h4>
...
```

In regular HTML, the class attribute is used to assign elements to classes, which is how elements are styled when using the Bootstrap CSS framework. Even though it might not appear so, JSX files are JavaScript files, and JavaScript configures classes through the className property. The differences between pure HTML and JSX can be jarring when you first begin React development, but they soon will become second nature.

■ **Tip** I provide a brief overview of working with the Bootstrap CSS framework in Chapter 3, where I explain the meaning of the classes to which the h4 element has been assigned in Listing 1-10, such as bg-primary, text-white, and p-2. You can ignore these classes for the moment, however, and just focus on the basic structure of the application.

React will write a warning message to the browser's JavaScript console if you forget you are working with JSX and use standard HTML instead. If you use the class attribute instead of className, for example, you will see the Invalid DOM property 'class'. Did you mean 'className'? warning. To see the browser's JavaScript console, press the F12 key and select the Console or JavaScript Console tab.

Displaying Dynamic Content

All web applications need to display dynamic content to the user, and React makes this easy by supporting the *expressions* feature. An expression is a fragment of JavaScript that is evaluated when a component's render method is called and provides the means to display data to the user. Many expressions are used to display data values defined by the component to keep track of the state of the application, known as *state data*. State data and expressions are easier to understand when you see an example, and Listing 1-11 adds both to the App component.

Listing 1-11. Adding State Data and Data Bindings in the App.js File in the src Folder

```
import React, { Component } from 'react';
export default class App extends Component {

    constructor(props) {
        super(props);
        this.state = {
            userName: "Adam"
        }
    }
```

```
    render() {
        return (
            <div>
                <h4 className="bg-primary text-white text-center p-2">
                    { this.state.userName }'s To Do List
                </h4>
            </div>
        )
    };
}
```

The constructor is a special method that is invoked when the component is initialized, and calling the super method within the constructor is required to ensure that the component is set up properly, as I explain in Chapter 11. The props parameter defined by the constructor is important in React development because it allows one component to configure another, which you will see shortly.

■ **Tip**   The term *props* is short for *properties*, and it reflects the way React creates the HTML content that is displayed in the browser, as I explain in Chapter 3.

React components have a special property named state, which is used to define state data, like this:

```
...
this.state = {
    userName: "Adam"
}
...
```

The this keyword refers to the current object and is used to access its properties and methods. The highlighted statement assigns an object with a userName property to this.state, which is all that is required to set up state data. Once state data has been defined, it can be included in the content generated by the component in an expression, like this:

```
...
<h4 className="bg-primary text-white text-center p-2">
    { this.state.userName }'s To Do List
</h4>
...
```

Expressions are denoted with curly braces (the { and } characters). When the render method is invoked, the expression is evaluated, and its result is included in the content presented to the user. The expression in Listing 1-11 reads the value of the userName state data property, producing the result shown in Figure 1-4.

Figure 1-4. *Using state data and expressions in the App.js file in the src Folder*

Understanding State Data Changes

The dynamic nature of a React application is based on changes to state data, which React responds to by invoking the component's render method again, which causes the expressions to be re-evaluated using the new state data values. In Listing 1-12, I have updated the App component so that the value of the userName state data property is changed.

Listing 1-12. Changing State Data in the App.js File in the src Folder

```
import React, { Component } from 'react';
export default class App extends Component {

    constructor(props) {
        super(props);
        this.state = {
            userName: "Adam"
        }
    }

    changeStateData = () => {
        this.setState({
            userName: this.state.userName === "Adam" ? "Bob" : "Adam"
        })
    }

    render() {
        return (
            <div>
                <h4 className="bg-primary text-white text-center p-2">
                    { this.state.userName }'s To Do List
                </h4>
                <button className="btn btn-primary m-2"
                        onClick={ this.changeStateData }>
                    Change
                </button>
            </div>
        )
    };
}
```

Save the changes to the App.js file, and you will see a button in the browser window. Clicking the button changes the username, as shown in Figure 1-5.

Figure 1-5. *Changing the username*

This example contains several important React features working together. The first is the onClick attribute on the button element.

```
...
<button className="btn btn-primary m-2" onClick={ this.changeStateData }>
    Change
</button>
...
```

The onClick attribute is assigned an expression that React evaluates when the button is clicked. Clicking a button triggers an *event*, and onClick is an example of an event-handler prop. The function or method that is specified by onClick will be invoked each time the button is clicked. The expression in Listing 1-12 specifies the changeStateData method, which is defined using the *fat arrow* syntax, which allows functions to be expressed concisely, as shown here:

```
...
changeStateData = () => {
    this.setState({ userName: this.state.userName === "Adam" ? "Bob" : "Adam" })
}
...
```

As I explain in Chapter 4, fat arrow functions are used to simplify responding to events, but they be used more widely and help keep the mix of HTML and JavaScript readable in a React application. The changeStateData method uses the setState method to set a new value for the userName property. When the setState method is called, React updates the component's state data with the new values and then invokes the render method so that the expressions will generate updated content. This is why clicking the button changes the name shown in the browser window from Adam to Bob. I didn't have to explicitly tell React that the value used by the expression changed—I just called the setState method to set the new value and left React to update the content in the browser.

■ **Tip** The this keyword is required whenever you use the properties and methods defined by a component, including the setState method. Forgetting to use this is a common error in React development, and it is the first thing to check if you don't get the behavior you expect.

Functions defined using the fat arrow syntax don't use the return keyword or require curly braces around the function body, which can result in simpler and clearer render methods, for example, as shown in Listing 1-13.

Listing 1-13. Redefining a Method Using a Fat Arrow Function in the App.js File in the src Folder

```
import React, { Component } from 'react';

export default class App extends Component {

    constructor(props) {
        super(props);
        this.state = {
            userName: "Adam"
        }
    }

    changeStateData = () => {
        this.setState({
            userName: this.state.userName === "Adam" ? "Bob" : "Adam"
        })
    }

    render = () =>
        <div>
            <h4 className="bg-primary text-white text-center p-2">
                { this.state.userName }'s To Do List
            </h4>
            <button className="btn btn-primary m-2"
                    onClick={ this.changeStateData }>
                Change
            </button>
        </div>
}
```

I use both styles to define functions and methods in this book. For the most part, you can choose between conventional JavaScript functions and fat arrow functions, although there are some important considerations explained in Chapter 12.

Adding the To-Do Application Features

Now that you have seen how React can display dynamic content, it is time to start adding the features required by the application, starting with additional state data and expressions, as shown in Listing 1-14.

Listing 1-14. Adding Application Features in the App.js File in the src Folder

```
import React, { Component } from 'react';

export default class App extends Component {

    constructor(props) {
        super(props);
```

```
        this.state = {
            userName: "Adam",
            todoItems: [{ action: "Buy Flowers", done: false },
                        { action: "Get Shoes", done: false },
                        { action: "Collect Tickets", done: true },
                        { action: "Call Joe", done: false }],
            newItemText: ""
        }
    }

    updateNewTextValue = (event) => {
        this.setState({ newItemText: event.target.value });
    }

    createNewTodo = () => {
        if (!this.state.todoItems
                .find(item => item.action === this.state.newItemText)) {
            this.setState({
                todoItems: [...this.state.todoItems,
                    { action: this.state.newItemText, done: false }],
                newItemText: ""
            });
        }
    }

    render = () =>
        <div>
            <h4 className="bg-primary text-white text-center p-2">
                {this.state.userName}'s To Do List
                ({ this.state.todoItems.filter(t => !t.done).length} items to do)
            </h4>
            <div className="container-fluid">
                <div className="my-1">
                    <input className="form-control"
                        value={ this.state.newItemText }
                        onChange={ this.updateNewTextValue } />
                    <button className="btn btn-primary mt-1"
                        onClick={ this.createNewTodo }>Add</button>
                </div>
            </div>
        </div>
}
```

Because React expressions are JavaScript, they can be used to inspect data values and generate results dynamically, like this expression:

```
...
<h4 className="bg-primary text-white text-center p-2">
    {this.state.userName}'s To Do List
    ({ this.state.todoItems.filter(t => !t.done).length} items to do)
</h4>
...
```

This expression filters the objects in the todoItems state data array so that only incomplete items are selected and then reads the value of the length property, which is the value that the binding will display to the user. The JSX format makes it easy to mix HTML elements and code like this, although complex expressions can be difficult to read and are often defined in a property or method to keep the HTML as simple as possible.

The changes in Listing 1-14 introduce an input element, which allows the user to enter the text for a new to-do item. The input element has two props, which are used to manage the content of the element and respond to changes, shown here:

```
...
<input className="form-control"
    value={ this.state.newItemText } onChange={ this.updateNewTextValue } />
...
```

The value prop is used to set the contents of the input element. In this case, the expression that the value prop contains will return the value of the newItemText state data property, which means that any change to the state data property will update the contents of the input element. The onChange prop tells React what to do when the change event is triggered, which will happen when the user types into the input element. This expression tells React to invoke the component's updateNewTextValue method, which uses the setState method to update the newItemText state data property. This may seem like a circular approach, but it ensures that React knows how to deal with changes performed by code and by the user.

The button element uses the onClick prop to tell React to invoke the createNewTodo method in response to the click event. The createNewTodo method checks that there an existing item with the same text and, if there is not, uses the setState method to add a new item to the todoItems array and resets the newItemText property, which has the effect of clearing the input element. The statement that adds the new item to the array does so with the JavaScript *spread* operator, which is a recent addition to the JavaScript language.

```
...
todoItems: [...this.state.todoItems,
    { action: this.state.newItemText, done: false }],
...
```

The spread operator is three periods, and it expands an array. The tools used for React development allow recent JavaScript features to be used and translates them into compatible code that can be understood by older web browsers. I describe the spread operator and other useful JavaScript features in Chapter 4.

To see the effect of the changes in Listing 1-14, enter a description of a task into the text field and click the Add button. React responds to the event by invoking the method specified by the button's onClick prop, which uses the value of the input element to create a new to-do item. You can't see the description of the task yet, but you will see that the number of incomplete tasks increases, as shown in Figure 1-6.

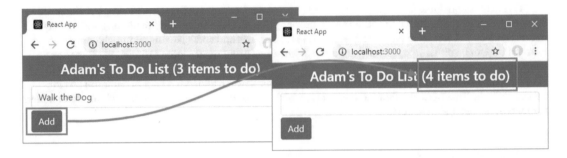

Figure 1-6. *Adding a new task*

Displaying the To-Do Items

The next step is to display each to-do item to the user so they can see details of the task and mark them complete when they are done, as shown in Listing 1-15.

Listing 1-15. Displaying To-Do Items in the App.js File in the src Folder

```
import React, { Component } from 'react';

export default class App extends Component {

    constructor(props) {
        super(props);
        this.state = {
            userName: "Adam",
            todoItems: [{ action: "Buy Flowers", done: false },
                        { action: "Get Shoes", done: false },
                        { action: "Collect Tickets", done: true },
                        { action: "Call Joe", done: false }],
            newItemText: ""
        }
    }

    updateNewTextValue = (event) => {
        this.setState({ newItemText: event.target.value });
    }

    createNewTodo = () => {
        if (!this.state.todoItems
                .find(item => item.action === this.state.newItemText)) {
            this.setState({
                todoItems: [...this.state.todoItems,
                    { action: this.state.newItemText, done: false }],
                newItemText: ""
            });
        }
    }
}
```

```
toggleTodo = (todo) => this.setState({ todoItems:
    this.state.todoItems.map(item => item.action === todo.action
        ? { ...item, done: !item.done } : item) });

todoTableRows = () => this.state.todoItems.map(item =>
    <tr key={ item.action }>
        <td>{ item.action}</td>
        <td>
            <input type="checkbox" checked={ item.done }
                onChange={ () => this.toggleTodo(item) } />
        </td>
    </tr> );

render = () =>
    <div>
        <h4 className="bg-primary text-white text-center p-2">
            {this.state.userName}'s To Do List
            ({ this.state.todoItems.filter(t => !t.done).length} items to do)
        </h4>
        <div className="container-fluid">
            <div className="my-1">
                <input className="form-control"
                    value={ this.state.newItemText }
                    onChange={ this.updateNewTextValue } />
                <button className="btn btn-primary mt-1"
                    onClick={ this.createNewTodo }>Add</button>
            </div>
            <table className="table table-striped table-bordered">
                <thead>
                    <tr><th>Description</th><th>Done</th></tr>
                </thead>
                <tbody>{ this.todoTableRows() }</tbody>
            </table>
        </div>
    </div>
}
```

So far, the emphasis in the App.js file has been embedding a JavaScript expression in fragments of HTML. But the JSX format allows HTML and JavaScript to be mixed freely, which means that JavaScript methods can return HTML content. You can see an example in Listing 1-15, where the todoTableRows method uses the JavaScript map method to produce a sequence of HTML elements for each object in the todoItems array, like this:

```
...
todoTableRows = () => this.state.todoItems.map(item =>
    <tr key={ item.action }>
        <td>{ item.action}</td>
        <td>
            <input type="checkbox" checked={ item.done }
                onChange={ () => this.toggleTodo(item) } />
        </td>
    </tr> );
...
```

Each item in the array is mapped to a `tr` element, which is the HTML element for a table row. Within the `tr` element is a set of `td` elements that define HTML table cells. The HTML content produced by the `map` method contains further JavaScript expressions that populate the `td` elements with state data values or functions that will be invoked to handle an event.

React does enforce some restrictions on the content it handles, such as the key prop added to each `tr` element by the `todoTableRows` method, shown here:

```
...
<tr key={ item.action }>
...
```

As you will learn in detail in Chapter 13, React invokes a component's `render` method when there is a change and compares the result with the HTML that is displayed in the browser so that only the differences are applied. React requires the key prop so that it can correlate the content is displayed with the data that produced it and manage changes efficiently.

The result of the changes in Listing 1-15 is that each to-do item is displayed with a checkbox that the user toggles to indicate that the task is complete. Each table row generated by the `todoTableRows` method contains an `input` element configured as a checkbox.

The result of the changes in Listing 1-15 is that the list of to-do items is displayed in a table and that checking an item as complete reduces the number displayed in the header, as shown in Figure 1-7.

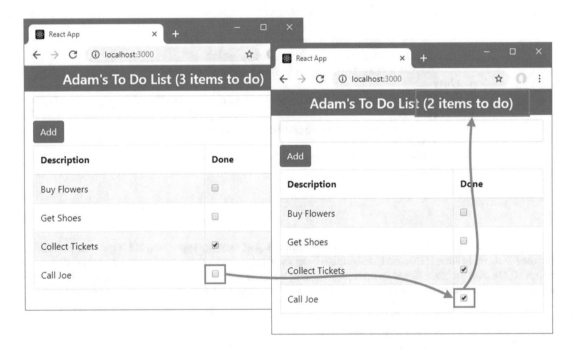

Figure 1-7. *Displaying the to-do items*

Introducing Additional Components

At the moment, all of the example application's functionality is contained in a single component, which can become difficult to manage as new features are added. To help keep components manageable, functionality is delegated up into separate components that are responsible for specific features. These are known as *child components*, while the component that delegated the functionality is known as the *parent*.

In this section, I am going to introduce several child components, each of which will be responsible for a single feature. I started by adding a file called TodoBanner.js to the src folder and using it to define the component shown in Listing 1-16.

Listing 1-16. The Contents of the TodoBanner.js File in the src Folder

```
import React, { Component } from 'react';

export class TodoBanner extends Component {

    render = () =>
        <h4 className="bg-primary text-white text-center p-2">
            { this.props.name }'s To Do List
            ({ this.props.tasks.filter(t => !t.done).length } items to do)
        </h4>
}
```

This component is responsible for displaying the banner. Parent components provide their children with data using *props*, and the data values are accessed through the props property, accessed via the this keyword. This component, which is called TodoBanner, expects to receive two props: a name prop, which contains the user's name, and a tasks prop, which contains the set of tasks and which is filtered to display the number that are incomplete. To display the value of the name prop, for example, the component uses an expression that contains this.props.name, like this:

```
...
{ this.props.name }'s To Do List
...
```

When React invokes the TodoBanner component's render method, the value of the name prop provided by the parent component will be included in the result. The other expression in the TodoBanner component's render method uses the JavaScript filter method to select the incomplete items and determine how many there are, showing that props can be used in expressions that do more than just display their value.

Next, I created a file called TodoRow.js in the src folder and used it to define the component shown in Listing 1-17.

Listing 1-17. The Contents of the TodoRow.js File in the src Folder

```
import React, { Component } from 'react';
export class TodoRow extends Component {

    render = () =>
        <tr>
            <td>{ this.props.item.action}</td>
            <td>
                <input type="checkbox" checked={ this.props.item.done }
```

```
                    onChange={ () => this.props.callback(this.props.item) }
                />
            </td>
        </tr>
    }
```

This component will be responsible for displaying a single row in the table, showing details of a to-do item. The data that is received by a child component through its props is read-only and must not be altered. To make changes, parent components can use *function props* to provide children with callback functions that are invoked when something important happens. This combination allows collaboration between components: data props allow a parent to provide data to a child, and function props allow a child to communicate with this parent.

The component in Listing 1-17 defines a data prop named item that is used to receive the to-do item to be displayed, and it defines a function prop named callback that provides a function that is invoked when the user toggles the checkbox. For the final child component, I added a file called TodoCreator.js to the src folder and added the code shown in Listing 1-18.

Listing 1-18. The Contents of the TodoCreator.js File in the src Folder

```
import React, { Component } from 'react';

export class TodoCreator extends Component {

    constructor(props) {
        super(props);
        this.state = { newItemText: "" }
    }

    updateNewTextValue = (event) => {
        this.setState({ newItemText: event.target.value});
    }

    createNewTodo = () => {
        this.props.callback(this.state.newItemText);
        this.setState({ newItemText: ""});
    }

    render = () =>
        <div className="my-1">
            <input className="form-control" value={ this.state.newItemText }
                onChange={ this.updateNewTextValue } />
            <button className="btn btn-primary mt-1"
                onClick={ this.createNewTodo }>Add</button>
        </div>
}
```

Child components can have their own state data, which is what this component uses to handle the content of its input element. The component invokes a function prop to notify its parent when the user clicks the Add button.

Using the Child Components

The components I defined in the previous section take responsibility for specific features of the to-do application. In Listing 1-19, I have updated the App component to use the three new components, each of which is configured using props to provide them with the data and callback functions they require.

Listing 1-19. Applying Child Components in the App.js File in the src Folder

```
import React, { Component } from 'react';
import { TodoBanner } from "./TodoBanner";
import { TodoCreator } from "./TodoCreator";
import { TodoRow } from "./TodoRow";

export default class App extends Component {

    constructor(props) {
        super(props);
        this.state = {
            userName: "Adam",
            todoItems: [{ action: "Buy Flowers", done: false },
                        { action: "Get Shoes", done: false },
                        { action: "Collect Tickets", done: true },
                        { action: "Call Joe", done: false }],
            //newItemText: ""
        }
    }

    updateNewTextValue = (event) => {
        this.setState({ newItemText: event.target.value });
    }

    createNewTodo = (task) => {
        if (!this.state.todoItems.find(item => item.action === task)) {
            this.setState({
                todoItems: [...this.state.todoItems, { action: task, done: false }]
            });
        }
    }

    toggleTodo = (todo) => this.setState({ todoItems:
        this.state.todoItems.map(item => item.action === todo.action
            ? { ...item, done: !item.done } : item) });

    todoTableRows = () => this.state.todoItems.map(item =>
        <TodoRow key={ item.action } item={ item } callback={ this.toggleTodo } />)

    render = () =>
        <div>
            <TodoBanner name={ this.state.userName } tasks={this.state.todoItems } />
            <div className="container-fluid">
                <TodoCreator callback={ this.createNewTodo } />
                <table className="table table-striped table-bordered">
```

```
                <thead>
                    <tr><th>Description</th><th>Done</th></tr>
                </thead>
                <tbody>{ this.todoTableRows() }</tbody>
            </table>
        </div>
    </div>
}
```

The new `import` statements declare dependencies on the child components, which ensures they are included in the application during the build process. Child components are used as custom HTML elements, with attributes and expressions defining the props that the component will receive, like this:

```
...
<TodoBanner name={ this.state.userName } tasks={this.state.todoItems } />
...
```

The expressions used to set the prop values provide a child component with access to specific data and methods defined by its parent. In this case, the `name` and `tasks` props are used to provide the `TodoBanner` component with the values of the `userName` and `todoItems` state data properties.

Adding the Finishing Touches

The basic features of the application are in place, and the set of components that provide those features are all working together. In this section, I add some finishing touches to complete the to-do application.

Managing the Visibility of Completed Tasks

At the moment, tasks always remain visible to the user even when they have been completed. To address this, I will present the user with separate lists of complete and incomplete tasks and allow the incomplete tasks to be hidden. I added a file called `VisibilityControl.js` to the `src` folder and used it to define the component shown in Listing 1-20.

Listing 1-20. The Contents of the VisibilityControl.js File in the src Folder

```
import React, { Component } from 'react';

export class VisibilityControl extends Component {

    render = () =>
        <div className="form-check">
            <input className="form-check-input" type="checkbox"
                checked={ this.props.isChecked }
                onChange={ (e) => this.props.callback(e.target.checked) } />
            <label className="form-check-label">
                Show { this.props.description }
            </label>
        </div>
}
```

Using props to receive data and callback functions from a parent makes it easy to add new features to an application. The component defined in Listing 1-20 is a general-purpose feature that has no knowledge of the content that it is being used to manage, and it works entirely through its props: the description prop provides the label text it displays, the isChecked prop provides the initial state for the checkbox, and the callback prop provides the function that is invoked when the user toggles the checkbox and triggers the change event.

In Listing 1-21, I have updated the App component to apply the VisibilityControl component as a child, along with the changes required to display the completed and incomplete tasks separately.

Listing 1-21. Managing Completed Tasks in the App.js File in the src Folder

```
import React, { Component } from 'react';
import { TodoBanner } from "./TodoBanner";
import { TodoCreator } from "./TodoCreator";
import { TodoRow } from "./TodoRow";
import { VisibilityControl } from "./VisibilityControl";

export default class App extends Component {

    constructor(props) {
        super(props);
        this.state = {
            userName: "Adam",
            todoItems: [{ action: "Buy Flowers", done: false },
                        { action: "Get Shoes", done: false },
                        { action: "Collect Tickets", done: true },
                        { action: "Call Joe", done: false }],
            showCompleted: true
        }
    }

    updateNewTextValue = (event) => {
        this.setState({ newItemText: event.target.value });
    }

    createNewTodo = (task) => {
        if (!this.state.todoItems.find(item => item.action === task)) {
            this.setState({
                todoItems: [...this.state.todoItems, { action: task, done: false }]
            });
        }
    }

    toggleTodo = (todo) => this.setState({ todoItems:
        this.state.todoItems.map(item => item.action === todo.action
            ? { ...item, done: !item.done } : item) });

    todoTableRows = (doneValue) => this.state.todoItems
        .filter(item => item.done === doneValue).map(item =>
            <TodoRow key={ item.action } item={ item }
                callback={ this.toggleTodo } />)
```

```
render = () =>
    <div>
        <TodoBanner name={ this.state.userName }
            tasks={this.state.todoItems } />
        <div className="container-fluid">
            <TodoCreator callback={ this.createNewTodo } />
            <table className="table table-striped table-bordered">
                <thead>
                    <tr><th>Description</th><th>Done</th></tr>
                </thead>
                <tbody>{ this.todoTableRows(false) }</tbody>
            </table>
            <div className="bg-secondary text-white text-center p-2">
                <VisibilityControl description="Completed Tasks"
                    isChecked={this.state.showCompleted}
                    callback={ (checked) =>
                        this.setState({ showCompleted: checked })} />
            </div>

            { this.state.showCompleted &&
                <table className="table table-striped table-bordered">
                    <thead>
                        <tr><th>Description</th><th>Done</th></tr>
                    </thead>
                    <tbody>{ this.todoTableRows(true) }</tbody>
                </table>
            }
        </div>
    </div>
}
```

The VisibilityControl component is configured so it changes the value of the App component's state data property named showCompleted when the user toggles the checkbox. To separate the complete and incomplete tasks, I added a parameter to the todoTableRows method and used the filter method to select objects from the state data array based on the value of the done property.

To display the completed tasks, I added a second table element. The table will be displayed only when the showCompleted property is true, so I placed the table and its content inside a data binding expression and used the && operator, like this:

```
...
{ this.state.showCompleted && <table className="table table-striped table-bordered">
...
```

When the expression is evaluated, the table element will be included in the component's content only if the showCompleted property is true. This is another example of how JSX mixes content and code. For the most part, JSX does a good job at blending elements and code statements, but it doesn't excel at everything, and the syntax required for conditional statements is awkward, as this example shows.

When you save the changes to the App.js file, you will see the separate sets of tasks. When you toggle the checkbox for a task, it will be moved to the other table, as shown in Figure 1-8. When you toggle the Show Completed Tasks checkbox, the second table will be hidden.

Figure 1-8. *Changing the task display*

Persistently Storing Data

The final change is to store the data so that the user's list is preserved when navigating away from the application. Later in the book, I demonstrate different ways of working with data stored on a server, but for this chapter I am going to keep the application simple and ask the browser to store the data using the Local Storage API, as shown in Listing 1-22.

■ **Tip** The Local Storage API is a standard browser feature and isn't specific to React development. See `https://developer.mozilla.org/en-US/docs/Web/API/Window/localStorage` for a good description of how local storage works.

Listing 1-22. Persistently Storing Data in the App.js File in the src Folder

```
import React, { Component } from 'react';
import { TodoBanner } from "./TodoBanner";
import { TodoCreator } from "./TodoCreator";
import { TodoRow } from "./TodoRow";
import { VisibilityControl } from "./VisibilityControl";

export default class App extends Component {

    constructor(props) {
        super(props);
        this.state = {
            userName: "Adam",
            todoItems: [{ action: "Buy Flowers", done: false },
                        { action: "Get Shoes", done: false },
                        { action: "Collect Tickets", done: true },
```

```
                      { action: "Call Joe", done: false }],
            showCompleted: true
        }
    }

    updateNewTextValue = (event) => {
        this.setState({ newItemText: event.target.value });
    }

    createNewTodo = (task) => {
        if (!this.state.todoItems.find(item => item.action === task)) {
            this.setState({
                todoItems: [...this.state.todoItems, { action: task, done: false }]
            }, () => localStorage.setItem("todos", JSON.stringify(this.state)));
        }
    }

    toggleTodo = (todo) => this.setState({ todoItems:
        this.state.todoItems.map(item => item.action === todo.action
            ? { ...item, done: !item.done } : item) });

    todoTableRows = (doneValue) => this.state.todoItems
        .filter(item => item.done === doneValue).map(item =>
            <TodoRow key={ item.action } item={ item }
                callback={ this.toggleTodo } />)

    componentDidMount = () => {
        let data = localStorage.getItem("todos");
        this.setState(data != null
            ? JSON.parse(data)
            : {
                userName: "Adam",
                todoItems: [{ action: "Buy Flowers", done: false },
                            { action: "Get Shoes", done: false },
                            { action: "Collect Tickets", done: true },
                            { action: "Call Joe", done: false }],
                showCompleted: true
            });
    }

    render = () =>
        <div>
            <TodoBanner name={ this.state.userName }
                tasks={this.state.todoItems } />
            <div className="container-fluid">
                <TodoCreator callback={ this.createNewTodo } />
                <table className="table table-striped table-bordered">
                    <thead>
                        <tr><th>Description</th><th>Done</th></tr>
                    </thead>
                    <tbody>{ this.todoTableRows(false) }</tbody>
                </table>
```

```
<div className="bg-secondary text-white text-center p-2">
    <VisibilityControl description="Completed Tasks"
        isChecked={this.state.showCompleted}
        callback={ (checked) =>
            this.setState({ showCompleted: checked })} />
</div>

{ this.state.showCompleted &&
    <table className="table table-striped table-bordered">
        <thead>
            <tr><th>Description</th><th>Done</th></tr>
        </thead>
        <tbody>{ this.todoTableRows(true) }</tbody>
    </table>
}
        </div>
    </div>
}
```

The Local Storage API is accessed through the localStorage object, and the component uses the setItem method to store the to-do items when a new to-do item is created. The local storage feature is only able to store string values, so I serialize the data objects as JSON before they can be stored. The setState method can accept a function that will be updated once the state data has been updated, as described in Chapter 11, and that ensures that the most recent data is stored.

Components have a well-defined lifecycle, which is described in Chapter 13, and can implement methods to receive notifications about important events. The component in the listing implements the componentDidMount method, which is invoked early in the component's life and provides a good opportunity to perform tasks such as loading data.

To retrieve the stored data, I have used the Local Storage API's getItem method. I use the setState method to update the component with the stored data or with some default data if there is no stored data available.

There is no visual change, but the application will persistently store any to-do items you create, which means they will still be available when you reload the browser window or navigate away to a different URL, such as the Apress home page, and then back to http://localhost:3000, as shown in Figure 1-9.

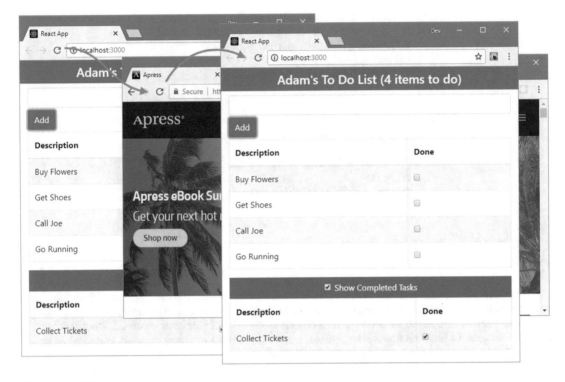

Figure 1-9. *Storing data*

Summary

In this chapter, I created a simple example application to introduce you to the React development process and to demonstrate some important React concepts. You saw that React development is focused on components, which are defined in JSX files that combine JavaScript code and HTML content. When you create a project, everything that is required to work with JSX files, build the application, and deliver it to the browser for testing is included so that you can get started quickly and easily.

You also learned that React applications can contain multiple components, each of which is responsible for a specific feature and which receive the data and callback functions they require using props.

Many more React features are available, as you can tell from the size of this book, but the basic application I created in this chapter has shown you the most essential characteristics of React development and will provide a foundation for later chapters. In the next chapter, I put React in context and describe the structure and content of this book.

CHAPTER 2

Understanding React

React is a flexible and powerful open-source framework for developing client-side applications; it takes cues from the world of server-side development and applies them to HTML elements, and it creates a foundation that makes building rich web applications easier. In this book, I explain how React works and demonstrate the different features it provides.

THIS BOOK AND THE REACT RELEASE SCHEDULE

The React team makes frequent releases, which means there is an ongoing stream of fixes and features. Minor releases tend not to break existing features and largely contain bug fixes. The major releases can contain substantial changes and may not offer backward compatibility.

It doesn't seem fair or reasonable to ask readers to buy a new edition of this book every few months, especially since the majority of React features are unlikely to change even in a major release. Instead, I am going to post updates following the major releases to the GitHub repository for this book, `https://github.com/Apress/pro-react-16`.

This is an ongoing experiment for me (and for Apress), and I don't yet know what form those updates may take—not least because I don't know what the major releases of React will contain—but the goal is to extend the life of this book by supplementing the examples it contains.

I am not making any promises about what the updates will be like, what form they will take, or how long I will produce them before folding them into a new edition of this book. Please keep an open mind and check the repository for this book when new React versions are released. If you have ideas about how the updates could be improved, then e-mail me at adam@adam-freeman.com and let me know.

Should I Use React?

React isn't the solution to every problem, and it is important to know when you should use React and when you should seek an alternative. React delivers the kind of functionality that used to be available only to server-side developers but is delivered entirely in the browser. The browser has to do a lot of work each time an HTML document to which React has been applied is loaded: data has to be loaded, components have to be created and composed, expressions have to be evaluated, and so on, creating the foundation for the features that I described in Chapter 1 and those that I explain throughout the rest of this book.

This kind of work takes time to perform, and the amount of time depends on the complexity of the React application and—critically—on the quality of the browser and the processing capability of the device.

A. Freeman, *Pro React 16*, https://doi.org/10.1007/978-1-4842-4451-7_2

You won't notice any performance issues when using the latest browsers on a capable desktop machine, but old browsers on underpowered smartphones can really slow down the initial setup of a React application.

The goal, therefore, is to perform this setup as infrequently as possible and deliver as much of the app as possible to the user when it is performed. This means giving careful thought to the kind of web application you build. In broad terms, there are two basic kinds of web application: *round-trip* and *single-page*.

Understanding Round-Trip Applications

For a long time, web apps were developed to follow a *round-trip* model. The browser requests an initial HTML document from the server. User interactions—such as clicking a link or submitting a form—leads the browser to request and receive a completely new HTML document. In this kind of application, the browser is essentially a rendering engine for HTML content, and all of the application logic and data resides on the server. The browser makes a series of stateless HTTP requests that the server handles by generating HTML documents dynamically.

A lot of current web development is still for round-trip applications, especially for line-of-business projects, not least because they put few demands on the browser and have the widest possible client support. But there are some serious drawbacks to round-trip applications: they make the user wait while the next HTML document is requested and loaded, they require a large server-side infrastructure to process all the requests and manage all the application state, and they can require more bandwidth because each HTML document has to be self-contained, which can lead to the same content being included in each response from the server. React is not well-suited to round-trip applications because the browser has to perform the initial setup process for each new HTML document that is received from the server.

Understanding Single-Page Applications

Single-page applications (SPAs) take a different approach. An initial HTML document is sent to the browser, but user interactions lead to HTTP requests for small fragments of HTML or data inserted into the existing set of elements being displayed to the user. The initial HTML document is never reloaded or replaced, and the user can continue to interact with the existing HTML while the HTTP requests are being performed asynchronously, even if that just means seeing a "data loading" message.

React is well-suited to single-page applications because the work that the browser has to perform to initialize the application has to be performed only once, after which the application runs in the browser, responding to user interaction and requesting the data or content that is required in the background.

COMPARING REACT TO VUE.JS AND ANGULAR

There are two main competitors to React: Angular and Vue.js. There are differences between them, but, for the most part, all of these frameworks are excellent, all of them work in similar ways, and all of them can be used to create rich and fluid client-side applications.

The real difference between these frameworks is the developer experience. Angular requires you to use TypeScript to be effective, for example, whereas it is just an option with React and Vue.js projects. React and Vue.js mix HTML and JavaScript together in a single file, which not everyone likes, although the way this is done differs for each framework.

My advice is simple: pick the framework that you like the look of the most and switch to one of the others if you don't get on with it. That may seem like an unscientific approach, but there isn't a bad choice to make, and you will find that many of the core concepts carry over between frameworks even if you change the one you use.

Understanding Application Complexity

The type of application isn't the only consideration when deciding whether React would be well-suited to a project. The complexity of a project is also important, and I often from readers who have embarked on a project using a client-side framework such as React, Angular, or Vue.js, when something much simpler would have been sufficient. A framework such as React requires a substantial time commitment to master (as the size of this book illustrates), and this effort isn't justified if you just need to validate a form or populate a `select` element programmatically.

In the excitement that surrounds client-side frameworks, it is easy to forget that browsers provide a rich set of APIs that can be used directly and that these are the same APIs that React relies on for all of its features. If you have a problem that is simple and self-contained, then you should consider using the browser APIs directly, starting with the Document Object Model (DOM) API. You will see that some of the examples in this book use the browser APIs directly, but a good place to start if you are new to browser development is `https://developer.mozilla.org`, which contains good documentation for all of the APIs that browsers support.

The drawback of the browser APIs, especially the DOM API, is that they can be awkward to work with and older browsers tend to implement features differently. A good alternative to working directly with the browser APIs, especially if you have to support older browsers, is jQuery (`https://jquery.org`). jQuery simplifies working with HTML elements and has excellent support for handling events, animations, and asynchronous HTTP requests.

React comes into its own in large applications, where there are complex workflows to implement, different types of users to deal with, and substantial volumes of data to be processed. In these situations, you can work directly with the browser APIs, but it becomes difficult to manage the code and hard to scale up the application. The features provided by React make it easier to build large and complex applications and to do so without getting bogged down in reams of unreadable code, which is often the fate of complex projects that don't adopt a framework.

What Do I Need to Know?

If you decide that React is the right choice for your project, then you should be familiar with the basics of web development, have an understanding of how HTML and CSS work, and have a working knowledge of JavaScript. If you are a little hazy on some of these details, I provide primers for the features I use in this book in Chapters 3 and 4. `https://developer.mozilla.org` is a good place to brush up on the fundamentals of HTML, CSS, and JavaScript.

How Do I Set Up My Development Environment?

The only development tools needed for React development are the ones you installed in Chapter 1 when you created your first application. Some later chapters require additional packages, but full instructions are provided. If you successfully built the application in Chapter 1, then you are set for React development and for the rest of the chapters in this book.

What Is the Structure of This Book?

This book is split into three parts, each of which covers a set of related topics.

Part 1: Getting Started with React

Part 1 of this book provides the information you need to get started with React development. It includes this chapter and primer/refresher chapters for the key technologies used in React development, including HTML, CSS, and JavaScript. Chapter 1 showed you how to create a simple React application, and Chapters 5–8 take you through the process of building a more realistic application, called SportsStore.

Part 2: Working with React

Part 2 of this book covers the core React features that are required in most projects. React provides a lot of built-in functionality, which I describe in depth, along with the way that custom code and content is added to a project to create bespoke features.

Part 3: Creating Complete React Applications

React relies on additional packages to provide the advanced features that are required by most complex applications. In Part 3 of this book, I introduce the most important of these packages, show you how they work, and explain how they add to the core React features.

Are There Lots of Examples?

There are *loads* of examples. The best way to learn React is by example, and I have packed as many of them into this book as I can, along with screenshots so you can see the effects of each feature. To maximize the number of examples in this book, I have adopted a simple convention to avoid listing the same code or content over and over. When I create a file, I will show its full contents, just as I have in Listing 2-1. I include the name of the file and its folder in the listing's header, and I show the changes that I have made in bold.

Listing 2-1. Using a Callback in the SimpleButton.js File in the src Folder

```
import React, { Component } from "react";

export class SimpleButton extends Component {

    constructor(props) {
        super(props);
        this.state = {
            counter: 0,
            hasButtonBeenClicked: false
        }
    }

    render = () =>
        <button onClick={ this.handleClick }
            className={ this.props.className }
            disabled={ this.props.disabled === "true"
                    || this.props.disabled === true }>
                { this.props.text} { this.state.counter }
                { this.state.hasButtonBeenClicked &&
                    <div>Button Clicked!</div>
                }
```

```
            </button>
    }

    handleClick = () => {
        this.setState({ counter: this.state.counter + 1 },
            () => this.setState({ hasButtonBeenClicked: this.state.counter > 0 }));
        this.props.callback();
    }
}
```

This is a listing from Chapter 11, which shows the contents of a file called SimpleButton.js that can be found in the src folder. Don't worry about the content of the listing or the purpose of the file; just be aware that this type of listing contains the complete contents of a file and that the changes you need to make to follow the example are shown in bold.

Some files in a React application can be long, but the feature that I am describing requires only a small change. Rather than list the complete file, I use an ellipsis (three periods in series) to indicate a partial listing, which shows just part of the file, as shown in Listing 2-2.

Listing 2-2. Making Multiple Updates in the SimpleButton.js File in the src Folder

```
...
handleClick = () => {
    for (let i = 0; i < 5; i++) {
        this.setState({ counter: this.state.counter + 1});
    }
    this.setState({ hasButtonBeenClicked: true });
    this.props.callback();
}
...
```

This is a later listing from Chapter 11, and it shows a set of changes that are applied to only one part of a much larger file. When you see a partial listing, you will know that the rest of the file does not have to change and that only the sections marked in bold are different.

In some cases, changes are required in different parts of a file, which makes it difficult to show as a partial listing. In this situation, I omit part of the file's contents, as shown in Listing 2-3.

Listing 2-3. Implementing a Lifecycle Method in the Message.js File in the src Folder

```
import React, { Component } from "react";
import { ActionButton } from "./ActionButton";

export class Message extends Component {

    // ...other methods omitted for brevity...

    componentDidMount() {
        console.log("componentDidMount Message Component");
    }

    componentDidUpdate() {
        console.log("componentDidUpdate Message Component");
    }
}
```

The changes are still marked in bold, and the parts of the file that are omitted from the listing are not affected by this example.

Where Can You Get the Example Code?

You can download the example projects for all the chapters in this book from `https://github.com/Apress/pro-react-16`. The download is available without charge and contains everything that you need to follow the examples without having to type in all of the code.

Where Can You Get Corrections for This Book?

You can find errata for this book at `https://github.com/Apress/pro-react-16`.

How Can You Contact Me?

If you have problems making the examples in this chapter work or if you find a problem in the book, then you can e-mail me at adam@adam-freeman.com, and I will try my best to help. Please check the errata for this book to see whether it contains a solution to your problem before contacting me.

Summary

In this chapter, I explained when React is a good choice for projects and outlined the alternatives and competitors. I also outlined the content and structure of this book, explained where to get updates, and explained how to contact me if you have problems with the examples in this book. In the next chapter, I provide a primer for the HTML and CSS features that I use in this book to explain React development.

CHAPTER 3

HTML, JSX, and CSS Primer

In this chapter, I provide a brief overview of HTML and explain how HTML content can be mixed with JavaScript code when using JSX, which is the superset of JavaScript supported by the React development tools that allows HTML to be mixed with code. I also introduce the Bootstrap CSS framework, which I use to style the content in the examples throughout this book.

■ **Note** Don't worry if not all the features described in this chapter make immediate sense. Some rely on recent additions to the JavaScript language that you may not have encountered before, which are described in Chapter 4 or explained in detail in other chapters.

Preparing for This Chapter

To create the project for this chapter, open a new command prompt, navigate to a convenient location, and run the command shown in Listing 3-1.

■ **Tip** You can download the example project for this chapter—and for all of the other chapters in this book—from https://github.com/Apress/pro-react-16.

Listing 3-1. Creating the Example Project

```
npx create-react-app primer
```

Once the project has been created, run the commands shown in Listing 3-2 to navigate to the project folder and install the Bootstrap CSS framework.

■ **Note**   When you create a new project, you may see warnings about security vulnerabilities. React development relies on a large number of packages, each of which has its own dependencies, and security issues will inevitably be discovered. For the examples in this book, it is important to use the package versions specified to ensure you get the expected results. For your own projects, you should review the warnings and update to versions that resolve the problems.

Listing 3-2.   Adding the Bootstrap Package to the Project

```
cd primer
npm install bootstrap@4.1.2
```

To include Bootstrap in the application, add the statement shown in Listing 3-3 to the index.js file.

Listing 3-3.   Including Bootstrap in the index.js File in the src Folder

```
import React from 'react';
import ReactDOM from 'react-dom';
import './index.css';
import App from './App';
import * as serviceWorker from './serviceWorker';
import 'bootstrap/dist/css/bootstrap.css';

ReactDOM.render(<App />, document.getElementById('root'));

// If you want your app to work offline and load faster, you can change
// unregister() to register() below. Note this comes with some pitfalls.
// Learn more about service workers: http://bit.ly/CRA-PWA
serviceWorker.unregister();
```

Preparing the HTML File and the Component

To prepare for the examples in the chapter, replace the contents of the index.html file in the public folder with the content shown in Listing 3-4.

Listing 3-4.   Replacing the Contents of the index.html File in the public Folder

```
<!DOCTYPE html>
<html lang="en">
  <head>
    <meta charset="utf-8" />
    <title>Primer</title>
  </head>
  <body>
    <h4 class="bg-primary text-white text-center p-2 m-1">
        Static HTML Element
    </h4>
```

```
    <div id="domParent"></div>
    <div id="root"></div>
  </body>
</html>
```

Replace the contents of the App.js file in the src folder with the code shown in Listing 3-5.

Listing 3-5. Replacing the Contents of the App.js File in the src folder

```
import React, { Component } from "react";

export default class App extends Component {
    render = () =>
        <h4 className="bg-primary text-white text-center p-2 m-1">
            Component Element
        </h4>
}
```

Running the Example Application

Ensure that all the changes are saved and use the command prompt to run the command shown in Listing 3-6 in the primer folder.

Listing 3-6. Starting the Development Tools

```
npm start
```

The React development tools will start, and once the initial preparations are complete, a new browser window will open and display the content shown in Figure 3-1.

Figure 3-1. *Running the example application*

Understanding HTML and DOM Elements

At the heart of all React web applications are HTML elements, which are used to describe the content that will be presented to the user. In a React application, the contents of the static index.html file in the public folder are combined with the HTML elements created dynamically by React to produce an HTML document that the browser displays to the user.

An HTML element tells the browser what kind of content each part of an HTML document represents. Here is an HTML element from the index.html file in the public folder:

```
...
<h4 class="bg-primary text-white text-center p-2 m-1">
        Static HTML Element
</h4>
...
```

As illustrated in Figure 3-2, this element has several parts: the start tag, the end tag, the attributes, and the content.

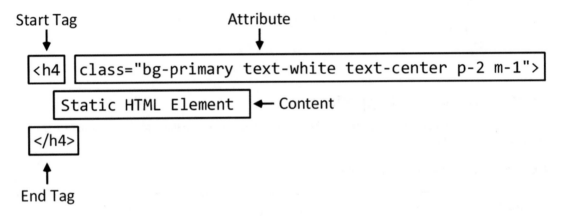

Figure 3-2. *The anatomy of an HTML element*

The *name* of this element (also referred to as the *tag name* or just the *tag*) is h4, and it tells the browser that the content between the tags should be treated as a header. There are a range of header elements, ranging from h1 to h6, where h1 is conventionally used for the most important content, h2 for slightly less important content, and so on.

When you define an HTML element, you start by placing the tag name in angle brackets (the < and > characters) and end an element by using the tag in a similar way, except that you also add a / character after the left-angle bracket (<), to create the *start tag* and *end tag*.

The tag indicates the purpose of the element, and there is a wide range of element types defined by the HTML specification. In Table 3-1, I have described the elements that I used most commonly in this book. For a complete list of tag types, you should consult the HTML specification.

Table 3-1. *Common HTML Elements Used in the Examples*

Element	Description
a	A link (more formally known as an anchor), which the user clicks to navigate to a new URL or a new location within the current document
button	A button, which can be clicked by the user to initiate an action
div	A generic element; often used to add structure to a document for presentation purposes
h1 to h6	A header
input	A field used to gather a single data item from the user
table	A table, used to organize content into rows and columns
tbody	The body of the table (as opposed to the header or footer)
td	A content cell in a table row
th	A header cell in a table row
thead	The header of a table
tr	A row in a table

Understanding Element Content

Whatever appears between the start and end tags is the element's content. An element can contain text (such as Static HTML Element in this case) or other HTML elements. In Listing 3-7, I have added a new HTML element that contains another element.

Listing 3-7. Adding a New Element in the index.html File in the public Folder

```
<!DOCTYPE html>
<html lang="en">
  <head>
    <meta charset="utf-8" />
    <title>Primer</title>
  </head>
  <body>
    <h4 class="bg-primary text-white text-center p-2 m-1">
        Static HTML Element
    </h4>
    <div class="text-center m-2">
      <div>This is a span element</div>
      <div>This is another span element</div>
    </div>
    <div id="domParent"></div>
    <div id="root"></div>
  </body>
</html>
```

The outer element is known as the *parent*, while the elements it contains are known as *children*. The additions in Listing 3-7 define a parent div element that has two children, also div elements. The content of each child div element is a text message, producing the result shown in Figure 3-3. Being able to create a hierarchy of elements is an essential HTML feature. It is one of the key building blocks for React applications, and it allows complex content to be created.

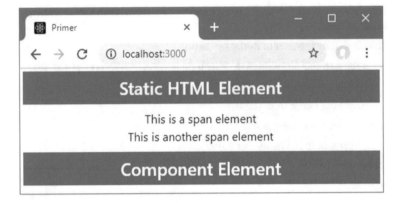

Figure 3-3. *Adding parent and child elements*

Understanding Element Content Restrictions

Some elements have restrictions on the types of elements that can be their children. The div elements in the example can contain any other element and are used to add structure to an HTML document, often so that content can be easily styled. Other elements have more specific roles that require specific types of elements to be used as children. For example, a tbody element, which you will see in later chapters and which represents the body of a table, can contain only one or more tr elements, each of which represents a table row.

■ **Tip** Don't worry about learning all of the HTML elements and their relationships. You will pick up everything you need to know as you follow the examples in later chapters, and most code editors will display a warning if you try to create invalid HTML.

Understanding Void Elements

Some elements are not allowed to contain anything at all. These are called *void* or *self-closing* elements, and they are written without a separate end tag, like this:

```
...
<input />
...
```

A void element is defined in a single tag, and you add a / character before the last angle bracket (the > character). The element shown here is the most common example of a void element, and it is used to gather data from the user in HTML forms. You will see many examples of void elements in later chapters.

Understanding Attributes

You can provide additional information to the browser by adding *attributes* to your elements. Here is the attribute that was applied to the h4 element illustrated in Figure 3-2:

```
...
<h4 class="bg-primary text-white text-center p-2 m-1">
        Static HTML Element
</h4>
...
```

Attributes are always defined as part of the start tag, and most attributes have a name and a value, separated by an equal sign, as illustrated in Figure 3-4.

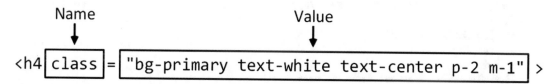

Figure 3-4. *The name and value of an attribute*

The name of this attribute is class, which is used to group related elements, typically so that their appearance can be managed consistently. This is why the class attribute has been used in this example, and the attribute value associates the h4 element with a number of classes that relate to styles provided by the Bootstrap CSS package, which I describe later in the chapter.

Creating HTML Elements Dynamically

The HTML elements defined in the index.html file are static. These elements are received and displayed by the browser just as they are defined, which you can see by right-clicking in the browser window and selecting Inspect or Inspect Element from the pop-up menu. The F12 developer tools will open and display the contents of the HTML document, which will include this element:

```
...
<h4 class="bg-primary text-white text-center p-2 m-1">
    Static HTML Element
</h4>
...
```

HTML elements can also be dynamically created using JavaScript and the Domain Object Model (DOM) API that all modern browsers support. In Listing 3-8, I have added some JavaScript to the index.html file that uses the DOM API to add a new element to the HTML document.

Listing 3-8. Creating an Element Dynamically in the index.html File in the public Folder

```
<!DOCTYPE html>
<html lang="en">
  <head>
    <meta charset="utf-8" />
    <title>Primer</title>
  </head>
  <body>
    <h4 class="bg-primary text-white text-center p-2 m-1">
        Static HTML Element
    </h4>
    <div class="text-center m-2">
      <div>This is a span element</div>
      <div>This is another span element</div>
    </div>
    <div id="domParent"></div>
    <div id="root"></div>
    <script>
      let element =  document.createElement("h4")
      element.className = "bg-primary text-white text-center p-2 m-1";
      element.textContent = "DOM API HTML Element";
      document.getElementById("domParent").appendChild(element);
    </script>
  </body>
</html>
```

The script element denotes a section of JavaScript code, which the browser will execute when it processes the contents of the index.html file and which creates a new HTML element, as shown in Figure 3-5.

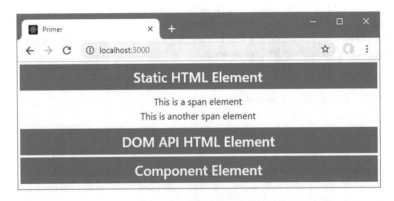

Figure 3-5. *Creating an element using the DOM API*

The first JavaScript statement in Listing 3-8 creates a new h4 element.

```
...
let element =  document.createElement("h4")
...
```

The document object represents the HTML document that the browser is displaying, and the createElement method returns an object that represents a new HTML element. The object that the DOM API provides to represent the new HTML element has properties that correspond to the attributes that are used when defining static HTML. The second JavaScript statement in Listing 3-8 uses the property that corresponds to the class attribute.

```
...
element.className = "bg-primary text-white text-center p-2 m-1";
...
```

Most of the properties defined by element objects have the same name as the attributes they correspond to. There are some exceptions, including className, which is used because the class keyword is reserved in many programming languages, including JavaScript.

The remaining JavaScript statements set the text content of the HTML element and add it to the HTML document so it is displayed by the browser. If you examine the new element by right-clicking in the browser window and selecting Inspect from the pop-up menu, you will see that the object created by the JavaScript statements in Listing 3-8 has been represented just like the static element from the index.html file.

```
...
<h4 class="bg-primary text-white text-center p-2 m-1">DOM API HTML Element</h4>
...
```

It is worth emphasizing that the index.html file does not contain this HTML element. Instead, it contains a series of JavaScript statements that instructed the browser to create the element and add it to the content presented to the user.

Creating Elements Dynamically Using a React Component

If you examine the contents of the App.js file, you will see that the render method of the App component combines aspects of the static and dynamic HTML elements from earlier sections:

```
...
import React, { Component } from "react";

export default class App extends Component {
    render = () =>
        <h4 className="bg-primary text-white text-center p-2 m-1">
            Component Element
        </h4>
}
...
```

React uses the DOM API to create the HTML elements specified by the render method, which it does by creating an object that is configured through its properties. The JSX format used for React development allows HTML elements to be defined declaratively, but the result is still JavaScript when the file is processed by the development tools, which is why the h4 element is configured using className and not class in the App render method. JSX lets elements appear to be configured using attributes, but they are just the means by which values are specified for properties, and this is why the term *prop* is used so much in React development.

■ **Note** No special steps are required to use JSX, which is supported by the tools added to the project by the `create-react-app` package. I explain how elements defined using JSX are transformed into JavaScript in Chapter 9.

Using Expressions in React Elements

The ability to use expressions to configure elements is one of the key features of React and JSX. Expressions are denoted by curly braces (the { and } characters), and the result is inserted into the content generated by a component. In Listing 3-9, I have used an expression to set the content of the h4 element rendered by the App component.

Listing 3-9. Using an Expression in the App.js File in the src Folder

```
import React, { Component } from "react";

const message = "This is a constant"

export default class App extends Component {

    render = () =>
        <h4 className="bg-primary text-white text-center p-2 m-1">
            { message }
        </h4>
}
```

I have defined a constant named message and used an expression to use the message value as the content for the h4 element. To simplify the example, I commented out the static HTML element and the DOM API code from the index.html file, as shown in Listing 3-10.

Listing 3-10. Removing Elements in the index.html File in the public Folder

```
<!DOCTYPE html>
<html lang="en">
  <head>
    <meta charset="utf-8" />
    <title>Primer</title>
  </head>
  <body>
    <!-- <h4 class="bg-primary text-white text-center p-2 m-1">
        Static HTML Element
    </h4>
    <div class="text-center m-2">
      <div>This is a span element</div>
      <div>This is another span element</div>
    </div>
    <div id="domParent"></div> -->
    <div id="root"></div>
```

```
<!-- <script>
  let element =  document.createElement("h4")
  element.className = "bg-primary text-white text-center p-2 m-1";
  element.textContent = "DOM API HTML Element";
  document.getElementById("domParent").appendChild(element);
</script> -->
  </body>
</html>
```

Save the changes, and you will see the value of the constant defined in Listing 3-9 displayed in the h4 element produced by the App component, as shown in Figure 3-6.

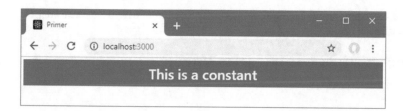

Figure 3-6. *Using an expression to set the content of an element*

Mixing Expressions and Static Content

Expressions can be combined with static values to create more complex results, as shown in Listing 3-11, which uses an expression to set part of the content for the h4 element.

Listing 3-11. Mixing an Expression with Static Content in the App.js File in the src Folder

```
import React, { Component } from "react";

const count = 4

export default class App extends Component {

    render = () =>
        <h4 className="bg-primary text-white text-center p-2 m-1">
            Number of things: { count }
        </h4>
}
```

The expression includes the count value in the content of the h4 element, which is combined with the static content, producing the result shown in Figure 3-7.

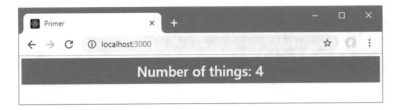

Figure 3-7. *Mixing an expression and static content*

Performing Computation in Expressions

Expressions can do more than inject values into the content rendered by a component and can be used for any computation, as shown in Listing 3-12.

Listing 3-12. Performing a Computation in the App.js File in the src Folder

```
import React, { Component } from "react";

const count = 4

export default class App extends Component {

    render = () =>
        <h4 className="bg-primary text-white text-center p-2 m-1">
            Number of things: { count % 2 === 0 ? "Even" : "Odd" }
        </h4>
}
```

This example uses the ternary operator to determine whether the count value is odd or even and produces the result shown in Figure 3-8.

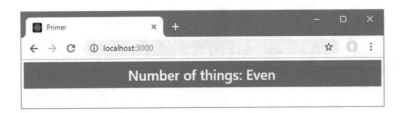

Figure 3-8. *Performing computation in an expression*

Expressions are well-suited to simple operations, but trying to include too much code in an expression results in a confusing component. For more complex operations, a function should be defined and invoked by the expression so that the function result is incorporated into the content produced by the component, as shown in Listing 3-13.

Listing 3-13. Defining a Function in the App.js File in the src Folder

```
import React, { Component } from "react";

const count = 4

function isEven() {
    return count % 2 === 0 ? "Even" : "Odd";
}

export default class App extends Component {

    render = () =>
        <h4 className="bg-primary text-white text-center p-2 m-1">
            Number of things: { isEven() }
        </h4>
}
```

When you use a function in an expression, you must invoke it with parentheses (the (and) characters), as shown in the listing, so that the result of the function is included in the content generated by the component.

Accessing Component Properties and Methods

The this keyword is required to specify properties and method defined by the component, as shown in Listing 3-14. As I explain in Part 2, there are different ways to create components, but the technique I use throughout this book is the one shown in the listing, which provides the widest range of features and is suitable for most projects.

Listing 3-14. Using the this Keyword in an Expression in the App.js File in the src Folder

```
import React, { Component } from "react";

export default class App extends Component {

    constructor(props) {
        super(props);
        this.state = {
            count: 4
        }
    }

    isEven() {
        return this.state.count % 2 === 0 ? "Even" : "Odd";
    }

    render = () =>
        <h4 className="bg-primary text-white text-center p-2 m-1">
            Number of things: { this.isEven() }
        </h4>
}
```

The component in this listing defines a constructor, which is how the initial state of the component is configured, as I explain in Chapter 4. The constructor assigns an object to the state property, with a count value of 4. The component also defines a method called isEven, which accesses the count value as this.state.count. The this keyword refers to the component instance, as explained in Chapter 4; state refers to the state property created in the constructor; and count selects the value to use in the computation. This this keyword is also used invoke the isEven method in the expression. The result is the same as the previous listing. Some methods require arguments, which can be specified as part of the expression, as shown in Listing 3-15.

Listing 3-15. Passing an Argument to a Method in the App.js File in the src Folder

```
import React, { Component } from "react";

export default class App extends Component {

    constructor(props) {
        super(props);
        this.state = {
            count: 4
        }
    }

    isEven(val) {
        return val % 2 === 0 ? "Even" : "Odd";
    }

    render = () =>
        <h4 className="bg-primary text-white text-center p-2 m-1">
            Number of things: { this.isEven(this.state.count) }
        </h4>
}
```

The expression in this example invokes the isEven method, using the count value as the argument. The result is the same as the previous listing.

Using Expressions to Set Prop Values

Expressions can also be used to set the value of props, which allows HTML elements and child components to be configured. In Listing 3-16, I have added a method to the App component whose result is used to set the className prop of the h4 element.

Listing 3-16. Setting a Prop Value in the App.js File in the src Folder

```
import React, { Component } from "react";

export default class App extends Component {

    constructor(props) {
        super(props);
        this.state = {
            count: 4
        }
    }
```

```
    isEven(val) {
        return val % 2 === 0 ? "Even" : "Odd";
    }

    getClassName(val) {
        return val % 2 === 0
            ? "bg-primary text-white text-center p-2 m-1"
            : "bg-secondary text-white text-center p-2 m-1"
    }

    render = () =>
        <h4 className={this.getClassName(this.state.count)}>
            Number of things: { this.isEven(this.state.count) }
        </h4>
}
```

The result is the same as the previous listing.

Using Expressions to Handle Events

Expressions are used to tell React how to respond to events when they are triggered by an element.
In Listing 3-17, I have added a button to the content returned by the App component and used the onClick
prop to tell React how to respond when the click event is triggered.

Listing 3-17. Handling an Event in the App.js File in the src Folder

```
import React, { Component } from "react";

export default class App extends Component {

    constructor(props) {
        super(props);
        this.state = {
            count: 4
        }
    }

    isEven(val) {
        return val % 2 === 0 ? "Even" : "Odd";
    }

    getClassName(val) {
        return val % 2 === 0
            ? "bg-primary text-white text-center p-2 m-1"
            : "bg-secondary text-white text-center p-2 m-1"
    }

    handleClick = () => this.setState({ count: this.state.count + 1});

    render = () =>
        <h4 className={this.getClassName(this.state.count)}>
            <button className="btn btn-info m-2" onClick={ this.handleClick }>
```

51

```
            Click Me
        </button>
        Number of things: { this.isEven(this.state.count) }
    </h4>
}
```

The button element is configured using the onClick prop, which tells React to invoke the handleClick method in response to the click event. Note that the method isn't specified using parentheses. Also, note that the handleClick method is defined using the fat arrow syntax; handling events is one of the few times where the way that a method is defined is important, as I explain in Chapter 12. Clicking the button updates the value of the count property, which changes the outcome of the other expressions in the render method, producing the effect shown in Figure 3-9.

Figure 3-9. *Handling an event*

Understanding Bootstrap

HTML elements tell the browser what kind of content they represent, but they don't provide any information about how that content should be displayed. The information about how to display elements is provided using *Cascading Style Sheets* (CSS). CSS consists of a comprehensive set of *properties* that can be used to configure every aspect of an element's appearance and a set of *selectors* that allow those properties to be applied.

One of the main problems with CSS is that some browsers interpret properties slightly differently, which can lead to variations in the way that HTML content is displayed on different devices. It can be difficult to track down and correct these problems, and CSS frameworks have emerged to help web app developers style their HTML content in a simple and consistent way.

The most popular CSS framework is Bootstrap, which was originally developed at Twitter but has become a widely used open source project. Bootstrap consists of a set of CSS classes that can be applied to elements to style them consistently and some optional JavaScript code that performs additional enhancement (but that I do not use in this book). I use Bootstrap in my own projects; it works well across browsers, and it is simple to use. I use the Bootstrap CSS styles in this book because they let me style my examples without having to define and then list my own custom CSS in each chapter. Bootstrap provides a lot more features than the ones I use in this book; see http://getbootstrap.com for full details.

I don't want to get into too much detail about Bootstrap because it isn't the topic of this book, but I do want to give you enough information so you can tell which parts of an example are React features and which are related to Bootstrap.

Applying Basic Bootstrap Classes

Bootstrap styles are applied via the className prop, which is the counterpart to the class attribute, and is used to group related elements. The className prop isn't just used to apply CSS styles, but it is the most common use, and it underpins the way that Bootstrap and similar frameworks operate. Here is an HTML element with a classNae prop, taken from Listing 3-9:

```
...
<h4 className="bg-primary text-white text-center p-2 m-1">
    { message }
</h4>
...
```

The className prop assigns the h4 element to five classes, whose names are separated by spaces: bg-primary, text-white, text-center, p-2, and m-1. These classes correspond to collections of styles defined by Bootstrap, as described in Table 3-2.

Table 3-2. *The h4 Element Classes*

Name	Description
bg-primary	This class applies a style context to provide a visual cue about the purpose of the element. See the "Using Contextual Classes" section.
text-white	This class applies a style that sets the text color for the element's content to white.
text-center	This class applies a style that horizontally centers the element's content.
p-2	This class applies a style that adds spacing around the element's content, as described in the "Using Margin and Padding" section.
m-1	This class applies a style that adds spacing around the element, as described in the "Using Margin and Padding" section.

Using Contextual Classes

One of the main advantages of using a CSS framework like Bootstrap is to simplify the process of creating a consistent theme throughout an application. Bootstrap defines a set of *style contexts* that are used to style related elements consistently. These contexts, which are described in Table 3-3, are used in the names of the classes that apply Bootstrap styles to elements.

Table 3-3. *The Bootstrap Style Contexts*

Name	Description
primary	Indicates the main action or area of content
secondary	Indicates the supporting areas of content
success	Indicates a successful outcome
info	Presents additional information
warning	Presents warnings
danger	Presents serious warnings
muted	De-emphasizes content
dark	Increases contrast by using a dark color
white	Increases contrast by using white

Bootstrap provides classes that allow the style contexts to be applied to different types of elements. The h4 element with which I started this section has been added to the bg-primary class, which sets the background color of an element to indicate that it is related to the main purpose of the application. Other classes are specific to a certain set of elements, such as btn-primary, which is used to configure button and a elements so they appear as buttons whose colors are consistent with other elements in the primary context. Some of these context classes must be applied in conjunction with other classes that configure the basic style of an element, such as the btn class, which is combined with the btn-primary class.

Using Margin and Padding

Bootstrap includes a set of utility classes that are used to add *padding*, which is space between an element's edge and its content, and *margin*, which is space between an element's edge and the surrounding elements. The benefit of using these classes is that they apply a consistent amount of spacing throughout the application.

The names of these classes follow a well-defined pattern. Here is the h4 element from Listing 3-9 again:

```
...
<h4 className="bg-primary text-white text-center p-2 m-1">
    { message }
...
```

The classes that apply margin and padding to elements follow a well-defined naming schema: first, the letter m (for margin) or p (for padding), followed by an optional letter selecting specific edges (t for top, b for bottom, l for left, or r for right), then a hyphen, and, finally, a number indicating how much space should be applied (0 for no spacing, or 1, 2, 3, 4 or 5 for increasing amounts). If there is no letter to specify edges, then the margin or padding will be applied to all edges. To help put this schema in context, the p-2 class to which the h4 element has been added applies padding level 2 to all of the element's edges.

Using Bootstrap to Create Grids

Bootstrap provides style classes that can be used to create different kinds of grid layout, ranging from one to twelve columns. I use the grid layout for many of the examples in this book, and I have created a simple grid layout in Listing 3-18.

Listing 3-18. Creating a Grid in the App.js File in the src Folder

```
import React, { Component } from "react";

export default class App extends Component {

    constructor(props) {
        super(props);
        this.state = {
            count: 4
        }
    }

    isEven(val) {
        return val % 2 === 0 ? "Even" : "Odd";
    }
```

```
getClassName(val) {
    return val % 2 === 0
        ? "bg-primary text-white text-center p-2 m-1"
        : "bg-secondary text-white text-center p-2 m-1"
}

handleClick = () => this.setState({ count: this.state.count + 1});

render = () =>
    <div className="container-fluid p-4">
        <div className="row bg-info text-white p-2">
            <div className="col font-weight-bold">Value</div>
            <div className="col-6 font-weight-bold">Even?</div>
        </div>
        <div className="row bg-light p-2 border">
            <div className="col">{ this.state.count }</div>
            <div className="col-6">{ this.isEven( this.state.count) }</div>
        </div>
        <div className="row">
            <div className="col">
                <button className="btn btn-info m-2"
                        onClick={ this.handleClick }>
                    Click Me
                </button>
            </div>
        </div>
    </div>
}
```

The Bootstrap grid layout system is simple to use. A top-level div element is assigned to the container class (or the container-fluid class if you want it to span the available space). You specify a column by applying the row class to a div element, which has the effect of setting up the grid layout for the content that the div element contains.

Each row defines 12 columns, and you specify how many columns each child element will occupy by assigning a class whose name is col- followed by the number of columns. For example, the class col-1 specifies that an element occupies one column, col-2 specifies two columns, and so on, right through to col-12, which specifies that an element fills the entire row. If you omit the number of columns and just assign an element to the col class, then Bootstrap will allocate an equal amount of the remaining columns. The grid in Listing 3-18 produces the layout shown in Figure 3-10.

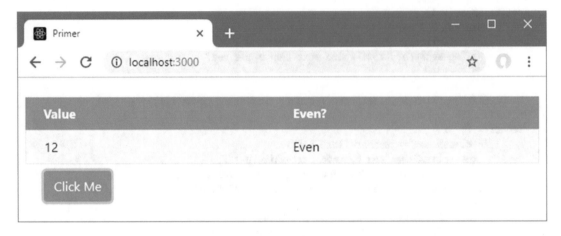

Figure 3-10. *Using a grid layout*

Using Bootstrap to Style Tables

Bootstrap includes support for styling table elements and their contents, which is a feature I use in some of the examples in later chapters. Table 3-4 lists the key Bootstrap classes for working with tables.

Table 3-4. *The Bootstrap CSS Classes for Tables*

Name	Description
table	Applies general styling to a table element and its rows
table-striped	Applies alternate-row striping to the rows in the table body
table-bordered	Applies borders to all rows and columns
table-sm	Reduces the spacing in the table to create a more compact layout

All these classes are applied directly to the table element, as shown in Listing 3-19, where I have replaced the grid layout with a table.

Listing 3-19. Using a Table Layout in the App.js File in the src Folder

```
import React, { Component } from "react";

export default class App extends Component {

    constructor(props) {
        super(props);
        this.state = {
            count: 4
        }
    }
```

```
    isEven(val) {
        return val % 2 === 0 ? "Even" : "Odd";
    }

    getClassName(val) {
        return val % 2 === 0
            ? "bg-primary text-white text-center p-2 m-1"
            : "bg-secondary text-white text-center p-2 m-1"
    }

    handleClick = () => this.setState({ count: this.state.count + 1});

    render = () =>
        <table className="table table-striped table-bordered table-sm">
            <thead   className="bg-info text-white">
                <tr><th>Value</th><th>Even?</th></tr>
            </thead>
            <tbody>
                <tr>
                    <td>{ this.state.count }</td>
                    <td>{ this.isEven(this.state.count) } </td>
                </tr>
            </tbody>
            <tfoot className="text-center">
                <tr>
                    <td colSpan="2">
                        <button className="btn btn-info m-2"
                                onClick={ this.handleClick }>
                            Click Me
                        </button>
                    </td>
                </tr>
            </tfoot>
        </table>
}
```

■ **Tip**   Notice that I have used the thead element when defining the tables in Listing 3-19. Browsers will automatically add any tr elements that are direct descendants of table elements to a tbody element if one has not been used. You will get odd results if you rely on this behavior when working with Bootstrap, and it is always a good idea to use the full set of elements when defining a table.

Figure 3-11 shows the result of using a table instead of a grid.

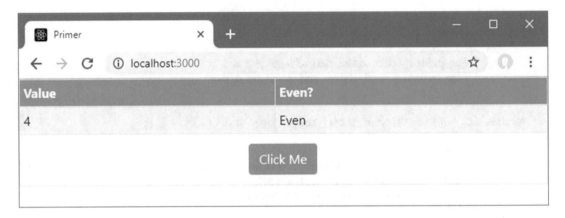

Figure 3-11. *Styling a table*

Using Bootstrap to Style Forms

Bootstrap includes styling for form elements, allowing them to be styled consistently with other elements in the application. In Listing 3-20, I have added form elements to the content produced by the App component.

Listing 3-20. Adding Form Elements in the App.js File in the src Folder

```
import React, { Component } from "react";

export default class App extends Component {

    render = () =>
        <div className="m-2">
            <div className="form-group">
                <label>Name:</label>
                <input className="form-control" />
            </div>
            <div className="form-group">
                <label>City:</label>
                <input className="form-control" />
            </div>
        </div>
}
```

The basic styling for forms is achieved by applying the form-group class to a div element that contains a label and an input element, where the input element is assigned to the form-control class. Bootstrap styles the elements so that the label is shown above the input element and the input element occupies 100 percent of the available horizontal space, as shown in Figure 3-12.

Figure 3-12. Styling form elements

Summary

In this chapter, I provided a brief overview of HTML and explained how it can be mixed with JavaScript code in React development, albeit with some changes and restrictions. I also introduced the Bootstrap CSS framework, which I use throughout this book but which is not directly related to React. You need to have a good grasp of HTML and CSS to be truly effective in web application development, but the best way to learn is by firsthand experience, and the descriptions and examples in this chapter will be enough to get you started and provide just enough background information for the examples ahead. In the next chapter, I continue the primer theme and introduce the most important JavaScript features used in this book.

CHAPTER 4

■ ■ ■

JavaScript Primer

In this chapter, I provide a quick tour of the most important features of the JavaScript language as they apply to React development. I don't have the space to describe JavaScript completely, so I have focused on the essentials that you'll need to get up to speed and follow the examples in this book.

JavaScript has been modernized in recent years with the addition of convenient language features and a substantial expansion of the utility functions available for common tasks such as array handling. Not all browsers support the latest features, and so the React development tools include the Babel package, which is responsible for transforming JavaScript written using the latest features into code that can be relied on to work in most mainstream browsers. This is means you are able to enjoy a modern development experience without needing to pay attention to dealing with the differences between browsers and keeping track of the features each supports. Table 4-1 summarizes the chapter.

Table 4-1. *Chapter Summary*

Problem	Solution	Listing
Provide instructions that will be executed by the browser	Use JavaScript statement	4
Delay execution of statements until they are required	Use JavaScript functions	5–7, 10–12
Define functions with variable numbers of parameters	Use default and rest parameters	8, 9
Express functions concisely	Use fat arrow functions	13
Define variables and constants	Use the let and const keywords	14, 15
Use the JavaScript primitive types	Use the string, number, or boolean keywords	16, 17, 19
Define strings that include other values	Use template strings	18
Execute statements conditionally	Use the if and else and switch keywords	20
Compare values and identities	Use the equality and identity operators	21, 22
Convert types	Use the type conversion keywords	23–25
Group related items	Define an array	26, 27
Read or change a value in an array	Use the index accessor notation	28, 29
Enumerate the contents of an array	Use a for loop or the forEach method	30

(*continued*)

© Adam Freeman 2019
A. Freeman, *Pro React 16*, https://doi.org/10.1007/978-1-4842-4451-7_4

Table 4-1. (*continued*)

Problem	Solution	Listing
Expand the contents of an array	Use the spread operator	31, 32
Process the contents of an array	Use the built-in array method	33
Gather related values into a single unit	Define an object using a literal or a class	34–36, 40
Define an operation that can be performed on the values of an object	Define a method	37, 39, 43, 44
Copy properties and value from one object to another	Use the Object.assign method or use the spread operator	41, 42
Group related features	Define a JavaScript module	45–54
Observe an asynchronous operation	Define a Promise and use the async and await keywords	55–58

Preparing for This Chapter

In this chapter, I continue working with the primer project created in Chapter 3. To prepare for this chapter, I added a file called example.js to the src folder and added the code shown in Listing 4-1.

■ **Tip** You can download the example project for this chapter—and for all the other chapters in this book—from https://github.com/Apress/pro-react-16.

Listing 4-1. The Contents of the example.js File in the src Folder

```
console.log("Hello");
```

To incorporate the example.js file into the application, I added the statement shown in Listing 4-2 to the index.js file in the src folder.

Listing 4-2. Importing a File in the index.js File in the src Folder

```
import React from 'react';
import ReactDOM from 'react-dom';
import './index.css';
import App from './App';
import * as serviceWorker from './serviceWorker';
import 'bootstrap/dist/css/bootstrap.css';

import "./example";

ReactDOM.render(<App />, document.getElementById('root'));

// If you want your app to work offline and load faster, you can change
// unregister() to register() below. Note this comes with some pitfalls.
// Learn more about service workers: http://bit.ly/CRA-PWA
serviceWorker.unregister();
```

Open a command prompt, navigate to the `primer` folder, and run the command shown in Listing 4-3 to start the React development tools.

Listing 4-3. Starting the Development Tools

```
npm start
```

The initial preparation of the project will take a moment, after which a new browser window or tab will open and navigate to `http://localhost:3000`, displaying the content shown in Figure 4-1.

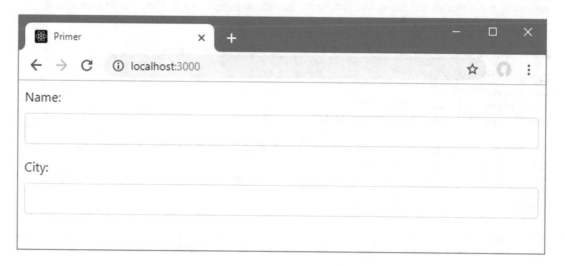

Figure 4-1. *Running the example application*

Open the browser's F12 development tools, which can usually be done by pressing F12 on the keyboard or right-clicking in the browser window and selecting Inspect from the pop-up menu. Inspect the Console tab, and you will see that the statement in the `example.js` file from Listing 4-1 has produced a simple result, as shown in Figure 4-2.

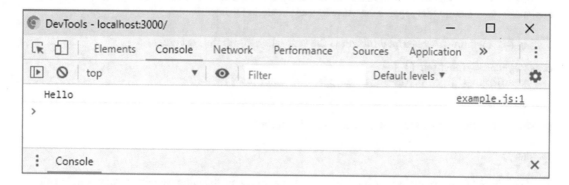

Figure 4-2. *A result in the browser's console*

All of the examples in this chapter produce text output and so rather than show screenshots of the Console tab, I will use just the text, like this:

```
Hello
```

Using Statements

The basic JavaScript building block is the *statement*. Each statement represents a single command, and statements are usually terminated by a semicolon (;). The semicolon is optional, but using them makes your code easier to read and allows for multiple statements on a single line. In Listing 4-4, I have added statements to the JavaScript file.

Listing 4-4. Adding JavaScript Statements in the example.js File in the src Folder

```
console.log("Hello");
console.log("Apples");
console.log("This is a statement");
console.log("This is also a statement");
```

The browser executes each statement in turn. In this example, all the statements simply write messages to the console. The results are as follows:

```
Hello
Apples
This is a statement
This is also a statement
```

Defining and Using Functions

When the browser receives JavaScript code, it executes the statements it contains in the order in which they are defined. This is what happened in the previous example. The statements in the example.js file were executed one by one, all of which wrote a message to the console, all in the order in which they were defined in example.js. You can also package statements into a *function*, which won't be executed until the browser encounters a statement that *invokes* that function, as shown in Listing 4-5.

Listing 4-5. Defining a JavaScript Function in the example.js File in the src Folder

```
const myFunc = function () {
    console.log("This statement is inside the function");
};

console.log("This statement is outside the function");

myFunc();
```

Defining a function simple: use the const keyword followed by the name you want to give the function, followed by the equal sign (=) and the function keyword, followed by parentheses (the (and) characters). The statements you want the function to contain are enclosed between braces (the { and } characters).

In the listing, I used the name myFunc, and the function contains a single statement that writes a message to the JavaScript console. The statement in the function won't be executed until the browser reaches another statement that calls the myFunc function, like this:

```
...
myFunc();
...
```

When you save the changes to the example.js file, the updated JavaScript code will be sent to the browser, where it is executed and produces the following output:

```
This statement is outside the function
This statement is inside the function
```

You can see that the statement inside the function isn't executed immediately, but other than demonstrating how functions are defined, this example isn't especially useful because the function is invoked immediately after it has been defined. Functions are much more useful when they are invoked in response to some kind of change or event, such as user interaction.

You can also define functions so you don't have to explicitly create and assign a variable, as shown in Listing 4-6.

Listing 4-6. Defining a Function in the example.js File in the src Folder

```
function myFunc() {
    console.log("This statement is inside the function");
}

console.log("This statement is outside the function");

myFunc();
```

The code works in the same way as Listing 4-5 but is more familiar for most developers. This example produces the same result as Listing 4-5.

Defining Functions with Parameters

JavaScript allows you to define parameters for functions, as shown in Listing 4-7.

Listing 4-7. Defining Functions with Parameters in the example.js File in the src Folder

```
function myFunc(name, weather) {
    console.log("Hello " + name + ".");
    console.log("It is " + weather + " today.");
}

myFunc("Adam", "sunny");
```

I added two parameters to the myFunc function, called name and weather. JavaScript is a dynamically typed language, which means you don't have to declare the data type of the parameters when you define the function. I'll come back to dynamic typing later in the chapter when I cover JavaScript variables. To invoke a function with parameters, you provide values as arguments when you invoke the function, like this:

```
...
myFunc("Adam", "sunny");
...
```

The results from this listing are as follows:

```
Hello Adam.
It is sunny today.
```

Using Default and Rest Parameters

The number of arguments you provide when you invoke a function doesn't need to match the number of parameters in the function. If you call the function with fewer arguments than it has parameters, then the value of any parameters you have not supplied values for is undefined, which is a special JavaScript value. If you call the function with more arguments than there are parameters, then the additional arguments are ignored.

The consequence of this is that you can't create two functions with the same name and different parameters and expect JavaScript to differentiate between them based on the arguments you provide when invoking the function. This is called *polymorphism*, and although it is supported in languages such as Java and C#, it isn't available in JavaScript. Instead, if you define two functions with the same name, then the second definition replaces the first.

There are two ways that you can modify a function to respond to a mismatch between the number of parameters it defines and the number of arguments used to invoke it. *Default parameters* deal with the situation where there are fewer arguments than parameters and allow you to provide a default value for the parameters for which there are no arguments, as shown in Listing 4-8.

Listing 4-8. Using a Default Parameter in the example.js File in the src Folder

```
function myFunc(name, weather = "raining") {
    console.log("Hello " + name + ".");
    console.log("It is " + weather + " today.");
}

myFunc("Adam");
```

The weather parameter in the function has been assigned a default value of raining, which will be used if the function is invoked with only one argument, producing the following results:

```
Hello Adam.
It is raining today.
```

Rest parameters are used to capture any additional arguments when a function is invoked with additional arguments, as shown in Listing 4-9.

Listing 4-9. Using a Rest Parameter in the example.js File in the src Folder

```javascript
function myFunc(name, weather, ...extraArgs) {
    console.log("Hello " + name + ".");
    console.log("It is " + weather + " today.");
    for (let i = 0; i < extraArgs.length; i++) {
        console.log("Extra Arg: " + extraArgs[i]);
    }
}

myFunc("Adam", "sunny", "one", "two", "three");
```

The rest parameter must be the last parameter defined by the function, and its name is prefixed with an ellipsis (three periods, . . .). The rest parameter is an array to which any extra arguments will be assigned. In the listing, the function prints out each extra argument to the console, producing the following results:

```
Hello Adam.
It is sunny today.
Extra Arg: one
Extra Arg: two
Extra Arg: three
```

Defining Functions That Return Results

You can return results from functions using the return keyword. Listing 4-10 shows a function that returns a result.

Listing 4-10. Returning a Result from a Function in the example.js File in the src Folder

```javascript
function myFunc(name) {
    return ("Hello " + name + ".");
}

console.log(myFunc("Adam"));
```

This function defines one parameter and uses it to produce a result. I invoke the function and pass the result as the argument to the console.log function, like this:

```
...
console.log(myFunc("Adam"));
...
```

Notice that you don't have to declare that the function will return a result or denote the data type of the result. The result from this listing is as follows:

```
Hello Adam.
```

Using Functions as Arguments to Other Functions

JavaScript functions can be treated as objects, which means you can use one function as the argument to another, as demonstrated in Listing 4-11.

Listing 4-11. Using a Function as an Arguments in the example.js File in the src Folder

```javascript
function myFunc(nameFunction) {
    return ("Hello " + nameFunction() + ".");
}

console.log(myFunc(function () {
    return "Adam";
}));
```

The myFunc function defines a parameter called nameFunction that it invokes to get the value to insert into the string it returns. I pass a function that returns Adam as the argument to myFunc, which produces the following output:

```
Hello Adam.
```

Functions can be chained together, building up more complex functionality from small and easily tested pieces of code, as shown in Listing 4-12.

Listing 4-12. Chaining Functions Calls in the example.js File in the src Folder

```javascript
function myFunc(nameFunction) {
    return ("Hello " + nameFunction() + ".");
}

function printName(nameFunction, printFunction) {
    printFunction(myFunc(nameFunction));
}

printName(function () { return "Adam" }, console.log);
```

This example produces the following output:

```
Hello Adam.
```

Using Arrow Functions

Arrow functions—also known as *fat arrow functions* or *lambda expressions*—are an alternative way of defining functions and are often used to define functions that are used only as arguments to other functions. Listing 4-13 replaces the functions from the previous example with arrow functions.

Listing 4-13. Using Arrow Functions in the example.js File in the src Folder

```
const myFunc = (nameFunction) => ("Hello " + nameFunction() + ".");

const printName = (nameFunction, printFunction) =>
    printFunction(myFunc(nameFunction));

printName(function () { return "Adam" }, console.log);
```

These functions perform the same work as the ones in Listing 4-12. There are three parts to an arrow function: the input parameters, then an equal sign and a greater-than sign (the "arrow"), and finally the function result. The return keyword and curly braces are required only if the arrow function needs to execute more than one statement. There are more examples of arrow functions later in this chapter, and you will see them used throughout the book.

■ **Note** In React development, you can decide which style of function you prefer to use, and you will see that I use both in the examples in this book. Care must be taken when defining functions that respond to events, however, as explained in Chapter 12.

Using Variables and Types

The let keyword is used to declare variables and, optionally, assign a value to the variable in a single statement—as opposed to the const keyword I used in earlier examples, which creates a constant value that cannot be modified.

When you use let or const, the variable or constant that you create can be accessed only in the region of code in which they are defined, which is known as the variable or constant's scope and which is demonstrated in Listing 4-14.

Listing 4-14. Using let to Declare Variables in the example.js File in the src Folder

```
function messageFunction(name, weather) {
    let message = "Hello, Adam";
    if (weather === "sunny") {
        let message = "It is a nice day";
        console.log(message);
    } else {
        let message = "It is " + weather + " today";
        console.log(message);
    }
    console.log(message);
}

messageFunction("Adam", "raining");
```

In this example, there are three statements that use the let keyword to define a variable called message. The scope of each variable is limited to the region of code that it is defined in, producing the following results:

```
It is raining today
Hello, Adam
```

This may seem like an odd example, but there is another keyword that can be used to declare variables: var. The let and const keywords are relatively new additions to the JavaScript specification that is intended to address some oddities in the way var behaves. Listing 4-15 takes the example from Listing 4-14 and replaces let with var.

USING LET AND CONST

It is good practice to use the const keyword for any value that you don't expect to change so that you receive an error if any modifications are attempted. This is a practice that I rarely follow, however—in part because I am still struggling to adapt to not using the var keyword and in part because I write code in a range of languages and there are some features that I avoid because they trip me up when I switch from one to another. If you are new to JavaScript, then I recommend trying to use const and let correctly and avoiding following my poor behavior.

Listing 4-15. Using var to Declare Variables in the example.js File in the src Folder

```
function messageFunction(name, weather) {
    var message = "Hello, Adam";
    if (weather === "sunny") {
        var message = "It is a nice day";
        console.log(message);
    } else {
        var message = "It is " + weather + " today";
        console.log(message);
    }
    console.log(message);
}

messageFunction("Adam", "raining");
```

When you save the changes in the listing, you will see the following results:

```
It is raining today
It is raining today
```

Some browsers will show repeated statements as a single line with a number next to them indicating how many times that output has occurred. This means you may see one statement with the number 2 next to it, indicating that it occurred twice.

The problem is that the var keyword creates variables whose scope is the containing function, which means that all the references to message are referring to the same variable. This can cause unexpected results for even experienced JavaScript developers and is the reason that the more conventional let keyword was introduced. The React development tools include warnings for common problems, which is why you will also see the following messages in the JavaScript console:

```
Line 4:  'message' is already defined  no-redeclare
Line 7:  'message' is already defined  no-redeclare
```

These messages can be cryptic until you get used to them, and the easiest way to learn more about them is to consult the documentation for the ESLint package, which applies a set of rules to JavaScript code and is used by the React development tools to create the warnings. The name of the rule is included in the warning, and the name of the rule that produced the warnings for Listing 4-15 is no-redeclare, which is described at https://eslint.org/docs/rules/no-redeclare.

USING VARIABLE CLOSURE

If you define a function inside another function—creating *inner* and *outer* functions—then the inner function is able to access the outer function's variables, using a feature called *closure*, like this:

```
function myFunc(name) {
    let myLocalVar = "sunny";
    let innerFunction = function () {
        return ("Hello " + name + ". Today is " + myLocalVar + ".");
    }
    return innerFunction();

}

console.log(myFunc("Adam"));
```

The inner function in this example is able to access the local variables of the outer function, including its parameter. This is a powerful feature that means you don't have to define parameters on inner functions to pass around data values, but caution is required because it is easy to get unexpected results when using common variable names like counter or index, where you may not realize that you are reusing a variable name from the outer function.

Using the Primitive Types

JavaScript defines a basic set of primitive types: string, number, boolean. This may seem like a short list, but JavaScript manages to fit a lot of flexibility into these types.

■ **Tip** I am simplifying here. There are three other primitives that you may encounter. Variables that have been declared but not assigned a value are undefined, while the null value is used to indicate that a variable has no value, just as in other languages. The final primitive type is Symbol, which is an immutable value that represents a unique ID but which is not widely used at the time of writing.

Working with Booleans

The boolean type has two values: true and false. Listing 4-16 shows both values being used, but this type is most useful when used in conditional statements, such as an if statement. There is no console output from this listing, although you will see warnings because the variables have been defined and not used.

Listing 4-16. Defining boolean Values in the example.js File in the src Folder

```
let firstBool = true;
let secondBool = false;
```

Working with Strings

You define string values using either the double quote or single quote characters, as shown in Listing 4-17.

Listing 4-17. Defining string Variables in the example.js File in the src Folder

```
let firstString = "This is a string";
let secondString = 'And so is this';
```

The quote characters you use must match. You can't start a string with a single quote and finish with a double quote, for example. There is no console output for this listing. JavaScript provides string objects with a basic set of properties and methods, the most useful of which are described in Table 4-2.

Table 4-2. *Useful string Properties and Methods*

Name	Description
length	This property returns the number of characters in the string.
charAt(index)	This method returns a string containing the character at the specified index.
concat(string)	This method returns a new string that concatenates the string on which the method is called and the string provided as an argument.
indexOf(term, start)	This method returns the first index at which term appears in the string or -1 if there is no match. The optional start argument specifies the start index for the search.
replace(term, newTerm)	This method returns a new string in which all instances of term are replaced with newTerm.
slice(start, end)	This method returns a substring containing the characters between the start and end indices.
split(term)	This method splits up a string into an array of values that were separated by term.
toUpperCase() toLowerCase()	These methods return new strings in which all the characters are uppercase or lowercase.
trim()	This method returns a new string from which all the leading and trailing whitespace characters have been removed.

Using Template Strings

A common programming task is to combine static content with data values to produce a string that can be presented to the user. The traditional way to do this is through string concatenation, which is the approach I have been using in the examples so far in this chapter, as follows:

```
...
let message = "It is " + weather + " today";
...
```

JavaScript also supports *template strings*, which allow data values to be specified inline, which can help reduce errors and result in a more natural development experience. Listing 4-18 shows the use of a template string.

Listing 4-18. Using a Template String in the example.js File in the src Folder

```
function messageFunction(weather) {
    let message = `It is ${weather} today`;
    console.log(message);
}

messageFunction("raining");
```

Template strings begin and end with backticks (the ` character), and data values are denoted by curly braces preceded by a dollar sign. This string, for example, incorporates the value of the weather variable into the template string:

```
...
let message = `It is ${weather} today`;
...
```

This example produces the following output:

```
It is raining today
```

Working with Numbers

The number type is used to represent both *integer* and *floating-point* numbers (also known as *real numbers*). Listing 4-19 provides a demonstration.

Listing 4-19. Defining number Values in the example.js File in the src Folder

```
let daysInWeek = 7;
let pi = 3.14;
let hexValue = 0xFFFF;
```

You don't have to specify which kind of number you are using. You just express the value you require, and JavaScript will act accordingly. In the listing, I have defined an integer value, defined a floating-point value, and prefixed a value with 0x to denote a hexadecimal value.

Using JavaScript Operators

JavaScript defines a largely standard set of operators. I've summarized the most useful in Table 4-3.

Table 4-3. *Useful JavaScript Operators*

Operator	Description
++, --	Pre- or post-increment and decrement
+, -, *, /, %	Addition, subtraction, multiplication, division, remainder
<, <=, >, >=	Less than, less than or equal to, more than, more than or equal to
==, !=	Equality and inequality tests
===, !==	Identity and nonidentity tests
&&, ||	Logical AND and OR (|| is used to coalesce null values)
=	Assignment
+	String concatenation
?:	Three-operand conditional statement

Using Conditional Statements

Many of the JavaScript operators are used in conjunction with conditional statements. In this book, I tend to use the if/else and switch statements. Listing 4-20 shows the use of both, which will be familiar to most developers.

Listing 4-20. Using Conditional Statements in the example.js File in the src Folder

```
let name = "Adam";

if (name === "Adam") {
    console.log("Name is Adam");
} else if (name === "Jacqui") {
    console.log("Name is Jacqui");
} else {
    console.log("Name is neither Adam or Jacqui");
}

switch (name) {
    case "Adam":
        console.log("Name is Adam");
        break;
    case "Jacqui":
        console.log("Name is Jacqui");
        break;
    default:
        console.log("Name is neither Adam or Jacqui");
        break;
}
```

This example produces the following results:

```
Name is Adam
Name is Adam
```

The Equality Operator vs. the Identity Operator

The equality and identity operators are of particular note. The equality operator will attempt to coerce (convert) operands to the same type to assess equality. This is a handy feature, as long as you are aware it is happening. Listing 4-21 shows the equality operator in action.

Listing 4-21. Using the Equality Operator in the example.js File in the src Folder

```
let firstVal = 5;
let secondVal = "5";

if (firstVal == secondVal) {
    console.log("They are the same");
} else {
    console.log("They are NOT the same");
}
```

The output from this example is as follows:

```
They are the same
```

JavaScript is converting the two operands into the same type and comparing them. In essence, the equality operator tests that values are the same irrespective of their type. This causes sufficient confusion that you will also see a warning in the JavaScript console:

```
Line 4:  Expected '===' and instead saw '=='    eqeqeq
```

A more predictable way of making comparisons is to use the identity operator (===, three equal signs, rather than the two of the equality operator), as shown in Listing 4-22.

Listing 4-22. Using the Identity Operator in the example.js File in the src Folder

```
let firstVal = 5;
let secondVal = "5";

if (firstVal === secondVal) {
    console.log("They are the same");
} else {
    console.log("They are NOT the same");
}
```

In this example, the identity operator will consider the two variables to be different. This operator doesn't coerce types. The result is as follows:

```
They are NOT the same
```

Explicitly Converting Types

The string concatenation operator (+) has precedence over the addition operator (also +), which means that JavaScript will concatenate variables in preference to adding. This can cause confusion because JavaScript will also convert types freely to produce a result—and not always the result that is expected, as shown in Listing 4-23.

Listing 4-23. String Concatenation Operator Precedence in the example.js File in the src Folder

```
let myData1 = 5 + 5;
let myData2 = 5 + "5";

console.log("Result 1: " + myData1);
console.log("Result 2: " + myData2);
```

These statements produce the following result:

```
Result 1: 10
Result 2: 55
```

The second result is the kind that causes confusion. What might be intended to be an addition operation is interpreted as string concatenation through a combination of operator precedence and over-eager type conversion. To avoid this, you can explicitly convert the types of values to ensure you perform the right kind of operation, as described in the following sections.

Converting Numbers to Strings

If you are working with multiple number variables and want to concatenate them as strings, then you can convert the numbers to strings with the toString method, as shown in Listing 4-24.

Listing 4-24. Using the number.toString Method in the example.js File in the src Folder

```
let myData1 = (5).toString() + String(5);

console.log("Result: " + myData1);
```

Notice that I placed the numeric value in parentheses, and then I called the toString method. This is because you have to allow JavaScript to convert the literal value into a number before you can call the methods that the number type defines. I have also shown an alternative approach to achieve the same effect, which is to call the String function and pass in the numeric value as an argument. Both of these techniques have the same effect, which is to convert a number to a string, meaning that the + operator is used for string concatenation and not addition. The output from this script is as follows:

```
Result: 55
```

There are some other methods that allow you to exert more control over how a number is represented as a string. I briefly describe these methods in Table 4-4. All of the methods shown in the table are defined by the number type.

Table 4-4. *Useful Number-to-String Methods*

Method	Description
toString()	This method returns a string that represents a number in base 10.
toString(2) toString(8) toString(16)	This method returns a string that represents a number in binary, octal, or hexadecimal notation.
toFixed(n)	This method returns a string representing a real number with n digits after the decimal point.
toExponential(n)	This method returns a string that represents a number using exponential notation with one digit before the decimal point and n digits after.
toPrecision(n)	This method returns a string that represents a number with n significant digits, using exponential notation if required.

Converting Strings to Numbers

The complementary technique is to convert strings to numbers so that you can perform addition rather than concatenation. You can do this with the Number function, as shown in Listing 4-25.

Listing 4-25. Converting Strings to Numbers in the example.js File in the src Folder

```
let firstVal = "5";
let secondVal = "5";

let result = Number(firstVal) + Number(secondVal);
console.log("Result: " + result);
```

The output from this script is as follows:

```
Result: 10
```

The Number function is strict in the way that is parses string values, but there are two other functions you can use that are more flexible and will ignore trailing non-number characters. These functions are parseInt and parseFloat. I have described all three methods in Table 4-5.

Table 4-5. *Useful String to Number Methods*

Method	Description
Number(str)	This method parses the specified string to create an integer or real value.
parseInt(str)	This method parses the specified string to create an integer value.
parseFloat(str)	This method parses the specified string to create an integer or real value.

Working with Arrays

JavaScript arrays work like arrays in most other programming languages. Listing 4-26 shows how you can create and populate an array.

Listing 4-26. Creating and Populating an Array in the example.js File in the src Folder

```
let myArray = new Array();
myArray[0] = 100;
myArray[1] = "Adam";
myArray[2] = true;
```

I have created a new array by calling new Array(). This creates an empty array, which I assign to the variable myArray. In the subsequent statements, I assign values to various index positions in the array. (There is no output from this listing.)

There are a couple of things to note in this example. First, I didn't need to declare the number of items in the array when I created it. JavaScript arrays will resize themselves to hold any number of items. The second point is that I didn't have to declare the data types that the array will hold. Any JavaScript array can hold any mix of data types. In the example, I have assigned three items to the array: a number, a string, and a boolean.

Using an Array Literal

The example in Listing 4-26 produces a warning because using new Array() isn't the standard way to create an array. Instead, the array literal style lets you create and populate an array in a single statement, as shown in Listing 4-27.

Listing 4-27. Using the Array Literal Style in the example.js File in the src Folder

```
let myArray = [100, "Adam", true];
```

In this example, I specified that the myArray variable should be assigned a new array by specifying the items I wanted in the array between square brackets ([and]). (There is no console output from this listing, although there will be a warning because the array is defined but not used.)

Reading and Modifying the Contents of an Array

You read the value at a given index using square braces ([and]), placing the index you require between the braces, as shown in Listing 4-28.

Listing 4-28. Reading the Data from an Array Index in the example.js File in the src Folder

```
let myArray = [100, "Adam", true];

console.log(`Index 0: ${myArray[0]}`);
```

You can modify the data held in any position in a JavaScript array simply by assigning a new value to the index. Just as with regular variables, you can switch the data type at an index without any problems. The output from the listing is as follows:

```
Index 0: 100
```

Listing 4-29 demonstrates how to modify the contents of an array.

Listing 4-29. Modifying the Contents of an Array in the example.js File in the src Folder

```
let myArray = [100, "Adam", true];
myArray[0] = "Tuesday";

console.log(`Index 0: ${myArray[0]}`);
```

In this example, I have assigned a string to position 0 in the array, a position that was previously held by a number and produces this output:

```
Index 0: Tuesday
```

Enumerating the Contents of an Array

You enumerate the content of an array using a for loop or using the forEach method, which receives a function that is called to process each element in the array. Both approaches are shown in Listing 4-30.

Listing 4-30. Enumerating the Contents of an Array in the example.js File in the src Folder

```
let myArray = [100, "Adam", true];

for (let i = 0; i < myArray.length; i++) {
    console.log(`Index ${i}: ${myArray[i]}`);
}

console.log("---");

myArray.forEach((value, index) => console.log(`Index ${index}: ${value}`));
```

The JavaScript for loop works just the same way as loops in many other languages. You determine how many elements there are in the array by using the length property.

The function passed to the forEach method is given two arguments: the value of the current item to be processed and the position of that item in the array. In this listing, I have used an arrow function as the argument to the forEach method, which is the kind of use for which they excel (and you will see used throughout this book). The output from the listing is as follows:

```
Index 0: 100
Index 1: Adam
Index 2: true
---
Index 0: 100
Index 1: Adam
Index 2: true
```

Using the Spread Operator

The spread operator is used to expand an array so that its contents can be used as function arguments. Listing 4-31 defines a function that accepts multiple arguments and invokes it using the values in an array with and without the spread operator.

Listing 4-31. Using the Spread Operator in the example.js File in the src Folder

```
function printItems(numValue, stringValue, boolValue) {
    console.log(`Number: ${numValue}`);
    console.log(`String: ${stringValue}`);
    console.log(`Boolean: ${boolValue}`);
}

let myArray = [100, "Adam", true];

printItems(myArray[0], myArray[1], myArray[2]);

printItems(...myArray);
```

The spread operator is an ellipsis (a sequence of three periods), and it causes the array to be unpacked and passed to the printItems function as individual arguments.

```
...
printItems(...myArray);
...
```

The spread operator also makes it easy to concatenate arrays, as shown in Listing 4-32.

Listing 4-32. Concatenating Arrays in the example.js File in the src Folder

```
let myArray = [100, "Adam", true];
let myOtherArray = [200, "Bob", false, ...myArray];

myOtherArray.forEach((value, index) => console.log(`Index ${index}: ${value}`));
```

Using the spread operator, I am able to specify myArray as an item when I define myOtherArray, with the result that the contents of the first array will be unpacked and added as items to the second array. This example produces the following results:

```
Index 0: 200
Index 1: Bob
Index 2: false
Index 3: 100
Index 4: Adam
Index 5: true
```

■ **Note**   Arrays can also be de-structured, whereby the individual elements of an array are assigned to different variables, so that [var1, var2] = [3, 4] assigns a value of 3 to var1 and 4 to var2. Array de-structuring is used by the hooks feature, which is described in Chapter 11.

Using the Built-in Array Methods

The JavaScript Array object defines a number of methods that you can use to work with arrays, the most useful of which are described in Table 4-6.

Table 4-6. *Useful Array Methods*

Method	Description
concat(otherArray)	This method returns a new array that concatenates the array on which it has been called with the array specified as the argument. Multiple arrays can be specified.
join(separator)	This method joins all the elements in the array to form a string. The argument specifies the character used to delimit the items.
pop()	This method removes and returns the last item in the array.
shift()	This method removes and returns the first element in the array.
push(item)	This method appends the specified item to the end of the array.
unshift(item)	This method inserts a new item at the start of the array.
reverse()	This method returns a new array that contains the items in reverse order.
slice(start,end)	This method returns a section of the array.
sort()	This method sorts the array. An optional comparison function can be used to perform custom comparisons.
splice(index, count)	This method removes count items from the array, starting at the specified index. The removed items are returned as the result of the method.
unshift(item)	This method inserts a new item at the start of the array.
every(test)	This method calls the test function for each item in the array and returns true if the function returns true for all of them and false otherwise.
some(test)	This method returns true if calling the test function for each item in the array returns true at least once.
filter(test)	This method returns a new array containing the items for which the test function returns true.
find(test)	This method returns the first item in the array for which the test function returns true.
findIndex(test)	This method returns the index of the first item in the array for which the test function returns true.
forEach(callback)	This method invokes the callback function for each item in the array, as described in the previous section.
includes(value)	This method returns true if the array contains the specified value.
map(callback)	This method returns a new array containing the result of invoking the callback function for every item in the array.
reduce(callback)	This method returns the accumulated value produced by invoking the callback function for every item in the array.

Since many of the methods in Table 4-6 return a new array, these methods can be chained together to process data, as shown in Listing 4-33.

Listing 4-33. Processing an Array in the example.js File in the src Folder

```
let products = [
    { name: "Hat", price: 24.5, stock: 10 },
    { name: "Kayak", price: 289.99, stock: 1 },
    { name: "Soccer Ball", price: 10, stock: 0 },
    { name: "Running Shoes", price: 116.50, stock: 20 }
];

let totalValue = products
    .filter(item => item.stock > 0)
    .reduce((prev, item) => prev + (item.price * item.stock), 0);

console.log(`Total value: $${totalValue.toFixed(2)}`);
```

I use the `filter` method to select the items in the array whose `stock` value is greater than zero and use the `reduce` method to determine the total value of those items, producing the following output:

```
Total value: $2864.99
```

Working with Objects

There are several ways to create objects in JavaScript. Listing 4-34 gives a simple example to get started.

Listing 4-34. Creating an Object in the example.js File in the src Folder

```
let myData = new Object();
myData.name = "Adam";
myData.weather = "sunny";

console.log(`Hello ${myData.name}.`);
console.log(`Today is ${myData.weather}.`);
```

I create an object by calling new `Object()`, and I assign the result (the newly created object) to a variable called myData. Once the object is created, I can define properties on the object just by assigning values, like this:

```
...
myData.name = "Adam";
...
```

Prior to this statement, my object doesn't have a property called name. When the statement has executed, the property does exist, and it has been assigned the value Adam. You can read the value of a property by combining the variable name and the property name with a period, like this:

```
...
console.log(`Hello ${myData.name}.`);
...
```

The result from the listing is as follows:

```
Hello Adam.
Today is sunny.
```

Using Object Literals

The previous example produces a warning because the standard way to define objects is to do so using the object literal format, which also allows properties to be defined in a single step, as shown in Listing 4-35.

Listing 4-35. Using the Object Literal Format in the example.js File in the src Folder

```
let myData = {
    name: "Adam",
    weather: "sunny"
};

console.log(`Hello ${myData.name}.`);
console.log(`Today is ${myData.weather}.`);
```

Each property that you want to define is separated from its value using a colon (:), and properties are separated using a comma (,). The effect is the same as in the previous example, and the result from the listing is as follows:

```
Hello Adam.
Today is sunny.
```

Using Variables as Object Properties

If you use a variable as an object property, JavaScript will use the variable name as the property name and the variable value as the property value, as shown in Listing 4-36.

Listing 4-36. Using a Variable in an Object Literal in the example.js File in the src Folder

```
let name = "Adam"

let myData = {
  name,
  weather: "sunny"
};

console.log(`Hello ${myData.name}.`);
console.log(`Today is ${myData.weather}.`);
```

The name variable is used to add a property to the myData object, such that the property is taken from the variable, name in this case, as its value, Adam. This is a useful technique when you want to combine a set of data values into an object, and you will see it used in examples in later chapters. The code in Listing 4-37 produces the following output:

```
Hello Adam.
Today is sunny.
```

Using Functions as Methods

One of the features that I like most about JavaScript is the way you can add functions to objects. A function defined on an object is called a *method*. Listing 4-37 shows how you can add methods in this manner.

Listing 4-37. Adding Methods to an Object in the example.js File in the src Folder

```javascript
let myData = {
    name: "Adam",
    weather: "sunny",
    printMessages: function () {
        console.log(`Hello ${myData.name}.`);
        console.log(`Today is ${myData.weather}.`);
    }
};

myData.printMessages();
```

In this example, I have used a function to create a method called printMessages. Notice that to refer to the properties defined by the object, I have to use the this keyword. When a function is used as a method, the function is implicitly passed the object on which the method has been called as an argument through the special variable this. The output from the listing is as follows:

```
Hello Adam.
Today is sunny.
```

You can also define methods without using the function keyword, as shown in Listing 4-38.

Listing 4-38. Defining a Method in the example.js File in the src Folder

```javascript
let myData = {
    name: "Adam",
    weather: "sunny",
    printMessages() {
        console.log(`Hello ${myData.name}.`);
        console.log(`Today is ${myData.weather}.`);
    }
};

myData.printMessages();
```

The output from this listing is as follows:

```
Hello Adam.
Today is sunny.
```

The fat arrow syntax can also be used to define methods, as shown in Listing 4-39.

Listing 4-39. Defining a Fat Arrow Method in the example.js File in the src Folder

```
let myData = {
    name: "Adam",
    weather: "sunny",
    printMessages: () => {
        console.log(`Hello ${myData.name}.`);
        console.log(`Today is ${myData.weather}.`);
    }
};

myData.printMessages();
```

■ **Tip** If you are returning an object literal as the result from a fat arrow function, then you must enclose the object in parentheses, e.g., myFunc = () => ({ data: "hello"}). You will receive an error if you omit the parentheses because the build tools will assume that the curly braces of the object literal are the start and end of a function body.

Using Classes

Classes are templates for objects, defining the properties and methods that new instances will possess. Classes are a recent addition to the JavaScript language, and they are used in React development to define components that have state data, as explained in Chapter 11. In Listing 4-40, I have replaced the object literal with a class.

Listing 4-40. Using a Class in the example.js File in the src Folder

```
class MyData {

    constructor() {
        this.name = "Adam";
        this.weather = "sunny";
    }

    printMessages = () => {
        console.log(`Hello ${this.name}.`);
        console.log(`Today is ${this.weather}.`);
    }
}

let myData = new MyData();
myData.printMessages();
```

Classes are defined using the class keyword. The constructor is a special method that is automatically invoked when an object is created from the class, which is known as *instantiating the class*. An object created from a class is said to be an *instance* of that class.

In JavaScript, the constructor is used to define the properties that instances will have, and the current object is referred to using the this keyword. The constructor in Listing 4-40 defines name and weather properties by assigning values to this.name and this.weather. Classes define methods by assigning functions to names, and in Listing 4-40, the class defines a printMessages method that is defined using the fat arrow syntax and that prints out messages to the console. Notice that the this keyword is required to access the values of the name and weather variables.

■ **Tip** There are other ways to use JavaScript classes, but I have focused on the way they are used in React development and in the examples throughout this book. See https://developer.mozilla.org/en-US/docs/Web/JavaScript/Reference/Classes for full details.

A new instance of the class is created using the new keyword, and a class can be used to create multiple objects, each of which has its own data values that are separate from the other instances. In the listing, the new keyword is used to create an object from the MyData class, which is then assigned to a variable named myData. The object's printMessages method is invoked, producing the following output:

```
Hello Adam.
Today is sunny.
```

In other languages and frameworks, classes are used for inheritance, where one class builds on the methods and properties defined by another. React development does not use class inheritance directly and uses an alternative approach, known as *composition*, to create complex features, as described in Chapter 14. The exception is when a React component is defined using a class, where the extends keyword must be used to ensure that the class inherits the core features required for a component. If you examine the contents of the App.js file, you will see that the component is defined using the class and extends keywords, like this:

```
...
import React, { Component } from "react";

export default class App extends Component {

    render = () =>
        <div className="m-2">
            <div className="form-group">
                <label>Name:</label>
                <input className="form-control" />
            </div>
            <div className="form-group">
                <label>City:</label>
                <input className="form-control" />
            </div>
        </div>
}
...
```

Copying Properties from One Object to Another

Some important features provided by React and the packages I describe in Part 3 rely on copying the properties from one object to another. JavaScript provides the Object.assign method for this purpose, as demonstrated in Listing 4-41.

Listing 4-41. Copying Object Properties in the example.js File in the src Folder

```
class MyData {

    constructor() {
        this.name = "Adam";
        this.weather = "sunny";
    }

    printMessages = () => {
        console.log(`Hello ${this.name}.`);
        console.log(`Today is ${this.weather}.`);
    }
}

let myData = new MyData();

let secondObject = {};

Object.assign(secondObject, myData);

secondObject.printMessages();
```

This example uses the literal form to create a new object that has no properties and uses the Object.assign method to copy the properties—and their values—from the myData object. This example produces the following output:

```
Hello Adam.
Today is sunny.
```

The destructuring operator—which is the same as the spread operator—can be used to copy properties from one object to another, and a technique I use in later chapters is to copy all of the existing properties using the destructuring operator and then define a new value for some of them, as shown in Listing 4-42.

Listing 4-42. Copying Using a Spread in the example.js File in the src Folder

```
class MyData {

    constructor() {
        this.name = "Adam";
        this.weather = "sunny";
    }

    printMessages = () => {
        console.log(`Hello ${this.name}.`);
```

```
            console.log(`Today is ${this.weather}.`);
    }
}

let myData = new MyData();

let secondObject = { ...myData, weather: "cloudy"};

console.log(`myData: ${ myData.weather}, secondObject: ${secondObject.weather}`);
```

This example copies the properties from the myData object and provides a new value for the weather property, producing the following output:

```
myData: sunny, secondObject: cloudy
```

Capturing Parameter Names from Objects

When an object is received as a function or method parameter, it can be awkward to navigate through the properties to get the data required. As a simple example, Listing 4-43 defines a structure of objects that are navigated to get data values.

Listing 4-43. Navigating Object Properties in the example.js File in the src Folder

```
const myData = {
    name: "Bob",
    location: {
        city: "Paris",
        country: "France"
    },
    employment: {
        title: "Manager",
        dept: "Sales"
    }
}

function printDetails(data) {
    console.log(`Name: ${data.name}, City: ${data.location.city},
        Role: ${data.employment.title}`);
}

printDetails(myData);
```

The printDetails function has to navigate through the object to get the name, city, and title properties it requires. The same outcome can be achieved more elegantly by capturing specific properties as named parameters, as shown in Listing 4-44.

Listing 4-44. Capturing Named Parameters in the example.js File in the src Folder

```
const myData = {
    name: "Bob",
    location: {
        city: "Paris",
        country: "France"
    },
    employment: {
        title: "Manager",
        dept: "Sales"
    }
}

function printDetails({ name, location: { city }, employment: { title }}) {
    console.log(`Name: ${name}, City: ${city}, Role: ${title}`);
}

printDetails(myData);
```

This example applies the technique described in Listing 4-36 to select specific properties from the object. This listing and Listing 4-43 produce the same output.

```
Name: Bob, City: Paris, Role: Manager
```

Understanding JavaScript Modules

React applications are too complex to define in a single JavaScript file. To break up an application into more manageable chunks, JavaScript supports *modules*, which contain JavaScript code that other parts of the application depend on. In the sections that follow, I explain the different ways that modules can be defined and used.

Creating and Using a JavaScript Module

There are already JavaScript modules in the example project, but the best way to understand how they work is to create and use a new module. I added a file called sum.js in the src folder and added the code shown in Listing 4-45.

Listing 4-45. The Contents of the sum.js File in the src Folder

```
export default function(values) {
    return values.reduce((total, val) => total + val, 0);
}
```

The sum.js file contains a function that accepts an array of values and uses the JavaScript array reduce method to sum them and return the result. What's important about this example is not what it does but the fact that the function is defined in its own file, which is the basic building block for a module.

There are two keywords used in Listing 4-45 that you will often encounter when defining modules: export and default. The export keyword is used to denote the features that will be available outside the module. By default, the contents of the JavaScript file are private and must be explicitly shared using the export keyword before they can be used in the rest of the application. The default keyword is used when the module contains a single feature, such as the function defined in Listing 4-45. Together, the export and default keywords are used to specify that the only function in the sum.js file is available for use in the rest of the application.

Using the JavaScript Module

Another keyword is required to use a module: the import keyword. In Listing 4-46, I used the import keyword to access the function defined in the previous section so that it can be used in the example.js file.

Listing 4-46. Using a JavaScript Module in the example.js File in the src Folder

```
import additionFunction from "./sum";

let values = [10, 20, 30, 40, 50];

let total = additionFunction(values);

console.log(`Total: ${total}`);
```

The import keyword is used to declare a dependency on the module. The import keyword can be used in a number of different ways, but this is the format you will use most often when working with modules you have created yourself, and the key parts are illustrated in Figure 4-3.

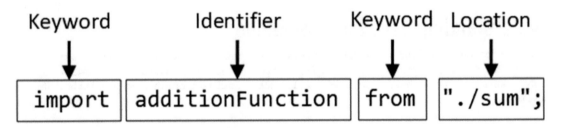

Figure 4-3. Declaring a dependency on a module

The import keyword is followed by an identifier, which is the name by which the function will be known when it is used, and the identifier in this example is additionFunction.

■ **Tip** Notice that it is the import statement in which the identifier is applied, which means that the code that consumes the function from the module chooses the name by which it will be known and that multiple import statements for the same module in different parts of the application can use different names to refer to the same function. See the next section for details of how the module can specify the names of the features it contains.

The from keyword follows the identifier, which is then followed by the location of the module. It is important to pay close attention to the location because different behaviors are created by different location formats, as described in the sidebar.

During the build process, the React tools will detect the import statement and include the function from the sum.js file in the JavaScript file that is sent to the browser so that it can execute the application. The identifier used in the import statement can be used to access the function in the module, in just the same way that locally defined functions are used.

```
...
let total = additionFunction(values);
...
```

If you examine the browser's JavaScript console, you will see that the code in Listing 4-42 uses the module's function to produce the following result:

```
Total: 150
```

UNDERSTANDING MODULE LOCATIONS

The location of a module changes the way that the build tools will look for the module when creating the JavaScript file that is sent to the browser. For modules you have defined yourself, the location is specified as a relative path; it starts with one or two periods, which indicates that the path is relative to the current file or to the current file's parent directory. In Listing 4-46, the location starts with a period.

```
...
import additionFunction from "./sum";
...
```

This location tells the build tools that there is a dependency on the sum module, which can be found in the same folder as the file that contains the import statement. Notice that the file extension is not included in the location.

If you omit the initial period, then the import statement declares a dependency on a module in the node_modules folder, which is where packages are installed during the project setup. This kind of location is used to access features provided by third-party packages, including the React packages, which is why you will see statements like this in React projects:

```
...
import React, { Component } from "react";
...
```

The location for this import statement doesn't start with a period and will be interpreted as a dependency on the react module in the project's node_modules folder, which is the package that provides the core React application features.

Exporting Named Features from a Module

A module can assign names to the features it exports, which is the approach I have taken for most of the examples in this book. In Listing 4-47, I have given a name to the function that is exported by the sum module.

Listing 4-47. Exporting a Named Feature in the sum.js File in the src Folder

```
export function sumValues (values) {
    return values.reduce((total, val) => total + val, 0);
}
```

The function provides the same feature but is exported using the name sumValues and no longer uses the default keyword. In Listing 4-48, I have imported the feature using its new name in the example.js file.

Listing 4-48. Importing a Named Feature in the example.js File in the src Folder

```
import { sumValues } from "./sum";

let values = [10, 20, 30, 40, 50];

let total = sumValues(values);

console.log(`Total: ${total}`);
```

The name of the feature to be imported is specified in curly braces (the { and } characters) and is used by this name in the code. A module can export default and named features, as shown in Listing 4-49.

Listing 4-49. Exporting Named and Default Features in the sum.js File in the src Folder

```
export function sumValues (values) {
    return values.reduce((total, val) => total + val, 0);
}

export default function sumOdd(values) {
    return sumValues(values.filter((item, index) => index % 2 === 0));
}
```

The new feature is exported using the default keyword. In Listing 4-50, I have imported the new feature as the default export from the module.

Listing 4-50. Importing a Default Feature in the example.js File in the src Folder

```
import oddOnly, { sumValues } from "./sum";

let values = [10, 20, 30, 40, 50];

let total = sumValues(values);
let odds = oddOnly(values);

console.log(`Total: ${total}, Odd Total: ${odds}`);
```

This is the pattern you will see at the start of the React components in the examples throughout this book because the core React features required for JSX are the default export from the react module and the Component class is a named feature:

```
...
import React, { Component } from "react";
...
```

The example in Listing 4-50 produces the following output:

```
Total: 150, Odd Total: 90
```

Defining Multiple Named Features in a Module

Modules can contain more than one named function or value, which is useful for grouping related features. To demonstrate, I created a file called operations.js to the src folder and added the code shown in Listing 4-51.

Listing 4-51. The Contents of the operations.js File in the src Folder

```
export function multiply(values) {
    return values.reduce((total, val) => total * val, 1);
}

export function subtract(amount, values) {
    return values.reduce((total, val) => total - val, amount);
}

export function divide(first, second) {
    return first / second;
}
```

This module defines three functions to which the export keyword has been applied. Unlike the previous example, the default keyword is not used, and each function has its own name. When importing from a module that contains multiple features, the names of the required features are specified as a comma-separated list between the braces, as shown in Listing 4-52.

Listing 4-52. Importing Named Features in the example.js File in the src Folder

```
import oddOnly, { sumValues } from "./sum";
import { multiply, subtract } from "./operations";

let values = [10, 20, 30, 40, 50];

let total = sumValues(values);
let odds = oddOnly(values);

console.log(`Total: ${total}, Odd Total: ${odds}`);
console.log(`Multiply: ${multiply(values)}`);
console.log(`Subtract: ${subtract(1000, values)}`);
```

The braces that follow the `import` keyword surround the list of functions that I want to use, which is the `multiply` and `subtract` functions in this case, separated by commas. I only declare dependencies on the functions that I require, and there is no dependency on the `divide` function, which is defined in the module but not used. This example produces the following output:

```
Total: 150, Odd Total: 90
Multiply: 12000000
Subtract: 850
```

Changing Module Feature Names

When importing named features from modules, you may find that there are two modules that use the same name or that the name used by the module doesn't produce readable code when it is imported. You can select a new name using the as keyword, as shown in Listing 4-53.

Listing 4-53. Assigning a Name to a Feature in the example.js File in the src Folder

```
import oddOnly, { sumValues } from "./sum";
import { multiply, subtract as deduct } from "./operations";

let values = [10, 20, 30, 40, 50];

let total = sumValues(values);
let odds = oddOnly(values);

console.log(`Total: ${total}, Odd Total: ${odds}`);
console.log(`Multiply: ${multiply(values)}`);
console.log(`Subtract: ${deduct(1000, values)}`);
```

I used the as keyword to specify that the `subtract` function should be given the name `deduct` when imported into the `example.js` file. This listing produces the same output as Listing 4-53.

Importing an Entire Module

Listing the names of all the functions in a module gets out of hand for complex modules. A more elegant approach is to import all the features provided by a module and just use the features you require, as shown in Listing 4-54.

Listing 4-54. Importing an Entire Module in the example.js File in the src Folder

```
import oddOnly, { sumValues } from "./sum";
import * as ops from "./operations";

let values = [10, 20, 30, 40, 50];

let total = sumValues(values);
let odds = oddOnly(values);

console.log(`Total: ${total}, Odd Total: ${odds}`);
console.log(`Multiply: ${ops.multiply(values)}`);
console.log(`Subtract: ${ops.subtract(1000, values)}`);
```

An asterisk is used to import everything in a module, followed by the as keyword and an identifier through which the module functions and values will be accessed. In this case, the identifier is ops, which means that the multiply, subtract, and divide functions can be accessed as ops.multiply, ops.subtract, and ops.divide. This listing produces the same output as Listing 4-53.

Understanding JavaScript Promises

A promise is a background activity that will be completed at some point in the future. The most common use for promises in this book is requesting data using an HTTP request, which is performed asynchronously and produces a result when a response is received from the web server.

Understanding the Asynchronous Operation Problem

The classic asynchronous operation for a web application is an HTTP request, which is typically used to get the data and content that a user requires. I explain how to make HTTP requests in Part 3 of this book, but I need something simpler for this chapter, so I added a file called async.js to the src folder with the code shown in Listing 4-55.

Listing 4-55. The Contents of the async.js File in the src Folder

```
import { sumValues } from "./sum";

export function asyncAdd(values) {
    setTimeout(() => {
        let total = sumValues(values);
        console.log(`Async Total: ${total}`);
        return total;
    }, 500);
}
```

The setTimeout function invokes a function asynchronously after a specified delay. In the listing, the asyncAdd function receives a parameter that is passed to the sumValues function defined in the sum module after a delay of 500 milliseconds, creating a background operation that doesn't complete immediately for the examples in this chapter and acting as a placeholder for more useful operations, such as making an HTTP request. In Listing 4-56, I have updated the example.js file to use the asyncAdd function.

Listing 4-56. Performing Background Work in the example.js File in the src Folder

```
import { asyncAdd } from "./async";

let values = [10, 20, 30, 40, 50];

let total = asyncAdd(values);

console.log(`Main Total: ${total}`);
```

The problem this example demonstrates is that the result from the asyncAdd function isn't produced until after the statements in the example.js file have been executed, which you can see in the output shown in the browser's JavaScript console:

```
Main Total: undefined
Async Total: 150
```

The browser executes the statements in the example.js file and invokes the asyncAdd function as instructed. The browser moves on to the next statement in the example.js file, which writes a message to the console using the result provided by asyncAdd—but this happens before the asynchronous task has been completed, which is why the output is undefined. The asynchronous task subsequently completes, but it is too late for the result to be used by the example.js file.

Using a JavaScript Promise

To solve the problem in the previous section, I need a mechanism that allows me to observe the asynchronous task so that I can wait for it to complete and then write out the result. This is the role of the JavaScript Promise, which I have applied to the asyncAdd function in Listing 4-57.

Listing 4-57. Using a Promise in the async.js File in the src Folder

```
import { sumValues } from "./sum";

export function asyncAdd(values) {
    return new Promise(callback =>
        setTimeout(() => {
            let total = sumValues(values);
            console.log(`Async Total: ${total}`);
            callback(total);
        }, 500));
}
```

It can be difficult to unpack the functions in this example. The new keyword is used to create a Promise, which accepts the function that is to be observed. The observed function is provided with a callback that is invoked when the asynchronous task has completed and that accepts the result of the task as an argument. Invoking the callback function is known as *resolving the promise.*

The Promise object that has become the result of the asyncAdd function allows the asynchronous task to be observed so that follow-up work can be performed when the task completes, as shown in Listing 4-58.

Listing 4-58. Observing a Promise in the example.js File in the src Folder

```
import { asyncAdd } from "./async";

let values = [10, 20, 30, 40, 50];

asyncAdd(values).then(total => console.log(`Main Total: ${total}`));
```

The then method accepts a function that will be invoked when the callback is used. The result passed to the callback is provided to the then function. In this case, that means the total isn't written to the browser's JavaScript console until the asynchronous task has completed and produces the following output:

```
Async Total: 150
Main Total: 150
```

Simplifying the Asynchronous Code

JavaScript provides two keywords—async and await—that support asynchronous operations without having to work directly with promises. In Listing 4-59, I have applied these keywords in the example.js file.

■ **Caution** It is important to understand that using async/await doesn't change the way that an application behaves. The operation is still performed asynchronously, and the result will not be available until the operation completes. These keywords are just a convenience to simplify working with asynchronous code so that you don't have to use the then method.

Listing 4-59. Using async and await in the example.js File in the src Folder

```
import { asyncAdd } from "./async";

let values = [10, 20, 30, 40, 50];

async function doTask() {
    let total = await asyncAdd(values);
    console.log(`Main Total: ${total}`);
}

doTask();
```

These keywords can be applied only to functions, which is why I added the doTask function in this listing. The async keyword tells JavaScript that this function relies on functionality that requires a promise. The await keyword is used when calling a function that returns a Promise and has the effect of assigning the result provided to the Promise object's callback and then executing the statements that follow, producing the following result:

```
Async Total: 150
Main Total: 150
```

Summary

In this chapter, I provided a brief primer on JavaScript, focusing on the core functionality that will get you started for React development. In the next chapter, I start the process of building a more complex and realistic project, called SportsStore.

CHAPTER 5

SportsStore: A Real Application

In Chapter 2, I built a quick and simple React application. Small and focused examples allow me to demonstrate specific features, but they can lack context. To help overcome this problem, I am going to create a simple but realistic e-commerce application.

My application, called SportsStore, will follow the classic approach taken by online stores everywhere. I will create an online product catalog that customers can browse by category and page, a shopping cart where users can add and remove products, and a checkout where customers can enter their details and place their orders. I will also create an administration area that includes create, read, update, and delete (CRUD) facilities for managing products and orders—and I will protect it so that only logged-in administrators can make changes. Finally, I show you how to prepare a React application for deployment.

My goal in this chapter and those that follow is to give you a sense of what real React development is like by creating as realistic an example as possible. I want to focus on React and the related packages that are used in most projects, of course, and so I have simplified the integration with external systems, such as the database, and omitted others entirely, such as payment processing.

The SportsStore example is one that I use in all of my books, not least because it demonstrates the ways in which different frameworks, languages, and development styles can be used to achieve the same result. You don't need to have read any of my other books to follow this chapter, but you will find the contrasts interesting if you already own my *Pro ASP.NET Core MVC 2* or *Pro Angular 6* book, for example.

The React features that I use in the SportsStore application are covered in-depth in later chapters. Rather than duplicate everything here, I tell you just enough to make sense of the example application and refer you to other chapters for in-depth information. You can either read the SportsStore chapters from end to end to get a sense of how React works or jump to and from the detail chapters to get into the depth.

Either way, don't expect to understand everything right away—React applications have a lot of moving parts and depend on a lot of packages, and the SportsStore application is intended to show you how they fit together without diving too deeply into the details that the rest of the book describes.

■ **Tip** You can download the example project for this chapter—and for all the other chapters in this book—from https://github.com/Apress/pro-react-16.

Preparing the Project

To create the project, open a new command prompt, navigate to a convenient location, and run the command shown in Listing 5-1.

Listing 5-1. Creating the SportsStore Project

```
npx create-react-app sportsstore
```

The create-react-app tool will create a new React project named sportsstore with the packages, configuration files, and placeholder content required to start development. The project setup process may take some time to complete because there is a large number of NPM packages to download and install.

■ **Note**   When you create a new project, you may see warnings about security vulnerabilities. React development relies on a large number of packages, each of which has its own dependencies, and security issues will inevitably be discovered. For the examples in this book, it is important to use the package versions specified to ensure you get the expected results. For your own projects, you should review the warnings and update to versions that resolve the problems.

Installing Additional NPM Packages

Additional packages are required for the SportsStore project, in addition to the core React libraries and development tools installed by the create-react-app package. Run the commands shown in Listing 5-2 to navigate to the sportsstore folder and add the packages. (The npm install command can be used to add multiple packages in one go, but the result is a long command where it is easy to omit a package. To avoid errors, I add packages individually throughout this book.)

■ **Note**   It is important to use the version numbers shown in the listing. You may see warnings about unmet peer dependencies as you add the packages, but these can be ignored.

Listing 5-2. Installing Additional Packages

```
cd sportsstore
npm install bootstrap@4.1.2
npm install @fortawesome/fontawesome-free@5.6.1
npm install redux@4.0.1
npm install react-redux@6.0.0
npm install react-router-dom@4.3.1
npm install axios@0.18.0
npm install graphql@14.0.2
npm install apollo-boost@0.1.22
npm install react-apollo@2.3.2
```

Don't be put off by the number of additional packages that are required. React focuses on a core set of the features that are required by web applications and relies on supporting packages to create complete applications. To provide some context, the packages added in Listing 5-2 are described in Table 5-1, and I cover them in depth in Part 3 of this book.

Table 5-1. *The Packages Required for the SportsStore Project*

Name	Description
bootstrap	This package provides the CSS styles that I used to present HTML content throughout the book.
fontawesome-free	This package provides icons that can be included in HTML content. I have used the free package, but there is a more comprehensive paid-for option available, too.
redux	This package provides a data store, which simplifies the process of coordinating the different parts of the application. See Chapter 19 for details.
react-redux	This package integrates a Redux data store into a React application, as described in Chapters 19 and 20.
react-router-dom	This package provides URL routing, which allows the content presented to the user to be selected based on the browser's current URL, as described in Chapters 21 and 22.
axios	This package is used to make HTTP requests and will be used to access RESTful and GraphQL services, as described in Chapters 23–25.
graphql	This package contains the reference implementation of the GraphQL specification.
apollo-boost	This package contains a client used to consume a GraphQL service, as described in Chapter 25.
react-apollo	This package is used to integrate the GraphQL client into a React application, as described in Chapter 25.

Further packages are required to create the back-end services that the SportsStore application will consume. Using the command prompt, run the commands shown in Listing 5-3 in the sportsstore folder. These packages are installed using the --save-dev argument, which indicates they are used during development and will not be part of the SportsStore application when it is deployed.

Listing 5-3. Adding Further Packages

```
npm install --save-dev json-server@0.14.2
npm install --save-dev jsonwebtoken@8.1.1
npm install --save-dev express@4.16.4
npm install --save-dev express-graphql@0.7.1
npm install --save-dev cors@2.8.5
npm install --save-dev faker@4.1.0
npm install --save-dev chokidar@2.0.4
npm install --save-dev npm-run-all@4.1.3
npm install --save-dev connect-history-api-fallback@1.5.0
```

You won't need these packages for applications that consume data from existing services, but I need to create a complete infrastructure for the SportsStore application. Table 5-2 briefly describes the purpose of each package installed in Listing 5-3.

Table 5-2. *The Additional Packages Required by the SportsStore Project*

Name	Description
json-server	This package will be used to provide a RESTful web service in Chapter 6.
jsonwebtoken	This package will be used to authenticate users in Chapter 8.
graphql	This package will be used to define the schema for the GraphQL server in Chapter 7.
express	This package will be used to host the back-end servers.
express-graphql	This package will be used to create a GraphQL server.
cors	This package is used to enable cross-origin request sharing (CORS) requests.
faker	This package generates fake data for testing and is used in Chapter 6.
chokidar	This package monitors files for changes.
npm-run-all	This package is used to run multiple NPM scripts in a single command.
connect-history-api-fallback	This package is used to respond to HTTP requests with the index.html file and is used in the production server in Chapter 8.

Adding the CSS Stylesheets to the Project

To use the Bootstrap and Font Awesome packages, I need to add import statements to the application's index.js file. The purpose of the index.js file is to start the application, as described in Chapter 9, and adding the import statements shown in Listing 5-4 ensures that the styles I require can be applied to the HTML content presented by the SportsStore application.

Listing 5-4. Adding CSS Stylesheets in the index.js File in the src Folder

```
import React from 'react';
import ReactDOM from 'react-dom';
import './index.css';
import App from './App';
import * as serviceWorker from './serviceWorker';
import "bootstrap/dist/css/bootstrap.css";
import "@fortawesome/fontawesome-free/css/all.min.css";

ReactDOM.render(<App />, document.getElementById('root'));

// If you want your app to work offline and load faster, you can change
// unregister() to register() below. Note this comes with some pitfalls.
// Learn more about service workers: http://bit.ly/CRA-PWA
serviceWorker.unregister();
```

Preparing the Web Service

Once the basic structure of the application is in place, I will add support for consuming data from a web service. In preparation, I added a file called data.js to the sportsstore folder with the content shown in Listing 5-5.

Listing 5-5. The Contents of the data.js File in the sportsstore Folder

```
module.exports = function () {
    return {
        categories: ["Watersports", "Soccer", "Chess"],
        products: [
            { id: 1, name: "Kayak", category: "Watersports",
                description: "A boat for one person", price: 275 },
            { id: 2, name: "Lifejacket", category: "Watersports",
                description: "Protective and fashionable", price: 48.95 },
            { id: 3, name: "Soccer Ball", category: "Soccer",
                description: "FIFA-approved size and weight", price: 19.50 },
            { id: 4, name: "Corner Flags", category: "Soccer",
                description: "Give your playing field a professional touch",
                price: 34.95 },
            { id: 5, name: "Stadium", category: "Soccer",
                description: "Flat-packed 35,000-seat stadium", price: 79500 },
            { id: 6, name: "Thinking Cap", category: "Chess",
                description: "Improve brain efficiency by 75%", price: 16 },
            { id: 7, name: "Unsteady Chair", category: "Chess",
                description: "Secretly give your opponent a disadvantage",
                price: 29.95 },
            { id: 8, name: "Human Chess Board", category: "Chess",
                description: "A fun game for the family", price: 75 },
            { id: 9, name: "Bling Bling King", category: "Chess",
                description: "Gold-plated, diamond-studded King", price: 1200 }
        ],
        orders: []
    }
}
```

The code in Listing 5-5 creates three data collections that will be used by the application. The products collection contains the products for sale to the customer, the categories collection contains the set of categories into which the products are organized, and the orders collection contains the orders that customers have placed (but is currently empty).

I added a file called server.js to the sportsstore folder with the code shown in Listing 5-6. This is the code that creates the web service that will provide the application with data. I add features to the back-end server, such as authentication and support for GraphQL, in later chapters.

Listing 5-6. The Contents of the server.js File in the sportsstore Folder

```
const express = require("express");
const jsonServer = require("json-server");
const chokidar = require("chokidar");
const cors = require("cors");
```

```
const fileName = process.argv[2] || "./data.js"
const port = process.argv[3] || 3500;

let router = undefined;

const app = express();

const createServer = () => {
    delete require.cache[require.resolve(fileName)];
    setTimeout(() => {
        router = jsonServer.router(fileName.endsWith(".js")
            ? require(fileName)() : fileName);
    }, 100)
}

createServer();

app.use(cors());
app.use(jsonServer.bodyParser)
app.use("/api", (req, resp, next) => router(req, resp, next));

chokidar.watch(fileName).on("change", () => {
    console.log("Reloading web service data...");
    createServer();
    console.log("Reloading web service data complete.");
});

app.listen(port, () => console.log(`Web service running on port ${port}`));
```

To ensure that the web service is started alongside the React development tools, I changed the scripts section of the package.json file, as shown in Listing 5-7.

Listing 5-7. Enabling the Web Service in the package.json File in the sportsstore Folder

```
...
"scripts": {
  "start": "npm-run-all --parallel reactstart webservice",
  "reactstart": "react-scripts start",
  "webservice": "node server.js",
  "build": "react-scripts build",
  "test": "react-scripts test",
  "eject": "react-scripts eject"
},
...
```

This change uses the npm-run-all package to run the React development server and the web service at the same time.

Running the Example Application

To start the application and the web service, use the command prompt to run the command shown in Listing 5-8 in the sportsstore folder.

Listing 5-8. Starting the Application

```
npm start
```

There will be a pause while the initial compilation is completed, and then a new browser window will open displaying the placeholder content shown in Figure 5-1.

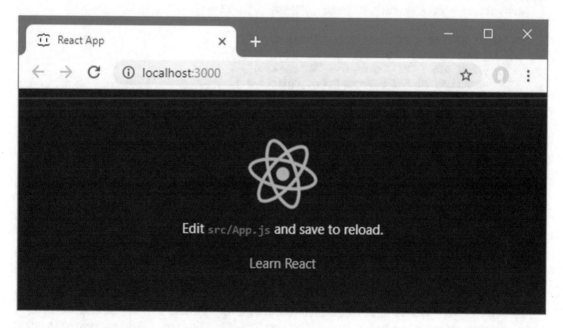

Figure 5-1. *Running the example application*

To make sure that the web service is running, open a new browser window and request the URL http://localhost:3500/api/products/1. The browser will display a JSON representation of one of the products defined in Listing 5-5, as follows:

```
{ "id":1, "name":"Kayak", "category":"Watersports",
   "description":"A boat for one person","price":275 }
```

Creating the Data Store

The starting point for SportsStore is the data store, which will be the repository for the data presented to the user and the supporting details required to coordinate application features, such as pagination.

I am going to start with a data store that uses local placeholder data. Later, I will add support for getting the data from a web service, but static data is a good place to start because it keeps the focus on the React application. The SportsStore data store will be created using the Redux package, which is the most popular data store for React projects and which I describe in Chapters 19 and 20. To get started, I created the src/data folder and added to it a file called placeholderData.js, with the content shown in Listing 5-9.

Listing 5-9. The Contents of the placeholderData.js File in the src/data Folder

```
export const data = {
    categories: ["Watersports", "Soccer", "Chess", "Running"],
    products: [
        { id: 1, name: "P1", category: "Watersports",
            description: "P1 (Watersports)", price: 3 },
        { id: 2, name: "P2", category: "Watersports",
            description: "P2 (Watersports)", price: 4 },
        { id: 3, name: "P3", category: "Running",
            description: "P3 (Running)", price: 5 },
        { id: 4, name: "P4", category: "Chess",
            description: "P4 (Chess)", price: 6 },
        { id: 5, name: "P5", category: "Chess",
            description: "P6 (Chess)", price: 7 },
    ]
}
```

Creating the Data Store Actions and Action Creators

Redux data stores separate reading data from the operations that change it. This can feel awkward at first, but it is similar to other parts of React development, such as component state data and using GraphQL, and it quickly becomes second nature.

Actions are objects that are sent to the data store to make changes to the data it contains. Actions have types, and action objects are created using *action creators*. The only action I need at the moment will load the data into the store, initially using the placeholder data defined in Listing 5-9 but eventually from a web service. There are different ways you can structure the actions for a data store, but it is worth identifying the common themes that are shared between different types of data to avoid code duplication later. I added a file called Types.js in the src/data folder and used it to list the data types in the store and the set of actions that can be performed on them, as shown in Listing 5-10.

Listing 5-10. The Contents of the Types.js File in the src/data Folder

```
export const DataTypes = {
    PRODUCTS: "products",
    CATEGORIES: "categories"
}

export const ActionTypes = {
    DATA_LOAD: "data_load"
}
```

There are two data types—PRODUCTS and CATEGORIES—and a single action, DATA_LOAD, which will populate the data store. There is no requirement to defined action types this way, but using constant values avoids typos when specifying action types elsewhere in the application.

Next, I need to define an *action creator* function, which will create an action object that can be processed by the data store to alter the data it contains. I added a file called ActionCreators.js to the src/ data folder, with the code shown in Listing 5-11.

Listing 5-11. The Contents of the ActionCreators.js File in the src/data Folder

```
import { ActionTypes} from "./Types";
import { data as phData} from "./placeholderData";

export const loadData = (dataType) => ({
    type: ActionTypes.DATA_LOAD,
    payload: {
        dataType: dataType,
        data: phData[dataType]
    }
});
```

The use of action creators is described in Chapter 19, but the only requirement for the objects produced by action creators is they must have a type property whose value specifies the type of change required to the data store. It is a good idea to use a common set of properties in action objects so that they can be handled consistently, and the action creator defined in Listing 5-11 returns an action object that has a payload property, which is the convention I will use for all of the SportsStore data store actions.

The payload property for the action object in Listing 5-11 has a dataType property that indicates the type of data that the action relates to and a data property that provides the data to be added to the data store. The value for the data property is obtained from the placeholder data at the moment, but I replace this with data obtained from a web service in Chapter 6.

Actions are processed by data store *reducers*, which are functions that receive the current contents of the data store and an action object and use them to make changes. I added a file called ShopReducer.js to the src/data folder and defined the reducer shown in Listing 5-12.

Listing 5-12. The Contents of the ShopReducer.js File in the src/data Folder

```
import { ActionTypes } from "./Types";
export const ShopReducer = (storeData, action) => {
    switch(action.type) {
        case ActionTypes.DATA_LOAD:
            return {
                ...storeData,
                [action.payload.dataType]: action.payload.data
            };
        default:
            return storeData || {};
    }
}
```

Reducers are required to create and return new objects that incorporate any required changes. If the action type isn't recognized, the reducer must return the data store object it received unchanged. The reducer in Listing 5-12 handles the DATA_LOAD action by creating a new object with all the properties of the old store plus the new data received in the action. Reducers are described in more detail in Chapter 19.

As the final step for creating the data store, I added a file called `DataStore.js` to the `src/data` folder and added the code shown in Listing 5-13.

Listing 5-13. The Contents of the DataStore.js File in the src/data Folder

```
import { createStore } from "redux";
import { ShopReducer } from "./ShopReducer";

export const SportsStoreDataStore = createStore(ShopReducer);
```

The Redux package provides the `createStore` function, which sets up a new data store using a reducer. This is enough to create a data store to get started with, but I will add additional features later so that further operations can be performed and so that data can be loaded from a web service.

Creating the Shopping Features

The first part of the application that will be seen by users is the storefront, which will present the available products in a two-column layout that allows filtering by category, as shown in Figure 5-2.

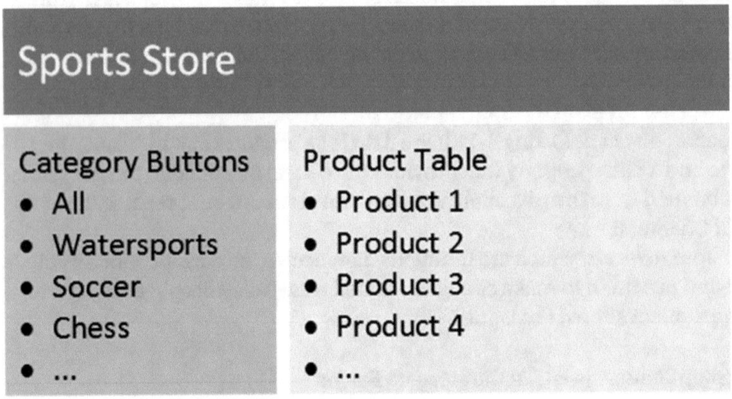

Figure 5-2. *The basic structure of the application*

I am going to structure the application so that the browser's URL is used to select the content presented to the user. To get started, the application will support the URLs described in Table 5-3, which will allow the user to see the products for sale and filter them by category.

Table 5-3. *The SportsStore URLs*

Name	Description
/shop/products	This URL will display all of the products to the user, regardless of category.
/shop/products/chess	This URL will display the products in a specific category. In this case, the URL will select the Chess category.

■ **Note** I have adopted the British term *shop* for the part of the application that offers products for sale to customers. I want to avoid confusion between the data store, in which the application's data is kept, and the product store, from which the user makes purchases.

Responding to the browser's URL in the application is known as *URL routing*, which is provided by the React Router package added in Listing 5-2, and which is described in detail in Chapters 21 and 22.

Creating the Product and Category Components

Components are the building blocks for React applications and are responsible for the content presented to the user. I created the src/shop folder and added to it a file called ProductList.js with the contents shown in Listing 5-14.

Listing 5-14. The Contents of the ProductList.js File in the src/shop Folder

```
import React, { Component } from "react";

export class ProductList extends Component {

    render() {
        if (this.props.products == null || this.props.products.length === 0) {
            return <h5 className="p-2">No Products</h5>
        }
        return this.props.products.map(p =>
                <div className="card m-1 p-1 bg-light" key={ p.id }>
                    <h4>
                        { p.name }
                        <span className="badge badge-pill badge-primary float-right">
                            ${ p.price.toFixed(2) }
                        </span>
                    </h4>
                    <div className="card-text bg-white p-1">
                        { p.description }
                    </div>
                </div>
            )
    }
}
```

Components are created to perform small tasks or display small amounts of content and are combined to create more complex features. The ProductList component defined in Listing 5-14 is responsible for displaying details of a list of products, whose details are received through a prop named product. Props are used to configure components and allow them to do their work—such as display details of a product—without getting involved in where the data comes from. The ProductList component generates HTML content that includes the value of each product's name, price, and description properties, but it doesn't have knowledge of how those products are defined in the application or whether they have been defined locally or retrieved from a remote server.

Next, I added a file called `CategoryNavigation.js` to the `src/shop` folder and defined the component shown in Listing 5-15.

Listing 5-15. The Contents of the CategoryNavigation.js File in the src/shop Folder

```
import React, { Component } from "react";
import { Link } from "react-router-dom";

export class CategoryNavigation extends Component {

    render() {
        return <React.Fragment>
            <Link className="btn btn-secondary btn-block"
                to={ this.props.baseUrl }>All</Link>
            { this.props.categories && this.props.categories.map(cat =>
                <Link className="btn btn-secondary btn-block" key={ cat }
                    to={ `${this.props.baseUrl}/${cat.toLowerCase()}` }>
                    { cat }
                </Link>
            )}
        </React.Fragment>
    }
}
```

The selection of a category will be handled by navigating to a new URL, which is done using the `Link` component provided by the React Router package. When the user clicks a `Link`, the browser is asked to navigate to a new URL without sending any HTTP requests or reloading the application. The details included in the new URL, such as the selected category in this case, allow different parts of the application to work together.

The `CategoryNavigation` component receives the array of categories through a prop named `categories`. The component checks to ensure that the array has been defined and uses the `map` method to generate the content for each array item. React requires a key prop to be applied to the elements generated by the `map` method so that changes to the array can be handled efficiently, as explained in Chapter 10. The result is a `Link` component for each category that is received in the array with an additional `Link` so that the user can select all products, regardless of category. The `Link` components are styled so they appear as buttons, and the URLs that the browser will navigate to are the combination of a prop called `baseUrl` and the name of the category.

To bring together the product table and the category buttons, I added a file called `Shop.js` to the `src/shop` folder and added the code shown in Listing 5-16.

Listing 5-16. The Contents of the Shop.js File in the src/shop Folder

```
import React, { Component } from "react";
import { CategoryNavigation } from "./CategoryNavigation";
import { ProductList } from "./ProductList";

export class Shop extends Component {

    render() {
        return <div className="container-fluid">
            <div className="row">
                <div className="col bg-dark text-white">
```

```
                    <div className="navbar-brand">SPORTS STORE</div>
                </div>
            </div>
            <div className="row">
                <div className="col-3 p-2">
                    <CategoryNavigation baseUrl="/shop/products"
                        categories={ this.props.categories } />
                </div>
                <div className="col-9 p-2">
                    <ProductList products={ this.props.products } />
                </div>
            </div>
        </div>
    }
}
```

A component can delegate responsibility for part of its content to other components. In its render method, the Shop component defined in Listing 5-16 contains HTML elements that set up a grid structure using Bootstrap CSS classes but delegates responsibility for populating some of the grid cells to the CategoryNavigation and ProductList components. These delegated components are expressed as custom HTML elements in the render method, where the element tag matches the name of the component, like this:

```
...
<ProductList products={ this.props.products } />
...
```

A relationship is created between the two components: the Shop component is the parent of the ProductList, and the ProductList component is the child of the Shop. Parents configure their child components by providing props, and in Listing 5-16, the Shop component passes on the products prop it received from its parent to its ProductList child component, which will be used to display the list of products to the user. The relationships between components and the ways they can be used to create complex features are described in Part 2 of this book.

Connecting to the Data Store and the URL Router

The Shop component and its CategoryNavigation and ProductList children need access to the data store. To connect these components to the features they require, I added a file called ShopConnector.js to the src/shop folder with the code shown in Listing 5-17.

Listing 5-17. The Contents of the ShopConnector.js File in the src/shop Folder

```
import React, { Component } from "react";
import { Switch, Route, Redirect }
    from "react-router-dom";
import { connect } from "react-redux";
import { loadData } from "../data/ActionCreators";
import { DataTypes } from "../data/Types";
import { Shop } from "./Shop";
```

```
const mapStateToProps = (dataStore) => ({
    ...dataStore
})

const mapDispatchToProps = {
    loadData
}

const filterProducts = (products = [], category) =>
    (!category || category === "All")
        ? products
        : products.filter(p => p.category.toLowerCase() === category.toLowerCase());

export const ShopConnector = connect(mapStateToProps, mapDispatchToProps)(
    class extends Component {
        render() {
            return <Switch>
                <Route path="/shop/products/:category?"
                    render={ (routeProps) =>
                        <Shop { ...this.props } { ...routeProps }
                            products={ filterProducts(this.props.products,
                                routeProps.match.params.category) } />} />
                <Redirect to="/shop/products" />
            </Switch>
        }

        componentDidMount() {
            this.props.loadData(DataTypes.CATEGORIES);
            this.props.loadData(DataTypes.PRODUCTS);
        }
    }
)
```

Don't worry if the code in Listing 5-17 seems impenetrable at the moment. The code is more complex than earlier listings because this component brings together and consolidates several features so they can be used more easily elsewhere in the project, as shown in Figure 5-3.

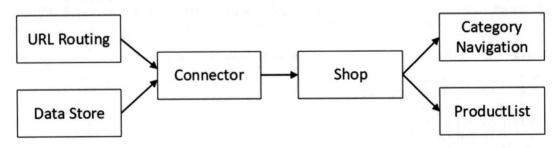

Figure 5-3. *Connecting an application to its services*

The advantage of this approach is that it simplifies adding features or making changes to the application because the components that present content to the user receive their data via props without the need to obtain it directly from the data store or the URL routing system. The disadvantage is that the component that connects the rest of the application to its services can be difficult to write and maintain, as it must combine the features of different packages and present them to its children. The complexity of this component will increase until the end of Chapter 6, when I consolidate the code around the final set of SportsStore shopping features.

The component in Listing 5-17 connects the Redux data store and the URL router to the Shop component. The Redux package provides the connect function, which is used to link a component to a data store so that its props are either values from the data store or functions that dispatch data store actions when they are invoked, as described in Chapter 20. It is the connect function that has led to much of the code in Listing 5-17 because it requires mappings between the data store and the component's props, which can be verbose. The mappings in Listing 5-17 give the Shop component access to all of the properties defined in the data store, which consists of the product and category data at present but will include other features later.

■ **Tip** You can be more specific in the data store properties you map to props, as demonstrated in Chapter 20, but I have mapped all of the products, which is a useful approach when you start developing a new project because it means you don't have to remember to map new properties each time you enhance the data store.

The product data must be filtered using the selected category, which is accessed through the features provided by the React Router package. A Route is used to select the component that will be displayed to the user when the browser navigates to a specific URL. The Route in Listing 5-17 matches the URLs from Table 5-3, like this:

```
...
<Route path="/shop/products/:category?" render={ (routeProps) =>
...
```

The path prop tells the Route to wait until the browser navigates to the /shop/products URL. If there is an additional segment in the URL, such as /shop/products/running, then the contents of that segment will be assigned to a parameter named category, which is how the user's category selection will be determined.

When the browser navigates to a URL that matches the path prop, the Route displays the content specified by the render prop, like this:

```
...
<Route path="/shop/products/:category?" render={ (routeProps) =>
    <Shop { ...this.props } { ...routeProps }
        products={ filterProducts(this.props.products,
            routeProps.match.params.category) } />} />
...
```

This is the point at which the data store and the URL routing features are combined. The Shop component needs to know which category the user has selected, which is available through the argument passed to the Route component's render prop. The category is combined with the data from the data store both of which are passed on to the Shop component. The order in which props are applied to a component allows props to be overridden, which I have relied on to replace the products data obtained from the data store with the result from the filterProduct function, which selects only the products in the category chosen by the user.

The Route is used in conjunction with Switch and Redirect components, both of which are part of the React Router package and which combine to redirect the browser to /shop/products if the browser's current URL isn't matched by the Route.

The ShopConnector component uses the componentDidMount method to load the data into the data store. The componentDidMount method is part of the React component lifecycle, which is described in detail in Chapter 13.

Adding the Shop to the Application

In Listing 5-18, I have set up the data store and the URL routing features and incorporated the ShopConnector component into the application.

Listing 5-18. Adding Routing and a Data Store to the App.js File in the src Folder

```
import React, { Component } from "react";
import { SportsStoreDataStore } from "./data/DataStore";
import { Provider } from "react-redux";
import { BrowserRouter as Router, Route, Switch, Redirect }
    from "react-router-dom";
import { ShopConnector } from "./shop/ShopConnector";

export default class App extends Component {

    render() {
        return <Provider store={ SportsStoreDataStore }>
            <Router>
                <Switch>
                    <Route path="/shop" component={ ShopConnector } />
                    <Redirect to="/shop" />
                </Switch>
            </Router>
        </Provider>
    }
}
```

The data store is applied to the application using a Provider, with the store prop being assigned the data store created in Listing 5-13. The URL routing features are applied to the application using the Router component, which I have supplemented using the Switch, Route, and Redirect components. The Redirect will navigate to the /shop URL, which matches the path prop of the Route and displays the ShopConnector component, producing the result shown in Figure 5-4. Clicking a category button redirects the browser to a new URL, such as /shop/products/watersports, which has the effect of filtering the products that are displayed.

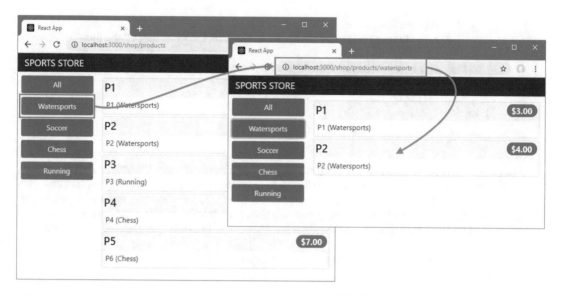

Figure 5-4. *Creating the basic shopping features*

Improving the Category Selection Buttons

The category selection buttons work but don't clearly reflect the current category to the user. To remedy this, I added a file called ToggleLink.js to the src folder and used it to define the component shown in Listing 5-19.

■ **Tip** I added this component to the src folder because I will use it for other parts of the application once the shop has been completed. There are no hard-and-fast rules about how a React project is organized, but I tend to keep related files grouped together in folders.

Listing 5-19. The Contents of the ToggleLink.js File in the src Folder

```
import React, { Component } from "react";
import { Route, Link } from "react-router-dom";

export class ToggleLink extends Component {

    render() {
        return <Route path={ this.props.to } exact={ this.props.exact }
                children={ routeProps => {

            const baseClasses = this.props.className || "m-2 btn btn-block";
            const activeClass = this.props.activeClass || "btn-primary";
            const inActiveClass = this.props.inActiveClass || "btn-secondary"
```

```
            const combinedClasses =
                `${baseClasses} ${routeProps.match ? activeClass : inActiveClass}`

            return <Link to={ this.props.to } className={ combinedClasses }>
                    { this.props.children }
                </Link>
        }} />
    }
}
```

The React Router package provides a component that indicates when a specific URL has been matched, but it doesn't work well with the Bootstrap CSS classes, as I describe in Chapter 22, where I explain how the ToggleLink component works in detail. For this chapter, it is enough to know that the Route component can be used to provide access to the URL routing system in order to get details about the current route. In Listing 5-20, I have updated the CategoryNavigation component to use the ToggleLink component.

Listing 5-20. Using ToggleLinks in the CategoryNavigation.js File in the src/shop Folder

```
import React, { Component } from "react";
//import { Link } from "react-router-dom";
import { ToggleLink } from "../ToggleLink";

export class CategoryNavigation extends Component {

    render() {
        return <React.Fragment>
            <ToggleLink to={ this.props.baseUrl } exact={ true }>All</ToggleLink>
            { this.props.categories && this.props.categories.map(cat =>
                <ToggleLink key={ cat }
                    to={ `${this.props.baseUrl}/${cat.toLowerCase()}` }>
                    { cat }
                </ToggleLink>
            )}
        </React.Fragment>
    }
}
```

The effect is to clearly indicate which category has been selected, as shown in Figure 5-5.

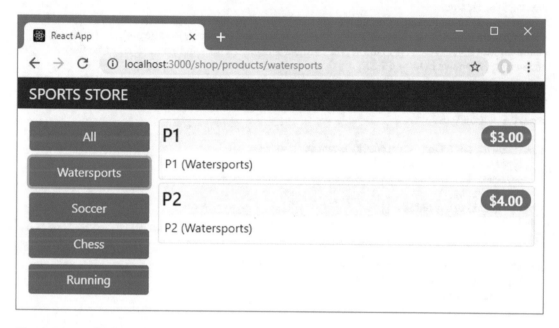

Figure 5-5. *Highlighting the selected component*

Adding the Shopping Cart

The shopping cart will allow the user to select several products in a single purchase before checking out. In the sections that follow, I add extend the data store to keep track of the user's product selections and create components that provide detailed and summary cart views.

Extending the Data Store

To extend the data store to add support for tracking the user's product selections, I added the action types shown in Listing 5-21.

Listing 5-21. Defining Action Types in the Types.js File in the src/data Folder

```
export const DataTypes = {
    PRODUCTS: "products",
    CATEGORIES: "categories"
}

export const ActionTypes = {
    DATA_LOAD: "data_load",
    CART_ADD: "cart_add",
    CART_UPDATE: "cart_update",
    CART_REMOVE: "cart_delete",
    CART_CLEAR: "cart_clear"
}
```

The new actions will allow products to be added and removed from the cart and for the entire cart content to be cleared.

You can define action creators and reducers for different parts of the application in the same file, but breaking them into separate files can make development easier, especially in large projects. I added a file called CartActionCreators.js to the src/data folder and used it to define action creators for the new action types, as shown in Listing 5-22.

Listing 5-22. The Contents of the CartActionCreators.js File in the src/data Folder

```
import { ActionTypes} from "./Types";

export const addToCart = (product, quantity) => ({
    type: ActionTypes.CART_ADD,
    payload: {
        product,
        quantity: quantity || 1
    }
});

export const updateCartQuantity = (product, quantity) => ({
    type: ActionTypes.CART_UPDATE,
    payload: { product, quantity }
})

export const removeFromCart = (product) => ({
    type: ActionTypes.CART_REMOVE,
    payload: product
})

export const clearCart = () => ({
    type: ActionTypes.CART_CLEAR
})
```

The action objects created by the functions in Listing 5-22 have a payload property that carries the data required to execute the action. To define a reducer that will process cart-related actions, I added a file called CartReducer.js in the src/data folder and defined the function shown in Listing 5-23.

Listing 5-23. The Contents of the CartReducer.js File in the src/data Folder

```
import { ActionTypes } from "./Types";

export const CartReducer = (storeData, action) => {
    let newStore = { cart: [], cartItems: 0, cartPrice: 0, ...storeData }
    switch(action.type) {
        case ActionTypes.CART_ADD:
            const p = action.payload.product;
            const q = action.payload.quantity;

            let existing = newStore.cart.find(item => item.product.id === p.id);
            if (existing) {
                existing.quantity += q;
            } else {
```

```
                    newStore.cart = [...newStore.cart, action.payload];
                }
                newStore.cartItems += q;
                newStore.cartPrice += p.price * q;
                return newStore;

        case ActionTypes.CART_UPDATE:
                newStore.cart = newStore.cart.map(item => {
                    if (item.product.id === action.payload.product.id) {
                        const diff = action.payload.quantity - item.quantity;
                        newStore.cartItems += diff;
                        newStore.cartPrice+= (item.product.price * diff);
                        return action.payload;
                    } else {
                        return item;
                    }
                });
                return newStore;

        case ActionTypes.CART_REMOVE:
                let selection = newStore.cart.find(item =>
                    item.product.id === action.payload.id);
                newStore.cartItems -= selection.quantity;
                newStore.cartPrice -= selection.quantity * selection.product.price;
                newStore.cart = newStore.cart.filter(item => item !== selection );
                return newStore;

        case ActionTypes.CART_CLEAR:
                return { ...storeData, cart: [], cartItems: 0, cartPrice: 0}

        default:
                return storeData || {};
    }
}
```

The reducer for the cart actions keeps track of the user's product selection by adding a cart property to the data store and assigning it an array of objects that have product and quantity properties. There are also cartItems and cartPrice properties that keep track of the number of items in the cart and their total price.

■ **Tip** It is important to keep the structure of your data store flat because changes deep in an object hierarchy won't be detected and displayed to the user. It is for this reason that the cart, cartItems, and cartPrice properties are defined alongside the products and categories properties in the data store, rather than grouped together into a single structure.

By default, the Redux data store uses only one reducer, but it is easy to combine multiple reducers to suit your project. There is built-in support for dividing up responsibilities for the data store between multiple reducers, as described in Chapter 19, but this splits up the data so each reducer can see only part of the model. For the SportsStore application, I want each reducer to have access to the complete data store, so

I added a file called CommonReducer.js to the src/data folder and used it to define the function shown in Listing 5-24.

Listing 5-24. The Contents of the CommonReducer.js File in the src/data Folder

```
export const CommonReducer = (...reducers) => (storeData, action) => {
    for (let i = 0; i < reducers.length; i++ ) {
        let newStore = reducers[i](storeData, action);
        if (newStore !== storeData) {
            return newStore;
        }
    }
    return storeData;
}
```

The commonReducer function combines multiple reducers into a single function and asks each of them to handle actions. Reducers return new objects when they modify the contents of the data store, which makes it easy to detect when an action has been handled. The result is that the SportsStore data store can support multiple reducers where the first to change the data store is considered to have processed the action. In Listing 5-25, I have updated the data store configuration to use the commonReducer function to combine the shop and cart reducers.

Listing 5-25. Combining Reducers in the DataStore.js File in the src/data Folder

```
import { createStore } from "redux";
import { ShopReducer } from "./ShopReducer";
import { CartReducer } from "./CartReducer";
import { CommonReducer } from "./CommonReducer";

export const SportsStoreDataStore
    = createStore(CommonReducer(ShopReducer, CartReducer));
```

Creating the Cart Summary Component

To show the user a summary of their shopping cart, I added a file called CartSummary.js in the src/shop folder and used it to define the component shown in Listing 5-26.

Listing 5-26. The Contents of the CartSummary.js File in the src/shop Folder

```
import React, { Component } from "react";
import { Link } from "react-router-dom";

export class CartSummary extends Component {

    getSummary = () => {
        if (this.props.cartItems > 0) {
            return <span>
                { this.props.cartItems } item(s),
                ${ this.props.cartPrice.toFixed(2)}
            </span>
```

```
        } else {
            return <span>Your cart: (empty) </span>
        }
    }

    getLinkClasses = () => {
        return `btn btn-sm bg-dark text-white
            ${ this.props.cartItems === 0 ? "disabled": ""}`;
    }

    render() {
        return <div className="float-right">
            <small>
                { this.getSummary() }
                <Link className={ this.getLinkClasses() }
                        to="/shop/cart">
                    <i className="fa fa-shopping-cart"></i>
                </Link>
            </small>
        </div>
    }
}
```

The component defined in Listing 5-26 receives the data it requires through cartItems and cartPrice props, which are used to create a summary of the component, along with a Link that will navigate to the / shop/cart URL when clicked. The Link is disabled when the value of the items prop is zero to prevent the user from progressing without selecting at least one product.

■ **Tip**   The i element used as the content of the Link applies a cart icon from the Font Awesome package added to the project in Listing 5-2. See https://fontawesome.com for more details and the full range of icons available.

React handles many aspects of web application development well, but there are some common tasks that are harder to achieve than you might be used to. One example is conditional rendering, where a data value is used to select different content to present to the user or different values for props. The cleanest approach in React is to define a method that uses JavaScript to return a result expressed as HTML, like the getSummary and getLinkClasses methods in Listing 5-26, which are invoked in the component's render method. The other approach is to use the && operator inline, which works well for simple expressions.

In Listing 5-27, I connected the cart-related additions from the data store to the rest of the application, along with the action creator functions.

Listing 5-27. Connecting the Cart in the ShopConnector.js File in the src/shop Folder

```
import React, { Component } from "react";
import { Switch, Route, Redirect }
    from "react-router-dom";
import { connect } from "react-redux";
import { loadData } from "../data/ActionCreators";
import { DataTypes } from "../data/Types";
```

```
import { Shop } from "./Shop";
import { addToCart, updateCartQuantity, removeFromCart, clearCart }
    from "../data/CartActionCreators";

const mapStateToProps = (dataStore) => ({
    ...dataStore
})

const mapDispatchToProps = {
    loadData,addToCart, updateCartQuantity, removeFromCart, clearCart
}

const filterProducts = (products = [], category) =>
    (!category || category === "All")
        ? products
        : products.filter(p => p.category.toLowerCase() === category.toLowerCase());

export const ShopConnector = connect(mapStateToProps, mapDispatchToProps)(
    class extends Component {
        render() {
            return <Switch>
                <Route path="/shop/products/:category?"
                    render={ (routeProps) =>
                        <Shop { ...this.props } { ...routeProps }
                            products={ filterProducts(this.props.products,
                                routeProps.match.params.category) } />} />
                <Redirect to="/shop/products" />
            </Switch>
        }

        componentDidMount() {
            this.props.loadData(DataTypes.CATEGORIES);
            this.props.loadData(DataTypes.PRODUCTS);
        }
    }
)
```

In Listing 5-28, I added a CartSummary to the content rendered by the Shop component, which will ensure that details of the user's selections are shown above the list of products.

Listing 5-28. Adding the Summary in the Shop.js File in the src/shop Folder

```
import React, { Component } from "react";
import { CategoryNavigation } from "./CategoryNavigation";
import { ProductList } from "./ProductList";
import { CartSummary } from "./CartSummary";

export class Shop extends Component {

    render() {
        return <div className="container-fluid">
            <div className="row">
```

```
            <div className="col bg-dark text-white">
                <div className="navbar-brand">SPORTS STORE</div>
                <CartSummary { ...this.props } />
            </div>
        </div>
        <div className="row">
            <div className="col-3 p-2">
                <CategoryNavigation baseUrl="/shop/products"
                    categories={ this.props.categories } />
            </div>
            <div className="col-9 p-2">
                <ProductList products={ this.props.products }
                    addToCart={ this.props.addToCart } />
            </div>
        </div>
    </div>
    }
}
```

To allow the user to add a product to the cart, I added a button alongside the description of each product produced by the ProductList component, as shown in Listing 5-29.

Listing 5-29. Adding a Button in the ProductList.js File in the src/shop Folder

```
import React, { Component } from "react";

export class ProductList extends Component {

    render() {
        if (this.props.products == null || this.props.products.length === 0) {
            return <h5 className="p-2">No Products</h5>
        }
        return this.props.products.map(p =>
                <div className="card m-1 p-1 bg-light" key={ p.id }>
                    <h4>
                        { p.name }
                        <span className="badge badge-pill badge-primary float-right">
                            ${ p.price.toFixed(2) }
                        </span>
                    </h4>
                    <div className="card-text bg-white p-1">
                        { p.description }
                        <button className="btn btn-success btn-sm float-right"
                            onClick={ () => this.props.addToCart(p) } >
                                Add To Cart
                        </button>
                    </div>
                </div>
            )
    }
}
```

React provides props that are used to register handlers for events, as described in Chapter 12. The handler for the click event, which is triggered when an element is clicked, is onClick, and the function that is specified invokes the addToCart prop, which is mapped to the data store action creator of the same name.

The result is that each product is shown with an Add To Cart button. When the button is clicked, the data store is updated, and the summary of the user's selections reflects the additional item and the new total price, as shown in Figure 5-6.

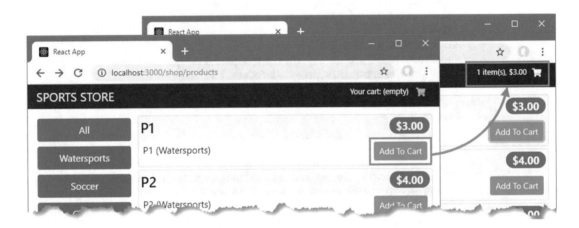

Figure 5-6. *Adding a product to the cart*

Adding the Cart Detail Component

To provide the user with a detailed view of their selections, I added a file called CartDetails.js to the src/shop folder and used it to define the component shown in Listing 5-30.

Listing 5-30. The Contents of the CartDetails.js File in the src/shop Folder

```
import React, { Component } from "react";
import { Link } from "react-router-dom";
import { CartDetailsRows } from "./CartDetailsRows";

export class CartDetails extends Component {

    getLinkClasses = () => `btn btn-secondary m-1
        ${this.props.cartItems === 0 ? "disabled": ""}`;

    render() {
        return <div className="m-3">
            <h2 className="text-center">Your Cart</h2>
            <table className="table table-bordered table-striped">
                <thead>
                    <tr>
                        <th>Quantity</th>
                        <th>Product</th>
                        <th className="text-right">Price</th>
```

```
                    <th className="text-right">Subtotal</th>
                    <th/>
                </tr>
            </thead>
            <tbody>
                <CartDetailsRows cart={ this.props.cart}
                    cartPrice={ this.props.cartPrice }
                    updateQuantity={ this.props.updateCartQuantity }
                    removeFromCart={ this.props.removeFromCart } />
            </tbody>
        </table>
        <div className="text-center">
            <Link className="btn btn-primary m-1" to="/shop">
                Continue Shopping
            </Link>
            <Link className={ this.getLinkClasses() } to="/shop/checkout">
                Checkout
            </Link>
        </div>
    </div>
    }
}
```

The CartDetails component presents a table to the user, along with Link components that return to the product list or navigate to the /shop/checkout URL, which starts the checkout process.

The CartDetails component relies on a CartDetailsRows component to display details of the user's product selection. To create this component, I added a file called CartDetailsRows.js to the src/shop folder and used it to define the component shown in Listing 5-31.

Listing 5-31. The Contents of the CartDetailsRows.js File in the src/shop Folder

```
import React, { Component } from "react";

export class CartDetailsRows extends Component {

    handleChange = (product, event) => {
        this.props.updateQuantity(product, event.target.value);
    }

    render() {
        if (!this.props.cart || this.props.cart.length === 0) {
            return <tr>
                <td colSpan="5">Your cart is empty</td>
            </tr>
        } else {
            return <React.Fragment>
                { this.props.cart.map(item =>
                    <tr key={ item.product.id }>
                        <td>
                            <input type="number" value={ item.quantity }
                                onChange={ (ev) =>
```

```
                                  this.handleChange(item.product, ev) } />
                </td>
                <td>{ item.product.name }</td>
                <td>${ item.product.price.toFixed(2) }</td>
                <td>${ (item.quantity * item.product.price).toFixed(2) }</td>
                <td>
                    <button className="btn btn-sm btn-danger"
                        onClick={ () =>
                                this.props.removeFromCart(item.product)}>
                            Remove
                    </button>
                </td>
            </tr>
        )}
        <tr>
            <th colSpan="3" className="text-right">Total:</th>
            <th colSpan="2">${ this.props.cartPrice.toFixed(2) }</th>
        </tr>
        </React.Fragment>
    }
  }
}
```

The render method must return a single top-level element, which is inserted into the HTML in place of the component's element when the HTML document is produced, as explained in Chapter 9. It isn't always possible to return a single HTML element without disrupting the content layout, such as in this example, where multiple table rows are required. For these situations, the React.Fragment element is used. This element is discarded when the content is processed and the elements it contains are added to the HTML document.

Adding the Cart URL to the Routing Configuration

In Listing 5-32, I have updated the routing configuration in the ShopConnector component to add support for the /shop/cart URL.

Listing 5-32. Adding a New URL in the ShopConnector.js File in the src/shop Folder

```
import React, { Component } from "react";
import { Switch, Route, Redirect }
    from "react-router-dom"
import { connect } from "react-redux";
import { loadData } from "../data/ActionCreators";
import { DataTypes } from "../data/Types";
import { Shop } from "./Shop";
import { addToCart, updateCartQuantity, removeFromCart, clearCart }
    from "../data/CartActionCreators";
import { CartDetails } from "./CartDetails";

const mapStateToProps = (dataStore) => ({
    ...dataStore
})
```

```
const mapDispatchToProps = {
    loadData,
    addToCart, updateCartQuantity, removeFromCart, clearCart
}

const filterProducts = (products = [], category) =>
    (!category || category === "All")
        ? products
        : products.filter(p => p.category.toLowerCase() === category.toLowerCase());

export const ShopConnector = connect(mapStateToProps, mapDispatchToProps)(
    class extends Component {
        render() {
            return <Switch>
                <Route path="/shop/products/:category?"
                    render={ (routeProps) =>
                        <Shop { ...this.props } { ...routeProps }
                            products={ filterProducts(this.props.products,
                                routeProps.match.params.category) } />} />
                <Route path="/shop/cart" render={ (routeProps) =>
                    <CartDetails { ...this.props } { ...routeProps }  />} />
                <Redirect to="/shop/products" />
            </Switch>
        }

        componentDidMount() {
            this.props.loadData(DataTypes.CATEGORIES);
            this.props.loadData(DataTypes.PRODUCTS);
        }
    }
)
```

The new Route handles the /shop/cart URL by displaying the CartDetails component, which receives props from both the data store and the routing system. In Listing 5-33, I have updated the Shop component to define a wrapper function around the addToCart action creator that also navigates to the new URL.

Listing 5-33. Navigating to the Cart in the Shop.js File in the src/shop Folder

```
import React, { Component } from "react";
import { CategoryNavigation } from "./CategoryNavigation";
import { ProductList } from "./ProductList";
import { CartSummary } from "./CartSummary";

export class Shop extends Component {

    handleAddToCart = (...args) => {
        this.props.addToCart(...args);
        this.props.history.push("/shop/cart");
    }
```

```
    render() {
        return <div className="container-fluid">
            <div className="row">
                <div className="col bg-dark text-white">
                    <div className="navbar-brand">SPORTS STORE</div>
                    <CartSummary { ...this.props } />
                </div>
            </div>
            <div className="row">
                <div className="col-3 p-2">
                    <CategoryNavigation baseUrl="/shop/products"
                        categories={ this.props.categories } />
                </div>
                <div className="col-9 p-2">
                    <ProductList products={ this.props.products }
                        addToCart={ this.handleAddToCart } />
                </div>
            </div>
        </div>
    }
}
```

The result is that clicking the Add To Cart button for a product displays the updated cart, which provides the user with the choice to return to the product list and make further selections, edit the contents of the cart, or start the checkout process, as shown in Figure 5-7.

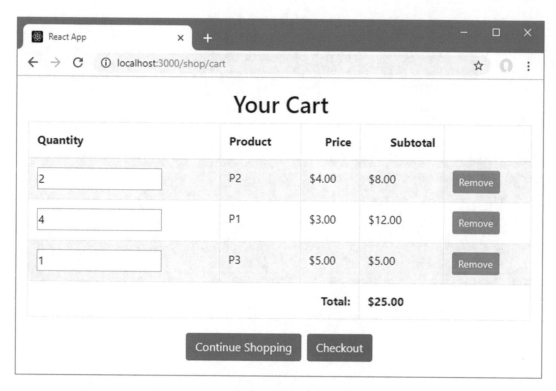

Figure 5-7. *Integrating the cart into the SportsStore project*

The Checkout button returns the user to the `/store/products` URL at the moment, but I add support for checking out in Chapter 6.

Summary

In this chapter, I started development of a realistic React project. The first part of the chapter was spent setting up the Redux data store, which introduces a range of terms—actions, action creators, reducers—that you may not be familiar with but which will soon become second nature. I also set up the React Router package so that the browser's URL can be used to select the content and data that is presented to the user. The foundation these features provides takes time to set up, but you will see that it starts to pay dividends as I add further features to SportsStore. In the next chapter, I add further features to the SportsStore application.

CHAPTER 6

SportsStore: REST and Checkout

In this chapter, I continue adding features to the SportsStore application I created in Chapter 5. I add support for retrieving data from a web service, presenting larger amounts of data in pages and checking out and placing orders.

Preparing for This Chapter

No preparation is required for this chapter, which uses the SportsStore project created in Chapter 5. To start the React development tools and the RESTful web service, open a command prompt, navigate to the sportsstore folder, and run the command shown in Listing 6-1.

■ **Tip** You can download the example project for this chapter—and for all the other chapters in this book—from https://github.com/Apress/pro-react-16.

Listing 6-1. Starting the Development Tools and Web Service

```
npm start
```

The initial build process will take a few seconds, after which a new browser window or tab will open and display the SportsStore application, as shown in Figure 6-1.

© Adam Freeman 2019
A. Freeman, *Pro React 16*, https://doi.org/10.1007/978-1-4842-4451-7_6

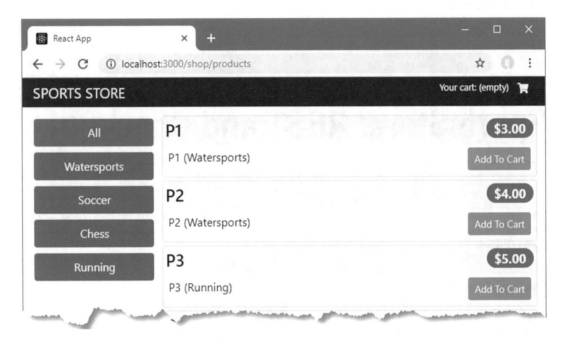

Figure 6-1. *Running the SportsStore application*

Consuming the RESTful Web Service

The basic structure of the SportsStore application is taking shape, and I have enough functionality in place to remove the placeholder data and start using the RESTful web service. In Chapter 7, I use GraphQL, which is a more flexible (and complex) alternative to REST web services, but regular web services are common, and I am going to use a REST web service to provide the SportsStore application with its product data and to submit orders at the end of the checkout process.

I describe REST in more detail in Chapter 23, but for this chapter, I need just one basic HTTP request to get started. Open a new browser tab and request `http://localhost:3500/api/products`. The browser will send an HTTP GET request to the web service that was created in Chapter 5 and started by the command in Listing 6-1. The GET method combined with the URL tells the web service that a list of the products is required and produces the following result:

```
...
[{"id":1,"name":"Kayak","category":"Watersports",
    "description":"A boat for one person","price":275},
 {"id":2,"name":"Lifejacket","category":"Watersports",
    "description":"Protective and fashionable","price":48.95},
 {"id":3,"name":"Soccer Ball","category":"Soccer",
    "description":"FIFA-approved size and weight","price":19.5},
 {"id":4,"name":"Corner Flags","category":"Soccer",
    "description":"Give your playing field a professional touch","price":34.95},
 {"id":5,"name":"Stadium","category":"Soccer",
    "description":"Flat-packed 35,000-seat stadium","price":79500},
```

```
{"id":6,"name":"Thinking Cap","category":"Chess",
    "description":"Improve brain efficiency by 75%","price":16},
{"id":7,"name":"Unsteady Chair","category":"Chess",
    "description":"Secretly give your opponent a disadvantage","price":29.95},
{"id":8,"name":"Human Chess Board","category":"Chess",
    "description":"A fun game for the family","price":75},
{"id":9,"name":"Bling Bling King","category":"Chess",
    "description":"Gold-plated, diamond-studded King","price":1200}]
...
```

The web service responds to requests using the JSON data format, which is easy to deal with in a React application since it is similar to the JavaScript object literal form described in Chapter 4. In the sections that follow, I'll create a foundation for working with the web service and use it to replace the static data that is currently displayed by the SportsStore application.

Creating a Configuration File

Projects often require different URLs in production and development. To avoid hard-coding the URLs into individual JavaScript files, I added a file called Urls.js to the src/data folder and used it to define the configuration data shown in Listing 6-2.

Listing 6-2. The Contents of the Urls.js File in the src/data Folder

```
import { DataTypes } from "./Types";

const protocol = "http";
const hostname = "localhost";
const port = 3500;

export const RestUrls = {
    [DataTypes.PRODUCTS]: `${protocol}://${hostname}:${port}/api/products`,
    [DataTypes.CATEGORIES]: `${protocol}://${hostname}:${port}/api/categories`
}
```

When I prepare the SportsStore application for deployment in Chapter 8, I will be able to configure the URLs required to access the web service in one place. I have used the data types already defined for the data store for consistency, which helps keeps references to the different types of data consistent and reduces the risk of a typo.

Creating a Data Source

I added a file called RestDataSource.js to the src/data folder and added the code shown in Listing 6-3. I want to consolidate the code that is responsible for sending HTTP requests to the web service and processing the results, allowing me to keep it contained in one place in the project.

Listing 6-3. The Contents of the RestDataSource.js File in the src/data Folder

```
import Axios from "axios";
import { RestUrls } from "./Urls";

export class RestDataSource {

    GetData = (dataType) =>
        this.SendRequest("get", RestUrls[dataType]);

    SendRequest = (method, url) => Axios.request({ method, url });
}
```

The RestDataSource class uses the Axios package to make HTTP requests to the web service. Axios is described in Chapter 23 and is a popular package for handling HTTP because it provides a consistent API and automatically processes responses to transform JSON into JavaScript objects. In Listing 6-3, the GetData method uses Axios to send an HTTP request to the web service to get all of the available objects for a specified data type. The result from the GetData method is a Promise that is resolved when the response is received from the web service.

Extending the Data Store

HTTP requests sent by JavaScript code are performed asynchronously. This doesn't fit well with the default behavior of the Redux data store, which responds to changes only when an action is processed by a reducer.

Redux data stores can be extended to support asynchronous operations using a middleware function, which inspects the actions that are sent to the data store and alters them before they are processed. In Chapter 20, I create data store middleware that intercepts actions and delays them while it performs asynchronous requests to get data.

For the SportsStore application, I am going to take a different approach and add support for actions whose payload is a Promise, which I described briefly in Chapter 4. The middleware will wait until the Promise is resolved and then pass on the action using the outcome of the Promise as the payload. I added a file called AsyncMiddleware.js to the src/data folder and added the code shown in Listing 6-4.

Listing 6-4. The Contents of the AsyncMiddleware.js File in the src/data Folder

```
const isPromise = (payload) =>
    (typeof(payload) === "object" || typeof(payload) === "function")
        && typeof(payload.then) === "function";

export const asyncActions = () => (next) => (action) => {
    if (isPromise(action.payload)) {
        action.payload.then(result => next({...action, payload: result}));
    } else {
        next(action)
    }
}
```

The code in Listing 6-4 contains a function that checks to see whether an action's payload is a Promise, which it does by looking for function or objects that have a then function. The asyncAction function will be used as the data store middleware, and it calls then on the Promise to wait for it to be resolved, at which point it uses the result to replace the payload and passes it on, using the next function, which continues the normal path through the data store. Actions whose payloads are not a `Promise` are passed on immediately. In Listing 6-5, I have added the middleware to the data store.

Listing 6-5. Adding Middleware in the DataStore.js File in the src/data Folder

```
import { createStore, applyMiddleware } from "redux";
import { ShopReducer } from "./ShopReducer";
import { CartReducer } from "./CartReducer";
import { CommonReducer } from "./CommonReducer";
import { asyncActions } from "./AsyncMiddleware";

export const SportsStoreDataStore
    = createStore(CommonReducer(ShopReducer, CartReducer),
        applyMiddleware(asyncActions));
```

The `applyMiddleware` is used to wrap the middleware so that it receives the actions, and the result is passed as an argument to the `createStore` function that creates the data store. The effect is that the `asyncActions` function defined in Listing 6-4 will be able to inspect all of the actions sent to the data store and seamlessly deal with those with a `Promise` payload.

Updating the Action Creator

In Listing 6-6, I removed the placeholder data from the store action creator and replaced it with a `Promise` that sends a request using the data source.

Listing 6-6. Using a Promise in the ActionCreators.js File in the src/data Folder

```
import { ActionTypes} from "./Types";
//import { data as phData} from "./placeholderData";
import { RestDataSource } from "./RestDataSource";

const dataSource = new RestDataSource();

export const loadData = (dataType) => ({
    type: ActionTypes.DATA_LOAD,
    payload: dataSource.GetData(dataType)
        .then(response => ({ dataType, data: response.data}))
});
```

When the action object created by the `loadData` function is received by the data store, the middleware defined in Listing 6-5 will wait for the response to be received from the web service and then pass on the action for normal processing, with the result that the SportsStore application displays data obtained remotely, as shown in Figure 6-2.

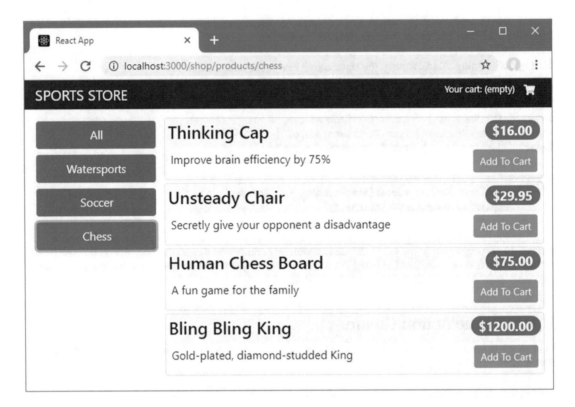

Figure 6-2. *Using data from a web service*

Paginating Data

The SportsStore application is now receiving data from the web service, but most applications have to deal with larger amounts of data, which must be presented to the user in pages. In Listing 6-7, I have used the Faker.js package to generate a larger number of products to replace the data presented by the web service.

Listing 6-7. Increasing the Amount of Data in the data.js File in the sportsstore Folder

```
var faker = require("faker");
var data = [];
var categories = ["Watersports", "Soccer", "Chess", "Running"];
faker.seed(100);
for (let i = 1; i <= 503; i++) {
    var category = faker.helpers.randomize(categories);
    data.push({
        id: i,
        name: faker.commerce.productName(),
        category: category,
        description: `${category}: ${faker.lorem.sentence(3)}`,
        price: Number(faker.commerce.price())
    })
}
```

```
module.exports = function () {
    return {
        categories: categories,
        products: data,
        orders: []
    }
}
```

The Faker.js package is an excellent tool for easily generating data for development and testing, providing contextual data through an API described at https://github.com/Marak/Faker.js. When you save the data.js file, the change will be detected by the server code created in Chapter 5 and loaded into the web service. Reload the SportsStore application in the browser window, and you will see all of the new products shown in a single list, as shown in Figure 6-3. The user can still filter the products using the category buttons, but there is still too much data presented in one go.

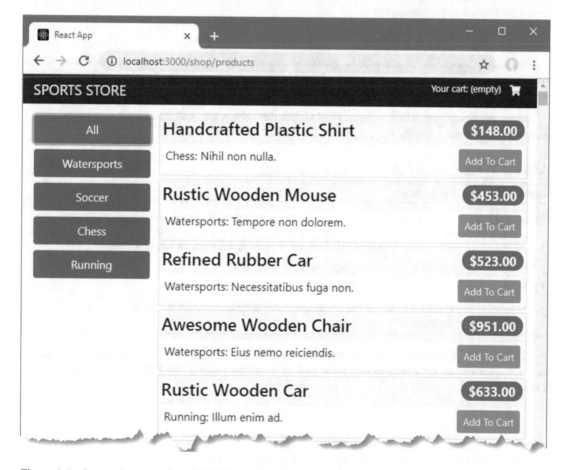

Figure 6-3. *Generating more data for testing pagination*

■ **Tip**   The code in Listing 6-7 creates 503 product objects. It is a good idea to use numbers of objects that are not divisible by the size of the pages you intend to support so that you can be sure that your code deals with a few stragglers on the last page.

Understanding the Web Service Pagination Support

Pagination requires support from the server so that it provides the client with the means to request a subset of the available data and information about how much data is available. There is no standard approach to providing pagination, and you should consult the documentation for the server or service you are using.

The json-server package that provides the RESTful web service for the SportsStore application supports pagination through query strings. Open a new browser window and request the URL shown in Listing 6-8 to see how pagination works.

Listing 6-8. Requesting a Page of Data

```
http://localhost:3500/api/products?category_like=watersports&_page=2&_limit=3&_sort=name
```

The query string for this URL—the part that follows the ? character—asks the web service to return a page of products from a specific category, using the fields described in Table 6-1.

Table 6-1. *The Query String Fields Required for Pagination*

Name	Description
category_like	This field filters the results to include only those objects whose category property matches the field value, which is Watersports in the example URL. If the category field is omitted, then products from all categories will be included in the results.
_page	This field selects the page number.
_limit	This field selects the page size.
_sort	This field specifies the property by which the objects will be sorted before being paginated.

The URL in Listing 6-8 asks the web service to return the second page containing three products from the set that have a category value of Watersports, sorted by the name property, producing the following results:

```
...
[
 {"id":469,"name":"Awesome Fresh Pants","category":"Watersports",
    "description":"Watersports: Quia quam aut.","price":864},
 {"id":19,"name":"Awesome Frozen Car","category":"Watersports",
    "description":"Watersports: A rerum mollitia.","price":314},
  {"id":182,"name":"Awesome Granite Fish", "category":"Watersports",
      description":"Watersports: Hic omnis incidunt.","price":521}
]
...
```

The web service response contains headers that help the client make future requests. Use the browser to request the URL shown in Listing 6-9.

Listing 6-9. Making a Simpler Pagination Request

```
http://localhost:3500/api/products?_page=2&_limit=3
```

The simpler URL makes the result headers easier to understand. Use the browser's F12 developer tools to inspect the response, and you will see that it contains the following headers:

```
...
X-Total-Count: 503
Link: <http://localhost:3500/api/products?_page=1&_limit=3>; rel="first",
      <http://localhost:3500/api/products?_page=1&_limit=3>; rel="prev",
      <http://localhost:3500/api/products?_page=3&_limit=3>; rel="next",
      <http://localhost:3500/api/products?_page=168&_limit=3>; rel="last"
...
```

These are not the only headers in the response, but they have been added specifically to help the client with future pagination requests. The X-Total-Count header provides the total number of objects that are matched by the request URL, which is useful for determining the total number of pages. Since there is no category field in the URL in Listing 6-9, the server has reported that 503 objects are available.

The Link header provides a set of URLs that can be used to query the first and last pages, and the pages before and after the current pages, although clients are not required to use the Link header to formulate subsequent requests.

Changing the HTTP Request and Action

In Listing 6-10, I changed the formulation of the URL for the request that obtains the product data to include request parameters, which will be used to request pages and specify a category. The Axios package will use the parameters to add query string to the request URL.

Listing 6-10. Adding URL Parameters in the RestDataSource.js File in the src/data/rest Folder

```
import Axios from "axios";
import { RestUrls } from "./Urls";

export class RestDataSource {

    GetData = async(dataType, params) =>
        this.SendRequest("get", RestUrls[dataType], params);

    SendRequest = (method, url, params) => Axios.request({
                method, url, params
    });
}
```

In Listing 6-11, I have updated the action created by the loadData action creator so that it includes parameters and adds additional information from the response to the data store.

Listing 6-11. Changing the Action in the ActionCreators.js File in the src/data Folder

```
import { ActionTypes } from "./Types";
import { RestDataSource } from "./RestDataSource";

const dataSource = new RestDataSource();

export const loadData = (dataType, params) => (
    {
        type: ActionTypes.DATA_LOAD,
        payload: dataSource.GetData(dataType, params).then(response =>
            ({ dataType,
                data: response.data,
                total: Number(response.headers["x-total-count"]),
                params
            })
        )
    })
```

When the Promise is resolved by the data store middleware, the action object that is sent to the reducer will contain payload.total and payload.params properties. The total property will contain the value of the X-Total-Count header, which I will use to create the pagination navigation controls. The params property will contain the parameters used to make the request, which I will use to determine when the user has made a change that requires an HTTP request for more data. In Listing 6-12, I have updated the reducer that processes the DATA_LOAD action so that the new action properties are added to the data store.

Listing 6-12. Adding Data Store Properties in the ShopReducer.js File in the src/data Folder

```
import { ActionTypes } from "./Types";

export const ShopReducer = (storeData, action) => {
    switch(action.type) {
        case ActionTypes.DATA_LOAD:
            return {
                ...storeData,
                [action.payload.dataType]: action.payload.data,
                [`${action.payload.dataType}_total`]: action.payload.total,
                [`${action.payload.dataType}_params`]: action.payload.params
            };
        default:
            return storeData || {};
    }
}
```

Creating the Data Loading Component

To create a component that takes care of obtaining the product data, I added a file called DataGetter.js to the src/data folder and used it to define the component shown in Listing 6-13.

Listing 6-13. The Contents of the DataGetter.js File in the src/data Folder

```
import React, { Component } from "react";
import { DataTypes } from "../data/Types";

export class DataGetter extends Component {

    render() {
        return <React.Fragment>{ this.props.children }</React.Fragment>
    }

    componentDidUpdate = () => this.getData();
    componentDidMount = () => this.getData();

    getData = () => {
        const dsData = this.props.products_params || {} ;
        const rtData = {
            _limit: this.props.pageSize || 5,
            _sort: this.props.sortKey || "name",
            _page: this.props.match.params.page || 1,
            category_like: (this.props.match.params.category || "") === "all"
                ? "" : this.props.match.params.category
        }

        if (Object.keys(rtData).find(key => dsData[key] !== rtData[key])) {
            this.props.loadData(DataTypes.PRODUCTS, rtData);
        }
    }
}
```

This component renders the content its parent provides between the start and end tags using the children props. This is useful for defining components that provide services to the application but that don't present content to the user. In this case, I need a component that can receive details of the current route and its parameters and also access the data store. The component's componentDidMount and componentDidUpdate methods, both part of the component lifecycle described in Chapter 13, call the getData method, which gets the parameters from the URL and compares them with those in the data store that were added after the last request. If there has been a change, a new action is dispatched that will load the data the user requires.

In addition to the category and page number, which are taken from the URL, the action is created with _sort and _limit parameters that order the results and set the data size. The values used for sorting and for setting the page size will be obtained from the data store.

Updating the Store Connector Component

To introduce the pagination support into the application, I updated the ShopConnector component, which is responsible for connecting the shop features in the application to the data store and the URL router. The changes in Listing 6-14 add the DataGetter component and remove the category filter for product data (since the products will already be filtered by the web service).

Listing 6-14. Adding Pagination in the ShopConnector.js File in the src/shop Folder

```
import React, { Component } from "react";
import { Switch, Route, Redirect }
    from "react-router-dom"
import { connect } from "react-redux";
import { loadData } from "../data/ActionCreators";
import { DataTypes } from "../data/Types";
import { Shop } from "./Shop";
import { addToCart, updateCartQuantity, removeFromCart, clearCart }
    from "../data/CartActionCreators";
import { CartDetails } from "./CartDetails";
import { DataGetter } from "../data/DataGetter";

const mapStateToProps = (dataStore) => ({
    ...dataStore
})

const mapDispatchToProps = {
    loadData,
    addToCart, updateCartQuantity, removeFromCart, clearCart
}

// const filterProducts = (products = [], category) =>
//      (!category || category === "All")
//          ? products
//          : products.filter(p =>
//              p.category.toLowerCase() === category.toLowerCase());

export const ShopConnector = connect(mapStateToProps, mapDispatchToProps)(
    class extends Component {
        render() {
            return <Switch>
                <Redirect from="/shop/products/:category"
                    to="/shop/products/:category/1" exact={ true } />
                <Route path={ "/shop/products/:category/:page" }
                    render={ (routeProps) =>
                        <DataGetter { ...this.props } { ...routeProps }>
                            <Shop { ...this.props } { ...routeProps }  />
                        </DataGetter>
                    } />
                <Route path="/shop/cart" render={ (routeProps) =>
                        <CartDetails { ...this.props } { ...routeProps }  />} />
                <Redirect to="/shop/products/all/1" />
            </Switch>
        }

        componentDidMount() {
            this.props.loadData(DataTypes.CATEGORIES);
            //this.props.loadData(DataTypes.PRODUCTS);
        }
    }
)
```

I have updated the routing configuration to support pagination. The first routing change is the addition of a Redirect, which matches URLs that have a category but no page and redirects them to the URL for the first page of the selected category. I also changed the existing Redirect so that it redirects any unmatched URLs to /shop/products/all.

The result is a block of code that looks more complicated than it is. When the ShopConnector component is asked to render its content, it uses a Route to match the URL and get category and parameters, like this:

```
...
<Route path={ "/shop/products/:category/:page" }
...
```

Immediately before the Route is a Redirect that matches URLs that have one segment and redirects the browser to a URL that will select the first page:

```
...
<Redirect from="/shop/products/:category"
          to="/shop/products/:category/1" exact={ true } />
...
```

This redirection ensures that there is always category and page values to work with. The other Redirect matches any other URLs and redirects them to the URL for the first page of the products, unfiltered by category.

```
...
<Redirect to="/shop/products/all/1" />
...
```

Updating the All Category Button

The routing components used in Listing 6-14 require a corresponding change to the All category button so that it is highlighted when no category has been selected, as shown in Listing 6-15.

Listing 6-15. Updating the All Button in the CategoryNavigation.js File in the src/shop Folder

```
import React, { Component } from "react";
import { ToggleLink } from "../ToggleLink";

export class CategoryNavigation extends Component {

    render() {
        return <React.Fragment>
            <ToggleLink to={ `${this.props.baseUrl}/all` } exact={ false }>
                All
            </ToggleLink>
            { this.props.categories && this.props.categories.map(cat =>
                <ToggleLink key={ cat }
                    to={ `${this.props.baseUrl}/${cat.toLowerCase()}`}>
                    { cat }
                </ToggleLink>
            )}
```

```
        </React.Fragment>
    }
}
```

I have added /all to the URL matched by the ToggleLink component and set the exact prop to false so that URLs such as /shop/products/all/1 will be matched. The effect is that the application requests individual pages of data from the web service, which is also responsible for filtering based on category. Each time the user clicks a category button, the DataGetter component requests new data, as shown in Figure 6-4.

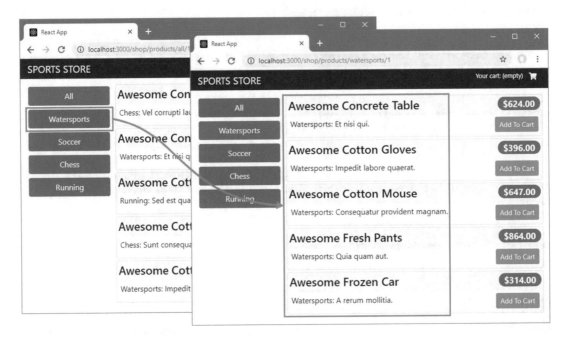

Figure 6-4. *Requesting pages of data from the web service*

Creating the Pagination Controls

The next step is to create a component that will allow the user to navigate to different pages and change the page size. Listing 6-16 defines new data store action types that will be used to change the page size and specify the property that will be used for sorting results.

Listing 6-16. Adding New Action Types in the Types.js File in the src/data Folder

```
export const DataTypes = {
    PRODUCTS: "products",
    CATEGORIES: "categories"
}

export const ActionTypes = {
    DATA_LOAD: "data_load",
    DATA_SET_SORT_PROPERTY: "data_set_sort",
    DATA_SET_PAGESIZE: "data_set_pagesize",
```

```
        CART_ADD: "cart_add",
        CART_UPDATE: "cart_update",
        CART_REMOVE: "cart_delete",
        CART_CLEAR: "cart_clear"
}
```

In Listing 6-17, I added new action creators that create actions using the new types.

Listing 6-17. Defining Creators in the ActionCreators.js File in the src/data Folder

```
import { ActionTypes } from "./Types";
import { RestDataSource } from "./RestDataSource";

const dataSource = new RestDataSource();

export const loadData = (dataType, params) => (
    {
        type: ActionTypes.DATA_LOAD,
        payload: dataSource.GetData(dataType, params).then(response =>
            ({ dataType,
               data: response.data,
               total: Number(response.headers["x-total-count"]),
               params
            })
        )
    })

export const setPageSize = (newSize) =>
    ({ type: ActionTypes.DATA_SET_PAGESIZE, payload: newSize});

export const setSortProperty = (newProp) =>
    ({ type: ActionTypes.DATA_SET_SORT_PROPERTY, payload: newProp});
```

In Listing 6-18, I extended the reducer to support the new actions.

Listing 6-18. Supporting New Actions in the ShopReducer.js File in the src/data Folder

```
import { ActionTypes } from "./Types";

export const ShopReducer = (storeData, action) => {
    switch(action.type) {
        case ActionTypes.DATA_LOAD:
            return {
                ...storeData,
                [action.payload.dataType]: action.payload.data,
                [`${action.payload.dataType}_total`]: action.payload.total,
                [`${action.payload.dataType}_params`]: action.payload.params
            };
```

```
        case ActionTypes.DATA_SET_PAGESIZE:
            return { ...storeData, pageSize: action.payload }
        case ActionTypes.DATA_SET_SORT_PROPERTY:
            return { ...storeData, sortKey: action.payload }
        default:
            return storeData || {};
    }
}
```

To produce the HTML elements that will allow the user to use the pagination features, I added a file called PaginationControls.js to the src folder and used it to define the component shown in Listing 6-19.

Listing 6-19. The Contents of the PaginationControls.js File in the src Folder

```
import React, { Component } from "react";
import { PaginationButtons } from "./PaginationButtons";

export class PaginationControls extends Component {

    constructor(props) {
        super(props);
        this.pageSizes = this.props.sizes || [5, 10, 25, 100];
        this.sortKeys = this.props.keys || ["Name", "Price"];
    }

    handlePageSizeChange = (ev) => {
        this.props.setPageSize(ev.target.value);
    }

    handleSortPropertyChange = (ev) => {
        this.props.setSortProperty(ev.target.value);
    }

    render() {
        return <div className="m-2">
                <div className="text-center m-1">
                    <PaginationButtons currentPage={this.props.currentPage}
                        pageCount={this.props.pageCount}
                        navigate={ this.props.navigateToPage }/>
                </div>
                <div className="form-inline justify-content-center">
                    <select className="form-control"
                            onChange={ this.handlePageSizeChange }
                            value={ this.props.pageSize|| this.pageSizes[0] }>
                        { this.pageSizes.map(s =>
                            <option value={s} key={s}>{s} per page</option>
                        )}
                    </select>
                    <select className="form-control"
                            onChange={ this.handleSortPropertyChange }
                            value={ this.props.sortKey || this.sortKeys[0] }>
                        { this.sortKeys.map(k =>
```

```
                <option value={k.toLowerCase()} key={k}>
                    Sort By { k }
                </option>
            )}
        </select>
    </div>
</div>
    }
}
```

The `PaginationControls` component uses `select` elements to allow the user to change the page size and the property used to sort the results. The `option` elements that provide the individual values that can be selected can be configured using props, which will allow me to reuse this component for the administration features in Chapter 7. If no props are supplied, then default values suitable for paginating products are used.

The `onChange` prop is applied to the `select` elements to respond to user changes, which are handled by methods that receive the event triggered by the change and invoke function props that are received from the parent component.

The process of generating the buttons that will allow movement between pages has been delegated to a component named `PaginationButtons`. To create this component, I added a file called `PaginationButtons.js` to the `src` folder and added the code shown in Listing 6-20.

Listing 6-20. The Contents of the PaginationButtons.js File in the src Folder

```
import React, { Component } from "react";

export class PaginationButtons extends Component {

    getPageNumbers = () => {
        if (this.props.pageCount < 4) {
            return [...Array(this.props.pageCount + 1).keys()].slice(1);
        } else if (this.props.currentPage <= 4) {
            return [1, 2, 3, 4, 5];
        } else  if (this.props.currentPage > this.props.pageCount - 4) {
            return [...Array(5).keys()].reverse()
                .map(v => this.props.pageCount - v);
        } else {
            return [this.props.currentPage -1, this.props.currentPage,
                this.props.currentPage + 1];
        }
    }

    render() {
        const current = this.props.currentPage;
        const pageCount = this.props.pageCount;
        const navigate = this.props.navigate;
        return <React.Fragment>
            <button onClick={ () => navigate(current  - 1) }
                disabled={ current === 1 } className="btn btn-secondary mx-1">
                    Previous
            </button>
```

```
                  { current > 4 &&
                      <React.Fragment>
                          <button className="btn btn-secondary mx-1"
                              onClick={ () => navigate(1)}>1</button>
                          <span className="h4">...</span>
                      </React.Fragment>
                  }
                  { this.getPageNumbers().map(num =>
                      <button className={ `btn mx-1 ${num === current
                              ? "btn-primary": "btn-secondary"}`}
                          onClick={ () => navigate(num)} key={ num }>
                              { num }
                      </button>)}
                  { current <= (pageCount - 4) &&
                      <React.Fragment>
                          <span className="h4">...</span>
                          <button className="btn btn-secondary mx-1"
                                  onClick={ () => navigate(pageCount)}>
                              { pageCount }
                          </button>
                      </React.Fragment>
                  }
                  <button onClick={ () => navigate(current + 1) }
                      disabled={ current === pageCount }
                      className="btn btn-secondary mx-1">
                          Next
                  </button>
              </React.Fragment>
          }
      }
```

Creating the pagination buttons is a complex process, and it is easy to get bogged down in the detail. The approach I have taken in Listing 6-20 aims to strike a balance between simplicity and providing the user with enough context to navigate through large amounts of data.

To connect the pagination controls to the product data in the store, I added a file called ProductPageConnector.js to the src/shop folder and defined the component shown in Listing 6-21.

Listing 6-21. The Contents of the ProductPageConnector.js File in the src/shop Folder

```
import { connect } from "react-redux";
import { withRouter } from "react-router-dom";
import { setPageSize, setSortProperty } from "../data/ActionCreators";

const mapStateToProps = dataStore => dataStore;
const mapDispatchToProps = { setPageSize, setSortProperty };

const mergeProps = (dataStore, actionCreators, router) => ({
    ...dataStore, ...router, ...actionCreators,
    currentPage: Number(router.match.params.page),
```

```
    pageCount: Math.ceil((dataStore.products_total
        | dataStore.pageSize || 5)/(dataStore.pageSize || 5)),
    navigateToPage: (page) => router.history
        .push(`/shop/products/${router.match.params.category}/${page}`),
})

export const ProductPageConnector = (PageComponent) =>
    withRouter(connect(mapStateToProps, mapDispatchToProps,
        mergeProps)(PageComponent))
```

As I explained earlier, the complexity in a React application often coalesces where different features are combined, which is the connector components in the SportsStore application. The code in Listing 6-21 creates a higher-order component (known as a *HOC* and described in Chapter 14), which is a function that provides features to another component through its props. The HOC is named ProductPageConnector, and it combines data store properties, action creators, and route parameters to provide the pagination control components with access to the features they require. The connect function is the same one I used in Chapter 5 to connect a component to the data store, and it has been used in conjunction with the withRouter function, which is its counterpart from the React Router package and which provides a component with the route details from the closest Route. In Listing 6-22, I have applied the higher-order component to the PaginationControls component and added the result to the content presented to the user.

Listing 6-22. Adding Pagination Controls in the Shop.js File in the src/shop Folder

```
import React, { Component } from "react";
import { CategoryNavigation } from "./CategoryNavigation";
import { ProductList } from "./ProductList";
import { CartSummary } from "./CartSummary";
import { ProductPageConnector } from "./ProductPageConnector";
import { PaginationControls } from "../PaginationControls";

const ProductPages = ProductPageConnector(PaginationControls);

export class Shop extends Component {

    handleAddToCart = (...args) => {
        this.props.addToCart(...args);
        this.props.history.push("/shop/cart");
    }

    render() {
        return <div className="container-fluid">
            <div className="row">
                <div className="col bg-dark text-white">
                    <div className="navbar-brand">SPORTS STORE</div>
                    <CartSummary { ...this.props } />
                </div>
            </div>
            <div className="row">
                <div className="col-3 p-2">
                    <CategoryNavigation baseUrl="/shop/products"
                        categories={ this.props.categories } />
                </div>
```

```
        <div className="col-9 p-2">
            <ProductPages />
            <ProductList products={ this.props.products }
                addToCart={ this.handleAddToCart } />
        </div>
    </div>
  </div>
  }
}
```

The result is a series of buttons allowing the user to move between pages, alongside select elements that change the sort property and the page size, as shown in Figure 6-5.

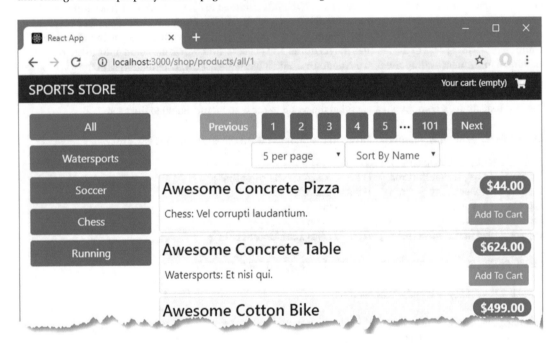

Figure 6-5. *Adding support for paginating products*

Adding the Checkout Process

The core features of the application are in place, allowing the user to filter and navigate through the product data and add items to a basket that are displayed in summary and detailed views. Once the user completes the checkout process, a new order must be sent to the web service, which will complete the shopping, reset the user's cart, and display a summary message. In the sections that follow, I add support for checking out and placing an order.

Extending the REST Data Source and the Data Store

As I explain in Chapter 23, when a RESTful web service receives an HTTP request, it uses a combination of the request method (also known as the *verb*) and the URL to determine what operation should be performed. To send an order to the web service, I am going to send a POST request to the web service's /orders URL. To keep the new features consistent with the existing application, I started by adding a constant that identifies the data type for orders and a new action for storing the order, as shown in Listing 6-23.

Listing 6-23. Adding Types in the Types.js File in the src/data Folder

```
export const DataTypes = {
    PRODUCTS: "products",
    CATEGORIES: "categories",
    ORDERS: "orders"
}

export const ActionTypes = {
    DATA_LOAD: "data_load",
    DATA_STORE: "data_store",
    DATA_SET_SORT_PROPERTY: "data_set_sort",
    DATA_SET_PAGESIZE: "data_set_pagesize",
    CART_ADD: "cart_add",
    CART_UPDATE: "cart_update",
    CART_REMOVE: "cart_delete",
    CART_CLEAR: "cart_clear"
}
```

The new data type allows me to define the URL for placing the order, as shown in Listing 6-24. I also use it in Chapter 7 when I add support for administration features.

Listing 6-24. Adding a New URL in the Urls.js File in the src/data Folder

```
import { DataTypes } from "./Types";

const protocol = "http";
const hostname = "localhost";
const port = 3500;

export const RestUrls = {
    [DataTypes.PRODUCTS]: `${protocol}://${hostname}:${port}/api/products`,
    [DataTypes.CATEGORIES]: `${protocol}://${hostname}:${port}/api/categories`,
    [DataTypes.ORDERS]: `${protocol}://${hostname}:${port}/api/orders`
}
```

In Listing 6-25, I added a method to the REST data source that receives the order object and sends it to the web service.

Listing 6-25. Adding a Method in the RestDataSource.js File in the src/data Folder

```
import Axios from "axios";
import { RestUrls } from "./Urls";

export class RestDataSource {

    constructor(err_handler) {
        this.error_handler = err_handler || (() => {});
    }

    GetData = (dataType, params) =>
        this.SendRequest("get", RestUrls[dataType], params);

    StoreData = (dataType, data) =>
        this.SendRequest("post", RestUrls[dataType], {}, data);

    SendRequest = (method, url, params, data) =>
        Axios.request({ method, url, params, data });
}
```

The Axios package will receive a data object and take care of formatting it so that it can be sent to the web service. In Listing 6-26, I added a new action creator that uses a Promise to send an order to the web service. The web service will return the stored data, which will include a unique identifier.

Listing 6-26. Adding a Creator to the ActionCreators.js File in the src/data Folder

```
import { ActionTypes, DataTypes } from "./Types";
import { RestDataSource } from "./RestDataSource";

const dataSource = new RestDataSource();

export const loadData = (dataType, params) => (
    {
        type: ActionTypes.DATA_LOAD,
        payload: dataSource.GetData(dataType, params).then(response =>
            ({ dataType,
                data: response.data,
                total: Number(response.headers["x-total-count"]),
                params
            })
        )
    })

export const setPageSize = (newSize) => {
    return ({ type: ActionTypes.DATA_SET_PAGESIZE, payload: newSize});
}

export const setSortProperty = (newProp) =>
    ({ type: ActionTypes.DATA_SET_SORT_PROPERTY, payload: newProp});
```

```
export const placeOrder = (order) => ({
    type: ActionTypes.DATA_STORE,
    payload: dataSource.StoreData(DataTypes.ORDERS, order).then(response => ({
        dataType: DataTypes.ORDERS, data: response.data
    }))
})
```

To process the result and add the order to the data store, I added the reducer shown in Listing 6-27.

Listing 6-27. Storing an Order in the ShopReducer.js File in the src/data Folder

```
import { ActionTypes, DataTypes } from "./Types";

export const ShopReducer = (storeData, action) => {
    switch(action.type) {
        case ActionTypes.DATA_LOAD:
            return {
                ...storeData,
                [action.payload.dataType]: action.payload.data,
                [`${action.payload.dataType}_total`]: action.payload.total,
                [`${action.payload.dataType}_params`]: action.payload.params
            };
        case ActionTypes.DATA_SET_PAGESIZE:
            return { ...storeData, pageSize: action.payload }
        case ActionTypes.DATA_SET_SORT_PROPERTY:
            return { ...storeData, sortKey: action.payload }
        case ActionTypes.DATA_STORE:
            if (action.payload.dataType === DataTypes.ORDERS) {
                return { ...storeData, order: action.payload.data }
            }
            break;
        default:
            return storeData || {};
    }
}
```

Creating the Checkout Form

To complete a SportsStore order, the user must complete a form with their personal details, which means that I must present the user with a form. React supports two ways to use form elements: *controlled* and *uncontrolled*. For a controlled element, React manages the element's content and responds to its change events. The select elements used for configuring pagination fall into this category. For the checkout form, I am going to use uncontrolled elements, which are not closely managed by React and rely more on the browser's functionality. The key to using uncontrolled for elements is a feature called *refs*, described in Chapter 16, which allow a React component to keep track of the HTML elements that are produced by its render method after they have been displayed to the user. For the checkout form, the advantage of using refs is that I can validate the form using the HTML5 validation API, which I describe in Chapter 15. The validation API requires direct access to the form elements, which wouldn't be possible without the use of refs.

■ **Note**   There are packages available for creating and validating forms in React applications, but they can be awkward to use and apply restrictions on the appearance of the form or the structure of the data that it produces. It is easy to create custom forms and validation using the features described in Chapters 15 and 16, which is the approach I have taken for the SportsStore chapter.

Creating the Validated Form

I am going to create a reusable form with validation that will generate the fields required programmatically. I created the src/forms folder and added to it a file called ValidatedForm.js, which I used to define the component shown in Listing 6-28.

Listing 6-28. The Contents of the ValidatedForm.js File in the src/forms Folder

```
import React, { Component } from "react";
import { ValidationError } from "./ValidationError";
import { GetMessages } from "./ValidationMessages";

export class ValidatedForm extends Component {

    constructor(props) {
        super(props);
        this.state = {
            validationErrors: {}
        }
        this.formElements = {};
    }

    handleSubmit = () => {
        this.setState(state => {
            const newState = { ...state, validationErrors: {} }
            Object.values(this.formElements).forEach(elem => {
                if (!elem.checkValidity()) {
                    newState.validationErrors[elem.name] = GetMessages(elem);
                }
            })
            return newState;
        }, () => {
            if (Object.keys(this.state.validationErrors).length === 0) {
                const data =  Object.assign(...Object.entries(this.formElements)
                    .map(e => ({[e[0]]: e[1].value})) )
                this.props.submitCallback(data);
            }
        });
    }
```

```
    registerRef = (element) => {
        if (element !== null) {
            this.formElements[element.name] = element;
        }
    }

    renderElement = (modelItem) => {
        const name = modelItem.name || modelItem.label.toLowerCase();
        return <div className="form-group" key={ modelItem.label }>
            <label>{ modelItem.label }</label>
            <ValidationError errors={ this.state.validationErrors[name] } />
            <input className="form-control" name={ name } ref={ this.registerRef }
                { ...this.props.defaultAttrs } { ...modelItem.attrs } />
        </div>
    }

    render() {
        return <React.Fragment>
            { this.props.formModel.map(m => this.renderElement(m))}
            <div className="text-center">
                <button className="btn btn-secondary m-1"
                        onClick={ this.props.cancelCallback }>
                    { this.props.cancelText || "Cancel" }
                </button>
                <button className="btn btn-primary m-1"
                        onClick={ this.handleSubmit }>
                    { this.props.submitText || "Submit"}
                </button>
            </div>
        </React.Fragment>
    }
}
```

The ValidatedForm component receives a data model and uses it to create a form that is validated using the HTML5 API. Each form element is rendered with a label and a ValidationError component that displays validation messages to the user. The form is displayed with buttons that cancel or submit the form using callback functions provided as props. The submit callback will not be invoked unless all of the elements meet their validation constraints.

When the submit callback is invoked, it will receive an object whose properties are the name attribute values for the form elements and whose values are the data entered into each field by the user.

Defining the Form

To create the component that is used to display error messages, I added a file called ValidationError.js to the src/forms folder and added the code shown in Listing 6-29.

Listing 6-29. The Contents of the ValidationError.js File in the src/forms Folder

```
import React, { Component } from "react";
export class ValidationError extends Component {

    render() {
        if (this.props.errors) {
            return this.props.errors.map(err =>
                <h6 className="text-danger" key={err}>
                    { err }
                </h6>
            )
        }
        return null;
    }
}
```

The validation API presents validation errors in an awkward way, as explained in Chapter 16. To create messages that can be shown to the user, I added a file called `ValidationMessages.js` in the `src/forms` folder and defined the function shown in Listing 6-30.

Listing 6-30. The Contents of the ValidationMessages.js File in the src/forms Folder

```
export const GetMessages = (elem) => {
    const messages = [];
    if (elem.validity.valueMissing) {
        messages.push("Value required");
    }
    if (elem.validity.typeMismatch) {
        messages.push(`Invalid ${elem.type}`);
    }
    return messages;
}
```

To use the validated form for checking out, I added a file called `Checkout.js` to the `src/shop` folder and defined the component shown in Listing 6-31.

Listing 6-31. The Contents of the Checkout.js File in the src/shop Folder

```
import React, { Component } from "react";
import { ValidatedForm } from "../forms/ValidatedForm";

export class Checkout extends Component {

    constructor(props) {
        super(props);
        this.defaultAttrs = { type: "text", required: true };
        this.formModel = [
                { label: "Name"},
                { label: "Email", attrs: { type: "email" }},
                { label: "Address" },
                { label: "City"},
```

```
                { label: "Zip/Postal Code", name: "zip"},
                { label: "Country"}]
    }

    handleSubmit = (formData) => {
        const order = { ...formData, products: this.props.cart.map(item =>
            ({ quantity: item.quantity, product_id: item.product.id})) }
        this.props.placeOrder(order);
        this.props.clearCart();
        this.props.history.push("/shop/thanks");
    }

    handleCancel = () => {
        this.props.history.push("/shop/cart");
    }

    render() {
        return <div className="container-fluid">
            <div className="row">
                <div className="col bg-dark text-white">
                    <div className="navbar-brand">SPORTS STORE</div>
                </div>
            </div>
            <div className="row">
                <div className="col m-2">
                    <ValidatedForm formModel={ this.formModel }
                        defaultAttrs={ this.defaultAttrs }
                        submitCallback={ this.handleSubmit }
                        cancelCallback={ this.handleCancel }
                        submitText="Place Order"
                        cancelText="Return to Cart" />
                </div>
            </div>
        </div>
    }
}
```

The Checkout component uses a ValidatedForm to present the user with fields for their name, email, and address. Each form element will be created with the required attribute, and the type attribute of the input element for the email address is set to email. These attributes are used by the HTML5 constraint validation API and will prevent the user from placing an order unless they provide a value for all fields and enter a valid email address into the email field (although it should be noted that only the format of the email address is validated).

The handleSubmit method will be invoked when the user submits valid form data. This method receives the form data and combines it with details of the user's cart before calling the placeOrder and clearCart action creators and then navigating to the /shop/thanks URL.

Creating the Thank You Component

To present the user with confirmation of their order and to complete the checkout process, I added a file called Thanks.js to the src/shop folder and defined the component shown in Listing 6-32.

Listing 6-32. The Contents of the Thanks.js File in the src/shop Folder

```
import React, { Component } from "react";
import { Link } from "react-router-dom";

export class Thanks extends Component {

    render() {
        return <div>
            <div className="col bg-dark text-white">
                <div className="navbar-brand">SPORTS STORE</div>
            </div>
            <div className="m-2 text-center">
                <h2>Thanks!</h2>
                <p>Thanks for placing your order.</p>
                <p>Your order is #{ this.props.order ? this.props.order.id : 0 }</p>
                <p>We'll ship your goods as soon as possible.</p>
                <Link to="/shop" className="btn btn-primary">
                    Return to Store
                </Link>
            </div>
        </div>
    }
}
```

The Thanks component displays a simple message and includes the value of the id property from the order object, which it obtains through its order prop. This component will be connected to the data store, and the order object it contains will have an id value that is assigned by the RESTful web service.

Applying the New Components

To add the new components to the application, I altered the routing configuration in the ShopConnector component, as shown in Listing 6-33.

Listing 6-33. Adding New Routes in the ShopConnector.js File in the src/shop Folder

```
import React, { Component } from "react";
import { Switch, Route, Redirect }
    from "react-router-dom"
import { connect } from "react-redux";
import { loadData, placeOrder } from "../data/ActionCreators";
import { DataTypes } from "../data/Types";
import { Shop } from "./Shop";
import { addToCart, updateCartQuantity, removeFromCart, clearCart }
    from "../data/CartActionCreators";
import { CartDetails } from "./CartDetails";
```

```
import { DataGetter } from "../data/DataGetter";
import { Checkout } from "./Checkout";
import { Thanks } from "./Thanks";

const mapStateToProps = (dataStore) => ({
    ...dataStore
})

const mapDispatchToProps = {
    loadData,
    addToCart, updateCartQuantity, removeFromCart, clearCart,
    placeOrder
}

export const ShopConnector = connect(mapStateToProps, mapDispatchToProps)(
    class extends Component {
        render() {
            return <Switch>
                <Redirect from="/shop/products/:category"
                    to="/shop/products/:category/1" exact={ true } />
                <Route path={ "/shop/products/:category/:page" }
                    render={ (routeProps) =>
                        <DataGetter { ...this.props } { ...routeProps }>
                            <Shop { ...this.props } { ...routeProps } />
                        </DataGetter>
                    } />
                <Route path="/shop/cart" render={ (routeProps) =>
                        <CartDetails { ...this.props } { ...routeProps } />} />
                <Route path="/shop/checkout" render={ routeProps =>
                    <Checkout { ...this.props } { ...routeProps } /> } />
                <Route path="/shop/thanks" render={ routeProps =>
                    <Thanks { ...this.props } { ...routeProps } /> } />
                <Redirect to="/shop/products/all/1" />
            </Switch>
        }

        componentDidMount() {
            this.props.loadData(DataTypes.CATEGORIES);
        }
    }
)
```

The result allows the user to check out. To test the new features, navigate to http://localhost:3000, add one or more products to the cart, and click the Checkout button, which will present the form shown in Figure 6-6. If you click the Place Order button before filling out the form, you will see validation warnings, as shown in the figure.

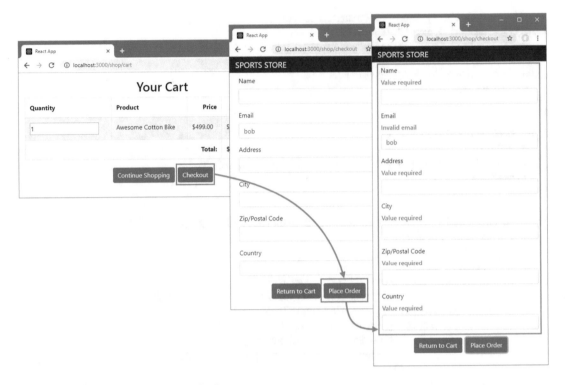

Figure 6-6. *Validation errors when checking out*

■ **Note**   Validation is performed only when the user clicks the button. See Chapters 15 and 16 for examples of validating the contents of a form element after each keystroke.

If you have filled all the fields and entered a valid email address, your order will be placed when you click the Place Order button, displaying the summary shown in Figure 6-7.

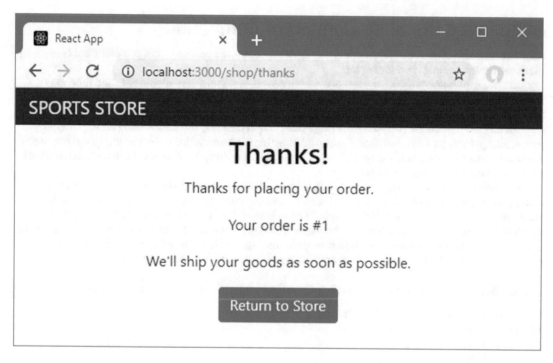

Figure 6-7. Placing an order

Open a new browser tab and request `http://localhost:3500/api/orders`, and the response will show the JSON representation of the order you place, like this:

```
...
[{
  "name":"Bob Smith","email":"bob@example.com",
  "address":"123 Main Street","city":"New York","zip":"NY 10036",
  "country":"USA","products":[{"quantity":1,"product_id":318}],"id":1
}]
...
```

Each time you place an order, it will be assigned an `id` by the RESTful web service, which will then be displayed in the order summary.

■ **Tip** The data used by the web service is regenerated each time that the development tools are started with the `npm start` command, which makes it easy to reset the application. In Chapter 8, I switch the SportsStore application to a persistent database as part of the preparations for deployment.

Simplifying the Shop Connector Component

All of the features required by the shopping part of the SportsStore application are complete, but I am going to make one more change in this chapter.

A React application is driven by its props, which provide components with the data and functions they require. When features like URL routing and a data store are used, the point where their capabilities are translated into props can become complex. For the SportsStore application, that is the ShopConnector component, which incorporates data store properties, action creators, and URL routing for the shopping part of the application. The advantage of consolidating these features is that the other shopping components are simpler to write, maintain, and test. The disadvantage is that consolidation results in code that is hard to read and where errors are likely to arise.

As I added features to the application, I added a new Route that selected a component and provided it with access to props from the data store and the URL router. I could have been more specific about the props each component received, which is the practice I have followed in many of the examples later in the book. For the SportsStore project, however, I gave every component access to all of the props, which is an approach that makes development easier and which allows the routing code to be tidied up once all of the features have been added. In Listing 6-34, I have simplified the connector for the shopping features.

Listing 6-34. Simplifying the Code in the ShopConnector.js File in the src/connectors Folder

```
import React, { Component } from "react";
import { Switch, Route, Redirect }
    from "react-router-dom"
import { connect } from "react-redux";
import * as ShopActions from "../data/ActionCreators";
import { DataTypes } from "../data/Types";
import { Shop } from "../shop/Shop";
import  * as CartActions from "../data/CartActionCreators";
import { CartDetails } from "../shop/CartDetails";
import { DataGetter } from "../data/DataGetter";
import { Checkout } from "../shop/Checkout";
import { Thanks } from "../shop/Thanks";

const mapDispatchToProps = { ...ShopActions, ...CartActions};

export const ShopConnector = connect(ds => ds, mapDispatchToProps)(
    class extends Component {

        selectComponent = (routeProps) => {
            const wrap = (Component, Content) =>
                <Component { ...this.props}  { ...routeProps}>
                    { Content && wrap(Content)}
                </Component>
            switch (routeProps.match.params.section) {
                case "products":
                    return wrap(DataGetter, Shop);
                case "cart":
                    return wrap(CartDetails);
                case "checkout":
                    return wrap(Checkout);
```

```
            case "thanks":
                return wrap(Thanks);
            default:
                return <Redirect to="/shop/products/all/1" />
        }
    }

    render() {
        return <Switch>
            <Redirect from="/shop/products/:category"
                to="/shop/products/:category/1" exact={ true } />
            <Route path={ "/shop/:section?/:category?/:page?"}
                render = { routeProps => this.selectComponent(routeProps) } />
        </Switch>
    }

    componentDidMount = () => this.props.loadData(DataTypes.CATEGORIES);
    }
)
```

In Chapter 9, I explain how JSX is translated into JavaScript, but it is easy to forget that all components can be restructured to rely less on the declarative nature of HTML elements and more on pure JavaScript. In Listing 6-34, I have collapsed the multiple Route components into one whose render function selects the component that should be displayed to the user and provides it with props from the data store and URL router. I have also changed the import statements for the action creators and used the spread operator when mapping them to function props, which I didn't do earlier because I wanted to show how I connected each data store feature to the rest of the application.

Summary

In this chapter, I continued the development of the SportsStore folder, adding support for working with the RESTful web server, scaling up the amount of data that the application can deal with, and adding support for checking out and placing orders. In the next chapter, I add the administration features to the SportsStore application.

CHAPTER 7

SportsStore: Administration

In this chapter, I add the administration features to the SportsStore application, providing the tools required to manage orders and products. I use GraphQL in this chapter rather than expanding the RESTful web service I used for the customer-facing part of SportsStore. GraphQL is an alternative to conventional web services that puts the client in control of the data it receives, although it requires more initial setup and can be more complex to use.

Preparing for This Chapter

This chapter builds on the SportsStore project created in Chapter 5 and modified in Chapter 6. To prepare for this chapter, I am going to generate a number of fake orders so there is data to work with, as shown in Listing 7-1.

■ **Tip** You can download the example project for this chapter—and for all the other chapters in this book—from https://github.com/Apress/pro-react-16.

Listing 7-1. Altering the Application Data in the data.js File in the sportsstore Folder

```
var faker = require("faker");
faker.seed(100);
var categories = ["Watersports", "Soccer", "Chess"];
var products = [];
for (let i = 1; i <= 503; i++) {
    var category = faker.helpers.randomize(categories);
    products.push({
        id: i,
        name: faker.commerce.productName(),
        category: category,
        description: `${category}: ${faker.lorem.sentence(3)}`,
        price: Number(faker.commerce.price())
    })
}
var orders = [];
for (let i = 1; i <= 103; i++) {
    var fname = faker.name.firstName(); var sname = faker.name.lastName();
```

```
    var order = {
        id: i, name: `${fname} ${sname}`,
        email: faker.internet.email(fname, sname),
        address: faker.address.streetAddress(), city: faker.address.city(),
        zip: faker.address.zipCode(), country: faker.address.country(),
        shipped: faker.random.boolean(), products:[]
    }
    var productCount = faker.random.number({min: 1, max: 5});
    var product_ids = [];
    while (product_ids.length < productCount) {
        var candidateId = faker.random.number({ min: 1, max: products.length});
        if (product_ids.indexOf(candidateId) === -1) {
            product_ids.push(candidateId);
        }
    }
    for (let j = 0; j < productCount; j++) {
        order.products.push({
            quantity: faker.random.number({min: 1, max: 10}),
            product_id: product_ids[j]
        })
    }
    orders.push(order);
}

module.exports = () => ({ categories, products, orders })
```

Running the Example Application

Open a new command prompt, navigate to the sportsstore folder, and run the command shown in Listing 7-2.

Listing 7-2. Running the Example Application

```
npm start
```

The React development tools and the RESTful web service will start. Once the development tools have compiled the SportsStore application, a new browser window will open and display the content shown in Figure 7-1.

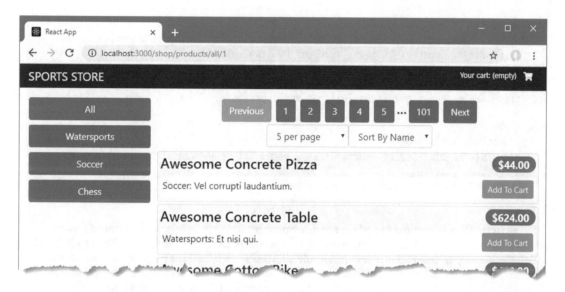

Figure 7-1. *Running the example application*

Creating a GraphQL Service

The administration features that I add to the SportsStore application in this chapter will use GraphQL instead of a RESTful web service. Few real applications would need to mix REST and GraphQL for the same data, but I want to demonstrate both approaches to remote services.

GraphQL isn't specific to React development, but it is so closely associated with React that I included an introduction to GraphQL in Chapter 24 and demonstrated the different ways a GraphQL service can be consumed by a React application in Chapter 25.

■ **Tip** I am going to create a custom GraphQL server for the SportsStore application so that I can share data with the RESTful web service provided by the excellent `json-server` package. As I explain in Chapter 24, there are open source and commercial GraphQL servers available.

Defining the GraphQL Schema

GraphQL requires that all of its operations are defined in a schema. To define the schema for the queries the service will support, I created a file called serverQueriesSchema.graphql in the sportsstore folder with the content shown in Listing 7-3.

Listing 7-3. The Contents of serverQueriesSchema.graphql in the sportsstore Folder

```
type product { id: ID!, name: String!, description: String! category: String!
            price: Float! }

type productPage { totalSize: Int!, products(sort: String, page: Int, pageSize: Int): [product]}

type orderPage { totalSize: Int, orders(sort: String, page: Int, pageSize: Int): [order]}
```

```
type order {
    id: ID!, name: String!, email: String!, address: String!, city: String!,
    zip: String!, country: String!, shipped: Boolean, products: [productSelection]
}

type productSelection { quantity: Int!, product: product }

type Query {
    product(id: ID!): product
    products(category: String, sort: String, page: Int, pageSize: Int): productPage
    categories: [String]
    orders(onlyUnshipped: Boolean): orderPage
}
```

The GraphQL specification includes a schema language used to define the features that a service provides. The schema in Listing 7-3 defines queries for products, categories, and orders. The product and order queries support pagination and return results that include a totalSize property that reports the number of items available so the client can present the user with pagination controls. The products can be filtered by category, and the orders can be filtered so that only unshipped orders are shown.

In GraphQL, changes are performed using *mutations*, following the theme of separating operations to read and write data that is common to much of React development. I added a file called serverMutationsSchema.graphql to the sportsstore folder and used it to define the mutations shown in Listing 7-4.

Listing 7-4. The Contents of the serverMutationsSchema.graphql File in the sportsstore Folder

```
input productStore {
    name: String!, description: String!, category: String!, price: Float!
}

input productUpdate {
    id: ID!, name: String, description: String, category: String, price: Float
}

type Mutation {
    storeProduct(product: productStore): product
    updateProduct(product: productUpdate): product
    deleteProduct(id: ID!): product
    shipOrder(id: ID!, shipped: Boolean!): order
}
```

The schema in Listing 7-4 defines mutations for storing new products, updating and deleting existing products, and marking orders as shipped or unshipped.

Defining the GraphQL Resolvers

The schema in a GraphQL service is implemented by a resolver. To provide the resolver for the queries, I added a file called serverQueriesResolver.js in the sportsstore folder with the code shown in Listing 7-5.

Listing 7-5. The Contents of the serverQueriesResolver.js File in the sportsstore Folder

```
const paginateQuery = (query, page = 1, pageSize = 5) =>
    query.drop((page - 1) * pageSize).take(pageSize);


const product = ({id}, {db}) => db.get("products").getById(id).value();

const products = ({ category }, { db }) => ({
    totalSize: () => db.get("products")
        .filter(p => category ? new RegExp(category, "i").test(p.category) : p)
        .size().value(),
    products: ({page, pageSize, sort}) => {
        let query = db.get("products");
        if (category) {
            query = query.filter(item =>
                new RegExp(category, "i").test(item.category))
        }
        if (sort) { query = query.orderBy(sort) }
        return paginateQuery(query, page, pageSize).value();
    }
})

const categories = (args, {db}) => db.get("categories").value();

const resolveProducts = (products, db) =>
    products.map(p => ({
        quantity: p.quantity,
        product: product({ id: p.product_id} , {db})
    }))

const resolveOrders = (onlyUnshipped, { page, pageSize, sort}, { db }) => {
    let query = db.get("orders");
    if (onlyUnshipped) { query = query.filter({ shipped: false}) }
    if (sort) { query = query.orderBy(sort) }
    return paginateQuery(query, page, pageSize).value()
        .map(order => ({ ...order, products: () =>
            resolveProducts(order.products, db) }));
}

const orders = ({onlyUnshipped = false}, {db}) => ({
    totalSize: () => db.get("orders")
        .filter(o => onlyUnshipped ? o.shipped === false : o).size().value(),
    orders: (...args) => resolveOrders(onlyUnshipped, ...args)
})

module.exports = { product, products, categories, orders }
```

The code in Listing 7-5 implements the queries defined in Listing 7-3. You can see an example of a stand-alone custom GraphQL server in Chapter 24, but the code in Listing 7-5 relies on the Lowdb database that the json-server package uses for data storage and that is described in detail at https://github.com/typicode/lowdb.

Each query is resolved using a series of functions invoked when the client requests specific fields, ensuring that the server has to load and process only the data that is needed. For the orders query, for example, the chain of functions ensures that the server only has to query the database for the related product objects if the client asks for them, avoiding retrieving data that is not required.

To implement the mutations, I added a file called serverMutationsResolver.js to the sportsstore folder and added the code shown in Listing 7-6.

Listing 7-6. The Contents of the serverMutationsResolver.js File in the sportsstore Folder

```
const storeProduct = ({ product}, {db }) =>
    db.get("products").insert(product).value();

const updateProduct = ({ product }, { db }) =>
    db.get("products").updateById(product.id, product).value();

const deleteProduct = ({ id }, { db }) => db.get("products").removeById(id).value();

const shipOrder = ({ id, shipped }, { db }) =>
    db.get("orders").updateById(id, { shipped: shipped}).value()

module.exports = {
    storeProduct, updateProduct, deleteProduct, shipOrder
}
```

Each of the functions defined in Listing 7-6 corresponds to a mutation defined in Listing 7-4. The code required to implement the mutation is simpler than the queries because the queries required additional statements to filter and page data.

Updating the Server

In Chapter 5, I added the packages required to create a GraphQL server to the SportsStore project. In Listing 7-7, I have used these packages to add support for GraphQL to the back-end server that has been providing the SportsStore application with its RESTful web service.

Listing 7-7. Adding GraphQL in the server.js File in the sportsstore Folder

```
const express = require("express");
const jsonServer = require("json-server");
const chokidar = require('chokidar');
const cors = require("cors");
const fs = require("fs");
const { buildSchema } = require("graphql");
const graphqlHTTP = require("express-graphql");
const queryResolvers  = require("./serverQueriesResolver");
const mutationResolvers = require("./serverMutationsResolver");

const fileName = process.argv[2] || "./data.js"
const port = process.argv[3] || 3500;
```

```
let router = undefined;
let graph = undefined;

const app = express();

const createServer = () => {
    delete require.cache[require.resolve(fileName)];
    setTimeout(() => {
        router = jsonServer.router(fileName.endsWith(".js")
                ? require(fileName)() : fileName);
        let schema = fs.readFileSync("./serverQueriesSchema.graphql", "utf-8")
            + fs.readFileSync("./serverMutationsSchema.graphql", "utf-8");
        let resolvers = { ...queryResolvers, ...mutationResolvers };
        graph = graphqlHTTP({
            schema: buildSchema(schema), rootValue: resolvers,
            graphiql: true, context: { db: router.db }
        })
    }, 100)
}

createServer();

app.use(cors());
app.use(jsonServer.bodyParser)
app.use("/api", (req, resp, next) => router(req, resp, next));
app.use("/graphql", (req, resp, next) => graph(req, resp, next));

chokidar.watch(fileName).on("change", () => {
    console.log("Reloading web service data...");
    createServer();
    console.log("Reloading web service data complete.");
});

app.listen(port, () => console.log(`Web service running on port ${port}`));
```

The additions load the schema and resolvers and use them to create a GraphQL service that shares a database with the existing RESTful web service. Stop the development tools and run the command shown in Listing 7-8 in the sportsstore folder to start them again, which will also start the GraphQL server.

Listing 7-8. Starting the Development Tools and Services

```
npm start
```

To make sure that the GraphQL server is running, navigate to `http://localhost:3500/graphql`, which will display the tool shown in Figure 7-2.

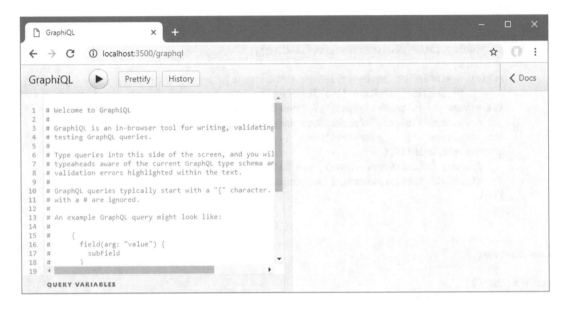

Figure 7-2. *The GraphiQL browser*

The package I used to create the GraphQL server includes the GraphiQL browser, which makes it easy to explore a GraphQL service. Replace the welcome message in the left part of the window with the GraphQL mutation shown in Listing 7-9.

■ **Note**   The data used by the RESTful web service and GraphQL service is reset each time the `npm start` command 2 is used, which means that the change made by the mutation in Listing 7-9 will be lost when you next start the server. I convert the SportsStore application to a persistent database as part of the deployment preparations in Chapter 8.

Listing 7-9. A GraphQL Mutation

```
mutation {
    updateProduct(product: {
        id: 272, price: 100
    }) { id, name, category, price }
}
```

Click the Execute Query button to send the mutation to the GraphQL server, which will update a product in the database and produce the following result:

```
...
{
  "data": {
    "updateProduct": {
      "id": "272",
      "name": "Awesome Concrete Pizza",
      "category": "Soccer",
      "price": 100
    }
  }
}
...
```

Navigate back to `http://localhost:3000` (or reload the browser tab if it is still open), and you will see that the price of the first product shown in the list has changed, as shown in Figure 7-3.

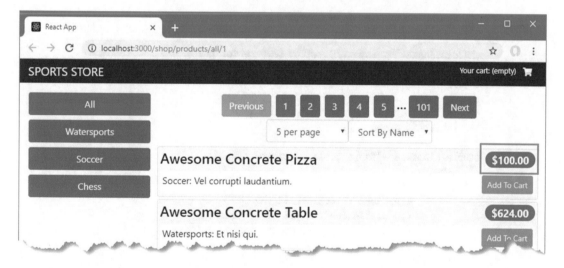

Figure 7-3. *The effect of a GraphQL mutation*

Creating the Order Administration Features

GraphQL requires more work at the server to create the schema and write the resolvers, but the benefit is that the client can be much simpler than one that uses a RESTful web service. In part, this is because of the way that GraphQL uses well-defined but flexible queries, but it is also because the GraphQL client package provides a lot of useful features that I had to create manually in Chapters 5 and 6.

■ **Note**   The way that I use GraphQL in the SportsStore chapter is the simplest approach, but it hides the detail of how GraphQL works. In Chapter 25, I demonstrate how to use GraphQL directly over HTTP and also how to integrate GraphQL into an application that uses a data store.

Defining the Order Table Component

I am going to start by creating a display of the orders. To define the component that displays the order data, I added a file called OrdersTable.js in the src/admin folder and added the code shown in Listing 7-10.

Listing 7-10. The Contents of the OrdersTable.js File in the src/admin Folder

```
import React, { Component } from "react";
import { OrdersRow } from "./OrdersRow";
import { PaginationControls } from "../PaginationControls";

export class OrdersTable extends Component {

    render = () =>
        <div>
            <h4 className="bg-info text-white text-center p-2">
                { this.props.totalSize } Orders
            </h4>

            <PaginationControls keys={["ID", "Name"]}
                { ...this.props } />

            <table className="table table-sm table-striped">
                <thead>
                    <tr><th>ID</th>
                        <th>Name</th><th>Email</th>
                        <th className="text-right">Total</th>
                        <th className="text-center">Shipped</th>
                    </tr>
                </thead>
                <tbody>
                    { this.props.orders.map(order =>
                        <OrdersRow key={ order.id }
                            order={ order} toggleShipped={ () =>
                                this.props.toggleShipped(order.id, !order.shipped) }
                        />
                    )}
                </tbody>
            </table>
        </div>
}
```

The OrdersTable component displays the total number of orders and renders a table where responsibility for each row is delegated to the OrdersRow component, which I defined by adding a file called OrdersRow.js to the src/admin folder with the code shown in Listing 7-11.

Listing 7-11. The Contents of the OrdersRow.js File in the src/admin Folder

```
import React, { Component } from "react";

export class OrdersRow extends Component {

    calcTotal = (products) => products.reduce((total, p) =>
        total += p.quantity * p.product.price, 0).toFixed(2)

    getShipping = (order) => order.shipped
        ? <i className="fa fa-shipping-fast text-success" />
        : <i className="fa fa-exclamation-circle text-danger" />

    render = () =>
        <tr>
            <td>{ this.props.order.id }</td>
            <td>{this.props.order.name}</td>
            <td>{ this.props.order.email }</td>
            <td className="text-right">
                ${ this.calcTotal(this.props.order.products) }
            </td>
            <td className="text-center">
                <button className="btn btn-sm btn-block bg-muted"
                        onClick={ this.props.toggleShipped }>
                    { this.getShipping(this.props.order )}
                    <span>
                        { this.props.order.shipped
                            ? " Shipped" : " Pending"}
                    </span>
                </button>
            </td>
        </tr>
}
```

Defining the Connector Component

When a GraphQL client queries its server, it provides values for any parameters the query defines and specifies the data fields that it wants to receive. This is the biggest difference from most RESTful web services, and it means that GraphQL clients receive only the data values they require. It does mean, however, that a client-side query has to be defined before data can be retrieved from the server. I like to define queries separately from components, and I added a file called clientQueries.js to the src/admin folder with the content shown in Listing 7-12.

Listing 7-12. The Contents of the clientQueries.js File in the src/admin Folder

```
import gql from "graphql-tag";

export const ordersSummaryQuery = gql`
    query($onlyShipped: Boolean, $page:Int, $pageSize:Int, $sort:String) {
        orders(onlyUnshipped: $onlyShipped) {
            totalSize,
```

```
            orders(page: $page, pageSize: $pageSize, sort: $sort) {
                id, name, email, shipped
                products {
                    quantity, product { price }
                }
            }
        }
    }`
```

GraphQL queries are defined as JavaScript string literals in the client application but must be processed using the gql function from the graphql-tag package. The query in Listing 7-12 targets the server's orders query and will accept variables that are used for the query's onlyShipped, page, pageSize, and sort parameters. The client query selects only the fields it requires and incorporates details of the product data related to each order, which is included in the query results generated by the server's resolver for the orders query.

The GraphQL client package, React-Apollo, provides the graphql function, which is the counterpart to the connect and withRouter functions used earlier and which connects a component to the GraphQL features by creating a *higher-order component*, which is a function that provides features to a component, as described in Chapter 14. To create the connection between the OrdersTable component and the query defined in Listing 7-12, I added a file called OrdersConnector.js to the src/admin folder and added the code shown in Listing 7-13.

Listing 7-13. The Contents of the OrdersConnector.js File in the src/admin Folder

```
import { graphql } from "react-apollo";
import { ordersSummaryQuery } from "./clientQueries";
import { OrdersTable } from "./OrdersTable";

const vars = {
    onlyShipped: false, page: 1, pageSize: 10, sort: "id"
}

export const OrdersConnector = graphql(ordersSummaryQuery,
    {
        options: (props) => ({ variables: vars }),
        props: ({data: { loading, orders, refetch }}) => ({
            totalSize: loading ? 0 : orders.totalSize,
            orders: loading ? []: orders.orders,
            currentPage: vars.page,
            pageCount: loading ? 0 : Math.ceil(orders.totalSize / vars.pageSize),
            navigateToPage: (page) => { vars.page = Number(page); refetch(vars)},
            pageSize: vars.pageSize,
            setPageSize: (size) => { vars.pageSize = Number(size); refetch(vars)},
            sortKey: vars.sort,
            setSortProperty: (key) => { vars.sort = key; refetch(vars)},
        })
    }
)(OrdersTable)
```

The graphql function accepts arguments for the query and a configuration object and returns a function that is used to wrap a component and provide it access to the query features. There are many properties supported by the configuration object, but I require only two. The first is the options property, which is used to create the set of variables that will be applied to the GraphQL query, using a function that receives the props applied by the parent component.

■ **Tip** The Apollo GraphQL client caches the results from queries so that it doesn't send duplicate requests to the server, which is useful when using components with routing, for example.

The second is the props property, which is used to create the props that will be passed to the display component and is provided with a data object that combines details of the query progress, the response from the server, and the functions used to refresh the query.

I selected three properties from the data object and used them to create the props for the OrdersTable component. The loading property is true while the query is sent to the server and the response is awaited, which allows me to use placeholder values until the GraphQL response is received. The results of the query are assigned to a property given the query name, which is orders in this case. The response from a query is structured like this:

```
...
{ "orders":
  { "totalSize":103,
    "orders":[
      {"id":"1","name":"Velva Dietrich","email":"Velva_Dietrich@yahoo.com",
       "shipped":false, "products":[{"quantity":8,"product":{"price":84 },
      {"quantity":7,"product":{"price":125}, {"quantity":3,"product":{"price":352}
         ...other data values omitted for brevity...
  }
}
...
```

To get the total number of available orders, for example, I read the value of the orders.totalSize property, like this:

```
...
totalSize: loading ? 0 : orders.totalSize,
...
```

The value of the totalSize prop is zero until the result from the server has been received and is then assigned the value of orders.totalSize.

The third property I selected from the data object is refetch, which is a function that resends the query and which I use to respond to pagination changes.

```
...
navigateToPage: (page) => { vars.page = Number(page); refetch(vars)},
...
```

I pass all of the query variables to the refetch function for brevity, but any values the function receives are merged with the original variables, which can be useful for more complex queries.

■ **Tip** There is also a `fetchMore` function available that can be used to retrieve data and merge it with existing results, which is useful for components that gradually build up the data they present to the user. I have taken a simpler approach for the SportsStore application, and each page of data replaces the previous query results.

Configuring the GraphQL Client

Access to the GraphQL client features is provided through the `ApolloProvider` component. To configure the GraphQL client and to create a convenient placeholder for other administration features, I created the `src/admin` folder and added to it a file called `Admin.js`, which I used to define the component shown in Listing 7-14.

Listing 7-14. The Contents of the Admin.js File in the src/admin Folder

```
import React, { Component } from "react";
import  ApolloClient from "apollo-boost";
import { ApolloProvider} from "react-apollo";
import { GraphQlUrl } from "../data/Urls";
import { OrdersConnector } from "./OrdersConnector"

const graphQlClient = new ApolloClient({
    uri: GraphQlUrl
});

export class Admin extends Component {

    render() {
        return <ApolloProvider client={ graphQlClient }>
            <div className="container-fluid">
                <div className="row">
                <div className="col bg-info text-white">
                    <div className="navbar-brand">SPORTS STORE</div>
                </div>
                </div>
                <div className="row">
                    <div className="col p-2">
                        <OrdersConnector />
                    </div>
                </div>
            </div>
            </ApolloProvider>
    }
}
```

To get started with the administration features, I am going to display an `OrdersTable` component, which I will create in the next section. I'll return to `Admin` and use URL routing to display additional features. To set the URL that will be used to communicate with the GraphQL server, I added the statement shown in Listing 7-15 to the `Urls.js` file.

Listing 7-15. Adding a URL in the Urls.js File in the src/data Folder

```
import { DataTypes } from "./Types";

const protocol = "http";
const hostname = "localhost";
const port = 3500;

export const RestUrls = {
    [DataTypes.PRODUCTS]: `${protocol}://${hostname}:${port}/api/products`,
    [DataTypes.CATEGORIES]: `${protocol}://${hostname}:${port}/api/categories`,
    [DataTypes.ORDERS]: `${protocol}://${hostname}:${port}/api/orders`
}

export const GraphQlUrl = `${protocol}://${hostname}:${port}/graphql`;
```

GraphQL requires only one URL because, unlike REST, it doesn't use the URL or the HTTP method to describe an operation. In Chapter 8, I will change the URLs used by the application as I prepare the project for deployment.

To incorporate the new features into the application, I added the route shown in Listing 7-16 to the App component.

Listing 7-16. Adding a Route in the App.js File in the src Folder

```
import React, { Component } from "react";
import { SportsStoreDataStore } from "./data/DataStore";
import { Provider } from "react-redux";
import { BrowserRouter as Router, Route, Switch, Redirect }
    from "react-router-dom";
import { ShopConnector } from "./shop/ShopConnector";
import { Admin } from "./admin/Admin";

export default class App extends Component {

    render() {
        return <Provider store={ SportsStoreDataStore }>
            <Router>
                <Switch>
                    <Route path="/shop" component={ ShopConnector } />
                    <Route path="/admin" component={ Admin } />
                    <Redirect to="/shop" />
                </Switch>
            </Router>
        </Provider>
    }
}
```

Save the changes to the files and navigate to http://localhost:3000/admin, and you will see the results shown in Figure 7-4.

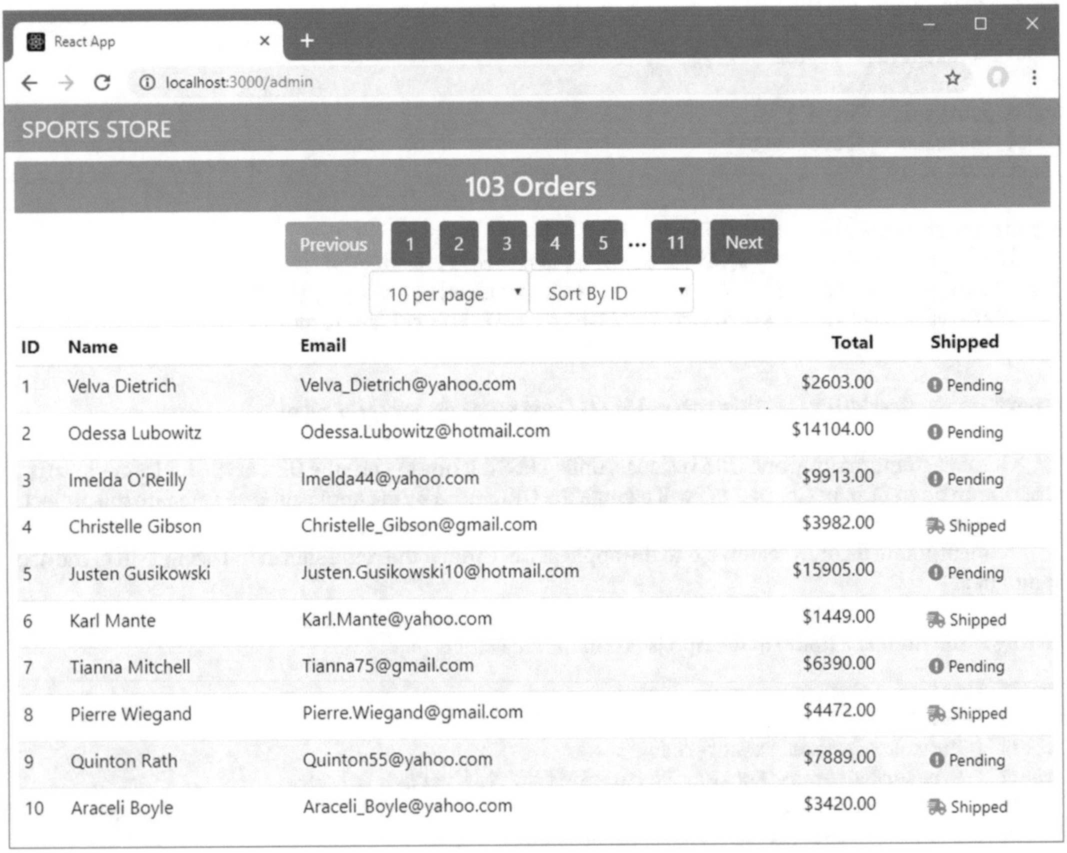

Figure 7-4. *Making a GraphQL query from a component*

Configuring the Mutation

The same basic approach for queries can be applied to integrate mutations into a React application. To allow the administrator to mark orders as shipped, I added a file called `clientMutations.js` to the `src/admin` folder with the content shown in Listing 7-17.

Listing 7-17. The Contents of the clientMutations.js File in the src/admin Folder

```
import gql from "graphql-tag";

export const shipOrder = gql`
    mutation($id: ID!, $shipped: Boolean!) {
        shipOrder(id: $id, shipped: $shipped) {
            id, shipped
        }
    }`
```

The GraphQL targets the `shipOrder` mutation, which updates the `shipped` property of an order specified by the value of its `id` property. In Listing 7-18 I have used the `graphql` function to provide access to the mutation and its results.

Listing 7-18. Applying a Mutation in the OrdersConnector.js File in the src/admin Folder

```
import { graphql, compose } from "react-apollo";
import { ordersSummaryQuery } from "./clientQueries";
import { OrdersTable } from "./OrdersTable";
import { shipOrder } from "./clientMutations";

const vars = {
    onlyShipped: false, page: 1, pageSize: 10, sort: "id"
}

export const OrdersConnector = compose(
    graphql(ordersSummaryQuery,
        {
            options: (props) => ({ variables: vars }),
            props: ({data: { loading, orders, refetch }}) => ({
                totalSize: loading ? 0 : orders.totalSize,
                orders: loading ? []: orders.orders,
                currentPage: vars.page,
                pageCount: loading ? 0 : Math.ceil(orders.totalSize / vars.pageSize),
                navigateToPage: (page) => { vars.page = Number(page); refetch(vars)},
                pageSize: vars.pageSize,
                setPageSize: (size) =>
                    { vars.pageSize = Number(size); refetch(vars)},
                sortKey: vars.sort,
                setSortProperty: (key) => { vars.sort = key; refetch(vars)},
            })
        }
    ),
    graphql(shipOrder, {
        props: ({ mutate }) => ({
            toggleShipped: (id, shipped) => mutate({ variables: { id, shipped }})
        })
    })
)(OrdersTable);
```

The React-Apollo package provides the compose function that simplifies combining queries and mutations. The existing query is combined with another call to the graphql function, which is passed the mutation from Listing 7-17. When using a mutation, the props property in the configuration object receives a function named mutate, which I use to create a prop called toggleShipped, corresponding to the prop used by the OrdersRow component to change the status of an order. To see the result, click the Shipped/Pending indicator for an order in the table, and its status will be changed, as shown in Figure 7-5.

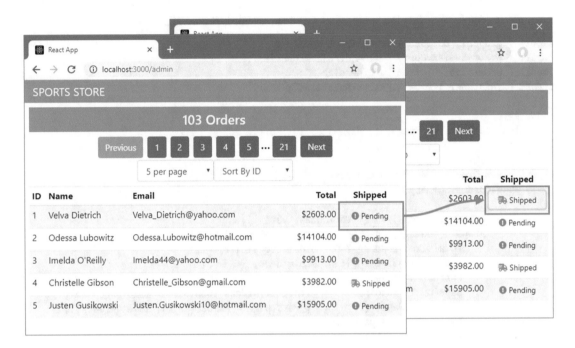

Figure 7-5. *Using a mutation*

The Apollo client automatically updates its cache of data when there is a change, which means that the change to the value of the shipped property is automatically reflected in the data displayed by the OrdersTable component.

Creating the Product Administration Features

To provide administration of the products presented to the user, I added a file called ProductsTable.js to the src/admin folder and used it to define the component shown in Listing 7-19.

Listing 7-19. The Contents of the ProductsTable.js File in the src/admin Folder

```
import React, { Component } from "react";
import { Link } from "react-router-dom";
import { PaginationControls } from "../PaginationControls";
import { ProductsRow } from "./ProductsRow";

export class ProductsTable extends Component {

    render = () =>
        <div>
            <h4 className="bg-info text-white text-center p-2">
                { this.props.totalSize } Products
            </h4>
```

```
        <PaginationControls keys={["ID", "Name", "Category"]}
            { ...this.props } />

        <table className="table table-sm table-striped">
            <thead>
                <tr><th>ID</th>
                    <th>Name</th><th>Category</th>
                    <th className="text-right">Price</th>
                    <th className="text-center"></th>
                </tr>
            </thead>
            <tbody>
                { this.props.products.map(prod =>
                    <ProductsRow key={ prod.id} product={ prod }
                        deleteProduct={ this.props.deleteProduct } />
                )}
            </tbody>
        </table>
        <div className="text-center">
            <Link to="/admin/products/create" className="btn btn-primary">
                Create Product
            </Link>
        </div>
    </div>
}
```

The ProductsTable component receives an array of objects through its products prop and uses the ProductsRow component to generate a table row for each of them. There is also a Link styled as a button that will be used to navigate to the component that will allow new products to be created.

To create the ProductsRow component that is responsible for a single table row, I added a file called ProductsRow.js to the src/admin folder and added the code shown in Listing 7-20.

Listing 7-20. The Contents of the ProductsRow.js File in the src/admin Folder

```
import React, { Component } from "react";
import { Link } from "react-router-dom";

export class ProductsRow extends Component {

    render = () =>
        <tr>
            <td>{ this.props.product.id }</td>
            <td>{this.props.product.name}</td>
            <td>{ this.props.product.category }</td>
            <td className="text-right">
                ${ this.props.product.price.toFixed(2) }
            </td>
            <td className="text-center">
                <button className="btn btn-sm btn-danger mx-1"
                    onClick={ () =>
                        this.props.deleteProduct(this.props.product.id) }>
                            Delete
```

```
            </button>
            <Link to={`/admin/products/${this.props.product.id}`}
                className="btn btn-sm btn-warning">
                    Edit
            </Link>
        </td>
    </tr>
}
```

Table cells are rendered for the id, name, category, and price properties. There is a button that invokes a function prop named deleteProduct that will remove a product from the database, and there is a Link that will navigate to the component used to edit product details.

Connecting the Product Table Component

To connect the product table component to the GraphQL data, I added the queries shown in Listing 7-21 to the clientQueries.js file, which also include the query I will require for editing a product. These queries correspond to the server-side GraphQL defined at the start of the chapter.

Listing 7-21. Adding Queries in the clientQueries.js File in the src/admin Folder

```
import gql from "graphql-tag";

export const ordersSummaryQuery = gql`
    query($onlyShipped: Boolean, $page:Int, $pageSize:Int, $sort:String) {
        orders(onlyUnshipped: $onlyShipped) {
            totalSize,
            orders(page: $page, pageSize: $pageSize, sort: $sort) {
                id, name, email, shipped
                products {
                    quantity, product { price }
                }
            }
        }
    }`


export const productsList = gql`
    query($page: Int, $pageSize: Int, $sort: String) {
        products {
            totalSize,
            products(page: $page, pageSize: $pageSize, sort: $sort) {
                id, name, category, price
            }
        }
    }`


export const product = gql`
    query($id: ID!) {
        product(id: $id) {
            id, name, description, category, price
        }
    }`
```

The query assigned to the constant named `productsList` will retrieve the `id`, `name`, `category`, and `price` properties for a page of products. The query assigned to the constant named `product` will retrieve the `id`, `name`, `description`, `category`, and `price` properties of a single `product` object. To add support for deleting, creating, and editing objects, I added the mutations shown in Listing 7-22 to the `clientMutations.js` file.

Listing 7-22. Adding Mutations in the clientMutations.js File in the src/admin Folder

```
import gql from "graphql-tag";

export const shipOrder = gql`
    mutation($id: ID!, $shipped: Boolean!) {
        shipOrder(id: $id, shipped: $shipped) {
            id, shipped
        }
    }`

export const storeProduct = gql`
    mutation($product: productStore) {
        storeProduct(product: $product) {
            id, name, category, description, price
        }
    }`

export const updateProduct = gql`
    mutation($product: productUpdate) {
        updateProduct(product: $product) {
            id, name, category, description, price
        }
    }`

export const deleteProduct = gql`
    mutation($id: ID!) {
        deleteProduct(id: $id) {
            id
        }
    }`
```

The new mutations correspond to the server-side GraphQL defined at the start of the chapter and allow the client to store a new product, edit an existing product, and delete a product.

Having defined the queries and mutations, I added a file called `ProductsConnector.js` to the `src/admin` folder and defined the higher-order component shown in Listing 7-23.

Listing 7-23. The Contents of the ProductsConnector.js File in the src/admin Folder

```
import { graphql, compose } from "react-apollo";
import { ProductsTable } from "./ProductsTable";
import { productsList } from "./clientQueries";
import { deleteProduct } from "./clientMutations";

const vars = {
    page: 1, pageSize: 10, sort: "id"
}
```

```
export const ConnectedProducts = compose(
    graphql(productsList,
        {
            options: (props) => ({ variables: vars }),
            props: ({data: { loading, products, refetch }}) => ({
                totalSize: loading ? 0 : products.totalSize,
                products: loading ? []: products.products,
                currentPage: vars.page,
                pageCount: loading ? 0
                    : Math.ceil(products.totalSize / vars.pageSize),
                navigateToPage: (page) => { vars.page = Number(page); refetch(vars)},
                pageSize: vars.pageSize,
                setPageSize: (size) =>
                    { vars.pageSize = Number(size); refetch(vars)},
                sortKey: vars.sort,
                setSortProperty: (key) => { vars.sort = key; refetch(vars)},
            })
        }
    ),
    graphql(deleteProduct,
        {
            options: {
                update: (cache, { data: { deleteProduct: { id }}}) => {
                    const queryDetails = { query: productsList, variables: vars };
                    const data = cache.readQuery(queryDetails)
                    data.products.products =
                        data.products.products.filter(p => p.id !== id);
                    data.products.totalSize = data.products.totalSize - 1;
                    cache.writeQuery({...queryDetails, data });
                }
            },
            props: ({ mutate }) => ({
                deleteProduct: (id) => mutate({ variables: { id }})
            })
        })
)(ProductsTable);
```

The code in Listing 7-23 is similar to the corresponding code for the orders administration features. One key difference is that mutations that remove objects do not automatically update the local cached data. For this type of mutation, an update function must be defined that modifies the cached data directly, like this:

```
...
update: (cache, { data: { deleteProduct: { id }}}) => {
    const queryDetails = { query: productsList, variables: vars };
    const data = cache.readQuery(queryDetails)
    data.products.products = data.products.products.filter(p => p.id !== id);
    data.products.totalSize = data.products.totalSize - 1;
    cache.writeQuery({...queryDetails, data });
}
...
```

This function reads the cached data, removes an object, reduces the totalSize to reflect the deletion, and then writes the data back to the cache, which will have the effect of updating the product list without needing to query the server.

■ **Tip** The downside of this approach is that it doesn't repaginate the data to reflect the deletion, which means that the page displays fewer items until the user navigates to another page. In the next section, I demonstrate how to address this by clearing the cached data, which leads to an additional GraphQL query but ensures that the application is consistent.

Creating the Editor Components

To allow the user to create a new product, I added a file called ProductEditor.js to the src/admin folder and defined the component shown in Listing 7-24.

Listing 7-24. The Contents of the ProductEditor.js File in the src/admin Folder

```
import React, { Component } from "react";
import { Query } from "react-apollo";
import { ProductCreator } from "./ProductCreator";
import { product } from "./clientQueries";

export class ProductEditor extends Component {

    render = () =>
        <Query query={ product } variables={ {id: this.props.match.params.id} } >
            { ({ loading, data }) => {
                if (!loading) {
                    return <ProductCreator {...this.props } product={data.product}
                        mode="edit" />
                }
                return null;
            }}
        </Query>
}
```

The Query component is provided as an alternative to the graphql function and allows GraphQL queries to be performed declaratively, with the results and other client features presented through a *render prop function*, which is described in Chapter 14. The ProductEditor component defined in Listing 7-24 will obtain the id of the product that the administrator wants to edit and obtains it using the Query component, which is configured using its query and variables props. The render prop function receives an object with loading and data properties, which have the same purpose as for the graphql function I used earlier. The ProductEditor component renders no content while the loading property is true and then displays a ProductCreator component, passing the data received from the query through the prop named product.

The ProductCreator component will do double duty in the SportsStore application. When used on its own, it will present the administrator with an empty form that will be sent to the storeProduct mutation. When it is used by the ProductEditor component, it will show details of an existing product and send the form data to the updateProduct mutation. To define the component, I added a file called ProductCreator.js to the src/admin folder with the code shown in Listing 7-25.

Listing 7-25. The Contents of the ProductCreator.js File in the src/admin Folder

```
import React, { Component } from "react";
import { ValidatedForm } from "../forms/ValidatedForm";
import { Mutation } from "react-apollo";
import { storeProduct, updateProduct } from "./clientMutations";

export class ProductCreator extends Component {

    constructor(props) {
        super(props);
        this.defaultAttrs = { type: "text", required: true };
        this.formModel = [
            { label: "Name" }, { label: "Description" },
            { label: "Category" },
            { label: "Price", attrs: { type: "number"}}
        ];
        this.mutation = storeProduct;
        if (this.props.mode === "edit" ) {
            this.mutation = updateProduct;
            this.formModel = [ { label: "Id", attrs: { disabled: true }},
                    ...this.formModel]
                .map(item => ({ ...item, attrs: { ...item.attrs,
                    defaultValue: this.props.product[item.label.toLowerCase()]} }));
        }
    }

    navigate = () => this.props.history.push("/admin/products");

    render = () => {
        return <div className="container-fluid">
            <div className="row">
                <div className="col bg-dark text-white">
                    <div className="navbar-brand">SPORTS STORE</div>
                </div>
            </div>
            <div className="row">
                <div className="col m-2">
                    <Mutation mutation={ this.mutation }>
                        { (saveMutation, {client }) => {
                            return <ValidatedForm formModel={ this.formModel }
                                defaultAttrs={ this.defaultAttrs }
                                submitCallback={ data => {
                                    saveMutation({variables: { product:
                                        { ...data, price: Number(data.price) }}});
                                    if (this.props.mode !== "edit" ) {
                                        client.resetStore();
                                    }
                                    this.navigate();
                                }}
```

```
                        cancelCallback={ this.navigate }
                        submitText="Save" cancelText="Cancel" />
                }}
            </Mutation>
        </div>
    </div>
</div>
    }
}
```

The ProductCreator component relies on the ValidatedForm that I created in Chapter 6 to handle checkout from the shopping part of the application. The form is configured with the fields required to edit a product, which will include the values obtained from the GraphQL query when they are provided through the product prop.

The counterpart to the Query component is Mutation, which allows a mutation to be used within the render function. The render prop function receives a function that is invoked to send the mutation to the server and that accepts an object that provides the variables for the mutation, like this:

```
...
<Mutation mutation={ this.mutation }>
    { (saveMutation, {client }) => {
        return <ValidatedForm formModel={ this.formModel }
            defaultAttrs={ this.defaultAttrs }
        submitCallback={ data => {
            saveMutation({variables: { product:
                { ...data, price: Number(data.price) }}});
                if (this.props.mode !== "edit" ) {
                    client.resetStore();
                }
                this.navigate();
        }}
            cancelCallback={ this.navigate }
            submitText="Save" cancelText="Cancel" />
    }
    }
</Mutation>
...
```

I have highlighted the section of code that sets up the function prop that is passed to the ValidatedForm component and that sends the mutation when it is invoked. When an object is updated, the Apollo client automatically updates its cached data to reflect the change, just as when I marked orders as shipped earlier in the chapter. New objects are not automatically processed, which means that the application has to take responsibility for managing the cache. The approach I took for deleting an object was to update the existing cache, but that is a much more complex process for a new item because it means trying to work out whether it should be displayed on the current page and, if so, where in the sort order it would appear. As a simpler alternative, I have received a client parameter from the render prop function, which allows me to clear the cached data through its resetStore method. When the navigate function sends the browser back to the product list, a fresh GraphQL will be sent to the server, which ensures that the data is consistently paged and sorted, albeit at the cost of an additional query.

Updating the Routing Configuration

The final step is to update the routing configuration to add navigation buttons that allow the order and product administration features to be selected, as shown in Listing 7-26.

Listing 7-26. Updating the Routing Configuration in the Admin.js File in the src/admin Folder

```
import React, { Component } from "react";
import  ApolloClient from "apollo-boost";
import { ApolloProvider} from "react-apollo";
import { GraphQlUrl } from "../data/Urls";
import { OrdersConnector } from "./OrdersConnector";
import { Route, Redirect, Switch } from "react-router-dom";
import { ToggleLink } from "../ToggleLink";
import { ConnectedProducts } from "./ProductsConnector";
import { ProductEditor } from "./ProductEditor";
import { ProductCreator } from "./ProductCreator";

const graphQlClient = new ApolloClient({
    uri: GraphQlUrl
});

export class Admin extends Component {

    render() {
        return <ApolloProvider client={ graphQlClient }>
            <div className="container-fluid">
                <div className="row">
                <div className="col bg-info text-white">
                    <div className="navbar-brand">SPORTS STORE</div>
                </div>
                </div>
            </div>
            <div className="row">
                <div className="col-3 p-2">
                    <ToggleLink to="/admin/orders">Orders</ToggleLink>
                    <ToggleLink to="/admin/products">Products</ToggleLink>
                </div>
                <div className="col-9 p-2">
                    <Switch>
                        <Route path="/admin/orders" component={ OrdersConnector } />
                        <Route path="/admin/products/create"
                            component={ ProductCreator} />
                        <Route path="/admin/products/:id"
                            component={ ProductEditor} />
                        <Route path="/admin/products"
                            component={ ConnectedProducts } />
                        <Redirect to="/admin/orders" />
                    </Switch>
```

```
                </div>
            </div>
        </div>
        </ApolloProvider>
    }
}
```

Save the changes, and you will see the layout shown in Figure 7-6. Clicking the Products button will display a paged table of products, which can be deleted and edited using the buttons in each table row.

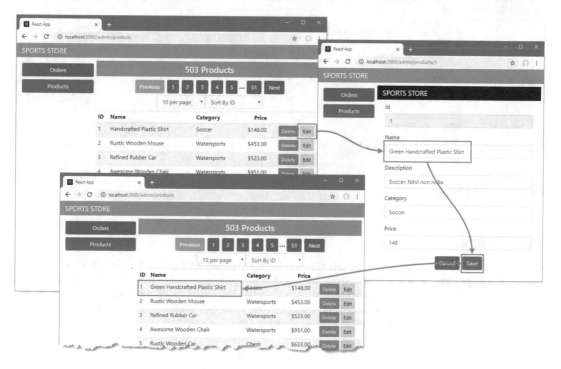

Figure 7-6. *The product administration features*

Clicking the Create Product button will display an editor that allows new products to be defined, as shown in Figure 7-7.

Figure 7-7. *Creating a new product*

Summary

In this chapter, I added the administration features to the SportsStore application. I started by creating a GraphQL service with the queries and mutations required to manage the order and products data. I used the GraphQL service to expand the application features, relying on the GraphQL client to manage the data in the application so that I didn't need to create and manage a data store. In the next chapter, I add authentication for the administration features and prepare the application for deployment.

CHAPTER 8

■ ■ ■

SportsStore: Authentication and Deployment

In this chapter, I add authentication to the SportsStore application to protect the administration features from unauthorized use. I also prepare the SportsStore application for deployment into a Docker container, which can be used on most hosting platforms.

Preparing for This Chapter

To prepare for this chapter, I am going to add support for authentication and authorization to the simple server that provides the RESTful web service and GraphQL service. At the moment, any client can perform any operation, which means that shoppers could change prices, create products, and perform other tasks that should be restricted to administrators. Table 8-1 lists the combination of HTTP methods and URLs that should be publicly accessible; everything else will be protected, including all GraphQL queries and mutations.

Table 8-1. *The Publicly Accessible HTTP Methods and URL Combinations*

HTTP Method	URL	Description
GET	/api/products	This combination is used to request pages of products for shoppers.
GET	/api/categories	This combination is used to request the set of categories and is used to provide shoppers with navigation buttons.
POST	/api/orders	This combination is used to submit orders.
POST	/login	This combination will be used to submit a username and password for authentication.

■ **Tip** You can download the example project for this chapter—and for all the other chapters in this book—from https://github.com/Apress/pro-react-16.

© Adam Freeman 2019
A. Freeman, *Pro React 16*, https://doi.org/10.1007/978-1-4842-4451-7_8

To implement the authentication and provide the means for authorization, I added a file called authMiddleware.js to the sportsstore folder and added the code shown in Listing 8-1.

Listing 8-1. The Contents of the authMiddleware.js File in the sportsstore Folder

```
const jwt = require("jsonwebtoken");

const APP_SECRET = "myappsecret", USERNAME = "admin", PASSWORD = "secret";

const anonOps = [{ method: "GET", urls: ["/api/products", "/api/categories"]},
                 { method: "POST", urls: ["/api/orders"]}]

module.exports = function (req, res, next) {
    if (anonOps.find(op => op.method === req.method
            && op.urls.find(url => req.url.startsWith(url)))) {
        next();
    } else if (req.url === "/login" && req.method === "POST") {
        if (req.body.username === USERNAME && req.body.password === PASSWORD) {
            res.json({
                success: true,
                token: jwt.sign({ data: USERNAME, expiresIn: "1h" }, APP_SECRET)
            });
        } else {
            res.json({ success: false });
        }
        res.end();
    } else {
        let token = req.headers["authorization"];
        if (token != null && token.startsWith("Bearer<")) {
            token = token.substring(7, token.length - 1);
            jwt.verify(token, APP_SECRET);
            next();
        } else {
            res.statusCode = 401;
            res.end();
        }
    }
}
```

The code in Listing 8-1 will inspect each request received by the HTTP server that delivers the RESTful web service and the GraphQL service. A 401 unauthorized response is returned if a request isn't for one of the unsecured combinations of HTTP method and URL. The /login URL is used for authentication, with the hardwired credentials shown in Table 8-2.

Table 8-2. *The Credentials Used by the SportsStore Application*

Name	Description
name	admin
password	secret

■ **Caution** All of the server-side code in the SportsStore project can be used for real projects except Listing 8-1, which contains hard-coded credentials and is unsuitable for anything other than basic development and testing.

To add the middleware to the server, I added the statements shown in Listing 8-2 to the server.js file.

Listing 8-2. Adding Middleware in the server.js File in the sportsstore Folder

```
const express = require("express");
const jsonServer = require("json-server");
const chokidar = require('chokidar');
const cors = require("cors");
const fs = require("fs");
const { buildSchema } = require("graphql");
const graphqlHTTP = require("express-graphql");
const queryResolvers  = require("./serverQueriesResolver");
const mutationResolvers = require("./serverMutationsResolver");
const auth = require("./authMiddleware");

const fileName = process.argv[2] || "./data.js"
const port = process.argv[3] || 3500;

let router = undefined;
let graph = undefined;

const app = express();

const createServer = () => {
    delete require.cache[require.resolve(fileName)];
    setTimeout(() => {
        router = jsonServer.router(fileName.endsWith(".js")
                ? require(fileName)() : fileName);
        let schema =  fs.readFileSync("./serverQueriesSchema.graphql", "utf-8")
            + fs.readFileSync("./serverMutationsSchema.graphql", "utf-8");
        let resolvers = { ...queryResolvers, ...mutationResolvers };
        graph = graphqlHTTP({
            schema: buildSchema(schema), rootValue: resolvers,
            graphiql: true, context: { db: router.db }
        })
    }, 100)
}

createServer();

app.use(cors());
app.use(jsonServer.bodyParser)
app.use(auth);
app.use("/api", (req, resp, next) => router(req, resp, next));
```

```
app.use("/graphql", (req, resp, next) => graph(req, resp, next));

chokidar.watch(fileName).on("change", () => {
    console.log("Reloading web service data...");
    createServer();
    console.log("Reloading web service data complete.");
});

app.listen(port, () => console.log(`Web service running on port ${port}`));
```

Open a new command prompt, navigate to the sportsstore folder, and run the command shown in Listing 8-3 to start the React development tools, the RESTful web service, and the GraphQL service.

Listing 8-3. Starting the Development Tool and Web Services

```
npm start
```

Once the project has been compiled, a new browser window will open and show the SportsStore shopping features, as shown in Figure 8-1.

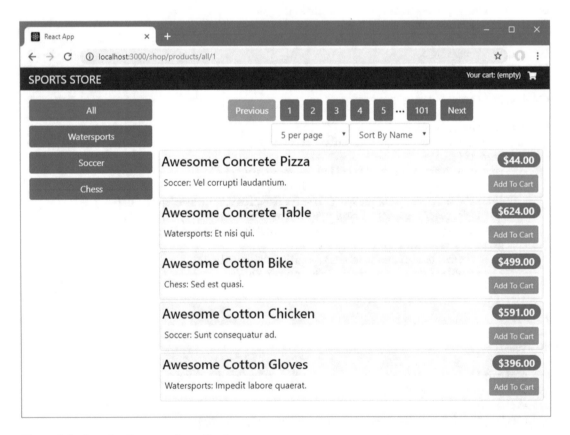

Figure 8-1. *Running the example application*

Adding Authentication for GraphQL Requests

The introduction of the authentication middleware has broken the administration features, which rely on HTTP requests that are no longer publicly accessible. If you navigate to http://localhost:3000/admin, you will see the effect of the 401 – Not Authorized response that the server makes to the GraphQL HTTP requests, as shown in Figure 8-2.

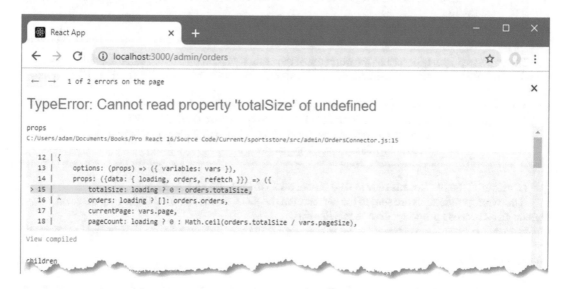

Figure 8-2. *Encountering an error*

In the sections that follow, I explain how the SportsStore application will authenticate users and implement the required features to prevent the error shown in the figure and restore the administration features for authenticated users.

Understanding the Authentication System

When the server authenticates a user, it will return a JSON Web Token (JWT) that the application must include in subsequent HTTP requests to show that authentication has been successfully performed. You can read the JWT specification at https://tools.ietf.org/html/rfc7519, but for the purposes of the SportsStore project, it is enough to know that the application can authenticate the user by sending a POST request to the /login URL, including a JSON-formatted object in the request body that contains name and password properties. There is only one set of valid credentials in the authentication code defined in Listing 8-1, which I have repeated in Table 8-3. You should not hard-code credentials in real projects, but this is the username and password that you will need for the SportsStore application.

Table 8-3. *The Authentication Credentials Supported by the RESTful Web Service*

Username	Password
admin	secret

If the correct credentials are sent to the /login URL, then the response from the server will contain a JSON object like this:

```
{
  "success": true,
  "token":"eyJhbGciOiJIUzI1NiIsInR5cCI6IkpXVCJ9.eyJkYXRhIjoiYWRtaW4iLCJleHBpcmVz
          SW4iOiIxaCIsImlhdCI6MTQ3ODk1NjI1Mn0.lJaDDrSu-bHBtdWrzO312p_DG5tKypGv6cA
          NgOyzlg8"
}
```

The success property describes the outcome of the authentication operation, and the token property contains the JWT, which should be included in subsequent requests using the Authorization HTTP header in this format:

```
Authorization: Bearer<eyJhbGciOiJIUzI1NiIsInR5cCI6IkpXVCJ9.eyJkYXRhIjoiYWRtaW4iLC
               JleHBpcmVzSW4iOiIxaCIsImlhdCI6MTQ3ODk1NjI1Mn0.lJaDDrSu-bHBtd
               WrzO312p_DG5tKypGv6cANgOyzlg8>
```

I configured the JWT tokens returned by the server so they expire after one hour.

If the wrong credentials are sent to the server, then the JSON object returned in the response will contain just a success property set to false, like this:

```
{
  "success": false
}
```

Creating the Authentication Context

The SportsStore application needs to be able to determine whether the user has been authenticated and keep track of the web token that must be included in HTTP requests, ensuring that the administration features are shown only after successful authentication.

This is the type of information that is often required in multiple places in an application, to ensure that components can easily collaborate. For the SportsStore application, I am going to use the React *context* feature, which allows functionality to be easily shared between components in a simple and lightweight way and which is described in Chapter 14. I created the src/auth folder and added to it a file called AuthContext.js with the code shown in Listing 8-4.

Listing 8-4. The Contents of the AuthContext.js File in the src/auth Folder

```
import React from "react";

export const AuthContext = React.createContext({
    isAuthenticated: false,
    webToken: null,
    authenticate: (username, password) => {},
    signout: () => {}
})
```

The React.createContext method is used to create a context, and the object it receives is used for default values, which is why the authenticate and signout functions are empty. The real functionality for a context is provided by a provider component, which I defined by creating a file called `AuthProviderImpl.js` in the `src/auth` folder and adding the code shown in Listing 8-5.

Listing 8-5. The Contents of the AuthProviderImpl.js File in the src/auth Folder

```
import React, { Component } from "react";
import Axios from "axios";
import { AuthContext } from "./AuthContext";
import { authUrl } from "../data/Urls";

export class AuthProviderImpl extends Component {

    constructor(props) {
        super(props);
        this.state = {
            isAuthenticated: false,
            webToken: null
        }
    }

    authenticate = (credentials) => {
        return Axios.post(authUrl,  credentials).then(response => {
            if (response.data.success === true) {
                this.setState({
                    isAuthenticated: true,
                    webToken:response.data.token
                })
                return true;
            } else {
                throw new Error("Invalid Credentials");
            }
        })
    }

    signout = () => {
        this.setState({ isAuthenticated: false, webToken: null });
    }

    render = () =>
        <AuthContext.Provider value={ {...this.state,
                authenticate: this.authenticate, signout: this.signout}}>
            { this.props.children }
        </AuthContext.Provider>
}
```

This component uses the React context feature in its render method to provide an implementation of the `AuthContext` properties and functions, which it does through the `value` prop of the special `AuthContext.Provider` element. The effect is to share access to the state data and the `authenticate` and `signout` methods directly to any descendant component that applies the corresponding `AuthContext.Consumer` element, which I will use shortly.

The implementation of the `authenticate` method uses the Axios package to send a POST request to validate credentials that will be obtained from the user. The result of the `authenticate` method is a

Promise that will be resolved when the server responds to confirm the credentials and will be rejected if the credentials are incorrect.

To define the URL used to perform authentication, I added the URL shown in Listing 8-6.

Listing 8-6. Adding a URL in the Urls.js File in the src/data Folder

```
import { DataTypes } from "./Types";

const protocol = "http";
const hostname = "localhost";
const port = 3500;

export const RestUrls = {
    [DataTypes.PRODUCTS]: `${protocol}://${hostname}:${port}/api/products`,
    [DataTypes.CATEGORIES]: `${protocol}://${hostname}:${port}/api/categories`,
    [DataTypes.ORDERS]: `${protocol}://${hostname}:${port}/api/orders`
}

export const GraphQlUrl = `${protocol}://${hostname}:${port}/graphql`;

export const authUrl = `${protocol}://${hostname}:${port}/login`;
```

To apply the context to the SportsStore application, I made the changes shown in Listing 8-7 to the App.js file.

Listing 8-7. Adding a Context Provider to the App.js File in the src Folder

```
import React, { Component } from "react";
import { SportsStoreDataStore } from "./data/DataStore";
import { Provider } from "react-redux";
import { BrowserRouter as Router, Route, Switch, Redirect }
    from "react-router-dom";
import { ShopConnector } from "./shop/ShopConnector";
import { Admin } from "./admin/Admin";
import { AuthProviderImpl } from "./auth/AuthProviderImpl";

export default class App extends Component {

    render() {
        return <Provider store={ SportsStoreDataStore }>
            <AuthProviderImpl>
                <Router>
                    <Switch>
                        <Route path="/shop" component={ ShopConnector } />
                        <Route path="/admin" component={ Admin } />
                        <Redirect to="/shop" />
                    </Switch>
                </Router>
            </AuthProviderImpl>
        </Provider>
    }
}
```

To make it easier to consume the features defined by the AuthContext, I added a file called AuthWrapper.js to the src/auth folder and defined the higher-order component shown in Listing 8-8.

Listing 8-8. The Contents of the AuthWrapper.js File in the src/auth Folder

```
import React, { Component } from "react";
import { AuthContext } from "./AuthContext";

export const authWrapper = (WrappedComponent) =>
    class extends Component {
        render = () =>
            <AuthContext.Consumer>
                { context =>
                    <WrappedComponent { ...this.props } { ...context } />
                }
            </AuthContext.Consumer>
    }
```

The context features rely on a render prop function, which can be difficult to integrate directly into components. Using the authWrapper function will allow a component to receive the features defined by the AuthContext as props. (Higher-order components and render prop functions are both described in Chapter 14.)

Creating the Authentication Form

To allow the user to provide their credentials, I added a file called AuthPrompt.js to the src/auth folder and used it to define the component shown in Listing 8-9.

Listing 8-9. The Contents of the AuthPrompt.js File in the src/auth Folder

```
import React, { Component } from "react";
import { withRouter } from "react-router-dom";
import { authWrapper } from "./AuthWrapper";
import { ValidatedForm } from "../forms/ValidatedForm";

export const AuthPrompt = withRouter(authWrapper(class extends Component {

    constructor(props) {
        super(props);
        this.state = {
            errorMessage: null
        }
        this.defaultAttrs = { required: true };
        this.formModel = [
            { label: "Username", attrs: { defaultValue: "admin"}},
            { label: "Password", attrs: { type: "password"} },
        ];
    }

    authenticate = (credentials) => {
        this.props.authenticate(credentials)
            .catch(err => this.setState({ errorMessage: err.message}))
            .then(this.props.history.push("/admin"));
    }
```

```
    render = () =>
        <div className="container-fluid">
            <div className="row">
                <div className="col bg-dark text-white">
                    <div className="navbar-brand">SPORTS STORE</div>
                </div>
            </div>
            <div className="row">
                <div className="col m-2">
                    { this.state.errorMessage != null &&
                        <h4 className="bg-danger text-center text-white m-1 p-2">
                            { this.state.errorMessage }
                        </h4>
                    }
                    <ValidatedForm formModel={ this.formModel }
                        defaultAttrs={ this.defaultAttrs }
                        submitCallback={ this.authenticate }
                        submitText="Login"
                        cancelCallback={ () => this.props.history.push("/")}
                        cancelText="Cancel"
                    />
                </div>
            </div>
        </div>
)))
```

This component receives routing features from the withRouter function and authentication features from the authWrapper function, both of which will be presented through the component's props. The ValidatedForm I defined in Chapter 6 is used to present the user with username and password fields, both of which require values. When the form data is submitted, the authenticate method forwards the details for authentication. If authentication is successful, then the history object provided by the URL routing system (described in Chapters 21 and 22) is used to redirect the user to the /admin URL. An error message is displayed if authentication fails.

Guarding the Authentication Features

To prevent access to the administration features until the user has been authenticated, I made the changes shown in Listing 8-10 to the Admin component.

Listing 8-10. Guarding Features in the Admin.js File in the src/admin Folder

```
import React, { Component } from "react";
import  ApolloClient from "apollo-boost";
import { ApolloProvider} from "react-apollo";
import { GraphQlUrl } from "../data/Urls";
import { OrdersConnector } from "./OrdersConnector"
import { Route, Redirect, Switch } from "react-router-dom";
import { ToggleLink } from "../ToggleLink";
import { ConnectedProducts } from "./ProductsConnector";
import { ProductEditor } from "./ProductEditor";
import { ProductCreator } from "./ProductCreator";
```

```
import { AuthPrompt } from "../auth/AuthPrompt";
import { authWrapper } from "../auth/AuthWrapper";

// const graphQlClient = new ApolloClient({
//     uri: GraphQlUrl
// });

export const Admin = authWrapper(class extends Component {

    constructor(props) {
        super(props);
        this.client = new ApolloClient({
            uri: GraphQlUrl,
            request: gqloperation => gqloperation.setContext({
                headers: {
                    Authorization: `Bearer<${this.props.webToken}>`
                },
            })
        })
    }

    render() {
        return <ApolloProvider client={ this.client }>
            <div className="container-fluid">
                <div className="row">
                <div className="col bg-info text-white">
                    <div className="navbar-brand">SPORTS STORE</div>
                </div>
                </div>
                <div className="row">
                    <div className="col-3 p-2">
                        <ToggleLink to="/admin/orders">Orders</ToggleLink>
                        <ToggleLink to="/admin/products">Products</ToggleLink>
                        { this.props.isAuthenticated &&
                            <button onClick={ this.props.signout }
                                className=
                                    "btn btn-block btn-secondary m-2 fixed-bottom col-3">
                                Log Out
                            </button>
                        }
                    </div>
                    <div className="col-9 p-2">
                        <Switch>
                            {
                                !this.props.isAuthenticated &&
                                    <Route component={ AuthPrompt } />
                            }
                            <Route path="/admin/orders" component={ OrdersConnector } />
                            <Route path="/admin/products/create"
                                component={ ProductCreator} />
                            <Route path="/admin/products/:id"
```

```
                          component={ ProductEditor} />
                <Route path="/admin/products"
                    component={ ConnectedProducts } />
                <Redirect to="/admin/orders" />
            </Switch>
        </div>
    </div>
    </div>
    </ApolloProvider>
    }
})
```

The Admin component is wrapped with the authWrapper function so it has access to the authentication features. The ApolloClient object is created in the constructor so that I can add a function that modifies each request to add an Authorization header to each GraphQL HTTP request.

There are two new code fragments in the render method. The first displays a logout button if the user is authenticated. The second fragment checks the authentication status and produces a Route component that displays the AuthPrompt component, regardless of the URL. (A Route component without a path property will always display its component and can be used with a Switch to prevent other Route components from being evaluated.)

Adding a Navigation Link for the Administration Features

To make it easier to use the administration features, I added a Link to the CategoryNavigation component, as shown in Listing 8-11.

Listing 8-11. Adding a Link in the CategoryNavigation.js File in the src/shop Folder

```
import React, { Component } from "react";
import { ToggleLink } from "../ToggleLink";
import { Link } from "react-router-dom";

export class CategoryNavigation extends Component {

    render() {
        return <React.Fragment>
            <ToggleLink to={ `${this.props.baseUrl}/all` } exact={ false }>
                All
            </ToggleLink>
            { this.props.categories && this.props.categories.map(cat =>
                <ToggleLink key={ cat }
                    to={ `${this.props.baseUrl}/${cat.toLowerCase()}`}>
                    { cat }
                </ToggleLink>
            )}
            <Link className="btn btn-block btn-secondary fixed-bottom m-2 col-3"
                to="/admin">
                Administration
            </Link>
        </React.Fragment>
    }
}
```

To see the authentication feature, navigate to `http://localhost:3000` and click the new Administration button. The guard will ensure that the authentication form is displayed. Enter **secret** into the password field and click the Login button to perform authentication, which will then display the administration features, as shown in Figure 8-3. Click the Log Out button to return to the unauthenticated state.

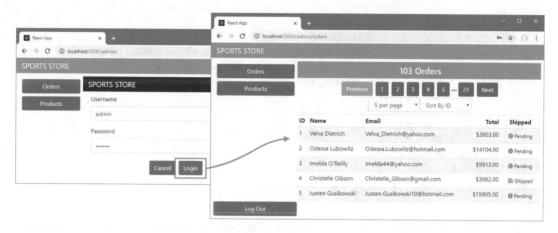

Figure 8-3. *Authenticating to use the administration features*

Preparing the Application for Deployment

In the sections that follow, I prepare the SportsStore application so that it can be deployed.

Enabling Lazy Loading for the Administration Features

When the application is deployed, the individual JavaScript files will be combined into a single file that the browser can download more efficiently. Most of the users will be shoppers, which means they are unlikely to require the administration features. To prevent them from downloading code that is unlikely to be used, I have enabled lazy loading on the `import` statement that incorporates the top-level administration component into the rest of the application, as shown in Listing 8-12.

Listing 8-12. Using Lazy Loading in the App.js File in the src Folder

```
import React, { Component, lazy, Suspense } from "react";
import { SportsStoreDataStore } from "./data/DataStore";
import { Provider } from "react-redux";
import { BrowserRouter as Router, Route, Switch, Redirect }
    from "react-router-dom";
import { ShopConnector } from "./shop/ShopConnector";
//import { Admin } from "./admin/Admin";
import { AuthProviderImpl } from "./auth/AuthProviderImpl";

const Admin = lazy(() => import("./admin/Admin"));

export default class App extends Component {
```

```
    render() {
        return <Provider store={ SportsStoreDataStore }>
            <AuthProviderImpl>
                <Router>
                    <Switch>
                        <Route path="/shop" component={ ShopConnector } />
                        <Route path="/admin" render={
                            routeProps =>
                                <Suspense fallback={ <h3>Loading...</h3> }>
                                    <Admin { ...routeProps } />
                                </Suspense>
                        } />
                        <Redirect to="/shop" />
                    </Switch>
                </Router>
            </AuthProviderImpl>
        </Provider>
    }
}
```

The Suspense component is used to denote content that should be loaded only when it is required and is combined with the lazy function. Together, these ensure that the Admin component will not be loaded until it is required. The lazy loading feature is a recent addition to React and, at the time of writing, doesn't support lazily loading named exports from files. To accommodate this requirement, I changed the definition of the Admin component as shown in Listing 8-13.

Listing 8-13. Changing the Export in the Admin.js File in the src/admin Folder

```
import React, { Component } from "react";
import  ApolloClient from "apollo-boost";
import { ApolloProvider} from "react-apollo";
import { GraphQlUrl } from "../data/Urls";
import { OrdersConnector } from "./OrdersConnector"
import { Route, Redirect, Switch } from "react-router-dom";
import { ToggleLink } from "../ToggleLink";
import { ConnectedProducts } from "./ProductsConnector";
import { ProductEditor } from "./ProductEditor";
import { ProductCreator } from "./ProductCreator";
import { AuthPrompt } from "../auth/AuthPrompt";
import { authWrapper } from "../auth/AuthWrapper";

export default authWrapper(class extends Component {

    // ...constructor and render method omitted for brevity...

})
```

Creating the Data File

The data file that is used by the RESTful and GraphQL services uses JavaScript to generate the same data each time the server is started. This has been useful during development because it has made it easy to return to a known state, but it isn't suitable for a production application.

The json-server package will create a persistent database when it is provided with a JSON file, so I added a file called productionData.json to the sportsstore folder with the content shown in Listing 8-14.

Listing 8-14. The Contents of the productionData.json File in the sportsstore Folder

```
{
    "products": [
        { "id": 1, "name": "Kayak", "category": "Watersports",
            "description": "A boat for one person", "price": 275 },
        { "id": 2, "name": "Lifejacket", "category": "Watersports",
            "description": "Protective and fashionable", "price": 48.95 },
        { "id": 3, "name": "Soccer Ball", "category": "Soccer",
            "description": "FIFA-approved size and weight", "price": 19.50 },
        { "id": 4, "name": "Corner Flags", "category": "Soccer",
            "description": "Give your playing field a professional touch",
            "price": 34.95 },
        { "id": 5, "name": "Stadium", "category": "Soccer",
            "description": "Flat-packed 35,000-seat stadium", "price": 79500 },
        { "id": 6, "name": "Thinking Cap", "category": "Chess",
            "description": "Improve brain efficiency by 75%", "price": 16 },
        { "id": 7, "name": "Unsteady Chair", "category": "Chess",
            "description": "Secretly give your opponent a disadvantage",
            "price": 29.95 },
        { "id": 8, "name": "Human Chess Board", "category": "Chess",
            "description": "A fun game for the family", "price": 75 },
        { "id": 9, "name": "Bling Bling King", "category": "Chess",
            "description": "Gold-plated, diamond-studded King", "price": 1200 }
    ],
    "categories": ["Watersports", "Soccer", "Chess"],
    "orders": []
}
```

Configuring the Request URLs

When I deploy the application, I will replace the React development HTTP server with one that combines serving static HTML and JavaScript files, as well as providing the RESTful and GraphQL services. To prepare for combining all the services on a single port, I changed the format of the URLs that the SportsStore uses, as shown in Listing 8-15.

Listing 8-15. Changing URLs in the Urls.js File in the src/data Folder

```
import { DataTypes } from "./Types";

// const protocol = "http";
// const hostname = "localhost";
// const port = 3500;
```

```
export const RestUrls = {
    [DataTypes.PRODUCTS]: `/api/products`,
    [DataTypes.CATEGORIES]: `/api/categories`,
    [DataTypes.ORDERS]: `/api/orders`
}

export const GraphQlUrl = `/graphql`;
export const authUrl = `/login`;
```

Building the Application

To create the optimized version of the application suitable for production use, open a new command prompt, navigate to the sportsstore folder, and run the command shown in Listing 8-16.

Listing 8-16. Building the Application for Deployment

```
npm run build
```

The build process can take a moment to complete, and the result is an optimized set of files in the build folder.

Creating the Application Server

The React development HTTP server isn't suitable for production. In Listing 8-17, I have extended the server that has been providing the RESTful and GraphQL services so that it will also serve the files from the build folder.

Listing 8-17. Configuring the Server in the server.js File in the sportsstore Folder

```
const express = require("express");
const jsonServer = require("json-server");
const chokidar = require('chokidar');
const cors = require("cors");
const fs = require("fs");
const { buildSchema } = require("graphql");
const graphqlHTTP = require("express-graphql");
const queryResolvers  = require("./serverQueriesResolver");
const mutationResolvers = require("./serverMutationsResolver");
const auth = require("./authMiddleware");
const history = require("connect-history-api-fallback");

const fileName = process.argv[2] || "./data.js"
const port = process.argv[3] || 3500;

let router = undefined;
let graph = undefined;

const app = express();
```

```
const createServer = () => {
    delete require.cache[require.resolve(fileName)];
    setTimeout(() => {
        router = jsonServer.router(fileName.endsWith(".js")
                ? require(fileName)() : fileName);
        let schema =  fs.readFileSync("./serverQueriesSchema.graphql", "utf-8")
            + fs.readFileSync("./serverMutationsSchema.graphql", "utf-8");
        let resolvers = { ...queryResolvers, ...mutationResolvers };
        graph = graphqlHTTP({
            schema: buildSchema(schema), rootValue: resolvers,
            graphiql: true, context: { db: router.db }
        })
    }, 100)
}

createServer();

app.use(history());
app.use("/", express.static("./build"));
app.use(cors());
app.use(jsonServer.bodyParser)
app.use(auth);
app.use("/api", (req, resp, next) => router(req, resp, next));
app.use("/graphql", (req, resp, next) => graph(req, resp, next));

chokidar.watch(fileName).on("change", () => {
    console.log("Reloading web service data...");
    createServer();
    console.log("Reloading web service data complete.");
});

app.listen(port, () => console.log(`Web service running on port ${port}`));
```

The `connect-history-api-fallback` package responds to any HTTP request with the contents of the `index.html` file. This is useful for applications that use URL routing because it means that users can navigate directly to the URLs to which the application navigates using the HTML5 History API.

Testing the Production Build and Server

To ensure that the production build is working and that the server has been configured correctly, run the command shown in Listing 8-18 in the `sportsstore` folder.

Listing 8-18. Testing the Production Build

```
node server.js ./productionData.json 4000
```

Once the server has started, open a new browser window and navigate to `http://localhost:4000`; you will see the familiar content shown in Figure 8-4.

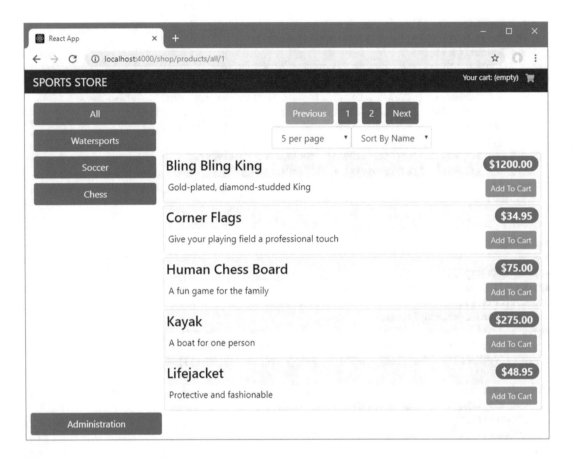

Figure 8-4. *Testing the application*

Containerizing the SportsStore Application

To complete this chapter, I am going to create a container for the SportsStore application so that it can be deployed into production. At the time of writing, Docker is the most popular way to create containers, which is a pared-down version of Linux with just enough functionality to run the application. Most cloud platforms or hosting engines have support for Docker, and its tools run on the most popular operating systems.

Installing Docker

The first step is to download and install the Docker tools on your development machine, which is available from `www.docker.com/products/docker`. There are versions for macOS, Windows, and Linux, and there are some specialized versions to work with the Amazon and Microsoft cloud platforms. The free Community edition is sufficient for this chapter.

■ **Caution** One drawback of using Docker is that the company that produces the software has gained a reputation for making breaking changes. This may mean that the example that follows may not work as intended with later versions. If you have problems, check the repository for this book for updates (https://github.com/Apress/pro-react-16) or contact me at adam@adam-freeman.com.

Preparing the Application

The first step is to create a configuration file for NPM that will be used to download the additional packages required by the application for use in the container. I created a file called deploy-package.json in the sportsstore folder with the content shown in Listing 8-19.

Listing 8-19. The Contents of the deploy-package.json File in the sportsstore Folder

```
{
    "name": "sportsstore",
    "description": "SportsStore",
    "repository": "https://github.com/Apress/pro-react-16",
    "license": "0BSD",

    "devDependencies": {
      "graphql": "^14.0.2",
      "chokidar": "^2.0.4",
      "connect-history-api-fallback": "^1.5.0",
      "cors": "^2.8.5",
      "express": "^4.16.4",
      "express-graphql": "^0.7.1",
      "json-server": "^0.14.2",
      "jsonwebtoken": "^8.1.1"
    }
}
```

The devDependencies section species the packages required to run the application in the container. All of the packages that are used in the browser have been included in the JavaScript files produced by the build command. The other fields describe the application, and their main use is to prevent warning when the container is created.

Creating the Docker Container

To define the container, I added a file called Dockerfile (with no extension) to the sportsstore folder and added the content shown in Listing 8-20.

Listing 8-20. The Contents of the Dockerfile File in the sportsstore Folder

```
FROM node:10.14.1

RUN mkdir -p /usr/src/sportsstore

COPY build /usr/src/sportsstore/build
```

```
COPY authMiddleware.js /usr/src/sportsstore/
COPY productionData.json /usr/src/sportsstore/
COPY server.js /usr/src/sportsstore/
COPY deploy-package.json /usr/src/sportsstore/package.json

COPY serverQueriesSchema.graphql /usr/src/sportsstore/
COPY serverQueriesResolver.js /usr/src/sportsstore/
COPY serverMutationsSchema.graphql /usr/src/sportsstore/
COPY serverMutationsResolver.js /usr/src/sportsstore/

WORKDIR /usr/src/sportsstore

RUN echo 'package-lock=false' >> .npmrc

RUN npm install

EXPOSE 80

CMD ["node", "server.js", "./productionData.json", "80"]
```

The contents of the Dockerfile use a base image that has been configured with Node.js and copies the files required to run the application, including the bundle file containing the application and the file that will be used to install the NPM packages required to run the application in deployment.

To speed up the containerization process, I created a file called .dockerignore in the sportsstore folder with the content shown in Listing 8-21. This tells Docker to ignore the node_modules folder, which is not required in the container and takes a long time to process.

Listing 8-21. The Contents of the .dockerignore File in the sportsstore Folder

```
node_modules
```

Run the command shown in Listing 8-22 in the sportsstore folder to create an image that will contain the SportsStore application, along with all the packages it requires.

Listing 8-22. Building the Docker Image

```
docker build . -t sportsstore  -f  Dockerfile
```

An image is a template for containers. As Docker processes the instructions in the Docker file, the NPM packages will be downloaded and installed, and the configuration and code files will be copied into the image.

Running the Application

Once the image has been created, create and start a new container using the command shown in Listing 8-23.

Listing 8-23. Starting the Docker Container

```
docker run -p 80:80 sportsstore
```

You can test the application by opening `http://localhost` in the browser, which will display the response provided by the web server running in the container, as shown in Figure 8-5.

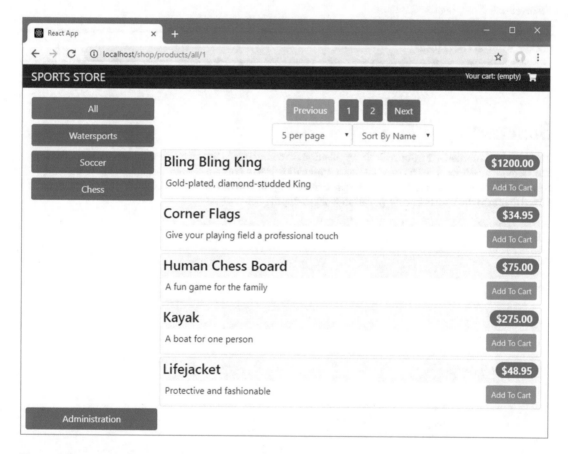

Figure 8-5. *Running the containerized SportsStore application*

To stop the container, run the command shown in Listing 8-24.

Listing 8-24. Listing the Containers

```
docker ps
```

You will see a list of running containers, like this (I have omitted some fields for brevity):

CONTAINER ID	IMAGE	COMMAND	CREATED
ecc84f7245d6	sportsstore	"node server.js"	33 seconds ago

Using the value in the Container ID column, run the command shown in Listing 8-25.

Listing 8-25. Stopping the Container

```
docker stop ecc84f7245d6
```

The application is ready to deploy to any platform that supports Docker.

Summary

This chapter completes the SportsStore application, showing how a React application can be prepared for deployment and how easy it is to put a React application into a container such as Docker. That's the end of this part of the book. In Part 2, I begin the process of digging into the details and show you how the features I used to create the SportsStore application work in depth.

PART II

Working with React

CHAPTER 9

Understanding React Projects

In Part 1 of this book, I created the SportsStore application to demonstrate how different React features can be combined with other packages to create a realistic application. In this part of the book, I dig into the detail of the built-in React features. In this chapter, I describe the structure of a React project and explain the tools that are provided for developers and the process by which code and content is compiled, packaged, and sent to the browser. Table 9-1 puts this chapter in context.

Table 9-1. *Putting React Projects in Context*

Question	Answer
What are they?	The `create-react-app` package is used to create projects and set up the tools that are required for effective React development.
Why are they useful?	Projects created with the `create-react-app` package are designed for the development of complex applications and provide a complete set of tools for development, testing, and deployment.
How are they used?	A project is created using the `npx create-react-app` package, and the development tools are started using the `npm start` command.
Are there any pitfalls or limitations?	The `create-react-app` package is "opiniated," which means that it provides a specific way of working with few configuration options. This can be frustrating if you are used to a different workflow.
Are there any alternatives?	You don't have to use `create-react-app` to create projects. There are alternative packages available as noted later in this chapter.

© Adam Freeman 2019
A. Freeman, *Pro React 16*, https://doi.org/10.1007/978-1-4842-4451-7_9

Table 9-2 summarizes the chapter.

Table 9-2. *Chapter Summary*

Problem	Solution	Listing
Create a new React project	Use the `create-react-app` package and add optional packages	1–3
Transform HTML to JavaScript	Use the JSX format to mix HTML and code statements	6
Include static content	Add files to the `src` folder and incorporate them into the application using the `import` keyword	9–10
Include static content outside of the development tools	Add files to the public folder and define references using the `PUBLIC_URL` property	11–13
Disabling linting messages	Add comments to JavaScript files	15–19
Configure the React development tools	Create an `.env` file and set configuration properties	20
Debug React applications	Use the React Devtools browser extension or use the browser debugger	22–26

Preparing for This Chapter

To create the example project for this chapter, open a new command prompt, navigate to a convenient location, and run the command shown in Listing 9-1.

Listing 9-1. Creating the Project

```
npx create-react-app projecttools
```

■ **Tip** You can download the example project for this chapter—and for all the other chapters in this book—from https://github.com/Apress/pro-react-16.

■ **Note** When you create a new project, you may see warnings about security vulnerabilities. React development relies on a large number of packages, each of which has its own dependencies, and security issues will inevitably be discovered. For the examples in this book, it is important to use the package versions specified to ensure you get the expected results. For your own projects, you should review the warnings and update to versions that resolve the problems.

Run the commands shown in Listing 9-2 to navigate to the project folder and add the Bootstrap package to the project.

Listing 9-2. Adding the Bootstrap CSS Framework

```
cd projecttools
npm install bootstrap@4.1.2
```

To include the Bootstrap CSS stylesheet in the application, add the statement shown in Listing 9-3 to the index.js file, which can be found in the src folder.

Listing 9-3. Including Bootstrap in the index.js File in the src Folder

```
import React from 'react';
import ReactDOM from 'react-dom';
import './index.css';
import App from './App';
import * as serviceWorker from './serviceWorker';
import 'bootstrap/dist/css/bootstrap.css';

ReactDOM.render(<App />, document.getElementById('root'));

// If you want your app to work offline and load faster, you can change
// unregister() to register() below. Note this comes with some pitfalls.
// Learn more about service workers: http://bit.ly/CRA-PWA
serviceWorker.unregister();
```

Using the command prompt, run the command shown in Listing 9-4 in the projecttools folder to start the development tools.

■ **Caution**   Notice that the development tools are started using the npm command and not the npx command that was used in Listing 9-1.

Listing 9-4. Starting the Development Tools

```
npm start
```

Once the initial preparation for the project is complete, a new browser window will open and display the URL http://localhost:3000 and display the placeholder content shown in Figure 9-1.

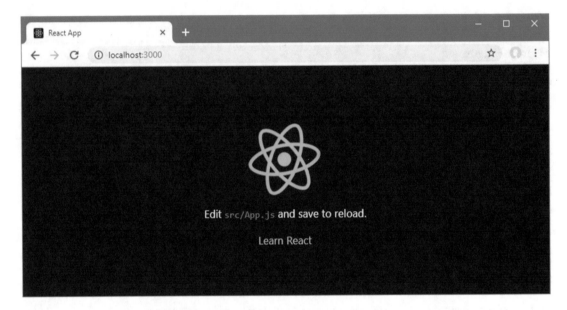

Figure 9-1. *Running the example application*

Understanding the React Project Structure

When you create a new project, you will start with a basic set of React application files, some placeholder content, and a complete set of development tools. Figure 9-2 shows the contents of the projecttools folder.

Figure 9-2. *The contents of a new project*

■ **Note** You don't have to use the create-react-app package to create React projects, but it is the most common approach, and it takes care of configuring the build tools that support the features described in this chapter. You can create all of the files and configure the tools directly, if you prefer, or use one of the other techniques available for creating a project, which are described at https://reactjs.org/docs/create-a-new-react-app.html.

Table 9-3 describes each of the files in the project, and I provide more details about the most important files in the sections that follow.

Table 9-3. *The Project Files and Folders*

Name	Description
node_modules	This folder contains the packages that the application and development tools require, as described in the "Understanding the Packages Folder" section.
public	This folder is used for static content and includes the index.html file that is used to respond to HTTP requests, as described in the "Understanding Static Content" section.
src	This folder contains the application code and content, as described in the "Understanding the Source Code Folder" section.
.gitignore	This file is used to exclude files and folders from the Git revision control package.
package.json	This folder contains the set of top-level package dependencies for the project, as described in the "Understanding the Packages Folder" section.
package-lock.json	This file contains a complete list of the package dependencies for the project, as described in the "Understanding the Packages Folder" section.
README.md	This file contains information about the project tools, and the same content can be found at https://github.com/facebook/create-react-app.

Understanding the Source Code Folder

The src folder is the most important in the project because it is where the application's code and content files are placed and where you will define the custom features required by your project. The create-react-app package adds files to jump-start development, as described in Table 9-4.

Table 9-4. *The Files in the src Folder*

Name	Description
index.js	This file is responsible for configuring and starting the application.
index.css	This file contains the global CSS styles for the application. See the "Understanding Static Content" section for details of using CSS files.
App.js	This file contains the top-level React component. Components are described in Chapters 10 and 11.
App.css	This file contains the placeholder CSS styles for new projects. See the "Understanding Static Content" section for details.
App.test.js	This file contains unit tests for the top-level component. See Chapter 17 for details of unit testing.
registerServiceWorker.js	This file is used by progressive web applications, which can work offline. I do not describe progressive applications in this book, but you can find details at https://facebook.github.io/create-react-app/docs/making-a-progressive-web-app.
logo.svg	This image file contains the React logo and is displayed by the placeholder component added to the project when it is created. See the "Understanding Static Content section.

Understanding the Packages Folder

JavaScript application development depends on a rich ecosystem of packages, ranging from those that contain the code that will be sent to the browser to small packages that are used behind the scenes during development for a specific task. A lot of packages are required in a React project: the example project created at the start of this chapter, for example, requires more than 900 packages.

There is a complex hierarchy of dependencies between these packages that is too difficult to manage manually and that is handled using a *package manager*. React projects can be created using two different package managers: NPM, which is the Node Package Manager and that was installed alongside Node.js in Chapter 1, and Yarn, which is a recent competitor designed to improve package management. I use NPM throughout this book for simplicity.

■ **Tip**   You should use NPM to follow the examples in this book, but you can find details of Yarn at `https://yarnpkg.com` if you want to use it in your own projects.

When a project is created, the package manager is given an initial list of packages required for React development, each of which is inspected to get the set of packages it depends on. The process is performed again to get the dependencies of those packages and repeated until a complete list of packages is built up. The package manager downloads and installs all of the packages and installs them into the node_modules folder.

The initial set of packages is defined in the package.json file using the dependencies and devDependencies properties. The dependencies section is used to list the packages that the application will require to run. The devDependencies section is used to list the packages that are required for development but that are not deployed as part of the application.

You may see different details in your project, but here is the dependencies section from the package.json file from my example project:

```
...
"dependencies": {
    "bootstrap": "^4.1.2",
    "react": "^16.7.0",
    "react-dom": "^16.7.0",
    "react-scripts": "2.1.2"
},
...
```

Only three packages are required in the dependencies section for a React project: the react package contains the main features, the react-dom package contains the features required for web applications, and the react-scripts package contains the development tool commands that I describe in this chapter. The fourth package is the Bootstrap CSS framework, added to the project in Listing 9-2. For each package, the package.json file includes details of the version numbers that are acceptable, using the format described in Table 9-5.

Table 9-5. *The Package Version Numbering System*

Format	Description
16.7.0	Expressing a version number directly will accept only the package with the exact matching version number, e.g., 16.7.0.
*	Using an asterisk accepts any version of the package to be installed.
>16.7.0 >=16.7.0	Prefixing a version number with > or >= accepts any version of the package that is greater than or greater than or equal to a given version.
<16.7.0 <=16.7.0	Prefixing a version number with < or <= accepts any version of the package that is less than or less than or equal to a given version.
~16.7.0	Prefixing a version number with a tilde (the ~ character) accepts versions to be installed even if the patch level number (the last of the three version numbers) doesn't match. For example, specifying ~16.7.0 will accept version 16.7.1 or 16.7.2 (which would contain patches to version 16.7.0) but not version 16.8.0 (which would be a new minor release).
^16.7.0	Prefixing a version number with a caret (the ^ character) will accept versions even if the minor release number (the second of the three version numbers) or the patch number doesn't match. For example, specifying ^16.7.0 will allow versions 16.8.0 and 16.9.0, for example, but not version 17.0.0.

The version numbers specified in the dependencies section of the package.json file will accept minor updates and patches.

UNDERSTANDING GLOBAL AND LOCAL PACKAGES

Package managers can install packages so they are specific to a single project (known as a *local install*) or so they can be accessed from anywhere (known as a *global install*). Few packages require global installs, but one exception is the create-react-app package that I installed in Chapter 1 as part of the preparations for this book. The create-react-app package requires a global install because it is used to create new projects. The individual packages required for the project are installed locally, into the node_modules folder.

All the packages required for development are automatically downloaded and installed into the node_modules folder when you create a React project, but Table 9-6 lists some NPM commands that you may find useful during development. All of these commands should be run inside the project folder, which is the one that contains the package.json file.

Table 9-6. *Useful NPM Commands*

Command	Description
npx create-react-app <name>	This command creates a new React project.
npm install	This command performs a local install of the packages specified in the package.json file.
npm install package@version	This command performs a local install of a specific version of a package and updates the package.json file to add the package to the dependencies section.
npm install --save-dev package@version	This command performs a local install of a specific version of a package and updates the package.json file to add the package to the devDependencies section, which is used to add packages to the project that are required for development but are not part of the application.
npm install --global package@version	This command will perform a global install of a specific version of a package.
npm list	This command will list all of the local packages and their dependencies.
npm run	This command will execute one of the scripts defined in the package.json file, as described next.

The last command described in Table 9-6 is an oddity, but package managers have traditionally included support for running commands that are defined in the scripts section of the package.json file. In a React project, this feature is used to provide access to the tools that are used during development and that prepare the application for deployment. Here is the scripts section of the package.json file in the example project:

```
...
"scripts": {
  "start": "react-scripts start",
  "build": "react-scripts build",
  "test": "react-scripts test",
  "eject": "react-scripts eject"
},
...
```

These commands are summarized in Table 9-7, and I demonstrate their use in later sections.

Table 9-7. *The Commands in the Scripts Section of the package.json File*

Name	Description
start	This command starts the development tools, as described in the "Using the React Development Tools" section.
build	This command performs the build process.
test	This command runs the unit tests, as described in Chapter 17.
eject	This command copies the configuration files for all the development tools into the project folder. This is a one-way operation and should be used only when the default configuration of the development tools is unsuitable for a project.

The commands in Table 9-7 are executed by using npm run followed by the name of the command that you require, and this must be done in the folder that contains the package.json file. So, if you want to run the build command in the example project, you would navigate to the projecttools folder and type npm run build. The exception is the start command, which is executed using npm start.

Using the React Development Tools

The development tools added to a project automatically detect changes in the src folder, compile the application, and package the files ready to be used by the browser. These are tasks you could perform manually, but having automatic updates makes for a more pleasant development experience. If they are not already running, start the development tools by opening a command prompt, navigating to the projecttools folder, and running the command shown in Listing 9-5.

Listing 9-5. Starting the Development Tools

```
npm start
```

The key package used by the development tools is *webpack*, which is the backbone for many JavaScript development tools and frameworks. Webpack is a *module bundler*, which means that it packages JavaScript modules for use in a browser—although that's a bland description for an important function, and it is one of the key tools that you will rely on while developing a React application.

When you run the command in Listing 9-5, you will see a series of messages as webpack prepares the bundles required to run the example application. Webpack starts with the index.js file and loads all of the modules for which there are import statements to create a set of dependencies. This process is repeated for each of the modules that index.js depends on, and webpack keeps working its way through the application until it has a complete set of dependencies for the entire application, which is then combined into a single file, known as the *bundle*.

The bundling process can take a moment, but it needs to be performed only when you start the development tools. Once the initial preparation has been completed, you will see a message like this one, which tells you that the application has been compiled and bundled:

```
...
Compiled successfully!

You can now view projecttools in the browser.

  Local:            http://localhost:3000/
  On Your Network:  http://192.168.0.77:3000/

Note that the development build is not optimized.
To create a production build, use npm run build.
...
```

As the initial process completes, a new browser window will be opened for http://localhost:3000, showing the placeholder content in Figure 9-3.

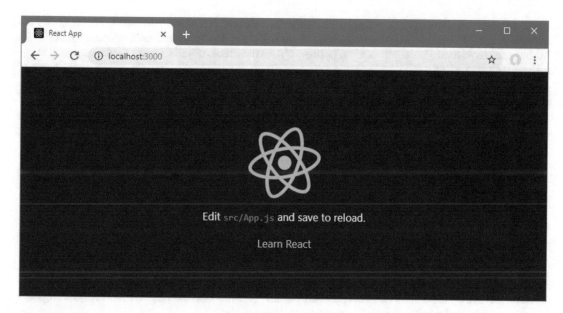

Figure 9-3. *Using the development tools*

Understanding the Compilation and Transformation Process

Webpack is responsible for the build process, and one of the key steps is code transformation performed by the *Babel* package. Babel has two important tasks in a React project: transforming JSX content and transforming JavaScript code that uses the latest JavaScript features into code that can be executed by older browsers.

Understanding the JSX Transformation

As I explained in Chapter 3, the JSX format is a superset of JavaScript that allows HTML to be mixed with regular code statements. JSX doesn't support entirely standard HTML, and the most obvious difference is that attributes such as class in pure HTML are expressed as className in a JSX file. The reason for these oddities is that the content of a JSX file is converted into calls to the React API by Babel during the build process so that every HTML element is translated into a call to the React.createElement method.
In Listing 9-6, I have replaced the placeholder content in the App.js file with a component whose render method returns some simple HTML elements.

Listing 9-6. Replacing the Placeholder Content in the App.js File in the src Folder

```
import React, { Component } from "react";

export default class extends Component {

    render = () =>
        <h4 className="bg-primary text-white text-center p-3">
            This is an HTML element
        </h4>
}
```

227

During the transformation process, the h4 element is replaced with a call to the `React.createElement` method, producing a result that is entirely JavaScript and that requires no special understanding of JSX by the browser. As a simple demonstration, Listing 9-7 uses the `React.createElement` method directly to achieve the same result.

Listing 9-7. Using the React API Directly in the App.js File in the src Folder

```
import React, { Component } from "react";

export default class extends Component {

    render = () => React.createElement("h4",
                    { className: "bg-primary text-white text-center p-3" },
                    "This is an HTML element")
}
```

Listing 9-6 and Listing 9-7 produce the same result, and when Babel processes the contents of the `App.js` file from Listing 9-6, it produces the code from Listing 9-7. When React executes the JavaScript code in the browser, it then uses the DOM API to create the HTML element, as demonstrated in Chapter 3. This may seem like a circular approach, but the JSX transformation is performed only during the build process and is intended to make writing React features easier.

Understanding the JavaScript Language Transformation

After years of stagnation, the JavaScript language has been revitalized and modernized with features that simplify development and provide features that are common in other programming languages, such as those features described in Chapter 4. Not all recent language features are supported by all browsers, especially older browsers or those used in corporate environments where updates are often rolled out slowly (if at all). Babel solves this problem by translating modern features into code that uses features that are supported by a much wider range of browsers, including those that pre-date the JavaScript renaissance.

In Listing 9-8, I have returned the `App.js` file to use HTML elements and used recent JavaScript features to set the content of the h4 element.

Listing 9-8. Using Modern JavaScript Features in the App.js File in the src Folder

```
import React, { Component } from "react";

let name = "Adam";
const city = "London";

export default class extends Component {

    message = () => `Hello ${name} from ${city}`;

    render = () =>
        <h4 className="bg-primary text-white text-center p-3">
            { this.message() }
        </h4>
}
```

This component relies on several recent JavaScript features: the `class` and `extends` keywords for defining classes, the `let` and `const` keywords for defining variables and constants, and a lambda function and template string in the `message` method. When you save the changes, the React development tools will automatically compile and bundle the JavaScript code and send it to the browser, producing the content shown in Figure 9-4.

Figure 9-4. *Using modern language features*

To see how Babel has handled the modern JavaScript features, open the F12 developer tools, select the Sources tab, and locate the `main.chunk.js` item in the tree on the left side of the window, as shown in Figure 9-5. For the version of Chrome that was current at the time of writing, the file is under the `localhost:3000 > static/js` part of the tree.

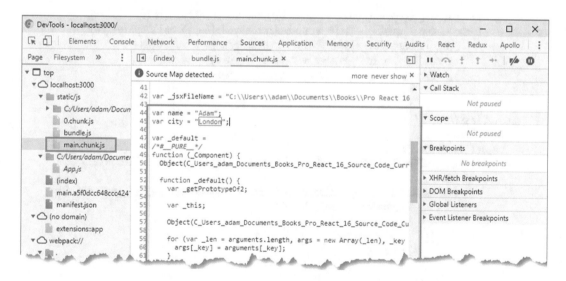

Figure 9-5. *Locating the compiled source code*

■ **Tip**   The Google Chrome developer tools change often, and you may have to hunt around to locate the code produced by Babel. Using Ctrl+F and searching for *London* is a good way to locate the code you are looking for. An alternative approach is to paste the code from Listing 9-8 into the interpreter at `https://babeljs.io/repl`, which will produce a similar result.

If you scroll down—or search for *London,* as noted earlier—then you will see the code that Babel has produced. All the features that are not supported by older browsers are replaced with backward-compatible code, like this:

```
...
var name = "Adam";
var city = "London";

var App = function (_Component) {
    _inherits(App, _Component);

    function App() {
        var _ref;

        var _temp, _this, _ret;

        _classCallCheck(this, App);

        for (var _len = arguments.length, args = Array(_len), _key = 0;
                _key < _len; _key++) {
            args[_key] = arguments[_key];
        }

        return _ret = (_temp = (_this = _possibleConstructorReturn(this,
            (_ref = App.__proto__ || Object.getPrototypeOf(App)).call.apply(_ref,
                [this].concat(args))), _this), _this.message = function () {
                    return "Hello " + name + " from " + city;
                }, _temp), _possibleConstructorReturn(_this, _ret);
    }

    _createClass(App, [{
        key: "render",
        value: function render() {
            return __WEBPACK_IMPORTED_MODULE_0_react___default.a.createElement(
                "div",
                { className: "h1 bg-primary text-white text-center p-3", __source: {
                        fileName: _jsxFileName,
                        lineNumber: 12
                    },
                    __self: this
                },
                this.message()
            );
        }
    }]);
    return App;
}
...
```

You don't have to understand how this code works in detail, not least because some of it is convoluted and difficult to read. What's important is how the features used in the App.js file are handled, such as the let and const keywords, which are replaced with the traditional var keyword.

```
...
var name = "Adam";
var city = "London";
...
```

You can also see that the template string has been replaced with string concatenation, as shown here:

```
...
return "Hello " + name + " from " + city;
...
```

Some of the features, such as classes, are handled using functions that Babel adds to the bundle sent to the browser. The JSX HTML fragment is translated into a call to the React.createElement method.

The translation of modern features is complex, but recent additions to the JavaScript language are largely syntactic sugar intended to make coding more pleasant for the developer. Translating these features robs the code of these leasing features and requires some contortions to create an equivalent effect that older browsers can execute.

UNDERSTANDING THE LIMITS OF BABEL

Babel is an excellent tool, but it deals only with JavaScript language features. Babel is not able to add support for recent JavaScript APIs to browsers that do not implement them. You can still use these APIs—as I demonstrated in Part 1 when I used the Local Storage API—but doing so restricts the range of browsers that can run the application.

Understanding the Development HTTP Server

To simplify the development process, the project incorporates the webpack-dev-server package, which is an HTTP server that is integrated with webpack. The server is configured to start listening for HTTP requests on port 3000 as soon as the initial bundling process is complete. When an HTTP request is received, the development HTTP server returns the contents of the public/index.html file. When it processes the index.html file, the development server makes some important additions, which you can see by right-clicking in the browser window and selecting View Page Source from the pop-up menu.

```html
<!DOCTYPE html>
<html lang="en">
  <head>
    <meta charset="utf-8">
    <meta name="viewport" content="width=device-width,
        initial-scale=1, shrink-to-fit=no">
    <meta name="theme-color" content="#000000">
    <link rel="manifest" href="/manifest.json">
    <link rel="shortcut icon" href="/favicon.ico">
    <title>React App</title>
  </head>
```

```
<body>
  <noscript>
    You need to enable JavaScript to run this app.
  </noscript>
  <div id="root"></div>
  <script src="/static/js/bundle.js"></script>
  <script src="/static/js/0.chunk.js"></script>
  <script src="/static/js/main.chunk.js"></script>
  <script src="/main.a5f0dcc648ccc4241725.hot-update.js"></script>
</body>
</html>
```

The development server adds `script` elements that tell the browser to load the files that contain the React framework, the application code, static content (such as CSS), and some additional features that support the development tools and automatically reload the browser when a change has been detected.

Understanding Static Content

There are two ways to include static content, such as images or CSS stylesheets in a React application. In most circumstances, the best approach is to add the files you need to the src folder and then declare dependencies on them in your code files using `import` statements.

To demonstrate how static content in the src folder is handled, I replaced the contents of the App.css file, which was added to the project when it was created, with the CSS style shown in Listing 9-9.

Listing 9-9. Replacing the Styles in the App.css File in the src Folder

```
img {
  background-color: lightcyan;
  width: 50%;
}
```

The style I defined selects `img` elements and sets the background color and width. In Listing 9-10, I added dependencies to two static files in the src folder to the App component, including the CSS file I updated in the previous listing and the placeholder image added to the project when it is created.

■ **Tip** The `index.css` file is imported by the `index.js` file, which is the JavaScript file responsible for starting the React application. You can define global styles in the CSS file, and they will be included in the content sent to the browser.

Listing 9-10. Declaring a Static Dependency in the App.js File in the src Folder

```
import React, { Component } from "react";
import "./App.css";
import reactLogo from "./logo.svg";
```

```
let name = "Adam";
const city = "London";

export default class extends Component {

    message = () => `Hello ${name} from ${city}`;

    render = () =>
        <div className="text-center">
            <h4 className="bg-primary text-white text-center p-3">
                { this.message() }
            </h4>
            <img src={ reactLogo } alt="reactLogo" />
        </div>
}
```

To import content that doesn't need to be referred to in order to be used, such as a CSS stylesheet, the import keyword is followed by the file name, which must include the file extension, like this:

```
...
import "./App.css";
...
```

To import content that will be referred to in an HTML element, such an image, then the form of the import statement that assigns a name to the imported feature must be used, like this statement:

```
...
import reactLogo from "./logo.svg";
...
```

This statement imports the logo.svg file and assigns it the name reactLogo, which I can then use in an expression in an img element, like this:

```
...
<img src={ reactLogo } alt="reactLogo" />
...
```

When you use the import keyword to declare a dependency on static content, the decision about how to handle the content is left to the development tools. For files that are smaller than 10Kb, the content will be included in the bundle.js file, along with the JavaScript code required to add the content to the HTML document. This is what happens with the App.css file that was imported in Listing 9-10: the contents of the CSS file will be included in the bundle.js file, along with the code required to create a style element.

For larger files—and any SVG files of any size—the imported file is requested in a separate HTTP request. The relative path specified by the import statement is automatically replaced by a URL that will locate the file, and the file name is changed so that it includes a checksum, which ensures that stale data won't be cached by the browser.

You can see the effect of the static content used in Listing 9-10 by saving the changes to the App.js file, waiting for the browser to reload, and then using the F12 developer's tools to examine the Elements tab, which will show the following HTML (although I have omitted the large number of Bootstrap CSS styles for brevity):

```
<html lang="en">
  <head>
    <meta charset="utf-8">
    <link rel="shortcut icon" href="/favicon.ico">
    <meta name="viewport" content="width=device-width,
        initial-scale=1, shrink-to-fit=no">
    <meta name="theme-color" content="#000000">
    <link rel="manifest" href="/manifest.json">
    <title>React App</title>
    <style type="text/css">
      img { background-color: lightcyan; width: 50% }
    </style>
  </head>
  <body>
    <noscript>You need to enable JavaScript to run this app.</noscript>
    <div id="root">
        <div class="text-center">
          <h4 class="bg-primary text-white text-center p-3">
            Hello Adam from London
          </h4>
          <img src="/static/media/logo.5d5d9eef.svg" alt="reactLogo">
        </div>
    </div>
    <script src="/static/js/bundle.js"></script>
    <script src="/static/js/1.chunk.js"></script>
    <script src="/static/js/main.chunk.js"></script>
    <script src="/main.00ec8a0c115561c18137.hot-update.js"></script>
  </body>
</html>
```

You can see that the CSS styles have been unpacked from the JavaScript bundle and added to the HTML document through a style element, whereas the image file is accessed through the URL /static/media/logo.5d5d9eef.svg. During the build process, large files are automatically copied into the location specified by the URLs that are included in the application's code, which means you don't have to worry about them being available. The changes in Listing 9-10 produce the result shown in Figure 9-6.

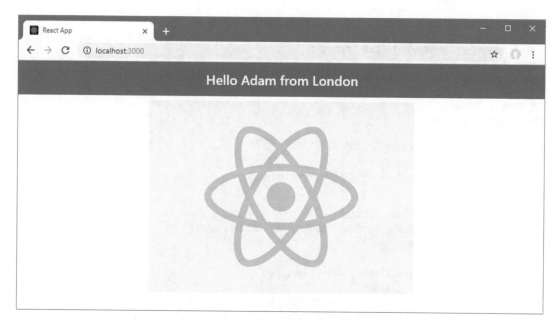

Figure 9-6. *Static content in the src folder*

Using the Public Folder for Static Content

There are several advantages to using the src folder for static content, but you may find that it isn't always suitable for every project, especially where static content isn't available at build time and cannot be processed by the React development tools. In these situations, you can put static content in the public folder, although this means you are responsible for ensuring the application has the files it requires. To demonstrate the use of the public folder, I added to it a file called static.css, with the content shown in Listing 9-11.

Listing 9-11. The Contents of the static.css File in the public Folder

```
img {
    border: 8px solid black;
}
```

Open a new command prompt, navigate to the projecttools folder, and run the command shown in Listing 9-12, which will copy the logo.svg file from the src folder into the public folder.

Listing 9-12. Copying an Image File into the Public Folder

```
cp src/logo.svg public/
```

In Listing 9-13, I have added HTML elements to the content rendered by the App component for the image and stylesheet in the public folder.

Listing 9-13. Accessing Static Files in the App.js File in the src Folder

```
import React, { Component } from "react";
import "./App.css";
import reactLogo from "./logo.svg";

let name = "Adam";
const city = "London";

export default class extends Component {

    message = () => `Hello ${name} from ${city}`;

    render = () =>
        <div className="text-center">
            <h4 className="bg-primary text-white text-center p-3">
                { this.message() }
            </h4>
            <img src={ reactLogo } alt="reactLogo" />
            <link rel="stylesheet"
                    href={ process.env.PUBLIC_URL + "/static.css"} />
            <img src={ process.env.PUBLIC_URL + "/logo.svg" } alt="reactLogo" />
        </div>
}
```

To specify the URL for the static files, the process.env.PUBLIC_URL property is combined with the file name in an expression. Notice that I have added a link element for the stylesheet because I cannot rely on the code in the bundle.js file to create the styles automatically. The result of the elements added to the component is shown in Figure 9-7.

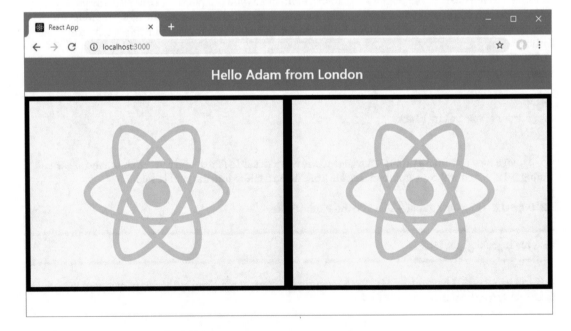

Figure 9-7. *Static content in the public folder*

Understanding the Error Display

One effect of the immediacy provided by the automatic-reload feature is that you will tend to stop watching the console output during development because your focus will naturally gravitate to the browser window. The risk is that the content displayed by the browser remains static when the code contains errors because the compilation process can't produce a new module to send to the browser through the HMR feature. To address this, the bundle produced by webpack includes an integrated error display that shows details of problems in the browser window. To demonstrate the way that an error is handled, I added the statement shown in Listing 9-14 to the App.js file.

Listing 9-14. Creating an Error in the App.js File in the src Folder

```
import React, { Component } from "react";
import "./App.css";
import reactLogo from "./logo.svg";

let name = "Adam";
const city = "London";

not a valid statement

export default class extends Component {

    message = () => `Hello ${name} from ${city}`;

    render = () =>
        <div className="text-center">
            <h4 className="bg-primary text-white text-center p-3">
                { this.message() }
            </h4>
            <img src={ reactLogo } alt="reactLogo" />
            <link rel="stylesheet"
                    href={ process.env.PUBLIC_URL + "/static.css"} />
            <img src={ process.env.PUBLIC_URL + "/logo.svg" } alt="reactLogo" />
        </div>
}
```

The addition isn't a valid JavaScript statement. When the change to the file is saved, the build process tries to compile the code and generates the following error message at the command prompt:

```
...
Failed to compile.

./src/App.js
  Line 8:  Parsing error: Unexpected token, expected ";"

   6 | const city = "London";
   7 |
>  8 | not a valid statement
     |     ^
   9 |
  10 | export default class extends Component {
```

11 |
...

The same error message is displayed in the browser window so you will realize there is a problem even if you are not paying attention to the command-line messages. If you click the stack trace, then the browser will send an HTTP request to the development server, which will try to figure out which code editor you are using and highlight the problem, as shown in Figure 9-8.

■ **Tip** You may need to configure the React development tools to specify your editor, as described in the "Configuring the Development Tools" section, and not all editors are supported. Figure 9-8 shows Visual Studio Code, which is one of the editors for which support is provided.

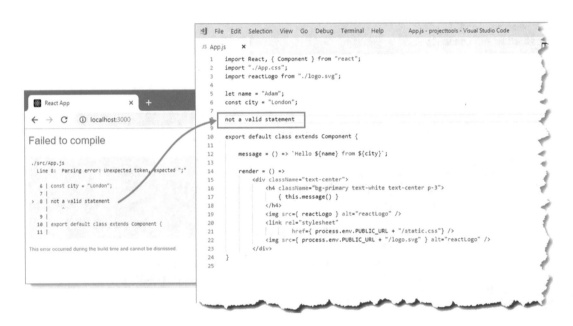

Figure 9-8. *Following an error to the source code file*

Understanding the Linter

The React development tools include a linter, which is responsible for checking the code and content in a project conform to a set of rules. When you create a project using the `create-react-app` package, the ESLint package is used as the linter with a set of rules that are intended to help programmers avoid common errors. As a demonstration, I added a variable to the `App.js` file, as shown in Listing 9-15. (This change also has the effect of removing the statement that causes the compiler error in the previous section).

Listing 9-15. Adding a Variable in the App.js File in the src Folder

```
import React, { Component } from "react";
import "./App.css";
import reactLogo from "./logo.svg";
```

```
let name = "Adam";
const city = "London";

let error = "not a valid statement";

export default class extends Component {

    message = () => `Hello ${name} from ${city}`;

    render = () =>
        <div className="text-center">
            <h4 className="bg-primary text-white text-center p-3">
                { this.message() }
            </h4>
            <img src={ reactLogo } alt="reactLogo" />
            <link rel="stylesheet"
                    href={ process.env.PUBLIC_URL + "/static.css"} />
            <img src={ process.env.PUBLIC_URL + "/logo.svg" } alt="reactLogo" />
        </div>
}
```

When you save the file, you will see the following warning displayed at the command line and also in the browser's JavaScript console:

```
...
Compiled with warnings.

./src/App.js
  Line 8:  'error' is assigned a value but never used  no-unused-vars
...
```

The linter cannot be disabled or reconfigured, which means that you will receive linting warnings for a fixed set of rules, including the no-unused-vars rule, which is the one broken by Listing 9-15. You can see the set of rules that are applied in React projects at https://github.com/facebook/create-react-app/tree/master/packages/eslint-config-react-app.

When you receive a warning, a search for the rule name will provide you with a description of the problem. In this case, a search for no-unused-vars will lead you to https://eslint.org/docs/rules/no-unused-vars, which explains that variables cannot be defined and not used.

Disabling Linting for Individual Statements and Files

Although the linter cannot be disabled, you can add comments to files to prevent warnings. In Listing 9-16, I have disabled the no-unused-var rule for a single statement by adding a comment.

Listing 9-16. Disabling a Single Linting Rule in the App.js File in the src Folder

```
import React, { Component } from "react";
import "./App.css";
import reactLogo from "./logo.svg";
```

```
let name = "Adam";
const city = "London";

// eslint-disable-next-line no-unused-vars
let error = "not a valid statement";

export default class extends Component {

    message = () => `Hello ${name} from ${city}`;

    render = () =>
        <div className="text-center">
            <h4 className="bg-primary text-white text-center p-3">
                { this.message() }
            </h4>
            <img src={ reactLogo } alt="reactLogo" />
            <link rel="stylesheet"
                    href={ process.env.PUBLIC_URL + "/static.css"} />
            <img src={ process.env.PUBLIC_URL + "/logo.svg" } alt="reactLogo" />
        </div>
}
```

If you want to disable every rule for a next statement, then you can omit the rule name, as shown in Listing 9-17.

Listing 9-17. Disabling All Linting Rules in the App.js File in the src Folder

```
...
// eslint-disable-next-line
let error = "not a valid statement";
...
```

If you want to disable a rule for an entire file, then you can add a comment to the top of the file, as shown in Listing 9-18.

Listing 9-18. Disabling a Single Rule for a File in the App.js File in the src Folder

```
/* eslint-disable no-unused-vars */

import React, { Component } from "react";
import "./App.css";
import reactLogo from "./logo.svg";

let name = "Adam";
const city = "London";

let error = "not a valid statement";

export default class extends Component {

    message = () => `Hello ${name} from ${city}`;
```

```
render = () =>
    <div className="text-center">
        <h4 className="bg-primary text-white text-center p-3">
            { this.message() }
        </h4>
        <img src={ reactLogo } alt="reactLogo" />
        <link rel="stylesheet"
                href={ process.env.PUBLIC_URL + "/static.css"} />
        <img src={ process.env.PUBLIC_URL + "/logo.svg" } alt="reactLogo" />
    </div>
}
```

If you want to disable linting for all rules for a single file, then you can omit the rule name from the comment, as shown in Listing 9-19.

Listing 9-19. Disabling All Rules for a File in the App.js File in the src Folder

```
...
/* eslint-disable */

import React, { Component } from 'react';
import "./App.css";
import reactLogo from "./logo.svg";

let name = "Adam";
const city = "London";
...
```

The linter will ignore the contents of the App.js file but will still check the contents of the other files in the project.

USING TYPESCRIPT OR FLOW

Linting isn't the only way to detect common errors and a good complementary technique is *static type checking*, in which you add details of the data types for variables and function results to your code to create a policy that is enforced by the compiler. For example, you might specify that a function always returns a string or that its first parameter can only be a number. When the application is compiled, the code that uses that function is checked to ensure that it only passes number values as arguments and treats the result only as a string.

There are two common ways to add static type checking to a React project. The first is to use TypeScript, which is a superset of JavaScript produced by Microsoft. TypeScript makes working with JavaScript more like C# or Java and includes support for static type checking. If you want to use TypeScript, then use the --scripts-version argument when you create the project, like this:

```
...
npx create-react-app projecttools --scripts-version=react-scripts-ts
...
```

The `react-scripts-ts` value produces a project that is set up with the TypeScript tools and features. You can learn more about TypeScript at `https://www.typescriptlang.org`.

An alternative is a package called Flow, which is focused solely on type checking and doesn't have the broader features of TypeScript. You can learn more about Flow at `https://flow.org`

Configuring the Development Tools

The React development tools provide a small number of configuration options, although these won't be required in most projects. The available options are described in Table 9-8.

***Table 9-8.** The React Development Tools Configuration Options*

Name	Description
BROWSER	This option is used to specify the browser that is opened when the development tools complete the initial build process. You can specify a browser by specifying its path or disable this feature by using none.
HOST	This option is used to specify the hostname that the development HTTP server binds to, which defaults to `localhost`.
PORT	This option is used to specify the port that the development HTTP server uses, which defaults to 3000.
HTTPS	When set to `true`, this option enables SSL for the development HTTP server, which generates a self-signed certificate. The default is `false`.
PUBLIC_URL	This option is used to change the URL used to request content from the `public` folder, as described in the *Understanding Static Content* section.
CI	When set to `true`, this option treats all warnings as errors in the build process. The default value is `false`.
REACT_EDITOR	This option is used to specify the editor for the feature that opens the code file when you click on a stack trace in the browser, as described in the *Understanding the Error Display* section.
CHOKIDAR_USEPOLLING	This option should be set to `true` when the development tools cannot detect changes to the `src` folder, which may happen if you are working in a virtual machine or a container.
GENERATE_SOURCEMAP	Settings this option to `false` disables the generation of source maps, which the browser uses to correlate the bundled JavaScript code with the source files in the project during debugging. The default is `true`.
NODE_PATH	This setting is used to specify the locations that will be searched for Node.js modules.

These options are specified either by setting environment variables or by creating an `.env` file, which is the approach that I find most reliable. To demonstrate the configuration process, I added a file called `.env` to the `projecttools` folder and added the configuration statements shown in Listing 9-20.

Listing 9-20. The Contents of the .env File in the projecttools Folder

```
PORT=3500
HTTPS=true
```

I used the PORT option to specify port 3500 for receiving requests and the HTTPS option to enable SSL in the development server. To see the effect of the changes, stop the development tools and run the command shown in Listing 9-21 to start them again.

Listing 9-21. Starting the React Development Tools

```
npm start
```

When the initial build process is complete, the browser window that is opened will navigate to https:// localhost:3500. Most browsers will display a warning about the self-signed certificate and then display the web application once you have clicked on the Advanced link (or its equivalent) and told the browser to proceed, as shown in Figure 9-9.

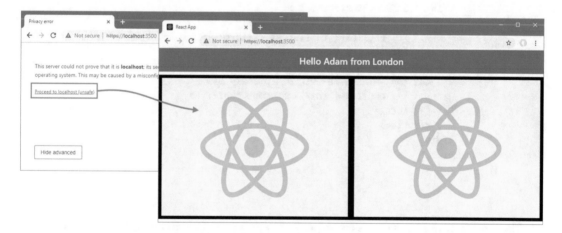

Figure 9-9. *Configuring the Development Tools*

Debugging React Applications

Not all problems can be detected by the compiler or the linter, and code that compiles perfectly can behave in unexpected ways. There are two ways to understand the behavior of your application, as described in the sections that follow. To help demonstrate the debugging features, I added a file called Display.js to the src folder and used it to define the component shown in Listing 9-22.

Listing 9-22. The Contents of the Display.js File in the src Folder

```
import React, {Component } from "react";

export class Display extends Component {
```

243

```
constructor(props) {
    super(props);
    this.state = {
        counter: 1
    }
}

incrementCounter = () => {
    this.setState({ counter: this.state.counter + 1 });
}

render() {
    return (
        <div>
            <h2 className="bg-primary text-white text-center p-2">
                <div>Props Value: { this.props.value }</div>
                <div>Local Value: { this.state.counter } </div>
            </h2>
            <div className="text-center">
                <button className="btn btn-primary m-2"
                        onClick={ this.props.callback }>
                    Parent
                </button>
                <button  className="btn btn-primary m-2"
                        onClick={ this.incrementCounter }>
                    Local
                </button>
            </div>
        </div>
    )
}
}
```

The component displays its own state property and a prop value it receives from its parents. It displays two button elements, one of which changes the state property and one of which invokes a callback provided as a prop. In Listing 9-23, I replaced the existing contents of the App component to prepare for the debugging section.

Listing 9-23. Replacing the Contents of the App.js File in the src Folder

```
import React, { Component } from "react";
import { Display } from "./Display";

export default class App extends Component {

    constructor(props) {
        super(props);
        this.state = {
            city: "London"
        }
    }
```

```
changeCity = () => {
    this.setState({ city: this.state.city === "London" ? "New York" : "London"})
}

render() {
    return (
        <Display value={ this.state.city } callback={ this.changeCity } />
    );
}
}
```

When you save the changes to the JavaScript files, the application will be compiled, and you will see the content shown in Figure 9-10.

■ **Note**   You may find that the browser doesn't update automatically when the HTTPS option is set to true in the .env file. You can reload the browser manually to see the changes or disable this option and restart the development tools.

Figure 9-10. Adding functionality to the example application

Exploring the Application State

The React Devtools browser extension is an excellent tool for exploring the state of a React application. There are versions available for Google Chrome and Mozilla Firefox, and details of the project—including support for other platforms and details of a stand-alone version—can be found at https://github.com/facebook/react-devtools. Once you have installed the extension, you will see an additional tab in the browser's developer tools window, which is accessed by pressing the F12 button (which is why these are also known as the F12 tools).

The React tab in the F12 tools window allows you to explore and alter the application's structure and state. You can see the set of components that provide the application functionality, along with their state data and their props.

For the example application, if you open the React tab and expand the application structure in the left pane, you will see the App and Display components in the left pane, displayed with the view of the HTML elements presented by the application. When you select a component in the left page, its props and state data are displayed in the right pane, as shown in Figure 9-11.

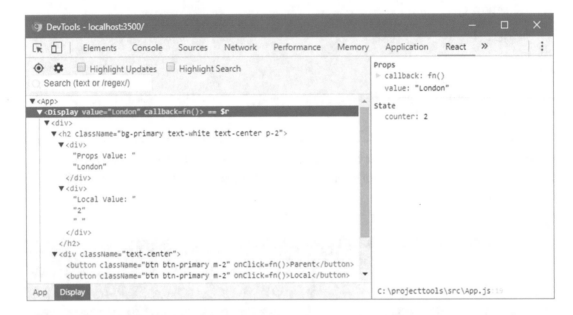

Figure 9-11. Exploring components using the React Devtools

If you click the buttons in the browser window, you will see the values displayed by the React Devtools change, reflecting the live state of the application. You can also click a state data value and change its values through React Devtools, which allows the state of the application to be manipulated directly.

■ **Tip** There are also debugging tools for the Redux data store package, which I describe in Chapter 19 and which is often used to manage the data for complex projects.

Using the Browser Debugger

Modern browsers include sophisticated debuggers that can be used to control the execution of an application and examine its state. The React development tools include support for creating source maps, which allow the browser to correlate the minified and bundled code that it is executing with the developer-friendly source code required for productive debugging.

Some browsers let you navigate through the application's source code using these source maps and create breakpoints, which will halt the execution of the application when they are reached and pass control to the debugger. As I write this, the ability to create breakpoints is a fragile feature that doesn't work on Chrome and has mixed reliability in other browsers. As a consequence, the most reliable way to pass control of the application to the debugger is to use the JavaScript debugger keyword, as shown in Listing 9-24.

Listing 9-24. Triggering the Debugger in the App.js File in the src Folder

```
import React, { Component } from "react";
import { Display } from "./Display";

export default class App extends Component {

    constructor(props) {
        super(props);
        this.state = {
            city: "London"
        }
    }

    changeCity = () => {
        debugger
        this.setState({ city: this.state.city === "London" ? "New York" : "London"})
    }

    render() {
        return (
            <Display value={ this.state.city } callback={ this.changeCity } />
        );
    }
}
```

To use the debugger effectively, disable the HTTPS option in the .env file, as shown in Listing 9-25. If you do not disable this option, you will only see the code generated by Babel and not your original source code.

Listing 9-25. Disabling Secure Connections in the .env File in the projecttools Folder

```
PORT=3500
HTTPS=false
```

Stop the development tools and start them again by running the command shown in Listing 9-26 in the projecttools folder.

Listing 9-26. Starting the Development Tools

```
npx start
```

The application will be executed as normal, but when the Parent button is clicked and the changeCity method is invoked, the browser will encounter the debugger keyword and halt the execution of the application. You can then use the controls in the F12 tools window to inspect the variables and their values at the point at which execution was stopped and manually control execution, as shown in Figure 9-12. The browser is executing the minified and bundled code created by the development tools but displaying the corresponding code from the source map.

■ **Tip** Most browsers ignore the `debugger` keyword unless the F12 tools window is open, but it is good practice to remove it at the end of a debugging session.

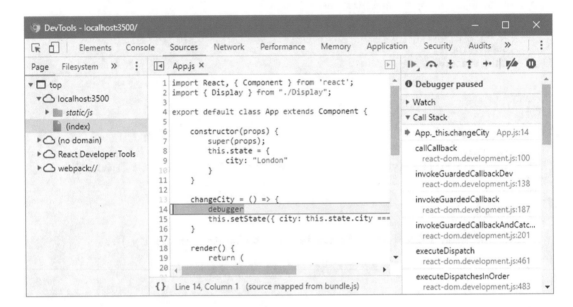

Figure 9-12. *Using the browser debugger*

Summary

In this chapter, I described the structure of React projects created with the `create-react-app` package and explained the purpose of the files and folders used in React development. I also explained how the React development tools are used, how applications are bundled for use in the browser, how the error display and linter help avoid common problems, and how you can debug applications when you don't receive the results you are expecting. In the next chapter, I introduce components, which are the key building block for React applications.

CHAPTER 10

■ ■ ■

Components and Props

In this chapter, I describe the key building block in React applications: the component. I focus on the simplest type of component in this chapter, which is the *stateless component*. I describe the more complex alternative, stateful components, in Chapter 11. I also explain how the props feature works in this chapter, which allows one component to provide another with the data it requires to render its content and the functions it should invoke when something important happens. Table 10-1 puts stateless components and props in context.

Table 10-1. *Putting Stateless Components and Props in Context*

Question	Answer
What are they?	Components are the key building blocks in React applications. Stateless components are JavaScript functions that render content that React can present to the user. Props are the means by which one component provides data to another so that it can adapt the content it renders.
Why are they useful?	Components are useful because they provide access to the React support for creating features by combining JavaScript, HTML, and other components. Props are useful because they allow components to adapt the content they produce.
How are they used?	Stateless components are defined as JavaScript functions that return a React element, which is usually defined using HTML in the JSX format. Props are defined as properties on elements.
Are there any pitfalls or limitations?	React requires components to behave in specific ways, such as returning a single React element and always returning a result, and it can take time to become used to these restrictions. The most common pitfall with props is specifying literal values when a JavaScript expression was required.
Are there any alternatives?	Components are the key building block in React applications, and there is no way to avoid their use. There are alternative to props that can be useful in larger and more complex projects, as described in Chapter 14 and in Part 3.

© Adam Freeman 2019
A. Freeman, *Pro React 16*, https://doi.org/10.1007/978-1-4842-4451-7_10

Table 10-2 summarizes the chapter.

Table 10-2. *Chapter Summary*

Problem	Solution	Listing
Add content to a React application	Define a function that returns HTML elements or invokes the `React.createElement` method	1–9
Add additional features to a React application	Define components and compose them in a parent-child relationship using elements that correspond to the component name	10–14
Configure a child component	Define props when applying the component	15–19
Render HTML elements for each object in a data array	Use the map method to create elements, ensuring that they have a `key` prop	20–24
Render multiple elements from a component	Use the `React.Fragment` element or use elements without tags	25–28
Render no content	Return `null`	29
Receive notifications from a child component	Configure the component with a function prop	31–34
Pass on props to a child	Use the prop values received from the parent or use the destructuring operator	35–39
Define default prop values	Use the `defaultProps` property	40, 41
Check prop types	Use the `propTypes` property	42–44

Preparing for This Chapter

To create the example project for this chapter, open a new command prompt, navigate to a convenient location, and run the command shown in Listing 10-1.

■ **Tip**   You can download the example project for this chapter—and for all the other chapters in this book—from `https://github.com/Apress/pro-react-16`.

Listing 10-1. Creating the Example Project

```
npx create-react-app components
```

Run the commands shown in Listing 10-2 to navigate to the project folder and add the Bootstrap package to the project.

Listing 10-2. Adding the Bootstrap CSS Framework

```
cd components
npm install bootstrap@4.1.2
```

To include the Bootstrap CSS stylesheet in the application, add the statement shown in Listing 10-3 to the index.js file, which can be found in the src folder.

Listing 10-3. Including Bootstrap in the index.js File in the src Folder

```
import React from 'react';
import ReactDOM from 'react-dom';
import './index.css';
import App from './App';
import * as serviceWorker from './serviceWorker';
import 'bootstrap/dist/css/bootstrap.css';

ReactDOM.render(<App />, document.getElementById('root'));

// If you want your app to work offline and load faster, you can change
// unregister() to register() below. Note this comes with some pitfalls.
// Learn more about service workers: http://bit.ly/CRA-PWA
serviceWorker.unregister();
```

Using the command prompt, run the command shown in Listing 10-4 in the components folder to start the development tools.

Listing 10-4. Starting the Development Tools

```
npm start
```

Once the initial preparation for the project is complete, a new browser window will open and display the URL http://localhost:3000 and display the placeholder content shown in Figure 10-1.

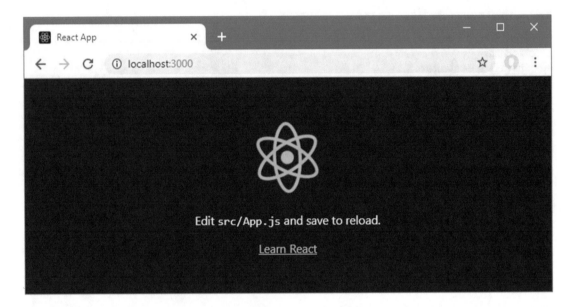

Figure 10-1. *Running the example application*

Understanding Components

The best place to start with components is by defining one and seeing how it works. In Listing 10-5,
I replaced the contents of the App.js file with a simple component.

Listing 10-5. Defining a Component in the App.js File in the src Folder

```
export default function App() {
    return "Hello Adam";
}
```

This is an example of a *stateless component*, and it is just about as simple as a component can
be: a function that returns content that React will display to the user, which is known as *rendering*.
When the application starts, the code in the index.js file is executed, including the statement that
renders the App component. React invokes the function and displays the result to the user, as shown
in Figure 10-2.

Figure 10-2. *Defining and applying a component*

As simple as the result might be, it reveals the key purpose of components, which is to provide React with content to display to the user.

Rendering HTML Content

When a component renders a string value, it is included as text content in the parent element. Components become more useful when they return HTML content, which is most easily done by taking advantage of JSX and the way it allows HTML to be mixed with JavaScript code. In Listing 10-6, I changed the result of the component so that it renders a fragment of HTML.

■ **Tip** You must declare a dependency on React from the react module when you use JSX, as shown in the listing. You will receive a warning if you forget.

Listing 10-6. Rendering HTML in the App.js File in the src Folder

```
import React from "react";

export default function App() {
    return   <h1 className="bg-primary text-white text-center p-2">
                Hello Adam
            </h1>
}
```

You remember to use the return keyword inside the component's function to render the result. This can feel awkward, but remember that the HTML fragment in a JSX file is converted to a call to the createElement method, which produces an object that React can display to the user.

The use of the return keyword makes sense when you consider what the code looks like once the HTML fragment has been replaced with the createElement method during the build process.

```
...
import React from "react";

export default function App() {
    return React.createElement("h1",
                { className: "bg-primary text-white text-center p-2" },
                "Hello Adam");
}
...
```

The component function returns the result from the React.createElement method, which is an element that React can use to add content to the Domain Object Model (DOM).

If you want to start the HTML on a separate line from the return keyword, then you can use parentheses to enclose the result, as shown in Listing 10-7.

Listing 10-7. Using Parentheses in the App.js File in the src Folder

```
import React from "react";

export default function App() {
    return (
        <h1 className="bg-primary text-white text-center p-2">
            Hello Adam
        </h1>
    )
}
```

This allows the HTML elements to be consistently indented, although the dangling (and) characters can strike some developers as awkward.

Functional components can also be defined using the fat arrow syntax, which omits the return keyword, as shown in Listing 10-8.

Listing 10-8. Using a Fat Arrow Function in the App.js File in the src Folder

```
import React from "react";

export default () =>
    <h1 className="bg-primary text-white text-center p-2">
        Hello Adam
    </h1>
```

The fat arrow function is exported without a name, which works in the example application because the statement in the index.js file that imports the component from the App.js file uses the default export, like this:

```
...
import App from './App';
...
```

Exporting a fat arrow function by name and as the default requires an additional statement, as shown in Listing 10-9.

Listing 10-9. Creating a Named and Default Export in the App.js File in the src Folder

```
import React from "react";

export const App = () =>
    <h1 className="bg-primary text-white text-center p-2">
        Hello Adam
    </h1>

export default App;
```

The fat arrow function is assigned to a const that is exported by name, and a separate statement uses the name to create the default export, which allows the component to be imported by name and as the default.

■ **Note**   I have included this example because module exports cause confusion, but in real projects they use either named or default exports throughout and don't have to accommodate both styles of working. I prefer using named exports, and that is the approach I have taken in the examples in this book.

I use regular functions in this chapter and use parentheses where they help make the HTML content more readable, but all of the examples in this section produce the same result, as shown in Figure 10-3.

Figure 10-3.   *Returning HTML content*

Rendering Other Components

One of the most important React features is that the content rendered by a component can contain other components, allowing features to be combined to create complex applications. I added a file called Message.js to the src folder and used it to define the component shown in Listing 10-10.

Listing 10-10.   The Contents of the Message.js File in the src Folder

```
import React from "react";

export function Message() {
    return   <h4 className="bg-success text-white text-center p-2">
                This is a message
            </h4>
}
```

The Message component renders an h4 element that contains a message. In Listing 10-11, I have updated the App component so that it renders the Message content as part of its content.

Listing 10-11.   Rendering Another Component in the App.js File in the src Folder

```
import React from "react";
import { Message } from "./Message";
```

255

```
export default function App() {
    return (
        <div>
            <h1 className="bg-primary text-white text-center p-2">
                Hello Adam
            </h1>
            <Message />
        </div>
    )
}
```

The import statement declares a dependency on the Message component, which is rendered using a Message element. When React receives the content rendered by the App component, it will contain the Message element, which it will deal with by invoking the Message component's function and replacing the Message element with the content it renders, producing the result shown in Figure 10-4.

Figure 10-4. *Rendering other content*

When one component uses another like this, a parent-child relationship is formed. In this example, the App component is the parent to the Message component, and the Message component is the child of the App component. A component can apply the same component more than once by defining multiple elements for the child component, as shown in Listing 10-12.

Listing 10-12. Applying a Child Component in the App.js File in the src Folder

```
import React from "react";
import { Message } from "./Message";

export default function App() {
    return (
        <div>
            <h1 className="bg-primary text-white text-center p-2">
                Hello Adam
            </h1>
```

```
        <Message />
        <Message />
        <Message />
    </div>
)
}
```

Each time that React encounters the Message element, it invokes the Message component and uses the content it renders to replace the Message element, as shown in Figure 10-5.

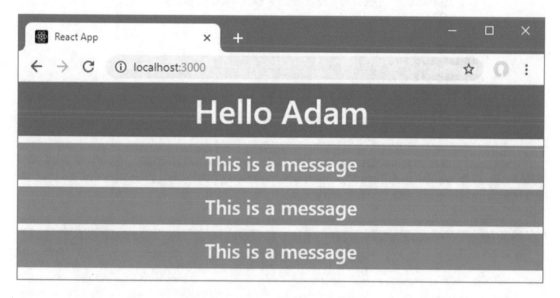

Figure 10-5. *Applying multiple children*

A component can have children of different types, which means that one component can take advantage of the features that multiple components offer. I created another simple component by adding a file called Summary.js to the src folder with the code shown in Listing 10-13.

Listing 10-13. The Contents of the Summary.js File in the src Folder

```
import React from "react";

export function Summary() {
    return  <h4 className="bg-info text-white text-center p-2">
                This is a summary
            </h4>
}
```

In Listing 10-14, I have updated the App component to declare a dependency on the Summary component and render its contents using a Summary element.

Listing 10-14. Adding a Child Component in the App.js File in the src Folder

```
import React from "react";
import { Message } from "./Message";
import { Summary } from "./Summary";

export default function App() {
    return (
        <div>
            <h1 className="bg-primary text-white text-center p-2">
                Hello Adam
            </h1>
            <Message />
            <Message />
            <Message />
            <Summary />
        </div>
    )
}
```

When React processes the content rendered by the App component, it encounters the elements for the child components, invokes their function, and replaces the Message and Summary elements with the content they render. The result is shown in Figure 10-6.

Figure 10-6. Using different child components

Understanding Props

Being able to render content from multiple children isn't that useful when each component renders identical content. Fortunately, React supports *props*—short for *properties*—which allows a parent component to provide data to its children, which they can use to render their content. In the sections that follow, I explain how props work and demonstrate the different ways they can be used.

Defining Props in the Parent Component

Props are defined by adding properties to the custom HTML elements that apply components. The name of the property is the name of the prop, and the value can be a static value or an expression. In Listing 10-15, I have added props to the Message elements used by the App component.

Listing 10-15. Defining Props in the App.js File in the src Folder

```
import React from "react";
import { Message } from "./Message";
import { Summary } from "./Summary";

export default function App() {
    return (
        <div>
            <h1 className="bg-primary text-white text-center p-2">
                Hello Adam
            </h1>
            <Message greeting="Hello" name="Bob" />
            <Message greeting="Hola" name={ "Alice" + "Smith" } />
            <Message greeting="Hi there" name="Dora" />
            <Summary />
        </div>
    )
}
```

I have provided two props, greeting and name, for each Message component. Most of the prop values are static values, which are expressed as literal strings. The value for the greeting prop on the second Message element is an expression, which concatenates two string values. (You will see a linter warning about the expression in Listing 10-15 because concatenating string literal values is on the list of poor practices that the linter is configured to detect. The linter warning can be ignored for this purposes of this chapter.)

DEFINING PROPS

Props can be used to pass static values or the results of dynamic expressions to child components. Static values are quoted literally, like this:

```
...
<Message greeting="Hello" name="Bob" />
...
```

This prop provides the child component with the value Bob for its name prop. If you want to use the result of a JavaScript expression as the value for the prop, then use a data binding expression, like this:

```
...
<Message greeting="Hola" name={ "Alice" + "Smith" } />
...
```

React will evaluate the expression and use the result, which is the concatenation of two strings in this example, as the value for the prop. A common mistake is to put the JavaScript expression in quotes, like this:

```
...
<Message greeting="Hola" name="{ "Alice" + "Smith" }" />
...
```

React will interpret this as a request to use the static value { "Alice" + "Smith" } as the value for the prop. When using expressions for props, you must remember not to use quotes. If you prefer not to use JSX and want to create React elements using pure JavaScript, then props are provided as the second argument to the createElement method, like this:

```
...
React.createElement(Message, { greeting: "Hola",  name: "Alice" + "Smith"})
...
```

If you don't get the results you expect, in JSX or pure JavaScript, the React Devtools browser extension (described in Chapter 9) can display the props that are received by each component in the application, which makes it easy to see where things have gone wrong.

Receiving Props in the Child Component

Props are received in components by defining a parameter called props (although that is just a convention, and you can give the parameter any legal JavaScript name). The props object has a property for each of the props, which is assigned the prop value. As an example, these props from Listing 10-15:

```
...
<Message greeting="Hello" name="Bob" />
...
```

will be translated into an object like this:

```
...
{
    greeting: "Hello",
    name: "Bob"
}
...
```

In Listing 10-16, I have changed the Message component so that it defines a prop parameter and uses the values provided by the parent component in the result it produces.

Listing 10-16. Using Props in the Message.js File in the src Folder

```
import React from "react";

export function Message(props) {
    return    <h4 className="bg-success text-white text-center p-2">
                {props.greeting}, {props.name}
            </h4>
}
```

The child component doesn't need to worry about whether a prop value was specified statically or with an expression and uses the props like any other JavaScript object. In the listing, I used the greeting and name props in an expression to set the contents of the h4 element rendered by the component, producing the result shown in Figure 10-7.

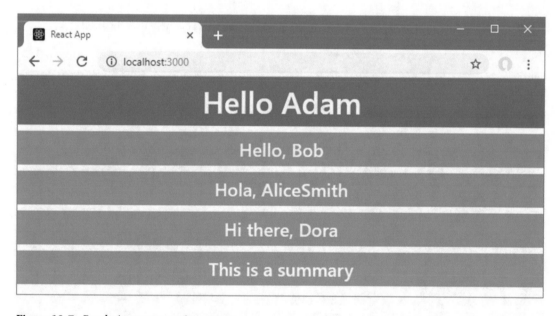

Figure 10-7. Rendering content using props

Combining JavaScript and Props to Render Content

The prop values provided to each Message element defined by the App component in Listing 10-16 results in different content, allowing the same functionality to be employed by the parent component in different ways.

Selectively Rendering Content

Components can use the JavaScript if keyword to inspect a prop and render different content based on its value. In Listing 10-17, I used the if statement to alter the content rendered by the Message component.

Listing 10-17. Selectively Rendering in the Message.js File in the src Folder

```
import React from "react";

export function Message(props) {
    if (props.name === "Bob") {
        return   <h4 className="bg-warning p-2">{props.greeting}, {props.name}</h4>
    } else {
        return   <h4 className="bg-success text-white text-center p-2">
                {props.greeting}, {props.name}
            </h4>
    }
}
```

If the value of the name prop is Bob, the component will render an h4 element with different class memberships, as shown in Figure 10-8.

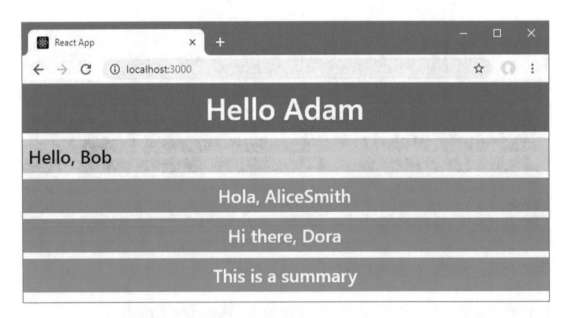

Figure 10-8. *Using an if statement to select content*

This type of selective rendering, where only the value of a prop changes, can be expressed with less duplication by separating the value of the property from the rest of the HTML, as shown in Listing 10-18.

Listing 10-18. Selecting a Property Value in the Message.js File in the src Folder

```
import React from "react";

export function Message(props) {

    let classes = props.name === "Bob" ? "bg-warning p-2"
        : "bg-success text-white text-center p-2";

    return  <h4 className={ classes }>
                {props.greeting}, {props.name}
            </h4>
}
```

I have used the JavaScript ternary conditional operator to select the classes that the h4 element will be assigned to and applied those classes with an expression for the className property. The result is the same as Listing 10-17 but without duplicating the unchanging parts of the HTML element.

A switch statement can be used when a component needs to select content from a more complex list, as shown in Listing 10-19.

Listing 10-19. Using a switch Statement in the Message.js File in the src Folder

```
import React from "react";

export function Message(props) {
    let classes;
    switch (props.name) {
        case "Bob":
            classes = "bg-warning p-2";
            break;
        case "Dora":
            classes = "bg-secondary text-white text-center p-2"
            break;
        default:
            classes = "bg-success text-white text-center p-2"
    }
    return  <h4 className={ classes }>
                {props.greeting}, {props.name}
            </h4>
}
```

This example uses the switch statement on the props.name value to select the classes for the h4 element, producing the result shown in Figure 10-9.

Figure 10-9. *Using a switch statement to select content*

Rendering Arrays

Components often have to create HTML elements for each element in an array, often to display items in a list or as rows in a table. The technique required for dealing with arrays causes confusion and is worth approaching carefully. To prepare, I updated the App component so that it configures the Summary component with a prop, as shown in Listing 10-20. (I also removed elements to keep the example simple.)

Listing 10-20. Adding a Prop in the App.js File in the src Folder

```
import React from "react";
//import { Message } from "./Message";
import { Summary } from "./Summary";

export default function App() {
    return (
        <div>
            <h1 className="bg-primary text-white text-center p-2">
                Hello Adam
            </h1>
            <Summary names={ ["Bob", "Alice", "Dora"]} />
        </div>
    )
}
```

The names prop provides the Summary component with an array of string values. In Listing 10-21, I have changed the content rendered by the Summary component so that it produces elements for each of the values in the array.

Listing 10-21. Rendering an Array in the Summary.js File in the src Folder

```
import React from "react";

function createInnerElements(names) {
    let arrayElems  = [];
    for (let i = 0; i < names.length; i++) {
        arrayElems.push(
            <div>
                {`${names[i]} contains ${names[i].length} letters`}
            </div>
        )
    }
    return arrayElems;
}

export function Summary(props) {
    return  <h4 className="bg-info text-white text-center p-2">
                { createInnerElements(props.names)}
            </h4>
}
```

The component function uses an expression to set the content of the h4 element, which it does by invoking the createInnerElements function. The createInnerElements function uses a JavaScript for loop to enumerate the contents of the names array and adds a div element to a result array.

```
...
arrayElems.push(<div>{`${names[i]} contains ${names[i].length} letters`}</div>)
...
```

The content of each div element is set with another expression, which uses a template string to create a message specific to each element in the array. The array of div elements is returned as the result of the createInnerElements function and used as the content for the h4 element, producing the result shown in Figure 10-10.

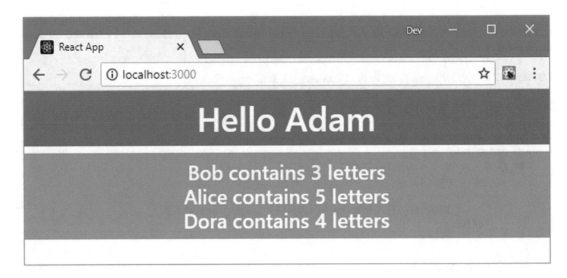

Figure 10-10. *Creating React elements for the objects in an array*

Using the Map Method to Process Array Objects

Although the for loop is the way that most programmers are used to enumerating arrays, it isn't the most elegant way to deal with arrays in React. The map method, described in Chapter 4, can be used to transform objects in an array into HTML elements, as shown in Listing 10-22.

Listing 10-22. Transforming an Array in the Summary.js File in the src Folder

```
import React from "react";

function createInnerElements(names) {
    return names.map(name =>
        <div>
            {`${name} contains ${name.length} letters`}
        </div>
    )
}

export function Summary(props) {
    return   <h4 className="bg-info text-white text-center p-2">
                { createInnerElements(props.names)}
            </h4>
}
```

The argument to the map method is a function that is invoked for each object in the array. Each time the function passed to the map method is invoked, the next item in the array is passed to the function, which I use to create the element that represents that object. The result from each call to the function is added to an array that is used as the map result. The code in Listing 10-22 produces the same result as Listing 10-21.

■ **Tip** You don't have to use fat arrow functions with the map method, but it produces a more concise component.

Now that the createInnerElement function contains a single line of code, I can further simplify the component by moving the statement that creates the inner elements into the component function, as shown in Listing 10-23.

Listing 10-23. Simplifying the Code in the Summary.js File in the src Folder

```
import React from "react";

export function Summary(props) {
    return (
        <h4 className="bg-info text-white text-center p-2">
            {   props.names.map(name =>
                    <div>
                        {`${name} contains ${name.length} letters`}
                    </div>
                )
            }
        </h4>
    )
}
```

This change doesn't alter the output and produces the same result as Listing 10-21 and Listing 10-22.

RECEIVING OTHER ARGUMENTS WHEN USING THE MAP METHOD

In Listing 10-23, the function I passed to the map method receives the current array object as its argument. The map method also provides two additional arguments: the zero-based index of the current object in the array and the complete array of objects. You can see an example of the array index in the "Rendering Multiple Elements" section later in this chapter.

Adding the Key Prop

One final change is required to complete the example. React requires a key prop to be added to elements that are generated for the objects in an array so that changes can be handled efficiently, as I explain in Chapter 13. The value of the key prop should be an expression whose value identifies the object uniquely within the array, as shown in Listing 10-24.

Listing 10-24. Adding the Key Prop in the Summary.js File in the src Folder

```
import React from "react";

export function Summary(props) {
    return (
        <h4 className="bg-info text-white text-center p-2">
            {   props.names.map(name =>
                <div key={ name }>
                    {`${name} contains ${name.length} letters`}
                </div>
                )
            }
        </h4>
    )
}
```

I used the value of the name variable, to which each object in the array is assigned when the function passed to the map method is invoked and which allows React to differentiate between the elements created from the array objects.

React will display elements that do not have a key prop, as the earlier examples in this section demonstrate, but a warning will be displayed in the browser's JavaScript console.

Rendering Multiple Elements

React requires components to return a single top-level element, although that element is able to contain as many other elements as the application requires. The Summary component, for example, returns a top-level h4 element that contains a series of div elements that are generated for the elements in the names prop.

There are times when the requirement for a single top-level element causes a problem. The HTML specification applies restrictions on how elements can be combined, which can conflict with the single element React requirement. To demonstrate the problem, I have changed the content rendered by the App component so that it contains a table, where the contents for each tr element are produced by a child component, as shown in Listing 10-25.

Listing 10-25. Rendering a Table in the App.js File in the src Folder

```
import React from "react";
import { Summary } from "./Summary";

let names = ["Bob", "Alice", "Dora"]

export default function App() {
    return (
        <table className="table table-sm table-striped">
            <thead>
                <tr><th>#</th><th>Name</th><th>Letters</th></tr>
            </thead>
            <tbody>
```

```
            { names.map((name, index) =>
                    <tr key={ name }>
                        <Summary index={index} name={name} />
                    </tr>
                )}
            </tbody>
        </table>
    )
}
```

The Summary component is passed index and name props. In Listing 10-26, I have updated the Summary component so that it generates a series of table cells using the prop values.

Listing 10-26. Rendering Table Cells in the Summary.js File in the src Folder

```
import React from "react";

export function Summary(props) {
    return   <td>{ props.index + 1} </td>
            <td>{ props.name } </td>
            <td>{ props.name.length } </td>
}
```

The Summary component renders a set of td elements because that's what the HTML specification requires as the children of td elements. But when you save the changes, you will see the following error:

```
...
Syntax error: src/Summary.js: Adjacent JSX elements must be wrapped
 in an enclosing tag (5:12)

  3 | export function Summary(props) {
  4 |     return   <td>{ props.index + 1} </td>
> 5 |             <td>{ props.name } </td>
    |             ^
  6 |             <td>{ props.name.length } </td>
  7 | }
...
```

This error message indicates that the content rendered by the component doesn't meet the React requirement of a single top-level element. There isn't an HTML element that can be used to wrap the td elements and still be a legal addition to the table. For these situations, React provides a special element, as shown in Listing 10-27.

Listing 10-27. Wrapping Elements in the Summary.js File in the src Folder

```
import React from "react";

export function Summary(props) {
    return   <React.Fragment>
                <td>{ props.index + 1} </td>
```

```
            <td>{ props.name } </td>
            <td>{ props.name.length } </td>
        </React.Fragment>
}
```

When React processes the elements rendered by the Summary component, it discards the React.Fragment element and uses the remaining content to replace the Summary element that applied the component, as shown in Figure 10-11.

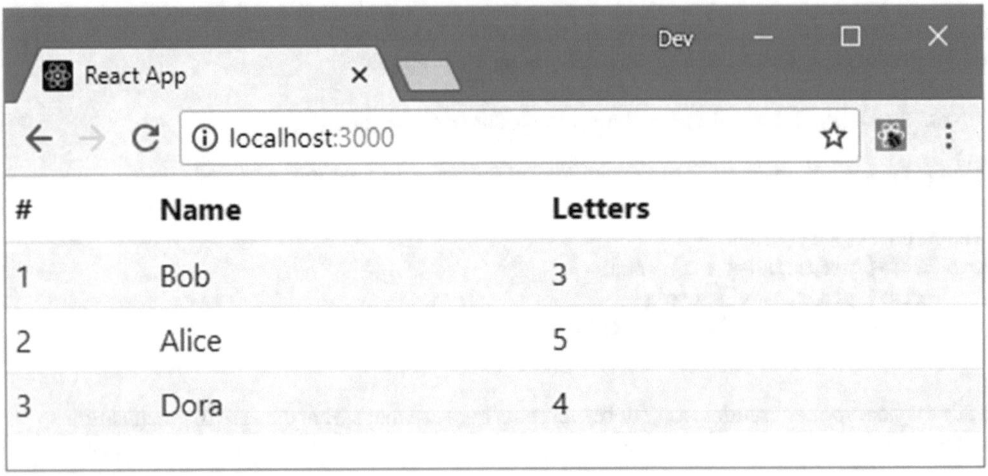

Figure 10-11. *Rendering multiple elements*

React supports an alternative syntax for these situations, which is to use an enclosing element without a tag name, as shown in Listing 10-28.

Listing 10-28. Wrapping Elements in the Summary.js File in the src Folder

```
import React from "react";

export function Summary(props) {
    return <>
            <td>{ props.index + 1} </td>
            <td>{ props.name } </td>
            <td>{ props.name.length } </td>
        </>
}
```

This is equivalent to Listing 10-27 and produces the same result. I use the React.Fragment for the examples in this book or wrap multiple elements in a div where that produces a legal combination of HTML elements.

Rendering No Content

A component must always return a result, even when it doesn't produce any content for React to display. In these situations, the component's function should return null, and in Listing 10-29, I have modified the Summary component so that it doesn't produce any content when the length of its name prop is less than four characters.

Listing 10-29. Rendering No Content in the Summary.js File in the src Folder

```
import React from "react";

export function Summary(props) {
    if (props.name.length >= 4) {
        return   <React.Fragment>
                    <td>{ props.index + 1} </td>
                    <td>{ props.name } </td>
                    <td>{ props.name.length } </td>
                </React.Fragment>
    } else {
        return null;
    }
}
```

The parent component still applies the Summary element three times, each of which results in the Summary component's function being invoked, but only two of those invocations produce a result, as shown in Figure 10-12.

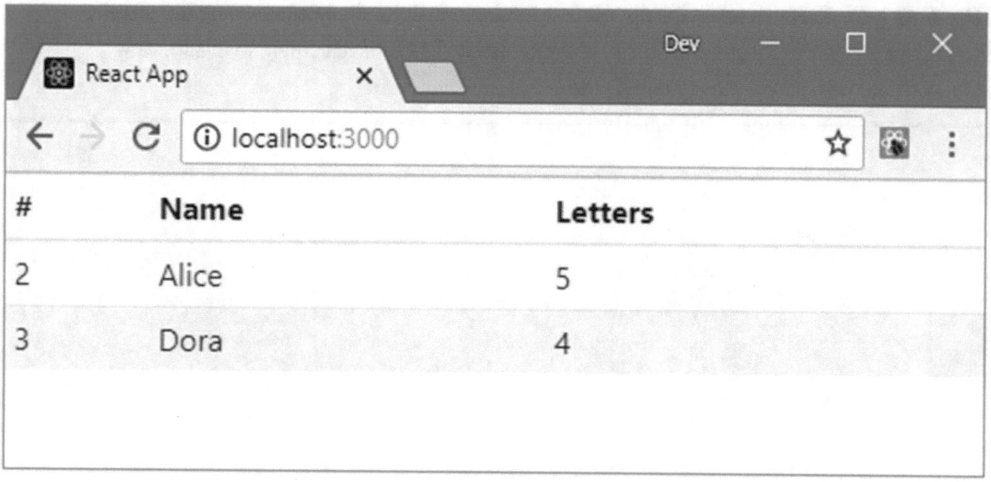

Figure 10-12. *Rendering no content*

Attempting to Change Props

Props are read-only and must not be changed by a component. When React creates the props object, it configures its properties so that an error is displayed if any changes are made. In Listing 10-30, I have added a statement to the Summary component that changes the value of the name prop.

Listing 10-30. Changing a Prop Value in the Summary.js File in the src Folder

```
import React from "react";

export function Summary(props) {
    props.name = `Name: ${props.name}`;
    if (props.name.length >= 4) {
        return  <React.Fragment>
                    <td>{ props.index + 1} </td>
                    <td>{ props.name } </td>
                    <td>{ props.name.length } </td>
                </React.Fragment>
    } else {
        return null;
    }
}
```

When you save the changes and the browser reloads, you will see the error message shown in Figure 10-13. This is a runtime error, which means that no warning is displayed by the compiler at the command prompt.

■ **Tip** This error isn't displayed when the application has been built for deployment using the process described in Chapter 8, which means you should test thoroughly during development to ensure your components don't inadvertently try to change a prop.

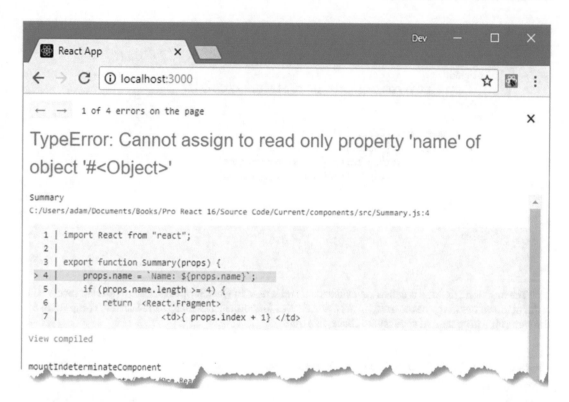

Figure 10-13. *Attempting to modify a prop*

Using Function Props

All of the props I have used so far in this chapter have been *data props*, which provide a child component with a read-only data value. React also supports function props, where the parent component provides a child with a function that it can invoke to notify the parent that something important has happened. The parent component can respond by changing the value of the data props, which will trigger an update and allow the child to present updated content to the user.

To show how this works, I have defined a function in the file that contains the App component that changes the order of the values that are used for the name props for the Summary elements, as shown in Listing 10-31.

Listing 10-31. Defining a Change Function in the App.js File in the src Folder

```
import React from "react";
import { Summary } from "./Summary";
import ReactDOM from "react-dom";

let names = ["Bob", "Alice", "Dora"]

function reverseNames() {
    names.reverse();
    ReactDOM.render(<App />, document.getElementById('root'));
}
```

```
export default function App() {
    return (
        <table className="table table-sm table-striped">
            <thead>
                <tr><th>#</th><th>Name</th><th>Letters</th></tr>
            </thead>
            <tbody>
                { names.map((name, index) =>
                    <tr key={ name }>
                        <Summary index={index} name={name}
                            reverseCallback={reverseNames} />
                    </tr>
                )}
            </tbody>
        </table>
    )
}
```

The function I defined is called reverseNames, and it uses the JavaScript reverse method to reverse the order of the values in the names array. The reverseNames function is provided to the Summary component as the value for a prop named reverseCallback, like this:

```
...
<Summary index={index} name={name} reverseCallback={reverseNames} />
...
```

The Summary component will receive a prop object with three properties: the index prop provides the index of the current object being processed by the map method, the name prop provides the current value from the array, and the reverseCallback prop provides the function that will reverse the order of the array's contents. In Listing 10-32, I have updated the Summary component to make use of the function it receives as a prop. (I have also removed the statement that attempts to change the prop value and removed the if statement that prevents the component for rendering content for short names.)

Listing 10-32. Using a Function Prop in the Summary.js File in the src Folder

```
import React from "react";

export function Summary(props) {
    return (
        <React.Fragment>
            <td>{ props.index + 1} </td>
            <td>{ props.name } </td>
            <td>{ props.name.length } </td>
            <td>
                <button className="btn btn-primary btn-sm"
                    onClick={ props.reverseCallback }>
                        Change
                </button>
            </td>
        </React.Fragment>
    )
}
```

The component renders a button element whose onClick prop selects the function prop it receives from its parent. I describe the onClick prop in Chapter 12, but, as you have seen in earlier chapters, this property tells React how to respond when the user clicks an element, and, in this case, the expression tells React to invoke the reverseCallback prop, which is the function that has been provided by the parent component.

The result is that clicking a button element causes React to invoke the changeValues function defined in the App.js file, which reverses the order of the values used for the name props, producing the result shown in Figure 10-14.

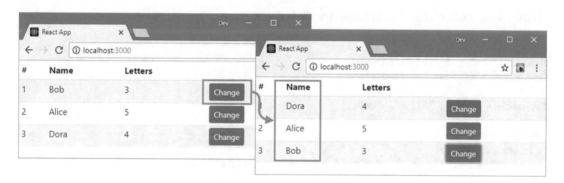

Figure 10-14. *Using a function received as a prop*

UNDERSTANDING THE UPDATE STATEMENT

When the Summary component invokes the function prop, the reverseCallback function is called, and this statement from Listing 10-31 is executed:

```
...
ReactDOM.render(<App />, document.getElementById('root'));
...
```

The render method is used to add a component's content to the Document Object Model (DOM) displayed by the browser and is used in the index.js file to start the application; it is described in Chapter 13. This is not a feature that is normally used directly, but I needed to be able to perform an update in response to the function prop being invoked. I describe the features that are normally used to perform updates in Chapter 11. For the moment, it is enough to know that calling this method updates the HTML elements displayed to the user, reflecting the change in the data values used for prop values.

Invoking Prop Functions with Arguments

In Listing 10-32, the expression for the onClick property specifies the function prop, like this:

```
...
<button className="btn btn-primary btn-sm" onClick={ props.reverseCallback } >
    Change
</button>
...
```

When the function is selected by an expression, it will be passed an event object, which I describe in Chapter 12 and which provides the function that is invoked with details of the HTML element that triggered the event.

This isn't always useful when invoking a function prop, because it requires the parent to have sufficient knowledge of the child component to make sense of the event and act accordingly. Often, a more helpful approach can be to provide a custom argument to the function that gives the parent component the detail it needs directly. In Listing 10-33, I added a function to the App.js file that moves a specified name to the front of the array and updated the App component so it passes the function to its children using a prop.

Listing 10-33. Adding a Function in the App.js File in the src Folder

```
import React from "react";
import { Summary } from "./Summary";
import ReactDOM from "react-dom";

let names = ["Bob", "Alice", "Dora"]

function reverseNames() {
    names.reverse();
    ReactDOM.render(<App />, document.getElementById('root'));
}

function promoteName(name) {
    names = [name, ...names.filter(val => val !== name)];
    ReactDOM.render(<App />, document.getElementById('root'));
}

export default function App() {
    return (
        <table className="table table-sm table-striped">
            <thead>
                <tr><th>#</th><th>Name</th><th>Letters</th></tr>
            </thead>
            <tbody>
                { names.map((name, index) =>
                    <tr key={ name }>
                        <Summary index={index} name={name}
                            reverseCallback={reverseNames}
                            promoteCallback={promoteName} />
                    </tr>
                )}
            </tbody>
        </table>
    )
}
```

The new function receives the name that should be moved to the start of the array as its parameter. In Listing 10-34, I added another button element to the content rendered by the Summary component and used the onClick property to invoke the new function prop.

Listing 10-34. Invoking a Function Prop in the Summary.js File in the src Folder

```
import React from "react";

export function Summary(props) {
    return (
        <React.Fragment>
            <td>{ props.index + 1} </td>
            <td>{ props.name } </td>
            <td>{ props.name.length } </td>
            <td>
                <button className="btn btn-primary btn-sm"
                    onClick={ props.reverseCallback }>
                        Change
                </button>
                <button className="btn btn-info btn-sm m-1"
                    onClick={ () => props.promoteCallback(props.name) }>
                        Promote
                </button>
            </td>
        </React.Fragment>
    )
}
```

Instead of making the App component work out which name has been selected, the function prop is invoked with an argument.

```
...
<button className="btn btn-info btn-sm m-1"
        onClick={ () => props.promoteCallback(props.name) }>
    Promote
</button>
...
```

The onClick expression is a fat arrow function that calls the function prop when it is invoked. It important that you define a function like this, and if you simply specify the function prop directly in the expression, you won't get the results you expect, as described in the sidebar. Clicking one of the Promote buttons will move the corresponding name to the first position in the array so that it is displayed at the top of the table, as shown in Figure 10-15.

Figure 10-15. *Invoking a function prop with an argument*

AVOIDING THE PREMATURE INVOCATION PITFALL

When you need to invoke a function prop with an argument, you should always specify a fat arrow function that invokes the prop, like this:

```
...
<button onClick={ () => props.promoteCallback(props.name) }>
    Promote
</button>
...
```

You will almost certainly forget to do this at least once and call the function prop directly in the expression, like this:

```
...
<button onClick={ props.promoteCallback(props.name) }>
    Promote
</button>
...
```

React will evaluate the expression when the component renders its content, which will invoke the prop even though the user hasn't clicked the button element. This is rarely the intended effect and can cause unexpected behaviors or produce an error, depending on what the prop does when it is invoked. In the case of the component in Listing 10-34, for example, the effect is to create a "Maximum Update Depth Exceeded" error, which occurs because the function prop asks React to re-render the components, which causes the Summary component to render content, which invokes the prop again. This continues until React halts execution and reports an error.

Passing on Props to Child Components

React applications are created by combining components, creating a series of parent-child relationships. This arrangement often requires a component to receive a data value or callback function from its parent and pass it on to its children. To demonstrate how a prop is passed on, I added a file called `CallbackButton.js` to the `src` folder and used it to define the component shown in Listing 10-35.

Listing 10-35. The Contents of the CallbackButton.js File in the src Folder

```
import React from "react";

export function CallbackButton(props) {
    return (
        <button className={`btn btn-${props.theme} btn-sm m-1`}
                onClick={ props.callback }>
            { props.text}
        </button>
    )
}
```

This component renders a `button` element whose text content is set using a prop named `text` and that invokes a function provided through the prop named `callback` when clicked. There is also a `theme` prop that is used to select the Bootstrap CSS style for the `button` element.

In Listing 10-36, I have updated the `Summary` component to use the `CallbackButton` component, which it configures by passing on props from its parent and adding additional props of its own.

Listing 10-36. Adding a Component in the Summary.js File in the src Folder

```
import React from "react";
import { CallbackButton } from "./CallbackButton";

export function Summary(props) {
    return (
        <React.Fragment>
            <td>{ props.index + 1} </td>
            <td>{ props.name } </td>
            <td>{ props.name.length } </td>
            <td>
                <CallbackButton theme="primary"
                    text="Reverse" callback={ props.reverseCallback } />
                <CallbackButton theme="info" text="Promote"
                    callback={ () => props.promoteCallback(props.name)} />
            </td>
        </React.Fragment>
    )
}
```

The component that receives the props doesn't know—or care—where they originated, and they are received through the same `props` argument, producing the result shown in Figure 10-16.

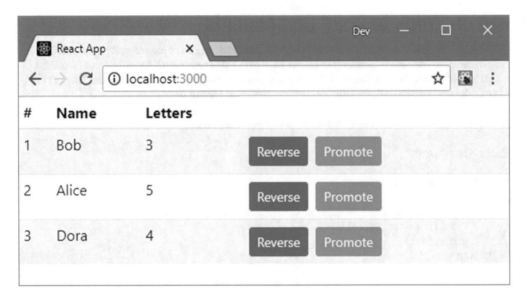

Figure 10-16. *Passing on props*

Passing On All Props to Child Components

The destructuring operator can be used if a component's parent provides props that have the same names as the props expected by the component's child. To demonstrate, I added a file called SimpleButton.js to the src folder and used it to define the component shown in Listing 10-37.

Listing 10-37. The Contents of the SimpleButton.js File in the src Folder

```
import React from "react";

export function SimpleButton(props) {
    return (
        <button onClick={ props.callback } className={props.className}>
            { props.text}
        </button>
    )
}
```

The SimpleButton component expects callback, className, and text props. When the SimpleButton component is applied by the CallbackButton component, there is overlap between the props provided by the parent, which means that the destructuring operator can be used to pass on props, as shown in Listing 10-38.

Listing 10-38. Passing on Props in the CallbackButton.js File in the src Folder

```
import React from "react";
import { SimpleButton } from "./SimpleButton";
```

```
export function CallbackButton(props) {
    return (
        <SimpleButton {...props} className={`btn btn-${props.theme} btn-sm m-1`} />
    )
}
```

The {...props} expression passes on all of the props received from the parent component, which are supplemented by the className prop. If a component wants to withhold specific props from its children, then a slightly different approach can be used, as shown in Listing 10-39.

Listing 10-39. Selectively Passing on Props in the CallbackButton.js File in the src Folder

```
import React from "react";
import { SimpleButton } from "./SimpleButton";

export function CallbackButton(props) {
    let { theme, ...childProps} = props;
    return (
        <SimpleButton { ...childProps }
            className={`btn btn-${props.theme} btn-sm m-1`} />
    )
}
```

The rest operator is used in a statement that creates a childProps object that contains all of the parent's props except theme. The destructuring operator is used to pass the props from the childProps object to the child component.

Providing Default Prop Values

As the number of props used in an application grows, you may find yourself repeating the same set of prop values, even though the values are the same each time. An alternative approach is to define a set of defaults and override only them when you need to use a different value. In Listing 10-40, I defined a set of default prop values for the CallbackButton component.

Listing 10-40. Defining Default Values in the CallbackButton.js File in the src Folder

```
import React from "react";
import { SimpleButton } from "./SimpleButton";

export function CallbackButton(props) {
    let { theme, ...childProps} = props;
    return (
        <SimpleButton {...childProps}
            className={`btn btn-${props.theme} btn-sm m-1`} />
    )
}

CallbackButton.defaultProps = {
    text: "Default Text",
    theme: "warning"
}
```

A property called defaultProps is added to the component and assigned an object that provides default values for props that are used if the parent component doesn't provide a value. In Listing 10-41, I changed the Summary component so that it relies on the default props for one CallbackButton element but provides values for the other.

Listing 10-41. Relying on Prop Defaults in the Summary.js File in the src Folder

```
import React from "react";
import { CallbackButton } from "./CallbackButton";

export function Summary(props) {
    return (
        <React.Fragment>
            <td>{ props.index + 1} </td>
            <td>{ props.name } </td>
            <td>{ props.name.length } </td>
            <td>
                <CallbackButton callback={props.reverseCallback} />
                <CallbackButton theme="info" text="Promote"
                    callback={ () => props.promoteCallback(props.name)} />
            </td>
        </React.Fragment>
    )
}
```

The first CallbackButton element relies on the default values, producing the result shown in Figure 10-17.

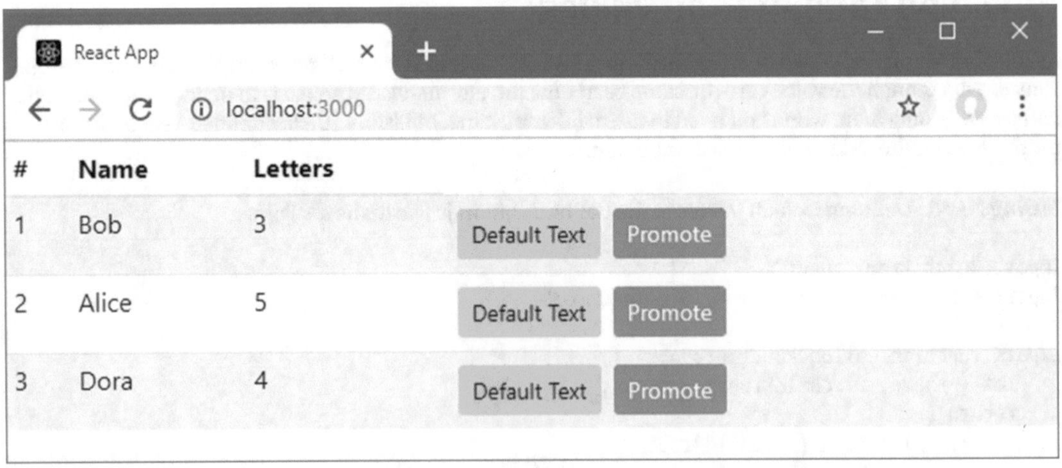

Figure 10-17. Using default prop values

Type Checking Prop Values

Props are unable to indicate what data types they are expecting to receive and have no way to signal to their ancestor components when they are unable to use a data value received as a prop. To help avoid these problems, React allows a component to declare the types it expects for its props, as shown in Listing 10-42.

Listing 10-42. Declaring Prop Types in the SimpleButton.js File in the src Folder

```
import React from "react";
import PropTypes from "prop-types";

export function SimpleButton(props) {
    return (
        <button onClick={ props.callback } className={props.className}>
            { props.text}
        </button>
    )
}

SimpleButton.defaultProps = {
    disabled: false
}

SimpleButton.propTypes = {
    text: PropTypes.string,
    theme: PropTypes.string,
    callback: PropTypes.func,
    disabled: PropTypes.bool
}
```

A propTypes property is added to the component and assigned an object whose property names correspond to prop names and whose values specify the type that the component expects. Types are specified using PropTypes values, which are imported from the prop-types package, and the most useful PropTypes values are described in Table 10-3.

■ **Tip** You can combine any of the types in Table 10-3 with isRequired to generate a warning if a value for that prop isn't supplied by the parent component: PropTypes.bool.isRequired.

Table 10-3. Useful PropTypes Values

Name	Description
array	This value specifies that a prop should be an array.
bool	This value specifies that a prop should be a bool.
func	This value specifies that a prop should be a function.
number	This value specifies that a prop should be a number value.
object	This value specifies that a prop should be an object.
string	This value specifies that a prop should be a string.

To demonstrate how types are checked, in Listing 10-43, I have added a value to the `CallbackButton` element for the `disabled` prop, using a string value rather than the `bool` specified in Listing 10-42.

Listing 10-43. Providing the Wrong Type in the Summary.js File in the src Folder

```
import React from "react";
import { CallbackButton } from "./CallbackButton";

export function Summary(props) {
    return (
        <React.Fragment>
            <td>{ props.index + 1} </td>
            <td>{ props.name } </td>
            <td>{ props.name.length } </td>
            <td>
                <CallbackButton callback={props.reverseCallback} />
                <CallbackButton theme="info" text="Promote"
                    callback={ () => props.promoteCallback(props.name)}
                    disabled="true" />
            </td>
        </React.Fragment>
    )
}
```

This is a common error, where a string literal value is used where a `bool` or `number` is expected. It can be hard to figure out where the problem is, especially since the prop is defined by an ancestor of the component where the problem occurs. Using a prop type makes the problem obvious. When you save the changes, the browser will reload, and you will see the following message displayed in the browser's JavaScript console:

```
...
index.js:2178 Warning: Failed prop type: Invalid prop `disabled` of type `string` supplied
to `SimpleButton`, expected `boolean`.
...
```

To resolve the problem, I could change the prop value so that it sends the expected type to the component. An alternative approach is to make the component more flexible so that it is able to deal with both `Boolean` and `string` values for the `disabled` prop. Given how common it is to create `string` prop values when `Boolean` values are required, this is a good idea, especially if you are writing components that are going to be used by other development teams. In Listing 10-44, I have added support to the `SimpleButton` component for dealing with both types and updated its `propTypes` configuration to reflect the change.

■ **Note**   The prop type checks are performed only during development and are disabled when the application is prepared for deployment. See Chapter 8 for an example of preparing an application for deployment.

Listing 10-44. Accepting Multiple Prop Types in the SimpleButton.js File in the src Folder

```
import React from "react";
import PropTypes from "prop-types";
```

```
export function SimpleButton(props) {
    return (
        <button onClick={ props.callback } className={props.className}
                disabled={ props.disabled === "true" || props.disabled === true }>
            { props.text}
        </button>
    )
}

SimpleButton.defaultProps = {
    disabled: false
}

SimpleButton.propTypes = {
    text: PropTypes.string,
    theme: PropTypes.string,
    callback: PropTypes.func,
    disabled: PropTypes.oneOfType([PropTypes.bool, PropTypes.string])
}
```

There are two useful PropTypes methods that can be used to specify multiple types or specific values, as described in Table 10-4.

Table 10-4. *Useful PropTypes Methods*

Name	Description
oneOfType	This method accepts an array of PropTypes values that the component is willing to receive.
oneOf	This method accepts an array of values that the component is willing to receive.

In Listing 10-44, I used the oneOfType method to tell React that the disabled property can accept both Boolean and string values. The component is able to process the value I provided for the disabled property in Listing 10-43, which disables the button elements, as shown in Figure 10-18.

■ **Tip** The alternative approach would have been to change the prop value to a Boolean when applying the component, which can be done using an expression for the disabled property: disabled={ true }.

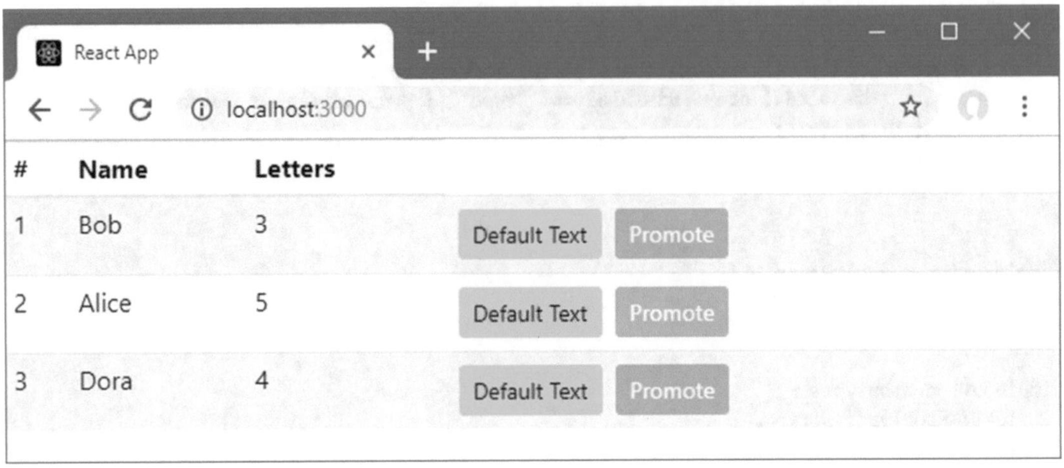

Figure 10-18. *Accepting multiple prop types*

Summary

In this chapter, I introduced stateless components, which are the simplest version of the key building block in React applications. I demonstrated how stateless components are defined, how they render content, and how components can be combined to create more complex features. I also explained how a parent component is able to pass on data to its children using props and showed you how props can also be used for functions, which provides the basic features required for communication between components. I finished this chapter by showing you the features that define default values and types for props. In the next chapter, I explain how to create components that have state data.

CHAPTER 11

Stateful Components

In this chapter, I introduce the stateful component, which builds on the features described in Chapter 10 and adds state data that is unique to each component and that can be used to alter the rendered output. Table 11-1 puts stateful components in context.

Table 11-1. *Putting Stateful Components in Context*

Question	Answer
What are they?	Components are the key building blocks in React applications. Stateful components have their own data that can be used to alter the content the component renders.
Why are they useful?	Stateful components make it easier to keep track of the application state provided by each component and provide the means to alter the data values and reflect the change in the content presented to the user.
How are they used?	Stateful components are defined using a class or by adding hooks to a functional component.
Are there any pitfalls or limitations?	Care must be taken to ensure that state data is modified correctly, as described in the "Modifying State Data" section of this chapter.
Are there any alternatives?	Components are the key building block in React applications, and there is no way to avoid their use. There are alternative to props that can be useful in larger and more complex projects, as described in later chapters.

Table 11-2 summarizes the chapter.

Table 11-2. *Chapter Summary*

Problem	Solution	Listing
Add state data to a component	Define a class whose constructor sets the state property or call the useState function to create a property and function for a single state property	4–5, 12, 13
Modify state data	Call the setState function or call the function returned by useState	6–11
Share data between components	Lift the state data to an ancestor component and distribute it using props	14–18
Define prop types and default values in a class-based component	Apply the properties to the class or define static properties within the class	19–20

Preparing for This Chapter

In this chapter, I continue using the components project created in Chapter 10. To prepare for this chapter, I changed the content rendered by the Summary component so that it uses the SimpleButton component directly as shown in Listing 11-1, rather than the CallbackButton that I used to describe how props are distributed.

■ **Tip**　You can download the example project for this chapter—and for all the other chapters in this book—from https://github.com/Apress/pro-react-16.

Listing 11-1.　Changing the Content in the Summary.js File in the src Folder

```
import React from "react";
//import { CallbackButton } from "./CallbackButton";
import { SimpleButton } from "./SimpleButton";

export function Summary(props) {
    return (
        <React.Fragment>
            <td>{ props.index + 1} </td>
            <td>{ props.name } </td>
            <td>{ props.name.length } </td>
            <td>
                <SimpleButton
                    className="btn btn-warning btn-sm m-1"
                    callback={ props.reverseCallback }
                    text={ `Reverse (${ props.name })`}
                />
                <SimpleButton
                    className="btn btn-info btn-sm m-1"
                    callback={ () => props.promoteCallback(props.name)}
                    text={ `Promote (${ props.name})`}
                />
            </td>
        </React.Fragment>
    )
}
```

In Listing 11-2, I have removed the types and default values for the SimpleButton component's props, which I will restore at the end of the chapter.

Listing 11-2.　Removing Properties in the SimpleButton.js File in the src Folder

```
import React from "react";

export function SimpleButton(props) {
    return (
```

```
    <button onClick={ props.callback } className={props.className}
        disabled={ props.disabled === "true" || props.disabled === true }>
      { props.text}
    </button>
  )
}
```

Open a command prompt, navigate to the components folder, and run the command shown in Listing 11-3 to start the React development tools.

Listing 11-3. Starting the Development Tools

```
npm start
```

After the initial build process, a new browser window will open and display the contents shown in Figure 11-1.

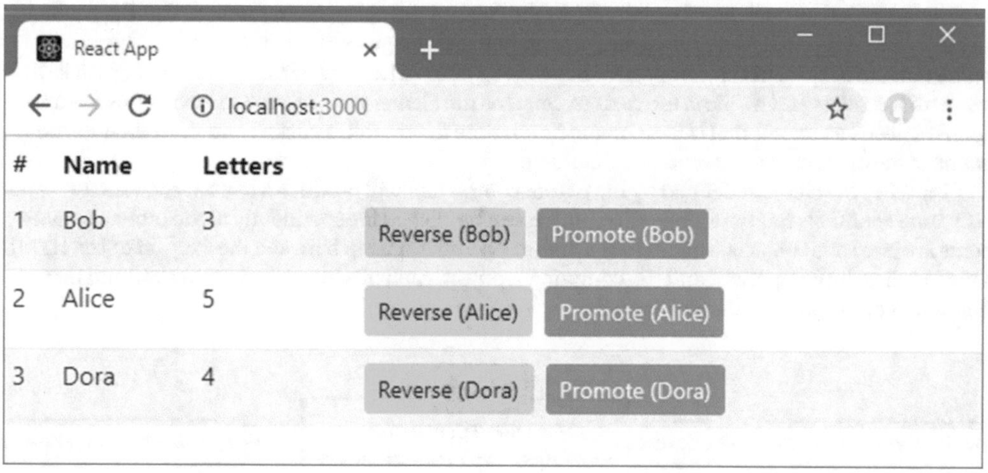

Figure 11-1. *Running the example application*

Understanding the Different Component Types

In the sections that follow, I explain the differences between the types of component that React supports. Understanding how stateful components work will be easier when you see the key difference from the stateless components described in Chapter 10.

Understanding Stateless Components

As you saw in Chapter 10, stateless components consist of a function that React invokes in response to custom HTML elements, passing the prop values as an argument. The same set of prop values on the custom HTML element will result in the same prop argument and produce the same result, as shown in Figure 11-2.

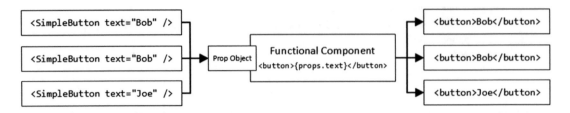

Figure 11-2. *Predictable results from a stateless component*

A stateless component will always render the same HTML elements given the same set of prop values, regardless of how often the function is invoked. It depends entirely on the prop values provided by the parent component to render its content. This means that React can keep invoking the same function regardless of how many SimpleButton elements there are in the application and just has to keep track of which props are associated with each SimpleButton element.

Understanding Stateful Components

A *stateful component* has its own data that influences the content the component renders. This data, which is known as *state data*, is separate from the parent component and the props it provides.

Imagine that the SimpleButton component has to keep track of how many times the user has clicks the button element it renders and displays the current count as the element's content. To provide this feature, the component needs a counter that is incremented each time the button is clicked and must include the current value of the counter when it renders its content.

Each SimpleButton element defined by the parent component will produce a button element for which a separate counter is required since each button can be clicked independently of the others. Stateful components are JavaScript objects, and there is a one-to-one relationship between the SimpleButton HTML element that applies the component and the component object, each of which has its own state and may render different output, as shown in Figure 11-3.

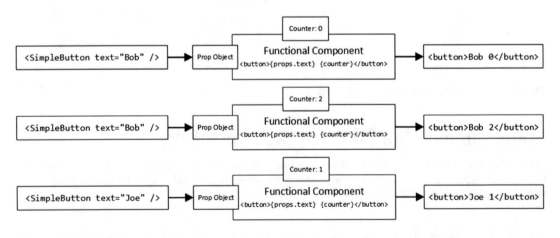

Figure 11-3. *Stateful components with a counter*

There is no longer any certainty that providing the same prop to a stateful component will render the same result because each component object can have different values for its state data and use it to generate different results.

As you will learn, stateful components have many features that are not available in stateless components, and you will find that these features are easier to understand if you remember that each stateful component is a JavaScript object with its own state data and is associated with a single custom HTML element.

Creating a Stateful Component

To get started, I am going to convert one the existing SimpleButton component in the example application from a stateless to stateful component, which will let me explain the basics before moving on to more complicated features.

Defining a stateful component is done using a class, which is a template that describes the functionality that each component object will have, as described in Chapter 4. In Listing 11-4, I have replaced the SimpleButton component's function with a class.

■ **Note**   This is a stateful component that doesn't have any state data. I explain how to define the component and then show you how to add state data in the "Adding State Data" section.

Listing 11-4. Introducing a Class in the SimpleButton.js File in the src Folder

```
import React, { Component } from "react";

export class SimpleButton extends Component {

    render() {
        return (
            <button onClick={ this.props.callback }
                    className={ this.props.className }
                    disabled={ this.props.disabled === "true"
                        || this.props.disabled === true   }>
                { this.props.text}
            </button>
        )
    }
}
```

In the sections that follow, I describe each of the changes made in Listing 11-4 and explain how they are used to create a stateful component.

Understanding the Component Class

When you define a stateful component, you use the class and extends keywords to denote a class that inherits the functionality provided by the Component class defined in the react package, like this:

```
...
export class SimpleButton extends Component {
...
```

This combination of keywords defines a class called SimpleButton that extends the Component class provided by React. The export keyword makes the SimpleButton class available for use outside of the JavaScript file in which it is defined, just as it did when the component was defined as a function.

Understanding the Import Statement

To extend from the Component class, an import is used, as follows:

```
...
import React, { Component } from "react";
...
```

As I explained in Chapter 4, there are two types of import in this statement. The default export from the react package is imported and assigned the name React, which allows JSX to work. The react package also has an export named Component that is imported using curly braces (the { and } characters). It is important that you use the import statement exactly as shown when you create a stateful component.

Understanding the render Method

The main purpose of a stateful component is to render content for React to display. The difference is that this is done in a method called render, which is invoked when React wants the component to render. The render method must return a React element, which can be created using the React.createElement method or, more typically, as a fragment of HTML.

```
...
render() {
    return (
        <button onClick={ this.props.callback }
                className={ this.props.className }
                disabled={ this.props.disabled === "true"
                    || this.props.disabled === true }>
            { this.props.text}
        </button>
    )
}
...
```

Understanding Stateful Component Props

One of the most noticeable differences when you start working with stateful components is that you must use the this keyword to access prop values, as follows:

```
...
return (
    <button onClick={ this.props.callback }
            className={ this.props.className }
            disabled={ this.props.disabled === "true"
                || this.props.disabled === true }>
```

```
        { this.props.text}
    </button>
)
...
```

The this keyword refers to the component's JavaScript object. When using a stateful component, you must use the this keyword to access the props property, and you will see an error like this one displayed on the command line, the browser's JavaScript console, and the browser window if you forget:

```
./src/SimpleButton.js   Line 7:   'props' is not defined   no-undef
```

Although I have redefined the component, I haven't changed the content that it renders or changed the way it behaves, and the result is just the same as when the component was defined as a function, as shown in Figure 11-4.

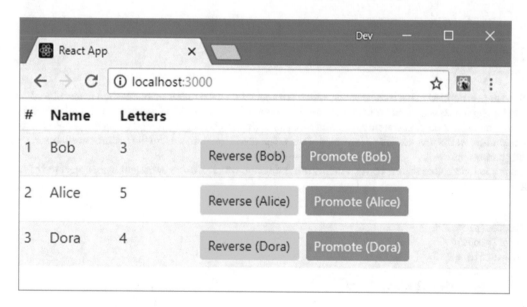

Figure 11-4. *Introducing a stateful component*

Adding State Data

The most import feature of stateful components is that each instance of the component can have its own data, known as *state data*. In Listing 11-5, I have added state data to the SimpleButton component.

Listing 11-5. Adding State Data in the SimpleButton.js File in the src Folder

```
import React, { Component } from "react";

export class SimpleButton extends Component {

    constructor(props) {
        super(props);
```

293

```
        this.state = {
            counter: 0,
            hasButtonBeenClicked: false
        }
    }

    render() {
        return (
            <button onClick={ this.props.callback }
                className={ this.props.className }
                disabled={ this.props.disabled === "true"
                        || this.props.disabled === true  }>
                    { this.props.text} { this.state.counter }
                    { this.state.hasButtonBeenClicked &&
                        <div>Button Clicked!</div>
                    }
            </button>
        )
    }
}
```

State data is defined using a *constructor*, which is a special method that is invoked when a new object is created using the class and that must follow the form shown in the listing: the constructor should define a props parameter, and the first statement should be a call to the special super method using the props object as an argument, which invokes the constructor of the Component class and sets up the features available in a stateful component.

Once you have called super, you can define the state data, which is done by assigning an object to this. state.

```
...
constructor(props) {
    super(props);
    this.state = {
        counter: 0,
        hasButtonBeenClicked: false
    }
}
...
```

The state data is defined as properties on the object. There is one property in this example, and it creates state data properties called counter, whose value is 0, and hasButtonBeenClicked, whose value is false.

Reading State Data

Accessing state data is done by reading the properties you have defined through this.state, similar to the way that props are accessed.

```
...
render() {
    return (
        <button onClick={ this.props.callback }
```

```
            className={ this.props.className }
            disabled={ this.props.disabled === "true"
                    || this.props.disabled === true  }>
              { this.props.text} { this.state.counter }
              { this.state.hasButtonBeenClicked &&
                  <div>Button Clicked!</div>
              }
        </button>
    )
}
...
```

The render method in Listing 11-5 sets the contents of the button element so that it contains a prop value and the value of the counter state data property, producing the effect shown in Figure 11-5. The additional div element I defined in Listing 11-5 won't be shown until the value of the hasButtonBeenClicked property is true, which I demonstrate in the next section.

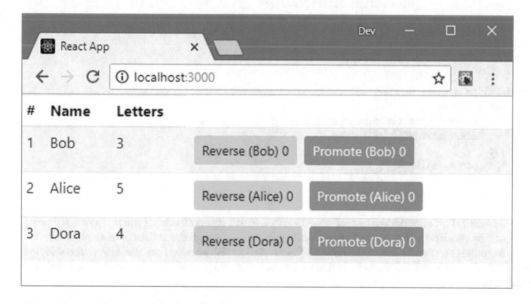

Figure 11-5. *Defining and reading state data*

Modifying State Data

The use of state data makes sense only when it can be modified because that's what allows component objects to render different content. React requires a specific technique for modifying state data, as shown in Listing 11-6.

Listing 11-6. Modifying State Data in the SimpleButton.js File in the src Folder

```
import React, { Component } from "react";

export class SimpleButton extends Component {
```

```
    constructor(props) {
        super(props);
        this.state = {
            counter: 0,
            hasButtonBeenClicked: false
        }
    }

    render() {
        return (
            <button onClick={ this.handleClick }
                className={ this.props.className }
                disabled={ this.props.disabled === "true"
                            || this.props.disabled === true  }>
                    { this.props.text} { this.state.counter }
                    { this.state.hasButtonBeenClicked &&
                        <div>Button Clicked!</div>
                    }
            </button>
        )
    }

    handleClick = () => {
        this.setState({
            counter: this.state.counter + 1,
            hasButtonBeenClicked: true
        });
        this.props.callback();
    }
}
```

React doesn't allow state data to be modified directly and will report an error if you try to assign a new value directly to a state property. Instead, modifications are made through the setState method, which is inherited from the Component class. In the listing, I have added a method called handleClick that is selected by the button element's onClick expression and that uses the setState method to increment the counter state property.

■ **Tip** Methods that are selected by the onClick property have to be defined in a specific way. I explain how the onClick property is used and how its methods are defined in Chapter 12.

The argument to the setState method is an object whose properties specify the state data to be updated, like this:

```
...
this.setState({
    counter: this.state.counter + 1,
    hasButtonBeenClicked: true
});
...
```

This statement tells React that the counter property should be modified by incrementing the current value and that the hasButtonBeenClicked property should be true. Notice that I have not used the increment operator (++) for counter because that would assign a new value to the property and result in an error.

▪ **Tip**   You only have to define properties for the values you want to change when using the setState method. React will merge the changes you specify with the rest of the component's state data and leave unchanged any property for which a value has not been provided.

Although using the setState method can feel awkward, the advantage is that React takes care of re-rendering the application to reflect the impact of the change, which means that I don't have manually invoke the ReactDOM.render method as I did in Chapter 11. The effect is that clicking the buttons increments the associated component's counter state data, as shown in Figure 11-6. (Clicking the buttons reorders the rows in the table, which means that the button you have clicked may be moved to a new position.)

Figure 11-6. *Modifying state data*

Clicking a button changes the state of one of the component objects and leaves the other five component objects unchanged.

Avoiding the State Data Modification Pitfalls

React performs changes to state data asynchronously and may choose to group together several updates to improve performance, which means that the effect of a call to the setState may not take effect in the way you expect. There are some common pitfalls when updating state data, which I describe in the sections that follow, along with details of how to avoid them.

▪ **Tip**   The React Devtools browser extension shows you the state data for a stateful component, which can be a useful way of seeing how the application responds to changes and tracking down problems when you don't get the behavior you expect.

Avoiding the Dependent Value Pitfall

State data values are often related, and a common problem is to assume that the effect of each change is applied individually, as shown in Listing 11-7.

Listing 11-7. Performing Related State Changes in the SimpleButton.js File in the src Folder

```
import React, { Component } from "react";

export class SimpleButton extends Component {

    constructor(props) {
        super(props);
        this.state = {
            counter: 0,
            hasButtonBeenClicked: false
        }
    }

    render() {
        return (
            <button onClick={ this.handleClick }
                className={ this.props.className }
                disabled={ this.props.disabled === "true"
                        || this.props.disabled === true   }>
                    { this.props.text} { this.state.counter }
                    { this.state.hasButtonBeenClicked &&
                        <div>Button Clicked!</div>
                    }
            </button>
        )
    }

    handleClick = () => {
        this.setState({
            counter: this.state.counter + 1,
            hasButtonBeenClicked: this.state.counter > 0
        });
        this.props.callback();
    }
}
```

The update to the hasButtonBeenClicked property assumes the counter property will have been changed before its expression is evaluated. React doesn't apply changes individually, and the expression for the hasButtonBeenClicked property is evaluated using the current counter value. This problem also arises when related updates are performed using separate calls to the setState method, as shown in Listing 11-8.

Listing 11-8. Making Dependent Updates in the SimpleButton.js File in the src Folder

```
import React, { Component } from "react";

export class SimpleButton extends Component {
```

```
    constructor(props) {
        super(props);
        this.state = {
            counter: 0,
            hasButtonBeenClicked: false
        }
    }

    render() {
        return (
            <button onClick={ this.handleClick }
                className={ this.props.className }
                disabled={ this.props.disabled === "true"
                        || this.props.disabled === true }>
                    { this.props.text} { this.state.counter }
                    { this.state.hasButtonBeenClicked &&
                        <div>Button Clicked!</div>
                    }
            </button>
        )
    }

    handleClick = () => {
        this.setState({ counter: this.state.counter + 1 });
        this.setState({ hasButtonBeenClicked: this.state.counter > 0 });
        this.props.callback();
    }
}
```

React will batch these updates together for efficiency, which creates the same result as Listing 11-6 and means that the hasButtonBeenClicked property won't be true until the button has been clicked twice, as shown in Figure 11-7.

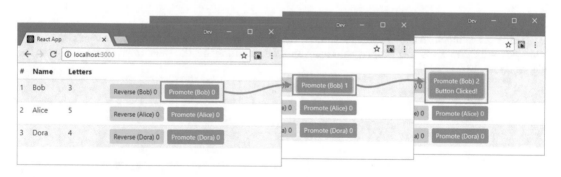

Figure 11-7. *The dependent value pitfall*

When you have a series of dependent changes to make, you can pass a function to the setState method that will be invoked when the state data has been updated and that can be used to perform tasks that rely on the changed state values, as shown in Listing 11-9.

Listing 11-9. Using a Callback in the SimpleButton.js File in the src Folder

```
import React, { Component } from "react";

export class SimpleButton extends Component {

    constructor(props) {
        super(props);
        this.state = {
            counter: 0,
            hasButtonBeenClicked: false
        }
    }

    render() {
        return (
            <button onClick={ this.handleClick }
                className={ this.props.className }
                disabled={ this.props.disabled === "true"
                           || this.props.disabled === true   }>
                    { this.props.text} { this.state.counter }
                    { this.state.hasButtonBeenClicked &&
                        <div>Button Clicked!</div>
                    }
            </button>
        )
    }

    handleClick = () => {
        this.setState({ counter: this.state.counter + 1 },
            () => this.setState({ hasButtonBeenClicked: this.state.counter > 0 }));
        this.props.callback();
    }
}
```

Using the callback function ensures that the value of the hasButtonBeenClicked value won't be changed until the new counter property has been applied, ensuring that the values are in sync, as shown in Figure 11-8.

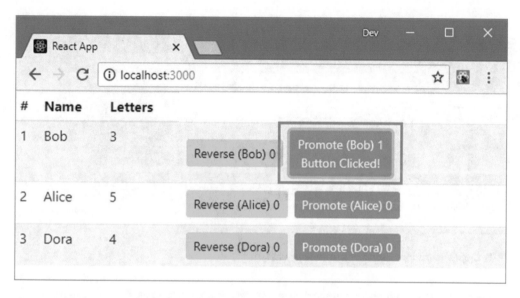

Figure 11-8. *Forcing state changes to be performed in sequence*

Avoiding the Missing Updates Pitfall

The way that React applies updates means that multiple changes to the same state data property are ignored and only the most recent value is applied, as demonstrated in Listing 11-10.

Listing 11-10. Making Multiple Updates in the SimpleButton.js File in the src Folder

```
...
handleClick = () => {
    for (let i = 0; i < 5; i++) {
        this.setState({ counter: this.state.counter + 1});
    }
    this.setState({ hasButtonBeenClicked: true });
    this.props.callback();
}
...
```

In real projects, multiple updates are usually done while processing data, rather than in a for loop, so that a state change is performed for each object in an array, for example. This listing shows the effect of repeatedly modifying the same property: rather than incrementing the counter value five times, clicking a button increments the value by one, as shown in Figure 11-9.

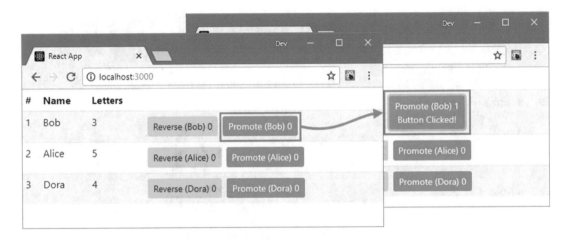

Figure 11-9. *Applying multiple updates to a state property*

If you need to perform multiple updates and have each take effect in sequence, then you can use the version of the setState method that accepts a function as its first argument. The function is provided with the current state data and a props object, as shown in Listing 11-11.

▪ **Tip** This version of the setState method is also useful for updating nested state properties, which you can see demonstrated in Chapter 14.

Listing 11-11. Making Multiple Updates in the SimpleButton.js File in the src Folder

```
...
handleClick = () => {
    for (let i = 0; i < 5; i++) {
        this.setState((state, props) => { return { counter: state.counter + 1 }});
    }
    this.setState({ hasButtonBeenClicked: true });
    this.props.callback();
}
...
```

The function passed to the setState method returns an update object using the same format as earlier examples. The difference is that the state data object reflects all of the previous changes that have been grouped together and can be used for repeated updates, producing the effect shown in Figure 11-10.

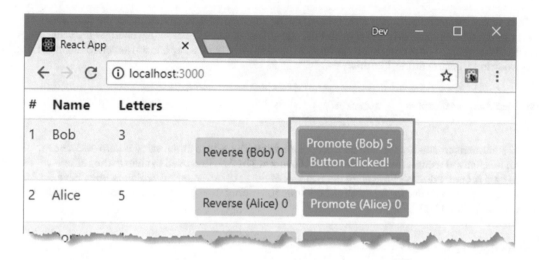

Figure 11-10. *Applying multiple updates to a state property*

Defining Stateful Components Using Hooks

Not all developers like using classes to define stateful components and so React provides an alternative approach, called *hooks*, which allow functional components to define state data. In Listing 11-12, I added a file called HooksButton.js to the src folder and re-created the stateful component from Listing 11-11 as a function that uses hooks.

Listing 11-12. The Contents of the HooksButton.js File in the src Folder

```
import React, { useState } from "react";

export function HooksButton(props) {
    const [counter, setCounter] = useState(0);
    const [hasButtonBeenClicked, setHasButtonBeenClicked] = useState(false);

    const handleClick = () => {
        setCounter(counter + 5);
        setHasButtonBeenClicked(true);
        props.callback();
    }

    return (
        <button onClick={ handleClick }
            className={ props.className }
            disabled={ props.disabled === "true" || props.disabled === true }>
                { props.text} { counter }
                { hasButtonBeenClicked && <div>Button Clicked!</div>}
        </button>
    )
}
```

The useState function is used to create state data. Its argument is the initial value for the state data property, and it returns a property that provides the current value and a function that changes the value and triggers an update. The property and the function are returned in an array and are assigned meaningful names using array destructuring, like this:

```
...
const [counter, setCounter] = useState(0);
...
```

This statement creates a state data property named counter whose initial value is zero and whose value can be changed using a function named setCounter. The function used to change the value of a state data property doesn't have all of the features of the setState method, which is why I have incremented the value by five in the handleClick function, rather than performing a series of individual updates, as in Listing 11-11.

```
...
const handleClick = () => {
    setCounter(counter + 5);
    setHasButtonBeenClicked(true);
    props.callback();
}
...
```

In Listing 11-13, I have updated the Summary so it uses the HooksButton component.

Listing 11-13. Using the Hooks Component in the Summary.js File in the src Folder

```
import React from "react";
import { SimpleButton } from "./SimpleButton";
import { HooksButton } from "./HooksButton";

export function Summary(props) {
    return (
        <React.Fragment>
            <td>{ props.index + 1 } </td>
            <td>{ props.name } </td>
            <td>{ props.name.length } </td>
            <td>
                <SimpleButton
                    className="btn btn-warning btn-sm m-1"
                    callback={ props.reverseCallback }
                    text={ `Reverse (${ props.name })`} />
                <HooksButton
                    className="btn btn-info btn-sm m-1"
                    callback={ () => props.promoteCallback(props.name)}
                    text={ `Promote (${ props.name})`} />
            </td>
        </React.Fragment>
    )
}
```

The use of hooks is not visible to the Summary component, which provides data and functions via props as normal. This example produces the same result, as shown in Figure 11-10.

SHOULD YOU USE HOOKS OR CLASSES?

Hooks offer an alternative approach to creating stateful components for developers who don't like to use classes. Depending on your personal preference, either this will be an important feature that suits your coding style or you will carry on defining classes and forget about hooks entirely.

The hooks and classes features will both be supported in future versions of React and so you can use whichever suits you best or mix and match freely if you prefer. I like the hooks features, but, aside from describing some related hooks features in Chapter 13, all of the examples in this book use classes. In part that is because the hooks feature is new—but it is also because I have been using class-based programming languages for a long time and using classes to define components suits my way of thinking about code, even for simple stateless components.

If you prefer using hooks but can't work out how to express the book examples without using a class, then e-mail me at adam@adam-freeman.com, and I will try to point you in the right direction.

Lifting Up State Data

At the moment, each SimpleButton and HooksButton component exists in isolation and has its own state data, so clicking a button affects only the state value of a single component and leaves the others unchanged.

A different approach is needed when components need access to the same data. In this situation, the state data is *lifted up*, which means it is moved to the first common ancestor component and distributed back down to the components that require it using props.

■ **Tip** There are alternative approaches available for sharing data between React components. Chapter 13 describes the context feature, and more complex projects can benefit from using a data store (see Chapters 19 and 20) or URL routing (see Chapters 21 and 22).

If I want the SimpleButton and HooksButton components in the same table row to share a counter value, for example, I need to define the state data property in the first common ancestor, which is the Summary component. In Listing 11-14, I have converted Summary to be a class-based stateful component that defines a counter value.

Listing 11-14. Lifting Up State Data in the Summary.js File in the src Folder

```
import React, { Component } from "react";
import { SimpleButton } from "./SimpleButton";
import { HooksButton } from "./HooksButton";
```

```
export class Summary extends Component {

    constructor(props) {
        super(props);
        this.state = {
            counter: 0
        }
    }

    incrementCounter = (increment) => {
        this.setState((state) => { return { counter: state.counter + increment}});
    }

    render() {
        const props = this.props;
        return (
            <React.Fragment>
                <td>{ props.index + 1} </td>
                <td>{ props.name } </td>
                <td>{ props.name.length } </td>
                <td>
                    <SimpleButton
                        className="btn btn-warning btn-sm m-1"
                        callback={ props.reverseCallback }
                        text={ `Reverse (${ props.name })`}
                        counter={ this.state.counter }
                        incrementCallback={this.incrementCounter }
                    />
                    <HooksButton
                        className="btn btn-info btn-sm m-1"
                        callback={ () => props.promoteCallback(props.name)}
                        text={ `Promote (${ props.name})`}
                        counter={ this.state.counter }
                        incrementCallback={this.incrementCounter }
                    />
                </td>
            </React.Fragment>
        )
    }
}
```

The Summary component defines a counter property and passes it on to its child components as a prop.
The component also defines an incrementCounter method that child components will invoke to change
the counter property, which is passed on using a prop named incrementCallback. This is required not only
because state data is not modified directly but also because props are read-only. The incrementCounter
method uses the setState method with a function so that it can be invoked repeatedly by child components.

■ **Tip**   I defined a props property in the render method so that I don't have to change all the references to
use the this keyword, which is a useful shortcut when converting a function component to use a class.

In Listing 11-15, I removed the counter state data property from the SimpleButton component and used the counter and incrementCounter props instead.

Listing 11-15. Replacing State Data with Props in the SimpleButton.js File in the src Folder

```
import React, { Component } from "react";

export class SimpleButton extends Component {

    constructor(props) {
        super(props);
        this.state = {
            // counter: 0,
            hasButtonBeenClicked: false
        }
    }

    render() {
        return (
            <button onClick={ this.handleClick }
                className={ this.props.className }
                disabled={ this.props.disabled === "true"
                        || this.props.disabled === true  }>
                    { this.props.text} { this.props.counter }
                    { this.state.hasButtonBeenClicked &&
                        <div>Button Clicked!</div>
                    }
            </button>
        )
    }

    handleClick = () => {
        this.props.incrementCallback(5);
        this.setState({ hasButtonBeenClicked: true });
        this.props.callback();
    }
}
```

A corresponding set of changes is required to the HooksButton component, which will share the same set of props, as shown in Listing 11-16.

Listing 11-16. Replacing State Data with Props in the HooksButton.js File in the src Folder

```
import React, { useState } from "react";

export function HooksButton(props) {
    //const [counter, setCounter] = useState(0);
    const[ hasButtonBeenClicked, setHasButtonBeenClicked] = useState(false);
```

```
const handleClick = () => {
    //setCounter(counter + 5);
    props.incrementCallback(5);
    setHasButtonBeenClicked(true);
    props.callback();
}

return (
    <button onClick={ handleClick }
        className={ props.className }
        disabled={ props.disabled === "true" || props.disabled === true }>
            { props.text} { props.counter }
            { hasButtonBeenClicked && <div>Button Clicked!</div>}
    </button>
)
}
```

Lifting the counter state property to the parent component means that the two buttons presented to the user in each table row share their parent's state data, such that clicking one of the button elements causes both to be updated, as shown in Figure 11-11.

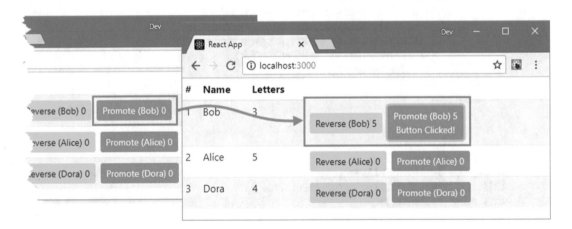

Figure 11-11. *Lifting state data*

Not every item of state data has to be lifted, and the individual components still have their own local state data, such that the hasButtonBeenClicked property remains local and independent from the other components.

Lifting Up State Data Further

State data can be lifted up further than the parent component. If I want all the SimpleButton and HooksButton components to share the same counter property, then I can lift it up to the App component, as shown in Listing 11-17, in which I have made the stateful using the hooks feature.

Listing 11-17. Lifting State Data in the App.js File in the src Folder

```
import React, { useState } from "react";
import { Summary } from "./Summary";
import ReactDOM from "react-dom";

let names = ["Bob", "Alice", "Dora"]

function reverseNames() {
    names.reverse();
    ReactDOM.render(<App />, document.getElementById('root'));
}

function promoteName(name) {
    names = [name, ...names.filter(val => val !== name)];
    ReactDOM.render(<App />, document.getElementById('root'));
}

export default function App() {
    const [counter, setCounter] = useState(0);

    const incrementCounter = (increment) => setCounter(counter + increment);

    return (
        <table className="table table-sm table-striped">
            <thead>
                <tr><th>#</th><th>Name</th><th>Letters</th></tr>
            </thead>
            <tbody>
                { names.map((name, index) =>
                    <tr key={ name }>
                        <Summary index={index} name={name}
                            reverseCallback={reverseNames}
                            promoteCallback={promoteName}
                            counter={ counter }
                            incrementCallback={ incrementCounter }
                        />
                    </tr>
                )}
            </tbody>
        </table>
    )
}
```

The App component defines the counter state property and the incrementCounter method that modifies it by calling the setCounter function. In Listing 11-18, I have removed the state data from the Summary component and passed on the props that are received from the App component to the children.

Listing 11-18. Removing State Data in the Summary.js File in the src Folder

```
import React, { Component } from "react";
import { SimpleButton } from "./SimpleButton";
import { HooksButton } from "./HooksButton";

export class Summary extends Component {

    // constructor(props) {
    //     super(props);
    //     this.state = {
    //         counter: 0
    //     }
    // }

    // incrementCounter = (increment) => {
    //     this.setState((state) => { return { counter: state.counter + increment}});
    // }

    render() {
        const props = this.props;
        return (
            <React.Fragment>
                <td>{ props.index + 1 } </td>
                <td>{ props.name } </td>
                <td>{ props.name.length } </td>
                <td>
                    <SimpleButton
                        className="btn btn-warning btn-sm m-1"
                        callback={ props.reverseCallback }
                        text={ `Reverse (${ props.name })` }
                        { ...this.props }
                    />
                    <HooksButton
                        className="btn btn-info btn-sm m-1"
                        callback={ () => props.promoteCallback(props.name)}
                        text={ `Promote (${ props.name})` }
                        { ...this.props }
                    />
                </td>
            </React.Fragment>
        )
    }
}
```

No constructor is required when a stateful component doesn't have state data, and you will receive a warning if you define a constructor that doesn't do anything except pass on props to the base class using super. I used the destructuring operator to pass on the props received from the App component to the SimpleButton and HooksButton components.

Now that the state data has been lifted up to the App component, all of the SimpleButton components that are descendants of the App component share a counter value, as shown in Figure 11-12.

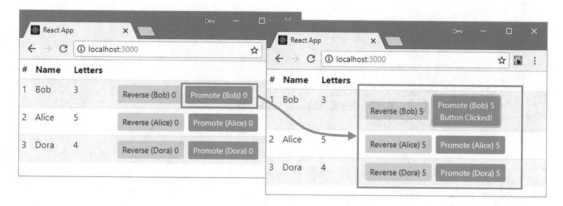

Figure 11-12. *Lifting state data to the top-level component*

No changes are required to the SimpleButton and HooksButton components, which are unaware of where the state data is defined and receive the data values and the callback functions required to change it as props.

Defining Prop Types and Default Values

At the start of the chapter, I removed the prop default values and types so I could focus on the transition from stateless to stateful components. Class-based components support these features in the same way as functional components, as shown in Listing 11-19.

Listing 11-19. Adding Prop Types and Values in the SimpleButton.js File in the src Folder

```
import React, { Component } from "react";
import PropTypes from "prop-types";

export class SimpleButton extends Component {

    constructor(props) {
        super(props);
        this.state = {
            // counter: 0,
            hasButtonBeenClicked: false
        }
    }

    render() {
        return (
            <button onClick={ this.handleClick }
                className={ this.props.className }
                disabled={ this.props.disabled === "true"
                        || this.props.disabled === true }>
                    { this.props.text} { this.props.counter }
                    { this.state.hasButtonBeenClicked &&
                        <div>Button Clicked!</div>
                    }
```

```
            </button>
        )
    }

    handleClick = () => {
        this.props.incrementCallback(5);
        this.setState({ hasButtonBeenClicked: true });
        this.props.callback();
    }

}

SimpleButton.defaultProps = {
    disabled: false
}

SimpleButton.propTypes = {
    text: PropTypes.string,
    theme: PropTypes.string,
    callback: PropTypes.func,
    disabled: PropTypes.oneOfType([PropTypes.bool, PropTypes.string ])
}
```

You can also define types and default prop values using class properties that have been decorated with the static keyword, as shown in Listing 11-20. The static keyword defines a property that applies to the component's class rather than objects created from that class and is transformed by the build process into the same form used in Listing 11-19.

Listing 11-20. Defining Static Properties in the SimpleButton.js File in the src Folder

```
import React, { Component } from "react";
import PropTypes from "prop-types";

export class SimpleButton extends Component {

    constructor(props) {
        super(props);
        this.state = {
            // counter: 0,
            hasButtonBeenClicked: false
        }
    }

    render() {
        return (
            <button onClick={ this.handleClick }
                className={ this.props.className }
                disabled={ this.props.disabled === "true"
                        || this.props.disabled === true }>
```

```
                    { this.props.text} { this.props.counter }
                    { this.state.hasButtonBeenClicked &&
                        <div>Button Clicked!</div>
                    }
            </button>
        )
    }

    handleClick = () => {
        this.props.incrementCallback(5);
        this.setState({ hasButtonBeenClicked: true });
        this.props.callback();
    }

    static defaultProps = {
        disabled: false
    }

    static propTypes = {
        text: PropTypes.string,
        theme: PropTypes.string,
        callback: PropTypes.func,
        disabled: PropTypes.oneOfType([PropTypes.bool, PropTypes.string ])
    }
}
```

These changes don't alter the appearance of the example application, but they ensure that the component will receive only the prop types it expects and that a default value for the `disabled` prop is available.

Summary

In this chapter, I introduced the stateful component, which has its own data values that can be used to alter the rendered output. I explained that stateful components are defined using classes and showed you how to define state data in a constructor. I also showed you the different ways that state data can be modified and how to avoid the most common pitfalls. In the next chapter, I explain how React deals with events.

CHAPTER 12

■ ■ ■

Working with Events

In this chapter, I describe the React support for events, which are generated by HTML elements, typically in response to user interaction. The React event features will be familiar if you have used the DOM event API features, but there are some important differences that can confuse the unwary developer. Table 12-1 puts the React event features in context.

Table 12-1. *Putting React Events in Context*

Question	Answer
What are they?	React events are triggered by elements to report important occurrences, most often user interaction.
Why are they useful?	Events allow components to respond to interaction with the content they render, which forms the foundation for interactive applications.
How are they used?	Interest in an event is indicated by adding properties to the elements rendered by a component. When an event in which a component is interested is triggered, the function specified by the property is invoked, allowing the component to update its state, invoke a function prop, or otherwise reflect the effect of the event.
Are there any pitfalls or limitations?	React events are similar to the events provided by the DOM API but with some differences that can present pitfalls for the unwary, especially when it comes to event phases, as described in the "Managing Event Propagation" section. Not all of the events defined by the DOM API are supported (see `https://reactjs.org/docs/events.html` for a list of events that React supports).
Are there any alternatives?	There is no alternative to using events, which provide an essential link between user interaction and the content rendered by a component.

Table 12-2 summarizes the chapter.

Table 12-2. *Chapter Summary*

Problem	Solution	Listing
Handle an event	Add the prop that corresponds to the event name and use the expression to process the event	6–10
Determine the event type	Use the event object's `type` property	11
Prevent an event from being reset before it is used	Use the event object's `persist` method	12, 13
Invoke event handlers with a custom argument	Define an inline function in the prop expression that invokes the handler method with the required data	14, 15
Prevent an event's default behavior	Use the event object's `preventDefault` method	16
Manage the propagation of an event	Determine the event phase	17–23
Stop an event	Use the event object's `stopPropagation` method	24

Preparing for This Chapter

To create the example project for this chapter, open a new command prompt, navigate to a convenient location, and run the command shown in Listing 12-1.

■ **Tip** You can download the example project for this chapter—and for all the other chapters in this book—from `https://github.com/Apress/pro-react-16`.

Listing 12-1. Creating the Example Project

```
npx create-react-app reactevents
```

Run the commands shown in Listing 12-2 to navigate to the `reactevents` folder and add the Bootstrap package to the project.

Listing 12-2. Adding the Bootstrap CSS Framework

```
cd reactevents
npm install bootstrap@4.1.2
```

To include the Bootstrap CSS stylesheet in the application, add the statement shown in Listing 12-3 to the `index.js` file, which can be found in the `src` folder.

Listing 12-3. Including Bootstrap in the index.js File in the src Folder

```
import React from 'react';
import ReactDOM from 'react-dom';
import './index.css';
import App from './App';
import * as serviceWorker from './serviceWorker';
import 'bootstrap/dist/css/bootstrap.css';

ReactDOM.render(<App />, document.getElementById('root'));

// If you want your app to work offline and load faster, you can change
// unregister() to register() below. Note this comes with some pitfalls.
// Learn more about service workers: http://bit.ly/CRA-PWA
serviceWorker.unregister();
```

Next, replace the contents of the App.js file with the code shown in Listing 12-4, which will provide the starting point for the examples in this chapter. The listing replaces the existing functional component with one that uses a class.

Listing 12-4. The Contents of the App.js File in the src Folder

```
import React, { Component } from 'react';

export default class App extends Component {

    constructor(props) {
        super(props);
        this.state = {
            message: "Ready"
        }
    }

    render() {
        return  (
            <div className="m-2">
                <div className="h4 bg-primary text-white text-center p-2">
                    { this.state.message }
                </div>
                <div className="text-center">
                    <button className="btn btn-primary">Click Me</button>
                </div>
            </div>
        )
    }
}
```

Using the command prompt, run the commands shown in Listing 12-5 in the reactevents folder to start the development tools.

Listing 12-5. Starting the Development Tools

```
npm start
```

Once the initial preparation for the project is complete, a new browser window will open and display the URL http://localhost:3000, which will display the content shown in Figure 12-1.

Figure 12-1. *Running the example application*

Understanding Events

Events are triggered by HTML elements to signal important changes, such as when the user clicks a button or types into a text field. Handling events in React is similar to using the Domain Object Model API, although there are important differences. In Listing 12-6, I have added an event handler that is invoked when the button element is clicked.

Listing 12-6. Adding an Event Handler in the App.js File in the src Folder

```
import React, { Component } from 'react';

export default class App extends Component {

    constructor(props) {
        super(props);
        this.state = {
            message: "Ready"
        }
    }

    render() {
        return (
            <div className="m-2">
                <div className="h4 bg-primary text-white text-center p-2">
                    { this.state.message }
                </div>
```

```
        <div className="text-center">
            <button className="btn btn-primary"
                onClick={ () => this.setState({ message: "Clicked!"})}>
                    Click Me
            </button>
        </div>
    </div>
)
    }
}
```

Events are handled using properties that share the name of the corresponding DOM API property, expressed in camel case. The DOM API onclick property is expressed as onClick in React applications and specifies how to handle the click event, which is triggered when the user clicks an element. The expression for an event handling property is a function that will be invoked when the specified event is triggered, like this:

```
...
<button className="btn btn-primary"
        onClick={ () => this.setState({ message: "Clicked!"})}>
    Click Me
</button>
...
```

This is an example of an inline function, which calls the setState method to change the value of the message state data property. When the button element is clicked, the click event is triggered, and React will invoke the inline function, producing the result shown in Figure 12-2.

Figure 12-2. *Handling an event*

Invoking a Method to Handle an Event

Stateful components can define methods and use them to respond to events, which helps avoid duplicating code in expressions when several elements handle the same event in the same way. For simple methods that don't change the state of the application or access other component features, the method can be specified as shown in Listing 12-7.

Listing 12-7. Adding an Event Handling Method in the App.js File in the src Folder

```
import React, { Component } from 'react';

export default class App extends Component {

    constructor(props) {
        super(props);
        this.state = {
            message: "Ready"
        }
    }

    handleEvent() {
        console.log("handleEvent method invoked");
    }

    render() {
        return   <div className="m-2">
                    <div className="h4 bg-primary text-white text-center p-2">
                        { this.state.message }
                    </div>
                    <div className="text-center">
                        <button className="btn btn-primary"
                            onClick={ this.handleEvent }>
                                Click Me
                        </button>
                    </div>
                </div>
    }
}
```

Notice that the onClick expression doesn't include parentheses, which would cause React to invoke the function when the render method is invoked, as explained in the sidebar. The handleEvent method doesn't change the state of the application and just writes out a message to the browser's JavaScript console. If you click the button in the browser window, you will see the following output shown in the console:

---

handleEvent method invoked

AVOIDING THE EVENT FUNCTION INVOCATION PITFALLS

The value assigned to an event handling property, such as onClick, must be an expression that returns a function that React can invoke to handle an event. There are two common mistakes when using an event handling property. The first mistake is to enclose the function you require in quotes rather than braces, like this:

```
...
<button className="btn btn-primary" onClick="this.handleEvent" >
...
```

This provides React with a string value instead of a function and produces an error in the browser's JavaScript console. The other common mistake is to use an expression that invokes the function you require.

```
...
<button className="btn btn-primary" onClick={ this.handleEvent() } >
...
```

This expression results in React invoking the handleEvent method when the component object is created and not when an event is triggered. You won't receive an error or warning for this mistake, which makes the problem harder to spot.

Accessing Component Features in an Event Handling Method

Additional work is required if you need to access the component's features in a method that handles an event. The value of the this keyword isn't set by default when JavaScript class methods are invoked, which means that there is no way for statements in the handleEvent method to access the component's methods and properties. In Listing 12-8, I have added a statement to the handleEvent method that invokes the setState method, which is accessed using the this keyword.

Listing 12-8. Accessing Component Features in the App.js File in the src Folder

```
import React, { Component } from 'react';

export default class App extends Component {

    constructor(props) {
        super(props);
        this.state = {
            message: "Ready"
        }
    }

    handleEvent() {
        this.setState({ message: "Clicked!"});
    }
```

```
render() {
    return   <div className="m-2">
                   <div className="h4 bg-primary text-white text-center p-2">
                      { this.state.message }
                   </div>
                   <div className="text-center">
                       <button className="btn btn-primary"
                           onClick={ this.handleEvent }>
                             Click Me
                       </button>
                   </div>
              </div>
    }
}
```

The handleEvent method will be invoked when the button is clicked, but the following error will be produced because this is undefined:

```
Uncaught TypeError: Cannot read property 'setState' of undefined
```

To ensure that a value is assigned to this, event handling methods can be expressed using the JavaScript public class fields syntax, as shown in Listing 12-9.

Listing 12-9. Redefining an Event Handling Method in the App.js File in the src Folder

```
import React, { Component } from 'react';

export default class App extends Component {

    constructor(props) {
        super(props);
        this.state = {
            message: "Ready"
        }
    }

    handleEvent = () => {
        this.setState({ message: "Clicked!"});
    }

    render() {
        return   <div className="m-2">
                       <div className="h4 bg-primary text-white text-center p-2">
                          { this.state.message }
                       </div>
                       <div className="text-center">
                           <button className="btn btn-primary"
```

```
                            onClick={ this.handleEvent }>
                                Click Me
                        </button>
                    </div>
                </div>
            }
        }
    }
```

The name of the method is followed by the equal sign, open and close parentheses, the fat arrow symbol, and then the message body, as shown in the listing. This is an awkward syntax, but I prefer it to the alternatives (described in the sidebar), and this is the approach I use throughout this chapter and the rest of the book. When you click the button element, the handleEvent method is provided with a value for this, producing the result shown in Figure 12-3.

Figure 12-3. *Binding for an event handler*

ALTERNATIVE WAYS TO ACCESS COMPONENT FEATURES

There are two alternative ways to provide an event handling method with a value for this. The first is to use an inline function in the expression for the event property.

```
...
<button className="btn btn-primary"
        onClick={ () => this.handleEvent() }>
    Click Me
</button>
...
```

Notice that the event handler method is invoked by the expression, which means that open and close parentheses are required after the method name. The other approach is to add a statement to the constructor for each of the component's event handler methods.

```
...
constructor(props) {
    super(props);
```

```
    this.state = {
        message: "Ready"
    }
    this.handleEvent = this.handleEvent.bind(this);
}
...
```

All three approaches take a while to get used to—and all are a little inelegant—and you should follow the approach that you find most comfortable.

Receiving an Event Object

When an event is triggered, React provides a SyntheticEvent object that describes the event to the handler object. The SyntheticEvent is a wrapper around the Event object provided by the DOM API that defines the same features but with additional code to ensure that events are described consistently in different browsers. The SyntheticEvent object has the basic properties and methods described in Table 12-3. (There are further methods and properties that I describe in later sections.)

REACT EVENTS VERSUS DOM EVENTS

React events provide an essential link between a component and the content it renders—but React events are not DOM events, even though they appear the same most of the time. If you go beyond the most commonly used features, you will encounter important differences that can produce unexpected results.

First, React doesn't support all events, which means that there some DOM API events that don't have corresponding React properties that components can use. You can see the set of events that React supports at https://reactjs.org/docs/events.html. The most commonly used events are included in the list, but not every event is available.

Second, React doesn't allow components to create and publish custom events. The React model for interaction between components is through function props, described in Chapter 10, and custom events are not distributed when the Event.dispatchEvent method is used.

Third, React provides a custom object as a wrapper around the DOM event objects, which doesn't always behave in the same way as the DOM event. You can access the DOM event through the wrapper, but this should be done with caution because it can cause unexpected side effects.

Finally, React intercepts DOM events in their bubble phase (described later in this chapter) and feeds them through the hierarchy of components, providing components with the opportunity to respond to events and update the content they render. This means some of the features provided by the event wrapper object don't work as expected, especially when it comes to propagation, as described in the "Managing Event Propagation" section.

Table 12-3. *The Basic Properties and Methods Defined by the SyntheticEvent Object*

Name	Description
nativeEvent	This property returns the Event object provided by the DOM API.
target	This property returns the object that represents the element that is the source of the event.
timeStamp	This property returns a timestamp that indicates when the event was triggered.
type	This property returns a string that indicates the event type.
isTrusted	This property returns true when the event has been initiated by the browser and false when the event object has been created in code.
preventDefault()	This method is called to prevent an events default behavior, as described in the "Preventing Default Behavior" section.
defaultPrevented	This property returns true if the preventDefault method has been called on the event object and false otherwise.
persist()	This method is called to present React from reusing the event object, which is important for asynchronous operations, as described in the "Avoiding the Event Reuse Pitfall" section.

In Listing 12-10, I have updated the handleEvent method so that it uses the event object that React provides to update the component's state.

Listing 12-10. Receiving an Event Object in the App.js File in the src Folder

```
import React, { Component } from 'react';

export default class App extends Component {

    constructor(props) {
        super(props);
        this.state = {
            message: "Ready"
        }
    }

    handleEvent = (event) => {
        this.setState({ message: `Event: ${event.type} `});
    }

    render() {
        return   <div className="m-2">
                     <div className="h4 bg-primary text-white text-center p-2">
                         { this.state.message }
                     </div>
                     <div className="text-center">
                         <button className="btn btn-primary"
                             onClick={ this.handleEvent }>
                                 Click Me
                         </button>
```

```
                </div>
            </div>
        }
    }
```

I have added an event parameter to the handleEvent method, which I use to include the value of the type property in the message that is displayed to the user, as shown in Figure 12-4.

Figure 12-4. *Receiving an event object*

Differentiating Between Event Types

React always provides a SyntheticEvent object when it invokes an event handling function, which can cause confusion if you are accustomed to using the instanceof keyword to differentiate between events created by the DOM API. In Listing 12-11, I have changed the button element so the handleEvent method is used to respond to MouseUp and MouseDown events.

Listing 12-11. Differentiating Events in the App.js File in the src Folder

```
import React, { Component } from 'react';

export default class App extends Component {

    constructor(props) {
        super(props);
        this.state = {
            message: "Ready"
        }
    }

    handleEvent = (event) => {
        if (event.type === "mousedown") {
            this.setState({ message: "Down"});
        } else {
            this.setState({ message: "Up"});
        }
    }
```

```
render() {
    return   <div className="m-2">
                  <div className="h4 bg-primary text-white text-center p-2">
                      { this.state.message }
                  </div>
                  <div className="text-center">
                      <button className="btn btn-primary"
                          onMouseDown={ this.handleEvent }
                          onMouseUp={ this.handleEvent } >
                              Click Me
                      </button>
                  </div>
             </div>
    }
}
```

The handleEvent method uses the type property to determine which event is being handled and updates the message value accordingly. When you press the mouse button down, a mousedown event is triggered, and when you release, a mouseup event is triggered, as shown in Figure 12-5.

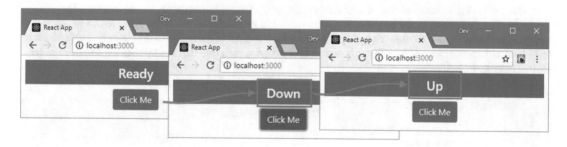

Figure 12-5. *Differentiating event types*

Avoiding the Event Reuse Pitfall

React reuses SyntheticEvent objects and resets all the properties to null once an event has been handled. This can cause problems if you are relying on asynchronous updates to state data, as described in Chapter 11. Listing 12-12 demonstrates the problem.

Listing 12-12. Using an Event Object Asynchronously in the App.js File in the src Folder

```
import React, { Component } from 'react';

export default class App extends Component {

    constructor(props) {
        super(props);
        this.state = {
            message: "Ready",
            counter: 0
        }
    }
```

```
handleEvent = (event) => {
    this.setState({ counter: this.state.counter + 1},
        () => this.setState({ message: `${event.type}: ${this.state.counter}`}));
}

render() {
    return  <div className="m-2">
                <div className="h4 bg-primary text-white text-center p-2">
                    { this.state.message }
                </div>
                <div className="text-center">
                    <button className="btn btn-primary"
                        onClick={ this.handleEvent } >
                            Click Me
                    </button>
                </div>
            </div>
    }
}
```

The handleEvent method uses the setState method's callback feature to update the message property after an update to the counter property has been applied. The value assigned to the message property includes the event object's type property, which is a problem because that property will be set to null by the time the setState callback function is invoked, which you can see by clicking the button, as shown in Figure 12-6.

Figure 12-6. Asynchronously using event objects

The persist method is used to prevent React from resetting the event object, as shown in Listing 12-13.

Listing 12-13. Persisting an Event Object in the App.js File in the src Folder

```
...
handleEvent = (event) => {
    event.persist();
    this.setState({ counter: this.state.counter + 1},
        () => this.setState({ message: `${event.type}: ${this.state.counter}`}));
}
...
```

328

The result is that the event's properties can be read from the setState method's callback function, producing the result shown in Figure 12-7.

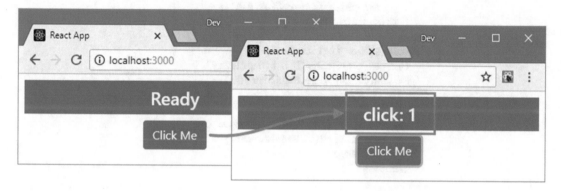

Figure 12-7. *Persisting an event*

Invoking Event Handlers with a Custom Argument

Event handlers are often more useful if they are provided with a custom argument, instead of the SythenticEvent object that React provides by default. To demonstrate why the event object isn't always useful, I added another button element to the content rendered by the App component and set up the event handler so that it uses the event to determine which button has been clicked, as shown in Listing 12-14.

Listing 12-14. Identifying the Source of an Event in the App.js File in the src Folder

```
import React, { Component } from 'react';

export default class App extends Component {

    constructor(props) {
        super(props);
        this.state = {
            message: "Ready",
            counter: 0,
            theme: "secondary"
        }
    }

    handleEvent = (event) => {
        event.persist();
        this.setState({
            counter: this.state.counter + 1,
            theme: event.target.innerText === "Normal" ? "primary" : "danger"
        }, () => this.setState({ message: `${event.type}: ${this.state.counter}` }));
    }
```

```
render() {
    return  <div className="m-2">
                <div className={ `h4 bg-${this.state.theme}
                        text-white text-center p-2`}>
                    { this.state.message }
                </div>
                <div className="text-center">
                    <button className="btn btn-primary"
                        onClick={ this.handleEvent } >
                            Normal
                    </button>
                    <button className="btn btn-danger m-1"
                        onClick={ this.handleEvent } >
                            Danger
                    </button>
                </div>
            </div>
    }
}
```

The problem with this approach is that the event handler has to understand the significance of the content rendered by the component. In this case, that means knowing that the value of the innerText property can be used to work out the source of the event and determine the value for the theme state data property. This can be difficult to manage if the content rendered by the component changes or if there are multiple interactions that can produce the same result. A more elegant approach is to use an inline expression for the event handler property that invokes the handler method and provides it with the information it needs, as shown in Listing 12-15.

Listing 12-15. Invoking a Handler with a Custom Argument in the App.js File in the src Folder

```
import React, { Component } from 'react';

export default class App extends Component {

    constructor(props) {
        super(props);
        this.state = {
            message: "Ready",
            counter: 0,
            theme: "secondary"
        }
    }

    handleEvent = (event, newTheme) => {
        event.persist();
        this.setState({
            counter: this.state.counter + 1,
            theme: newTheme
        }, () => this.setState({ message: `${event.type}: ${this.state.counter}`}));
    }
```

```
render() {
    return  <div className="m-2">
                <div className={ `h4 bg-${this.state.theme}
                        text-white text-center p-2`}>
                    { this.state.message }
                </div>
                <div className="text-center">
                    <button className="btn btn-primary"
                        onClick={ (e) => this.handleEvent(e, "primary") } >
                            Normal
                    </button>
                    <button className="btn btn-danger m-1"
                        onClick={ (e) => this.handleEvent(e, "danger") } >
                            Danger
                    </button>
                </div>
            </div>
    }
}
```

The result is the same, but the handleEvent method doesn't have to inspect the element that triggered the event in order to set the theme property. To see the effect of setting the theme, click either of the button elements, as shown in Figure 12-8.

■ **Tip** If your handler method doesn't need the event object, then you can use the inline expression to call the handler without it: () => handleEvent("primary").

Figure 12-8. *Using a custom argument*

Preventing Default Behavior

Some events have behavior that the browser performs by default. The default behavior for clicking a checkbox, for example, is to toggle the status of that checkbox. The preventDefault method can be called on event objects to prevent the default behavior, and to demonstrate, I added a checkbox element to the content that will be toggled only after one of the button elements has been clicked, as shown in Listing 12-16.

Listing 12-16. Preventing Default Behavior in the App.js File in the src Folder

```
import React, { Component } from 'react';

export default class App extends Component {

    constructor(props) {
        super(props);
        this.state = {
            message: "Ready",
            counter: 0,
            theme: "secondary"
        }
    }

    handleEvent = (event, newTheme) => {
        event.persist();
        this.setState({
            counter: this.state.counter + 1,
            theme: newTheme
        }, () => this.setState({ message: `${event.type}: ${this.state.counter}`}));
    }

    toggleCheckBox = (event) => {
        if (this.state.counter === 0) {
            event.preventDefault();
        }
    }

    render() {
        return   <div className="m-2">
                    <div className="form-check">
                        <input className="form-check-input" type="checkbox"
                            onClick={ this.toggleCheckBox }/>
                        <label>This is a checkbox</label>
                    </div>

                    <div className={ `h4 bg-${this.state.theme}
                        text-white text-center p-2`}>
                        { this.state.message }
                    </div>
                    <div className="text-center">
                        <button className="btn btn-primary"
                            onClick={ (e) => this.handleEvent(e, "primary") } >
                                Normal
                        </button>
                        <button className="btn btn-danger m-1"
                            onClick={ (e) => this.handleEvent(e, "danger") } >
                                Danger
                        </button>
                    </div>
                </div>
    }
}
```

The onClick property on the input element tells React to invoke the toggleCheckBox method when the user clicks the checkbox. The preventDefault method is called on the event if the value of the counter state data property is zero, with the result that the checkbox cannot be toggled until after a button has been clicked, as shown in Figure 12-9.

Figure 12-9. *Preventing event default behavior*

Managing Event Propagation

Events have a lifecycle that allows an element's ancestors to receive events triggered by their descendants and also to intercept events before they reach an element. In the sections that follow, I describe how events are propagated through HTML elements and explain the effect this has on React applications, using the properties and methods defined by the SyntheticEvent that are described in Table 12-4.

Table 12-4. *The SyntheticEvent Properties and Methods for Event Propagation*

Name	Description
eventPhase	This property returns the propagation phase of an event. However, the way that React handles events means this property is not useful, as described in the "Determining the Event Phase" section.
bubbles	This property returns true if the event will enter the bubble phase.
currentTarget	This property returns an object that represents the element whose event handler is processing the event.
stopPropagation()	This method is called to stop event propagation, as described in the "Stopping Event Propagation" section.
isPropagationStopped()	This method returns true if stopPropagation has been called on an event.

Understanding the Target and Bubble Phases

When an event is first triggered, it enters the *target phase*, where event handlers applied to the element that is the source of the event are invoked. Once those event handlers are complete, the event enters the *bubble phase*, where the event works its way up the chain of ancestor elements and is used to invoke any handlers that have been applied for that type of event. To help demonstrate these phases, I added a file called ThemeButton.js to the src folder and used it to define the component shown in Listing 12-17.

Listing 12-17. The Contents of the ThemeButton.js File in the src Folder

```
import React, { Component } from "react";

export class ThemeButton extends Component {

    handleClick = (event) => {
        console.log(`ThemeButton: Type: ${event.type} `
            + `Target: ${event.target.tagName} `
            + `CurrentTarget: ${event.currentTarget.tagName}`);
        this.props.callback(this.props.theme);
    }

    render() {
        return  <span className="m-1" onClick={ this.handleClick }>
                    <button className={`btn btn-${this.props.theme}`}
                        onClick={ this.handleClick }>
                            Select {this.props.theme } Theme
                    </button>
                </span>
    }
}
```

This component renders a span element that contains a button and is provided with a theme prop, which specifies a Bootstrap CSS theme name, and a callback prop that is invoked to select the prop. The onClick property has been applied to both the span and button elements. In Listing 12-18, I updated the App component to use the ThemeButton component and to remove some of the code used in earlier examples.

Listing 12-18. Applying a Component in the App.js File in the src Folder

```
import React, { Component } from 'react';
import { ThemeButton } from "./ThemeButton";

export default class App extends Component {

    constructor(props) {
        super(props);
        this.state = {
            message: "Ready",
            counter: 0,
            theme: "secondary"
        }
    }

    selectTheme = (newTheme) => {
        this.setState({
            theme: newTheme,
            message: `Theme: ${newTheme}`
        });
    }
```

```
render() {
    return (
        <div className="m-2">
            <div className={ `h4 bg-${this.state.theme}
                    text-white text-center p-2`}>
                { this.state.message }
            </div>
            <div className="text-center">
                <ThemeButton theme="primary" callback={ this.selectTheme } />
                <ThemeButton theme="danger" callback={ this.selectTheme } />
            </div>
        </div>
    )
}
}
```

Click either of the button elements, and you will see the following output in the browser's JavaScript console:

```
...
ThemeButton: Type: click Target: BUTTON CurrentTarget: BUTTON
ThemeButton: Type: click Target: BUTTON CurrentTarget: SPAN
...
```

There are two messages in the console because there are two onClick properties in the content rendered by the ThemeButton component. The first message is generated during the target phase when the event is processed by the handlers of the element that triggered it, which is the button element in this example. The event then enters the bubble phase, where it propagates up through the button element's ancestor and invokes any suitable event handlers. In the example, the span element that is the parent of the button also has an onClick property, which results in two calls to the handleClick method and two messages written to the console.

■ **Tip** Not all types of event have a bubble phase. As a rule of thumb, events that are specific to a single element—such as gaining and losing focus—do not bubble. Events that apply to multiple elements—such as clicking a region of the screen that is occupied by multiple elements—will bubble. You can check to see whether a specific event is going to go through the bubble phase by reading the bubbles property of the event object.

The bubble phase extends beyond the content rendered by the component and propagates throughout the entire hierarchy of HTML elements. To demonstrate, I added onClick handlers to elements rendered by the App component that will receive the click event when it bubbles up from the button element rendered by the ThemeButton component, as shown in Listing 12-19.

Listing 12-19. Adding Event Handlers in the App.js File in the src Folder

```
import React, { Component } from 'react';
import { ThemeButton } from "./ThemeButton";
```

```
export default class App extends Component {

    constructor(props) {
        super(props);
        this.state = {
            message: "Ready",
            counter: 0,
            theme: "secondary"
        }
    }

    selectTheme = (newTheme) => {
        this.setState({
            theme: newTheme,
            message: `Theme: ${newTheme}`
        });
    }

    handleClick= (event) => {
        console.log(`App: Type: ${event.type} `
            + `Target: ${event.target.tagName} `
            + `CurrentTarget: ${event.currentTarget.tagName}`);
    }

    render() {
        return (
            <div className="m-2" onClick={ this.handleClick }>
                    <div className={ `h4 bg-${this.state.theme}
                        text-white text-center p-2`}>
                      { this.state.message }
                    </div>
                    <div className="text-center" onClick={ this.handleClick }>
                        <ThemeButton theme="primary" callback={ this.selectTheme } />
                        <ThemeButton theme="danger" callback={ this.selectTheme } />
                    </div>
            </div>
        )
    }
}
```

I added the onClick property to two div elements, and when you click one of the buttons, you will see the following series of messages displayed in the browser's JavaScript console (some browsers group the last two messages together since they are the same):

```
...
ThemeButton: Type: click Target: BUTTON CurrentTarget: BUTTON
ThemeButton: Type: click Target: BUTTON CurrentTarget: SPAN
App: Type: click Target: BUTTON CurrentTarget: DIV
App: Type: click Target: BUTTON CurrentTarget: DIV
...
```

The SyntheticEvent object provides the currentTarget property, which returns the element whose event handler is being invoked, as opposed to the target property, which returns the element that triggered the event.

```
...
console.log(`ThemeButton: Type: ${event.type} `
    + `Target: ${event.target.tagName} `
    + `CurrentTarget: ${event.currentTarget.tagName}`);
...
```

These messages show the target and bubble phases of the click event as it is propagated up the hierarchy of HTML elements, as shown in Figure 12-10.

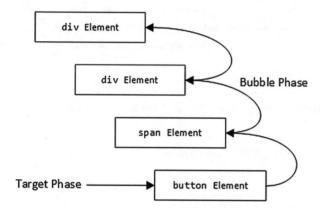

Figure 12-10. *The target and bubble phases of the event*

EVENTS AND ELEMENTS THAT APPLY COMPONENTS

Event handling is performed by the HTML elements that are rendered by components and excludes the custom HTML elements that are used to apply components. Adding event handler properties, such as onClick to the ThemeButton element, for example, has no effect. No error is reported, but the custom element is excluded from the HTML that is displayed by the browser, and the handler will never be invoked.

Understanding the Capture Phase

The capture phase provides an opportunity for elements to process events before the target phase. During the capture phase, the browser starts with the body element and works its way down the hierarchy of elements toward the target, following the opposite path to the bubble phase, and gives each element the chance to process the event, as shown in Figure 12-11.

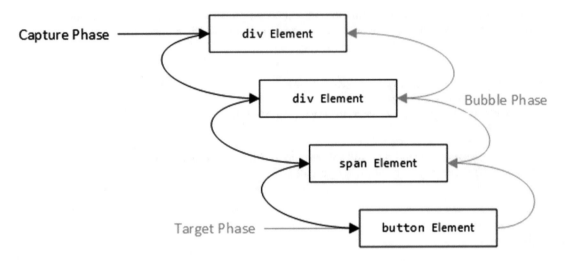

Figure 12-11. *The event capture phase*

A separate property is required to tell React that an event handler should be applied in the capture phase, as shown in Listing 12-20.

Listing 12-20. Capturing an Event in the ThemeButton.js File in the src Folder

```
import React, { Component } from "react";

export class ThemeButton extends Component {

    handleClick = (event) => {
        console.log(`ThemeButton: Type: ${event.type} `
            + `Target: ${event.target.tagName} `
            + `CurrentTarget: ${event.currentTarget.tagName}`);
        this.props.callback(this.props.theme);
    }

    render() {
        return   <span className="m-1" onClick={ this.handleClick }
                    onClickCapture={ this.handleClick }>
                <button className={`btn btn-${this.props.theme}`}
                    onClick={ this.handleClick }>
                        Select {this.props.theme } Theme
                </button>
            </span>
    }
}
```

For each event handling property, such as onClick, there is a corresponding capture property, onClickCapture, that receives events in the capture phase. In the listing, I applied the onClickCapture property to the span element and specified the handleClick method in the expression. The result is that the span element will receive `click` events in the `capture` and `bubble` phases as the event works its way down the hierarchy of HTML elements and goes back up again. Clicking either of the `button` elements will produce an additional message in the browser's JavaScript console.

```
...
ThemeButton: Type: click Target: BUTTON CurrentTarget: SPAN
ThemeButton: Type: click Target: BUTTON CurrentTarget: BUTTON
ThemeButton: Type: click Target: BUTTON CurrentTarget: SPAN
App: Type: click Target: BUTTON CurrentTarget: DIV
App: Type: click Target: BUTTON CurrentTarget: DIV
...
```

Determining the Event Phase

The `handleClick` method defined by the `ThemeButton` component will handle events several times for each `click` event, and it moves from the capture to the target and then the bubble phase. Each time the `handleClick` method is called, it invokes the function prop provided by the parent component, which has the effect of repeatedly changing the value of the `App` component's `theme` state property. This is a harmless effect, but in real projects, repeatedly invoking a callback can cause problems, and it is bad practice for a child component to assume that props can be invoked without issue. To highlight the problem, I added a statement to the `ThemeButton` component's `handleEvent` method that writes a message to the browser's JavaScript console when the function prop is invoked, as shown in Listing 12-21.

Listing 12-21. Adding a Debugging Message in the ThemeButton.js File in the src Folder

```
import React, { Component } from "react";

export class ThemeButton extends Component {

    handleClick = (event) => {
        console.log(`ThemeButton: Type: ${event.type} `
            + `Target: ${event.target.tagName} `
            + `CurrentTarget: ${event.currentTarget.tagName}`);
        console.log("Invoked function prop");
        this.props.callback(this.props.theme);
    }

    render() {
        return  <span className="m-1" onClick={ this.handleClick }
                    onClickCapture={ this.handleClick }>
                    <button className={`btn btn-${this.props.theme}`}
                        onClick={ this.handleClick }>
                        Select {this.props.theme } Theme
                    </button>
                </span>
    }
}
```

Click one of the button's presented by the example application, and you will see that the function prop is invoked for each of the three phases that the click event goes through.

```
...
ThemeButton: Type: click Target: BUTTON CurrentTarget: SPAN
Invoked function prop
ThemeButton: Type: click Target: BUTTON CurrentTarget: BUTTON
Invoked function prop
ThemeButton: Type: click Target: BUTTON CurrentTarget: SPAN
Invoked function prop
App: Type: click Target: BUTTON CurrentTarget: DIV
App: Type: click Target: BUTTON CurrentTarget: DIV
...
```

The SytheticEvent object that React uses defines an eventPhase property, which returns the value of the corresponding property from the native DOM API event object. Unfortunately, the value of that property always indicates that the event is in the bubble phase because React intercepts the native event and uses it to simulate the three propagation phases. As a consequence, a little more work is required to identify event phases.

The first step is to identify events in the capture phase, which can be done by using a different handler method or providing an additional argument to the common handler, which is the approach that I have taken in Listing 12-22.

Listing 12-22. Identifying Capture Phase Events in the ThemeButton.js File in the src Folder

```
import React, { Component } from "react";

export class ThemeButton extends Component {

    handleClick = (event, capturePhase = false) => {
        console.log(`ThemeButton: Type: ${event.type} `
            + `Target: ${event.target.tagName} `
            + `CurrentTarget: ${event.currentTarget.tagName}`);
        if (capturePhase) {
            console.log("Skipped function prop: capture phase");
        } else {
            console.log("Invoked function prop");
            this.props.callback(this.props.theme);
        }
    }

    render() {
        return <span className="m-1" onClick={ this.handleClick }
                    onClickCapture={ (e) => this.handleClick(e, true) }>
                <button className={`btn btn-${this.props.theme}`}
                    onClick={ this.handleClick }>
                        Select {this.props.theme } Theme
                </button>
            </span>
    }
}
```

I used an inline expression for the onClickCapture property that receives the SythenticEvent object and uses it to invoke the handleClick method, along with an additional argument that indicates the event is in the capture phase. Within the handleClick method, I check the value of the capturePhase parameter to identify events in their capture phase.

Separating the target and bubble phases is more difficult because events in both phases are handled by the onClick property. The most reliable way to determine the phase is to see whether the values for the target and currentTarget properties are different and to see whether the bubbles property is true. If the object returned by the currentTarget is different from the target value and the event has a bubble phase, then it is reasonable to assume that the event is bubbling, as shown in Listing 12-23.

Listing 12-23. Identifying Bubble Phase Events in the ThemeButton.js File in the src Folder

```
import React, { Component } from "react";

export class ThemeButton extends Component {

    handleClick = (event, capturePhase = false) => {
        console.log(`ThemeButton: Type: ${event.type} `
            + `Target: ${event.target.tagName} `
            + `CurrentTarget: ${event.currentTarget.tagName}`);
        if (capturePhase) {
            console.log("Skipped function prop: capture phase");
        } else if (event.bubbles && event.currentTarget !== event.target) {
            console.log("Skipped function prop: bubble phase");
        } else {
            console.log("Invoked function prop");
            this.props.callback(this.props.theme);
        }
    }

    render() {
        return   <span className="m-1" onClick={ this.handleClick }
                    onClickCapture={ (e) => this.handleClick(e, true) }>
                    <button className={`btn btn-${this.props.theme}`}
                    onClick={ this.handleClick }>
                        Select {this.props.theme } Theme
                    </button>
                </span>
    }
}
```

When you click a button, you will see the following sequence of messages in the browser's JavaScript console, indicating that each phase has been identified and that the function prop has been called only in the target phase.

```
...
ThemeButton: Type: click Target: BUTTON CurrentTarget: SPAN
Skipped function prop: capture phase
ThemeButton: Type: click Target: BUTTON CurrentTarget: BUTTON
Invoked function prop
ThemeButton: Type: click Target: BUTTON CurrentTarget: SPAN
Skipped function prop: bubble phase
```

```
App: Type: click Target: BUTTON CurrentTarget: DIV
App: Type: click Target: BUTTON CurrentTarget: DIV
...
```

These messages also confirm the order of the event's phases: capture, target, and then bubble.

Stopping Event Propagation

Understanding event phases can also be important if you want to disrupt the normal propagation sequence and prevent elements from receiving events. In Listing 12-24, I have changed the ThemeButton component so that it intercepts click events in the capture phase and stops them from reaching the target element.

Listing 12-24. Stopping Event Propagation in the ThemeButton.js File in the src Folder

```
import React, { Component } from "react";

export class ThemeButton extends Component {

    handleClick = (event, capturePhase = false) => {
        console.log(`ThemeButton: Type: ${event.type} `
            + `Target: ${event.target.tagName} `
            + `CurrentTarget: ${event.currentTarget.tagName}`);
        if (capturePhase) {
            if (this.props.theme === "danger") {
                event.stopPropagation();
                console.log("Stopped event");
            } else {
                console.log("Skipped function prop: capture phase");
            }
        } else if (event.bubbles && event.currentTarget !== event.target) {
            console.log("Skipped function prop: bubble phase");
        } else {
            console.log("Invoked function prop");
            this.props.callback(this.props.theme);
        }
    }

    render() {
        return  <span className="m-1" onClick={ this.handleClick }
                    onClickCapture={ (e) => this.handleClick(e, true) }>
                    <button className={`btn btn-${this.props.theme}`}
                        onClick={ this.handleClick }>
                        Select {this.props.theme } Theme
                    </button>
                </span>
    }
}
```

The onClickCapture property on the span element will invoke the handleClick method when it receives a click event in the capture phase. The stopPropagation method is called when the value of the theme prop is danger, which prevents the event from reaching the button element and has the effect of preventing the user from selecting the danger theme, as illustrated in Figure 12-12.

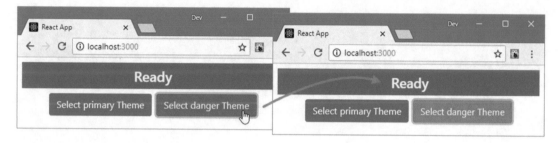

Figure 12-12. *Stopping an event*

Summary

In this chapter, I described the features that React provides for working with events. I demonstrated the different ways that handler functions can be defined, showed you how to work with event objects, and showed how to use custom arguments instead. I also explained how React events are not the same as DOM API events, even though they are similar and closely related. I finished the chapter by introducing the event lifecycle and showing you how events are propagated. In the next chapter, I describe the component lifecycle and explain how state data changes are reconciled.

CHAPTER 13

Reconciliation and Lifecycles

In this chapter, I explain how React uses a process called *reconciliation* to efficiently deal with content produced by components. The reconciliation process is part of a larger lifecycle that React provides for components, and I describe the different lifecycle stages and show you how stateful components can implement methods to become active lifecycle participants. Table 13-1 puts reconciliation and the component lifecycle in context.

Table 13-1. *Putting Reconciliation and Lifecycle Text in Context*

Question	Answer
What is it?	Reconciliation is the process of efficiently handling the content produced by components to minimize changes to the Document Object Model (DOM). Reconciliation is part of a larger lifecycle that is applied to stateful components.
Why is it useful?	The reconciliation process helps application performance, while the broader component lifecycle provides a consistent model for application development and provides useful features for advanced projects.
How is it used?	The reconciliation process is performed automatically, and no explicit action is required. All stateful components go through the same lifecycle and can participate actively by implementing specific methods (for class-based components) or the effect hook (for functional components).
Are there any pitfalls or limitations?	Care must be taken to write components so they fit into the overall lifecycle, which includes being able to render content even though it may not be used to update the DOM.
Are there any alternatives?	No, the lifecycle and the reconciliation process are fundamental React features.

© Adam Freeman 2019
A. Freeman, *Pro React 16*, https://doi.org/10.1007/978-1-4842-4451-7_13

Table 13-2 summarizes the chapter.

Table 13-2. *Chapter Summary*

Problem	Solution	Listing
Trigger reconciliation	Call the `forceUpdate` method	15, 16
Respond to lifecycle stages	Implement the method that corresponds to the lifecycle stage	17–20
Receive notifications in a functional component	Use the effect hook	21–23
Prevent updates	Implement the `shouldComponentUpdate` method	24, 25
Set state data from props	Implement the `getDerivedStateFromProps` method	26, 27

Preparing for This Chapter

To create the example project for this chapter, open a new command prompt, navigate to a convenient location, and run the command shown in Listing 13-1.

■ **Tip** You can download the example project for this chapter—and for all the other chapters in this book—from `https://github.com/Apress/pro-react-16`.

Listing 13-1. Creating the Example Project

```
npx create-react-app lifecycle
```

Run the commands shown in Listing 13-2 to navigate to the `lifecycle` folder and add the Bootstrap package to the project.

Listing 13-2. Adding the Bootstrap CSS Framework

```
cd lifecycle
npm install bootstrap@4.1.2
```

To include the Bootstrap CSS stylesheet in the application, add the statement shown in Listing 13-3 to the `index.js` file, which can be found in the `src` folder.

Listing 13-3. Including Bootstrap in the index.js File in the src Folder

```
import React from 'react';
import ReactDOM from 'react-dom';
import './index.css';
```

```
import App from './App';
import * as serviceWorker from './serviceWorker';
import 'bootstrap/dist/css/bootstrap.css';

ReactDOM.render(<App />, document.getElementById('root'));

// If you want your app to work offline and load faster, you can change
// unregister() to register() below. Note this comes with some pitfalls.
// Learn more about service workers: http://bit.ly/CRA-PWA
serviceWorker.unregister();
```

Creating the Example Components

Some basic components are needed for the examples in this chapter. Add a file called ActionButton.js to the src folder and add the content shown in Listing 13-4.

Listing 13-4. The Contents of the ActionButton.js File in the src Folder

```
import React, { Component } from "react";

export class ActionButton extends Component {

    render() {
        console.log(`Render ActionButton (${this.props.text}) Component `);
        return <button className="btn btn-primary m-2"
                        onClick={ this.props.callback }>
                    { this.props.text }
                </button>
    }
}
```

This component renders a button that invokes a function prop in response to the click event. Next, add a file called Message.js to the src folder and add the content shown in Listing 13-5.

Listing 13-5. The Contents of the Message.js File in the src Folder

```
import React, { Component } from "react";
import { ActionButton } from "./ActionButton";

export class Message extends Component {

    render() {
        console.log(`Render Message Component `);
        return (
            <div>
                <ActionButton theme="primary"  {...this.props} />
                <div className="h5 text-center p-2">
                    { this.props.message }
                </div>
```

```
            </div>
        )
    }
}
```

This component displays a message received as a prop and passes on a function prop as the callback for an `ActionButton`, as defined in Listing 13-4. Next, add a file called `List.js` to the `src` folder and add the content shown in Listing 13-6.

Listing 13-6. The Contents of the List.js File in the src Folder

```
import React, { Component } from "react";
import { ActionButton } from "./ActionButton";

export class List extends Component {

    constructor(props) {
        super(props);
        this.state = {
            names: ["Bob", "Alice", "Dora"]
        }
    }

    reverseList = () => {
        this.setState({ names: this.state.names.reverse()});
    }

    render() {
        console.log("Render List Component");
        return (
            <div>
                <ActionButton callback={ this.reverseList }
                    text="Reverse Names" />
                { this.state.names.map((name, index) => {
                    return <h5 key={ name }>{ name }</h5>
                })}

            </div>
        )
    }
}
```

This component has its own state data, which it uses to render a list. An `ActionButton` component is provided with the `reverseList` method as its function prop, which reverses the order of the items in the list.

The final change is to replace the contents of the `App.js` file with the code shown in Listing 13-7, which renders content that uses the other components and defines the state data that the `Message` component requires.

Listing 13-7. The Contents of the App.js File in the src Folder

```
import React, { Component } from 'react';
import { Message } from "./Message";
import { List } from "./List";

export default class App extends Component {

    constructor(props) {
        super(props);
        this.state = {
            counter: 0
        }
    }

    incrementCounter = () => {
        this.setState({ counter: this.state.counter + 1 });
    }

    render() {
        console.log("Render App Component");
        return   <div className="container text-center">
                     <div className="row p-2">
                         <div className="col-6">
                             <Message message={ `Counter: ${this.state.counter}`}
                                 callback={ this.incrementCounter }
                                 text="Increment Counter" />
                         </div>
                         <div className="col-6">
                             <List />
                         </div>
                     </div>
                 </div>

    }
}
```

The content rendered by the App component displays the Message and List components side by side using the Bootstrap CSS grid features. The counter property is incremented by the incrementCounter method, which is used as the function prop for the Message component. Using the command prompt, run the command shown in Listing 13-8 in the lifecycle folder to start the development tools.

Listing 13-8. Starting the Development Tools

```
npm start
```

Once the initial preparation for the project is complete, a new browser window will open and display the URL http://localhost:3000, which will display the content shown in Figure 13-1.

Figure 13-1. *Running the example application*

Understanding How Content Is Rendered

The starting point for the rendering process is the statement in the index.js file that invokes the ReactDOM. render method.

```
...
ReactDOM.render(<App />, document.getElementById('root'));
...
```

This method starts the initial rendering process. React creates a new instance of the App component, which is specified by the first argument to the ReactDOM.render method, and invokes its render method. The content rendered by the App component includes Message and List elements, and React creates instances of these components and calls their render methods. The process continues to the ActionButton elements in the content rendered by the Message and List elements, creating two instances of the ActionButton component and calling the render method for each of them. The result of calling the render method on each component is a hierarchy of HTML elements that are inserted into the element selected by the second argument to the ReactDOM.render method, creating the content shown in Figure 13-1. The result of the initial rendering process is a hierarchy of component objects and HTML elements, as shown in Figure 13-2.

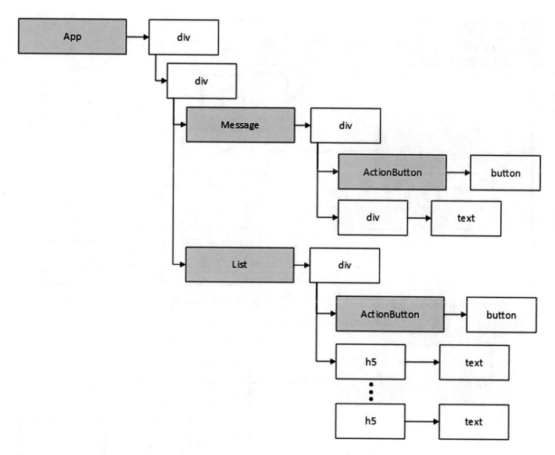

Figure 13-2. *Components and their content*

React uses the browser's API to add HTML elements to the Document Object Model (DOM) so they can be presented to user, as shown in Figure 13-3, and creates a mapping between the components and the content they render.

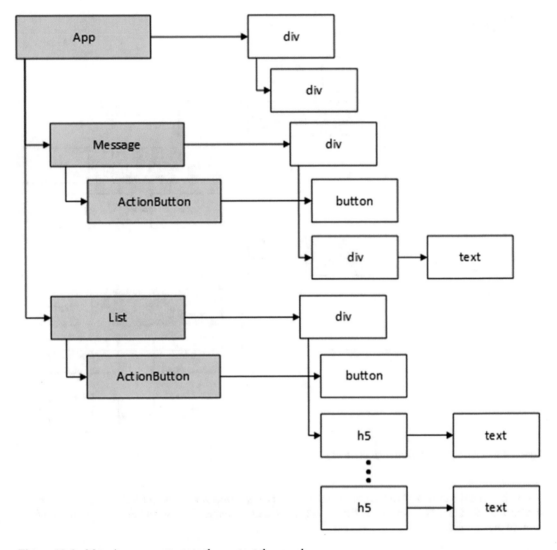

Figure 13-3. Mapping components to the content they render

The browser doesn't know—or care—about the components, and its only job is to present the HTML elements in the DOM. React is responsible for managing the components and dealing with the content that is rendered.

Each of the components in the example application has a `console.log` statement in its `render` method, and the messages displayed in the browser's JavaScript console show that each of the five component objects is asked to render its content.

```
...
Render App Component
Render Message Component
Render ActionButton (Increment Counter) Component
```

```
Render List Component
Render ActionButton (Reverse Names) Component
...
```

There are messages from one App component, one Message component, one List component, and two ActionButton components, matching the structure illustrated in Figures 13-2 and 13-3.

Understanding the Update Process

When the application first starts, React asks all the components to render their content so that it can be displayed to the user. Once the content is displayed, the application is in the *reconciled* state, where the content displayed to the user is consistent with the state of the components.

When the application is reconciled, React waits for something to change. In most applications, changes are caused by user interaction, which triggers an event and results in a call to the setState method. The setState method updates a component's state data, but it also marks the component as "stale," meaning that the HTML content displayed to the user may be out-of-date. A single event may result in multiple state data changes, and once they have all been processed, React invokes the render method for each dirty component and its children. To see the effect of a change, click the Increment Counter button in the browser window, as shown in Figure 13-4.

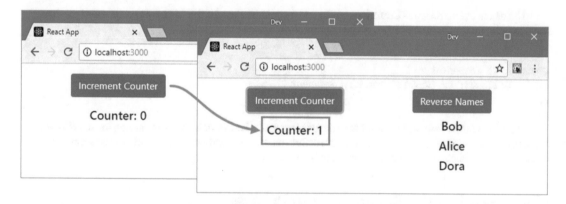

Figure 13-4. *Clicking a button to trigger a change*

The handler that responds to the click event updates App component's counter state data property. Since App is the top-level component, that means the render method is invoked on all of the application's components, which can be seen in the messages displayed in the browser's JavaScript console.

```
...
Render App Component
Render Message Component
Render ActionButton (Increment Counter) Component
Render List Component
Render ActionButton (Reverse Names) Component
...
```

React only updates the components that are affected by a change, minimizing the amount of work that the application has to do before it is reconciled again. You can see how this works by clicking the Reverse Names button, as shown in Figure 13-5.

Figure 13-5. *Clicking a button to trigger a limited change*

The click event from this button results in a state data change for the List component and produces the following messages in the browser's JavaScript console:

```
...
Render List Component
Render ActionButton (Reverse Names) Component
...
```

The List component and its child ActionButton are marked as stale, but the change hasn't affected the App and Message components or the other ActionButton. React assumes that the content rendered these components is still current and doesn't need to be updated.

Understanding the Reconciliation Process

Although React will invoke the render method of any component that has been marked as stale, it doesn't always use the content that is produced. Making changes to the HTML elements in the Domain Object Model is an expensive operation and so React compares the content returned by the components with the previous results so that it can ask the browser to perform the smallest number of operations, a process known as *reconciliation*.

To demonstrate how React minimizes the changes it makes, I have made a change to the content rendered by the Message component, as shown in Listing 13-9.

Listing 13-9. Changing Content in the Message.js File in the src Folder

```
import React, { Component } from "react";
import { ActionButton } from "./ActionButton";
```

```
export class Message extends Component {

    render() {
        console.log(`Render Message Component `);
        return (
            <div>
                <ActionButton theme="primary" {...this.props} />
                <div id="messageDiv" className="h5 text-center p-2">
                    { this.props.message }
                </div>
            </div>
        )
    }
}
```

The addition of the id attribute makes it easier to manipulate the div element. Using the F12 developer tools, switch to the Console tab, enter the statement shown in Listing 13-10, and press Enter. All browsers allow JavaScript arbitrary statements to be executed, and in Google Chrome this is done by entering code into the prompt at the bottom of the Console tab.

Listing 13-10. Manipulating an HTML Element

```
document.getElementById("messageDiv").classList.add("bg-info")
```

This statement uses the DOM API to select the div element rendered by the Message component and assign it to the bg-info class, which selects a background color defined by the Bootstrap CSS framework. When you click the Increment Counter button, the content of the div element is updated, but the color doesn't change, because React has compared the content returned by the Message component's render method with the previous result and detected that only the content of the div element is different, as illustrated in Figure 13-6.

Figure 13-6. *The effect of reconciliation*

React compares the content produced by components with its own cache of previous results, known as the virtual DOM, which is defined in a format that allows for efficient comparisons. The effect is that React doesn't have to query the elements in the DOM to figure out the set of changes.

■ **Tip** Don't confuse the term *virtual DOM*, which is specific to React, with *shadow DOM*, which is a recent browser feature that allows content to be scoped to a specific part of the HTML document.

A second example is required to confirm the reconciliation behavior, demonstrating how React handles a more complex change. In Listing 13-11, I have added state data to the Message component and used it to alternate between two different element types.

Listing 13-11. Alternating Elements in the Message.js File in the src Folder

```
import React, { Component } from "react";
import { ActionButton } from "./ActionButton";

export class Message extends Component {

    constructor(props) {
        super(props);
        this.state = {
            showSpan: false
        }
    }

    handleClick = (event) => {
        this.setState({ showSpan: !this.state.showSpan });
        this.props.callback(event);
    }

    getMessageElement() {
        let div = <div id="messageDiv" className="h5 text-center p-2">
                        { this.props.message }
                    </div>
        return this.state.showSpan ? <span>{ div } </span> : div;
    }

    render() {
        console.log(`Render Message Component `);
        return (
            <div>
                <ActionButton theme="primary" {...this.props}
                    callback={ this.handleClick } />
                { this.getMessageElement() }
            </div>
        )
    }
}
```

The component alternates between displaying a div element directly or wrapping it in a span element. Save the changes and execute the statement shown in Listing 13-12 in the browser's JavaScript console to set the background color of the div element. Notice that I have defined the callback property after passing on props to the ActionButton component using the spread operator. The Message component receives a callback property from its parent, so I have to define my replacement afterward to override it.

■ **Caution** Don't change the top-level element in components in real projects because it causes React to replace elements in the DOM without performing a detailed comparison to detect changes.

Listing 13-12. Manipulating an HTML Element

```
document.getElementById("messageDiv").classList.add("bg-info")
```

When you click the Increment Counter button, the Message component's render method will return content that includes the span element. Click the button a second time, and the render method will return to the original content, but the background color will not be shown, as illustrated in Figure 13-7.

Figure 13-7. *Reconciling different types of element*

React compares the output from the render method with the previous results and detects the introduction of the span element. React doesn't investigate the content of the new span element to perform a more detailed comparison and just uses it to replace the existing div element that the browser is displaying.

Understanding List Reconciliation

React has special support for handling elements that display arrays of data. Most operations on lists leave most of the elements in the array, although they can often be in a different location, such as when the objects are sorted. To ensure that React is able to minimize the number of changes it has to make to display a change, elements generated from arrays are required to have a key prop, such as the one defined by the List component.

```
...
render() {
    console.log("Render List Component");
    return (
        <div>
            <ActionButton callback={ this.reverseList }
                text="Reverse Names" />
            { this.state.names.map((name, index) => {
                return <h5 key={ name }>{ name }</h5>
            })}
        </div>
    )
}
...
```

The value of the key prop must be unique within the set of elements so that React can identify each one. To demonstrate how React minimizes the changes required to update lists, I added an attribute to the h5 elements rendered by the List component, as shown in Listing 13-13.

■ **Tip**   Key values should be stable, such that they should continue to refer to the same object even after operations that make changes to the array. A common mistake is to use the position of an object in the array as its index, which is not stable because many operations on arrays affect the order of objects.

Listing 13-13. Adding an Attribute in the List.js File in the src Folder

```
import React, { Component } from "react";
import { ActionButton } from "./ActionButton";

export class List extends Component {

    constructor(props) {
        super(props);
        this.state = {
            names: ["Bob", "Alice", "Dora"]
        }
    }

    reverseList = () => {
        this.setState({ names: this.state.names.reverse()});
    }

    render() {
        console.log("Render List Component");
        return (
            <div>
                <ActionButton callback={ this.reverseList }
                    text="Reverse Names" />
                { this.state.names.map((name, index) => {
                    return <h5 id={ name.toLowerCase() } key={ name }>{ name }</h5>
                })}
            </div>
        )
    }
}
```

The addition of the id attribute makes it easy to manipulate the element using the browser's JavaScript console, using the same approach as earlier examples. Use the JavaScript console to execute the statements shown in Listing 13-14, which assign the h5 elements to classes that apply Bootstrap background colors.

Listing 13-14. Adding Classes to Elements

```
document.getElementById("bob").classList.add("bg-primary")
document.getElementById("alice").classList.add("bg-secondary")
document.getElementById("dora").classList.add("bg-info")
```

Click the Reverse Names button, and you will see that the order of the h5 elements is changed, but no elements are destroyed and re-created, as shown in Figure 13-8.

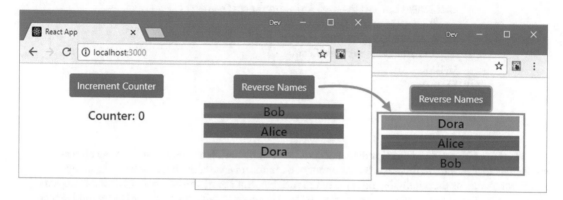

Figure 13-8. *Reordering elements in a list*

Explicitly Triggering Reconciliation

The reconciliation process relies on React being notified of changes through the setState method, which allows it to determine which data is stale. It isn't always possible to call the setState method if you need to respond to changes that have occurred outside of the application, such as when external data has arrived. For these situations, React provides the forceUpdate method, which can be used to explicitly trigger an update and ensures that any changes are reflected in the content presented to the user. To demonstrate explicit reconciliation, I added a file called ExternalCounter.js to the src folder and used it to define the component shown in Listing 13-15.

■ **Caution**   It is worth considering the design of your application if you find yourself using the forceUpdate method. The forceUpdate method is a blunt instrument and its use can often be avoided by extending the use of state data or by applying one of the composition techniques described in Chapter 14.

Listing 13-15. The Contents of the ExternalCounter.js File in the src Folder

```
import React, {Component } from "react";
import { ActionButton } from "./ActionButton";

let externalCounter = 0;

export class ExternalCounter extends Component {

    incrementCounter = () => {
        externalCounter++;
        this.forceUpdate();
    }
}
```

```
    render() {
        return (
            <div>
                <ActionButton callback={ this.incrementCounter }
                    text="External Counter" />
                <div  className="h5 text-center p-2">
                    External: { externalCounter }
                </div>
            </div>
        )
    }
}
```

This is an obvious candidate for data that could readily be handled as state data, but not all real-world situations are clear-cut. In this case, the component depends on a variable that is outside the control of React, which means that changing the value of the variable won't mark the component as state and start the reconciliation process. Instead, the incrementCounter method calls the forceUpdate method, which explicitly starts reconciliation and ensures that the new value is incorporated in the content displayed to the user. To incorporate the new component into the applications, I made the changes shown in Listing 13-16 to the App component.

Listing 13-16. Adding a New Component in the App.js File in the src Folder

```
import React, { Component } from 'react';
import { Message } from "./Message";
import { List } from "./List";
import { ExternalCounter } from './ExternalCounter';

export default class App extends Component {

    constructor(props) {
        super(props);
        this.state = {
            counter: 0
        }
    }

    incrementCounter = () => {
        this.setState({ counter: this.state.counter + 1 });
    }

    render() {
        console.log("Render App Component");
        return   <div className="container text-center">
                    <div className="row p-2">
                        <div className="col-4">
                            <Message message={ `Counter: ${this.state.counter}`}
                                callback={ this.incrementCounter }
                                text="Increment Counter" />
                        </div>
```

```
                    <div className="col-4">
                        <List />
                    </div>
                    <div className="col-4">
                        <ExternalCounter />
                    </div>
                </div>
            </div>
        }
    }
```

The new component is displayed on the right side of the application's layout, and clicking the External Counter button explicitly marks that component as stale and triggers the reconciliation process, as shown in Figure 13-9.

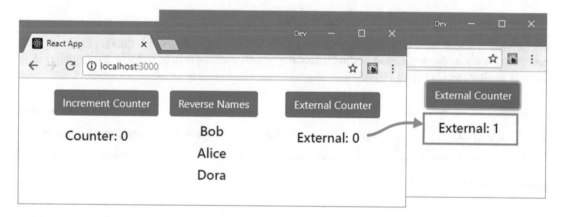

Figure 13-9. *Explicitly starting reconciliation*

Understanding the Component Lifecycle

Most class-based stateful components implement a constructor and the render method. The constructor is used to receive props from the parent and to define state data. The render method is used to produce content, both when the application starts and when React is responding to an update.

The constructor and render method are part of a larger component lifecycle that stateful components can participate in by implementing methods that React invokes to signal changes in the lifecycle. In the sections that follow, I explain the different stages of the component lifecycle and the methods for each of them. For quick reference, Table 13-3 lists the commonly used lifecycle methods. There are also three advanced methods that I describe in the "Using the Advanced Lifecycle Methods" section.

■ **Note** See the "Using the Effect Hook" section for details of how the hooks feature provides access to the lifecycle features for functional components.

Table 13-3. *The Stateful Component Lifecycle Methods*

Name	Description
constructor	This special method is called when a new instance of the component class is created.
render	This method is called when React requires content from the component.
componentDidMount	This method is called after the initial content rendered by the component has been processed.
componentDidUpdate	This method is called after React has completed the reconciliation process following an update.
componentWillUnmount	This method is called before a component is destroyed.
componentDidCatch	This method is used to handle errors, as described in Chapter 14.

Understanding the Mounting Phase

The process by which React creates a component and renders its content for the first time is called *mounting*, and there are three commonly used methods that components implement to participate in the mounting process, as illustrated in Figure 13-10.

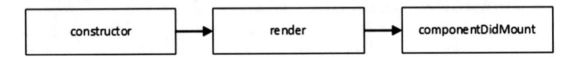

Figure 13-10. *The mounting phase*

The constructor is called when React needs to create a new instance of a component, which gives the component an opportunity to receive the props from its parents, define its state data, and perform other preparatory work.

Next, the render method is called so that the component provides React with the content that will be added to the DOM. Finally, React calls the componentDidMount method, which tells the component that its content has been added to the DOM.

The componentDidMount method is typically used to perform Ajax requests to get data from web services, which I demonstrate in Part 3. For the purposes of this chapter, I implemented the componentDidMount method in the Message component and used it to write a message to the browser's JavaScript console, as shown in Listing 13-17.

Listing 13-17. Implementing a Lifecycle Method in the Message.js File in the src Folder

```
import React, { Component } from "react";
import { ActionButton } from "./ActionButton";

export class Message extends Component {
```

```
    constructor(props) {
        super(props);
        this.state = {
            showSpan: false
        }
    }

    handleClick = (event) => {
        this.setState({ showSpan: !this.state.showSpan });
        this.props.callback(event);
    }

    getMessageElement() {
        let div = <div id="messageDiv" className="h5 text-center p-2">
                        { this.props.message }
                  </div>
        return this.state.showSpan ? <span>{ div } </span> : div;
    }

    render() {
        console.log(`Render Message Component `);
        return (
            <div>
                <ActionButton theme="primary" {...this.props}
                    callback={ this.handleClick } />
                { this.getMessageElement() }
            </div>
        )
    }

    componentDidMount() {
        console.log("componentDidMount Message Component");
    }
}
```

Save the changes to the Message component and examine the messages displayed in the browser's JavaScript console as the application is updated, and you will see that the componentDidMount method was invoked.

```
...
Render App Component
Render Message Component
Render ActionButton (Increment Counter) Component
Render List Component
Render ActionButton (Reverse Names) Component
Render ActionButton (External Counter) Component
componentDidMount Message Component
...
```

You can see that the componentDidMount method has been called after all the component's render methods have been invoked. The componentDidMount method is invoked when React needs a new instance of the component, which includes application startup. But mounting will also occur when React creates an instance of a component while the application is running, such as when content is conditionally rendered, as shown in Listing 13-18.

Listing 13-18. Conditionally Displaying a Component in the App.js File in the src Folder

```
import React, { Component } from 'react';
import { Message } from "./Message";
import { List } from "./List";
import { ExternalCounter } from './ExternalCounter';

export default class App extends Component {

    constructor(props) {
        super(props);
        this.state = {
            counter: 0,
            showMessage: true
        }
    }

    incrementCounter = () => {
        this.setState({ counter: this.state.counter + 1 });
    }

    handleChange = () => {
        this.setState({ showMessage: !this.state.showMessage });
    }

    render() {
        console.log("Render App Component");
        return (
            <div className="container text-center">
                <div className="row p-2">
                    <div className="col-4">
                        <div className="form-check">
                            <input type="checkbox" className="form-check-input"
                                checked={ this.state.showMessage }
                                onChange={ this.handleChange } />
                            <label className="form-check-label">Show</label>
                        </div>
                        { this.state.showMessage &&
                            <Message message={ `Counter: ${this.state.counter}`}
                                callback={ this.incrementCounter }
                                text="Increment Counter" />
                        }
                    </div>
                </div>
```

```
            <div className="col-4">
                <List />
            </div>
            <div className="col-4">
                <ExternalCounter />
            </div>
        </div>
    </div>
)
    }
}
```

I added a checkbox and used the onChange property to register the handleChange method to receive change events, which are triggered when the checkbox is toggled. The checkbox is used to control visibility of the Message component, as shown in Figure 13-11.

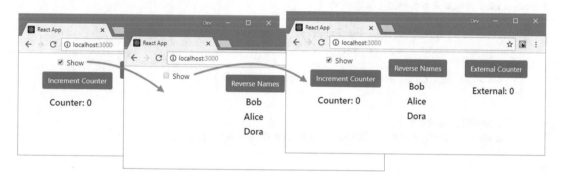

Figure 13-11. *Controlling the visibility of a component*

Each time the checkbox is toggled on, React creates a new Message object and goes through the mounting process, calling each of the methods in turn: constructor, render, and componentDidMount. This can be seen in the messages displayed in the browser's JavaScript console.

Understanding the Update Phase

The process by which React responds to changes and goes through reconciliation is known as the *update phase*, which invokes calling the render method to get content from the component and then calling the componentDidUpdate after the reconciliation process is complete, as shown in Figure 13-12.

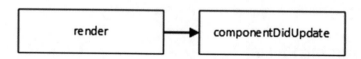

Figure 13-12. *The update phase*

The main use of the componentDidUpdate method is to directly manipulate the HTML elements in the DOM using the React refs feature, which I describe in Chapter 16. For this chapter, I have implemented the method in the Message component and used it to write a message to the browser's JavaScript console, as shown in Listing 13-19.

■ **Tip**   The componentDidUpdate method is called even if the reconciliation process determines that the content generated by the component has not changed.

Listing 13-19.   Implementing a Lifecycle Method in the Message.js File in the src Folder

```
import React, { Component } from "react";
import { ActionButton } from "./ActionButton";

export class Message extends Component {

    // ...other methods omitted for brevity...

    componentDidMount() {
        console.log("componentDidMount Message Component");
    }

    componentDidUpdate() {
        console.log("componentDidUpdate Message Component");
    }
}
```

After the initial rendering that is performed during the mounting phase, any subsequent calls to the render method will be followed by a call to the componentDidUpdate method once React has completed the reconciliation process and updated the DOM. Clicking the Increment Counter button will start the update phase and produce the following message in the browser's JavaScript console:

```
...
Render App Component
Render Message Component
Render ActionButton (Increment Counter) Component
Render List Component
Render ActionButton (Reverse Names) Component
Render ActionButton (External Counter) Component
componentDidUpdate Message Component
...
```

Understanding the Unmounting Phase

When a component is about to be destroyed, React will call the componentWillUnmount method, which provides components with the opportunity to release resources, close network connections, and stop any asynchronous tasks. In Listing 13-20, I have implemented the componentWillUnmount method in the Message component and used it to write a message to the browser's JavaScript console.

Listing 13-20. Implementing a Lifecycle Method in the Message.js File in the src Folder

```
import React, { Component } from "react";
import { ActionButton } from "./ActionButton";

export class Message extends Component {

    // ...other methods omitted for brevity...

    componentDidMount() {
        console.log("componentDidMount Message Component");
    }

    componentDidUpdate() {
        console.log("componentDidUpdate Message Component");
    }

    componentWillUnmount() {
        console.log("componentWillUnmount Message Component");
    }
}
```

You can trigger the unmounting phase by unchecking the checkbox that I added in Listing 13-20. When React reconciles the new content rendered by the App component, it determines that the Message component is no longer required and calls the componentWillUnmount method before destroying the object, producing the following messages in the browser's JavaScript console:

```
...
Render App Component
Render List Component
Render ActionButton (Reverse Names) Component
Render ActionButton (External Counter) Component
componentWillUnmount Message Component
...
```

React will not reuse components once they have been unmounted. React will create a new object and perform the mounting sequence if another Message component is required, such as when the checkbox is toggled again. This means you can always rely on the constructor and the componentDidMount methods to initialize a component, and a component object will never be asked to recover from an unmounted state.

Using the Effect Hook

Components defined as functions are unable to implement methods and cannot participate in the lifecycle in the same way. For this type of component, the hooks feature provides the effect hook, which is roughly equivalent to the componentDidMount, componentDidUpdate, and componentWillUnmount methods. To show the use of the effect hook, I added a file called HooksMessage.js to the src folder and added the code shown in Listing 13-21.

Listing 13-21. The Contents of the HooksMessage.js File in the src Folder

```
import React, { useState, useEffect} from "react";
import { ActionButton } from "./ActionButton";

export function HooksMessage(props) {
    const [showSpan, setShowSpan] = useState(false);

    useEffect(() => console.log("useEffect function invoked"));

    const handleClick = (event) => {
        setShowSpan(!showSpan);
        props.callback(event);
    }

    const getMessageElement = () => {
        let div = <div id="messageDiv" className="h5 text-center p-2">
                        { props.message }
                    </div>
        return showSpan ? <span>{ div } </span> : div;
    }

    return (
        <div>
            <ActionButton theme="primary" {...props} callback={ handleClick } />
            { getMessageElement() }
        </div>
    )
}
```

This component provides the same functionality as the `Message` component but is expressed as a function that uses hooks. The `useEffect` function is used to register a function that will be invoked when the component is mounted, updated, and unmounted. The same function is invoked in all three situations, which reflects the nature of using a function for a component, as opposed to a class. In Listing 13-22, I have added the new component to the content rendered by the `App` component.

Listing 13-22. Rendering a New Component in the App.js File in the src Folder

```
import React, { Component } from 'react';
import { Message } from "./Message";
import { List } from "./List";
import { ExternalCounter } from './ExternalCounter';
import { HooksMessage } from './HooksMessage';

export default class App extends Component {

    constructor(props) {
        super(props);
        this.state = {
            counter: 0,
            showMessage: true
        }
    }
```

```
    incrementCounter = () => {
        this.setState({ counter: this.state.counter + 1 });
    }

    handleChange = () => {
        this.setState({ showMessage: !this.state.showMessage });
    }

    render() {
        console.log("Render App Component");
        return (
            <div className="container text-center">
                <div className="row p-2">
                    <div className="col-4">
                        <div className="form-check">
                            <input type="checkbox" className="form-check-input"
                                checked={ this.state.showMessage }
                                onChange={ this.handleChange } />
                            <label className="form-check-label">Show</label>
                        </div>
                        { this.state.showMessage &&
                            <div>
                                <Message message={ `Counter: ${this.state.counter}` }
                                    callback={ this.incrementCounter }
                                    text="Increment Counter" />
                                <HooksMessage
                                    message={ `Counter: ${this.state.counter}` }
                                    callback={ this.incrementCounter }
                                    text="Increment Counter" />
                            </div>
                        }
                    </div>
                    <div className="col-4">
                        <List />
                    </div>
                    <div className="col-4">
                        <ExternalCounter />
                    </div>
                </div>
            </div>
        )
    }
}
```

Save the changes to the components and examine the messages shown in the browser's JavaScript console to see the effect hook function being invoked when the component is mounted and updated, as follows:

```
...
Render List Component
ActionButton.js:6 Render ActionButton (Reverse Names) Component
ActionButton.js:6 Render ActionButton (External Counter) Component
```

```
Message.js:37 componentDidMount Message Component
HooksMessage.js:7 useEffect function invoked
...
```

The function passed to useState can return a cleanup function that will be invoked when the component is unmounted, providing a feature similar to the componentWillUnmount method, as shown in Listing 13-23.

Listing 13-23. Using a Cleanup Function in the HooksMessage.js File in the src Folder

```
import React, { useState, useEffect} from "react";
import { ActionButton } from "./ActionButton";

export function HooksMessage(props) {
    const [showSpan, setShowSpan] = useState(false);

    useEffect(() => {
        console.log("useEffect function invoked")
        return () => console.log("useEffect cleanup");
    });

    const handleClick = (event) => {
        setShowSpan(!showSpan);
        props.callback(event);
    }

    const getMessageElement = () => {
        let div = <div id="messageDiv" className="h5 text-center p-2">
                        { props.message }
                </div>
        return showSpan ? <span>{ div } </span> : div;
    }

    return (
        <div>
            <ActionButton theme="primary" {...props} callback={ handleClick } />
            { getMessageElement() }
        </div>
    )
}
```

Toggle the checkbox to unmount the components, and you will see the following message in the browser's JavaScript console:

```
...
Render ActionButton (Reverse Names) Component
ActionButton.js:6 Render ActionButton (External Counter) Component
Message.js:45 componentWillUnmount Message Component
HooksMessage.js:9 useEffect cleanup
...
```

Using the Advanced Lifecycle Methods

The features described in the previous sections are useful in many projects, especially using the componentDidMount method to request remote data, which I demonstrate in Part 3. React provides advanced lifecycle methods for class-based components that are useful in specific situations I describe in the sections that follow, although one of these methods is used in conjunction with the refs feature that I describe in Chapter 16. For quick reference, Table 13-4 describes the advanced lifecycle methods.

Table 13-4. *The Advanced Component Lifecycle Methods*

Name	Description
shouldComponentUpdate	This method allows a component to indicate that it does not need to be updated.
getDerivedStateFromProps	This method allows a component to set its state data values based on the props it receives.
getSnapshotBeforeUpdate	This method allows a component to capture information about its state before the reconciliation process updates the DOM. This method is used in conjunction with the ref feature, described in Chapter 16.

Preventing Unnecessary Component Updates

React's default behavior is to mark a component as stale and render its content whenever its state data changes. And, since a component's state can be passed on to its children as props, the descendant components are rendered as well, as you have seen in earlier examples.

Components can override the default behavior by implementing the shouldComponentUpdate method. This feature allows components to improve the application's performance by avoiding calls to the render method when they are not required.

The shouldComponentUpdate method is called in the update phase, and its result determines whether React will call the render method to get fresh content from the component, as illustrated in Figure 13-13. The arguments to the shouldComponentUpdate method are new props and state objects that can be inspected and compared to the existing values. React will continue with the update phase if the shouldComponentUpdate method returns true. If the shouldComponentUpdate method returns false, React will abandon the update phase for the component and will not call the render and componentDidUpdate methods.

Figure 13-13. *The advanced sequence of update methods*

In Listing 13-24, I have implemented the showComponentUpdate method in the Message component and used it to prevent updates if the value of the message prop has not changed. (I have also removed the lifecycle methods from earlier examples for the sake of brevity.)

Listing 13-24. Preventing Updates in the Message.js File in the src Folder

```
import React, { Component } from "react";
import { ActionButton } from "./ActionButton";

export class Message extends Component {

    constructor(props) {
        super(props);
        this.state = {
            showSpan: false
        }
    }

    handleClick = (event) => {
        this.setState({ showSpan: !this.state.showSpan });
        this.props.callback(event);
    }

    getMessageElement() {
        let div = <div id="messageDiv" className="h5 text-center p-2">
                        { this.props.message }
                  </div>
        return this.state.showSpan ? <span>{ div } </span> : div;
    }

    render() {
        console.log(`Render Message Component `);
        return (
            <div>
                <ActionButton theme="primary" {...this.props}
                        callback={ this.handleClick } />
                { this.getMessageElement() }
            </div>
        )
    }

    shouldComponentUpdate(newProps, newState) {
        let change = newProps.message !== this.props.message;
        if (change) {
            console.log(`shouldComponentUpdate ${this.props.text}: Update Allowed`)
        } else {
            console.log(`shouldComponentUpdate ${this.props.text}: Update Prevented`)
        }
        return change;
    }
}
```

In Listing 13-25, I have revised the App component so it renders two Message components, each of which receives and modifies a state data value as a prop.

Listing 13-25. Displaying Side-By-Side Components in the App.js File in the src Folder

```
import React, { Component } from 'react';
import { Message } from "./Message";
//import { List } from "./List";
//import { ExternalCounter } from './ExternalCounter';

export default class App extends Component {

    constructor(props) {
        super(props);
        this.state = {
            counterLeft: 0,
            counterRight: 0
        }
    }

    incrementCounter = (counter) => {
        if (counter === "left") {
            this.setState({ counterLeft: this.state.counterLeft + 1});
        } else {
            this.setState({ counterRight: this.state.counterRight+ 1});
        }
    }

    render() {
        console.log("Render App Component");
        return (
            <div className="container text-center">
                <div className="row p-2">
                    <div className="col-6">
                        <Message
                            message={ `Left: ${this.state.counterLeft}`}
                            callback={ () => this.incrementCounter("left") }
                            text="Increment Left Counter" />
                    </div>
                    <div className="col-6">
                        <Message
                            message={ `Right: ${this.state.counterRight}`}
                            callback={ () => this.incrementCounter("right") }
                            text="Increment Right Counter" />
                    </div>
                </div>
            </div>
        )
    }
}
```

The new content rendered by the App component displays the Message components side by side, as shown in Figure 13-14. Clicking either of the button elements increments the counter for that component.

Figure 13-14. *Displaying components side by side*

The default React behavior is to render both Message components when either of the counterLeft or counterRight state data values changes, which results in one of the components rendering content unnecessarily. The implementation of the shouldComponentUpdate method in Listing 13-25 overrides this behavior and ensures that only the component affected by the change is updated. If you click either of the buttons presented by the application, you will see a message in the browser's JavaScript console noting that shouldComponentUpdate prevented one of the components from being updated.

```
...
Render App Component
shouldComponentUpdate Increment Left Counter: Update Allowed
Render Message Component
Render ActionButton (Increment Left Counter) Component
shouldComponentUpdate Increment Right Counter: Update Prevented
...
```

Setting State Data from Prop Values

The getDerivedStateFromProps method is called before the render method in the mounting phase and before the shouldComponentUpdate method in the update phase, as shown in Figure 13-15. The getDerivedStateFromProps method provides components with the opportunity to inspect prop values and use them to update its state data before its content is rendered and is intended for use by components whose behavior is affected by changing prop values over time.

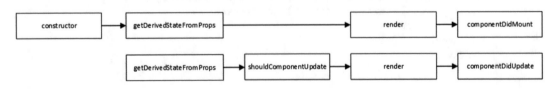

Figure 13-15. *Updating state data from props*

The getDerivedStateFromProps method is static, which means that it is unable to access any of the instance methods or properties via the this keyword. Instead, the method receives a props object, which contains the props values provided by the parent component, and a state object, which represents the current state data. The getDerivedStateFromProps method returns a new state data object that is derived from the prop data.

To demonstrate this method, I added a file called DirectionDisplay.js to the src folder and used it to define the component shown in Listing 13-26.

Listing 13-26. The Contents of the DirectionDisplay.js File in the src Folder

```
import React, { Component } from "react";

export class DirectionDisplay extends Component {

    constructor(props) {
        super(props);
        this.state = {
            direction: "up",
            lastValue: 0
        }
    }

    getClasses() {
        return (this.state.direction === "up" ? "bg-success" : "bg-danger")
            + " text-white text-center p-2 m-2";
    }

    render() {
        return <h5 className={ this.getClasses() }>
                    { this.props.value }
                </h5>
    }

    static getDerivedStateFromProps(props, state) {
        if (props.value !== state.lastValue) {
            return {
                lastValue: props.value,
                direction: state.lastValue > props.value ? "down" : "up"
            }
        }
        return state;
    }
}
```

This component displays a numeric value with a background color that indicates whether the current value is larger or smaller than the last value. The getDerivedStateFromProps method receives the new prop values and the component's current state data and uses them to create a new state data object that includes the direction in which the prop value has changed. In Listing 13-27, I have updated the App component so that it renders the DirectionDisplay component and buttons that change its prop data value.

Listing 13-27. Rendering a New Component in the App.js File in the src Folder

```
import React, { Component } from 'react';
//import { Message } from "./Message";
import { DirectionDisplay } from './DirectionDisplay';

export default class App extends Component {

    constructor(props) {
        super(props);
        this.state = {
            counter: 100
        }
    }

    changeCounter = (val) => {
        this.setState({ counter: this.state.counter + val })
    }

    render() {
        console.log("Render App Component");
        return (
            <div className="container text-center">
                <DirectionDisplay value={ this.state.counter } />
                <div className="text-center">
                    <button className="btn btn-primary m-1"
                        onClick={ () => this.changeCounter(-1)}>Decrease</button>
                    <button className="btn btn-primary m-1"
                        onClick={ () => this.changeCounter(1)}>Increase</button>
                </div>
            </div>
        )
    }
}
```

The result is that the background color selected by the DirectionDisplay component changes based on the output from the getDerivedStateFromProps method, as shown in Figure 13-16.

■ **Tip** Notice that I create a new state data object only if the value of the prop is different. Remember that React will trigger a component's update phase when an ancestor's state has changed, which means that the getDerivedStateFromProps method may be called even though none of the prop values on which the component depends has changed.

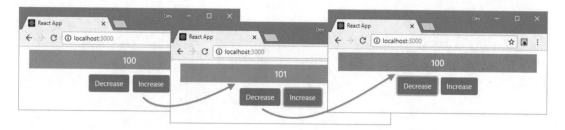

Figure 13-16. *Deriving state data from prop values*

Summary

In this chapter, I explained how React deals with the content rendered by components through the reconciliation process. I also described the broader component lifecycle and showed you how to receive notifications in stateful components by implementing methods. In the next chapter, I describe the different ways that components can be combined to create complex features.

CHAPTER 14

Composing Applications

In this chapter, I describe the different ways that components can be combined to create complex features. These composition patterns can be used together, and you will find that most problems can be tackled in several ways, which leaves you free to apply the approach with which you are most comfortable. Table 14-1 puts the chapter in context.

Table 14-1. *Putting Application Composition in Context*

Question	Answer
What is it?	Application composition is the combination of components to create complex features.
Why is it useful?	Composition makes development easier by allowing small and simple components to be written and tested before being combined to work together.
How is it used?	There are different patterns available, but the basic approach is to combine multiple components.
Are there any pitfalls or limitations?	The composition patterns can feel awkward if you are used to deriving functionality from classes, such as in C# or Java development. Many problems can be solved equally well by multiple patterns, which can lead to decision paralysis.
Are there any alternatives?	You could write monolithic components that implement all the features required by an application, although this results in a project that is different to test and maintain.

Table 14-2 summarizes the chapter.

Table 14-2. *Chapter Summary*

Problem	Solution	Listing
Display content received from the parent component	Use the `children` prop	8–9
Manipulate the components received via the `children` prop	Use the `React.children` prop	10, 11
Enhance an existing component	Create a specialized component or a higher-order component	12–18
Combine higher-order components	Chain the function calls together	19, 20
Provide a component with the content it should render	Use a render prop	21–24
Distribute data and functions without threading props	Use a context	25–34
Consume a context without using a render prop	Use the simplified context API for class-based components and the `useContext` hook for functional components	35, 36
Prevent errors from unmounting the application	Define an error boundary	37–39

Preparing for This Chapter

To create the example project for this chapter, open a new command prompt, navigate to a convenient location, and run the command shown in Listing 14-1.

■ **Tip** You can download the example project for this chapter—and for all the other chapters in this book—from `https://github.com/Apress/pro-react-16`.

Listing 14-1. Creating the Example Project

```
npx create-react-app composition
```

Run the commands shown in Listing 14-2 to navigate to the `composition` folder and add the Bootstrap package to the project.

Listing 14-2. Adding the Bootstrap CSS Framework

```
cd composition
npm install bootstrap@4.1.2
```

To include the Bootstrap CSS stylesheet in the application, add the statement shown in Listing 14-3 to the index.js file, which can be found in the src folder.

Listing 14-3. Including Bootstrap in the index.js File in the src Folder

```
import React from 'react';
import ReactDOM from 'react-dom';
import './index.css';
import App from './App';
import * as serviceWorker from './serviceWorker';
import 'bootstrap/dist/css/bootstrap.css';

ReactDOM.render(<App />, document.getElementById('root'));

// If you want your app to work offline and load faster, you can change
// unregister() to register() below. Note this comes with some pitfalls.
// Learn more about service workers: http://bit.ly/CRA-PWA
serviceWorker.unregister();
```

Creating the Example Components

Add a file called ActionButton.js to the src folder and add the content shown in Listing 14-4.

Listing 14-4. The Contents of the ActionButton.js File in the src Folder

```
import React, { Component } from "react";

export class ActionButton extends Component {

    render() {
        return (
            <button className={` btn btn-${this.props.theme} m-2` }
                    onClick={ this.props.callback }>
                { this.props.text }
            </button>
        )
    }
}
```

This is a similar button component to the one I used in Chapter 13, which accepts configuration settings via its prop, including a function that is invoked in response to the click event. Next, add a file called Message.js to the src folder and add the content shown in Listing 14-5.

Listing 14-5. The Contents of the Message.js File in the src Folder

```
import React, { Component } from "react";

export class Message extends Component {
```

```
    render() {
        return (
            <div className={`h5 bg-${this.props.theme } text-white p-2`}>
                { this.props.message }
            </div>
        )
    }
}
```

This component displays a message received as a prop. The final change is to replace the contents of the App.js file with the code shown in Listing 14-6, which renders content that uses the other components and defines the state data that the Message component requires.

Listing 14-6. The Contents of the App.js File in the src Folder

```
import React, { Component } from 'react';
import { Message } from "./Message";
import { ActionButton } from './ActionButton';

export default class App extends Component {

    constructor(props) {
        super(props);
        this.state = {
            counter: 0
        }
    }

    incrementCounter = () => {
        this.setState({ counter: this.state.counter + 1 });
    }

    render() {
        return   <div className="m-2 text-center">
                    <Message theme="primary"
                        message={ `Counter: ${this.state.counter}`} />
                    <ActionButton theme="secondary"
                        text="Increment" callback={ this.incrementCounter } />
                </div>
    }
}
```

The content rendered by the App component displays the Message and ActionButton components and configures them so that clicking the button will update the counter state data value, which has been passed as a prop to the Message component.

Using the command prompt, run the command shown in Listing 14-7 in the composition folder to start the development tools.

Listing 14-7. Starting the Development Tools

```
npm start
```

Once the initial preparation for the project is complete, a new browser window will open and display the URL `http://localhost:3000` and display the content shown in Figure 14-1.

Figure 14-1. *Running the example application*

Understanding the Basic Component Relationship

The components in the example project are simple, but they illustrate the basic relationship that underpins React development: parent components configure children with data props and receive notifications through function props, which leads to state data changes and triggers the update process, as shown in Figure 14-2.

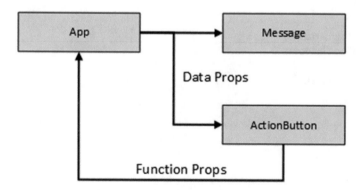

Figure 14-2. *The basic component relationship*

This relationship is the foundation for React development and is the basic pattern used to arrange features in applications. This pattern is easy to understand in a simple example, its use in more complex situations can be less obvious, and it can be hard to know how to locate and distribute the state data, props, and callbacks without duplicating code and data.

383

Using the Children Prop

React provides a special `children` prop that is used when a component needs to display content provided by its parent but doesn't know what that content will be in advance. This is a useful way of reducing duplication by standardizing features in a container that can be reused across an application. To demonstrate, I created a file called ThemeSelector.js in the src folder and used it to define the component shown in Listing 14-8.

Listing 14-8. The Contents of the ThemeSelector.js File in the src Folder

```
import React, { Component } from "react";

export class ThemeSelector extends Component {

    render() {
        return (
            <div className="bg-dark p-2">
                <div className="bg-info p-2">
                    { this.props.children }
                </div>
            </div>
        )
    }
}
```

This component renders two `div` elements that contain an expression whose value is the `children` prop. To show how the content for the children prop is provided, Listing 14-9 applies the `ThemeSelector` in the App component.

Listing 14-9. Using a Container Component in the App.js File in the src Folder

```
import React, { Component } from 'react';
import { Message } from "./Message";
import { ActionButton } from './ActionButton';
import { ThemeSelector } from './ThemeSelector';

export default class App extends Component {

    constructor(props) {
        super(props);
        this.state = {
            counter: 0
        }
    }

    incrementCounter = () => {
        this.setState({ counter: this.state.counter + 1 });
    }
```

```
render() {
    return   <div className="m-2 text-center">
                <ThemeSelector>
                    <Message theme="primary"
                        message={ `Counter: ${this.state.counter}`} />
                    <ActionButton theme="secondary"
                        text="Increment" callback={ this.incrementCounter } />
                </ThemeSelector>
            </div>
    }
}
```

The App component provides content for the ThemeSelector component by defining elements between its start and end tags. In this case, the elements apply the Message and ActionButton components. When React processes the content rendered by the App component, the content between the ThemeSelector tags is assigned to the props.children property, producing the result shown in Figure 14-3.

Figure 14-3. *A container component*

The ThemeSelector component doesn't add a lot of value at present, but you can see how it acts as a container for the content provided by the App component.

Manipulating Prop Children

Components that use the children prop are useful only when they are able to provide services to their children, which can be difficult when there is no advanced knowledge of what those children will provide. To help work around this limitation, React provides a number of methods that a container can use to manipulate its children, as described in Table 14-3.

Table 14-3. *The Container Children Methods*

Name	Description
React.Children.map	This method invokes a function for each child and returns an array of the function results.
React.Children.forEach	This method invokes a function for each child without returning an array.
React.Children.count	This method returns the number of children.
React.Children.only	This method throws an array if the collection of children it receives contains more than one child.
React.Children.toArray	This method returns an array of children, which can be used to reorder or remove elements.
React.cloneElement	This method is used to duplicate a child element and allows new props to be added by the container.

Adding Props to Container Children

A component can't manipulate the content it receives from the parent directly, so to provide the components received through the children prop with additional data or functions, the React.Children. map method is used in conjunction with the React.cloneElement method to duplicate the child components and assign additional props.

Listing 14-10 adds a select element to the content rendered by the ThemeSelector that updates a state data property and allows a user to choose one of the theme colors provided by the Bootstrap CSS framework, which is then passed on to the container's children as a prop.

Listing 14-10. Adding Theme Selection in the ThemeSelector.js File in the src Folder

```
import React, { Component } from "react";

export class ThemeSelector extends Component {

    constructor(props) {
        super(props);
        this.state = {
            theme: "primary"
        }
        this.themes = ["primary", "secondary", "success", "warning", "dark"];
    }

    setTheme = (event) => {
        this.setState({ theme : event.target.value });
    }

    render() {

        let modChildren = React.Children.map(this.props.children,
            (c => React.cloneElement(c, { theme: this.state.theme})));
```

```
        return (
            <div className="bg-dark p-2">
                <div className="form-group text-left">
                    <label className="text-white">Theme:</label>
                    <select className="form-control" value={ this.state.theme }
                            onChange={ this.setTheme }>
                        { this.themes.map(theme =>
                            <option key={ theme } value={ theme }>{theme}</option>) }
                    </select>
                </div>

                <div className="bg-info p-2">
                    { modChildren }
                </div>
            </div>
        )
    }
}
```

Because props are read-only, I can't use the React.Children.forEach method to simply enumerate the child components and assign a new property to their props object. Instead, I used the map method to enumerate the children and used the React.cloneElement method to duplicate each child with an additional prop.

```
...
let modChildren = React.Children.map(this.props.children,
    (c => React.cloneElement(c, { theme: this.state.theme})));
...
```

The cloneElement method accepts a child component and a props object, which is merged with the child component's existing props.

One consequence of using the map method to enumerate the child components into an array is that React expects each component to have a key prop and will report a warning in the browser's JavaScript console.

The result is that the props passed to the Message and ActionButton components are a combination of those defined by the App component and those added using the cloneElement method by the ThemeSelector component. When you choose a theme from the select element, an update is performed, and the selected theme is applied to the Message and ActionButton components, as shown in Figure 14-4.

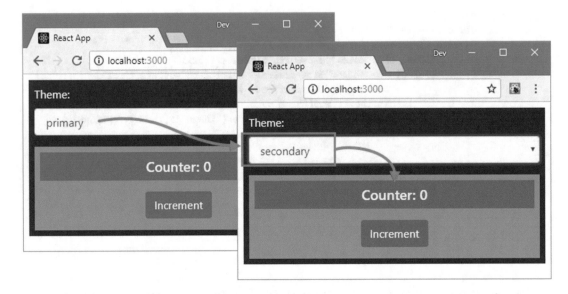

Figure 14-4. *Adding props to contained components*

Ordering or Omitting Components

Although a container doesn't have any advanced knowledge of its children, the toArray method described in Table 14-3 can be used to convert the children to an array that can be manipulated using the standard JavaScript features, such as sorting or adding and removing items. This type of operation can also be performed on the result from the React.Children.map method, also described in Table 14-3, which returns an array as well.

In Listing 14-11, I have added a button to the ThemeSelector component that reverses the order of the children when it is clicked, which I achieve by calling the reverse method on the array produced by the map method.

Listing 14-11. Reversing Children in the ThemeSelector.js File in the src Folder

```
import React, { Component } from "react";

export class ThemeSelector extends Component {

    constructor(props) {
        super(props);
        this.state = {
            theme: "primary",
            reverseChildren: false
        }
        this.themes = ["primary", "secondary", "success", "warning", "dark"];
    }
```

```
setTheme = (event) => {
    this.setState({ theme : event.target.value });
}

toggleReverse = () => {
    this.setState({ reverseChildren: !this.state.reverseChildren});
}

render() {

    let modChildren = React.Children.map(this.props.children,
        (c => React.cloneElement(c, { theme: this.state.theme})));

    if (this.state.reverseChildren) {
        modChildren.reverse();
    }

    return (
        <div className="bg-dark p-2">
            <button className="btn btn-primary" onClick={ this.toggleReverse }>
                Reverse
            </button>
            <div className="form-group text-left">
                <label className="text-white">Theme:</label>
                <select className="form-control" value={ this.state.theme }
                        onChange={ this.setTheme }>
                    { this.themes.map(theme =>
                        <option key={ theme } value={ theme }>{theme}</option>) }
                </select>
            </div>

            <div className="bg-info p-2">
                { modChildren }
            </div>
        </div>
    )
}
}
```

This type of operation is more typically used with lists of similar objects, such as products in an online store, but it can be applied to any children, as shown in Figure 14-5.

Figure 14-5. *Changing the order of child components in a container*

Creating a Specialized Component

Some components provide specialized versions of the features provided by another, more general, component. In some frameworks, specialization is handled by using features such as class inheritance, but React relies on the specialized component rendering the more general component and managing its behavior with props. To demonstrate, I added a file called GeneralList.js to the src folder and used it to define the component shown in Listing 14-12.

■ **Note** If you are used to class-based languages, such as C# or Java, you might expect to create a subclass using the same extends keyword that stateful components employ to inherit functionality from the React Component class. This is not how React is intended to be used, and you should compose components even though it can feel odd to do so at first.

Listing 14-12. The Contents of the GeneralList.js File in the src Folder

```
import React, { Component } from "react";

export class GeneralList extends Component {

    render() {
        return (
            <div className={`bg-${this.props.theme} text-white p-2`}>
                { this.props.list.map((item, index) =>
                    <div key={ item }>{ index + 1 }: { item }</div>
                )}
            </div>
```

```
        )
    }
}
```

This component receives a prop named `list`, which is processed using the array map method to render a series of div elements. To create a component that receives a list and allows it to be sorted, I can create a more specialized component that builds on the features provided by the GeneralList. I added a file called SortedList.js to the src folder and used it to define the component shown in Listing 14-13.

Listing 14-13. The Contents of the SortedList.js File in the src Folder

```
import React, { Component } from "react";
import { GeneralList } from "./GeneralList";
import { ActionButton } from "./ActionButton";

export class SortedList extends Component {

    constructor(props) {
        super(props);
        this.state = {
            sort: false
        }
    }

    getList() {
        return this.state.sort
            ? [...this.props.list].sort() : this.props.list;
    }

    toggleSort = () => {
        this.setState({ sort : !this.state.sort });
    }

    render() {
        return (
            <div>
                <GeneralList list={ this.getList() } theme="info" />
                <div className="text-center m-2">
                    <ActionButton theme="primary" text="Sort"
                        callback={this.toggleSort} />
                </div>
            </div>
        )
    }
}
```

The SortedList renders a GeneralList as part of its output and uses the list prop to control the presentation of the data, allowing the user to selected a sorted or unsorted list. In Listing 14-14, I have changed the layout of the App component to show the general and more specific components side by side.

Listing 14-14. Changing the Component Layout in the App.js File in the src Folder

```
import React, { Component } from 'react';
//import { Message } from "./Message";
//import { ActionButton } from './ActionButton';
//import { ThemeSelector } from './ThemeSelector';
import { GeneralList } from './GeneralList';
import { SortedList } from "./SortedList";

export default class App extends Component {

    constructor(props) {
        super(props);
        this.state = {
            // counter: 0
            names: ["Zoe", "Bob", "Alice", "Dora", "Joe"]
        }
    }

    // incrementCounter = () => {
    //     this.setState({ counter: this.state.counter + 1 });
    // }

    render() {
        return (
            <div className="container-fluid">
                <div className="row">
                    <div className="col-6">
                        <GeneralList list={ this.state.names } theme="primary" />
                    </div>
                    <div className="col-6">
                        <SortedList list={ this.state.names } />
                    </div>
                </div>
            </div>
        )
    }
}
```

The result is that the general list and the sortable list are both presented to the user, as shown in Figure 14-6.

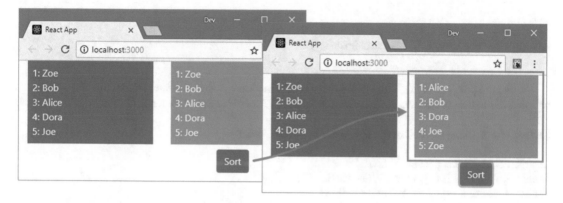

Figure 14-6. *General and more specialized components*

Creating Higher-Order Components

Higher-order components (HOCs) provide an alternative to specialized components and are useful when components require common code but may not render related content. HOCs are often used for *cross-cutting concerns*, a term that refers to tasks that span the entire application and would otherwise lead to the same features being implemented in several places. The most commonly encountered examples of cross-cutting concerns are authorization, logging, and data retrieval. To demonstrate the use of HOCs, I added a file called ProFeature.js to the src folder and used it to define the component shown in Listing 14-15.

Listing 14-15. The Contents of the ProFeature.js File in the src Folder

```
import React from "react";

export function ProFeature(FeatureComponent) {
    return function(props) {

        if (props.pro) {
            let { pro, ...childProps}  = props;
            return <FeatureComponent {...childProps} />
        } else {
            return (
                <h5 className="bg-warning text-white text-center">
                    This is a Pro Feature
                </h5>
            )
        }
    }
}
```

A HOC is a function that accepts a component and returns a new component that wraps around it to provide additional features. In Listing 14-15, the HOC is a function called ProFeature, and it accepts a component that should be presented to the user only when the value of the prop named pro is true, acting as a simple authorization feature. To display the component, the render method uses the component received as the function argument and passes on all of its props, except the one named pro.

```
...
let { pro, ...childProps} = props;
return <FeatureComponent {...childProps} />
...
```

When the pro prop is false, the ProFeature HOC function returns a header element that displays a warning. Listing 14-16 updates the App component to use ProFeature to protect one of its child components.

Listing 14-16. Using an HOC in the App.js File in the src Folder

```
import React, { Component } from 'react';
import { GeneralList } from './GeneralList';
import { SortedList } from "./SortedList";
import { ProFeature } from "./ProFeature";

const ProList = ProFeature(SortedList);

export default class App extends Component {

    constructor(props) {
        super(props);
        this.state = {
            names: ["Zoe", "Bob", "Alice", "Dora", "Joe"],
            cities: ["London", "New York", "Paris", "Milan", "Boston"],
            proMode: false
        }
    }

    toggleProMode = () => {
        this.setState({ proMode: !this.state.proMode});
    }

    render() {
        return (
            <div className="container-fluid">
                <div className="row">
                    <div className="col-12 text-center p-2">
                        <div className="form-check">
                            <input type="checkbox" className="form-check-input"
                                value={ this.state.proMode }
                                onChange={ this.toggleProMode } />
                            <label className="form-check-label">Pro Mode</label>
                        </div>
                    </div>
                </div>
                <div className="row">
                    <div className="col-3">
                        <GeneralList list={ this.state.names } theme="primary" />
                    </div>
```

```
        <div className="col-3">
            <ProList list={ this.state.names }
                    pro={ this.state.proMode } />
        </div>
        <div className="col-3">
            <GeneralList list={ this.state.cities } theme="secondary" />
        </div>
        <div className="col-3">
            <ProList list={ this.state.cities }
                pro={ this.state.proMode } />
        </div>
    </div>
  </div>
 )
 }
}
```

HOCs are used to create new components by invoking the function, like this:

```
...
const ProList = ProFeature(SortedList);
...
```

Because HOCs are functions, you can define additional arguments to configure behavior, but in this example, I pass the component that I want to wrap as the only argument. I assign the result from the function to a constant named ProList, which I use like any other component in the render method.

```
...
<ProList list={ this.state.cities } pro={ this.state.proMode } />
...
```

I defined the pro prop for the HOC and the list prop for the SortedList component that it wraps. The value of the pro prop is set by toggling a checkbox, with the effect shown in Figure 14-7.

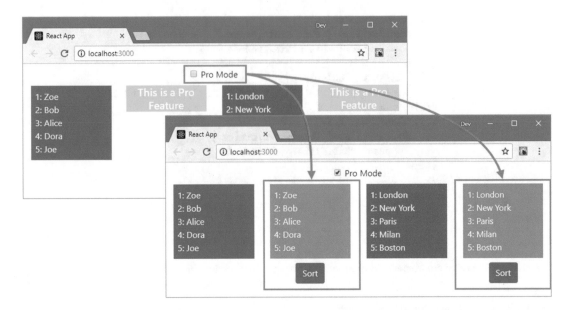

Figure 14-7. *Using higher-order components*

Creating Stateful Higher-Order Components

Higher-order components can be stateful, which allows for more complex features to be added to an application. I added a file called ProController.js to the src folder and used it to define the HOC shown in Listing 14-17.

Listing 14-17. The Contents of the ProController.js File in the src Folder

```
import React, { Component } from "react";
import { ProFeature } from "./ProFeature";

export function ProController(FeatureComponent) {

    const ProtectedFeature = ProFeature(FeatureComponent);

    return class extends Component {

        constructor(props) {
            super(props);
            this.state = {
                proMode: false
            }
        }

        toggleProMode = () => {
            this.setState({ proMode: !this.state.proMode});
        }
```

```
    render() {
        return (
            <div className="container-fluid">
                <div className="row">
                    <div className="col-12 text-center p-2">
                        <div className="form-check">
                            <input type="checkbox" className="form-check-input"
                                value={ this.state.proMode }
                                onChange={ this.toggleProMode } />
                            <label className="form-check-label">Pro Mode</label>
                        </div>
                    </div>
                </div>
                <div className="row">
                    <div className="col-12">
                        <ProtectedFeature {...this.props}
                            pro={ this.state.proMode } />
                    </div>
                </div>
            </div>
        )
    }
}
}
```

The HOC function returns a class-based stateful component that presents the checkbox and uses the ProFeature HOC to control visibility of the wrapped component. Listing 14-18 updates App component to use the ProController component.

Listing 14-18. Using a New HOC in the App.js File in the src Folder

```
import React, { Component } from 'react';
import { GeneralList } from './GeneralList';
import { SortedList } from "./SortedList";
//import { ProFeature } from "./ProFeature";
import { ProController } from "./ProController";

const ProList = ProController(SortedList);

export default class App extends Component {

    constructor(props) {
        super(props);
        this.state = {
            names: ["Zoe", "Bob", "Alice", "Dora", "Joe"],
            cities: ["London", "New York", "Paris", "Milan", "Boston"],
            //proMode: false
        }
    }
```

```
render() {
    return (
        <div className="container-fluid">
            <div className="row">
                <div className="col-3">
                    <GeneralList list={ this.state.names } theme="primary" />
                </div>
                <div className="col-3">
                    <ProList list={ this.state.names }  />
                </div>
                <div className="col-3">
                    <GeneralList list={ this.state.cities } theme="secondary" />
                </div>
                <div className="col-3">
                    <ProList list={ this.state.cities }  />
                </div>
            </div>
        </div>
    )
  }
}
```

Figure 14-8 shows the effect of HOC, which gives each protected component its own checkbox.

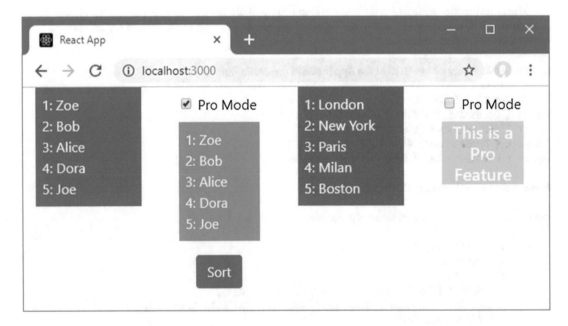

Figure 14-8. *A stateful higher-order component*

Combining Higher-Order Components

A useful feature of HOCs is they can be combined by changing only the function call that creates the wrapped component class. To demonstrate, I added a file called LogToConsole.js to the src folder and used it to define the HOC shown in Listing 14-19.

Listing 14-19. The Contents of the LogToConsole.js File in the src Folder

```
import React, { Component } from "react";

export function LogToConsole(FeatureComponent, label, logMount, logRender, logUnmount) {
    return class extends Component {

        componentDidMount() {
            if (logMount) {
                console.log(`${label}: mount`);
            }
        }

        componentWillUnmount() {
            if (logUnmount) {
                console.log(`${label}: unmount`);
            }
        }

        render() {
            if (logRender) {
                console.log(`${label}: render`);
            }
            return <FeatureComponent { ...this.props } />
        }
    }
}
```

The HOC function receives the component that will be wrapped, along with a label argument that is used to write messages to the browser's JavaScript console. There are three further arguments that specify whether log messages will be written when the component is mounted, rendered, and unmounted, following the stateful component lifecycle described in Chapter 11. To apply the new HOC, I have changed only the function that creates the wrapped component, as shown in Listing 14-20.

Listing 14-20. Combining HOCs in the App.js File in the src Folder

```
import React, { Component } from 'react';
import { GeneralList } from './GeneralList';
import { SortedList } from "./SortedList";
//import { ProFeature } from "./ProFeature";
import { ProController } from "./ProController";
import { LogToConsole } from "./LogToConsole";

const ProList = ProController(LogToConsole(SortedList, "Sorted", true, true, true));
```

```
export default class App extends Component {

    constructor(props) {
        super(props);
        this.state = {
            names: ["Zoe", "Bob", "Alice", "Dora", "Joe"],
            cities: ["London", "New York", "Paris", "Milan", "Boston"],
            //proMode: false
        }
    }
    render() {
        return (
            <div className="container-fluid">
                <div className="row">
                    <div className="col-3">
                        <GeneralList list={ this.state.names }
                            theme="primary" />
                    </div>
                    <div className="col-3">
                        <ProList list={ this.state.names }  />
                    </div>
                    <div className="col-3">
                        <GeneralList list={ this.state.cities }
                            theme="secondary" />
                    </div>
                    <div className="col-3">
                        <ProList list={ this.state.cities }  />
                    </div>
                </div>
            </div>
        )
    }
}
```

The effect is that the SortedList component is wrapped by the LogToConsole component, which is in turn wrapped by the ProFeature component. As you toggle the Pro Mode checkbox, you will see the following messages displayed in the browser's JavaScript console:

```
...
Sorted: render
Sorted: mount
Sorted: unmount
...
```

Using Render Props

A *render prop* is a function prop that provides a component with the content it should render, providing an alternative model of wrapping one component in another. In Listing 14-21, I have rewritten the ProFeature component so it uses a render prop.

Listing 14-21. Using a Render Prop in the ProFeature.js File in the src Folder

```
import React from "react";

export function ProFeature(props) {
    if (props.pro) {
        return props.render();
    } else {
        return (
            <h5 className="bg-warning text-white text-center">
                This is a Pro Feature
            </h5>
        )
    }
}
```

Components that use render props are defined in the normal way. The difference is in the render method, where a function prop named render is invoked to display content provided by the parent.

```
...
return props.render();
...
```

The parent component provides the function for the render prop when it applies the component. In Listing 14-22, I have changed the App component so it provides the ProFeature component with the function it requires. (I have also removed some of the content for sake of brevity.)

■ **Tip** The name of the prop that the parent uses to provide the function doesn't have to be render, although that is the convention. You can use any name, just as long as it is applied consistently in both the parent and the child components.

Listing 14-22. Using a Render Prop in the App.js File in the src Folder

```
import React, { Component } from 'react';
import { GeneralList } from './GeneralList';
import { SortedList } from "./SortedList";
import { ProFeature } from "./ProFeature";
// import { ProController } from "./ProController";
// import { LogToConsole } from "./LogToConsole";

// const ProList = ProController(LogToConsole(SortedList, "Sorted", true, true));

export default class App extends Component {

    constructor(props) {
        super(props);
```

```
        this.state = {
            names: ["Zoe", "Bob", "Alice", "Dora", "Joe"],
            cities: ["London", "New York", "Paris", "Milan", "Boston"],
            proMode: false
        }
    }

    toggleProMode = () => {
        this.setState({ proMode: !this.state.proMode});
    }

    render() {
        return (
            <div className="container-fluid">
                <div className="row">
                    <div className="col-12 text-center p-2">
                        <div className="form-check">
                            <input type="checkbox" className="form-check-input"
                                value={ this.state.proMode }
                                onChange={ this.toggleProMode } />
                            <label className="form-check-label">Pro Mode</label>
                        </div>
                    </div>
                </div>
                <div className="row">
                    <div className="col-6">
                        <GeneralList list={ this.state.names }
                            theme="primary" />
                    </div>
                    <div className="col-6">
                        <ProFeature pro={ this.state.proMode }
                            render={ () => <SortedList list={ this.state.names } /> }
                        />
                    </div>
                </div>
            </div>
        )
    }
}
```

The ProFeature component is provided with a pro prop that is used to determine whether a feature is displayed and with a render prop that is set to a function that returns a SortedList element.

```
...
<ProFeature pro={ this.state.proMode }
    render={ () => <SortedList list={ this.state.names } /> } />
...
```

When React renders the application's content, the ProFeature component's render method is invoked, which in turn invokes the render prop function, which leads to the creation of a new SortedList component. Using a render prop achieves the same result as the HOC, as shown in Figure 14-9.

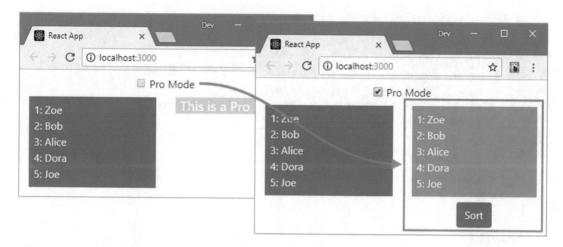

Figure 14-9. *Using a render prop*

Using a Render Prop with an Argument

Render props are regular JavaScript functions, which means they can be invoked with arguments. This can be a useful feature in its own right, but it also helps understand how the context feature works, which I describe in the next section.

Using an argument allows the component that invokes the render prop to provide props to the wrapper content. This is a technique that is more readily understood with an example. In Listing 14-23, I changed the ProFeature component so that it passes a string argument to the render prop function.

Listing 14-23. Adding an Argument in the ProFeature.js File in the src Folder

```
import React from "react";

export function ProFeature(props) {
    if (props.pro) {
        return props.render("Pro Feature");
    } else {
        return (
            <h5 className="bg-warning text-white text-center">
                This is a Pro Feature
            </h5>
        )
    }
}
```

The argument can be received by the component that defines the render prop function and used in the content that it produces, as shown in Listing 14-24.

Listing 14-24. Receiving a Render Prop Argument in the App.js File in the src Folder

```
import React, { Component } from 'react';
import { GeneralList } from './GeneralList';
import { SortedList } from "./SortedList";
import { ProFeature } from "./ProFeature";
```

403

```
export default class App extends Component {

    constructor(props) {
        super(props);
        this.state = {
            names: ["Zoe", "Bob", "Alice", "Dora", "Joe"],
            cities: ["London", "New York", "Paris", "Milan", "Boston"],
            proMode: false
        }
    }

    toggleProMode = () => {
        this.setState({ proMode: !this.state.proMode});
    }

    render() {
        return (
            <div className="container-fluid">
                <div className="row">
                    <div className="col-12 text-center p-2">
                        <div className="form-check">
                            <input type="checkbox" className="form-check-input"
                                value={ this.state.proMode }
                                onChange={ this.toggleProMode } />
                            <label className="form-check-label">Pro Mode</label>
                        </div>
                    </div>
                </div>

                <div className="row">
                    <div className="col-6">
                        <GeneralList list={ this.state.names }
                            theme="primary" />
                    </div>
                    <div className="col-6">
                        <ProFeature pro={ this.state.proMode }
                            render={ text =>
                                <React.Fragment>
                                    <h4 className="text-center">{ text }</h4>
                                    <SortedList list={ this.state.names } />
                                </React.Fragment>
                            } />
                    </div>
                </div>
            </div>
        )
    }
}
```

The content produced when the checkbox is selected shows how the ProFeature component is able to influence the content produced by the render prop function, as shown in Figure 14-10.

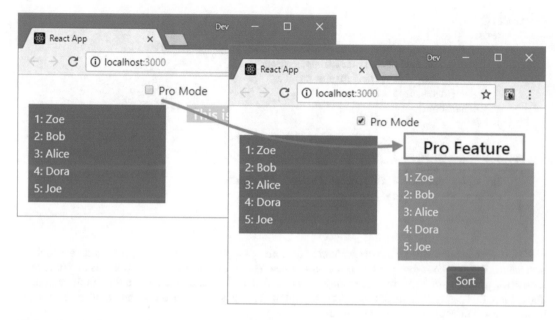

Figure 14-10. *Using a render prop with an argument*

Using Contexts for Global Data

The management of props can become difficult, regardless of how you choose to compose your application. As the complexity of the application increases, so does the number of components that need to cooperate. As the hierarchy of components grows, the state data gets lifted up higher in the application, further away from where that data is used, with the result that every component has to pass on props that it doesn't use directly but that its descendants rely on.

To help avoid this problem, React provides the *context* feature, which allows state data to be passed from where it is defined to where it is needed without having to be relayed through the intermediate components. To demonstrate, I am going to make the Pro Mode in the example application more granular so that it disables the Sort button rather than hides the data list entirely.

In Listing 14-25, I have added a property to the button element rendered by the `ActionButton` component that sets the `disabled` property based on a prop and changes the Bootstrap theme to make it more obvious when the button is disabled.

■ **Tip**   The Redux package is often used for more complex projects and can be easier to use in large applications. See Chapters 19 and 20 for details.

Listing 14-25.   Disabling a Button in the ActionButton.js File in the src Folder

```
import React, { Component } from "react";

export class ActionButton extends Component {
```

```
render() {
    return (
        <button className={ this.getClasses(this.props.proMode)}
                disabled={ !this.props.proMode }
            onClick={ this.props.callback }>
            { this.props.text }
        </button>
    )
}

getClasses(proMode) {
    let col = proMode ? this.props.theme : "danger";
    return `btn btn-${col} m-2`;
}
}
```

The proMode property that the ActionButton depends on is part of the App component's state, which also defines the checkbox that is used to change its value. The result is a chain of components that have to receive the proMode property from their parent and pass it on to their children. Even in the simple example application, this means that the SortedList component has to pass on the proMode data value even though it doesn't use it directly, as shown in Figure 14-11.

Figure 14-11. *Passing on props in the example application*

This is known as *prop drilling* or *prop threading*, where data values are passed through the component hierarchy to reach the point where they can be used. It is easy to forget to pass on a prop that is required by a descendant, and it can be hard work to figure out where the threading of a prop has missed a step in a complex application. In Listing 14-26, I have updated the App component to remove the ProFeature component from the previous section and to pass on the value of the proMode state property to the SortedList component as a prop, beginning the process of threading the prop.

Listing 14-26. Threading a Prop in the App.js File in the src Folder

```
import React, { Component } from 'react';
import { GeneralList } from './GeneralList';
import { SortedList } from "./SortedList";
//import { ProFeature } from "./ProFeature";

export default class App extends Component {
```

```
    constructor(props) {
        super(props);
        this.state = {
            names: ["Zoe", "Bob", "Alice", "Dora", "Joe"],
            cities: ["London", "New York", "Paris", "Milan", "Boston"],
            proMode: false
        }
    }

    toggleProMode = () => {
        this.setState({ proMode: !this.state.proMode});
    }

    render() {
        return (
            <div className="container-fluid">
                <div className="row">
                    <div className="col-12 text-center p-2">
                        <div className="form-check">
                            <input type="checkbox" className="form-check-input"
                                value={ this.state.proMode }
                                onChange={ this.toggleProMode } />
                            <label className="form-check-label">Pro Mode</label>
                        </div>
                    </div>
                </div>

                <div className="row">
                    <div className="col-6">
                        <GeneralList list={ this.state.names }
                            theme="primary" />
                    </div>
                    <div className="col-6">
                        <SortedList proMode={this.state.proMode}
                            list={ this.state.names } />
                    </div>
                </div>
            </div>
        )
    }
}
```

The SortedList component doesn't use the proMode prop directly, but it must be passed on to the ActionButton component, completing the prop threading, as shown in Listing 14-27.

Listing 14-27. Threading a Prop in the SortedList.js File in the src Folder

```
import React, { Component } from "react";
import { GeneralList } from "./GeneralList";
import { ActionButton } from "./ActionButton";

export class SortedList extends Component {
```

```
    constructor(props) {
        super(props);
        this.state = {
            sort: false
        }
    }

    getList() {
        return this.state.sort
            ? [...this.props.list].sort() : this.props.list;
    }

    toggleSort = () => {
        this.setState({ sort : !this.state.sort });
    }

    render() {
        return (
            <div>
                <GeneralList list={ this.getList() } theme="info" />
                <div className="text-center m-2">
                    <ActionButton theme="primary" text="Sort"
                        proMode={ this.props.proMode }
                        callback={this.toggleSort} />
                </div>
            </div>
        )
    }
}
```

The result is that the value of the proMode state value is passed from the App component, through the SortedList component, and is received and used by the ActionButton component, as shown in Figure 14-12.

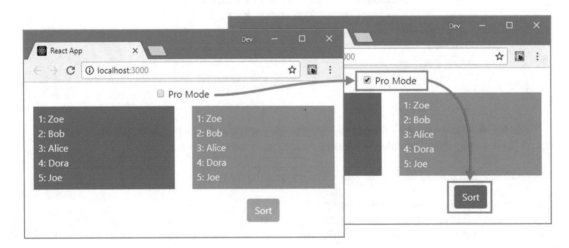

Figure 14-12. *Threading a prop through the application*

It is this problem that the context feature solves, allowing state data to be passed directly to the component that uses it, without needing to be threaded through the intermediate components that separate them in the hierarchy.

Defining the Context

The first step is to define the context, which is the mechanism by which the state data is distributed. Contexts can be defined anywhere in the application. I added a file called ProModeContext.js in the src folder with the code shown in Listing 14-28.

Listing 14-28. The Contents of the ProModeContext.js in the src Folder

```
import React from "react";

export const ProModeContext = React.createContext({
    proMode: false
})
```

The React.createContext method is used to create a new context and is provided with a data object that is used to specify the context's default values, which are overridden when the context is used, which I demonstrate shortly. In the listing, the context that I defined is called ProModeContext, and it defines a proMode property, which will be false by default.

Creating the Context Consumer

The next step is to consume the context where the data value is required, as shown in Listing 14-29.

Listing 14-29. Creating a Context Consumer in the ActionButton.js File in the src Folder

```
import React, { Component } from "react";
import { ProModeContext } from "./ProModeContext";

export class ActionButton extends Component {

    render() {
        return (
            <ProModeContext.Consumer>
                { contextData =>
                    <button
                        className={ this.getClasses(contextData.proMode)}
                        disabled={ !contextData.proMode }
                        onClick={ this.props.callback }>
                            { this.props.text }
                    </button>
                }
            </ProModeContext.Consumer>
        )
    }
```

```
    getClasses(proMode) {
        let col = proMode ? this.props.theme : "danger";
        return `btn btn-${col} m-2`;
    }
}
```

Consuming a context is similar to defining a render prop, with the addition of a custom HTML element to select the context that is required. First comes the HTML element whose tag name is the context name, followed by a period, followed by Consumer, like this:

```
...
return <ProModeContext.Consumer>

    // ...context can be consumed here...

</ProModeContext.Consumer>
...
```

Between the start and end tags of the HTML element is a function that receives the context object and renders the content that depends on it.

```
...
<ProModeContext.Consumer>
    { contextData =>
        <button
            className={ this.getClasses(contextData.proMode)}
            disabled={ !contextData.proMode }
            onClick={ this.props.callback }>
                { this.props.text }
        </button>
    }
</ProModeContext.Consumer>
...
```

The component can still access the component's state and prop data, which can be mixed freely with the data provided by the context. In this example, the callback prop is still used to handle click events, while the proMode context property is used to set the value of the className and disabled attributes.

Creating the Context Provider

The final step is to create a context provider, which associates the source state data with the context, as shown in Listing 14-30.

Listing 14-30. Creating a Context Provider in the App.js File in the src Folder

```
import React, { Component } from 'react';
import { GeneralList } from './GeneralList';
import { SortedList } from "./SortedList";
import { ProModeContext } from './ProModeContext';
```

```
export default class App extends Component {

    constructor(props) {
        super(props);
        this.state = {
            names: ["Zoe", "Bob", "Alice", "Dora", "Joe"],
            cities: ["London", "New York", "Paris", "Milan", "Boston"],
            //proMode: false,
            proContextData: {
                proMode: false
            }
        }
    }

    toggleProMode = () => {
        this.setState(state =>   state.proContextData.proMode
            = !state.proContextData.proMode);
    }

    render() {
        return (
            <div className="container-fluid">
                <div className="row">
                    <div className="col-12 text-center p-2">
                        <div className="form-check">
                            <input type="checkbox" className="form-check-input"
                                value={ this.state.proContextData.proMode }
                                onChange={ this.toggleProMode } />
                            <label className="form-check-label">Pro Mode</label>
                        </div>
                    </div>
                </div>
                <div className="row">
                    <div className="col-6">
                        <GeneralList list={ this.state.names }
                            theme="primary" />
                    </div>
                    <div className="col-6">
                        <ProModeContext.Provider value={ this.state.proContextData }>
                            <SortedList list={ this.state.names } />
                        </ProModeContext.Provider>
                    </div>
                </div>
            </div>
        )
    }
}
```

I don't want to expose all the App component's state data to the context consumers, so I have created a nested proContextData state object that has a proMode property. To apply the context, another custom HTML element is used, with the tag name of the context name, followed by a period, followed by Provider.

```
...
<ProModeContext.Provider value={ this.state.proContextData }>
    <SortedList list={ this.state.names } />
</ProModeContext.Provider>
...
```

The value property is used to provide the context with data values that override the defaults defined in Listing 14-28, which in this case is the proContextData state object.

■ **Tip**   Use the version of the setState method that accepts a function if you need to update a nested state property, as shown in Listing 14-28. See Chapter 11 for details of the different ways that setState can be used.

The components that are defined between the start and end ProModeContext.Provider tags are able to access the state data directly by using the ProModeContext.Consumer element. In the example application, this means that the App component's proMode state data property is available directly in the ActionButton component without being threaded through the SortedList component, as illustrated in Figure 14-13.

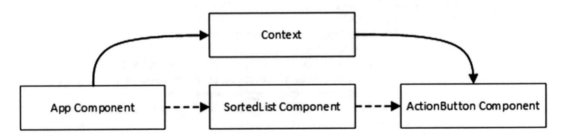

Figure 14-13. *The effect of using a context to distribute a state data property*

Changing Context Data Values in a Consumer

The data values in the context are read-only, but you can include a function in a context object that updates the source state data, creating the equivalent of a function prop. In Listing 14-31, I added a placeholder for the function that will be used if the provider applies the content without using the value property.

Listing 14-31. Adding a Function in the ProModeContext.js file in the src Folder

```
import React from "react";

export const ProModeContext = React.createContext({
    proMode: false,
    toggleProMode: () => {}
})
```

The function has an empty body and is used to prevent errors only if the default data object is received by a consumer. To demonstrate modifying a context data value, I am going to create a component that will render the checkbox used to toggle the pro mode. I added a file called ProModeToggle.js to the src folder and used it to define the component shown in Listing 14-32.

Listing 14-32. The Contents of the ProModeToggle.js File in the src Folder

```
import React, { Component } from "react";
import { ProModeContext } from "./ProModeContext";

export class ProModeToggle extends Component {

    render() {
        return <ProModeContext.Consumer>
            { contextData => (
                <div className="form-check">
                    <input type="checkbox" className="form-check-input"
                        value={ contextData.proMode }
                        onChange={ contextData.toggleProMode } />
                    <label className="form-check-label">
                        { this.props.label }
                    </label>
                </div>
                )
            }
        </ProModeContext.Consumer>
    }
}
```

This component is a context consumer and uses the proMode property to set the value of a checkbox and invokes the toggleProMode function when it changes. The component also uses a prop to set the content of a label element, just to show that a component that consumes a context is still able to receive props from its parent. In Listing 14-33, I have updated the App component so that it uses the ProModeToggle component and provides the context with a function.

■ **Caution** Avoid the temptation to create the object for a context in the provider's render method, which can be appealing because it avoids the need to create nested state objects and to assign methods to state properties. Creating a new object each time the render method is called undermines the change detection process that React applies to contexts and can lead to additional updates.

Listing 14-33. Expanding the Context in the App.js File in the src Folder

```
import React, { Component } from 'react';
import { GeneralList } from './GeneralList';
import { SortedList } from "./SortedList";
import { ProModeContext } from './ProModeContext';
import { ProModeToggle } from './ProModeToggle';
```

```
export default class App extends Component {

    constructor(props) {
        super(props);
        this.state = {
            names: ["Zoe", "Bob", "Alice", "Dora", "Joe"],
            cities: ["London", "New York", "Paris", "Milan", "Boston"],
            //proMode: false,
            proContextData: {
                proMode: false,
                toggleProMode: this.toggleProMode
            }
        }
    }

    toggleProMode = () => {
        this.setState(state =>  state.proContextData.proMode
            = !state.proContextData.proMode);
    }

    render() {
        return (
            <div className="container-fluid">
                <ProModeContext.Provider value={ this.state.proContextData }>
                    <div className="row">
                        <div className="col-12 text-center p-2">
                            <ProModeToggle label="Pro Mode" />
                        </div>
                    </div>
                    <div className="row">
                        <div className="col-6">
                            <GeneralList list={ this.state.names }
                                theme="primary" />
                        </div>
                        <div className="col-6">
                            <SortedList list={ this.state.names } />
                        </div>
                    </div>
                </ProModeContext.Provider>
            </div>
        )
    }
}
```

To provide an object that has both the state data and a function, I have added a property whose value is the toggleProMode method and that allows the context consumer to change the value of the state data property and, in doing so, trigger an update. Notice that I have lifted up the ProModeContext.Provider element so that the ProModeToggle and the SortedList component are both in scope. This is optional, and I could have given each child component its own context element, just as long as the value attributes used the same object. Using separate elements can be useful when you want to use multiple instances of the context with different groups of components, as shown in Listing 14-34.

Listing 14-34. Using Multiple Contexts in the App.js File in the src Folder

```
import React, { Component } from 'react';
//import { GeneralList } from './GeneralList';
import { SortedList } from "./SortedList";
import { ProModeContext } from './ProModeContext';
import { ProModeToggle } from './ProModeToggle';

export default class App extends Component {

    constructor(props) {
        super(props);
        this.state = {
            names: ["Zoe", "Bob", "Alice", "Dora", "Joe"],
            cities: ["London", "New York", "Paris", "Milan", "Boston"],
            proContextData: {
                proMode: false,
                toggleProMode: this.toggleProMode
            },
            superProContextData: {
                proMode: false,
                toggleProMode: this.toggleSuperMode
            }
        }
    }

    toggleProMode = () => {
        this.setState(state =>   state.proContextData.proMode
            = !state.proContextData.proMode);
    }

    toggleSuperMode = () => {
        this.setState(state =>   state.superProContextData.proMode
            = !state.superProContextData.proMode);
    }

    render() {
        return (
            <div className="container-fluid">
                <div className="row">
                    <div className="col-6 text-center p-2">
                        <ProModeContext.Provider value={ this.state.proContextData }>
                            <ProModeToggle label="Pro Mode" />
                        </ProModeContext.Provider>
                    </div>
                    <div className="col-6 text-center p-2">
                        <ProModeContext.Provider
                                value={ this.state.superProContextData }>
                            <ProModeToggle label="Super Pro Mode" />
                        </ProModeContext.Provider>
                    </div>
                </div>
```

```
<div className="row">
    <div className="col-6">
        <ProModeContext.Provider value={ this.state.proContextData }>
            <SortedList list={ this.state.names } />
        </ProModeContext.Provider>
    </div>
    <div className="col-6">
        <ProModeContext.Provider
                value={ this.state.superProContextData }>
            <SortedList list={ this.state.cities } />
        </ProModeContext.Provider>
    </div>
</div>
        </div>
    )
  }
}
```

The App component uses different contexts to manage two pro levels, as shown in Figure 14-14. Each context has its own data object, and React keeps track of the providers and consumers for each one.

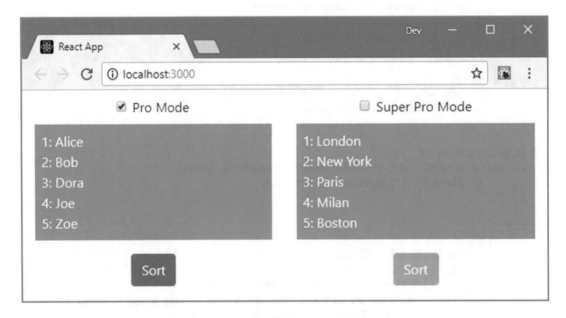

Figure 14-14. *Using multiple contexts*

Using the Simplified Context Consumer APIs

React offers an alternative means to access a context that can be easier to use than a render prop function, as shown in Listing 14-35.

Listing 14-35. Using the Simpler Context API in the ProModeToggle.js File in the src Folder

```
import React, { Component } from "react";
import { ProModeContext } from "./ProModeContext";

export class ProModeToggle extends Component {
    static contextType = ProModeContext;

    render() {
        return (
            <div className="form-check">
                <input type="checkbox" className="form-check-input"
                    value={ this.context.proMode }
                    onChange={ this.context.toggleProMode } />
                <label className="form-check-label">
                    { this.props.label }
                </label>
            </div>
        )
    }
}
```

A static property named contextType is assigned the context, which is then available throughout the component as this.context. This is a relatively recent addition to React, but it can be easier to use, with the caveat that a component can consume only one context.

Consuming a Context Using Hooks

The useContext hook provides the counterpart to the contextType property for functional components. In Listing 14-36, I have rewritten the ProModeToggle component to be defined as a function that relies on the useContext hook.

Listing 14-36. Using a Hook in the ProModeToggle.js File in the src Folder

```
import React, { useContext } from "react";
import { ProModeContext } from "./ProModeContext";

export function ProModeToggle(props) {

    const context = useContext(ProModeContext);

    return (
        <div className="form-check">
            <input type="checkbox" className="form-check-input"
                value={ context.proMode }
                onChange={ context.toggleProMode } />
            <label className="form-check-label">
                { props.label }
            </label>
        </div>
    )
}
```

417

The useContext function returns a context object through which the properties and functions can be accessed.

Defining Error Boundaries

When a component generates an error in its render method or in a lifecycle method, it propagates up the component hierarchy until it reaches the top of the application, at which point all of the application's components are unmounted. This means that any error can effectively terminate the application, which is rarely ideal, especially if the error is one that the application can recover from. To demonstrate the default error handling behavior, I changed the ActionButton component so it throws an error the second time the button element is clicked, as shown in Listing 14-37.

Listing 14-37. Throwing an Error in the ActionButton.js File in the src Folder

```
import React, { Component } from "react";
import { ProModeContext } from "./ProModeContext";

export class ActionButton extends Component {

    constructor(props) {
        super(props);
        this.state = {
            clickCount: 0
        }
    }

    handleClick = () => {
        this.setState({ clickCount: this.state.clickCount + 1});
        this.props.callback();
    }

    render() {
        return (
            <ProModeContext.Consumer>
                { contextData => {
                    if (this.state.clickCount > 1) {
                        throw new Error("Click Counter Error");
                    }
                    return <button
                        className={ this.getClasses(contextData.proMode)}
                        disabled={ !contextData.proMode }
                        onClick={ this.handleClick }>
                            { this.props.text }
                    </button>
                }}
            </ProModeContext.Consumer>
        )
    }
```

```
    getClasses(proMode) {
        let col = proMode ? this.props.theme : "danger";
        return `btn btn-${col} m-2`;
    }
}
```

To see the default behavior, enable one of the checkboxes and click the associated button. The order of the list will be changed when you click the first time. When you click again, the error will be thrown, and you will see the response shown in Figure 14-15. This message is shown during development but is disabled when the application is built for deployment, as demonstrated in Chapter 8. Click the close icon in the top right of the browser window, and you will see that all of the application's components have been unmounted, leaving an empty browser window.

Figure 14-15. *The default error handling*

The browser's JavaScript console displays a stack trace for the error.

```
...
Uncaught Error: Click Counter Error
    at ActionButton.js:23
    at updateContextConsumer (react-dom.development.js:13799)
    at beginWork (react-dom.development.js:13987)
    at performUnitOfWork (react-dom.development.js:16249)
...
```

Creating the Error Boundary Component

Class-based components can implement the componentDidCatch lifecycle method, which is invoked when a child component throws an error. The React convention is to use dedicated error-handling components, known as *error boundaries*, that intercept errors and either recover the application so it can continue execution or display a message to the user to indicate the nature of the problem. I added a file called ErrorBoundary.js to the src folder and used it to define the error boundary shown in Listing 14-38.

■ **Caution**   Error boundaries apply only to errors that are thrown in lifecycle methods and do not respond to errors thrown in event handlers. Error boundaries also cannot be used for asynchronous HTTP requests and a try/catch block must be used instead, as shown in Part 3.

Listing 14-38. The Contents of the ErrorBoundary.js File in the src Folder

```
import React, { Component } from "react";

export class ErrorBoundary extends Component {

    constructor(props) {
        super(props);
        this.state = {
            errorThrown: false
        }
    }

    componentDidCatch = (error, info) => this.setState({ errorThrown: true});

    render() {
        return (
            <React.Fragment>
                { this.state.errorThrown &&
                    <h3 className="bg-danger text-white text-center m-2 p-2">
                        Error Detected
                    </h3>
                }
                { this.props.children }
            </React.Fragment>
        )
    }
}
```

The componentDidCatch method receives the error object thrown by the problem component and an additional information object that provides the component's stack trace, which can be useful for logging.

When an error boundary is used, React will invoke the componentDidCatch method and then call the render method. The content rendered by the error boundary is handled using the mounting phase of the component lifecycle, as described in Chapter 13, so that new instances of all the components are created. This sequence allows the error boundary to change the content that is rendered to avoid problems or change the state of the application so that the error will not occur again. For this example, I have taken the third option, which is to render the same content but with a message noting that the error has been detected. This is an approach that can be used when the error has arisen because of a problem outside the scope of the application, such as when data cannot be obtained from a web service. Error boundaries are applied as container components, as shown in Listing 14-39.

Listing 14-39. Applying an Error Boundary in the SortedList.js File in the src Folder

```
import React, { Component } from "react";
import { GeneralList } from "./GeneralList";
import { ActionButton } from "./ActionButton";
import { ErrorBoundary } from "./ErrorBoundary";
```

```
export class SortedList extends Component {

    constructor(props) {
        super(props);
        this.state = {
            sort: false
        }
    }

    getList() {
        return this.state.sort
            ? [...this.props.list].sort() : this.props.list;
    }

    toggleSort = () => {
        this.setState({ sort : !this.state.sort });
    }

    render() {
        return (
            <div>
                <ErrorBoundary>
                    <GeneralList list={ this.getList() } theme="info" />
                    <div className="text-center m-2">
                        <ActionButton theme="primary" text="Sort"
                            proMode={ this.props.proMode }
                            callback={this.toggleSort} />
                    </div>
                </ErrorBoundary>
            </div>
        )
    }
}
```

The error boundary will handle errors thrown by any of the components it contains and any of their descendants. To see the effect, click one of the Sort buttons twice and close the error warning message to see the message indicating the error has been detected, as shown in Figure 14-16.

421

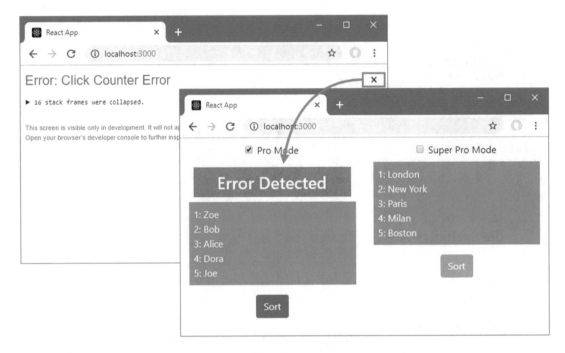

Figure 14-16. *The effect of an error boundary*

Summary

In this chapter, I described the different ways that components can be combined to compose applications, including containers, higher-order components, and render props. I also showed you how contexts can be used to distribute global data and avoid prop threading and how error boundaries can be used to handle problems in component lifecycle methods. In the next chapter, I describe the features that React provides for working with forms.

CHAPTER 15

■■■

Forms and Validation

Forms allow applications to collect data from the user. In this chapter, I explain how React works with form elements, using state properties to set their value and event handlers to respond to user interactions. I show you how to work with different element types and show you how to validate the data that the user provides in a form so that the application receives data it can use. Table 15-1 puts forms and validation in context.

Table 15-1. *Putting Forms and Validation in Context*

Question	Answer
What are they?	Forms are the basic mechanism that allows applications to prompt the user for data. Validation is the process of checking that data to ensure it can be used by the application.
Why are they useful?	Most applications require some degree of data entry from the user, such as e-mail addresses, payment details, or shipping addresses. Forms allow the user to enter that data, either in free-text form or by selecting from a range of predefined choices. Validation is used to ensure that the data is in a format that the application expects and can process.
How are they used?	In this chapter, I describe controlled form elements, whose value is set using the value or checked props and whose change events are handled to process user editing or selection. These features are also used for validation.
Are there any pitfalls or limitations?	There are differences in the way that different form elements behave and small deviations between React and the standard HTML form elements, as described in later sections.
Are there any alternatives?	Applications do not have to use form elements at all. In some applications, uncontrolled form elements, where React is not responsible for managing the element's data, may be a more suitable choice, as described in Chapter 16.

Table 15-2 summarizes the chapter.

Table 15-2. *Chapter Summary*

Problem	Solution	Listing
Add a form element to a component	Add the element to the content rendered by the component. Set the initial value of the element using the value prop and respond to changes using the onChange prop.	1–10, 12, 13
Determine the state of a checkbox	Inspect the checked property of the target element when handling the change event	11
Validate form data	Define validation rules and apply them when the user edits a field and triggers a change event	14–25

Preparing for This Chapter

To create the example project for this chapter, open a new command prompt, navigate to a convenient location, and run the command shown in Listing 15-1.

■ **Tip**   You can download the example project for this chapter—and for all the other chapters in this book—from https://github.com/Apress/pro-react-16.

Listing 15-1. Creating the Example Project

```
npx create-react-app forms
```

Run the commands shown in Listing 15-2 to navigate to the forms folder to add the Bootstrap package and a validation package to the project. (I use the validation package in the "Validating Form Data" section.)

Listing 15-2. Adding Packages to the Project

```
cd forms
npm install bootstrap@4.1.2
npm install validator@10.7.1
```

To include the Bootstrap CSS stylesheet in the application, add the statement shown in Listing 15-3 to the index.js file, which can be found in the src folder.

Listing 15-3. Including Bootstrap in the index.js File in the src Folder

```
import React from 'react';
import ReactDOM from 'react-dom';
import './index.css';
import App from './App';
```

```
import * as serviceWorker from './serviceWorker';
import 'bootstrap/dist/css/bootstrap.css';

ReactDOM.render(<App />, document.getElementById('root'));

// If you want your app to work offline and load faster, you can change
// unregister() to register() below. Note this comes with some pitfalls.
// Learn more about service workers: http://bit.ly/CRA-PWA
serviceWorker.unregister();
```

Defining the Example Components

Add a file called Editor.js to the src folder and add the content shown in Listing 15-4.

Listing 15-4. The Contents of the Editor.js File in the src Folder

```
import React, { Component } from "react";

export class Editor extends Component {

    render() {
        return <div className="h5 bg-info text-white p-2">
                    Form Will Go Here
                </div>
    }
}
```

I will use this component to display a form to the user. To start, however, this component renders a placeholder message. Next, add a file called Display.js to the src folder and add the content shown in Listing 15-5.

Listing 15-5. The Contents of the Display.js File in the src Folder

```
import React, { Component } from "react";

export class Display extends Component {

    formatValue = (data) => Array.isArray(data)
        ? data.join(", ") : data.toString();

    render() {
        let keys = Object.keys(this.props.data);
        if (keys.length === 0) {
            return <div className="h5 bg-secondary p-2 text-white">
                No Data
            </div>
        } else {
            return <div className="container-fluid bg-secondary p-2">
                    { keys.map(key =>
                        <div key={key} className="row h5 text-white">
```

```
                            <div className="col">{ key }:</div>
                            <div className="col">
                                { this.formatValue(this.props.data[key]) }
                            </div>
                        </div>
                    )}
                </div>
            }
        }
    }
}
```

This component receives a data prop and enumerates its properties and values in a grid. Finally, change the content in the App.js file to replace the content added when the project was created with the component shown in Listing 15-6.

Listing 15-6. The Contents of the App.js File in the src Folder

```
import React, { Component } from "react";
import { Editor } from "./Editor";
import { Display } from "./Display";

export default class App extends Component {

    constructor(props) {
        super(props);
        this.state = {
            formData: {}
        }
    }

    submitData = (newData) => {
        this.setState({ formData: newData});
    }

    render() {
        return <div className="container-fluid">
            <div className="row p-2">
                <div className="col-6">
                    <Editor submit={ this.submitData } />
                </div>
                <div className="col-6">
                    <Display data={ this.state.formData } />
                </div>
            </div>
        </div>
    }
}
```

Starting the Development Tools

Using the command prompt, run the command shown in Listing 15-7 in the forms folder to start the development tools.

Listing 15-7. Starting the Development Tools

```
npm start
```

Once the initial preparation for the project is complete, a new browser window will open and display the URL http://localhost:3000, which displays the content shown in Figure 15-1.

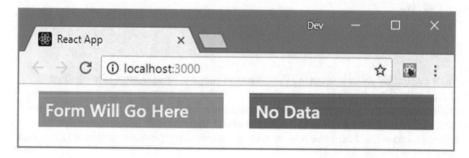

Figure 15-1. Running the example application

Using Form Elements

The simplest way to use form elements is to build on the React capabilities described in earlier chapters, using the state and event features. The result is known as a *controlled component*, and it will be familiar from earlier examples. In Listing 15-8, I have added an input element whose content is managed by React to the Editor component.

■ **Tip** There is also an approach called an *uncontrolled component*, which I describe in Chapter 16.

Listing 15-8. Adding a Form Element in the Editor.js File in the src Folder

```
import React, { Component } from "react";

export class Editor extends Component {

    constructor(props) {
        super(props);
        this.state = {
            name: ""
        }
    }
}
```

```
    updateFormValue = (event) => {
        this.setState({ [event.target.name]: event.target.value },
            () => this.props.submit(this.state));
    }

    render() {
        return <div className="h5 bg-info text-white p-2">
                    <div className="form-group">
                        <label>Name</label>
                        <input className="form-control"
                            name="name"
                            value={ this.state.name }
                            onChange={ this.updateFormValue } />
                    </div>
                </div>
    }
}
```

The input element's value attribute is set using the name state property, and changes are handled using the updateFormValue method, which has been selected using the onChange prop. Most forms require multiple fields and rather than define a different event handling method for each of them, it is a good idea to use one method and ensure that the form element is configured to indicate with which state value it is associated. In this example, I have used the name prop to specify the state property's name, which I then read from the event received by the handler method:

```
...
updateFormValue = (event) => {
    this.setState({ [event.target.name]: event.target.value },
        () => this.props.submit(this.state));
}
...
```

The contents of the square brackets (the [and] characters) are evaluated to get the property name for the state update, which allows me to use the name property from the event.target object with the setState method. Not all types of form element can be processed in the same way, as you will see in later examples, but this approach reduces the number of event handling methods in a component.

■ **Tip** Set the state property to the empty string ("") if you want to present an empty input element to the user. You can see examples of empty elements in Listing 15-8. Don't use null or undefined because these values cause React to generate a warning in the browser's JavaScript console.

Notice that I have used the callback option provided by the setState method to invoke the submit function prop after the state data has been updated, which allows me to send the form data to the parent component. This means that any change in the state data of the Editor component is also pushed to the App component so that it can be shown by the Display component, with the result that typing into the input element is immediately reflected in the content presented to the user, as shown in Figure 15-2. This may seem like needless duplication of state data, but it will allow me to more easily implement validation features later in this chapter.

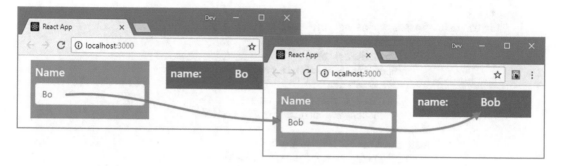

Figure 15-2. *Using a controlled component*

Using Select Elements

Once the basic structure is in place, a controller component can easily support additional form elements. In Listing 15-9, I have added two select elements to the Editor component.

Listing 15-9. Adding Select Elements in the Editor.js File in the src Folder

```
import React, { Component } from "react";

export class Editor extends Component {

    constructor(props) {
        super(props);
        this.state = {
            name: "Bob",
            flavor: "Vanilla",
            toppings: ["Strawberries"]
        }

        this.flavors = ["Chocolate", "Double Chocolate",
            "Triple Chocolate", "Vanilla"];
        this.toppings = ["Sprinkles", "Fudge Sauce",
                            "Strawberries", "Maple Syrup"]
    }

    updateFormValue = (event) => {
        this.setState({ [event.target.name]: event.target.value },
            () => this.props.submit(this.state));
    }

    updateFormValueOptions = (event) => {
        let options = [...event.target.options]
            .filter(o => o.selected).map(o => o.value);
        this.setState({ [event.target.name]: options },
            () => this.props.submit(this.state));
    }
```

```
render() {
    return <div className="h5 bg-info text-white p-2">
                <div className="form-group">
                    <label>Name</label>
                    <input className="form-control"
                        name="name"
                        value={ this.state.name }
                        onChange={ this.updateFormValue } />
                </div>
                <div className="form-group">
                    <label>Ice Cream Flavors</label>
                    <select className="form-control"
                            name="flavor" value={ this.state.flavor }
                            onChange={ this.updateFormValue } >
                        { this.flavors.map(flavor =>
                            <option value={ flavor } key={ flavor }>
                                { flavor }
                            </option>
                        )}
                    </select>
                </div>
                <div className="form-group">
                    <label>Ice Cream Toppings</label>
                    <select className="form-control" multiple={true}
                            name="toppings" value={ this.state.toppings }
                            onChange={ this.updateFormValueOptions }>
                        { this.toppings.map(top =>
                            <option value={ top } key={ top }>
                                { top }
                            </option>
                        )}
                    </select>
                </div>
            </div>
}
}
```

The select element is easy to work with, although care has to be taken for elements that display multiple values. For a basic select element, the value property is used to set the selected value, and selections are handled using the onChange property. The option elements presented by the select element can be specified as regular HTML elements or generated programmatically, in which case they will require a key property, like this:

```
...
<select className="form-control" name="flavor" value={ this.state.flavor }
        onChange={ this.updateFormValue } >
    { this.flavors.map(flavor =>
        <option value={ flavor } key={ flavor }>{ flavor }</option>
    )}
</select>
...
```

Changes to the `select` element that presents a single item for selection can be handled using the same method defined for the `input` element since the selected value is accessed through the `event.target.value` property.

Using Select Elements That Present Multiple Items

`Select` elements that allow multiple selections require a little more work. When defining the element, the `multiple` prop is set to `true` using an expression.

```
...
<select className="form-control" multiple={true} name="toppings"
    value={ this.state.toppings } onChange={ this.updateFormValueOptions }>
...
```

Using an expression avoids a common problem where assigning a string literal value to the `multiple` prop enables multiple elements, even when the string is `"false"`. Handling the user's selection requires a different handler method for the change event, as follows:

```
...
updateFormValueOptions = (event) => {
    let options = [...event.target.options]
        .filter(o => o.selected).map(o => o.value);
    this.setState({ [event.target.name]: options },
        () => this.props.submit(this.state));
}
...
```

The selections that the user has made are accessed through the `event.target.options` property, where the chosen items have a `selected` property whose value is `true`. In the listing, I create an array from the options, using the `filter` method to get the chosen items and the `map` method to get the `value` property, which leaves an array that contains the values from the `value` attribute of each chosen `option` element. Both `select` elements can be seen in Figure 15-3. (The data won't be shown by the `Display` component until you make a change.)

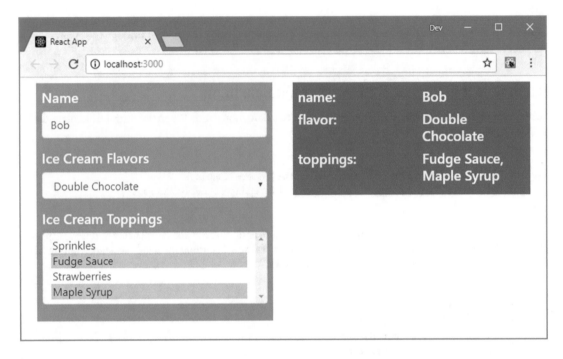

Figure 15-3. *Using select elements*

Using Radio Buttons

Working with radio buttons requires a similar process to text input elements, where the user's selection can be accessed through the target element's value property, as shown in Listing 15-10.

Listing 15-10. Using Radio Buttons in the Editor.js File in the src Folder

```
import React, { Component } from "react";

export class Editor extends Component {

    constructor(props) {
        super(props);
        this.state = {
            name: "Bob",
            flavor: "Vanilla"
        }

        this.flavors = ["Chocolate", "Double Chocolate",
            "Triple Chocolate", "Vanilla"];
        this.toppings = ["Sprinkles", "Fudge Sauce",
                         "Strawberries", "Maple Syrup"]
    }

    updateFormValue = (event) => {
        this.setState({ [event.target.name]: event.target.value },
            () => this.props.submit(this.state));
    }
```

```
render() {
    return <div className="h5 bg-info text-white p-2">
            <div className="form-group">
                <label>Name</label>
                <input className="form-control"
                    name="name"
                    value={ this.state.name }
                    onChange={ this.updateFormValue } />
            </div>

            <div className="form-group">
                <label>Ice Cream Flavors</label>
                { this.flavors.map(flavor =>
                    <div className="form-check" key={ flavor }>
                        <input className="form-check-input"
                            type="radio" name="flavor"
                            value={ flavor }
                            checked={ this.state.flavor === flavor }
                            onChange={ this.updateFormValue } />
                        <label className="form-check-label">
                            { flavor }
                        </label>
                    </div>
                )}
            </div>
        </div>
    }
}
```

Radio buttons allow the user to select a single value from a list of options. The choice represented by the radio button is specified by its value property, and its checked property is used to ensure the element is selected correctly, as shown in Figure 15-4.

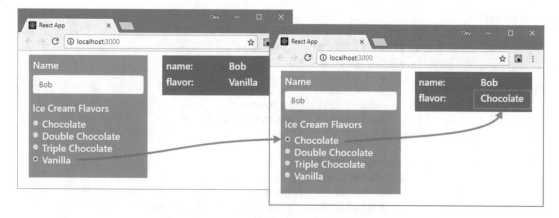

Figure 15-4. *Using radio buttons to present a choice*

Using Checkboxes

Checkboxes require a different approach because the checked property of the target element has to be read to determine whether the user has checked or unchecked the element, as shown in Listing 15-11.

Listing 15-11. Using a Checkbox in the Editor.js File in the src Folder

```
import React, { Component } from "react";

export class Editor extends Component {

    constructor(props) {
        super(props);
        this.state = {
            name: "Bob",
            flavor: "Vanilla",
            twoScoops: false
        }

        this.flavors = ["Chocolate", "Double Chocolate",
            "Triple Chocolate", "Vanilla"];
        this.toppings = ["Sprinkles", "Fudge Sauce",
                            "Strawberries", "Maple Syrup"]
    }

    updateFormValue = (event) => {
        this.setState({ [event.target.name]: event.target.value },
            () => this.props.submit(this.state));
    }

    updateFormValueCheck = (event) => {
        this.setState({ [event.target.name]: event.target.checked },
            () => this.props.submit(this.state));
    }

    render() {
        return <div className="h5 bg-info text-white p-2">
                    <div className="form-group">
                        <label>Name</label>
                        <input className="form-control"
                            name="name"
                            value={ this.state.name }
                            onChange={ this.updateFormValue } />
                    </div>

                    <div className="form-group">
                        <label>Ice Cream Flavors</label>
                        { this.flavors.map(flavor =>
                            <div className="form-check" key={ flavor }>
                                <input className="form-check-input"
                                    type="radio" name="flavor"
```

```
                            value={ flavor }
                            checked={ this.state.flavor === flavor }
                            onChange={ this.updateFormValue } />
                        <label className="form-check-label">
                            { flavor }
                        </label>
                    </div>
                )}
            </div>

            <div className="form-group">
                <div className="form-check">
                    <input className="form-check-input"
                        type="checkbox" name="twoScoops"
                        checked={ this.state.twoScoops }
                        onChange={ this.updateFormValueCheck } />
                    <label className="form-check-label">Two Scoops</label>
                </div>
            </div>
        </div>
    }
}
```

The checked property is used to specify whether the checkbox should be checked when it is displayed, and the checked property is used when handling the change event to determine whether the user has checked or unchecked the element, as shown in Figure 15-5.

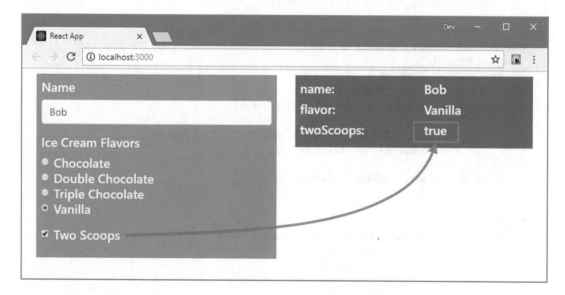

Figure 15-5. *Using a checkbox*

Using Checkboxes to Populate an Array

Checkboxes can also be used to populate an array, allowing users to choose from related options in a way that may be more familiar than a multi-option select element, as shown in Listing 15-12.

Listing 15-12. Using Related Checkboxes in the Editor.js File in the src Folder

```
import React, { Component } from "react";

export class Editor extends Component {

    constructor(props) {
        super(props);
        this.state = {
            name: "",
            flavor: "Vanilla",
            toppings: ["Strawberries"]
        }

        this.flavors = ["Chocolate", "Double Chocolate",
            "Triple Chocolate", "Vanilla"];
        this.toppings = ["Sprinkles", "Fudge Sauce",
                         "Strawberries", "Maple Syrup"]
    }

    updateFormValue = (event) => {
        this.setState({ [event.target.name]: event.target.value },
            () => this.props.submit(this.state));
    }

    updateFormValueCheck = (event) => {
        event.persist();
        this.setState(state => {
            if (event.target.checked) {
                state.toppings.push(event.target.name);
            } else {
                let index = state.toppings.indexOf(event.target.name);
                state.toppings.splice(index, 1);
            }
        }, () => this.props.submit(this.state));
    }

    render() {
        return <div className="h5 bg-info text-white p-2">
                    <div className="form-group">
                        <label>Name</label>
                        <input className="form-control"
                            name="name"
                            value={ this.state.name }
                            onChange={ this.updateFormValue } />
                    </div>
```

```
<div className="form-group">
    <label>Ice Cream Toppings</label>
    { this.toppings.map(top =>
        <div className="form-check" key={ top }>
            <input className="form-check-input"
                type="checkbox" name={ top }
                value={ this.state[top] }
                checked={ this.state.toppings.indexOf(top) > -1 }
                onChange={ this.updateFormValueCheck } />
            <label className="form-check-label">{ top }</label>
        </div>
    )}
</div>
            </div>
        }
    }
```

The elements are generated in the same way, but changes are required to the updateFormValueCheck method to manage the contents of the toppings array so that it contains only the user's chosen values. The standard JavaScript array features are used to remove a value from the array when the corresponding checkbox is unchecked and to add a value when the checkbox is checked, producing the result shown in Figure 15-6.

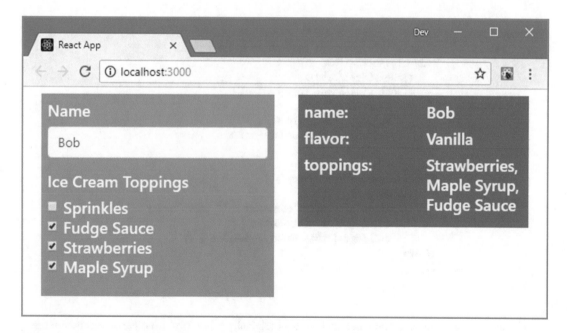

Figure 15-6. *Using checkboxes to populate an array*

Using Text Areas

The content of a textarea element is set and read using the value property, unlike regular HTML. In Listing 15-13, I have added a textarea element to the example application and used the onChange handler to respond to edits.

Listing 15-13. Using a Text Area in the Editor.js File in the src Folder

```
import React, { Component } from "react";

export class Editor extends Component {

    constructor(props) {
        super(props);
        this.state = {
            name: "Bob",
            order: ""
        }
    }

    updateFormValue = (event) => {
        this.setState({ [event.target.name]: event.target.value },
            () => this.props.submit(this.state));
    }

    render() {
        return <div className="h5 bg-info text-white p-2">
                    <div className="form-group">
                        <label>Name</label>
                        <input className="form-control"
                            name="name"
                            value={ this.state.name }
                            onChange={ this.updateFormValue } />
                    </div>

                    <div className="form-group">
                        <label>Order</label>
                        <textarea className="form-control" name="order"
                            value={ this.state.order }
                            onChange={ this.updateFormValue } />
                    </div>
                </div>
    }
}
```

Changes can be handled by the same method that I originally defined for text input elements, and the listing produces the result shown in Figure 15-7.

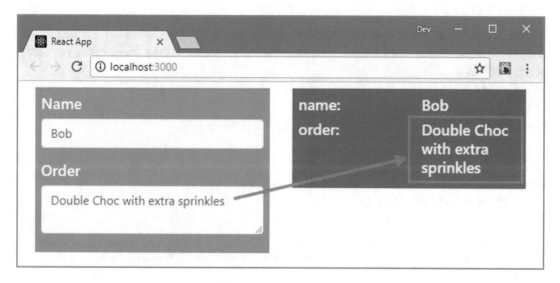

Figure 15-7. *Using a text area element*

Validating Form Data

Users will enter just about anything into form fields, either because they have made a mistake or because they are trying to skip through the form without filling it in, as noted in the sidebar. Validation checks the data that users provide to ensure that the application has data that it can work with. In the sections that follow, I show you how to perform form validation in a React application.

MINIMIZING THE USE OF FORMS

One reason that users will enter bad data into forms is they don't regard the result as valuable. This can occur when the form interrupts a process that is important to the user with something that is unimportant, such as an intrusive prompt to create an account when reading an article or when the same form is presented at the start of a process that the user performs often.

Validation won't help when the user doesn't value the form because they will simply enter bad data that passes the checks but that is still bad data. If you find that your intrusive prompt for an e-mail address results in a lot of a@a.com responses, then you should consider that your users don't think your weekly newsletter is as interesting as you do.

Use forms sparingly and only for processes that the user will regard as useful, such as providing a shipping address. For other forms, find an alternative way to solicit the data from the user that doesn't interrupt their workflow and doesn't annoy them each time they try to perform a task.

When validating forms, the different parts of the validation process can be distributed in a complex hierarchy of HTML and components. Instead of threading props to connect the different parts, I am going to use a context to keep track of validation problems. I added a file called ValidationContext.js to the src folder with the content shown in Listing 15-14. (Contexts are described in Chapter 14.)

■ **Note** The examples in this section rely on the `validator` package that was added to the project in Listing 15-2. If you skipped over the installation, you should go back and add the package before proceeding with the examples.

Listing 15-14. The Contents of the ValidationContext.js File in the src Folder

```
import React from "react";

export const ValidationContext = React.createContext({
    getMessagesForField: (field) => []
})
```

I am going to store the validation issues for each form element as an array and display messages for each of the issues alongside the element. The context provides access to a function that will return the validation messages for a specific field.

Defining the Validation Rules

Next, I added a file called `validation.js` to the `src` folder and added the code shown in Listing 15-15. This is the code that will validate the form data, using the `validator` package that was installed at the start of the chapter.

Listing 15-15. The Contents of the validation.js File in the src Folder

```
import validator from "validator";

export function ValidateData(data, rules) {
    let errors = {};
    Object.keys(data).forEach(field => {
        if (rules.hasOwnProperty(field)) {
            let fielderrors = [];
            let val = data[field];
            if (rules[field].required && validator.isEmpty(val)) {
                fielderrors.push("Value required");
            }
            if (!validator.isEmpty(data[field])) {
                if (rules[field].minlength
                        && !validator.isLength(val, rules[field].minlength)) {
                    fielderrors.push(`Enter at least ${rules[field].minlength}`
                        + " characters");
                }
                if (rules[field].alpha && !validator.isAlpha(val)) {
                    fielderrors.push("Enter only letters");
                }
                if (rules[field].email && !validator.isEmail(val)) {
                    fielderrors.push("Enter a valid email address");
                }
            }
```

```
            if (fielderrors.length > 0) {
                errors[field] = fielderrors;
            }
        }
    })
    return errors;
}
```

The ValidateData function will receive an object whose properties are the form values and an object that specifies the validation rules that are to be applied. The validation package provides methods that can be used to perform a wide range of checks, but I have focused on four validation checks for this example: ensuring that the user has supplied a value, ensuring a minimum length, ensuring a valid e-mail address, and ensuring that only alphabetic characters are used. Table 15-3 describes the methods provided by the validation package that I use in the examples that follow. See https://www.npmjs.com/package/validator for the full range of features provided by the validator package.

Table 15-3. *The validator Methods*

Name	Description
isEmpty	This method returns true if a value is an empty string.
isLength	This method returns true if a value exceeds a minimum length.
isAlpha	This method returns true if a value contains only letters.
isEmail	This method returns true if a value is a valid e-mail address.
isEqual	This method returns true if two values are the same.

Creating the Container Component

To create the validation component, I added a file called FormValidator.js to the src folder and used it to define the component shown in Listing 15-16.

Listing 15-16. The Contents of the FormValidator.js File in the src Folder

```
import React, { Component } from "react";
import { ValidateData } from "./validation";
import { ValidationContext } from "./ValidationContext";

export class FormValidator extends Component {

    constructor(props) {
        super(props);
        this.state = {
            errors: {},
            dirty: {},
            formSubmitted: false,
            getMessagesForField: this.getMessagesForField
        }
    }
```

```
    static getDerivedStateFromProps(props, state) {
        return {
            errors: ValidateData(props.data, props.rules)
        };
    }

    get formValid() {
        return Object.keys(this.state.errors).length === 0;
    }

    handleChange = (ev) => {
        let name = ev.target.name;
        this.setState(state => state.dirty[name] = true);
    }

    handleClick = (ev) => {
        this.setState({ formSubmitted: true }, () => {
            if (this.formValid) {
                this.props.submit(this.props.data)
            }
        });
    }

    getButtonClasses() {
        return this.state.formSubmitted && !this.formValid
            ? "btn-danger" : "btn-primary";
    }

    getMessagesForField = (field) => {
        return (this.state.formSubmitted || this.state.dirty[field]) ?
            this.state.errors[field] || [] : []
    }

    render() {
        return <React.Fragment>
            <ValidationContext.Provider value={ this.state }>
                <div onChange={ this.handleChange }>
                    { this.props.children }
                </div>
            </ValidationContext.Provider>

            <div className="text-center">
                <button className={ `btn ${ this.getButtonClasses() }`}
                        onClick={ this.handleClick }
                        disabled={ this.state.formSubmitted && !this.formValid } >
                    Submit
                </button>
            </div>
        </React.Fragment>
    }
}
```

The validation is performed in the getDerivedStateFromProps lifecycle method, which provides a component with a change to make changes to its state based on the props it receives. The component receives a data prop that contains the form data to be validated and a rules prop that defines the validation checks that should be applied and passes these to the ValidateData function defined in Listing 15-15. The result of the ValidateData function is assigned to the state.errors property and is an object with a property for each form field that has validation issues and an array of messages that should be presented to the user.

Form validation should not begin until the user has started to edit a field or has attempted to submit the form. Individual edits are handled by listening for the change event as it bubbles up from the form elements contained by the component, as described in Chapter 12.

```
...
<div onChange={ this.handleChange }>
    { this.props.children }
</div>
...
```

The handleChange method adds the value of the name prop of the change event's target element to the dirty state object (during validation, elements are regarded as *pristine* until the user starts editing, after which they are considered *dirty*). The component presents the user with a button element with a handler that changes the formSubmitted state property when it is clicked. If the button is clicked while there are invalid form elements, then it is disabled until the problems have been resolved and its color is changed to make it obvious that the data cannot be processed.

```
...
<button className={ `btn ${ this.getButtonClasses() }` }
        onClick={ this.handleClick }
        disabled={ this.state.formSubmitted && !this.formValid } >
    Submit
</button>
...
```

If the validation checks produce no errors, then the handleClick method invokes a function prop called submit and uses the validated data as the argument.

Displaying Validation Messages

To display validation messages alongside the form elements, I added a file called ValidationMessage.js to the src folder and used it to define the component shown in Listing 15-17.

Listing 15-17. The Contents of the ValidationMessage.js File in the src Folder

```
import React, { Component } from "react";
import { ValidationContext } from "./ValidationContext";

export class ValidationMessage extends Component {
    static contextType = ValidationContext;
```

```
    render() {
        return this.context.getMessagesForField(this.props.field).map(err =>
            <div className="small bg-danger text-white mt-1 p-1"
                    key={ err } >
                { err }
            </div>
        )
    }
}
```

This component consumes the context provided by the FormValidator component and uses it to get the validation messages for a single form field whose name is specified through the field prop. This component doesn't have any insight into the type of form element whose validation issues it reports or any knowledge of the overall validity of the form—it just requests the messages and displays them. If there are no messages to be displayed, then no content is rendered.

Applying the Form Validation

The final step is to apply the validation to the form, as shown in Listing 15-18. The FormValidator component must be an ancestor to the form fields so it can receive change events from them as they bubble up. It must also be an ancestor to the ValidationMessage components so that they have access to the validation messages through the shared context.

Listing 15-18. Applying Validation in the Editor.js File in the src Folder

```
import React, { Component } from "react";
import { FormValidator } from "./FormValidator";
import { ValidationMessage } from "./ValidationMessage";

export class Editor extends Component {

    constructor(props) {
        super(props);
        this.state = {
            name: "",
            email: "",
            order: ""
        }
        this.rules = {
            name: { required: true, minlength: 3, alpha: true },
            email: { required: true, email: true },
            order: { required: true }
        }
    }

    updateFormValue = (event) => {
        this.setState({ [event.target.name]: event.target.value });
    }
```

```
render() {
    return <div className="h5 bg-info text-white p-2">
              <FormValidator data={ this.state } rules={ this.rules }
                      submit={ this.props.submit }>
                  <div className="form-group">
                      <label>Name</label>
                      <input className="form-control"
                          name="name"
                          value={ this.state.name }
                          onChange={ this.updateFormValue } />
                      <ValidationMessage field="name" />
                  </div>

                  <div className="form-group">
                      <label>Email</label>
                      <input className="form-control"
                          name="email"
                          value={ this.state.email }
                          onChange={ this.updateFormValue } />
                      <ValidationMessage field="email" />
                  </div>

                  <div className="form-group">
                      <label>Order</label>
                      <textarea className="form-control"
                          name="order"
                          value={ this.state.order }
                          onChange={ this.updateFormValue } />
                      <ValidationMessage field="order" />
                  </div>
              </FormValidator>
          </div>
    }
}
```

In addition to applying the validation components, I added an email field and changed the updateFormValue method so that it doesn't automatically send the data for display. The result is shown in Figure 15-8. No validation messages are shown until you start editing a field or click the button, and you can't submit the data until the data you entered meets all of the validation requirements.

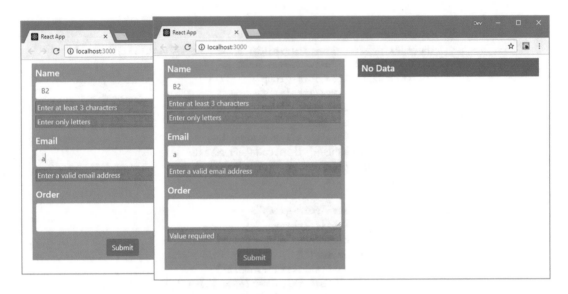

Figure 15-8. *Validating form data*

Validating Other Element and Data Types

Notice that the validation features don't deal directly with the input and textarea elements. Instead, the standard state and event features are used to bring the data under React's control, where it is validated and dealt with by components that have no knowledge or interest in where the data came from. This means that once the basic validation features are in place, they can be different types of form element and different types of data. Each project has its own validation requirements, but the examples in the sections that follow demonstrate some of the most commonly required approaches that you can adapt to your own needs.

Ensuring That a Checkbox Is Selected

A common validation requirement is to ensure that the user checks a box to accept terms and conditions. In Listing 15-19, I have added a check to the set of validations that ensures that a value is true, which will be the case when a checkbox element is checked.

Listing 15-19. Adding a Validation Option in the validation.js File in the src Folder

```
import validator from "validator";

export function ValidateData(data, rules) {
    let errors = {};
    Object.keys(data).forEach(field => {
        if (rules.hasOwnProperty(field)) {
            let fielderrors = [];
            let val = data[field];
            if (rules[field].true) {
                if (!val) {
                    fielderrors.push("Must be checked");
                }
```

```
        } else {
            if (rules[field].required && validator.isEmpty(val)) {
                fielderrors.push("Value required");
            }
            if (!validator.isEmpty(data[field])) {
                if (rules[field].minlength
                        && !validator.isLength(val, rules[field].minlength)) {
                    fielderrors.push(`Enter at least ${rules[field].minlength}`
                        + " characters");
                }
                if (rules[field].alpha && !validator.isAlpha(val)) {
                    fielderrors.push("Enter only letters");
                }
                if (rules[field].email && !validator.isEmail(val)) {
                    fielderrors.push("Enter a valid email address");
                }
            }
        }
        if (fielderrors.length > 0) {
            errors[field] = fielderrors;
        }
    }
})
return errors;
}
```

The validator package that I am using to perform the validation checks operates only on string values and reports an error if it is asked to check a Boolean. To avoid problems, I have treated the new validation check as a special case that cannot be combined with other rules. In Listing 15-20, I have removed some of the existing form elements and added a checkbox, along with a validation rule that ensures it is checked.

Listing 15-20. Validating a Checkbox in the Editor.js File in the src Folder

```
import React, { Component } from "react";
import { FormValidator } from "./FormValidator";
import { ValidationMessage } from "./ValidationMessage";

export class Editor extends Component {

    constructor(props) {
        super(props);
        this.state = {
            name: "",
            terms: false
        }
        this.rules = {
            name: { required: true, minlength: 3, alpha: true },
            terms: { true: true}
        }
    }
```

```
updateFormValue = (event) => {
    this.setState({ [event.target.name]: event.target.value });
}

updateFormValueCheck = (event) => {
    this.setState({ [event.target.name]: event.target.checked });
}

render() {
    return <div className="h5 bg-info text-white p-2">
                <FormValidator data={ this.state } rules={ this.rules }
                       submit={ this.props.submit }>
                   <div className="form-group">
                       <label>Name</label>
                       <input className="form-control"
                           name="name"
                           value={ this.state.name }
                           onChange={ this.updateFormValue } />
                       <ValidationMessage field="name" />
                   </div>

                <div className="form-group">
                    <div className="form-check">
                        <input className="form-check-input"
                            type="checkbox" name="terms"
                            checked={ this.state.terms }
                            onChange={ this.updateFormValueCheck } />
                        <label className="form-check-label">
                            Agree to terms
                        </label>
                    </div>
                    <ValidationMessage field="terms" />
                </div>
                </FormValidator>
            </div>
    }
}
```

The user is presented with a checkbox that must be checked before the form can be submitted, as shown in Figure 15-9.

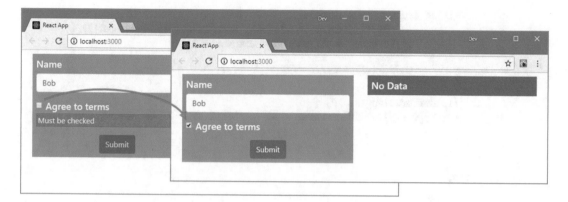

Figure 15-9. *Validating a checkbox*

Ensuring Matching Values

Some values require confirmation in two inputs, such as passwords and e-mail addresses for contact purposes. In Listing 15-21, I have added a validation rule that checks that two values are the same.

Listing 15-21. Ensuring Equal Values in the validation.js File in the src Folder

```
import validator from "validator";

export function ValidateData(data, rules) {
    let errors = {};
    Object.keys(data).forEach(field => {
        if (rules.hasOwnProperty(field)) {
            let fielderrors = [];
            let val = data[field];
            if (rules[field].true) {
                if (!val) {
                    fielderrors.push("Must be checked");
                }
            } else {
                if (rules[field].required && validator.isEmpty(val)) {
                    fielderrors.push("Value required");
                }
                if (!validator.isEmpty(data[field])) {
                    if (rules[field].minlength
                            && !validator.isLength(val, rules[field].minlength)) {
                        fielderrors.push(`Enter at least ${rules[field].minlength}`
                            + " characters");
                    }
                    if (rules[field].alpha && !validator.isAlpha(val)) {
                        fielderrors.push("Enter only letters");
                    }
                    if (rules[field].email && !validator.isEmail(val)) {
                        fielderrors.push("Enter a valid email address");
                    }
```

449

```
                    if (rules[field].equals
                            && !validator.equals(val, data[rules[field].equals])) {
                        fielderrors.push("Values don't match");
                    }
                }
            }
            if (fielderrors.length > 0) {
                errors[field] = fielderrors;
            }
        }
    })
    return errors;
}
```

In Listing 15-22, I have added two input elements to the Editor component and added a validation check to ensure that the user enters the same value in both fields.

Listing 15-22. Adding Related Elements in the Editor.js File in the src Folder

```
import React, { Component } from "react";
import { FormValidator } from "./FormValidator";
import { ValidationMessage } from "./ValidationMessage";

export class Editor extends Component {

    constructor(props) {
        super(props);
        this.state = {
            name: "",
            email: "",
            emailConfirm: ""
        }
        this.rules = {
            name: { required: true, minlength: 3, alpha: true },
            email: { required: true, email: true, equals: "emailConfirm"},
            emailConfirm: { required: true, email: true, equals: "email"}
        }
    }

    updateFormValue = (event) => {
        this.setState({ [event.target.name]: event.target.value });
    }
```

```
render() {
    return <div className="h5 bg-info text-white p-2">
            <FormValidator data={ this.state } rules={ this.rules }
                    submit={ this.props.submit }>
                <div className="form-group">
                    <label>Name</label>
                    <input className="form-control"
                        name="name"
                        value={ this.state.name }
                        onChange={ this.updateFormValue } />
                    <ValidationMessage field="name" />
                </div>

                <div className="form-group">
                    <label>Email</label>
                    <input className="form-control"
                        name="email"
                        value={ this.state.email }
                        onChange={ this.updateFormValue } />
                    <ValidationMessage field="email" />
                </div>

                <div className="form-group">
                    <label>Confirm Email</label>
                    <input className="form-control"
                        name="emailConfirm"
                        value={ this.state.emailConfirm }
                        onChange={ this.updateFormValue } />
                    <ValidationMessage field="emailConfirm" />
                </div>
            </FormValidator>
        </div>
    }
}
```

The result is that the form is valid only when the contents of the email and emailConfirm fields are the same, as shown in Figure 15-10.

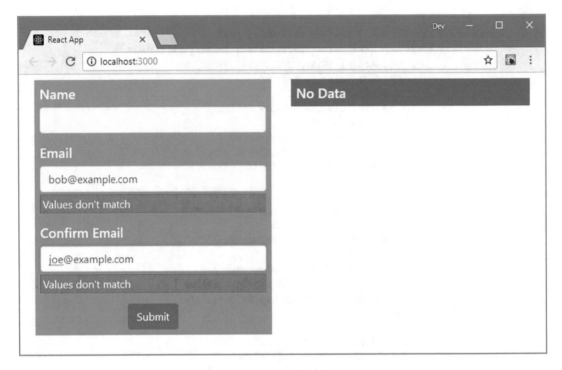

Figure 15-10. *Ensuring matching values*

Performing Whole-Form Validation

Some types of validation cannot be performed on individual values, such as ensuring that combinations of choices are consistent. This sort of validation can be performed only when the user has entered valid data into the form and submitted it, at which point an application can perform a final set of checks before processing the data.

Validation for individual fields can be applied in multiple forms using the same code, while validation on combinations of values tends to be specific to a single form. To avoid mixing general code with form-specific features, I added a file called wholeFormValidation.js to the src folder and used it to define the validation function shown in Listing 15-23.

Listing 15-23. The Contents of the wholeFormValidation.js File in the src Folder

```
export function ValidateForm(data) {
    let errors = [];
    if (!data.email.endsWith("@example.com")) {
        errors.push("Only example.com users allowed");
    }
    if (!data.email.toLowerCase().startsWith(data.name.toLowerCase())) {
        errors.push("Email address must start with name");
    }
```

```
    if (data.name.toLowerCase() === "joe") {
        errors.push("Go away, Joe")
    }
    return errors;
}
```

The ValidateForm function receives the form data and checks that e-mail addresses end with @example.com and that the name property isn't joe and that the email value begins with the name value. In Listing 15-24, I have extended the FormValidator component so that it receives a form validation function as a prop and uses it before submitting the form data.

Listing 15-24. Adding Support for Whole-Form Validation in the FormValidator.js File in the src Folder

```
import React, { Component } from "react";
import { ValidateData } from "./validation";
import { ValidationContext } from "./ValidationContext";

export class FormValidator extends Component {

    constructor(props) {
        super(props);
        this.state = {
            errors: {},
            dirty: {},
            formSubmitted: false,
            getMessagesForField: this.getMessagesForField
        }
    }

    static getDerivedStateFromProps(props, state) {
        state.errors = ValidateData(props.data, props.rules);
        if (state.formSubmitted && Object.keys(state.errors).length === 0) {
            let formErrors = props.validateForm(props.data);
            if (formErrors.length > 0) {
                state.errors.form = formErrors;
            }
        }
        return state;
    }

    get formValid() {
        return Object.keys(this.state.errors).length === 0;
    }

    handleChange = (ev) => {
        let name = ev.target.name;
        this.setState(state => state.dirty[name] = true);
    }
```

```
    handleClick = (ev) => {
        this.setState({ formSubmitted: true }, () => {
            if (this.formValid) {
                let formErrors = this.props.validateForm(this.props.data);
                if (formErrors.length === 0) {
                    this.props.submit(this.props.data)
                }
            }
        });
    }

    getButtonClasses() {
        return this.state.formSubmitted && !this.formValid
            ? "btn-danger" : "btn-primary";
    }

    getMessagesForField = (field) => {
        return (this.state.formSubmitted || this.state.dirty[field]) ?
            this.state.errors[field] || [] : []
    }

    render() {
        return <React.Fragment>
            <ValidationContext.Provider value={ this.state }>
                <div onChange={ this.handleChange }>
                    { this.props.children }
                </div>
            </ValidationContext.Provider>

            <div className="text-center">
                <button className={ `btn ${ this.getButtonClasses() }`}
                        onClick={ this.handleClick }
                        disabled={ this.state.formSubmitted && !this.formValid } >
                    Submit
                </button>
            </div>
        </React.Fragment>
    }
}
```

The changes start validating the entire form as soon as the user clicks the Submit button.
In Listing 15-25, I have updated the Editor component so that it provides the FormValidator with
a whole-form validation function and defines a new ValidationMessage component to display errors
that are form-specific.

Listing 15-25. Applying Whole-Form Validation in the Editor.js File in the src Folder

```
import React, { Component } from "react";
import { FormValidator } from "./FormValidator";
import { ValidationMessage } from "./ValidationMessage";
import { ValidateForm } from "./wholeFormValidation";
```

```
export class Editor extends Component {

    constructor(props) {
        super(props);
        this.state = {
            name: "",
            email: "",
            emailConfirm: ""
        }
        this.rules = {
            name: { required: true, minlength: 3, alpha: true },
            email: { required: true, email: true, equals: "emailConfirm"},
            emailConfirm: { required: true, email: true, equals: "email"}
        }
    }

    updateFormValue = (event) => {
        this.setState({ [event.target.name]: event.target.value });
    }

    render() {
        return <div className="h5 bg-info text-white p-2">
                    <FormValidator data={ this.state } rules={ this.rules }
                        submit={ this.props.submit }
                        validateForm={ ValidateForm }>

                    <ValidationMessage field="form" />

                    <div className="form-group">
                        <label>Name</label>
                        <input className="form-control"
                            name="name"
                            value={ this.state.name }
                            onChange={ this.updateFormValue } />
                        <ValidationMessage field="name" />
                    </div>

                    <div className="form-group">
                        <label>Email</label>
                        <input className="form-control"
                            name="email"
                            value={ this.state.email }
                            onChange={ this.updateFormValue } />
                        <ValidationMessage field="email" />
                    </div>
```

```
                    <div className="form-group">
                        <label>Confirm Email</label>
                        <input className="form-control"
                            name="emailConfirm"
                            value={ this.state.emailConfirm }
                            onChange={ this.updateFormValue } />
                        <ValidationMessage field="emailConfirm" />
                    </div>
                </FormValidator>
            </div>
        }
}
```

The user is presented with additional validation messages if they try to submit data that doesn't meet the conditions checked in Listing 15-23, as shown in Figure 15-11.

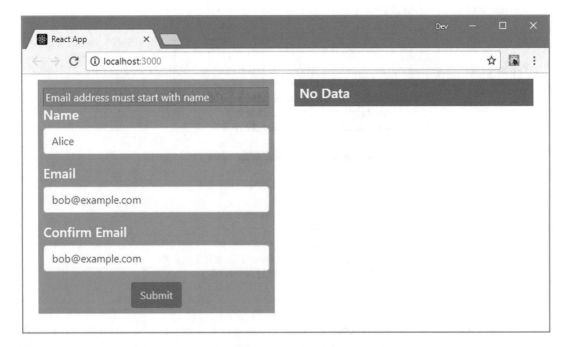

Figure 15-11. *Performing whole-form validation*

Summary

In this chapter, I showed you how to create controlled components, which are form elements whose content is managed through a state property and whose editing is processed by an event handler. I showed you different types of form element and demonstrated how form data can be validated. Controlled form components are only one type that React supports, and in the next chapter, I introduce the refs feature and explained how uncontrolled form elements can be used.

CHAPTER 16

■ ■ ■

Using Refs and Portals

Under normal circumstances, a component doesn't interact directly with the elements in the Document Object Model (DOM). Normal interaction is through props and event handlers, which make it possible to compose applications and for components to work together without knowledge of the content they deal with.

There are some situations where components need to interact with the elements in the DOM, and React provides two features for this purpose. The *refs* feature—short for references—provides access to the HTML elements rendered by a component after they have been added to the DOM. The *portals* feature provides access to HTML elements outside of the application's content.

These features should be used with caution because they undermine the isolation between components in an application, which makes it harder to write, test, and maintain. These features lead to "rabbit holing," where they fix one problem but introduce another, which leads to another fix and another problem and so on. If used injudiciously, these features produce components that duplicate the core functionality provided by React, which is rarely a beneficial result. Table 16-1 puts refs and portals in context.

Table 16-1. *Putting Refs and Portals in Context*

Question	Answer
What are they?	Refs are references to the elements in the DOM that have been rendered by a component. A portal allows content to be rendered outside of the application's content.
Why are they useful?	There are some features of HTML elements that cannot be easily managed without accessing the DOM directly, such as focusing an element. These features are also useful for integration with other frameworks and libraries.
How are they used?	Refs are created using the special ref attribute and can be created using the React.createRef method or using a callback function. Portals are created using the ReactDOM.createPortal method.
Are there any pitfalls or limitations?	These features are prone to misuse, such that they undermine component isolation and are used to duplicate features that are provided by React.
Are there any alternatives?	Refs and portals are advanced features that will not be required in many projects.

© Adam Freeman 2019
A. Freeman, *Pro React 16*, https://doi.org/10.1007/978-1-4842-4451-7_16

Table 16-2 summarizes the chapter.

Table 16-2. *Chapter Summary*

Problem	Solution	Listing
Access the HTML element objects created for a component	Use a ref	1–9, 11, 12, 18, 19
Use a form element without using state data and an event handler	Use uncontrolled form components	10, 13–15
Prevent data loss during updates	Use the getSnapshotBeforeUpdate method	16, 17
Access a child component's content	Use the refs prop or ref forwarding	20–23
Project content into a specific DOM element	Use a portal	24–26

Preparing for This Chapter

To create the example project for this chapter, open a new command prompt, navigate to a convenient location, and run the command shown in Listing 16-1.

■ **Tip**   You can download the example project for this chapter—and for all the other chapters in this book—from https://github.com/Apress/pro-react-16.

Listing 16-1. Creating the Example Project

```
npx create-react-app refs
```

Run the commands shown in Listing 16-2 to navigate to the refs folder to add the Bootstrap package.

Listing 16-2. Adding the Bootstrap CSS Framework

```
cd refs
npm install bootstrap@4.1.2
```

In this chapter, I create an example that relies on jQuery. Run the command shown in Listing 16-3 in the refs folder to add the jQuery package to the project.

Listing 16-3. Installing jQuery

```
npm install jquery@3.3.1
```

To include the Bootstrap CSS stylesheet in the application, add the statement shown in Listing 16-4 to the index.js file, which can be found in the src folder.

Listing 16-4. Including Bootstrap in the index.js File in the src Folder

```
import React from 'react';
import ReactDOM from 'react-dom';
import './index.css';
import App from './App';
import * as serviceWorker from './serviceWorker';
import 'bootstrap/dist/css/bootstrap.css';

ReactDOM.render(<App />, document.getElementById('root'));

// If you want your app to work offline and load faster, you can change
// unregister() to register() below. Note this comes with some pitfalls.
// Learn more about service workers: http://bit.ly/CRA-PWA
serviceWorker.unregister();
```

Add a file called Editor.js file in the src folder and add the code shown in Listing 16-5.

Listing 16-5. The Contents of the Editor.js File in the src Folder

```
import React, { Component } from "react";

export class Editor extends Component {

    constructor(props) {
        super(props);
        this.state = {
            name: "",
            category: "",
            price: ""
        }
    }

    handleChange = (event) => {
        event.persist();
        this.setState(state => state[event.target.name] = event.target.value);
    }

    handleAdd = () => {
        this.props.callback(this.state);
        this.setState({ name: "", category:"", price:""});
    }

    render() {
        return <React.Fragment>
            <div className="form-group p-2">
                <label>Name</label>
                <input className="form-control" name="name"
                    value={ this.state.name } onChange={ this.handleChange }
                    autoFocus={ true } />
            </div>
            <div className="form-group p-2">
```

```
            <label>Category</label>
            <input className="form-control" name="category"
                value={ this.state.category } onChange={ this.handleChange }  />
        </div>
        <div className="form-group p-2">
            <label>Price</label>
            <input className="form-control" name="price"
                value={ this.state.price } onChange={ this.handleChange }  />
        </div>
        <div className="text-center">
            <button className="btn btn-primary" onClick={ this.handleAdd }>
                Add
            </button>
        </div>
    </React.Fragment>
  }

}
```

The Editor component renders a series of input elements whose value are set using state data properties and whose change events are handled by the handleChange method. There is a button element whose click event invokes the handleAdd method, which invokes a function prop using the state data, which is then reset.

Next, add a file called ProductTable.js to the src folder and add the code shown in Listing 16-6.

Listing 16-6. The Contents of the ProductTable.js File in the src Folder

```
import React, { Component } from "react";

export class ProductTable extends Component {

    render() {
        return <table className="table table-sm table-striped">
            <thead><tr><th>Name</th><th>Category</th><th>Price</th></tr></thead>
            <tbody>
                {
                    this.props.products.map(p =>
                        <tr key={ p.name }>
                            <td>{ p.name }</td>
                            <td>{ p.category }</td>
                            <td>${ Number(p.price).toFixed(2) }</td>
                        </tr>
                    )
                }
            </tbody>
        </table>
    }
}
```

The ProductTable component renders a table that contains a row for each object received in the products prop. Next, replace the contents of the App.js file with the code shown in Listing 16-7.

Listing 16-7. Replacing the Contents of the App.js File in the src Folder

```
import React, { Component } from "react";
import { Editor } from "./Editor"
import { ProductTable } from "./ProductTable";

export default class App extends Component {

    constructor(props) {
        super(props);
        this.state = {
            products: []
        }
    }

    addProduct = (product) => {
        if (this.state.products.indexOf(product.name) === -1) {
            this.setState({ products: [...this.state.products, product ]});
        }
    }

    render() {
        return <div>
            <Editor callback={ this.addProduct } />
            <h6 className="bg-secondary text-white m-2 p-2">Products</h6>
                <div className="m-2">
                    {
                        this.state.products.length === 0
                            ? <div className="text-center">No Products</div>
                                : <ProductTable products={ this.state.products } />
                    }
                </div>
        </div>
    }
}
```

Using the command prompt, run the command shown in Listing 16-8 in the refs folder to start the development tools.

Listing 16-8. Starting the Development Tools

```
npm start
```

Once the initial preparation for the project is complete, a new browser window will open and display the URL http://localhost:3000, which displays the content shown in Figure 16-1. Fill out the form and click the Add button, and you will see a new entry displayed in the table.

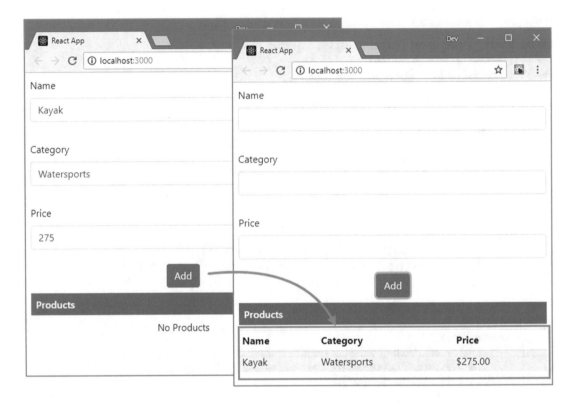

Figure 16-1. *Running the example application*

Creating Refs

Refs can be used when a component needs to access the DOM in order to use features of a specific HTML element. There are HTML features that cannot be achieved through the use of props, one of which is to ask an element to gain focus. The autoFocus attribute can be used to focus an element when content is first rendered, but the focus will switch to the button element once the user clicks it, which means that the user can't start typing to create another item until they refocus, either by clicking the input element or by using the Tab key.

A ref can be used to access the DOM and invoke the focus method on the input element when the event triggered by clicking the Add button is handled, as shown in Listing 16-9.

DON'T RUSH TO USE REFS

Being able to access the DOM is a natural expectation for web developers, and refs can seem like a feature that makes React development easier, especially if you are coming to React from a framework like Angular.

It is easy to get carried away with refs and end up with a component that duplicates the content handling features that should be performed by React. A component that makes excessive use of refs is difficult to manage, can create dependencies on specific browser features, and can be difficult to run on different platforms.

Use refs only as a last resort, and always consider if you can achieve the same result using the state and props features.

Listing 16-9. Using a Ref in the Editor.js File in the src Folder

```
import React, { Component } from "react";

export class Editor extends Component {

    constructor(props) {
        super(props);
        this.state = {
            name: "",
            category: "",
            price: ""
        }
        this.nameRef = React.createRef();
    }

    handleChange = (event) => {
        event.persist();
        this.setState(state => state[event.target.name] = event.target.value);
    }

    handleAdd = () => {
        this.props.callback(this.state);
        this.setState({ name: "", category:"", price:""},
            () => this.nameRef.current.focus());
    }

    render() {
        return <React.Fragment>
            <div className="form-group p-2">
                <label>Name</label>
                <input className="form-control" name="name"
                    value={ this.state.name } onChange={ this.handleChange }
                    autoFocus={ true } ref={ this.nameRef } />
            </div>
            <div className="form-group p-2">
                <label>Category</label>
                <input className="form-control" name="category"
                    value={ this.state.category } onChange={ this.handleChange }  />
            </div>
            <div className="form-group p-2">
                <label>Price</label>
                <input className="form-control" name="price"
                    value={ this.state.price } onChange={ this.handleChange }  />
            </div>
```

```
        <div className="text-center">
            <button className="btn btn-primary" onClick={ this.handleAdd }>
                Add
            </button>
        </div>
    </React.Fragment>
    }
}
```

Refs are created using the React.createRef method, which is invoked in the constructor so that the result can be used throughout the component. A ref is associated with an element using the special ref prop, with an expression that selects the ref for the element.

```
...
<input className="form-control" name="name"
    value={ this.state.name } onChange={ this.handleChange }
    autoFocus={ true } ref={ this.nameRef } />
...
```

The ref object returned by the createRef method defines just one property, named current, that returns the HTMLElement object that represents the element in the DOM. I use the current property in the handleAdd method to invoke the focus method after the state data update has been completed, like this:

```
...
this.setState({ name: "", category:"", price:""},
    () => this.nameRef.current.focus());
...
```

The result is that the name input element will regain the focus when the update triggered by the Add button is complete, allowing the user to start typing for the next new product without having to manually select the element, as shown in Figure 16-2.

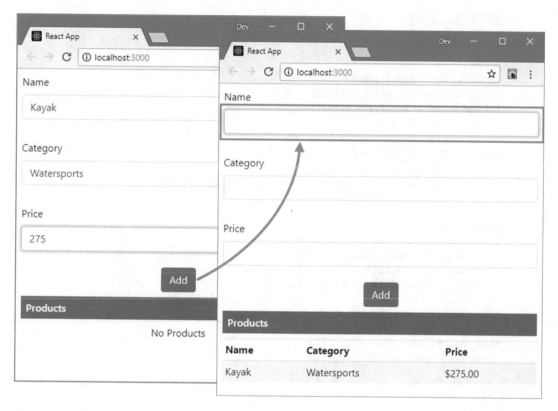

Figure 16-2. *Using a ref*

Using Refs to Create Uncontrolled Form Components

The example application uses the controlled form components technique that I introduced in Chapter 15, where React is responsible for the contents of each form element, using a state data property to store its value and an event handler to respond to changes.

Form elements already have the ability to store a value and respond to changes, but these features are not used by a controlled form component. An alternative technique is to create an *uncontrolled form component*, where a ref is used to access form elements and the browser is responsible for managing the element's value and responding to changes. In Listing 16-10, I have removed the state data used to manage the input elements rendered by the Editor component and used refs to create uncontrolled form components.

Listing 16-10. Creating Uncontrolled Form Components in the Editor.js File in the src Folder

```
import React, { Component } from "react";

export class Editor extends Component {

    constructor(props) {
        super(props);
        // this.state = {
```

465

```
        //      name: "",
        //      category: "",
        //      price: ""
        // }
        this.nameRef = React.createRef();
        this.categoryRef = React.createRef();
        this.priceRef = React.createRef();
    }

    // handleChange = (event) => {
    //     event.persist();
    //     this.setState(state => state[event.target.name] = event.target.value);
    // }

    handleAdd = () => {
        this.props.callback({
            name: this.nameRef.current.value,
            category: this.categoryRef.current.value,
            price: this.priceRef.current.value
        });
        this.nameRef.current.value = "";
        this.categoryRef.current.value = "";
        this.priceRef.current.value = "";
        this.nameRef.current.focus();
    }

    render() {
        return <React.Fragment>
            <div className="form-group p-2">
                <label>Name</label>
                <input className="form-control" name="name"
                    autoFocus={ true } ref={ this.nameRef } />
            </div>
            <div className="form-group p-2">
                <label>Category</label>
                <input className="form-control" name="category"
                    ref={ this.categoryRef } />
            </div>
            <div className="form-group p-2">
                <label>Price</label>
                <input className="form-control" name="price" ref={ this.priceRef } />
            </div>
            <div className="text-center">
                <button className="btn btn-primary" onClick={ this.handleAdd }>
                    Add
                </button>
            </div>
        </React.Fragment>
    }
}
```

The input elements values are not required until the user clicks the Add button. In the handleAdd method, which is invoked when the button is clicked, the refs for each of the input elements is used to read the value property. The result has the same appearance to the user as earlier examples, but behind the scenes, React is no longer responsible for managing the element values or responding to change events.

SETTING AN INITIAL VALUE FOR AN UNCONTROLLED ELEMENT

React isn't responsible for uncontrolled elements, but it can still provide an initial value, which is then managed by the browser. To set the value, use the defaultValue or defaultChecked attribute, but bear in mind that the value you specify will be used only when the element is first rendered and won't update the element when it is changed.

Creating Refs Using a Callback Function

The previous example shows how refs can be used in form elements, but the result isn't that different from the controlled form component with which I started the chapter. There is an alternative technique that can be used to create refs and that can produce more concise components, as shown in Listing 16-11, known as *callback refs*.

Listing 16-11. Using Callback Refs in the Editor.js File in the src Folder

```
import React, { Component } from "react";

export class Editor extends Component {

    constructor(props) {
        super(props);
        this.formElements = {
            name: { },
            category: { },
            price: { }
        }
    }

    setElement = (element) => {
        if (element !== null) {
            this.formElements[element.name].element = element;
        }
    }

    handleAdd = () => {
        let data = {};
        Object.values(this.formElements)
            .forEach(v => {
                data[v.element.name] = v.element.value;
                v.element.value = "";
            });
```

```
        this.props.callback(data);
        this.formElements.name.element.focus();
    }

    render() {
        return <React.Fragment>
            <div className="form-group p-2">
                <label>Name</label>
                <input className="form-control" name="name"
                    autoFocus={ true } ref={ this.setElement } />
            </div>
            <div className="form-group p-2">
                <label>Category</label>
                <input className="form-control" name="category"
                    ref={ this.setElement } />
            </div>
            <div className="form-group p-2">
                <label>Price</label>
                <input className="form-control" name="price"
                    ref={ this.setElement } />
            </div>
            <div className="text-center">
                <button className="btn btn-primary" onClick={ this.handleAdd }>
                    Add
                </button>
            </div>
        </React.Fragment>
    }
}
```

The value of the ref property of the input elements is set to a method, which is invoked when the content is rendered. Instead of dealing with a ref object, the specified method receives the HTMLElement object directly, instead of a reference object with a current property. In the listing, the setElement method receives the elements, which are added to the formElements object using the name value so that I can differentiate between the elements.

The function you provide for a callback ref will also be invoked with null as the argument if the element is unmounted. For this example, I don't need to do any tidying up if the elements are removed, so I just check for the null value in the setElement method.

```
...
setElement = (element) => {
    if (element !== null) {
        this.formElements[element.name].element = element;
    }
}
...
```

Once you have the function for the refs in place, forms can be easily generated programmatically, as shown in Listing 16-12, because refs don't have be created and assigned to elements individually.

Listing 16-12. Generating a Form Programmatically in the Editor.js File in the src Folder

```
import React, { Component } from "react";

export class Editor extends Component {

    constructor(props) {
        super(props);
        this.formElements = {
            name: { label: "Name", name: "name" },
            category: { label: "Category", name: "category" },
            price: { label: "Price", name: "price" }
        }
    }

    setElement = (element) => {
        if (element !== null) {
            this.formElements[element.name].element = element;
        }
    }

    handleAdd = () => {
        let data = {};
        Object.values(this.formElements)
            .forEach(v => {
                data[v.element.name] = v.element.value;
                v.element.value = "";
            });
        this.props.callback(data);
        this.formElements.name.element.focus();
    }

    render() {
        return <React.Fragment>
            {
                Object.values(this.formElements).map(elem =>
                    <div className="form-group p-2" key={ elem.name }>
                        <label>{ elem.label }</label>
                        <input className="form-control"
                            name={ elem.name }
                            autoFocus={ elem.name === "name" }
                            ref={ this.setElement }  />
                    </div>)
            }
            <div className="text-center">
                <button className="btn btn-primary" onClick={ this.handleAdd }>
                    Add
                </button>
            </div>
        </React.Fragment>
    }
}
```

469

The input elements are generated using the properties of the formElements object, where each property is assigned an object with label and name properties that are used in the render method to configure the element.

The code required to define and manage the form is more concise, but the effect is the same, and filling the form and clicking the Add button displays a new object, as shown in Figure 16-3.

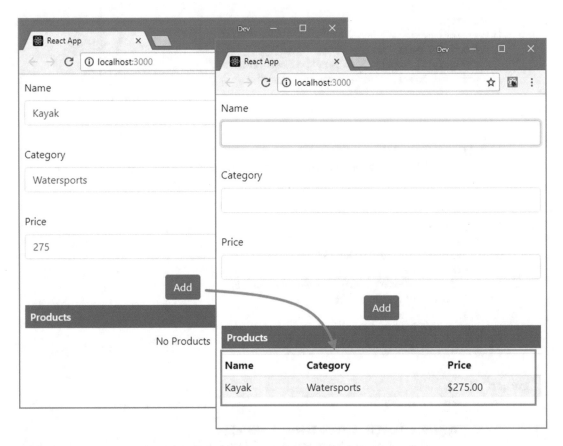

Figure 16-3. Programmatically creating form elements and refs

Validating Uncontrolled Form Components

Form elements have built-in validation support through the HTML Constraint Validation API, which can be accessed using refs. The validation API describes an element's validation status using an object like this one:

```
...
{
    valueMissing: true, tooShort: false, rangeUnderflow: false
}
...
```

The valueMissing property will be true when I have specified that the element must have a value but is empty. The tooShort property will be true when there are fewer characters in the element's value than specified by the validation rules. The rangeUnderflow property will be true for numeric values that are smaller than a specified minimum value.

To process this type of validation object, I added a file called ValidationMessages.js to the src folder and used it to define the function shown in Listing 16-13.

Listing 16-13. The Contents of the ValidationMessages.js File in the src Folder

```
export function GetValidationMessages(elem) {
    let errors = [];
    if (!elem.checkValidity()) {
        if (elem.validity.valueMissing) {
            errors.push("Value required");
        }
        if (elem.validity.tooShort) {
            errors.push("Value is too short");
        }
        if (elem.validity.rangeUnderflow) {
            errors.push("Value is too small");
        }
    }
    return errors;
}
```

The GetValidationMessages function receives an HTML element object and asks the browser for data validation by calling the element's checkValidity method. The checkValidity method returns true if the element's value is valid and false otherwise. If the element's value isn't valid, then the element's validity property is checked for the valueMissing, tooShort, and rangeUnderflow properties with true values and used to create an array of errors that can be shown to the user.

■ **Tip** The HTML validation features include a wider range of validation checks and validity properties than I use in this chapter. See https://developer.mozilla.org/en-US/docs/Web/Guide/HTML/HTML5/ Constraint_validation for a good description of the available features.

I added a file called ValidationDisplay.js in the src folder and used it to define a component that will display the validation messages for a single element, as shown in Listing 16-14.

Listing 16-14. The Contents of the ValidationDisplay.js File in the src Folder

```
import React, { Component } from "react";

export class ValidationDisplay extends Component {

    render() {
        return this.props.errors
            ? this.props.errors.map(err =>
                <div className="small bg-danger text-white mt-1 p-1"
                        key={ err } >
                    { err }
```

```
                </div>)
            : null
    }
}
```

This component receives an array of error messages that it should display and returns null to indicate no content if there are no error messages to show. In Listing 16-15, I have updated the Editor component so that validation attributes are applied to the form elements and validation checks are performed before the form data is used.

Listing 16-15. Applying Validation in the Editor.js File in the src Folder

```
import React, { Component } from "react";
import { ValidationDisplay } from "./ValidationDisplay";
import { GetValidationMessages } from "./ValidationMessages";

export class Editor extends Component {

    constructor(props) {
        super(props);
        this.formElements = {
            name: { label: "Name", name: "name",
                validation: { required: true, minLength: 3 }},
            category: { label: "Category", name:"category",
                validation: { required: true, minLength: 5 }},
            price: { label: "Price", name: "price",
                validation: { type: "number", required: true, min: 5 }}
        }
        this.state = {
            errors: {}
        }
    }

    setElement = (element) => {
        if (element !== null) {
            this.formElements[element.name].element = element;
        }
    }

    handleAdd = () => {
        if (this.validateFormElements()) {
            let data = {};
            Object.values(this.formElements)
                .forEach(v => {
                    data[v.element.name] = v.element.value;
                    v.element.value = "";
                });
            this.props.callback(data);
            this.formElements.name.element.focus();
        }
    }
```

```
validateFormElement = (name) => {
    let errors = GetValidationMessages(this.formElements[name].element);
    this.setState(state => state.errors[name] = errors);
    return errors.length === 0;
}

validateFormElements = () => {
    let valid = true;
    Object.keys(this.formElements).forEach(name => {
        if (!this.validateFormElement(name)) {
            valid = false;
        }
    })
    return valid;
}

render() {
    return <React.Fragment>
        {
            Object.values(this.formElements).map(elem =>
                <div className="form-group p-2" key={ elem.name }>
                    <label>{ elem.label }</label>
                    <input className="form-control"
                        name={ elem.name }
                        autoFocus={ elem.name === "name" }
                        ref={ this.setElement }
                        onChange={ () => this.validateFormElement(elem.name) }
                        { ...elem.validation} />
                    <ValidationDisplay
                        errors={ this.state.errors[elem.name] } />
                </div>)
        }
        <div className="text-center">
            <button className="btn btn-primary" onClick={ this.handleAdd }>
                Add
            </button>
        </div>
    </React.Fragment>
}
}
```

I included the validation attributes for each element in the objects that describes that element, like this:

```
...
name: { label: "Name", name: "name", validation: { required: true, minLength: 3 }},
...
```

The required attribute indicates that a value is required, and the minLength attribute specifies that the value should contain at least three characters. These attributes are applied to the input elements when they are created by the render method.

```
...
<input className="form-control" name={ elem.name }
    autoFocus={ elem.name === "name" } ref={ this.setElement }
    onChange={ () => this.validateFormElement(elem.name) }
    { ...elem.validation} />
...
```

I don't have to worry about the pristine/dirty element issue I described in Chapter 15 because validation isn't performed until the checkValidity method is invoked, which will happen in response to the change event, which I handle using the onChange event prop and the validateFormElement method, with the effect that validation for an element begins only when the user starts to type, as shown in Figure 16-4.

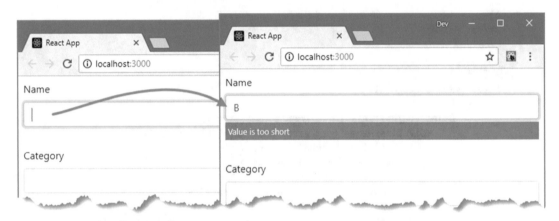

Figure 16-4. *Validating an element*

When the user clicks the Add button, the handleAdd method invokes the validateFormElements button, which validates all the elements and ensures that the form data isn't used until the problems are resolved, as shown in Figure 16-5. The effects of changes are shown immediately because each edit triggers a change event that causes the element's value to validated again.

Figure 16-5. *Validating all elements*

Understanding Refs and the Lifecycle

Refs are not assigned a value until React invokes a component's render method. If you are using the createRef method, the current property will not be assigned a value before the component has rendered its content. Similarly, callback refs won't invoke their method until the component has rendered.

The assignment of refs may seem late in the component lifecycle, but refs provide access to DOM elements, which are not created until the rendering phase, which means that React hasn't created the elements that refs refer to until the render method is invoked. The element associated with a ref can be accessed only in the componentDidMount and componentDidUpdate lifecycle methods because they occur after rendering has been completed and the DOM has been populated or updated.

One consequence of using refs is that a component can't rely on the state feature to preserve its context when React replaces the elements it renders in the DOM. React tries to minimize DOM changes, but you cannot rely on the same element being used throughout the life of an application. As noted in Chapter 13, changing the top-level element rendered by a component causes React to replace its elements in the DOM, as shown in Listing 16-16.

Listing 16-16. Rendering a Different Top-Level Element in the Editor.js File in the src Folder

```
import React, { Component } from "react";
import { ValidationDisplay } from "./ValidationDisplay";
import { GetValidationMessages } from "./ValidationMessages";

export class Editor extends Component {

    constructor(props) {
        super(props);
        this.formElements = {
            name: { label: "Name", name: "name",
```

```
            validation: { required: true, minLength: 3 }},
        category: { label: "Category", name:"category",
            validation: { required: true, minLength: 5 }},
        price: { label: "Price", name: "price",
            validation: { type: "number", required: true, min: 5 }}
    }
    this.state = {
        errors: {},
        wrapContent: false
    }
}

setElement = (element) => {
    if (element !== null) {
        this.formElements[element.name].element = element;
    }
}

handleAdd = () => {
    if (this.validateFormElements()) {
        let data = {};
        Object.values(this.formElements)
            .forEach(v => {
                data[v.element.name] = v.element.value;
                v.element.value = "";
            });
        this.props.callback(data);
        this.formElements.name.element.focus();
    }
}

validateFormElement = (name) => {
    let errors = GetValidationMessages(this.formElements[name].element);
    this.setState(state => state.errors[name] = errors);
    return errors.length === 0;
}

validateFormElements = () => {
    let valid = true;
    Object.keys(this.formElements).forEach(name => {
        if (!this.validateFormElement(name)) {
            valid = false;
        }
    })
    return valid;
}

toggleWrap = () => {
    this.setState(state => state.wrapContent = !state.wrapContent);
}
```

```
wrapContent(content) {
    return this.state.wrapContent
        ? <div className="bg-secondary p-2">
                <div className="bg-light">{ content }</div>
          </div>
        : content;
}

render() {
    return this.wrapContent(
        <React.Fragment>
                <div className="form-group text-center p-2">
                    <div className="form-check">
                        <input className="form-check-input"
                            type="checkbox"
                            checked={ this.state.wrapContent }
                            onChange={ this.toggleWrap } />
                        <label className="form-check-label">Wrap Content</label>
                    </div>
                </div>
            {
                Object.values(this.formElements).map(elem =>
                    <div className="form-group p-2" key={ elem.name }>
                        <label>{ elem.label }</label>
                        <input className="form-control"
                            name={ elem.name }
                            autoFocus={ elem.name === "name" }
                            ref={ this.setElement }
                            onChange={ () => this.validateFormElement(elem.name) }
                            { ...elem.validation} />
                        <ValidationDisplay
                             errors={ this.state.errors[elem.name] } />
                    </div>)
            }
            <div className="text-center">
                <button className="btn btn-primary" onClick={ this.handleAdd }>
                    Add
                </button>
            </div>
        </React.Fragment>)
    }
}
```

I have added a wrapContent state property that is set using a controlled checkbox and that wraps the content rendered by the component and ensures that React replaces the component's existing elements in the DOM with new ones. To see the effect, enter text into the Name field and check the Wrap Context checkbox, as shown in Figure 16-6.

Figure 16-6. *Replacing elements*

The input element into which you entered text has been destroyed, and its content has been lost. To make matters more confusing for the user, any validation errors that have been detected are part of the component's state data, which means they will be displayed alongside the new input element, even though the data value they describe is no longer visible.

To help avoid this problem, the stateful component lifecycle includes the getSnapshotBeforeUpdate method, which is called between the render and componentDidUpdate methods in the update phase, as shown in Figure 16-7.

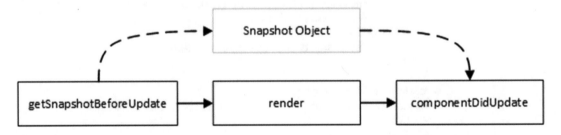

Figure 16-7. *The snapshot process*

This getSnapshotBeforeUpdate method allows a component to inspect its current content and generate a custom snapshot object before the render method is called. Once the update is complete, the componentDidUpdate method is called and provided with the snapshot object so that the component can modify the elements that are now in the DOM.

■ **Caution** A snapshot doesn't help preserve context if the component is unmounted and re-created, which can happen when an ancestor's content changes. In these situations, the componentWillUnmount method can be used to access refs, and the data can be preserved via a context, as described in Chapter 15.

In Listing 16-17, I have used the snapshot feature to capture the values entered into the input element before the update and restore those values after the update.

Listing 16-17. Taking a Snapshot in the Editor.js File in the src Folder

```
import React, { Component } from "react";
import { ValidationDisplay } from "./ValidationDisplay";
import { GetValidationMessages } from "./ValidationMessages";

export class Editor extends Component {

    constructor(props) {
        super(props);
        this.formElements = {
            name: { label: "Name", name: "name",
                validation: { required: true, minLength: 3 }},
            category: { label: "Category", name:"category",
                validation: { required: true, minLength: 5 }},
            price: { label: "Price", name: "price",
                validation: { type: "number", required: true, min: 5 }}
        }
        this.state = {
            errors: {},
            wrapContent: false
        }
    }

    // ...other methods omitted for brevity...

    getSnapshotBeforeUpdate(props, state) {
        return Object.values(this.formElements).map(item =>
            {return { name: [item.name], value: item.element.value }})
    }

    componentDidUpdate(oldProps, oldState, snapshot) {
        snapshot.forEach(item => {
            let element = this.formElements[item.name].element
            if (element.value !== item.value) {
                element.value = item.value;
            }
        });
    }
}
```

The getSnapshotBeforeUpdate method receives the component's props and state as they were before the update was triggered and returns an object that will be passed to the componentDidUpdate method after the update. In the example, I don't need to access props or state because the data I need to preserve is contained in the input elements. React doesn't mandate a specific format for the snapshot object, and the getSnapshotBeforeUpdate method can return data in any format that will be useful. In the example, the getSnapshotBeforeUpdate method returns an array of objects with name and value properties.

Once React has completed the update, it calls the componentDidUpdate and provides the snapshot as an argument, along with the old props and state data. In the example, I process the array of objects and set the values of the input elements. The result is that data entered into the input elements is preserved when the checkbox is toggled, as shown in Figure 16-8.

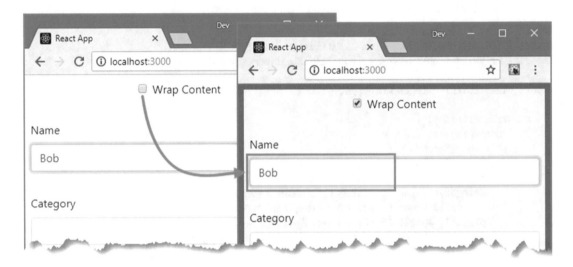

Figure 16-8. *Using snapshot data*

The getSnapshotBeforeUpdate and componentDidUpdate methods are called for every update, even when React hasn't replaced the component's elements in the DOM, which is why I apply a snapshot value only when an element's value differs from the snapshot value when the update has been completed.

UNDERSTANDING THE REFS RABBIT HOLE

There is an unintended consequence of using the HTML5 constraint validation API in the previous example. Validation is performed only when the user edits the contents of the text field and not when the value is set programmatically. When I use the snapshot data to set the value of a newly created input element, it will pass validation, even if the value previously failed validation. The effect is that the user can bypass validation by entering bad values into the name or category input elements, checking the wrap content checkbox, and clicking the Add button.

This is a problem that can be worked around, but the underlying issue is that using refs to access the DOM directly presents a series of small conflicts, each of which can be solved with the addition of a few lines of code. But these fixes often present other issues or compromises that require additional work, and the result is a fragile application made from complex components.

Working directly with the DOM can be essential in some projects, and there can be advantages to avoiding duplicating data and features that are already in the DOM. But use refs only when they are required because they can create as many problems as they solve.

Using Refs with Other Libraries or Frameworks

Some projects are moved to React gradually so that components have to interoperate with existing features that are written in another library or framework. The most common example is jQuery, which was the most popular choice for web application development before the era of frameworks like React and Angular and which is still widely used for simple projects. If you have an extensive set of features that are written in jQuery, for example, then you can apply them to the HTML elements rendered by a component using refs. To demonstrate, I am going to use jQuery to assign form elements with invalid elements to a class that will apply a Bootstrap style. I added a file called jQueryColorizer.js to the src folder and added the code shown in Listing 16-18.

■ **Note** This example requires the jQuery package that was added to the project in Listing 16-3. If you did not install jQuery, you should do so before proceeding.

Listing 16-18. The Contents of the jQueryColorizer.js in the src Folder

```
var $ = require('jquery');

export function ColorInvalidElements(rootElement) {
    $(rootElement)
        .find("input:invalid").addClass("border-danger")
            .removeClass("border-success")
        .end()
        .find("input:valid").removeClass("border-danger")
            .addClass("border-success");
}
```

The jQuery statement locates all the input elements that are assigned to the invalid pseudoclass and adds them to the border-danger class and adds any input elements in the valid pseudoclass to the border-success class. The valid and invalid classes are used by the HTML constraint validation API to indicate an element's validation status. In Listing 16-19, I have added a ref and used it to invoke the jQuery function from the App component.

MIXING FRAMEWORKS

Using refs to incorporate other frameworks is difficult and prone to problems. Like any use of refs, it should be done with caution and only when you are unable to rewrite the functionality in React. You may feel that you will save time by building on your existing code, but my experience is that any time saved will be spent trying to work around a long series of small problems that arise because the two frameworks work in different ways.

If you have to use another library or framework alongside React, then you should pay close attention to the way that the frameworks approach the DOM. You will find that React and the other framework expect to have complete control of the content they create, and unexpected results can arise when elements are added, removed, or changed in a way that the framework developers did not expect.

Listing 16-19. Invoking a Function in the App.js File in the src Folder

```
import React, { Component } from "react";
import { Editor } from "./Editor"
import { ProductTable } from "./ProductTable";
import { ColorInvalidElements } from "./jQueryColorizer";

export default class App extends Component {

    constructor(props) {
        super(props);
        this.state = {
            products: []
        }
        this.editorRef = React.createRef();
    }

    addProduct = (product) => {
        if (this.state.products.indexOf(product.name) === -1) {
            this.setState({ products: [...this.state.products, product ]});
        }
    }

    colorFields = () => {
        ColorInvalidElements(this.editorRef.current);
    }

    render() {
        return <div>
                <div className="text-center m-2">
                    <button className="btn btn-primary" onClick={ this.colorFields }>
                        jQuery
                    </button>
                </div>
                <div ref={ this.editorRef} >
                    <Editor callback={ this.addProduct } />
                </div>
                <h6 className="bg-secondary text-white m-2 p-2">Products</h6>
                    <div className="m-2">
                        {
                            this.state.products.length === 0
                                ? <div className="text-center">No Products</div>
                                : <ProductTable products={ this.state.products } />
                        }
                    </div>
            </div>
    }
}
```

The result is that clicking the jQuery button invokes the colorFields method, which uses the ref to provide the jQuery function with the HTML element it requires. The jQuery function applies borders to the input elements to indicate their validation status, as shown in Figure 16-9. (The difference in the border colors will not be evident in the printed edition of this book, and this is an example that is best run in the browser to see the effect.)

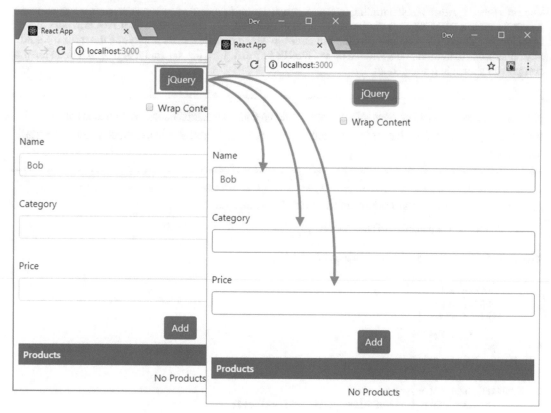

Figure 16-9. *Providing jQuery with an element via a ref*

ACCESSING COMPONENTS WITH REFS

In Listing 16-19, I added a div element around the Editor element. When React renders the content into the DOM, the Editor element won't be part of the HTML document, and adding the div element ensures that jQuery is able to access the application's content.

Refs do work with components, and if I had applied the ref prop to the Editor element, the value of the ref's current property will be assigned to the Editor object that React created when rendering the App component's content.

A ref to a component allows access to that component's state data and methods. It can be tempting to use refs to invoke a child component's methods because it produces a development experience that more closely resembles the way that objects are conventionally used.

Manipulating a component via a ref is bad practice. It produces tightly coupled components that end up working against React. The state data, props, and event features may feel less natural at first, but you will become accustomed to them, and the result is an application that takes full advantage of React and that is easier to write, test, and maintain.

Accessing a Child Component's Content

The `refs` prop is given special handling by React, which means that care must be taken when a component requires a ref to a DOM element rendered by one of its descendants. The simplest approach is to pass the ref object or callback function using a different name, in which case React will pass along the ref as it would any other prop. To demonstrate, I added a file called `FormField.js` to the `src` folder and used it to define the component shown in Listing 16-20.

■ **Note**   Accessing a child component's content should be done with caution because it creates tightly coupled components that are harder to write and test. Where possible, you should use props to communicate between components.

Listing 16-20. The Contents of the FormField.js File in the src Folder

```
import React, { Component } from "react";

export class FormField extends Component {

    constructor(props) {
        super(props);
        this.state = {
            fieldValue: ""
        }
    }

    handleChange = (ev) => {
        this.setState({ fieldValue: ev.target.value});
    }

    render() {
        return <div className="form-group">
            <label>{ this.props.label }</label>
            <input className="form-control" value={ this.state.fieldValue }
                onChange={ this.handleChange } ref={ this.props.fieldRef } />
        </div>
    }
}
```

This component renders a controlled `input` element and uses a prop called `fieldRef` to associate the `ref` received from the parent with the element. In Listing 16-21, I have replaced the content rendered by the App component to use the `FormField` component and provide it with a ref.

Listing 16-21. Replacing the Contents of the App.js File in the src Folder

```
import React, { Component } from "react";
import { FormField } from "./FormField";

export default class App extends Component {
```

```
    constructor(props) {
        super(props);
        this.fieldRef = React.createRef();
    }

    handleClick = () => {
        this.fieldRef.current.focus();
    }

    render() {
        return <div className="m-2">
                <FormField label="Name" fieldRef={ this.fieldRef } />
                <div className="text-center m-2">
                    <button className="btn btn-primary"
                            onClick={ this.handleClick }>
                        Focus
                    </button>
                </div>
            </div>
    }
}
```

The App component creates a ref and passes it to the FormField component using the fieldRef prop, which is then applied to the input element using ref. The result is that clicking the Focus button, rendered by the App component, will focus the input element, rendered by its child, as shown in Figure 16-10.

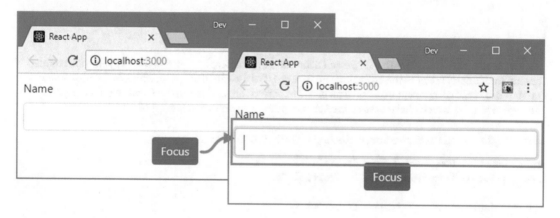

Figure 16-10. *Accessing a child's content*

Using Ref Forwarding

React provides an alternative approach to passing refs to children, known as *ref forwarding*, which allows ref to be used instead of a regular prop. In Listing 16-22, I have used ref forwarding for the FormField component.

Listing 16-22. Using Ref Forwarding in the FormField.js File in the src Folder

```
import React, { Component } from "react";

export const ForwardFormField = React.forwardRef((props, ref) =>
    <FormField { ...props } fieldRef={ ref } />
)

export class FormField extends Component {

    constructor(props) {
        super(props);
        this.state = {
            fieldValue: ""
        }
    }

    handleChange = (ev) => {
        this.setState({ fieldValue: ev.target.value});
    }

    render() {
        return <div className="form-group m-2">
            <label>{ this.props.label }</label>
            <input className="form-control" value={ this.state.fieldValue }
                onChange={ this.handleChange } ref={ this.props.fieldRef } />
        </div>
    }
}
```

The React.forwardRef method is passed a function that receives props and the ref value and renders content. In this case, I receive the ref value and forward it to the fieldRef prop, which is the prop name that the FormField component expects to receive. I exported the result from the forwardRef method as ForwardFormField, which I have used in the App component, as shown in Listing 16-23.

Listing 16-23. Using Ref Forwarding in the App.js File in the src Folder

```
import React, { Component } from "react";
import { ForwardFormField } from "./FormField";

export default class App extends Component {

    constructor(props) {
        super(props);
        this.fieldRef = React.createRef();
    }

    handleClick = () => {
        this.fieldRef.current.focus();
    }
```

```
    render() {
        return <div>
                <ForwardFormField label="Name" ref={ this.fieldRef } />
                <div className="text-center m-2">
                    <button className="btn btn-primary"
                            onClick={ this.handleClick }>
                        Focus
                    </button>
                </div>
            </div>
    }
}
```

This example produces the same effect as shown in Figure 16-10, with the advantage that the App component doesn't require any special knowledge of how the ref is handled inside the child component.

Using Portals

A portal allows a component to render its content into a specific DOM element, instead of being presented as part of its parent's content. This feature lets a component break out of the normal React component model but requires the target element to be created and managed outside of the application, meaning that you can't use portals to render the content into a different component. As a consequence, this feature is useful in a limited range of situations, such as when creating dialogs or model alerts to the user or when integrating React into content created by another framework or library. In Listing 16-24, I have added new HTML elements to the index.html file so that there is a DOM element outside of the content rendered by the example application that I can target with a portal.

Listing 16-24. Adding Elements in the index.html File in the public Folder

```
<!DOCTYPE html>
<html lang="en">

<head>
  <meta charset="utf-8">
  <meta name="viewport" content="width=device-width, initial-scale=1, shrink-to-fit=no">
  <meta name="theme-color" content="#000000">
  <link rel="manifest" href="%PUBLIC_URL%/manifest.json">
  <link rel="shortcut icon" href="%PUBLIC_URL%/favicon.ico">
  <title>React App</title>
</head>

<body>
  <noscript>
    You need to enable JavaScript to run this app.
  </noscript>

  <div class="container">
    <div class="row">
      <div class="col">
        <div id="root"></div>
      </div>
```

```
      <div class="col">
        <div id="portal" class="m-2">
          <h6 class="bg-info text-white text-center p-2">
            This is the portal target
          </h6>
        </div>
      </div>
    </div>
  </div>
</body>
</html>
```

The new elements are assigned to Bootstrap CSS grid classes so that the portal target element is shown alongside the content rendered by the application, as shown in Figure 16-11.

Figure 16-11. *Adding an Element to the HTML Document*

I added a file called `PortalWrapper.js` in the `src` folder and used it to define the component shown in Listing 16-25, which locates the target element in the DOM and uses it to create a portal.

Listing 16-25. The Contents of the PortalWrapper.js File in the src Folder

```
import React, { Component } from "react";
import ReactDOM from "react-dom";

export class PortalWrapper extends Component {

    constructor(props) {
        super(props);
        this.portalElement = document.getElementById("portal");
    }
```

```
    render() {
        return ReactDOM.createPortal(
            <div className="border p-3">{ this.props.children }</div>
        , this.portalElement);
    }
}
```

The PortalWrapper component is defined using the props.children property to create a container but returns its content using the ReactDOM.createPortal method, whose arguments are the content to render and the DOM target element. In this example, I use the DOM API's getElementById method to locate the target element added to the HTML file in Listing 16-24. In Listing 16-26, I have used the portal in the App component.

USING REFS FOR PORTALS

You cannot use a portal to render content to an element using a ref. Portals are used during the rendering process, and refs are not assigned elements until rendering is complete, which means that you won't be able to access an element via a ref early enough in the lifecycle for the ReactDOM. createPortal method. Use contexts, as described in Chapter 14, if you need coordination between components in different parts of the application or use one of the packages described in Part 3.

Listing 16-26. Using a Portal in the App.js File in the src Folder

```
import React, { Component } from "react";
import { ForwardFormField } from "./FormField";
import { PortalWrapper } from "./PortalWrapper";

export default class App extends Component {

    constructor(props) {
        super(props);
        this.fieldRef = React.createRef();
        this.portalFieldRef = React.createRef();
    }

    focusLocal = () => {
        this.fieldRef.current.focus();
    }

    focusPortal = () => {
        this.portalFieldRef.current.focus();
    }

    render() {
        return <div>
                <PortalWrapper>
                    <ForwardFormField label="Name" ref={ this.portalFieldRef } />
                </PortalWrapper>
```

```
            <ForwardFormField label="Name" ref={ this.fieldRef } />
            <div className="text-center m-2">
                <button className="btn btn-primary m-1"
                        onClick={ this.focusLocal }>
                    Focus Local
                </button>
                <button className="btn btn-primary m-1"
                        onClick={ this.focusPortal }>
                    Focus Portal
                </button>
            </div>
        </div>
    }
}
```

The PortalWrapper element is used to apply the new component as a container for a
ForwardFormField. The content displayed by the portal is treated as though it is part of the App components
content, such that events will bubble up as normal and refs can be assigned, even though the content of
the portal is being rendered outside the application. The App component is unaware that a portal is being
used, and clicking the Focus Local and Focus Portal buttons uses the same ref technique to focus the input
element presented by each ForwardFormField component, as shown in Figure 16-12.

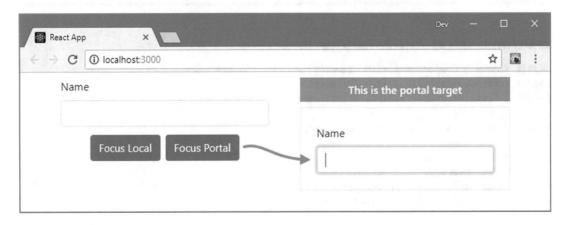

Figure 16-12. *Using a portal*

Summary

In this chapter, I described the React features for working directly with the DOM. I explained how refs
can provide access to content rendered by a component and how this makes uncontrolled form elements
possible. I also demonstrated a portal, which allows content to be rendered outside of the application's
component hierarchy. These features can be invaluable but should be used sparingly because they
undermine the normal React development model and result in closely coupled components. In the next
chapter, I show you how to perform unit testing on React components.

CHAPTER 17

■ ■ ■

Unit Testing

In this chapter, I show you how to test React components. I introduce a package that makes testing easier and demonstrate how it can be used to test components in isolation and test their interactions with their children. Table 17-1 puts unit testing in context.

Table 17-1. *Putting Unit Testing in Context*

Question	Answer
What is it?	React components require special support for testing so that their interactions with other parts of the application can be isolated and inspected.
Why is it useful?	Isolated unit tests are able to assess the basic logic provided by a component without being influenced by the interactions with the rest of the application.
How is it used?	Projects created with `create-react-app` are configured with basic test tools that are supplemented with packages that simplify the process of working with components.
Are there any pitfalls or limitations?	Effective unit testing can be difficult, and it can take time and effort to get to the point where unit tests are easily written and run and you are sure that you have isolated the correct part of the application for testing.
Are there any alternatives?	Unit testing is not a requirement and is not adopted in all projects.

DECIDING WHETHER TO UNIT TEST

Unit testing is a contentious topic. This chapter assumes you do want to do unit testing and shows you how to set up the tools and apply them to a React application. It isn't an introduction to unit testing, and I make no effort to persuade skeptical readers that unit testing is worthwhile. If would like an introduction to unit testing, then there is a good article here: `https://en.wikipedia.org/wiki/Unit_testing`.

I like unit testing, and I use it in my own projects—but not all of them and not as consistently as you might expect. I tend to focus on writing unit tests for features and functions that I know will be hard to write and that are likely to be the source of bugs in deployment. In these situations, unit testing helps structure my thoughts about how to best implement what I need. I find that just thinking about what I need to test helps produce ideas about potential problems, and that's before I start dealing with actual bugs and defects.

© Adam Freeman 2019
A. Freeman, *Pro React 16*, https://doi.org/10.1007/978-1-4842-4451-7_17

That said, unit testing is a tool and not a religion, and only you know how much testing you require. If you don't find unit testing useful or if you have a different methodology that suits you better, then don't feel you need to unit test just because it is fashionable. (However, if you don't have a better methodology and you are not testing at all, then you are probably letting users find your bugs, which is rarely ideal.)

Table 17-2 summarizes the chapter.

Table 17-2. *Chapter Summary*

Problem	Solution	Listing
Perform unit tests on React components	Use Jest (or one of the other test frameworks available) along with Enzyme to create the tests	9–11
Isolate a component for testing	Test using shallow rendering	12
Test a component along with its descendants	Test using full rendering	13
Test a component's behavior	Test using the Enzyme features for working with props, state, methods, and events	14–17

Preparing for This Chapter

For this chapter, I am going to use a new project. Open a new command prompt, navigate to a convenient location, and run the command shown in Listing 17-1 to create a project called testapp.

■ **Tip** You can download the example project for this chapter—and for all the other chapters in this book—from https://github.com/Apress/pro-react-16.

Listing 17-1. Creating the Example Project

```
npx create-react-app testapp
```

Run the commands shown in Listing 17-2 to navigate to the testapp folder to add the Bootstrap package.

Listing 17-2. Adding the Bootstrap CSS Framework

```
cd testapp
npm install bootstrap@4.1.2
```

To include the Bootstrap CSS stylesheet in the application, add the statement shown in Listing 17-3 to the `index.js` file, which can be found in the `testapp/src` folder.

Listing 17-3. Including Bootstrap in the index.js File in the src Folder

```
import React from 'react';
import ReactDOM from 'react-dom';
import './index.css';
import App from './App';
import * as serviceWorker from './serviceWorker';
import 'bootstrap/dist/css/bootstrap.css';

ReactDOM.render(<App />, document.getElementById('root'));

// If you want your app to work offline and load faster, you can change
// unregister() to register() below. Note this comes with some pitfalls.
// Learn more about service workers: http://bit.ly/CRA-PWA
serviceWorker.unregister();
```

The `create-react-app` tool creates projects that contain basic test tools, but there are some useful additions that make testing easier. Run the commands shown in Listing 17-4 in the `testapp` folder to add the testing packages to the project.

Listing 17-4. Adding Packages to the Example Project

```
npm install --save-dev enzyme@3.8.0
npm install --save-dev enzyme-adapter-react-16@1.7.1
```

Table 17-3 describes the packages that have been added to the project.

Table 17-3. *The Unit Testing Packages*

Name	Description
enzyme	Enzyme is a test package created by Airbnb that makes it easy to test components by exploring the content they render and examining their props and state.
enzyme-adapter-react-16	Enzyme requires an adapter for the specific version of React being used. This package is for the version of React used throughout this book.

Creating Components

I need some simple components to demonstrate how React applications can be unit tested. I added a file called `Result.js` to the `src` folder and used it to define the component shown in Listing 17-5.

Listing 17-5. The Contents of the Result.js File in the src Folder

```
import React from "react";

export const Result = (props) => {
    return <div className="bg-light text-dark border border-dark p-2 ">
        { props.result || 0 }
    </div>
}
```

Result is a simple functional component that displays the result of a calculation, received through its result prop. Next, I added a file called ValueInput.js to the src folder and used it to define the component shown in Listing 17-6.

Listing 17-6. The Contents of the ValueInput.js File in the src Folder

```
import React, { Component } from "react";

export class ValueInput extends Component {

    constructor(props) {
        super(props);
        this.state = {
            fieldValue: 0
        }
    }

    handleChange = (ev) => {
        this.setState({ fieldValue: ev.target.value },
            () => this.props.changeCallback(this.props.id, this.state.fieldValue));
    }

    render() {
        return <div className="form-group p-2">
            <label>Value #{this.props.id}</label>
            <input className="form-control"
                value={ this.state.fieldValue}
                onChange={ this.handleChange } />
        </div>
    }
}
```

This is a stateful component that renders an input element and invokes a callback function when there is a change. Listing 17-7 shows the changes I made to the App component to remove the placeholder content and use the new components.

Listing 17-7. Completing the Example Application in the App.js File in the src Folder

```
import React, { Component } from "react";
import { ValueInput } from "./ValueInput";
import { Result } from "./Result";

export default class App extends Component {

    constructor(props) {
        super(props);
        this.state = {
            title: this.props.title || "Simple Addition" ,
            fieldValues: [],
            total: 0
        }
    }

    updateFieldValue = (id, value) => {
        this.setState(state => {
            state.fieldValues[id] = Number(value);
            return state;
        });
    }

    updateTotal = () => {
        this.setState(state => ({
            total: state.fieldValues.reduce((total, val) => total += val, 0)
        }))
    }

    render() {
        return <div className="m-2">
                    <h5 className="bg-primary text-white text-center p-2">
                        { this.state.title }
                    </h5>
                    <Result result={ this.state.total } />
                    <ValueInput id="1" changeCallback={ this.updateFieldValue } />
                    <ValueInput id="2" changeCallback={ this.updateFieldValue } />
                    <ValueInput id="3" changeCallback={ this.updateFieldValue } />
                    <div className="text-center">
                    <button className="btn btn-primary" onClick={ this.updateTotal}>
                        Total
                    </button>
                    </div>
            </div>
    }
}
```

App creates three ValueInput components and configures them so that the values the user enters are stored in the fieldValues state array. A button is configured so that a click event invokes the updateTotal method, which sums the values from the ValueInput components and updates a state data value that is displayed by the Result component.

Running the Example Application

Use the command prompt to navigate to the testapp folder and run the command shown in Listing 17-8 to start the React developer tools.

Listing 17-8. Starting the Development Tools

```
npm start
```

A new browser window will open, and you will see the example application, as shown in Figure 17-1. Enter numeric values into the fields, and click the Total button to display a result.

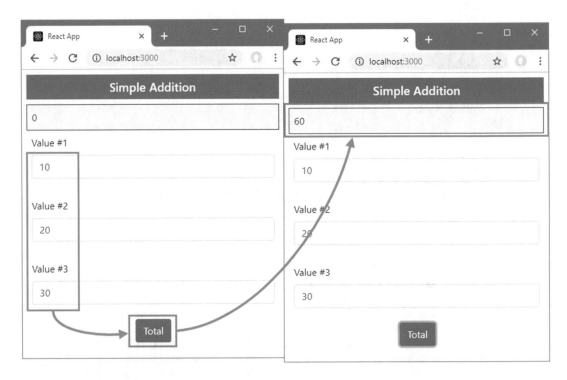

Figure 17-1. *Running the example application*

Running the Placeholder Unit Test

Projects created with create-react-app contain the Jest test runner, which is a tool that executes unit tests and reports the results. As part of the project setup process, a file called App.test.js is created, which contains the following code:

```
import React from 'react';
import ReactDOM from 'react-dom';
import App from './App';
```

```
it('renders without crashing', () => {
  const div = document.createElement('div');
  ReactDOM.render(<App />, div);
  ReactDOM.unmountComponentAtNode(div);
});
```

This is a basic unit test, which is encapsulated in the it function. The first argument to the function is a description of the test. The second argument is the test itself, which is a function that performs some work. In this case, the unit test renders the App component into a div element and then unmounts it. Open a new command prompt, navigate to the testapp folder, and run the command shown in Listing 17-9 to perform the unit test. (The test tools are designed so that you can have them running alongside the development tools.)

Listing 17-9. Running a Unit Test

```
npm run test
```

This command locates all the tests defined in the project and executes them. There is only one test at the moment, which produces the following results:

```
...
PASS  src/App.test.js
  √ renders without crashing (24ms)

Test Suites: 1 passed, 1 total
Tests:       1 passed, 1 total
Snapshots:   0 total
Time:        2.077s
Ran all test suites related to changed files.

Watch Usage
 › Press a to run all tests.
 › Press f to run only failed tests.
 › Press p to filter by a filename regex pattern.
 › Press t to filter by a test name regex pattern.
 › Press q to quit watch mode.
 › Press Enter to trigger a test run.
...
```

After the tests have been run, the testing tool enters watch mode. When a file changes, tests are located and executed, and the results displayed again. To see what happens when a unit test fails, add the statement shown in Listing 17-10 to the render method of the App component.

Listing 17-10. Making a Test Fail in the App.js File in the src Folder

```
...
render() {
    throw new Error("something went wrong");
    return <div className="m-2">
            <h5 className="bg-primary text-white text-center p-2">
                { this.state.title }
            </h5>
```

497

```
                    <Result result={ this.state.total } />
                    <ValueInput id="1" changeCallback={ this.updateFieldValue } />
                    <ValueInput id="2" changeCallback={ this.updateFieldValue } />
                    <ValueInput id="3" changeCallback={ this.updateFieldValue } />
                    <div className="text-center">
                    <button className="btn btn-primary" onClick={ this.updateTotal}>
                        Total
                    </button>
                    </div>
            </div>
        </div>
}
...
```

An error will be thrown when the render method is invoked, which is the behavior that the unit test is looking out for. When you save the change, the unit test will be performed again, but this time it will fail, giving you details of the problem that was detected.

```
...
renders without crashing

  something went wrong

    27 |
    28 |        render() {
  > 29 |            throw new Error("something went wrong");
       |                  ^
    30 |            return <div className="m-2">
    31 |                        <h5 className="bg-primary text-white text-center p-2">
    32 |                            Simple Addition
...
```

The error that is thrown by the component bubbles up to the it function in the unit test and is treated as a test failure. To restore the application to its working state, comment out the throw statement from the App component, as shown in Listing 17-11.

Listing 17-11. Removing the throw Statement in the App.js File in the src Folder

```
...
render() {
    //throw new Error("something went wrong");
    return <div className="m-2">
                <h5 className="bg-primary text-white text-center p-2">
                    { this.state.title }
                </h5>
                <Result result={ this.state.total } />
                <ValueInput id="1" changeCallback={ this.updateFieldValue } />
                <ValueInput id="2" changeCallback={ this.updateFieldValue } />
                <ValueInput id="3" changeCallback={ this.updateFieldValue } />
                <div className="text-center">
```

```
            <button className="btn btn-primary" onClick={ this.updateTotal}>
                Total
            </button>
        </div>
    </div>
}
...
```

When you save the change, the test will run again and will pass this time.

Testing a Component Using Shallow Rendering

Shallow rendering isolates a component from its children, allowing it to be tested on its own. It is an effective technique for testing the basic functions of a component without the effects caused by interaction with its content. To test the App component using shallow rendering, I added a file called appContent.test.js to the src folder and added the code shown in Listing 17-12.

■ **Tip** Jest will find tests in files whose name ends with test.js or spec.js or any file in a folder named __tests__ (two underscores before and after tests).

Listing 17-12. The Contents of the appContent.test.js File in the src Folder

```
import React from "react";
import Adapter from 'enzyme-adapter-react-16';
import Enzyme, { shallow } from "enzyme";
import App from "./App";
import { ValueInput } from "./ValueInput";

Enzyme.configure({ adapter: new Adapter() });

it("Renders three ValueInputs", () => {
    const wrapper = shallow(<App />);
    const valCount = wrapper.find(ValueInput).length;
    expect(valCount).toBe(3)
});
```

This is the first real unit test in this chapter, so I will explain each part and show you how they fit together.

The first statement configures the Enzyme package and applies the adapter that allows Enzyme to work with the correct version of React.

```
...
Enzyme.configure({ adapter: new Adapter() });
...
```

The Enzyme.configure method is passed a configuration object whose adapter property is assigned the imported contents of the adapter package. If you need to test a different version of React, you can see the list of adapters available at https://airbnb.io/enzyme.

The next step is the definition of the unit test. The it method doesn't need to be imported because it is defined globally by the Jest test package.

```
...
it("Renders three ValueInputs", () => {
...
```

The first argument should be a meaningful description of what the test aims to establish. In this case, the test checks that App renders three ValueInput components.

The next statement sets up the component, which is done using the shallow function imported from the enzyme package.

```
...
const wrapper = shallow(<App />);
...
```

The shallow function accepts the component element. A component is instantiated and is put through the lifecycle described in Chapter 13, and its contents are rendered. But, since this is shallow rendering, the child components are not used to rendered, leaving their elements in place in the output from the App component. That means that the App component's props and state data are used when rendering the content, but the child components are not processed, producing a result like this:

```
...
<div className="m-2">
    <h5 className="bg-primary text-white text-center p-2">
        Simple Addition
    </h5>
    <Result result={0} />
    <ValueInput id="1" changeCallback={[Function]} />
    <ValueInput id="2" changeCallback={[Function]} />
    <ValueInput id="3" changeCallback={[Function]} />
    <div className="text-center">
        <button className="btn btn-primary" onClick={[Function]}>
            Total
        </button>
    </div>
</div>
...
```

The output is presented in a wrapper object that can be inspected for testing. The Enzyme package provides a set of methods that can be used to inspect the content rendered from the DOM, modeled on the API provided by the popular jQuery DOM manipulation package. The most useful methods are described in Table 17-4, and the full set of features is described at https://airbnb.io/enzyme.

Table 17-4. *Useful Enzyme Methods for Inspecting Component Content*

Name	Description
find(selector)	This method finds all elements matched by the CSS selector, which will match element types, attributes, and classes.
findWhere(predicate)	This method finds all elements that are matched by the specified predicate.
first(selector)	Returns the first element that is matched by the selector. If the selector is omitted, then the first element of any type will be returned.
children()	Creates a new selection containing the children of the current element.
hasClass(class)	This method returns true if an element is a member of a specified class.
text()	This method returns the text content from an element.
html()	This method returns the deep rendered content from the component so that all of the descendant components are processed.
debug()	This method returns the shallow rendered content from the component.

These methods can be used to navigate through the content rendered by a component and to inspect the contents. The test in Listing 17-12 uses the find selector to select all the ValueInput elements rendered by the App component and uses the length property on the result to determine how many elements have been found.

```
...
const valCount = wrapper.find(ValueInput).length;
...
```

The final step in the test is to compare the result with the expected outcome, which is done using the global expect function provided by Jest.

```
...
expect(valCount).toBe(3)
...
```

The result of a test is passed to the expect function, and then a matcher method is invoked on the result. Jest supports an extensive array of matches, described at https://jestjs.io/docs/en/expect, and the most useful are shown in Table 17-5.

Table 17-5. *Useful Expect Matchers*

Name	Description
toBe(value)	This method asserts that a result is the same as the specified value (but need not be the same object).
toEqual(object)	This method asserts that a result is the same object as the specified value.
toMatch(regexp)	This method asserts that a result matches the specified regular expression.
toBeDefined()	This method asserts that the result has been defined.
toBeUndefined()	This method asserts that the result has not been defined.
toBeNull()	This method asserts that the result is null.
toBeTruthy()	This method asserts that the result is truthy.
toBeFalsy()	This method asserts that the result is falsy.
toContain(substring)	This method asserts that the result contains the specified substring.
toBeLessThan(value)	This method asserts that the result is less than the specified value.
toBeGreaterThan(value)	This method asserts that the result is more than the specified value.

Jest keeps track of which matches fail and reports the outcome when all the tests in the project have been run. The matcher in Listing 17-12 checks that there are three ValueInput components in the content rendered by App.

Jest runs the test in Listing 17-12 as soon as the file is saved, which produces the following results:

```
...
PASS  src/App.test.js
 PASS  src/App.shallow.test.js

Test Suites: 2 passed, 2 total
Tests:       2 passed, 2 total
Snapshots:   0 total
Time:        2.672s
Ran all test suites.

Watch Usage: Press w to show more.
...
```

There are now two tests in the project, and both of them are run. You can leave the tests to run automatically, or you can run one or more tests on demand using the options that are shown when the W key is pressed.

Testing a Component with Full Rendering

Full rendering processes all the descendent components. The descendent component elements are left in the rendered content, which means that the App component will produce the following content when it is fully rendered:

```
...
<App>
<div className="m-2">
  <h5 className="bg-primary text-white text-center p-2">
    Simple Addition
  </h5>
  <Result result={0}>
    <div className="bg-light text-dark border border-dark p-2 ">0</div>
  </Result>
  <ValueInput id="1" changeCallback={[Function]}>
    <div className="form-group p-2">
      <label>Value #1</label>
      <input className="form-control" value={0} onChange={[Function]} />
    </div>
  </ValueInput>
  <ValueInput id="2" changeCallback={[Function]}>
    <div className="form-group p-2">
      <label>Value #2</label>
      <input className="form-control" value={0} onChange={[Function]} />
    </div>
  </ValueInput>
  <ValueInput id="3" changeCallback={[Function]}>
    <div className="form-group p-2">
      <label>Value #3</label>
      <input className="form-control" value={0} onChange={[Function]} />
    </div>
  </ValueInput>
  <div className="text-center">
    <button className="btn btn-primary" onClick={[Function]}>Total</button>
  </div>
</div>
</App>
...
```

Full rendering is performed with the mount method, as shown in Listing 17-13.

Listing 17-13. Fully Rendering a Component in the appContent.test.js File in the src Folder

```
import React from "react";
import Adapter from 'enzyme-adapter-react-16';
import Enzyme, { shallow, mount } from "enzyme";
import App from "./App";
import { ValueInput } from "./ValueInput";

Enzyme.configure({ adapter: new Adapter() });
```

```
it("Renders three ValueInputs", () => {
    const wrapper = shallow(<App />);
    const valCount = wrapper.find(ValueInput).length;
    expect(valCount).toBe(3)
});

it("Fully renders three inputs", () => {
    const wrapper = mount(<App title="tester" />);
    const count = wrapper.find("input.form-control").length
    expect(count).toBe(3);
});

it("Shallow renders zero inputs", () => {
    const wrapper = shallow(<App />);
    const count = wrapper.find("input.form-control").length
    expect(count).toBe(0);
})
```

The first new test uses the Enzyme mount function to fully render App and its descendants. The wrapper returned by mount supports the methods described in Table 17-5, and the full set of features is described at https://airbnb.io/enzyme/docs/api/mount.html. I use the find method to locate input elements that have been assigned to the form-control class and use expect to make sure that there are three of them. The second new test locates the same elements but does so using shallow rendering and checks that there are no input elements in the content.

When the changes to the file are saved, the tests will be run and produce the following results:

```
...
PASS    src/App.test.js
PASS    src/appContent.test.js

Test Suites: 2 passed, 2 total
Tests:       4 passed, 4 total
Snapshots:   0 total
Time:        3.109s
Ran all test suites.

Watch Usage: Press w to show more.
...
```

Testing with Props, State, Methods, and Events

The content that a component renders can change in response to user input or updates in the application state. To help test the behavior of a component, Enzyme provides the methods described in Table 17-6.

Table 17-6. *Enzyme Methods for Testing Behavior*

Name	Description
instance()	This method returns the component object so that its methods can be invoked.
prop(key)	This method returns the value of the specified prop.
props()	This method returns all of the component's props.
setProps(props)	This method is used to specify new props, which are merged with the component's existing props before it is updated.
state(key)	This method is used to get a specified state value. If no value is specified, then all of the component's state data is returned.
setState(state)	This method changes the component's state data and then re-renders the component.
simulate(event, args)	This method dispatches an event to the component.
update()	This method forces the component to re-render its content.

The simplest test of behavior is to ensure that a component reflects its props. I created a file called appBehavior.test.js in the src folder and used it to define the test shown in Listing 17-14.

Listing 17-14. Testing a Prop in the appBehavior.test.js File in the src Folder

```
import React from "react";
import Adapter from 'enzyme-adapter-react-16';
import Enzyme, { shallow } from "enzyme";
import App from "./App";

Enzyme.configure({ adapter: new Adapter() });

it("uses title prop", () => {

    const titleVal = "test title"
    const wrapper = shallow(<App title={ titleVal } />);

    const firstTitle = wrapper.find("h5").text();
    const stateValue = wrapper.state("title");

    expect(firstTitle).toBe(titleVal);
    expect(stateValue).toBe(titleVal);
});
```

The App component is configured with a title prop when it is passed to the shallow method. The test checks that the prop is used to override the default value by locating the h5 element and getting its text content and also by reading the value of the title state property. The test passes only if both the contents of the h5 element and the state property are the same as the value of the title prop.

505

Testing the Effect of Methods

The `instance` method is used to obtain the component object, which can then be used to invoke its methods. In Listing 17-15, I have defined a test that invokes the `updateField` and `updateTotal` methods and checks the effect on the component's state data.

Listing 17-15. Invoking Methods in the appBehavior.test.js File in the src Folder

```
import React from "react";
import Adapter from 'enzyme-adapter-react-16';
import Enzyme, { shallow } from "enzyme";
import App from "./App";

Enzyme.configure({ adapter: new Adapter() });

it("uses title prop", () => {

    const titleVal = "test title"
    const wrapper = shallow(<App title={ titleVal } />);

    const firstTitle = wrapper.find("h5").text();
    const stateValue = wrapper.state("title");

    expect(firstTitle).toBe(titleVal);
    expect(stateValue).toBe(titleVal);
});

it("updates state data", () => {
    const wrapper = shallow(<App />);
    const values = [10, 20, 30];

    values.forEach((val, index) =>
        wrapper.instance().updateFieldValue(index + 1, val));
    wrapper.instance().updateTotal();

    expect(wrapper.state("total"))
        .toBe(values.reduce((total, val) => total + val), 0);
});
```

The new test shallow renders an App component and then calls the `updateFieldValue` method with an array of values before then invoking the `updateTotal` method. The `state` method is used to get the value of the total `state` property, which is compared to the sum of the values passed to the `updateFieldValue` method.

Testing the Effects of an Event

The `simulate` method is used to send an event to the component's event handlers. Care must be taken with this type of test because it is easy to end up testing React's ability to dispatch events rather than the component's ability to handle them. In most cases, it is more useful to invoke the methods that will be executed in response to an event. Listing 17-16 locates the `button` element rendered by the App component and triggers a `click` event in order to ensure that it leads to the total being calculated.

Listing 17-16. Simulating an Event in the appBehavior.test.js File in the src Folder

```
import React from "react";
import Adapter from 'enzyme-adapter-react-16';
import Enzyme, { shallow } from "enzyme";
import App from "./App";

Enzyme.configure({ adapter: new Adapter() });

it("uses title prop", () => {

    const titleVal = "test title"
    const wrapper = shallow(<App title={ titleVal } />);

    const firstTitle = wrapper.find("h5").text();
    const stateValue = wrapper.state("title");

    expect(firstTitle).toBe(titleVal);
    expect(stateValue).toBe(titleVal);
});

it("updates state data", () => {
    const wrapper = shallow(<App />);
    const values = [10, 20, 30];

    values.forEach((val, index) =>
        wrapper.instance().updateFieldValue(index + 1, val));
    wrapper.instance().updateTotal();

    expect(wrapper.state("total"))
        .toBe(values.reduce((total, val) => total + val), 0);
})

it("updates total when button is clicked", () => {
    const wrapper = shallow(<App />);
    const button = wrapper.find("button").first();

    const values = [10, 20, 30];
    values.forEach((val, index) =>
        wrapper.instance().updateFieldValue(index + 1, val));

    button.simulate("click")

    expect(wrapper.state("total"))
        .toBe(values.reduce((total, val) => total + val), 0);
})
```

The new test simulates the click event, the handler for which invokes the component's updateTotal method. To ensure that the event has been handled, the value of the total state data property is read.

Testing the Interaction Between Components

The ability to navigate the content rendered by a component can be combined with the methods described in Table 17-6 to test the interaction between components, as shown in Listing 17-17.

Listing 17-17. Testing Component Interaction in the appBehavior.test.js File in the src Folder

```
import React from "react";
import Adapter from 'enzyme-adapter-react-16';
import Enzyme, { shallow, mount } from "enzyme";
import App from "./App";
import { ValueInput } from "./ValueInput";

Enzyme.configure({ adapter: new Adapter() });

it("uses title prop", () => {

    const titleVal = "test title"
    const wrapper = shallow(<App title={ titleVal } />);

    const firstTitle = wrapper.find("h5").text();
    const stateValue = wrapper.state("title");

    expect(firstTitle).toBe(titleVal);
    expect(stateValue).toBe(titleVal);
});

it("updates state data", () => {
    const wrapper = shallow(<App />);
    const values = [10, 20, 30];

    values.forEach((val, index) =>
        wrapper.instance().updateFieldValue(index + 1, val));
    wrapper.instance().updateTotal();

    expect(wrapper.state("total"))
        .toBe(values.reduce((total, val) => total + val), 0);
})

it("updates total when button is clicked", () => {
    const wrapper = shallow(<App />);
    const button = wrapper.find("button").first();

    const values = [10, 20, 30];
    values.forEach((val, index) =>
        wrapper.instance().updateFieldValue(index + 1, val));

    button.simulate("click")

    expect(wrapper.state("total"))
        .toBe(values.reduce((total, val) => total + val), 0);
})
```

```
it("child function prop updates state", () => {
    const wrapper = mount(<App />);
    const valInput = wrapper.find(ValueInput).first();
    const inputElem = valInput.find("input").first();

    inputElem.simulate("change", { target: { value: "100"}});
    wrapper.instance().updateTotal();

    expect(valInput.state("fieldValue")).toBe("100");
    expect(wrapper.state("total")).toBe(100);
})
```

The new test locates the input element rendered by the first ValueInput and triggers its change event, supplying an argument that will provide the component's handler with the values it needs. The instance method is used to invoke the updateTotal method of the App component, and the state method is used to check that the state data for both the App and ValueInput components has been updated correctly.

Summary

In this chapter, I showed you how to perform unit tests on React components. I showed you how to run tests using Jest and how to perform those tests with shallow and full rendering, provided by the Enzyme package. I explained how to examine the content rendered by a component, how to invoke its methods, how to explore its state, and how to manage its props. Together, these features allow a component to be tested in isolation and in combination with its children. In the next part of the book, I describe how to supplement the core React features to create complete web applications.

PART III

Creating Complete Applications

CHAPTER 18

■ ■ ■

Creating Complete Applications

React provides an excellent set of features for presenting HTML content to the user and relies on third-party packages to provide the supporting functionality required to develop complete web applications. There are countless packages available for use with React, and in this part of the book, I introduce those that are most widely used and most likely to be needed by readers of this book. These packages are all open-source and freely available, and there are paid-for support options in some cases.

In this chapter, I build an example application using only the features described in Part 2 of this book. In the chapters that follow, I introduce the third-party packages and demonstrate the features they provide and explain the problems they solve. Table 18-1 provides a brief overview of the packages that are covered in this part of the book.

Table 18-1. *The Packages Described in This Part of the Book*

Name	Description
Redux	Redux provides a data store that manages data outside of an application's components. I use this package in Chapters 19 and 20.
React Redux	React Redux connects React components through its props to a Redux data store, allowing direct access to data without relying on prop threading. I use this package in Chapters 19 and 20.
React Router	React Router provides URL routing for React applications, allowing the components displayed to the user to be selected based on the browser's URL. I use this package in Chapters 21 and 22.
Axios	Axios provides a consistent API for making asynchronous HTTP requests. I use this package in Chapter 23 to consume a RESTful web service and in Chapter 25 to consume a GraphQL service.
Apollo Boost	Apollo is a client for consuming GraphQL services, which are more flexible than traditional RESTful web services. I use the Boost edition of this package, which provides sensible defaults for React applications, in Chapter 25 to consume a GraphQL service.
React Apollo	React Apollo connects React components to GraphQL queries and mutations, allowing a GraphQL service to be consumed through props.

© Adam Freeman 2019
A. Freeman, *Pro React 16*, https://doi.org/10.1007/978-1-4842-4451-7_18

There are credible alternatives for each of the packages I have selected, and I make suggestions in each chapter in case you can't get along with the packages that are covered. Please e-mail me at adam@adam-freeman.com if there is a package that interests you that I have not covered in this part of the book. Although I make no promises, I will try to include commonly requested packages in the next edition of this book or, if there is sufficient demand, in updates posted to this book's GitHub repository.

Creating the Project

Open a new command prompt, navigate to a convenient location, and run the command shown in Listing 18-1.

■ **Tip** You can download the example project for this chapter—and for all the other chapters in this book—from https://github.com/Apress/pro-react-16.

Listing 18-1. Creating the Example Project

```
npx create-react-app productapp
```

Run the commands shown in Listing 18-2 to navigate to the productapp folder to add the Bootstrap package.

Listing 18-2. Adding the Bootstrap CSS Framework

```
cd productapp
npm install bootstrap@4.1.2
```

To include the Bootstrap CSS stylesheet in the application, add the statement shown in Listing 18-3 to the index.js file, which can be found in the productapp/src folder.

Listing 18-3. Including Bootstrap in the index.js File in the src Folder

```
import React from 'react';
import ReactDOM from 'react-dom';
import './index.css';
import App from './App';
import * as serviceWorker from './serviceWorker';
import 'bootstrap/dist/css/bootstrap.css';

ReactDOM.render(<App />, document.getElementById('root'));

// If you want your app to work offline and load faster, you can change
// unregister() to register() below. Note this comes with some pitfalls.
// Learn more about service workers: http://bit.ly/CRA-PWA
serviceWorker.unregister();
```

Starting the Development Tools

Using the command prompt, run the command shown in Listing 18-4 in the `productapp` folder to start the development tools.

Listing 18-4. Starting the Development Tools

```
npm start
```

Once the initial preparation for the project is complete, a new browser window will open and display the URL `http://localhost:3000`, which shows the placeholder content in Figure 18-1.

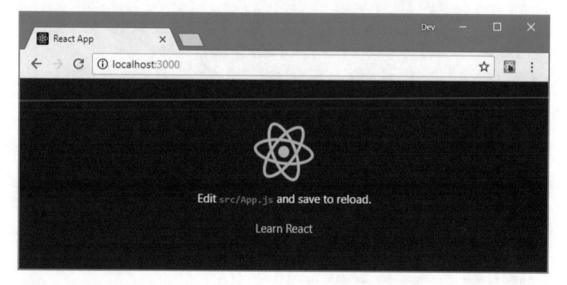

Figure 18-1. *Running the example application*

Creating the Example Application

The application in this chapter is simple but representative of a typical project built using only the features provided by React. The application presents the user with create, read, update, and delete (CRUD) features for two types of data, products and suppliers, and the user can toggle between the data that is being managed. Figure 18-2 shows how the application will appear once the components defined in the following sections have been created.

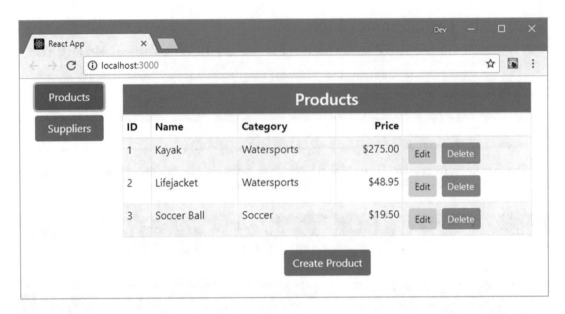

Figure 18-2. *The example application*

Example applications are contrived, of course, and my goal, in this case, is to show that the core React features are powerful but are not sufficient on their own to create complex web applications. Once the application has been defined, I highlight the problems that it contains, each of which I address using the tools and packages described in the following chapters.

Creating the Product Features

To get started with the application functionality, I added a file called ProductTableRow.js to the src folder and used it to define the component shown in Listing 18-5.

Listing 18-5. The Contents of the ProductTableRow.js File in the src Folder

```
import React, { Component } from "react";

export class ProductTableRow extends Component {

    render() {
        let p = this.props.product;
        return <tr>
            <td>{ p.id }</td>
            <td>{ p.name }</td>
            <td>{ p.category}</td>
            <td className="text-right">${ Number(p.price).toFixed(2) }</td>
            <td>
                <button className="btn btn-sm btn-warning m-1"
                    onClick={ () => this.props.editCallback(p) }>
                        Edit
                </button>
```

```
                <button className="btn btn-sm btn-danger m-1"
                    onClick={ () => this.props.deleteCallback(p) }>
                        Delete
                </button>
            </td>
        </tr>
    }
}
```

This component renders a single row in a table, with columns for id, name, category, and price properties, which are obtained from a prop object called product. There is a further column that displays Edit and Delete buttons that invoke function props named editCallback and deleteCallback, passing the product prop as an argument.

Creating the Product Table

I added a file called ProductTable.js to the src folder and used it to define the component shown in Listing 18-6.

Listing 18-6. The Contents of the ProductTable.js File in the src Folder

```
import React, { Component } from "react";
import { ProductTableRow } from "./ProductTableRow";

export class ProductTable extends Component {

    render() {
        return <table className="table table-sm table-striped table-bordered">
                <thead>
                    <tr>
                        <th colSpan="5"
                                className="bg-primary text-white text-center h4 p-2">
                            Products
                        </th>
                    </tr>
                    <tr>
                        <th>ID</th><th>Name</th><th>Category</th>
                        <th className="text-right">Price</th>
                        <th></th>
                    </tr>
                </thead>
                <tbody>
                    {
                        this.props.products.map(p =>
                            <ProductTableRow product={ p }
                                key={ p.id }
                                editCallback={ this.props.editCallback }
                                deleteCallback={ this.props.deleteCallback } />)
                    }
                </tbody>
            </table>
    }
}
```

517

This component renders a table, whose body is populated with `ProductTableRow` components for each object in an array prop named `products`. This component passes on the `deleteCallback` and `editCallback` function props to the `ProductTableRow` instances.

Creating the Product Editor

To allow the user to edit a product or provide values for a new product, I added a file called `ProductEditor.js` in the `src` folder and added the code shown in Listing 18-7.

Listing 18-7. The Contents of the ProductEditor.js File in the src Folder

```
import React, { Component } from "react";

export class ProductEditor extends Component {

    constructor(props) {
        super(props);
        this.state = {
            formData: {
                id: props.product.id || "",
                name: props.product.name || "",
                category: props.product.category || "",
                price: props.product.price || ""
            }
        }
    }

    handleChange = (ev) => {
        ev.persist();
        this.setState(state => state.formData[ev.target.name] =  ev.target.value);
    }

    handleClick = () => {
        this.props.saveCallback(this.state.formData);
    }

    render() {
        return <div className="m-2">
            <div className="form-group">
                <label>ID</label>
                <input className="form-control" name="id"
                    disabled
                    value={ this.state.formData.id }
                    onChange={ this.handleChange } />
            </div>
            <div className="form-group">
                <label>Name</label>
                <input className="form-control" name="name"
                    value={ this.state.formData.name }
                    onChange={ this.handleChange } />
            </div>
```

```
            <div className="form-group">
                <label>Category</label>
                <input className="form-control" name="category"
                    value={ this.state.formData.category }
                    onChange={ this.handleChange } />
            </div>
            <div className="form-group">
                <label>Price</label>
                <input className="form-control" name="price"
                    value={ this.state.formData.price }
                    onChange={ this.handleChange } />
            </div>
            <div className="text-center">
                <button className="btn btn-primary m-1" onClick={ this.handleClick }>
                    Save
                </button>
                <button className="btn btn-secondary"
                        onClick={ this.props.cancelCallback }>
                    Cancel
                </button>
            </div>
        </div>
    }
}
```

The ProductEditor component presents the user with fields for editing the properties of an object. The initial values for the fields are received from a prop named product and used to populate state data. There is a Save button that invokes a function prop named saveCallback when it is clicked, passing the state data values so that can be saved. There is also a Cancel button that invokes a function callback named cancelCallback when it is clicked.

Creating the Product Display Component

Next, I need a component that will switch between the table of products and the product editor. I added a file called ProductDisplay.js to the src folder and used it to define the component shown in Listing 18-8.

Listing 18-8. The Contents of the ProductDisplay.js File in the src Folder

```
import React, { Component } from "react";
import { ProductTable } from "./ProductTable"
import { ProductEditor } from "./ProductEditor";

export class ProductDisplay extends Component {

    constructor(props) {
        super(props);
        this.state = {
            showEditor: false,
            selectedProduct: null
        }
    }
}
```

```
    startEditing = (product) => {
        this.setState({ showEditor: true, selectedProduct: product })
    }

    createProduct = () => {
        this.setState({ showEditor: true, selectedProduct: {} })
    }

    cancelEditing = () => {
        this.setState({ showEditor: false, selectedProduct: null })
    }

    saveProduct = (product) => {
        this.props.saveCallback(product);
        this.setState({ showEditor: false, selectedProduct: null })
    }

    render() {
        if (this.state.showEditor) {
            return <ProductEditor
                key={ this.state.selectedProduct.id || -1 }
                product={ this.state.selectedProduct }
                saveCallback={ this.saveProduct }
                cancelCallback={ this.cancelEditing } />
        } else {
            return <div className="m-2">
                <ProductTable products={ this.props.products }
                    editCallback={ this.startEditing }
                    deleteCallback={ this.props.deleteCallback } />
                <div className="text-center">
                    <button className="btn btn-primary m-1"
                        onClick={ this.createProduct }>
                        Create Product
                    </button>
                </div>
            </div>
        }
    }
}
```

This component defines state data to determine whether the data table or the editor should be shown and, if it is the editor, which product the user wants to modify. This component passes on function props to both the ProductEditor and ProductTable components, as well as introducing its own functionality.

Creating the Supplier Functionality

The part of the application that deals with supplier data follows a similar pattern to the components created in earlier sections. I added a file called SupplierTableRow.js to the src folder and used it to define the component shown in Listing 18-9.

Listing 18-9. The Contents of the SupplierTableRow.js File in the src Folder

```
import React, { Component } from "react";

export class SupplierTableRow extends Component {

    render() {
        let s = this.props.supplier;
        return <tr>
            <td>{ s.id }</td>
            <td>{ s.name }</td>
            <td>{ s.city}</td>
            <td>{ s.products.join(", ") }</td>
            <td>
                <button className="btn btn-sm btn-warning m-1"
                    onClick={ () => this.props.editCallback(s) }>
                        Edit
                </button>
                <button className="btn btn-sm btn-danger m-1"
                    onClick={ () => this.props.deleteCallback(s) }>
                        Delete
                </button>
            </td>
        </tr>
    }
}
```

This component renders a table row with the id, name, city, and products properties of a prop object named supplier. There are also Edit and Delete buttons that invoke function props.

Creating the Supplier Table

To present a table of suppliers to the user, I added a file called SupplierTable.js to the src folder and added the code shown in Listing 18-10.

Listing 18-10. The Contents of the SupplierTable.js File in the src Folder

```
import React, { Component } from "react";
import { SupplierTableRow } from "./SupplierTableRow";

export class SupplierTable extends Component {

    render() {
        return <table className="table table-sm table-striped table-bordered">
            <thead>
                <tr>
                    <th>ID</th><th>Name</th><th>City</th>
                    <th>Products</th><th></th>
                </tr>
            </thead>
            <tbody>
```

```
                     {
                         this.props.suppliers.map(s =>
                             <SupplierTableRow supplier={ s }
                                 key={ s.id }
                                 editCallback={ this.props.editCallback }
                                 deleteCallback={ this.props.deleteCallback } />)
                     }
                 </tbody>
             </table>
      }
}
```

This component renders a table, mapping each object in the `suppliers` prop array into a `SupplierTableRow`. The props for the callbacks are received from the parent component and passed on.

Creating the Supplier Editor

To create the editor for suppliers, I added a file called `SupplierEditor.js` to the `src` folder and used it to define the component shown in Listing 18-11.

Listing 18-11. The Contents of the SupplierEditor.js File in the src Folder

```
import React, { Component } from "react";

export class SupplierEditor extends Component {

    constructor(props) {
        super(props);
        this.state = {
            formData: {
                id: props.supplier.id || "",
                name: props.supplier.name || "",
                city: props.supplier.city || "",
                products: props.supplier.products || [],
            }
        }
    }

    handleChange = (ev) => {
        ev.persist();
        this.setState(state =>
            state.formData[ev.target.name] =
                ev.target.name === "products"
                    ? ev.target.value.split(",") : ev.target.value);
    }

    handleClick = () => {
```

```
        this.props.saveCallback(
            {
                ...this.state.formData,
                products: this.state.formData.products.map(val => Number(val))
            });
    }

    render() {
        return <div className="m-2">
            <div className="form-group">
                <label>ID</label>
                <input className="form-control" name="id"
                    disabled
                    value={ this.state.formData.id }
                    onChange={ this.handleChange } />
            </div>
            <div className="form-group">
                <label>Name</label>
                <input className="form-control" name="name"
                    value={ this.state.formData.name }
                    onChange={ this.handleChange } />
            </div>
            <div className="form-group">
                <label>City</label>
                <input className="form-control" name="city"
                    value={ this.state.formData.city }
                    onChange={ this.handleChange } />
            </div>

            <div className="form-group">
                <label>Products</label>
                <input className="form-control" name="products"
                    value={ this.state.formData.products }
                    onChange={ this.handleChange } />
            </div>

            <div className="text-center">
                <button className="btn btn-primary m-1" onClick={ this.handleClick }>
                    Save
                </button>
                <button className="btn btn-secondary"
                        onClick={ this.props.cancelCallback }>
                    Cancel
                </button>
            </div>
        </div>
    }
}
```

Creating the Supplier Display Component

To manage the side of the application that deals with supplier data so that only the table or the editor is shown, I added a file called SupplierDisplay.js to the src folder and used it to define the component shown in Listing 18-12.

Listing 18-12. The Contents of the SupplierDisplay.js File in the src Folder

```
import React, { Component } from "react";
import { SupplierEditor } from "./SupplierEditor";
import { SupplierTable } from "./SupplierTable";

export class SupplierDisplay extends Component {

    constructor(props) {
        super(props);
        this.state = {
            showEditor: false,
            selected: null
        }
    }

    startEditing = (supplier) => {
        this.setState({ showEditor: true, selected: supplier })
    }

    createSupplier = () => {
        this.setState({ showEditor: true, selected: {} })
    }

    cancelEditing = () => {
        this.setState({ showEditor: false, selected: null })
    }

    saveSupplier= (supplier) => {
        this.props.saveCallback(supplier);
        this.setState({ showEditor: false, selected: null })
    }

    render() {
        if (this.state.showEditor) {
            return <SupplierEditor
                    key={ this.state.selected.id || -1 }
                    supplier={ this.state.selected }
                    saveCallback={ this.saveSupplier }
                    cancelCallback={ this.cancelEditing } />
        } else {
            return <div className="m-2">
                        <SupplierTable suppliers={ this.props.suppliers }
                            editCallback={ this.startEditing }
                            deleteCallback={ this.props.deleteCallback }
                    />
```

```
                 <div className="text-center">
                     <button className="btn btn-primary m-1"
                         onClick={ this.createSupplier }>
                             Create Supplier
                     </button>
                 </div>
            </div>
        }
    }
}
```

The SupplierDisplay component has its own state data for determining whether the editor or table component should be displayed.

Completing the Application

To allow the user to choose between the product or supplier features, I added a file called Selector.js to the src folder and added the code shown in Listing 18-13.

Listing 18-13. The Contents of the Selector.js File in the src Folder

```
import React, { Component } from "react";

export class Selector extends Component {

    constructor(props) {
        super(props);
        this.state = {
            selection: React.Children.toArray(props.children)[0].props.name
        }
    }

    setSelection = (ev) => {
        ev.persist();
        this.setState({ selection: ev.target.name});
    }

    render() {
        return <div className="container-fluid">
            <div className="row">
                <div className="col-2">
                    { React.Children.map(this.props.children, c =>
                        <button
                            name={ c.props.name }
                            onClick={ this.setSelection }
                            className={`btn btn-block m-2
                            ${this.state.selection === c.props.name
                                ? "btn-primary active": "btn-secondary"}`}>
                                    { c.props.name }
                        </button>
                    )}
```

```
            </div>
            <div className="col">
                {
                    React.Children.toArray(this.props.children)
                        .filter(c => c.props.name === this.state.selection)
                }
            </div>
        </div>
    </div>
    }
}
```

The Selector component is a container that renders a button for each of its children and displays only the one selected by the user. To provide the data that will be displayed by the application and implementation for the callback functions that operate on it, I added a file called ProductsAndSuppliers.js to the src folder and used it to define the component shown in Listing 18-14.

Listing 18-14. The Contents of the ProductsAndSuppliers.js File in the src Folder

```
import React, { Component } from 'react';
import { Selector } from './Selector';
import { ProductDisplay } from './ProductDisplay';
import { SupplierDisplay } from './SupplierDisplay';

export default class ProductsAndSuppliers extends Component {

    constructor(props) {
        super(props);
        this.state = {
            products: [
                { id: 1, name: "Kayak",
                category: "Watersports", price: 275 },
                { id: 2, name: "Lifejacket",
                    category: "Watersports", price: 48.95 },
                { id: 3, name: "Soccer Ball", category: "Soccer", price: 19.50 }
            ],
            suppliers: [
                { id: 1, name: "Surf Dudes", city: "San Jose", products: [1, 2] },
                { id: 2, name: "Field Supplies", city: "New York", products: [3] },
            ]
        }
        this.idCounter = 100;
    }

    saveData = (collection, item) => {
        if (item.id === "") {
            item.id = this.idCounter++;
            this.setState(state => state[collection]
                = state[collection].concat(item));
        } else {
```

```
            this.setState(state => state[collection]
                = state[collection].map(stored =>
                        stored.id === item.id ? item: stored))
        }
    }

    deleteData = (collection, item) => {
        this.setState(state => state[collection]
            = state[collection].filter(stored => stored.id !== item.id));
    }

    render() {
        return <div>
            <Selector>
                <ProductDisplay
                    name="Products"
                    products={ this.state.products }
                    saveCallback={ p => this.saveData("products", p) }
                    deleteCallback={ p => this.deleteData("products", p) } />
                <SupplierDisplay
                    name="Suppliers"
                    suppliers={ this.state.suppliers }
                    saveCallback={ s => this.saveData("suppliers", s) }
                    deleteCallback={ s => this.deleteData("suppliers", s) } />
            </Selector>
        </div>
    }
}
```

The component defines product and suppliers state data properties and defines methods that allow objects to be deleted or saved for each data category. The component renders a Selector and provides the category display components as its children.

The final step is to replace the contents of the App component so that the custom components defined in the previous sections are displayed to the user, as shown in Listing 18-15.

Listing 18-15. Adding Data and Methods to the App.js File in the src Folder

```
import React, { Component } from "react";
import ProductsAndSuppliers from "./ProductsAndSuppliers";

export default class App extends Component {

    render() {
        return <ProductsAndSuppliers/>
    }
}
```

Once you save the changes to the App component, the browser will display the completed example application. To make sure that everything works as it should, click the Suppliers button, click the Create Supplier button, and fill out the form. Click the Save button, and you should see a new entry in the table with the detail you entered, as shown in Figure 18-3.

Figure 18-3. *Testing the example application*

Understanding the Limitations of the Example Application

The example application shows how React components can be combined to create applications—but it also shows the limitations of the features that React provides.

The biggest limitation of the example application is that it uses statically defined data that is hard-coded into the App component. The same data is displayed each time the application is started, and changes are lost when the browser is reloaded or closed.

The most common way of persisting data outside of a web application is to use a web service, although modern browsers provide support for storing limited amounts of data locally. React doesn't include integrated support for working with web services, but there are some good choices, both for simple web services, which I describe in Chapter 23, and those that present more complex data, which I describe in Chapters 24 and 25.

The next limitation is that the state data has been lifted all the way to the top of the application. As I explained in Part 2, state data can be used to coordinate between components, and that state data can be lifted up to the common ancestor of components that need to access the same data.

The example application shows the downside of this approach, such that the important data—the products and suppliers arrays, in this case—end up being pushed to the top level of the application. React destroys components when they are unmounted and their state data is lost, which means that any component that is below the Selector in the example application is unsuitable for storing the application's data. As a result, all of the application's data has been defined in the App component, along with the methods that operate on that data. I exacerbated this problem with the structure I chose for the application, but the underlying issue is that a component's state is perfect for keeping track of the data required to manage the content presented to the user—such as whether a data table or an editor should be displayed—but isn't well-suited for managing the data that relates to the purpose of the application, often known as the *domain data* or *model data*.

The best way to prevent the model data from being pushed up to the top-level component is to put it in a separate data store, which leaves the React components to deal with the presentation of the data without having to manage it. I explain the use of a data store and show you how to create one in Chapters 19 and 20.

The application is also limited in the way that it requires the user to work through a specific sequence of tasks to get to specific features. In many applications, especially those designed to support a specific corporate function, users have to perform a small set of tasks and want to be able to start them as easily as possible. The example application only presents its features in response to clicking particular elements. In Chapters 21 and 22, I add support for URL routing, which makes it possible for users to navigate to specific features directly.

Summary

In this chapter, I created the example application that I will enhance throughout this part of the book. In the next chapter, I start that process by introducing a data store, which will allow the model data to be removed from the App component and distributed directly to the parts of the application that need it.

CHAPTER 19

■ ■ ■

Using a Redux Data Store

A *data store* moves the application's data outside of the React component hierarchy. Using a data store means that the data doesn't have to be lifted up to the top-level component and doesn't have to thread props to ensure access to that data where it is needed. The result is a more natural application structure, which leaves the React components to focus on what they are good at, which is rendering content for the user.

But data stores can be complex, and introducing them to an application can be a counterintuitive process. In this chapter, I introduce Redux, which is the most popular choice of data store for React projects, and show you to create a data store and integrate into an application. In Chapter 20, I explain how Redux works in more depth and explain some of its advanced features. Table 19-1 puts using a Redux data store in context.

Table 19-1. *Putting Redux Data Stores in Context*

Question	Answer
What is it?	A data store moves an application's data outside of the component hierarchy, which means that data doesn't have to be lifted up and then made available to descendants through prop threading.
Why is it useful?	Data stores can simplify the components in a project, producing an application that is easier to develop and test.
How is it used?	Data is moved into a dedicated part of the application that can be accessed directly by the components that require it. In the case of Redux, components are connected to the data store through props, which takes advantage of the nature of React, although the mapping process itself can be awkward and require close attention.
Are there any pitfalls or limitations?	Data stores can be complex and often work in counterintuitive ways. Some data store packages, including Redux, enforce specific methods of dealing with data that some developers find restrictive.
Are there any alternatives?	Not all applications need a data store. For smaller amounts of data, using component state features may be acceptable and the React context API, described in Chapter 14, can be used for basic data management features.

© Adam Freeman 2019
A. Freeman, *Pro React 16*, https://doi.org/10.1007/978-1-4842-4451-7_19

Table 19-2 summarizes the chapter.

Table 19-2. *Chapter Summary*

Problem	Solution	Listing
Create a data store	Define the initial data, action types, creators, and reducers	3–8, 13–21
Add a data store to a React application	Use the `Provider` component from the React-Redux package	9
Consume a data store in a React component	Use the `connect` function to map the component's props to the data store's data and action creators	10, 12
Dispatch multiple data store actions	Use the `dispatch` function directly when mapping data store action creators to component function props.	22

Preparing for This Chapter

In this chapter, I continue using the `productapp` project created in Chapter 18. To prepare for this chapter, open a new command prompt and run the commands shown in Listing 19-1 in the `productapp` folder.

■ **Tip** You can download the example project for this chapter—and for all the other chapters in this book—from `https://github.com/Apress/pro-react-16`.

Listing 19-1. Installing Packages

```
npm install redux@4.0.1
npm install react-redux@6.0.0
```

For quick reference, Table 19-3 describes the packages added to the project by the commands in Listing 19-1.

Table 19-3. *The Packages Added to the Project*

Name	Description
`redux`	This package contains the main Redux data store features.
`react-redux`	This package contains the integration features for using Redux with React.

Once the packages have been installed, run the command shown in Listing 19-2 in the `productapp` folder to start the React development tools.

Listing 19-2. Starting the Development Tools

```
npm start
```

Once the application has been compiled, the development HTTP server will start and display the content shown in Figure 19-1.

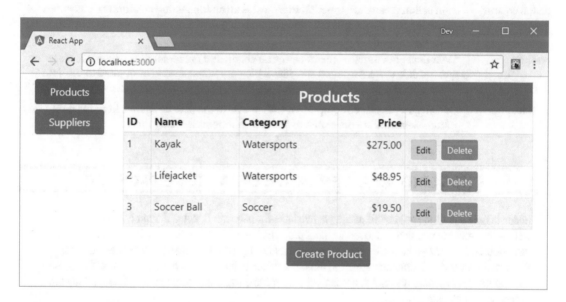

Figure 19-1. Running the example application

Creating a Data Store

Much like React, Redux imposes a specific flow for data and changes. And, like React, understanding how the different parts of Redux fit together can be difficult at first. There are two characteristics of Redux that cause confusion.

First, changes in Redux are not applied directly to the data in the store, even though that data is expressed as regular JavaScript objects. Instead, Redux relies on functions that accept a payload and update the data in the store, similar to the way that React components enforce the use of the setState method to update state data.

The second point of confusion is the terminology. There are a number of different parts in a Redux data store, and their names don't intuitively describe their purpose. For quick references as you get started with Redux, Table 19-4 describes the terms that you will encounter and that are explained in more detail the sections that follow, where I create a data store and integrate it into the example application.

Table 19-4. *Important Redux Terms*

Name	Description
action	An action describes an operation that will change the data in the store. Redux doesn't allow data to be modified directly and requires actions to specify changes.
action type	Actions are plain JavaScript objects that have a type parameter, which specifies the action type. This ensures that actions can be identified and processed correctly.
action creator	An action creator is a function that creates an action. Action creators are presented to React components as function props so that invoking the action creator function applies a change to the data store.
reducer	A reducer is a function that receives an action and processes the change it represents in the data store. An action specifies which operation should be applied to the data store, but it is the reducer that contains the JavaScript code that makes it happen.
selector	A selector provides a component with access to the data it requires from the data store. Selectors are presented to React components as data props.

CHOOSING AN ALTERNATIVE DATA STORE PACKAGE

Redux is only one of the data store packages available for use with React, although it is the most well-known and the one that is chosen by most projects. If you don't like the way that Redux works, then MobX (`https://github.com/mobxjs/mobx`) may be a good alternative. MobX works well with React and allows direct state changes. The main drawback is that it relies on decorators, which some developers find awkward and which are not yet part of the JavaScript specification (although they are widely used, including by Angular).

In Chapters 24 and 25, I introduce GraphQL and explain its use in retrieving data for applications. If you become a committed React user, then you may want to consider Relay (`https://facebook.github.io/relay`) for data management. Relay works only with GraphQL, which means that it isn't suitable for all projects, but it has some interesting features and integrates well with React.

Defining the Data Types

The example application contains similar sets of features applied to two types of data. In this situation, it is easy to end up with duplication in the code that manages the data store, performing essentially the same operation but on different collections of objects, with the effect that the data store is harder to write, harder to understand, and prone to errors introduced by copying the code for one type of data and incorrectly adapting it.

This is such a common problem that I am going to demonstrate a data store that consolidates as much common code as possible. The first step is to define constant values that will let me consistently identify the different types of data throughout the data store. I created the src/store folder and added to it a file called dataTypes.js with the statements shown in Listing 19-3.

Listing 19-3. The Contents of the dataTypes.js File in the src/store Folder

```
export const PRODUCTS = "products";
export const SUPPLIERS = "suppliers";
```

Defining the Initial Data

In later chapters, I show you how to get data from web services, but for the moment I am going to continue using statically defined data. To define the initial contents of the data store, I created a file called initialData.js in the store folder and added the statements shown in Listing 19-4.

■ **Note** As I add more features to the example application, I am going to create different sections of the data store to keep features separate. I am going to refer to the product and supplier data presented to the user as *model data* to differentiate it from the internal data used to coordinate between components, which I will refer to as *state data*.

Listing 19-4. The Contents of the initialData.js File in the src/store Folder

```
import { PRODUCTS, SUPPLIERS } from "./dataTypes";

export const initialData = {
    [PRODUCTS]: [
        { id: 1, name: "Trail Shoes", category: "Running", price: 100 },
        { id: 2, name: "Thermal Hat", category: "Running", price: 12 },
        { id: 3, name: "Heated Gloves", category: "Running", price: 82.50 }],
    [SUPPLIERS]: [
        { id: 1, name: "Zoom Shoes", city: "London", products: [1] },
        { id: 2, name: "Cosy Gear", city: "New York", products: [2, 3] }],
}
```

The initial state of the data store is defined as a regular JavaScript object; one of the characteristics of working with Redux is that it relies on pure JavaScript for many of its features. To make it clear when the data store is being used, I have used different details for the objects in the PRODUCTS and SUPPLIERS arrays.

Defining the Model Data Action Types

The next step is to describe the operations that can be performed on the data in the store, which are called *actions*. There can be a lot of actions in a complex application, and it can be helpful to define constant values to identify them. I added a file called modelActionTypes.js to the store folder and added the content shown in Listing 19-5.

Listing 19-5. The Contents of the modelActionTypes.js File in the src/store Folder

```
export const STORE  = "STORE";
export const UPDATE = "UPDATE";
export const DELETE = "DELETE";
```

To provide the functionality for the example application, I need three events: STORE to add objects to the data store, UPDATE to modify existing objects, and DELETE to remove objects.

The value assigned to the action types isn't important just as long as it is unique, and the simplest approach is to assign each action type a string value of its name.

Defining the Model Action Creators

Actions are objects that are sent from the application to the data store to request a change. An action has an action type and a data payload, where the action type specifies the operation and the payload provides the data that the operation requires. Actions are ordinary JavaScript objects that can define any combination of properties required to describe an operation. The convention is to define a type property to indicate the event type, and I will supplement this with dataType and payload properties to specify the data that the action should be applied to and the data required for the action.

Actions are created by *action creators*, which is the name given to functions that accept data from the application and return an action that describes a change to the data store. To define the action creators, I added a file called modelActionCreators.js to the store folder and added the code shown in Listing 19-6.

Listing 19-6. The Contents of the modelActionCreators.js File in the src/store Folder

```
import { PRODUCTS, SUPPLIERS } from "./dataTypes"
import { STORE, UPDATE, DELETE } from "./modelActionTypes";

let idCounter = 100;

export const saveProduct = (product) => {
    return createSaveEvent(PRODUCTS, product);
}

export const saveSupplier = (supplier) => {
    return createSaveEvent(SUPPLIERS, supplier);
}

const createSaveEvent = (dataType, payload)  => {
    if (!payload.id) {
        return {
            type: STORE,
            dataType: dataType,
            payload: { ...payload, id: idCounter++ }
        }
    } else {
        return {
            type: UPDATE,
            dataType: dataType,
            payload: payload
        }
    }
}

export const deleteProduct = (product) => ({
    type: DELETE,
    dataType: PRODUCTS,
    payload: product.id
})
```

```
export const deleteSupplier = (supplier) => ({
    type: DELETE,
    dataType: SUPPLIERS,
    payload: supplier.id
})
```

There are four action creators in the listing. The saveProduct and saveSupplier functions receive an object parameter and pass it to createSaveEvent, which inspects the value of the id property to determine whether a STORE or UPDATE action is required. The deleteProduct and deleteSupplier action creators are simpler and create a DELETE action whose payload is the id property value of the object to be deleted.

Defining the Reducer

Actions are applied to the data store by a JavaScript function called a *reducer*. Put another way, an action describes the type of change that is needed, and the reducer contains the logic to make it happen. I added a file called modelReducer.js to the store folder and added the code shown in Listing 19-7.

Listing 19-7. The Contents of the modelReducer.js File in the src/store Folder

```
import { STORE, UPDATE, DELETE } from "./modelActionTypes";
import { initialData } from "./initialData";

export default function(storeData, action) {
    switch (action.type) {
        case STORE:
            return {
                ...storeData,
                [action.dataType]:
                    storeData[action.dataType].concat([action.payload])
            }
        case UPDATE:
            return {
                ...storeData,
                [action.dataType]: storeData[action.dataType].map(p =>
                    p.id === action.payload.id ? action.payload : p)
            }
        case DELETE:
            return {
                ...storeData,
                [action.dataType]: storeData[action.dataType]
                    .filter(p => p.id !== action.payload)
            }
        default:
            return storeData || initialData;
    }
}
```

The reducer receives the current data from the data store and an action as its parameters. It inspects the action and uses it to create a new data object, which will replace the existing data in the data store.

There are two important rules to follow. First, the reducer must create a new object and not return the object received as a parameter because Redux will ignore any changes that have been made. Second, because the object that the reducer creates replaces the data in the store, it is important to copy the properties of the existing object, not just the one modified by the action. The simplest way to copy the properties is to use the spread operator, like this:

```
...
case STORE:
    return {
        ...store,
        [action.dataType]: store[action.dataType].concat([action.payload])
}
...
```

This ensures that all the properties are copied to the result object. The property for the data that is changed is then replaced with the data modified by the action.

Another important aspect of the reducer is that it will be invoked when the data store is created to get the initial data. This is handled by the default clause of the switch statement, as shown here:

```
...
default:
    return storeData || initialData;
...
```

Redux will report an error if the function returns undefined, and it is important to ensure that you return a useful result. In the listing, I return the initialData object that was defined in Listing 19-4.

AVOIDING CODE DUPLICATION IN THE REDUCER

Most data sets require a core set of common operations. This can be seen in the example application, where the product and supplier data both need store, update, and delete operations. This can result in code duplication when you define the data store, with similar action types, action creators, and reducer code. The approach I have taken in this section is to include a property in the actions that specifies which type of data an operation should be applied to, and then I relied on the JavaScript property accessor feature to select the appropriate data store property in the reducer, like this:

```
...
case STORE:
    return {
        ...store,
        [action.dataType]: store[action.dataType].concat([action.payload])
}
...
```

When the new data store object is created, JavaScript will evaluate the action.dataType property and use its value to define a new property on the object and access the property on the old data store, using the values I defined in Listing 19-5, so that a dataType value of PRODUCTS selects the products data and a value of SUPPLIERS selects the supplier data. You don't have to use this type of technique in your own projects, but it helps keep the code concise and manageable.

Creating the Data Store

Redux provides the `createStore` function, which creates the data store and prepares it for use. I added a file called `index.js` to the `store` folder and added the code shown in Listing 19-8.

■ **Tip**   You don't have to use the `index.js` file name, but doing so allows the data store to be imported using only the name of the folder, as shown in Listing 19-9.

Listing 19-8. The Contents of the index.js File in the src/store Folder

```
import { createStore } from "redux";
import modelReducer from "./modelReducer";

export default createStore(modelReducer);

export { saveProduct, saveSupplier, deleteProduct, deleteSupplier }
    from "./modelActionCreators";
```

The default export from the `index.js` file is the result of calling `createStore`, which accepts the reducer function as its argument. I also exported the action creators so that all of the data store's functionality can be accessed through a single `import` statement elsewhere in the application, which makes using the data store a little simpler.

Using the Data Store in the React Application

The actions, reducers, and selectors I created in the previous section are not yet integrated into the application, and there are no links between the components in the application and the data in the data store. In the sections that follow, I show you how to use the data store to replace the state data and methods that currently manage the application data.

Applying the Data Store to the Top-Level Component

The React-Redux package includes a React container component that provides access to a data store. This component, called `Provider`, is applied at the top of the component hierarchy so that the data store is available throughout the application. In Listing 19-9, I imported the data store from the `index.js` file created in Listing 19-8 and used the `Provider` component to apply the data store to the components in the application.

Listing 19-9. Applying the Data Store in the App.js File in the src Folder

```
import React, { Component } from "react";
import ProductsAndSuppliers from "./ProductsAndSuppliers";
import { Provider } from "react-redux";
import dataStore from "./store";

export default class App extends Component {

    render() {
```

```
    return (
        <Provider store={ dataStore }>
            <ProductsAndSuppliers/>
        </Provider>
    )
  }
}
```

The Provider component has a store prop that is used to specify the data store, which I assigned the name dataStore in the import statement.

Connecting the Product Data

The next step is to connect the data store to the components that require the data it contains and the action creators that operate on it. I am going to take the most direct approach, which is to use the features provided by the React-Redux package to connect the ProductDisplay component to the data store, as shown Listing 19-10.

Listing 19-10. Connecting to the Data Store in the ProductDisplay.js File in the src Folder

```
import React, { Component } from "react";
import { ProductTable } from "./ProductTable"
import { ProductEditor } from "./ProductEditor";
import { connect } from "react-redux";
import { saveProduct, deleteProduct } from "./store"

const mapStateToProps = (storeData) => ({
    products: storeData.products
})

const mapDispatchToProps = {
    saveCallback: saveProduct,
    deleteCallback: deleteProduct
}

const connectFunction = connect(mapStateToProps, mapDispatchToProps);

export const ProductDisplay = connectFunction(
        class extends Component {

        constructor(props) {
            super(props);
            this.state = {
                showEditor: false,
                selectedProduct: null
            }
        }

        startEditing = (product) => {
            this.setState({ showEditor: true, selectedProduct: product })
        }
```

```
    createProduct = () => {
        this.setState({ showEditor: true, selectedProduct: {} })
    }

    cancelEditing = () => {
        this.setState({ showEditor: false, selectedProduct: null })
    }

    saveProduct = (product) => {
        this.props.saveCallback(product);
        this.setState({ showEditor: false, selectedProduct: null })
    }

    render() {
        if (this.state.showEditor) {
            return <ProductEditor
                key={ this.state.selectedProduct.id || -1 }
                product={ this.state.selectedProduct }
                saveCallback={ this.saveProduct }
                cancelCallback={ this.cancelEditing } />
        } else {
            return <div className="m-2">
                <ProductTable products={ this.props.products }
                    editCallback={ this.startEditing }
                    deleteCallback={ this.props.deleteCallback } />
                <div className="text-center">
                    <button className="btn btn-primary m-1"
                        onClick={ this.createProduct }>
                        Create Product
                    </button>
                </div>
            </div>
        }
    }
})
```

The first step is to define a function that receives the data store and selects the props that will connect the component and the store, like this:

```
...
const mapStateToProps = (storeData) => ({
    products: storeData.products
})
...
```

This function is conventionally named mapStateToProps, and it returns an object that maps prop names for the connected component to data in the store. These mappings are known as *selectors* because they select the data that will be mapped to the component's prop. In this case, selector maps the store's products array to a prop named products.

The next step is to create the object that will map the function props that the component requires to data store action creators, like this:

```
...
const mapDispatchToProps = {
    saveCallback: saveProduct,
    deleteCallback: deleteProduct
}
...
```

The React-Redux package supports different ways of connecting action creators to function props, but this is the simplest, which is to create an object that maps prop names to action creator functions. When the component is connected to the data store, the action creator functions defined in this object will be wired up so that the reducer is automatically invoked. In this case, I mapped the saveProduct and deleteProduct action creators to function props named saveCallback and deleteCallback.

Once the mappings for data and function props have been defined, they are passed to the connect function, provided by the React-Redux package.

```
...
const connectFunction = connect(mapStateToProps, mapDispatchToProps);
...
```

The connect function creates a higher-order component (HOC) that passes on props connected to the data store merged with the props that are provided by the parent component.

■ **Tip**　Higher-order components are described in Chapter 14.

The final step is to pass a component to the function returned by connect, like this:

```
...
export const ProductDisplay = connectFunction(class extends Component {
...
```

The result is a component whose props are connected to the data store. When you save the changes in Listing 19-10, the application will display the data defined in Listing 19-4, as shown in Figure 19-2.

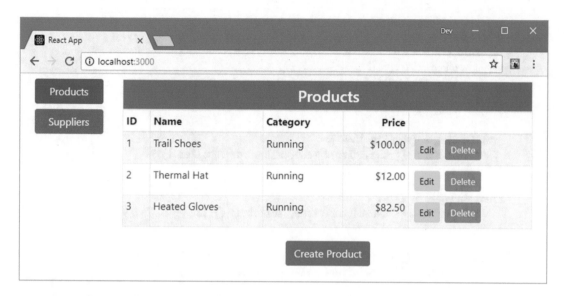

Figure 19-2. *Using a data store for product data*

Because the props provided by the data store replace those from the parent component, the ProductDisplay component operates entirely on the data store data, including creating, editing, and deleting objects.

Connecting the Supplier Data

The same process can be applied to connect the supplier data, as shown in Listing 19-11, where I have used the connect method to provide the SupplierDisplay component with access to the data store.

Listing 19-11. Connecting to the Data Store in the SupplierDisplay.js File in the src Folder

```
import React, { Component } from "react";
import { SupplierEditor } from "./SupplierEditor";
import { SupplierTable } from "./SupplierTable";
import { connect } from "react-redux";
import { saveSupplier, deleteSupplier} from "./store";

const mapStateToProps = (storeData) => ({
    suppliers: storeData.suppliers
})

const mapDispatchToProps = {
    saveCallback: saveSupplier,
    deleteCallback: deleteSupplier
}

const connectFunction = connect(mapStateToProps, mapDispatchToProps);

export const SupplierDisplay = connectFunction(
    class extends Component {
```

543

```
    constructor(props) {
        super(props);
        this.state = {
            showEditor: false,
            selected: null
        }
    }

    startEditing = (supplier) => {
        this.setState({ showEditor: true, selected: supplier })
    }

    createSupplier = () => {
        this.setState({ showEditor: true, selected: {} })
    }

    cancelEditing = () => {
        this.setState({ showEditor: false, selected: null })
    }

    saveSupplier= (supplier) => {
        this.props.saveCallback(supplier);
        this.setState({ showEditor: false, selected: null })
    }

    render() {
        if (this.state.showEditor) {
            return <SupplierEditor
                key={ this.state.selected.id || -1 }
                supplier={ this.state.selected }
                saveCallback={ this.saveSupplier }
                cancelCallback={ this.cancelEditing } />
        } else {
            return <div className="m-2">
                    <SupplierTable suppliers={ this.props.suppliers }
                        editCallback={ this.startEditing }
                        deleteCallback={ this.props.deleteCallback }
                    />
                    <div className="text-center">
                        <button className="btn btn-primary m-1"
                            onClick={ this.createSupplier }>
                                Create Supplier
                        </button>
                    </div>
            </div>
        }
    }
})
```

The result is that the SupplierDisplay component receives props that connect it to the data store, as illustrated in Figure 19-3.

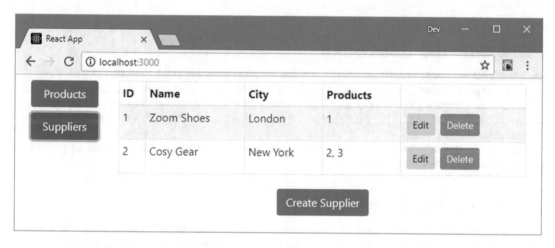

Figure 19-3. *Using a data store for supplier data*

With the data store in place, the ProductsAndSuppliers component is redundant, since its role was to provide the product and supplier data and the methods to store and delete it. In Listing 19-12, I have updated the App component to display the Selector, ProductDisplay, and SupplierDisplay components directly.

Listing 19-12. Displaying Content Directly in the App.js File in the src Folder

```
import React, { Component } from "react";
//import ProductsAndSuppliers from "./ProductsAndSuppliers";
import { Provider } from "react-redux";
import dataStore from "./store";
import { Selector } from "./Selector";
import { ProductDisplay } from "./ProductDisplay";
import { SupplierDisplay } from "./SupplierDisplay";

export default class App extends Component {

    render() {
        return (
            <Provider store={ dataStore }>
                <Selector>
                    <ProductDisplay name="Products" />
                    <SupplierDisplay name="Suppliers" />
                </Selector>
            </Provider>
        )
    }
}
```

Notice I don't have to provide props for the ProductDisplay and SupplierDisplay components to give them access to data and methods; these will be set up by the connect method that connects the components to the data store.

Expanding the Data Store

Data stores are not just for the data that is displayed to the user—they can also be used to store the state data that is used to coordinate and manage components. Expanding the data store to include state data will allow me to connect the model data in the store directly to the components that use it, which is not possible currently because ProductDisplay and SupplierDisplay maintain state data that is used to select the content presented to the user.

In the sections that follow, I move the state data and code that manages it into the data store so that I can further simplify the application.

Adding State Data to the Store

I want to keep the state data separate from the model data, so I am going to add some structure to the store. I like to represent the structure in the initial data that I used to populate the data store, although this is entirely to help me understand the shape of the data that I am working with and is not a requirement enforced by Redux.

To structure the store data, I moved the existing data to a property named modelData and added a new stateData section, as shown in Listing 19-13.

Listing 19-13. Expanding the Data in the initialData.js File in the src/store Folder

```
import { PRODUCTS, SUPPLIERS } from "./dataTypes";

export const initialData = {
    modelData: {
        [PRODUCTS]: [
            { id: 1, name: "Trail Shoes", category: "Running", price: 100 },
            { id: 2, name: "Thermal Hat", category: "Running", price: 12 },
            { id: 3, name: "Heated Gloves", category: "Running", price: 82.50 }],
        [SUPPLIERS]: [
            { id: 1, name: "Zoom Shoes", city: "London", products: [1] },
            { id: 2, name: "Cosy Gear", city: "New York", products: [2, 3] }],
    },
    stateData: {
        editing: false,
        selectedId: -1,
        selectedType: PRODUCTS
    }
}
```

My goal is to move the state data and logic in the ProductDisplay and SupplierDisplay components into the data store. These components track the user's selection for editing and whether the table or the editor component should be rendered. To provide this information in the store, I defined editing, selected and selectedType properties in the stateData section.

Defining the Action Types and Creators for State Data

Next, I need to define the actions for the state data in the store. When I set up the data store, I defined the action types and the creators in different files, but that's not a requirement, and both can be defined together. To separate the state data actions from the rest of the store, I added a file called stateActions.js to the src/store folder and used it to define the action types and creators shown in Listing 19-14.

Listing 19-14. The Contents of the stateActions.js File in the src/store Folder

```
import { PRODUCTS, SUPPLIERS } from "./dataTypes";

export const STATE_START_EDITING = "state_start_editing";
export const STATE_END_EDITING = "state_end_editing";
export const STATE_START_CREATING = "state_start_creating";

export const startEditingProduct = (product) => ({
    type: STATE_START_EDITING,
    dataType: PRODUCTS,
    payload: product
})

export const startEditingSupplier = (supplier) => ({
    type: STATE_START_EDITING,
    dataType: SUPPLIERS,
    payload: supplier
})

export const endEditing = () => ({
    type: STATE_END_EDITING
})

export const startCreatingProduct = () => ({
    type: STATE_START_CREATING, dataType: PRODUCTS
})

export const startCreatingSupplier = () => ({
    type: STATE_START_CREATING, dataType: SUPPLIERS
})
```

The action creators correspond to the methods defined by the ProductDisplay and SupplierDisplay components and allow a user to start editing an object, cancel editing, and start creating a new object.

Defining the State Data Reducer

To update the data store in response to an action, I need to define a reducer. Rather than add code to the existing reducer, I am going to define a separate function to deal with the state data. I added a file called stateReducer.js in the src/store folder and added the code shown in Listing 19-15.

Listing 19-15. The Contents of the stateReducer.js File in the src/store Folder

```
import { STATE_START_EDITING, STATE_END_EDITING, STATE_START_CREATING }
    from "./stateActions";
import { initialData } from "./initialData";

export default function(storeData, action) {
    switch(action.type) {
        case STATE_START_EDITING:
        case STATE_START_CREATING:
            return {
                ...storeData,
                editing: true,
                selectedId: action.type === STATE_START_EDITING
                    ? action.payload.id : -1,
                selectedType: action.dataType
            }
        case STATE_END_EDITING:
            return {
                ...storeData,
                editing: false
            }
        default:
            return storeData || initialData.stateData;
    }
}
```

The reducer for the state data keeps track of what the user is editing or creating, which echoes the approach taken by the existing components in the example application, although I am going to use a single set of properties to coordinate the editors for both types of model data in the application.

Incorporating the State Data Features into the Store

Redux provides the combineReducers function, which allows multiple reducers to be combined for use in a data store, with each reducer responsible for one section of the data store data. In Listing 19-16, I used the combineReducers function to combine the reducers for the model and state data.

Listing 19-16. Configuring the Data Store in the index.js File in the src/store Folder

```
import { createStore, combineReducers } from "redux";
import modelReducer from "./modelReducer";
import stateReducer from "./stateReducer";

export default createStore(combineReducers(
    {
        modelData: modelReducer,
        stateData: stateReducer
    }));

export { saveProduct, saveSupplier, deleteProduct, deleteSupplier }
    from "./modelActionCreators";
```

The argument for the createReducers function is an object whose property names correspond to sections of the data store and the reducers that will manage them. In the listing, I have made the original reducer responsible for the modelData section of the data store and have made the reducer defined in Listing 19-15 responsible for the stateData section. The combined reducers are passed to the createStore function to create the data store.

■ **Note** Each reducer operates on a separate part of the data store, but when an action is processed, each reducer is passed the action until one of them returns a new data store object, indicating that the action has been processed.

Adding structure to the data in the store requires a corresponding change to the initial state returned by the reducer function for the model data, as shown in Listing 19-17.

Listing 19-17. Changing the Initial State in the modelReducer.js File in the src/store Folder

```
import { STORE, UPDATE, DELETE } from "./modelActionTypes";
import { initialData } from "./initialData";

export default function(storeData, action) {
    switch (action.type) {
        case STORE:
            return {
                ...storeData,
                [action.dataType]:
                    storeData[action.dataType].concat([action.payload])
            }
        case UPDATE:
            return {
                ...storeData,
                [action.dataType]: storeData[action.dataType].map(p =>
                    p.id === action.payload.id ? action.payload : p)
            }
        case DELETE:
            return {
                ...storeData,
                [action.dataType]: storeData[action.dataType]
                    .filter(p => p.id !== action.payload)
            }
        default:
            return storeData || initialData.modelData;
    }
}
```

When the combineReducers function is used, each reducer is provided with only its section of the data in the store and is unaware of the rest of the data and the other reducers. This means I only need to change the source of the initial data and don't have to worry about navigating through the new data structure when applying an action.

Connecting the React Components to the Stored State Data

Now that the state data has been put into the data store, I can connect it to components. Rather than configure each component separately, I am going to define separate connector components that will take care of mapping data store features to component props. I created a file called EditorConnector.js in the src/store folder with the code shown in Listing 19-18.

UNDERSTANDING THE PRESENTER/CONNECTOR PATTERN

A common approach when using a data store is to use two different types of component. Presenter components are responsible for rendering content to the user and responding to user input. They receive data and function props but are not directly connected to the data store. Connector components—confusingly, also known as *container components*—exist to connect to the data store to provide presenter components with props. This is the general approach I have taken in this part of the chapter, although, as with much in the React/Redux world, implementation details can vary, and there is disagreement over how best to approach this kind of separation.

Listing 19-18. The Contents of the EditorConnector.js File in the src/store Folder

```
import { connect } from "react-redux";
import { endEditing } from "./stateActions";
import { saveProduct, saveSupplier } from "./modelActionCreators";
import { PRODUCTS, SUPPLIERS  } from "./dataTypes";

export const EditorConnector = (dataType, presentationComponent) => {

    const mapStateToProps = (storeData) => ({
        editing: storeData.stateData.editing
            && storeData.stateData.selectedType === dataType,
        product: (storeData.modelData[PRODUCTS]
            .find(p => p.id === storeData.stateData.selectedId)) || {},
        supplier:(storeData.modelData[SUPPLIERS]
            .find(s => s.id === storeData.stateData.selectedId)) || {}
    })

    const mapDispatchToProps = {
        cancelCallback: endEditing,
        saveCallback: dataType === PRODUCTS ? saveProduct: saveSupplier
    }

    return connect(mapStateToProps, mapDispatchToProps)(presentationComponent);
}
```

The EditorConnector is a higher-order component that provides a presentation component with the props required by both the ProductEditor and SupplierEditor components, which means that these components can be connected to the data store using the same code, rather than requiring separate uses of the connect function. To support both types of editor, the HOC function accepts a data type that is used to select the data and action creators that will be mapped to props.

■ **Tip** Notice that the segmentation of the data store created by the combineReducers function doesn't have any effect on data selection, which means I can select data from the entire store.

To provide the same service for the components that display the table components, I added a file called TableConnector.js to the src/store folder and used it to define the HOC shown in Listing 19-19.

Listing 19-19. The Contents of the TableConnector.js File in the src/store Folder

```
import { connect } from "react-redux";
import { startEditingProduct, startEditingSupplier } from "./stateActions";
import { deleteProduct, deleteSupplier } from "./modelActionCreators";
import { PRODUCTS, SUPPLIERS } from "./dataTypes";

export const TableConnector = (dataType, presentationComponent) => {

    const mapStateToProps = (storeData) => ({
        products: storeData.modelData[PRODUCTS],
        suppliers: storeData.modelData[SUPPLIERS]
    })

    const mapDispatchToProps = {
        editCallback: dataType === PRODUCTS
            ? startEditingProduct : startEditingSupplier,
        deleteCallback: dataType === PRODUCTS ? deleteProduct : deleteSupplier
    }

    return connect(mapStateToProps, mapDispatchToProps)(presentationComponent);
}
```

Applying the Connector Components

With the connector components in place, I can remove the state data and methods from the ProductDisplay and SupplierDisplay components. Listing 19-20 shows the simplification of the ProductDisplay component.

Listing 19-20. Using Connector Components in the ProductDisplay.js File in the src Folder

```
import React, { Component } from "react";
import { ProductTable } from "./ProductTable"
import { ProductEditor } from "./ProductEditor";
import { connect } from "react-redux";
//import { saveProduct, deleteProduct } from "./store"
import { EditorConnector } from "./store/EditorConnector";
import { PRODUCTS } from "./store/dataTypes";
import { TableConnector } from "./store/TableConnector";
import { startCreatingProduct } from "./store/stateActions";
```

551

```
const ConnectedEditor = EditorConnector(PRODUCTS, ProductEditor);
const ConnectedTable = TableConnector(PRODUCTS, ProductTable);

const mapStateToProps = (storeData) => ({
    editing: storeData.stateData.editing,
    selected: storeData.modelData.products
        .find(item =>  item.id === storeData.stateData.selectedId) || {}
})

const mapDispatchToProps = {
    createProduct: startCreatingProduct,
}

const connectFunction = connect(mapStateToProps, mapDispatchToProps);

export const ProductDisplay = connectFunction(
    class extends Component {

        // constructor(props) {
        //     super(props);
        //     this.state = {
        //         showEditor: false,
        //         selectedProduct: null
        //     }
        // }

        // startEditing = (product) => {
        //     this.setState({ showEditor: true, selectedProduct: product })
        // }

        // createProduct = () => {
        //     this.setState({ showEditor: true, selectedProduct: {} })
        // }

        // cancelEditing = () => {
        //     this.setState({ showEditor: false, selectedProduct: null })
        // }

        // saveProduct = (product) => {
        //     this.props.saveCallback(product);
        //     this.setState({ showEditor: false, selectedProduct: null })
        // }

        render() {
            if (this.props.editing) {
                return <ConnectedEditor key={ this.props.selected.id || -1 } />
                // return <ProductEditor
                //     key={ this.state.selectedProduct.id || -1 }
                //     product={ this.state.selectedProduct }
                //     saveCallback={ this.saveProduct }
                //     cancelCallback={ this.cancelEditing } />
```

```
        } else {
            return <div className="m-2">
                <ConnectedTable />
                {/* <ProductTable products={ this.props.products }
                    editCallback={ this.startEditing }
                    deleteCallback={ this.props.deleteCallback } />  */}
                <div className="text-center">
                    <button className="btn btn-primary m-1"
                        onClick={ this.props.createProduct }>
                        Create Product
                    </button>
                </div>
            </div>
        }
    }
})
```

The number of commented-out statements shows the amount of the ProductDisplay component that was dedicated to providing data and function props to its children, all of which is now handled through the data store and the connector components. There is no longer any need for local state data, so the constructor and all of the methods except render can be removed. The component does still require a connection to the data store, however, because it needs to know which child component to display and needs to generate key values for the editor components.

Listing 19-21 shows the simplified SupplierDisplay component, with the redundant statements removed rather than just commented out.

Listing 19-21. Using Connector Components in the SupplierDisplay.js File in the src Folder

```
import React, { Component } from "react";
import { SupplierEditor } from "./SupplierEditor";
import { SupplierTable } from "./SupplierTable";
import { connect } from "react-redux";
import { startCreatingSupplier } from "./store/stateActions";
import { SUPPLIERS } from "./store/dataTypes";
import { EditorConnector } from "./store/EditorConnector";
import { TableConnector } from "./store/TableConnector";

const ConnectedEditor = EditorConnector(SUPPLIERS, SupplierEditor);
const ConnectedTable = TableConnector(SUPPLIERS, SupplierTable);

const mapStateToProps = (storeData) => ({
    editing: storeData.stateData.editing,
    selected: storeData.modelData.suppliers
        .find(item => item.id === storeData.stateData.selectedId) || {}
})

const mapDispatchToProps = {
    createSupplier: startCreatingSupplier
}
```

```
const connectFunction = connect(mapStateToProps, mapDispatchToProps);

export const SupplierDisplay = connectFunction(
    class extends Component {

        render() {
            if (this.props.editing) {
                return <ConnectedEditor key={ this.props.selected.id || -1 } />
            } else {
                return <div className="m-2">
                    <ConnectedTable />
                    <div className="text-center">
                        <button className="btn btn-primary m-1"
                            onClick={ this.props.createSupplier }>
                                Create Supplier
                        </button>
                    </div>
                </div>
            }
        }
    }
})
```

OVER-SIMPLIFYING COMPONENTS

As I have pushed the use of the data store further into the component hierarchy, the differences between the components for product and supplier data have been reduced, and these components are converging. At this point, I could replace the `ProductDisplay` and `SupplierDisplay` components with a single component that deals with both data types and keep working toward driving the entire application from the data store. In practice, however, there comes a point where convergence no longer simplifies the application and starts simply moving complexity around. As you gain experience working with the data store, you will find the point where you are comfortable with the degree you rely on the data store and the amount of duplication in the components. Like much of React and Redux development, this is as much personal preference as it is good practice, and it is worth experimenting until you find an approach that suits you.

Dispatching Multiple Actions

There is a problem with the way that the example application uses the data store. If you create a new object or edit an existing one, clicking the Save button updates the data store but doesn't change the component displayed to the user, as shown in Figure 19-4, and you must click the Cancel button to update the data value that changes the selected component.

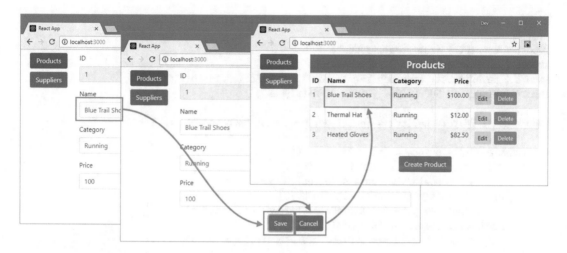

Figure 19-4. *Making a change using the example application*

The problem is that the connect function that maps action creators to props allows for only one action creator to be selected by default, but I need two action creators to solve this problem: the saveProduct or saveSupplier creators to update the model data and the endEditing creator to signal that editing is complete and the table should be presented to the user.

I can't define a new creator to perform both tasks because each action is handled by a single reducer and each reducer is responsible for an isolated part of the data in the store, which means that an action can lead to a change in the model data or the state data but not both.

Fortunately, the connect function provides an alternative way to map props to action creators that provides more flexibility. When the mapDispatchToProps argument to the connect method is an object, the connect function wraps each action creator function in a dispatch method, which is responsible for sending the action returned by the action creator to the reducer. This means that an object that maps a creator like this:

```
...
const mapDispatchToProps = {
    createSupplier: startCreatingSupplier
}
...
```

is transformed into an object like this:...

```
const mapDispatchToProps = {
    createSupplier: payload => dispatch(startCreatingSupplier(payload))
}
...
```

The action creator is invoked to get the action, which is then passed to the dispatch function so it can be processed by a reducer. Instead of defining an object and allowing the connect function to wrap each creator, you can define a function that accepts dispatch as its argument and produces props that explicitly handle action creation and dispatch, as shown in Listing 19-22.

Listing 19-22. Dispatching Actions in the EditorConnector.js File in the src Folder

```
import { connect } from "react-redux";
import { endEditing } from "./stateActions";
import { saveProduct, saveSupplier } from "./modelActionCreators";
import { PRODUCTS, SUPPLIERS  } from "./dataTypes";

export const EditorConnector = (dataType, presentationComponent) => {

    const mapStateToProps = (storeData) => ({
        editing: storeData.stateData.editing
            && storeData.stateData.selectedType === dataType,
        product: (storeData.modelData[PRODUCTS]
            .find(p => p.id === storeData.stateData.selectedId)) || {},
        supplier:(storeData.modelData[SUPPLIERS]
            .find(s => s.id === storeData.stateData.selectedId)) || {}
    })

    const mapDispatchToProps = dispatch => ({
        cancelCallback: () => dispatch(endEditing()),
        saveCallback: (data) => {
            dispatch((dataType === PRODUCTS ? saveProduct: saveSupplier)(data));
            dispatch(endEditing());
        }
    });

    return connect(mapStateToProps, mapDispatchToProps)(presentationComponent);
}
```

A function that dispatches an action is required as the value for each mapped prop and the implementation can simply invoke the action creator or, in the case of the saveCallback prop, create and dispatch multiple actions. The result is that he Save buttons rendered by the editor components invoke a function prop that dispatches actions that update the model data and the state data, as shown in Figure 19-5.

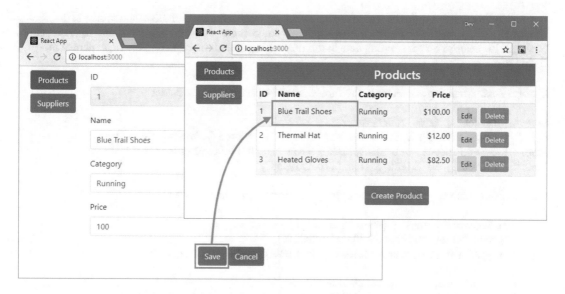

Figure 19-5. *Dispatching multiple actions*

Understanding the Need for References

You may have noticed that I keep track of the object that the user has selected using a combination of id property value and data type, like this:

```
...
stateData: {
    editing: false,
    selectedId: -1,
    selectedType: PRODUCTS
}
...
```

The table components pass a complete object to action creators that start the editing process, and you may wonder why I have chosen to only keep an ID reference to the selected object and not store the object itself, especially since this approach requires some additional work to obtain the object for the editor components.

```
...
const mapStateToProps = (storeData) => ({
    editing: storeData.stateData.editing
        && storeData.stateData.selectedType === dataType,
    product: (storeData.modelData[PRODUCTS]
        .find(p => p.id === storeData.stateData.selectedId)) || {},
    supplier:(storeData.modelData[SUPPLIERS]
        .find(s => s.id === storeData.stateData.selectedId)) || {}
})
...
```

The indirection is required because the data store represents the authoritative data source in the application, which may be altered by the selectors that connect the data to components. As a demonstration, I changed the selector for the supplier data in the TableConnector connector component, as shown in Listing 19-23.

Listing 19-23. Changing a Selector in the TableConnector.js File in the src Folder

```
import { connect } from "react-redux";
import { startEditingProduct, startEditingSupplier } from "./stateActions";
import { deleteProduct, deleteSupplier } from "./modelActionCreators";
import { PRODUCTS, SUPPLIERS } from "./dataTypes";

export const TableConnector = (dataType, presentationComponent) => {

    const mapStateToProps = (storeData) => ({
        products: storeData.modelData[PRODUCTS],
        suppliers: storeData.modelData[SUPPLIERS].map(supp => ({
            ...supp,
            products: supp.products.map(id =>
                storeData.modelData[PRODUCTS].find(p => p.id === Number(id)) || id)
                    .map(val => val.name || val)
        }))
    })

    const mapDispatchToProps = {
        editCallback: dataType === PRODUCTS
            ? startEditingProduct : startEditingSupplier,
        deleteCallback: dataType === PRODUCTS ? deleteProduct : deleteSupplier
    }

    return connect(mapStateToProps, mapDispatchToProps)(presentationComponent);
}
```

The new selector matches up the supplier and product data to replace each supplier object's products property with one that contains the name, rather than the id value, of the corresponding product, as shown in Figure 19-6.

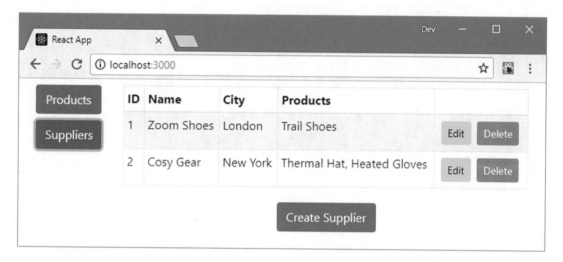

Figure 19-6. *Altering data in a selector*

Transforming data in a selector ensures consistency whenever the same view of the data is required, but it does mean that the connected component is no longer working with the original data from the data store. As a consequence, relying on the data received by one component to drive the behavior of another component can lead to problems, and it is for this reason that I used ID values to keep track of the objects that are selected by the user for editing.

Summary

In this chapter, I created a Redux data store and connected it to the components in the example application. I showed you how to define actions, action creators, reducers, and selectors, and I demonstrated how data store features can be presented to components as props. In the next chapter, I describe the advanced features Redux provides through its API.

CHAPTER 20

■ ■ ■

Using the Data Store APIs

In Chapter 19, I showed you how to use the Redux and React-Redux packages to create a data store and connect it to the example application. In this chapter, I describe the APIs that both packages provide for advanced use, allowing direct access to the data store and managing the connection between a component and the data features it requires. Table 20-1 puts the data store APIs in context.

Table 20-1. *Putting Data Store APIs in Context*

Question	Answer
What are they?	The Redux and React-Redux packages both define APIs that support advanced use, going beyond the basic techniques described in Chapter 19.
Why are they useful?	These APIs are useful for exploring how data stores work and how components can be connected to them. They can also be used to add features to a data store and to fine-tune an application's use of it.
How are they used?	The Redux API is used directly on the data store object or during its creation. The React-Redux API is used when connecting a component to the data store, either using the connect function or using its more flexible connectAdvanced alternative.
Are there any pitfalls or limitations?	The APIs described in this chapter require careful thought to ensure that you achieve the desired effect. It is easy to create an application that doesn't properly respond to data store changes or that updates too often.
Are there any alternatives?	You don't have to use the APIs described in this chapter, and most projects will be able to make effective use of a data store using only the basic techniques described in Chapter 19.

© Adam Freeman 2019

A. Freeman, *Pro React 16*, https://doi.org/10.1007/978-1-4842-4451-7_20

Table 20-2 summarizes the chapter.

Table 20-2. *Chapter Summary*

Problem	Solution	Listing
Access the Redux data store API	Use the methods defined by the data store object returned by the `createStore` method	2–4
Observe data store changes	Use the subscribe method	5
Dispatch actions	Use the dispatch method	6
Create a custom connector	Map the props of a component to the data store features	7–8
Add features to the data store	Create a reducer enhancer	9–11
Process actions before they are passed to the reducer	Create a middleware function	12–16
Extend the data store API	Create an enhancer function	17–19
Incorporate a component's props into a data store mapping	Use the optional argument to the connect function	20–24

Preparing for This Chapter

In this chapter, I continue working with the `productapp` project created in Chapter 18 and modified in Chapter 19. No changes are required for this chapter. Open a new command prompt, navigate to the `productapp` folder, and run the command shown in Listing 20-1 to start the development tools.

■ **Tip** You can download the example project for this chapter—and for all the other chapters in this book—from `https://github.com/Apress/pro-react-16`.

Listing 20-1. Starting the Development Tools

```
npm start
```

Once the development tools have started, a new browser window will open and display the content shown in Figure 20-1.

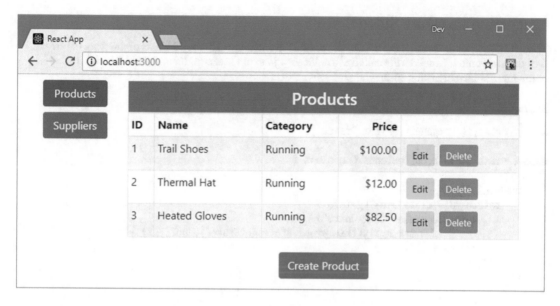

Figure 20-1. *Running the example application*

Using the Redux Data Store API

In most React applications, access to a Redux data store is mediated through the React-Redux package, which maps data store features to props. This is the most convenient way to use Redux, but there is also a full API that provides direct access to data store features, which I describe in the sections that follow, starting with the features that provide access to the data in the store.

In Chapter 19, I used the Redux createStore function to create a new data store so that I could pass it as a prop to the Provider component from the React-Redux package. The object returned by the createStore function can also be used directly through the four methods described in Table 20-3.

Table 20-3. *The Data Store Methods*

Name	Description
getState()	This method returns the data from the data store, as described in the "Obtaining the Data Store State" section.
subscribe(listener)	This method registers a function that will be invoked each time changes are made to the data store, as described in the "Observing Data Store Changes" section.
dispatch(action)	This method accepts an action, typically produced by an action creator, and sends it to the data store so that it can be processed by the reducer, as described in the "Dispatching Actions" section.
replaceReducer(next)	This method replaces the reducer used by the data store to process actions. This method is not useful in most project, and middleware provides a more useful mechanism for changing the behavior of the data store.

Obtaining the Data Store State

The getState method returns the data in the data store and allows for the contents of the store to be read. As a demonstration, I added a file called StoreAccess.js to the store folder and used it to define the component shown in Listing 20-2.

Listing 20-2. The Contents of the StoreAccess.js File in the src/store Folder

```
import React, { Component } from "react";

export class StoreAccess extends Component {

    render() {
        return <div className="bg-info">
            <pre className="text-white">
                { JSON.stringify(this.props.store.getState(), null, 2) }
            </pre>
        </div>
    }
}
```

The component receives the data store object as a prop and calls the getState method, which returns the data object for the store. To format the data, I use the JSON.stringify method, which serializes the JavaScript object to JSON and then formats the result so that it can be easily read. In Listing 20-3, I have added a grid layout so that the new component is displayed alongside the rest of the application functionality.

Listing 20-3. Displaying the Data Store Contents in the App.js File in the src Folder

```
import React, { Component } from "react";
import { Provider } from "react-redux";
import dataStore from "./store";
import { Selector } from "./Selector";
import { ProductDisplay } from "./ProductDisplay";
import { SupplierDisplay } from "./SupplierDisplay";
import { StoreAccess } from "./store/StoreAccess";

export default class App extends Component {

    render() {
        return <div className="container-fluid">
            <div className="row">
                <div className="col-3">
                    <StoreAccess store={ dataStore } />
                </div>
                <div className="col">
                    <Provider store={ dataStore }>
                        <Selector>
                            <ProductDisplay name="Products" />
                            <SupplierDisplay name="Suppliers" />
                        </Selector>
                    </Provider>
```

```
            </div>
        </div>
    </div>
    }
}
```

There can be a lot of data in a store, so I have displayed the JSON text so it will appear in its own column, as shown in Figure 20-2. Don't worry if you can't fit all of the text on-screen because I'll narrow the focus to a subset of the data shortly.

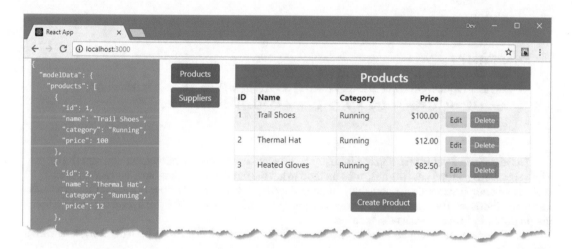

Figure 20-2. *Getting the contents of the data store*

If you examine the data that has been obtained through the getState method, you will see that everything is included so that both the contents of the modelData and stateData properties are available. The segmentation that is applied to reducers doesn't affect the data returned by the getState method, which provides access to everything in the data store.

Narrowing the Focus on Specific Data

To make it easier to keep track of the contents of the data store, I am going to focus on a subset of the data returned by the getState method, which will allow me to more easily demonstrate other Redux features. In Listing 20-4, I have changed the StoreAccess component so that it displays only the first product object and the set of state data variables.

Listing 20-4. Focusing the Data in the StoreAccess.js File in the src/store Folder

```
import React, { Component } from "react";

export class StoreAccess extends Component {

    constructor(props) {
        super(props);
        this.selectors = {
```

```
                product: (storeState) => storeState.modelData.products[0],
                state: (storeState) => storeState.stateData
            }
        }

        render() {
            return <div className="bg-info">
                <pre className="text-white">
                    { JSON.stringify(this.selectData(), null, 2) }
                </pre>
            </div>
        }

        selectData() {
            let storeState = this.props.store.getState();
            return Object.entries(this.selectors).map(([k, v]) => [k, v(storeState)])
                .reduce((result, [k, v]) => ({ ...result, [k]: v}), {});
        }
    }
```

I have defined a selectors object whose property values are functions that select data from the store. The selectData method uses the getState method to get the data from the data store and invokes each selector function to generate the data that is rendered by the component. (The use of the entries, map, and reduce methods produces an object with the same property names as the selectors prop with values that are produced by invoking each selector function.)

The changes to the component select a more manageable section of the data from the store, as shown in Figure 20-3.

Figure 20-3. *Selecting a subset of the store data*

Observing Data Store Changes

The object returned by the getState method is a snapshot of the data in the store, which isn't automatically updated when the store changes. The usual React change detection features don't work on the store because it is not part of a component's state data. As a consequence, changes made to the data in the store do not trigger a React update.

Redux provides the subscribe method to receive notifications when a change has been made to the data store, which allows the getState method to be called again to get a fresh snapshot of the data. In Listing 20-5, I have used the subscribe method in the StoreAccess component to ensure that the data displayed by the component is kept up-to-date.

Listing 20-5. Subscribing to Change Notifications in the StoreAccess.js File in the src/store Folder

```
import React, { Component } from "react";

export class StoreAccess extends Component {

    constructor(props) {
        super(props);
        this.selectors = {
            product: (storeState) => storeState.modelData.products[0],
            state: (storeState) => storeState.stateData
        }
        this.state = this.selectData();
    }

    render() {
        return <div className="bg-info">
            <pre className="text-white">
                { JSON.stringify(this.state, null, 2) }
            </pre>
        </div>
    }

    selectData() {
        let storeState = this.props.store.getState();
        return Object.entries(this.selectors).map(([k, v]) => [k, v(storeState)])
            .reduce((result, [k, v]) => ({ ...result, [k]: v}), {});
    }

    handleDataStoreChange() {
        let newData = this.selectData();
        Object.keys(this.selectors)
            .filter(key => this.state[key] !== newData[key])
            .forEach(key => this.setState({ [key]: newData[key]}));
    }

    componentDidMount() {
        this.unsubscriber =
            this.props.store.subscribe(() => this.handleDataStoreChange());
    }
```

```
componentWillUnmount() {
    this.unsubscriber();
}
}
```

I subscribe to updates in the componentDidMount method. The result from the subscribe method is a function that can be used to unsubscribe from updates, which I invoke in the componentWillUnmount method.

The argument to the subscribe method is a function that will be invoked when there have been changes to the data store. No argument is provided to the function, which is just a signal that there has been a change and that the getState method can be used to get the new contents of the data store.

Redux doesn't provide any information about what data has been changed and so I defined the handleStoreChange method to inspect the data obtained by each of the selector functions to see whether the data that the component renders has changed. I use the component state data feature to keep track of the displayed data and use the setState method to trigger updates. It is important to perform a state change only when the data displayed by the component has changed; otherwise, an update would be performed for every change made to the data store.

To see the effect of a change, click the Edit button for the Trail Shoes product, make a change to the Name field, and click the Save button. As you go through this process, the data displayed by the StoreAccess component will reflect the changes in the data store, as shown in Figure 20-4.

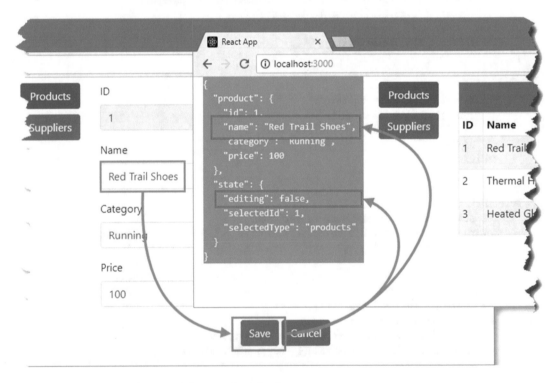

Figure 20-4. *Receiving change notifications from the data store*

Dispatching Actions

Actions can be dispatched using the `dispatch` method, which is the same `dispatch` to which the React-Redux package provided access in Chapter 19 when I needed to dispatch multiple actions.

As I explained in Chapter 19, actions are created through action creators. In Listing 20-6, I added a button to the `StoreAccess` component that uses an action creator to obtain an action object, which is then sent to the data store using the `dispatch` method.

Listing 20-6. Dispatching an Action in the StoreAccess.js File in the src/store Folder

```
import React, { Component } from "react";
import { startCreatingProduct } from "./stateActions";

export class StoreAccess extends Component {

    constructor(props) {
        super(props);
        this.selectors = {
            product: (storeState) => storeState.modelData.products[0],
            state: (storeState) => storeState.stateData
        }
        this.state = this.selectData();
    }

    render() {
        return <React.Fragment>
            <div className="text-center">
                <button className="btn btn-primary m-1"
                    onClick={ this.dispatchAction }>
                        Dispatch Action
                </button>
            </div>
            <div className="bg-info">
                <pre className="text-white">
                    { JSON.stringify(this.state, null, 2) }
                </pre>
            </div>
        </React.Fragment>
    }

    dispatchAction = () => {
        this.props.store.dispatch(startCreatingProduct())
    }

    selectData() {
        let storeState = this.props.store.getState();
        return Object.entries(this.selectors).map(([k, v]) => [k, v(storeState)])
            .reduce((result, [k, v]) => ({ ...result, [k]: v}), {});
    }
```

```
handleDataStoreChange() {
    let newData = this.selectData();
    Object.keys(this.selectors)
        .filter(key => this.state[key] !== newData[key])
        .forEach(key => this.setState({ [key]: newData[key]}));
}

componentDidMount() {
    this.unsubscriber =
        this.props.store.subscribe(() => this.handleDataStoreChange());
}

componentWillUnmount() {
    this.unsubscriber();
}
}
```

The button responds to the click event by invoking the dispatchAction method, which invokes the startCreatingProduct action creator and passes the result to the data store's dispatch method. The result is that clicking the button toggles the display to show the editor, as shown in Figure 20-5.

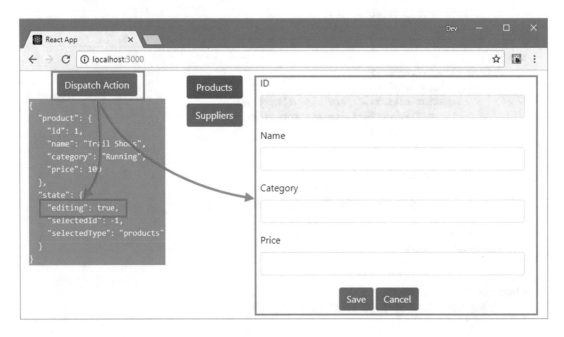

Figure 20-5. *Dispatching an action*

Creating a Connector Component

The ability to get the current data from the store, receive change notifications, and dispatch actions provides all the features to create a basic connector component that provides a rudimentary equivalent to the React-Redux package I used in the example application. To create the facility to connect components to the data store through the Redux API, I added a file called CustomConnector.js to the store folder and added the code shown in Listing 20-7.

___

■ **Caution**   I don't recommend using a custom connector in real projects. The React-Redux package has additional features and has been thoroughly tested, but combining core React features with the Redux data store API provides a useful example of how advanced features can be created.

___

Listing 20-7. The Contents of the CustomConnector.js File in the src/store Folder

```
import React, { Component } from "react";

export const CustomConnectorContext = React.createContext();

export class CustomConnectorProvider extends Component {

    render() {
        return <CustomConnectorContext.Provider value={ this.props.dataStore }>
            { this.props.children }
        </CustomConnectorContext.Provider>
    }
}

export class CustomConnector extends React.Component {
    static contextType = CustomConnectorContext;

    constructor(props, context) {
        super(props, context);
        this.state = this.selectData();
        this.functionProps = Object.entries(this.props.dispatchers)
            .map(([k, v]) => [k, (...args) => this.context.dispatch(v(...args))])
            .reduce((result, [k, v]) => ({...result, [k]: v}), {})
    }

    render() {
        return  React.Children.map(this.props.children, c =>
            React.cloneElement(c, { ...this.state, ...this.functionProps }))
    }

    selectData() {
        let storeState = this.context.getState();
        return Object.entries(this.props.selectors).map(([k, v]) =>
                [k, v(storeState)])
            .reduce((result, [k, v]) => ({ ...result, [k]: v}), {});
    }

    handleDataStoreChange() {
        let newData = this.selectData();
        Object.keys(this.props.selectors)
            .filter(key => this.state[key] !== newData[key])
            .forEach(key => this.setState({ [key]: newData[key]}));
    }
```

```
    componentDidMount() {
        this.unsubscriber =
            this.context.subscribe(() => this.handleDataStoreChange());
    }

    componentWillUnmount() {
        this.unsubscriber();
    }
}
```

I have used the context API to make the data store available through a `CustomConnectorProvider` component, which is received by a `CustomConnector` component that receives selector and action creator props. The selector props are processed to set the state of the component so that changes can be detected and processed, while the action creator props are wrapped in the `dispatch` method so they can be invoked as function props by the connected child components. To demonstrate the custom connector, I added the content shown in Listing 20-8 to the App component.

Listing 20-8. Using the Custom Connector in the App.js File in the src Folder

```
import React, { Component } from "react";
import { Provider } from "react-redux";
import dataStore, { deleteProduct } from "./store";
import { Selector } from "./Selector";
import { ProductDisplay } from "./ProductDisplay";
import { SupplierDisplay } from "./SupplierDisplay";
import { StoreAccess } from "./store/StoreAccess";
import { CustomConnector, CustomConnectorProvider } from "./store/CustomConnector";
import { startEditingProduct } from "./store/stateActions";
import { ProductTable } from "./ProductTable";

const selectors = {
    products: (store) => store.modelData.products
}

const dispatchers = {
    editCallback: startEditingProduct,
    deleteCallback: deleteProduct
}

export default class App extends Component {

    render() {
        return <div className="container-fluid">
            <div className="row">
                <div className="col-3">
                    <StoreAccess store={ dataStore } />
                </div>
                <div className="col">
                    <Provider store={ dataStore }>
                        <Selector>
                            <ProductDisplay name="Products" />
                            <SupplierDisplay name="Suppliers" />
```

```
                    </Selector>
                </Provider>
            </div>
        </div>
        <div className="row">
            <div className="col">
                <CustomConnectorProvider dataStore={ dataStore }>
                    <CustomConnector selectors={ selectors }
                            dispatchers={ dispatchers }>
                        <ProductTable/>
                    </CustomConnector>
                </CustomConnectorProvider>
            </div>
        </div>
    </div>
    }
}
```

I don't want to replace the existing application content, so I added a row to the Bootstrap grid layout and used it to display a `ProductTable` component that is connected to the data store using the components defined in Listing 20-8. The `CustomConnector` component is defined as the child of the `CustomConnectorProvider` component for brevity, and the effect is to map the selectors and action creators to props that are presented to the `ProductTable` component. The result is that the application displays a second table of products, both of which reflect changes to the data they display, as shown in Figure 20-6.

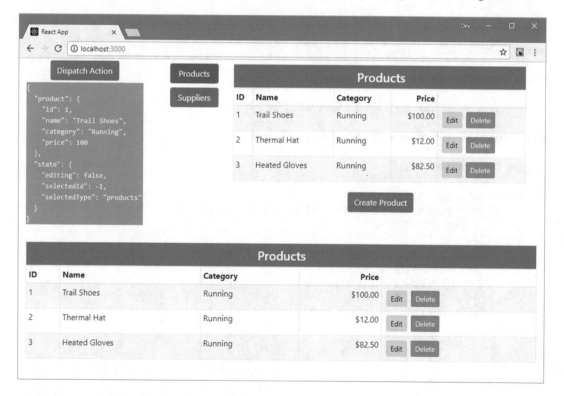

Figure 20-6. *Using a custom data store connector*

Enhancing Reducers

As I explained in Chapter 19, a reducer is a function that processes an action and updates the data store. A *reducer enhancer* is a function that accepts one or more normal reducers and uses them to add additional features to the data store.

Redux has no special awareness when a reducer enhancer is used because the result appears just like a regular reducer and is passed to the createStore method in just the same way, as this statement from the index.js file in the src/store folder shows:

```
...
export default createStore(combineReducers(
    {
        modelData: modelReducer,
        stateData: stateReducer
    }));
...
```

The combineReducers function is a reducer enhancer that comes built-in to Redux and that I used in Chapter 19 to keep the reducer logic for the model and state data separate.

Reducer enhancers are useful because they receive the actions before they are processed, which means they can alter actions, reject them, or handle them in special ways, such as processing them using multiple reducers, which is what the combineReducers function does.

To demonstrate a reducer enhancer, I added a file called customReducerEnhancer.js to the store folder and added the code shown in Listing 20-9.

Listing 20-9. The Contents of the customReducerEnhancer.js File in the src/store Folder

```
import { initialData } from "./initialData";

export const STORE_RESET = "store_clear";

export const resetStore = () => ({ type: STORE_RESET });

export function customReducerEnhancer(originalReducer) {

    let intialState = null;

    return (storeData, action) => {
        if (action.type === STORE_RESET && initialData != null) {
            return intialState;
        } else {
            const result = originalReducer(storeData, action);
            if (intialState == null) {
                intialState = result;
            }
            return result;
        }
    }
}
```

The customReducerEnhancer function accepts a reducer as its argument and returns a new reducer function that can be used by the data store. The enhancer function makes a note of the initial state of the data store, which is obtained by the first action that is sent to the reducers. A new action type, STORE_RESET, causes the enhancer function to return the initial data store state, which has the effect of resetting the data store. All other actions are passed on to the normal reducer. To help implement the store reset feature, Listing 20-9 defines a resetStore action creator function. In Listing 20-10, I have applied the reducer enhancer to the data store.

Listing 20-10. Applying a Reducer Enhancer in the index.js File in the src/store Folder

```
import { createStore, combineReducers } from "redux";
import modelReducer from "./modelReducer";
import stateReducer from "./stateReducer";
import { customReducerEnhancer } from "./customReducerEnhancer";

const enhancedReducer = customReducerEnhancer(
    combineReducers(
        {
            modelData: modelReducer,
            stateData: stateReducer
        })
);

export default createStore(enhancedReducer);

export { saveProduct, saveSupplier, deleteProduct, deleteSupplier }
    from "./modelActionCreators";
```

Reducer enhancers can be combined. In this listing, I use the reducer created by the combineReducers function as the argument to the customReducerEnhancer function. In Listing 20-11, I used the resetStore action creator to create an action when the user clicks the button rendered by the StoreAccess component.

Listing 20-11. Changing Actions in the StoreAccess.js File in the src/store Folder

```
import React, { Component } from "react";
//import { startCreatingProduct } from "./stateActions";
import { resetStore } from "./customReducerEnhancer";

export class StoreAccess extends Component {

    constructor(props) {
        super(props);
        this.selectors = {
            product: (storeState) => storeState.modelData.products[0],
            state: (storeState) => storeState.stateData
        }
        this.state = this.selectData();
    }
```

```
    render() {
        return <React.Fragment>
            <div className="text-center">
                <button className="btn btn-primary m-1"
                    onClick={ this.dispatchAction }>
                        Dispatch Action
                </button>
            </div>
            <div className="bg-info">
                <pre className="text-white">
                    { JSON.stringify(this.state, null, 2) }
                </pre>
            </div>
        </React.Fragment>
    }

    dispatchAction = () => {
        this.props.store.dispatch(resetStore())
    }

    // ...other methods omitted for brevity...
}
```

The effect of the enhancer is that the application's state and model data are reset when the user clicks the Dispatch Action button, with the result that any changes are discarded, as shown in Figure 20-7.

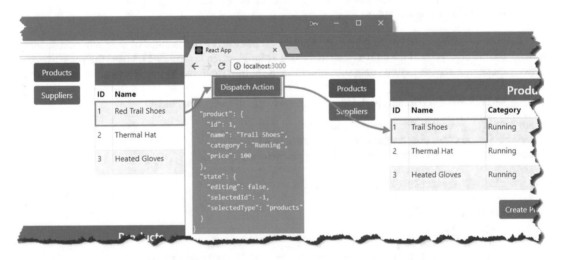

Figure 20-7. *Resetting the data in the store*

Using Data Store Middleware

Redux provides support for data store *middleware*, which are functions that receive actions after they have been passed to the dispatch method and before they reach the reducer, allowing them to be intercepted, transformed, or processed in some other way. The most common uses for middleware are to add support for actions that perform asynchronous tasks and to wrap actions in functions so they can be dispatched conditionally or in the future.

■ **Note** There are middleware packages available that address common project needs and that you should consider instead of writing custom code. The `redux-promise` package supports asynchronous actions (see `https://github.com/redux-utilities/redux-promise`), and the `redux-thunk` package supports action creators that return functions (see `https://github.com/reduxjs/redux-thunk`). I find, however, that neither of these packages works in just the way I require, so I prefer to create my own middleware.

To demonstrate the use of middleware, I added a file called `multiActionMiddleware.js` to the src/store folder and added the code shown in Listing 20-12.

Listing 20-12. The Contents of the multiActionMiddleware.js File in the src/store Folder

```
export function multiActions({dispatch, getState}) {
    return function receiveNext(next) {
        return function processAction(action) {
            if (Array.isArray(action)) {
                action.forEach(a => next(a));
            } else {
                next(action);
            }
        }
    }
}
```

Middleware is expressed as a set of functions that return other functions, and to make it easier to understand, I have used the function keyword in Listing 20-12. The outer function, multiActions, is called when the middleware is registered with the data store, and it receives the data store's dispatch and getState method, like this:

```
...
export function multiActions({dispatch, getState}) {
...
```

This provides the middleware with the ability to dispatch actions and to get the data currently in the data store. A data store can use multiple middleware components; actions are passed from one to the next in a chain, and then they are passed to the data store's dispatch method. The job of the multiActions function is to return a function that will be invoked once the middleware chain has been assembled and that provides the next middleware component in the chain.

```
...
export function multiActions({dispatch, getState}) {
    return function receiveNext(next) {
...
```

A middleware component will usually process an action and then pass it on to the next component in the chain by invoking the next function.

The result of the receiveNext function is to return the innermost function, which is invoked when an action has been dispatched to the data store and which I have called processAction in Listing 20-12.

```
...
export function multiActions({dispatch, getState}) {
    return function receiveNext(next) {
        return function processAction(action) {
...
```

This function is able to change or replace the action object before it is passed on to the next middleware component. It is also possible to short-circuit the chain by invoking the dispatch method received by the outer function or do nothing at all (in which case the action won't be processed by the data store). The middleware component that I defined in Listing 20-12 checks to see whether the action is an array, in which case it passes on each object contained in the array to the next middleware component for processing.

Defining the nested functions helps explain how a middleware component is defined, but the convention is to use fat arrow functions, as shown in Listing 20-13.

Listing 20-13. Using Fat Arrow Functions in the multiActionMiddleware.js File in the src/store Folder

```
export const multiActions = ({dispatch, getState}) => next => action => {
    if (Array.isArray(action)) {
        action.forEach(a => next(a));
    } else {
        next(action);
    }
}
```

This is the same functionality as Listing 20-12 but expressed more concisely. Redux provides an applyMiddlware function that is used to create the middleware chain for use with the data store and which I used in Listing 20-14 to add the new middleware component to the application.

Listing 20-14. Registering Middleware in the index.js File in the src/store Folder

```
import { createStore, combineReducers, applyMiddleware } from "redux";
import modelReducer from "./modelReducer";
import stateReducer from "./stateReducer";
import { customReducerEnhancer } from "./customReducerEnhancer";
import { multiActions } from "./multiActionMiddleware";

const enhancedReducer = customReducerEnhancer(
    combineReducers(
        {
            modelData: modelReducer,
            stateData: stateReducer
        })
);
```

```
export default createStore(enhancedReducer, applyMiddleware(multiActions));

export { saveProduct, saveSupplier, deleteProduct, deleteSupplier }
    from "./modelActionCreators";
```

The middleware function is passed as an argument to the Redux applyMiddleware function, whose result is then passed as an argument to the createStore function.

■ **Tip** Multiple middleware functions can be passed as separate arguments to the applyMiddleware function, which will chain them together in the order they have been specified.

Now that the data store can process arrays of actions, I can define action creators that generate more complex results and that allow connector components to be expressed more simply. I added a file called multiActionCreators.js in the src/store folder and used it to define the action creator shown in Listing 20-15.

Listing 20-15. The Contents of the multiActionCreators.js File in the src/store Folder

```
import { PRODUCTS } from "./dataTypes";
import { saveProduct, saveSupplier } from "./modelActionCreators";
import { endEditing } from "./stateActions";

export const saveAndEndEditing = (data, dataType) =>
    [dataType === PRODUCTS ? saveProduct(data) : saveSupplier(data), endEditing()];
```

It is not a requirement to put such action creators in a separate file, but this creator mixes actions that affect model and state data, and I prefer to keep them apart. The saveAndEndEditing action receives a data object and type and uses it to produce an array of actions that will be received by the middleware and dispatched in sequence. In Listing 20-16, I have replaced the statements in the EditorConnector component that used the dispatch method directly to send multiple events.

Listing 20-16. Dispatching Multiple Actions in the EditorConnector.js File in the src/store Folder

```
import { connect } from "react-redux";
import { endEditing } from "./stateActions";
//import { saveProduct, saveSupplier } from "./modelActionCreators";
import { PRODUCTS, SUPPLIERS  } from "./dataTypes";
import { saveAndEndEditing } from "./multiActionCreators";

export const EditorConnector = (dataType, presentationComponent) => {

    const mapStateToProps = (storeData) => ({
        editing: storeData.stateData.editing
            && storeData.stateData.selectedType === dataType,
        product: (storeData.modelData[PRODUCTS]
            .find(p => p.id === storeData.stateData.selectedId)) || {},
        supplier:(storeData.modelData[SUPPLIERS]
            .find(s => s.id === storeData.stateData.selectedId)) || {}
    })
```

```
const mapDispatchToProps = {
    cancelCallback: endEditing,
    saveCallback: (data) => saveAndEndEditing(data, dataType)
}

    return connect(mapStateToProps, mapDispatchToProps)(presentationComponent);
}
```

There is no change in the behavior of the application, but the code is more concise and easier to understand.

Enhancing the Data Store

Most projects will not need to modify the behavior of the data store, and if they do, the middleware features described in the previous chapter will be sufficient. But if middleware doesn't provide sufficient flexibility, a more advanced option is to use an *enhancer function*, which is a function that takes responsibility for creating the data store object and that can provide wrappers around the standard methods or define new ones.

The applyMiddleware function I used earlier is an enhancer function. This function replaces the data store's dispatch method so that it can channel actions through its chain of middleware components before they are passed to the reducer.

To demonstrate the use of enhancer functions, I am going to add a new method to the data store that dispatches actions asynchronously. I added a file called asyncEnhancer.js to the src/store folder and added the code shown in Listing 20-17.

Listing 20-17. The Contents of the asyncEnhancer.js File in the src/store Folder

```
export function asyncEnhancer(delay) {
    return function(createStoreFunction) {
        return function(...args) {
            const store = createStoreFunction(...args);
            return {
                ...store,
                dispatchAsync: (action) => new Promise((resolve, reject) => {
                    setTimeout(() => {
                        store.dispatch(action);
                        resolve();
                    }, delay);
                })
            };
        }
    }
}
```

The enhancer dispatches actions asynchronously, returning a Promise that is resolved once the action has been dispatched. There are currently no tasks in the example application that need asynchronous work, and so I have introduced a delay before dispatching actions to similar a background activity.

This is another Redux feature that requires a nested set of functions, which I defined using the function keyword so I can explain how they fit together. The outer function is invoked when the enhancer is applied to the data store and provides an opportunity to receive arguments that will configure the enhancer's behavior. The outermost function in Listing 20-17 receives the length of the delay that will be applied before an action is dispatched.

```
...
export function asyncEnhancer(delay) {
...
```

Now it gets more complex: the result of the outer function is a function that receives the createStore function. The word *function* appears too many times for the previous sentence to make immediate sense, and it is worth unpacking what happens.

To give enhancers complete control, Redux lets them replace the createStore function with a custom alternative. But most reducers will just need to add features to the standard data store and so Redux provides the existing createStore function.

```
...
export function asyncEnhancer(delay) {
    return function(createStoreFunction) {
...
```

When the enhancer is applied, this function will be invoked, and the result will be used to replace the standard createStore function, which takes us to the innermost function in Listing 20-17, which is the one that does all the work.

```
...
return function(...args) {
    const store = createStoreFunction(...args);
    return {
        ...store,
        dispatchAsync: (action) => new Promise((resolve, reject) => {

            // ...statements omitted for brevity...

        })
    };
}
...
```

When a data store is created, Redux invokes the function provided by the enhancer and uses the result as the data store object, ensuring that any additional features are available to the rest of the application. In this case, the enhancer uses the standard createStore function and then adds a dispatchAsync method to the result. The new method receives an action and dispatches it after a delay. Using the function keyword makes it easier to see the relationship between the nested functions, but enhancers are typically expressed using fat arrow functions, as shown in Listing 20-18. This is the same functionality but expressed more concisely.

Listing 20-18. Using Arrow Functions in the asyncEnhancer.js File in the src/store Folder

```
export const asyncEnhancer = delay => createStoreFunction => (...args) => {
    const store = createStoreFunction(...args);
    return {
        ...store,
        dispatchAsync: (action) => new Promise((resolve, reject) => {
            setTimeout(() => {
                store.dispatch(action);
                resolve();
```

```
            }, delay);
        })
    };
}
```

Applying the Enhancer

The standard createStore function can accept only a single enhancer function, and I am already using the applyMiddleware enhancer. Fortunately, reducer functions can be composed so that the result from one enhancer can be passed to another. To simplify the process of combining functions, Redux provides the compose function, which I have used in Listing 20-19 to apply the new enhancer to the data store.

Listing 20-19. Adding an Enhancer in the index.js File in the src/store Folder

```
import { createStore, combineReducers, applyMiddleware, compose } from "redux";
import modelReducer from "./modelReducer";
import stateReducer from "./stateReducer";
import { customReducerEnhancer } from "./customReducerEnhancer";
import { multiActions } from "./multiActionMiddleware";
import { asyncEnhancer } from "./asyncEnhancer";

const enhancedReducer = customReducerEnhancer(
    combineReducers(
        {
            modelData: modelReducer,
            stateData: stateReducer
        })
);

export default createStore(enhancedReducer,
    compose(applyMiddleware(multiActions), asyncEnhancer(2000)));

export { saveProduct, saveSupplier, deleteProduct, deleteSupplier }
    from "./modelActionCreators";
```

The result from the compose function is passed to createStore, and both enhancers are applied to the data store, adding middleware and the new dispatchAsync method. In Listing 20-20, I updated the StoreAccess component so that it uses the enhanced data store method when it dispatches an action and disables the button element until the background task is complete.

Listing 20-20. Using the Enhanced Data Store in the StoreAccess.js File in the src/store Folder

```
import React, { Component } from "react";
import { resetStore } from "./customReducerEnhancer";

export class StoreAccess extends Component {

    constructor(props) {
        super(props);
        this.selectors = {
```

```
        product: (storeState) => storeState.modelData.products[0],
        state: (storeState) => storeState.stateData
    }
    this.state = this.selectData();
    this.buttonRef = React.createRef();
}

render() {
    return <React.Fragment>
        <div className="text-center">
            <button className="btn btn-primary m-1" ref={ this.buttonRef }
                onClick={ this.dispatchAction }>
                    Dispatch Action
            </button>
        </div>
        <div className="bg-info">
            <pre className="text-white">
                { JSON.stringify(this.state, null, 2) }
            </pre>
        </div>
    </React.Fragment>
}

dispatchAction = () => {
    this.buttonRef.current.disabled = true;
    this.props.store.dispatchAsync(resetStore())
        .then(data => this.buttonRef.current.disabled = false);
}

// ...other methods omitted for brevity...
}
```

The result is that clicking the button dispatches the action, which will be processed after a two-second display. The component receives a Promise when it dispatches the action, which is resolved once it has been dispatched, allowing the component to enable the button element again, as shown in Figure 20-8.

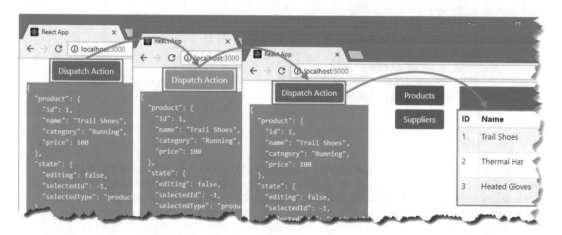

Figure 20-8. *Using an enhanced data store*

Using the React-Redux API

The previous sections demonstrated that you can work directly with the Redux API to connect components to the data store. For most projects, however, it is simpler and easier to use the React-Redux package as demonstrated in Chapter 19. In the sections that follow, I describe the advanced options that the React-Redux package provides for configuring how components are connected to the data store.

Advanced Connect Features

The connect method is typically used with two arguments, which select the data props and the function props, like this statement from the TableConnector component:

```
...
return connect(mapStateToProps, mapDispatchToProps)(presentationComponent);
...
```

The connect function can accept some additional arguments for advanced features and can receive arguments expressed in different ways. In this section, I explain the options for using the arguments you are already familiar with and introduce the new arguments and demonstrate their use.

Mapping Data Props

The first argument to the connect function selects the data from the store for the component's data props. Usually, the selectors are defined as a function that receives the value from the store's getState method and returns an object whose properties correspond to the prop names. The selector function is invoked when there is a change to the data store, and the higher-order component created by the connect function uses the shouldComponentUpdate lifecycle method (described in Chapter 13) to see whether any the changed values require the connector component to update.

The selection of data values is flexible and isn't just about mapping data store properties to props. In the TableConnector component, for example, I used the selector function to map data values from different parts of the store, like this:

```
...
const mapStateToProps = (storeData) => ({
    products: storeData.modelData[PRODUCTS],
    suppliers: storeData.modelData[SUPPLIERS].map(supp => ({
        ...supp,
        products: supp.products.map(id =>
            storeData.modelData[PRODUCTS].find(p => p.id === Number(id)) || id)
                .map(val => val.name || val)
    }))
})
...
```

The selector function can also be expressed with a second argument, which is used to receive the props provided for the connector component by its parent. This allows for the component's props to be used in selecting data and ensures that the selector function will be reevaluated when the component's props change as well as when there are changes to the data store. Listing 20-21 demonstrates the use of the additional argument.

Listing 20-21. Using an Additional Selector Argument in the TableConnector.js File in the src/store Folder

```
import { connect } from "react-redux";
import { startEditingProduct, startEditingSupplier } from "./stateActions";
import { deleteProduct, deleteSupplier } from "./modelActionCreators";
import { PRODUCTS, SUPPLIERS } from "./dataTypes";

export const TableConnector = (dataType, presentationComponent) => {

    const mapStateToProps = (storeData, ownProps) => {
        if (!ownProps.needSuppliers) {
            return { products: storeData.modelData[PRODUCTS] };
        } else {
            return {
                suppliers: storeData.modelData[SUPPLIERS].map(supp => ({
                    ...supp,
                    products: supp.products.map(id =>
                        storeData.modelData[PRODUCTS]
                            .find(p => p.id === Number(id)) || id)
                            .map(val => val.name || val)
                }))
            }
        }
    }

    const mapDispatchToProps = {
        editCallback: dataType === PRODUCTS
            ? startEditingProduct : startEditingSupplier,
        deleteCallback: dataType === PRODUCTS ? deleteProduct : deleteSupplier
    }

    return connect(mapStateToProps, mapDispatchToProps)(presentationComponent);
}
```

One problem with creating connectors that are applied to multiple components is that too much data is selected, which can lead to unnecessary updates when a change in the data store affects a prop that is used by one component but not another. The TableConnector component is a connector for both tables of product and supplier data, but only the supplier data requires the suppliers prop to be mapped from the data store. For the product table, not only does this mean that the computation of the suppliers property is wasted, but it causes updates when data that it does not display is changed.

The additional argument—which is conventionally named ownProps—allows each instance of a connector component to be customized through the standard React prop features. In Listing 20-21, I used the ownProps argument to decide which props are mapped to the data store based on the value of a prop named needSuppliers applied to the connector component. If the value is true, then a suppliers prop is mapped to the data store and the products prop is mapped otherwise.

In Listing 20-22, I have added the needSuppliers prop to the ConnectedTable component rendered by the SupplierDisplay component, which will ensure that it maps the data that its presentation component requires. The corresponding ConnectedTable component rendered by the ProductDisplay component doesn't have the needSuppliers prop and won't receive the data from the store.

Listing 20-22. Adding a Prop in the SupplierDisplay.js File in the src Folder

```
...
export const SupplierDisplay = connectFunction(
    class extends Component {

        render() {
            if (this.props.editing) {
                return <ConnectedEditor key={ this.props.selected.id || -1 } />
            } else {
                return <div className="m-2">
                    <ConnectedTable needSuppliers={ true } />
                    <div className="text-center">
                        <button className="btn btn-primary m-1"
                            onClick={ this.props.createSupplier }>
                                Create Supplier
                        </button>
                    </div>
                </div>
            }
        }
    }
})
...
```

There is no difference in the behavior of the application, but behind the scenes, each presentation component that is connected to the data store by the ConnectedTable components uses different props.

THE DANGERS OF PREMATURE OPTIMIZATION

Don't worry too much about optimizing updates until you find you have a performance problem. Almost all optimization adds complexity to a project, and you may find that the performance penalty incurred by your unoptimized code is not discernable or not enough of a problem to worry about. It is easy to get bogged down in trying to optimize away problems that may not exist, and a better approach is to write the clearest, simplest code you can and then optimize the parts that don't behave the way you require.

Mapping Function Props

As I explained in Chapter 19, the second connect argument, which maps between function props, can be specified as an object or a function. When an object is provided, the value of each of the object's properties is assumed to be an action creator function and is automatically wrapped in the dispatch method and mapped to a function prop. When a function is provided, the function is given the dispatch method and is responsible for using it to create function prop mappings.

■ **Tip** You can omit the second argument to the connect function, in which the dispatch method is mapped to a prop, also named dispatch, which allows the component to create actions and dispatch them directly.

If you specify a function, then you can also choose to receive the connector components props, as described in the previous section. This allows for advanced components to receive direction from their parent about the set of function props that are mapped to the data store. In Listing 20-23, I have used a function to configure function props and defined a second argument to receive the component's props.

Listing 20-23. Using Props in the TableConnector.js File in the src/store Folder

```
import { connect } from "react-redux";
import { startEditingProduct, startEditingSupplier } from "./stateActions";
import { deleteProduct, deleteSupplier } from "./modelActionCreators";
import { PRODUCTS, SUPPLIERS } from "./dataTypes";

export const TableConnector = (dataType, presentationComponent) => {

    const mapStateToProps = (storeData, ownProps) => {
        if (!ownProps.needSuppliers) {
            return { products: storeData.modelData[PRODUCTS] };
        } else {
            return {
                suppliers: storeData.modelData[SUPPLIERS].map(supp => ({
                    ...supp,
                    products: supp.products.map(id =>
                        storeData.modelData[PRODUCTS]
                            .find(p => p.id === Number(id)) || id)
                            .map(val => val.name || val)
                }))
            }
        }
    }

    const mapDispatchToProps = (dispatch, ownProps) => {
        if (!ownProps.needSuppliers) {
            return {
                editCallback: (...args) => dispatch(startEditingProduct(...args)),
                deleteCallback: (...args) => dispatch(deleteProduct(...args))
            }
        } else {
            return {
                editCallback: (...args) => dispatch(startEditingSupplier(...args)),
                deleteCallback: (...args) => dispatch(deleteSupplier(...args))
            }
        }
    }

    return connect(mapStateToProps, mapDispatchToProps)(presentationComponent);
}
```

Merging Props

The connect function accepts a third argument that is used to compose the props before they are passed to the presentation component. This argument, known as mergeProps, is a function that receives the mapped data props, the function props, and the connected components props and returns an object that merges them into the object used as the props for the presentation component.

By default, the props are composed starting with the props received from the parent, which are then combined with the data props and function props. This means a prop received from the parent will be replaced with a mapped data prop that has the same name, and both will be replaced if there is a mapped function prop with the same name. The mergeProps function can be used to change the priority when there is a name clash, as well as binding actions so they are dispatched using values received as props from the parent. Listing 20-24 shows how props can be merged explicitly using the mergeProps argument.

Listing 20-24. Merging Props in the EditorConnector.js File in the src/store Folder

```
import { connect } from "react-redux";
import { endEditing } from "./stateActions";
import { PRODUCTS, SUPPLIERS  } from "./dataTypes";
import { saveAndEndEditing } from "./multiActionCreators";

export const EditorConnector = (dataType, presentationComponent) => {

    const mapStateToProps = (storeData) => ({
        editing: storeData.stateData.editing
            && storeData.stateData.selectedType === dataType,
        product: (storeData.modelData[PRODUCTS]
            .find(p => p.id === storeData.stateData.selectedId)) || {},
        supplier:(storeData.modelData[SUPPLIERS]
            .find(s => s.id === storeData.stateData.selectedId)) || {}
    })

    const mapDispatchToProps = {
        cancelCallback: endEditing,
        saveCallback: (data) => saveAndEndEditing(data, dataType)
    }

    const mergeProps = (dataProps, functionProps, ownProps) =>
        ({ ...dataProps, ...functionProps, ...ownProps })

    return connect(mapStateToProps, mapDispatchToProps,
        mergeProps)(presentationComponent);
}
```

The mergeProps function in Listing 20-24 combines the properties from each prop's object. The properties are copied from the objects in the order specified, which means the function copies from ownProps last and also means props received from the parent will be used when there are props with the same name.

Setting Connection Options

The final argument to the connect method is conventionally named options and is an object used to configure the connection to the data store. The options object can be defined with properties whose names are shown in Table 20-4.

Table 20-4. *The Options Object Property Names*

Name	Description
pure	By default, a connector component will be updated only when its own props change or when one of the selected values from the data store changes, which allows the higher-order component (HOC) created by connect to prevent updates when no prop or data change has been made. Setting this property to false indicates that the connector component may rely on other data, and the HOC will not try to prevent updates. The default values for this property is true.
areStatePropsEqual	This function is used to override the default equality comparison for the mapStateToProps values to minimize updates when the pure property is true.
areOwnPropsEqual	This function is used to override the default equality comparison for the mapDispatchToProps values to minimize updates when the pure property is true.
areMergedPropsEqual	This function is used to override the default equality comparison for the mergeProps values to minimize updates when the pure property is true.
areStatesEqual	This function is used to override the default equality comparison for the entire component state to minimize updates when the pure property is true.

Summary

In this chapter, I described the APIs provided by Redux and the React-Redux package and demonstrated how they can be used. I showed you how to connect a component directly to the data store using the Redux API, how to enhance the data store and its reducers, and how to define middleware components. I also demonstrated the advanced options available when using the React-Redux package, which can be used to manage a component's connection to the data store. In the next chapter, I introduce URL routing to the example application.

CHAPTER 21

■ ■ ■

Using URL Routing

At the moment, the selection of content displayed to the user is controlled by the application's state data. Some of that state data is specific to a single component, such as the Selector component, which manages the choice between products and supplier data. The rest of the data is in the Redux data store and is used by the connected components to decide whether the data table or editor components are required and to obtain the data to populate those components' content.

In this chapter, I introduce a different approach to structuring the application, which is to select content based on the browser's URL, known as *URL routing*. Instead of button elements whose event handlers dispatch Redux actions, I am going to render anchor elements that navigate to new URLs and respond to those URLs by selecting content and presenting it to the user. For complex applications, URL routing can make it easier to structure a project and make it easy to scale up and maintain features. Table 21-1 puts URL routing in context.

Table 21-1. *Putting URL Routing in Context*

Question	Answer
What is it?	URL routing uses the browser's current URL to select the content presented to the user.
Why is it useful?	URL routing allows applications to be structured without the need for shared state data, which becomes encoded in the URL, which also makes it easier to change the structure of an application.
How is it used?	Navigation elements are rendered that change the browser's URL without triggering a new HTTP request. The new URL is used to select the content presented to the user.
Are there any pitfalls or limitations?	Thorough testing is required to ensure that all of the URLs to which the user can navigate are handled correctly and display the appropriate content.
Are there any alternatives?	URL routing is entirely optional, and there are other ways to compose an application and its data, as demonstrated in earlier chapters.

Table 21-2 summarizes the chapter.

Table 21-2. *Chapter Summary*

Problem	Solution	Listing
Create a navigation element	Use the Link component	4, 13
Respond to navigation	Use the Route component	5–6
Match a specific URL	Use the Route component's exact prop	7
Match several URLs	Specify the URLs as an array in the Route component's path prop or use a regular expression	8–9
Select a single route	Use the Switch component	10
Define a fallback route	Use the Redirect component	11, 12
Indicate the active route	Use the NavLink component	14, 15
Choose the mechanism used to represent the route in the URL	Select the router component	16

Preparing for This Chapter

In this chapter, I continue using the productapp project created in Chapter 18 and used most recently in Chapter 20. To prepare for this chapter, open a new command prompt, navigate to the productapp folder, and run the command shown in Listing 21-1 to add a package to the project. The React Router package is available for a range of application types. The package installed in Listing 21-1 is for web applications.

■ **Tip** You can download the example project for this chapter—and for all the other chapters in this book—from https://github.com/Apress/pro-react-16.

Listing 21-1. Adding a Package to the Project

```
npm install react-router-dom@4.3.1
```

To simplify the content presented to the user, I have removed some of the content rendered by the App component, as shown in Listing 21-2.

Listing 21-2. Simplifying Content in the App.js File in the src Folder

```
import React, { Component } from "react";
import { Provider } from "react-redux";
import dataStore from "./store";
import { Selector } from "./Selector";
import { ProductDisplay } from "./ProductDisplay";
import { SupplierDisplay } from "./SupplierDisplay";
```

```
export default class App extends Component {

    render() {
        return  <Provider store={ dataStore }>
                    <Selector>
                        <ProductDisplay name="Products" />
                        <SupplierDisplay name="Suppliers" />
                    </Selector>
                </Provider>
    }
}
```

Save the changes to the component JavaScript file and use the command prompt to run the command shown in Listing 21-3 in the productapp folder to start the React development tools.

Listing 21-3. Starting the Development Tools

```
npm start
```

The project will be compiled, and the development HTTP server will be started. A new browser window will open and display the application, as shown in Figure 21-1.

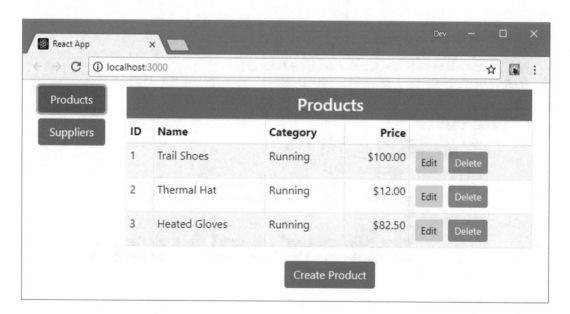

Figure 21-1. *Running the example application*

Getting Started with URL Routing

To get started, I am going to use URL routing in the Selector component so that it doesn't need its own state data to keep track of whether the user wants to work with products or suppliers.

There are two steps to setting up URL routing. The first step is to create the links that the user will click to navigate to a different part of the application. The second step is to select the content that will be displayed for each URL that the user can navigate to. These steps are performed using React components provided by the React-Router package, as shown in Listing 21-4.

Listing 21-4. Adding URL Routing in the Selector.js File in the src Folder

```
import React, { Component } from "react";
import { BrowserRouter as Router, Link, Route } from "react-router-dom";
import { ProductDisplay } from "./ProductDisplay";
import { SupplierDisplay } from "./SupplierDisplay";

export class Selector extends Component {

    // constructor(props) {
    //     super(props);
    //     this.state = {
    //         selection: React.Children.toArray(props.children)[0].props.name
    //     }
    // }

    // setSelection = (ev) => {
    //     ev.persist();
    //     this.setState({ selection: ev.target.name});
    // }

    render() {
        return <Router>
            <div className="container-fluid">
                <div className="row">
                    <div className="col-2">
                        <div><Link to="/products">Products</Link></div>
                        <div><Link to="/suppliers">Suppliers</Link></div>
                    </div>
                    <div className="col">
                        <Route path="/products" component={ ProductDisplay } />
                        <Route path="/suppliers" component={ SupplierDisplay} />
                    </div>
                </div>
            </div>
        </Router>
    }
}
```

Three components are required to set up a basic routing configuration. The Router component is used to provide access to the URL routing features. There are different ways of using the URL for navigation, each of which has its own React-Router component that I describe in the "Selecting and Configuring the Router" section. The convention is to import the component you require, which is `BrowserRouter` in this case, and assign it the name `Router`, which is then used as a container for the content that requires access to the routing features.

| **CHOOSING AN ALTERNATIVE ROUTING PACKAGE** |

React-Router is by far the most widely used routing package for React projects and is a good place to start for most applications. There are other routing packages available, but not all of them are specific to React and can require awkward adaptations.

If you can't get along with React-Router, then the best alternative is Backbone (`https://backbonejs.org`). This well-regarded package provides routing for any JavaScript application and works well with React.

Getting Started with the Link Component

The `Link` component renders an element that the user can click to navigate to a new URL, like this:

```
...
<div><Link to="/products">Products</Link></div>
...
```

The navigation URL is specified using the `to` prop, and this `Link` will navigate to the `/products` URL. Navigation URLs are specified relative to the application's starting URL, which is `http://localhost:3000` during development. That means that specifying `/products` for the `to` prop of a `Link` component tells it to render an element that will navigate to `http://localhost:3000/products`. These relative URLs will continue to work when the application is deployed and has a public URL.

Getting Started with the Route Component

The final component added to Listing 21-4 is `Route`, which waits until the browser navigates to a specific URL and then displays its content, like this:

```
...
<Route path="/products" component={ ProductDisplay } />
...
```

This `Route` component has been configured to wait until the browser navigates to the `/products` URL, at which point it will show the `ProductDisplay` component. For all other URLs, this `Route` component will not render any content.

The result of the changes in Listing 21-4 is not visually impressive, as Figure 21-2 shows, but it demonstrates the basic nature of URL routing. When the browser displays the application's starting URL, `http://localhost:3000`, no content is shown. When you click the `Products` or `Suppliers` links, the browser navigates to `http://localhost:3000/products` or `http://localhost:3000/suppliers`, and the `ProductDisplay` or `SupplierDisplay` components are shown.

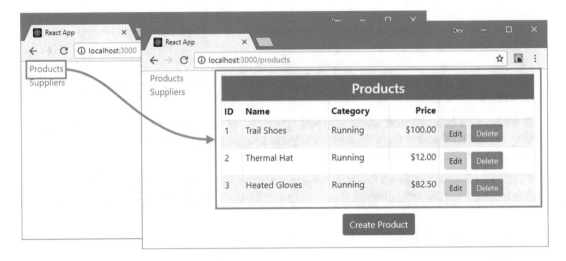

Figure 21-2. *Adding navigation elements*

Right-click either of navigation elements created by the Link components and select Inspect or Inspect Element from the pop-up menu, and you will see the HTML that has been rendered, which looks this:

```
...
<div><a href="/products">Products</a></div>
<div><a href="/suppliers">Suppliers</a></div>
...
```

The Link components have been rendered to produce anchor (elements whose tag is a) elements, and the value of the to prop has translated into URLs for the anchor element's href attributes. When you click one of the anchor elements, the browser navigates to a new URL, and the corresponding Route component displays its content. If the browser navigates to a URL for which no Route component has been configured, then no content is displayed, which is why a component was not shown until one of the links had been clicked.

■ **Caution** Do not try to create your own anchor elements for navigation because they will cause the browser to send an HTTP request to the server for the URL you specify with the effect that the application will be reloaded. The anchor elements rendered by the Link component have event handlers that change the URL using the HTML5 History API without triggering a new HTTP request.

Responding to Navigation

The Route component is used to implement an application's routing scheme, which it does by waiting until the browser navigates to a specific URL and displaying a component when it does. The mapping between URLs and components can be complex in real applications, and the matching of URLs and the selection of content by the Route component can be configured using the props described in Table 21-3, which I demonstrate in the sections that follow.

Table 21-3. *The Route Component Props*

Name	Description
path	The prop is used to specify the URL or URLs that the component should wait for.
exact	When this prop is true, only URLs that precisely equal the path prop are matched, as demonstrated in the "Restricting Matches with Props" section.
sensitive	When this prop is true, matching URLs is case-sensitive.
strict	When this prop is true, path values that end in a / will only match URLs whose corresponding segment also ends with a /.
component	This prop is used to specify a single component that will be displayed when the path prop matches the browser's current URL.
render	This prop is used to specify a function that returns the content that will be displayed when the path prop matches the browser's current URL.
children	This prop is used to specify a function that will always render content, even when the URL specified by the path prop doesn't match. This is useful for displaying content in descendent components or components that are not rendered in response to URL changes, as described in Chapter 22.

Selecting Components and Content

The component prop is used to specify a single component that will be displayed if the current URL is matched by the path prop. The component type is specified directly as the component prop value, like this:

```
...
<Route path="/products" component={ ProductDisplay } />
...
```

The value of the component prop should not be a function because it can lead to a new instance of the specified component being created each time that the application updates.

Using the render Prop

The advantage of the component prop is simplicity, and it works well for projects that have self-contained components that render all the required content and don't require props. The Route component provides the render prop for more complex content and to pass on props, as shown in Listing 21-5.

Listing 21-5. Using the render Prop in the Selector.js File in the src Folder

```
import React, { Component } from "react";
import { BrowserRouter as Router, Link, Route } from "react-router-dom";
import { ProductDisplay } from "./ProductDisplay";
import { SupplierDisplay } from "./SupplierDisplay";

export class Selector extends Component {

    render() {
        return <Router>
```

```
        <div className="container-fluid">
            <div className="row">
                <div className="col-2">
                    <div><Link to="/products">Products</Link></div>
                    <div><Link to="/suppliers">Suppliers</Link></div>
                </div>
                <div className="col">
                    <Route path="/products" render={ (routeProps) =>
                        <ProductDisplay myProp="myValue" /> } />
                    <Route path="/suppliers" render={ (routeProps) =>
                        <React.Fragment>
                            <h4 className="bg-info text-center text-white p-2">
                                Suppliers
                            </h4>
                            <SupplierDisplay />
                        </React.Fragment>
                    } />
                </div>
            </div>
        </div>
    </Router>
  }
}
```

The result of the function is the content that should be displayed by the Route component. In the listing, I passed on a prop to the ProductDisplay component and included the SupplierDisplay component in a larger fragment of content, as shown in Figure 21-3.

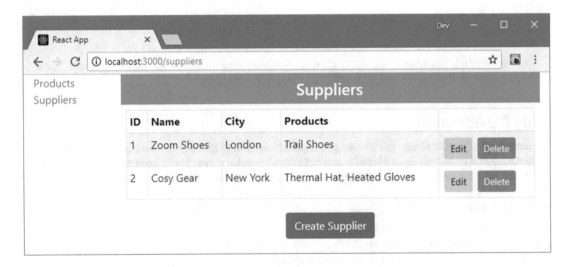

Figure 21-3. *Using the Route component's render prop*

■ **Tip** The function passed to the render prop receives an object that provides information about the state of the routing system, which I describe in Chapter 22.

Matching URLs

One of the most difficult aspects of using URL routing is making sure that the URLs you want to support are correctly matched by Route components. The Route component provides a range of features that allow you to expand or narrow the range of URLs that will be matched, which I describe in the sections that follow.

Matching Using Segments

The simplest way to match a URL is to provide one or more target segments to the Route component's path prop. This will match any URL that starts with the segments you specify, as shown in Listing 21-6.

Listing 21-6. Matching URLs in the Selector.js File in the src Folder

```
import React, { Component } from "react";
import { BrowserRouter as Router, Link, Route } from "react-router-dom";
//import { ProductDisplay } from "./ProductDisplay";
//import { SupplierDisplay } from "./SupplierDisplay";

export class Selector extends Component {

    renderMessage = (msg) => <h5 className="bg-info text-white m-2 p-2">{ msg }</h5>

    render() {
        return <Router>
            <div className="container-fluid">
                <div className="row">
                    <div className="col-2">
                        <div><Link to="/data/one">Link #1</Link></div>
                        <div><Link to="/data/two">Link #2</Link></div>
                        <div><Link to="/people/bob">Bob</Link></div>
                    </div>
                    <div className="col">
                        <Route path="/data"
                            render={ () => this.renderMessage("Route #1") } />
                        <Route path="/data/two"
                            render={ () => this.renderMessage("Route #2") } />
                    </div>
                </div>
            </div>
        </Router>
    }
}
```

I replaced the ProductDisplay and SupplierDisplay components with content generated by a method called renderMessage. There are three Link components, which target the URLs /data/one, data/two, and /people/bob.

The first Route component is configured with /data as its path prop. This will match any URL whose first segment is data, which means it will match the /data/one and /data/two URLs but not /people/bob. The second Route component has /data/two as the value of its path prop, so it will only match the /data/two URL. Each Route component evaluates its path prop independently, and you can see how they match URLs by clicking the navigation links, as shown in Figure 21-4.

Figure 21-4. *Matching URLs with the Route component*

One Route component matches the /data/one URL, both match the /data/two URL, and neither matches /people/bob, and so no content is displayed.

Restricting Matches with Props

The default behavior of the Route component can lead to over-matching, where a component matches a URL when you don't want it to. I might want to distinguish between the /data and /data/one URLs, for example, so that the first URL displays a list of data items and the second displays the details of a specific object. The default matching makes this difficult because a path prop of /data matches any URL whose first segment is /data, regardless of how many segments the URL contains in total.

To help restrict the range of URLs that a path will match, the Route component supports three additional props: exact, strict, and sensitive. The most useful of the three props is exact, which will match a URL only if it exactly matches the path prop value so that a URL of /data/one won't be matched by a path of /data, as shown in Listing 21-7.

Listing 21-7. Making Exact Matches in the Selector.js File in the src Folder

```
import React, { Component } from "react";
import { BrowserRouter as Router, Link, Route } from "react-router-dom";

export class Selector extends Component {

    renderMessage = (msg) => <h5 className="bg-info text-white m-2 p-2">{ msg }</h5>

    render() {
        return <Router>
            <div className="container-fluid">
                <div className="row">
                    <div className="col-2">
                        <div><Link to="/data">Data</Link></div>
                        <div><Link to="/data/one">Link #1</Link></div>
                        <div><Link to="/data/two">Link #2</Link></div>
                        <div><Link to="/people/bob">Bob</Link></div>
                    </div>
                    <div className="col">
                        <Route path="/data" exact={ true }
                            render={ () => this.renderMessage("Route #1") } />
```

```
            <Route path="/data/two"
                   render={ () => this.renderMessage("Route #2") } />
            </div>
          </div>
        </div>
      </Router>
    }
}
```

Setting the exact prop affects only the Route component to which it is applied. In the example, the exact prop prevents the first Route component from matching the /data/one and /data/two URLs, as shown in Figure 21-5.

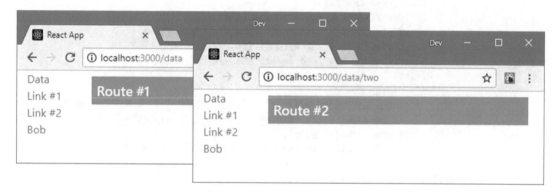

Figure 21-5. *Making exact matches*

When set to true, the strict prop is used to restrict matches for a path that has a trailing slash to URLs that have one too, so a path of /data/ will only match the /data/ URL and not /data. The strict prop does match URLs with additional segments, however, so that a path of /data/ will match /data/one.

The sensitive prop is used to control case sensitivity. When true, it will allow matches only when the case of the path prop matches the case of the URL, so a path of /data will not match a /Data URL.

Specifying Multiple URLs in a Path

The value of the Route component's path prop can be an array of URLs, which causes content to be displayed if any of them are matched. This can be useful when the same content is required in response to URLs that don't have a common structure (such as displaying the same component in response to /data/ list and /people/list) or when a specific number of exact matches are required, such as matching /data/ one and /data/two but not any other URL that starts with /data, as demonstrated in Listing 21-8.

■ **Note** At the time of writing, there is a mismatch with the prop types that are expected by the Route component that results in a JavaScript console warning when an array is used. This warning can be ignored and may be fixed by the time you read this chapter. See Chapters 10 and 11 for details of how the data types that a component expects for its props can be specified.

Listing 21-8. Using an Array of Paths in the Selector.js File in the src Folder

```
import React, { Component } from "react";
import { BrowserRouter as Router, Link, Route } from "react-router-dom";

export class Selector extends Component {

    renderMessage = (msg) => <h5 className="bg-info text-white m-2 p-2">{ msg }</h5>

    render() {
        return <Router>
            <div className="container-fluid">
                <div className="row">
                    <div className="col-2">
                        <div><Link to="/data">Data</Link></div>
                        <div><Link to="/data/one">Link #1</Link></div>
                        <div><Link to="/data/two">Link #2</Link></div>
                        <div><Link to="/people/bob">Bob</Link></div>
                    </div>
                    <div className="col">
                        <Route path={["/data/one", "/people/bob" ] }  exact={ true }
                            render={ () => this.renderMessage("Route #1") } />
                        <Route path={["/data", "/people" ] }
                            render={ () => this.renderMessage("Route #2") } />
                    </div>
                </div>
            </div>
        </Router>
    }
}
```

The path array is provided as an expression using curly braces. The path property of the first Route component is set to an array containing /data/one and /people/bob. These paths are combined with the exact prop to restrict the URLs that the component will match. The second Route component is configured to match more widely and will respond to any URL whose first segment is data or people, as shown in Figure 21-6.

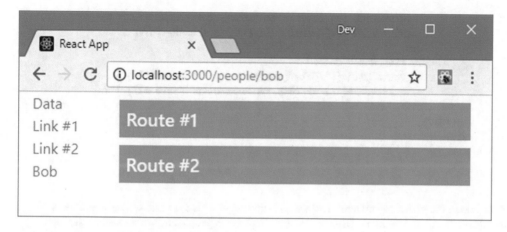

Figure 21-6. *Using an array to specify paths*

Matching URLs with Regular Expressions

Not all combinations of URLs can be expressed using individual segments, and the Route component supports regular expressions in its path prop for more complex matches, as shown in Listing 21-9.

REGULAR EXPRESSION CLARITY VERSUS CONCISENESS

Most programmers have a tendency to express routes with the fewest regular expressions possible, but the result can be a routing configuration that is hard to read and breaks easily when changes are required. When deciding how to match URLs, keep expressions simple and use a path array to expand the range of URLs that a Route can match without using regular expressions that are difficult to understand.

Listing 21-9. Using a Regular Expression in the Selector.js File in the src Folder

```
import React, { Component } from "react";
import { BrowserRouter as Router, Link, Route } from "react-router-dom";

export class Selector extends Component {

    renderMessage = (msg) => <h5 className="bg-info text-white m-2 p-2">{ msg }</h5>

    render() {
        return <Router>
            <div className="container-fluid">
                <div className="row">
                    <div className="col-2">
                        <div><Link to="/data">Data</Link></div>
                        <div><Link to="/data/one">Link #1</Link></div>
                        <div><Link to="/data/two">Link #2</Link></div>
                        <div><Link to="/data/three">Link #3</Link></div>
```

```
                    <div><Link to="/people/bob">Bob</Link></div>
                    <div><Link to="/people/alice">Alice</Link></div>
                </div>
                <div className="col">
                    <Route path={["/data/(one|three)", "/people/b*" ] }
                        render={ () => this.renderMessage("Route #1") } />
                </div>
            </div>
        </div>
    </Router>
  }
}
```

The first item in the path array matches URLs whose first segment is data and second segment is one or three. The second item matches URLs whose first segment is people and whose second segment starts with b. The result is that the Route component will match the /data/one, /data/two, and /people/bob URLs but not the /data/two and /people/alice URLs.

■ **Note** See https://github.com/pillarjs/path-to-regexp for the full range of regular expression features that can be used to match URLs.

Making a Single Route Match

Each Route component assesses its path prop independently; this can be useful but isn't ideal if you want just one component to be display based n the current URL. For these situations, the Redux-Router package provides the Switch component, which acts as a wrapper around multiple Route components, queries them in order, and displays the content rendered by the first one to match the current URL. Listing 21-10 shows the use of the Switch component.

Listing 21-10. Using the Switch Component in the Selector.js File in the src Folder

```
import React, { Component } from "react";
import { BrowserRouter as Router, Link, Route, Switch } from "react-router-dom";
import { ProductDisplay } from "./ProductDisplay";
import { SupplierDisplay } from "./SupplierDisplay";

export class Selector extends Component {

    renderMessage = (msg) => <h5 className="bg-info text-white m-2 p-2">{ msg }</h5>

    render() {
        return <Router>
            <div className="container-fluid">
                <div className="row">
                    <div className="col-2">
                        <div><Link to="/">Default URL</Link></div>
                        <div><Link to="/products">Products</Link></div>
                        <div><Link to="/suppliers">Suppliers</Link></div>
                    </div>
```

```
        <div className="col">
            <Switch>
                <Route path="/products" component={ ProductDisplay} />
                <Route path="/suppliers" component={ SupplierDisplay } />
                <Route render={ () =>
                    this.renderMessage("Fallback Route")} />
            </Switch>
        </div>
    </div>
</div>
</Router>
}
}
```

The Switch component checks its children in the order they are defined, which means that the Route components must be arranged so that the most specific URLs appear first. A Route component with no path prop will always match the current URL and can be used as the default by the Switch component, similar to the default clause in a regular JavaScript switch statement.

The changes in the listing associated the /products URL with the ProductDisplay component and the /suppliers URL with the SupplierDisplay component. Any other URL will cause a message to be rendered using the renderMessage method, as shown in Figure 21-7.

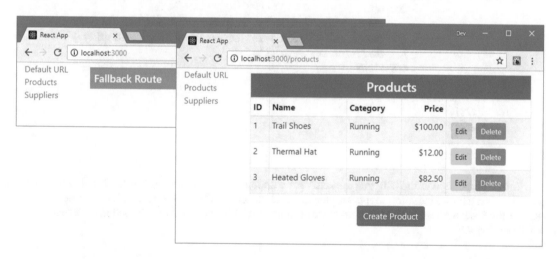

Figure 21-7. Using a Switch component

The use of the Switch component allows me to render content when the application first starts before the user has clicked one of the navigation links. However, this is only one way to select content for the default URL, and a more elegant approach is to use the Redirect component, as described in the next section.

Using Redirection as the Fallback Route

For some applications, it doesn't make sense to introduce a separate URL as a fallback, in which case the Redirect component can be used to automatically trigger navigation to a URL that can be handled by a Route component. In Listing 21-11, I have replaced the existing fallback with a redirection to the /product URL.

Listing 21-11. Using a Redirection in the Selector.js File in the src Folder

```
import React, { Component } from "react";
import { BrowserRouter as Router, Link, Route, Switch, Redirect }
    from "react-router-dom";
import { ProductDisplay } from "./ProductDisplay";
import { SupplierDisplay } from "./SupplierDisplay";

export class Selector extends Component {

    renderMessage = (msg) => <h5 className="bg-info text-white m-2 p-2">{ msg }</h5>

    render() {
        return <Router>
            <div className="container-fluid">
                <div className="row">
                    <div className="col-2">
                        <div><Link to="/">Default URL</Link></div>
                        <div><Link to="/products">Products</Link></div>
                        <div><Link to="/suppliers">Suppliers</Link></div>
                    </div>
                    <div className="col">
                        <Switch>
                            <Route path="/products" component={ ProductDisplay} />
                            <Route path="/suppliers" component={ SupplierDisplay } />
                            <Redirect to="/products" />
                        </Switch>
                    </div>
                </div>
            </div>
        </Router>
    }
}
```

The to prop specifies the URL that the Redirect component will navigate to. The Redirect component won't be used if the Route components are able to match the current URL. But if the Switch component reaches the Redirect component without having found a matching Route, then redirection to /products will be performed.

Performing Selective Redirection

The most common way to use the Redirect component is with just the to prop, but there are additional props available that can be used to restrict when redirection is performed, as described in Table 21-4.

Table 21-4. *The Redirect Component Props*

Name	Description
to	This prop specifies the location to which the browser should be redirected.
from	This prop restricts the redirection so that it is performed only when the current URL matches the specified path.
exact	When true, this prop restricts redirection so that it is performed only when the current URL exactly matches the from prop, performing the same role as the Route component's exact prop.
strict	When true, this prop restricts redirection so that it is performed only when the current URL ends with a / if the path also ends with a /, performing the same role as the Route component's strict prop.
push	When true, the redirection will add a new item to the browser's history. When false, the redirection will replace the current location.

Selectively redirecting to a new URL is a useful way of maintaining support for URLs that are no longer directly handled by a Route, as shown in Listing 21-12. (A similar effect can be achieved using a path array for a Route, but that can lead to complications when matching URL parameters, as described in Chapter 22.)

Listing 21-12. Selectively Redirecting URLs in the Selector.js File in the src Folder

```
import React, { Component } from "react";
import { BrowserRouter as Router, Link, Route, Switch, Redirect }
    from "react-router-dom";
import { ProductDisplay } from "./ProductDisplay";
import { SupplierDisplay } from "./SupplierDisplay";

export class Selector extends Component {

    renderMessage = (msg) => <h5 className="bg-info text-white m-2 p-2">{ msg }</h5>

    render() {
        return <Router>
            <div className="container-fluid">
                <div className="row">
                    <div className="col-2">
                        <div><Link to="/">Default URL</Link></div>
                        <div><Link to="/products">Products</Link></div>
                        <div><Link to="/suppliers">Suppliers</Link></div>
                        <div><Link to="/old/data">Old Link</Link></div>
                    </div>
                    <div className="col">
                        <Switch>
                            <Route path="/products" component={ ProductDisplay} />
                            <Route path="/suppliers" component={ SupplierDisplay } />
                            <Redirect from="/old/data" to="/suppliers" />
                            <Redirect to="/products" />
                        </Switch>
                    </div>
                </div>
```

```
                </div>
            </div>
        </Router>
    }
}
```

The new Redirect will perform a redirection from the /old/data URL to /suppliers. The order of selective Redirect components is important, and they must be placed before the nonselective redirections are performed; otherwise, the Switch will not reach them as it works its way through the list of routing components.

Rendering Navigation Links

The Link component is responsible for generating the elements that navigate to new URLs, which it does by rendering an anchor element with an event handler that changes the browser's URL without reloading the application. To configure its behavior, the Link component accepts the props described in Table 21-5.

Table 21-5. *The Link Component Props*

Name	Description
to	This prop is used to specify the location that clicking the link will navigate to.
replace	This prop is used to specify whether clicking the navigation link will add an entry to the browser's history or replace the current entry, which determines whether the user will be able to use the back button to return to the previous location. The default value is false.
innerRef	This prop is used to access a ref for the underlying HTML element. See Chapter 16 for details of refs.

The Link component will pass on any other props to the anchor element that it renders. The main use for this feature is to apply the className prop to the Link to style the navigation links, as shown in Listing 21-13.

Listing 21-13. Applying Classes in the Selector.js File in the src Folder

```
import React, { Component } from "react";
import { BrowserRouter as Router, Link, Route, Switch, Redirect }
    from "react-router-dom";
import { ProductDisplay } from "./ProductDisplay";
import { SupplierDisplay } from "./SupplierDisplay";

export class Selector extends Component {

    renderMessage = (msg) => <h5 className="bg-info text-white m-2 p-2">{ msg }</h5>

    render() {
        return <Router>
            <div className="container-fluid">
                <div className="row">
                    <div className="col-2">
```

```
            <Link className="m-2 btn btn-block btn-primary"
                to="/">Default URL</Link>
            <Link className="m-2 btn btn-block btn-primary"
                to="/products">Products</Link>
            <Link className="m-2 btn btn-block btn-primary"
                to="/suppliers">Suppliers</Link>
            <Link className="m-2 btn btn-block btn-primary"
                to="/old/data">Old Link</Link>
        </div>
        <div className="col">
            <Switch>
                <Route path="/products" component={ ProductDisplay} />
                <Route path="/suppliers" component={ SupplierDisplay } />
                <Redirect from="/old/data" to="/suppliers" />
                <Redirect to="/products" />
            </Switch>
        </div>
      </div>
    </div>
  </Router>
}
}
```

The Bootstrap CSS framework is able to style anchor elements as buttons, and the classes that I have applied in Listing 21-13 apply a button style that fills the available horizontal space and allows me to remove the div elements that I used to stack the navigation links vertically. When the Link components render their content, the result is a navigation link that appears as a button, as shown in Figure 21-8.

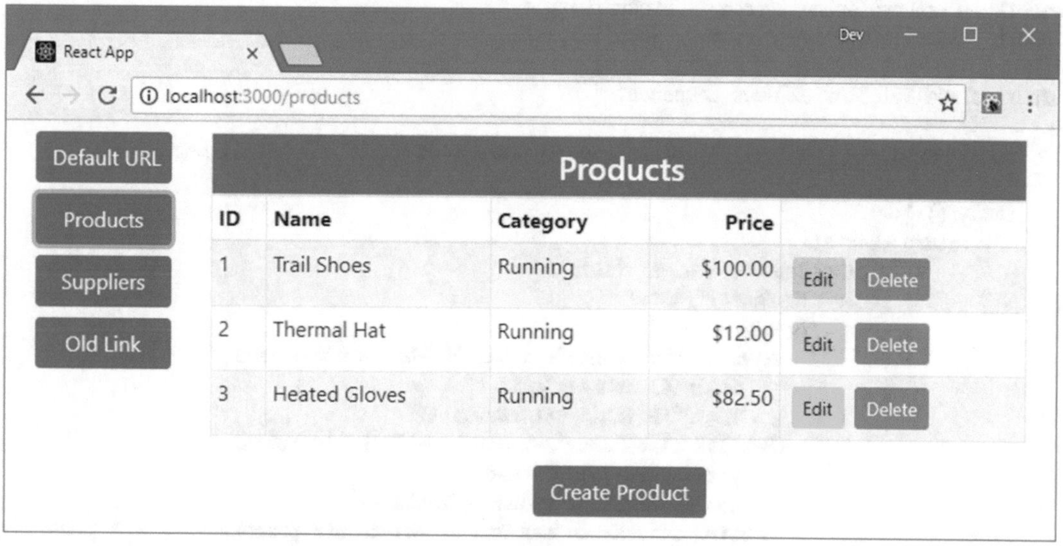

Figure 21-8. *Passing on classes to the navigation element*

Indicating the Active Route

The NavLink component builds on the basic Link features but will add a class or style to the anchor element when the value of its to property matches the current URL. Table 21-6 describes the properties provided by the NavLink component, which are defined in addition to those described in Table 21-5. In Listing 21-14, I have introduced NavLink components that apply the active class.

Table 21-6. *The NavLink Component Properties*

Name	Description
activeClassName	This prop specifies the classes that will be added to the anchor element when the link is active.
activeStyle	This prop specifies the styles that will be added to the anchor element when the link is active. Styles are specified as a JavaScript object whose properties are the style names.
exact	When true, this prop enforces exact matching, as described in the "Matching URLs" section.
strict	When true, this prop enforces strict matching, as described in the "Matching URLs" section.
isActive	This prop can be used to specify a custom function that determines whether the link is active. The function receives match and location arguments, as described in Chapter 22. The default behavior compares the current URL with the to prop.

Listing 21-14. Using NavLink Components in the Selector.js File in the src Folder

```
import React, { Component } from "react";
import { BrowserRouter as Router, NavLink, Route, Switch, Redirect }
    from "react-router-dom";
import { ProductDisplay } from "./ProductDisplay";
import { SupplierDisplay } from "./SupplierDisplay";

export class Selector extends Component {

    renderMessage = (msg) => <h5 className="bg-info text-white m-2 p-2">{ msg }</h5>

    render() {
        return <Router>
            <div className="container-fluid">
                <div className="row">
                    <div className="col-2">
                        <NavLink className="m-2 btn btn-block btn-primary"
                            activeClassName="active"
                            to="/">Default URL</NavLink>
                        <NavLink className="m-2 btn btn-block btn-primary"
                            activeClassName="active"
                            to="/products">Products</NavLink>
                        <NavLink className="m-2 btn btn-block btn-primary"
                            activeClassName="active"
                            to="/suppliers">Suppliers</NavLink>
                        <NavLink className="m-2 btn btn-block btn-primary"
                            activeClassName="active"
                            to="/old/data">Old Link</NavLink>
```

```
            </div>
            <div className="col">
                <Switch>
                    <Route path="/products" component={ ProductDisplay} />
                    <Route path="/suppliers" component={ SupplierDisplay } />
                    <Redirect from="/old/data" to="/suppliers" />
                    <Redirect to="/products" />
                </Switch>
            </div>
        </div>
    </div>
    </Router>
}
}
```

When the browser's URL matches the value of a component's to prop, the anchor element is added to the active class, which provides a useful indicator to the user, as shown in Figure 21-9.

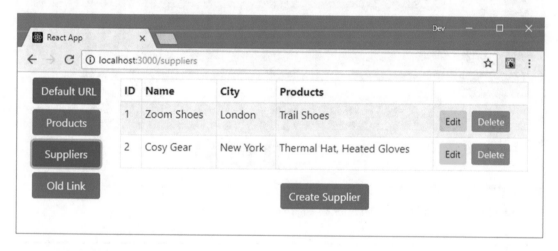

Figure 21-9. *Responding to route activation*

Notice that the Default URL button is always highlighted. The NavLink component relies on the Route URL matching, which means that a to prop of / will match any URL. The exact and strict props described in Table 21-6 have the same purpose as when applied to a Route, and Listing 21-15 shows the use of the exact prop to restrict matching.

Listing 21-15. Restricting NavLink Matching in the Selector.js File in the src Folder

```
...
<div className="col-2">
    <NavLink className="m-2 btn btn-block btn-primary"
        activeClassName="active" exact={ true }
        to="/">Default URL</NavLink>
    <NavLink className="m-2 btn btn-block btn-primary"
        activeClassName="active"
        to="/products">Products</NavLink>
```

```
    <NavLink className="m-2 btn btn-block btn-primary"
        activeClassName="active"
        to="/suppliers">Suppliers</NavLink>
    <NavLink className="m-2 btn btn-block btn-primary"
        activeClassName="active"
        to="/old/data">Old Link</NavLink>
</div>
...
```

The result is that the NavLink is no longer highlighted, as shown in Figure 21-10.

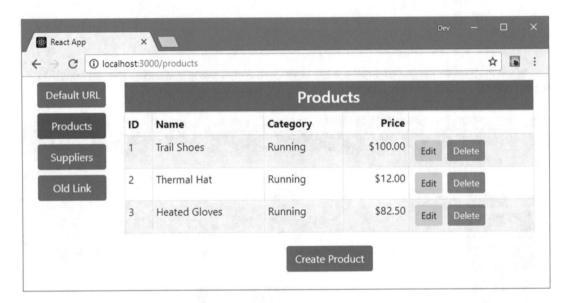

Figure 21-10. *Restricting URL matching for highlighting*

■ **Note**   The NavLink component doesn't allow classes to be removed when the activeClassName value is applied, which means that I can't accurately re-create the original effect from the example project. I demonstrate how to create this functionality with a custom navigation component in Chapter 22.

Selecting and Configuring the Router

URL routing relies on manipulating the browser's URL to perform navigation without sending HTTP requests to the server. In a web application, the core routing functionality is provided by either the BrowserRouter or HashRouter component; both are conventionally given the name Router when they are imported, like this:

```
...
import { BrowserRouter as Router, Link, Switch, Route, Redirect }
    from "react-router-dom";
...
```

BrowserRouter uses the HTML5 History API. This API provides natural URLs for routing, such as http://localhost:3000/products, which is the type of URL you have seen in the examples in this chapter. The BrowserRouter component can accept a range of props that configure its behavior, as described in Table 21-7. The default values for the props are suitable for most applications.

Table 21-7. *The BrowserRouter Props*

Name	Description
basename	This prop is used when the application isn't at the root of its URL, such as http://localhost:3000/myapp.
getUserConfirmation	This prop is used to specify the function used to obtain user confirmation for navigation with the Prompt component, described in Chapter 22.
forceRefresh	When true, this prop forces a complete refresh during navigation with an HTTP request sent to the server. This undermines the point of a rich client-side application and should be used only for testing and when browsers are unable to use the History API.
keyLength	Each change in navigation is given a unique key. This prop is used to specify the length of the key and defaults to six characters. The key is incorporated into the location objects that identify each navigation location, described in Chapter 22.
history	This prop allows a custom history object to be used. The history object is described in Chapter 22.

Using the HashRouter Component

Older browsers don't support the History API, and the navigation details have to be added as a fragment at the end of the URL, following the # character. Routing with URL fragments is provided by the HashRouter component, as shown in Listing 21-16.

Listing 21-16. Using the HashRouter Component in the Selector.js File in the src Folder

```
import React, { Component } from "react";
import { HashRouter as Router, NavLink, Route, Switch, Redirect }
    from "react-router-dom";
import { ProductDisplay } from "./ProductDisplay";
import { SupplierDisplay } from "./SupplierDisplay";

export class Selector extends Component {

    // ...methods omitted for brevity...
}
```

Using the as keyword to import the routing component means that only the import statement has to change. Save the changes to the file and navigate to http://localhost:3000, and you will see that the style of the URL has changed, as shown in Figure 21-11.

Figure 21-11. *Using hash routing*

■ **Tip** You may see a URL like `http://localhost:3000/suppliers/#/suppliers` when the browser first reloads. This happens because the browser reloads from its current URL, which is then assumed to be the base URL for the application. Manually navigate to `http://localhost:3000` and you should see the URL shown in the figure.

The part of the URL that is used for routing now follows the # character. URL routing still works the same way, but the URLs are less natural compared with those generated by the `BrowserRouter` component. The `HashRouter` component can be configured with the props shown in Table 21-8.

Table 21-8. *The HashRouter Component Props*

Name	Description
basename	This prop is used when the application isn't at the root of its URL, such as `http://localhost:3000/myapp`.
getUserConfirmation	This prop is used to specify the function used to obtain user confirmation for navigation with the `Prompt` component, described in Chapter 22.
hashType	This prop sets the style used to encode the routing in the URL. The options are `slash`, which creates the URL style shown in Figure 21-11; `noslash`, which omits the leading / after the # character; and `hashbang`, which creates URLs such as `#!/products` by inserting an exclamation mark after the # character.

Summary

In this chapter, I showed you how to use the React-Router package to add URL routing to a React application. I explained how routing can simplify applications by moving state data into the URL and how `Link` and `Route` components are used to create navigation elements and respond to URL changes. In the next chapter, I describe the advanced URL routing features.

CHAPTER 22

Advanced URL Routing

In this chapter, I describe the advanced features that are available for URL routing with the React-Router package. I show you how to create components that can participate in the routing process, how to navigate programmatically, how to generate routes programmatically, and how to use URL routing in components that are connected to the data store. Table 22-1 puts the advanced URL routing features in context.

Table 22-1. *Putting Advanced URL Routing in Context*

Question	Answer
What is it?	The advanced routing features provide programmatic access to the URL routing system.
Why is it useful?	These features allow components to be aware of the routing system and the currently active route.
How is it used?	Access to the advanced routing features is provided by props.
Are there any pitfalls or limitations?	These are advanced features, and care is required to ensure that they are properly integrated into components.
Are there any alternatives?	These are optional features. Applications can use the standard features described in Chapter 21 or avoid URL routing entirely.

Table 22-2 summarizes the chapter.

Table 22-2. *Chapter Summary*

Problem	Solution	Listing
Receive details of the routing system in a component	Use the props provided by the Route component or use the withRouter higher-order component	3, 4, 10–12, 19–23
Get details of the current navigation location	Use the location prop	5
Get URL segments from the current route	Add parameters to the URL	6–9
Navigate programmatically	Use the methods defined by the history prop	13, 14
Prompt the user before navigation	Use the Prompt component	15–17

Preparing for This Chapter

In this chapter, I continue using the productapp project from Chapter 21. To prepare for this chapter, change the router that is used by the application from HashRouter to BrowserRouter, so that the HTML5 History API is used for navigation, and simplified the Link and Router components, as shown in Listing 22-1.

■ **Tip** You can download the example project for this chapter—and for all the other chapters in this book—from https://github.com/Apress/pro-react-16.

Listing 22-1. Changing Routers and Routes in the Selector.js File in the src Folder

```
import React, { Component } from "react";
import { BrowserRouter as Router, NavLink, Route, Switch, Redirect }
    from "react-router-dom";
import { ProductDisplay } from "./ProductDisplay";
import { SupplierDisplay } from "./SupplierDisplay";

export class Selector extends Component {

    render() {
        return <Router>
            <div className="container-fluid">
                <div className="row">
                    <div className="col-2">
                        <NavLink className="m-2 btn btn-block btn-primary"
                            activeClassName="active"
                            to="/products">Products</NavLink>
                        <NavLink className="m-2 btn btn-block btn-primary"
                            activeClassName="active"
                            to="/suppliers">Suppliers</NavLink>
                    </div>
                    <div className="col">
                        <Switch>
                            <Route path="/products" component={ ProductDisplay} />
                            <Route path="/suppliers" component={ SupplierDisplay } />
                            <Redirect to="/products" />
                        </Switch>
                    </div>
                </div>
            </div>
        </Router>
    }
}
```

Open a command prompt, navigate to the productapp folder, and run the command shown in Listing 22-2 to start the development tools.

Listing 22-2. Starting the Development Tools

```
npm start
```

Once the application has been compiled, the development HTTP server will start and display the content shown in Figure 22-1.

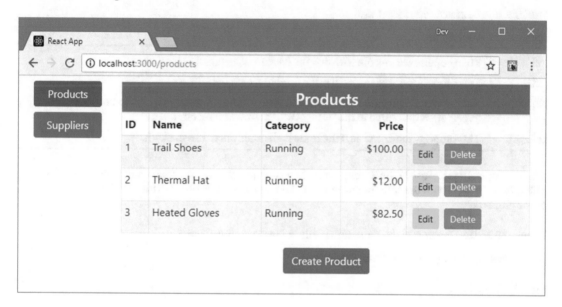

Figure 22-1. *Running the example application*

Creating Routing-Aware Components

When a Route displays a component, it provides it with context data that describes the current route and with access to an API that can be used for navigation, allowing components to be aware of the current location and to participate in routing. When the component prop is used, the Route passes the data and API to the component it displays as props, named match, location, and history. When the render prop is used, the render function is passed an object that has match, location, and history properties whose values are the same objects used as render props. The match, location, and history objects are described in Table 22-3.

Table 22-3. *The Props Provided by the Route Component*

Name	Description
match	This prop provides information about how the Route component matched the current browser URL.
location	This prop provides a representation of the current location and can be used for navigation instead of URLs expressed as strings.
history	This prop provides an API that can be used for navigation, as demonstrated in the "Navigating Programmatically" section.

Understanding the Match Prop

The match prop provides a component with details of how the parent Route matches the current URL. As I demonstrated in Chapter 21, a single Route can be used to match a range of URLs, and routing-aware components often need details about the current URL, which are available through the properties shown in Table 22-4.

Table 22-4. *The Match Prop Properties*

Name	Description
url	This property returns the URL that the Route has matched.
path	This property returns the path value used to match the URL.
params	This property returns the route params, which allow segments of a URL to be mapped to variables, as described in the "Using URL Parameters" section.
isExact	This property returns true if the route path exactly matches the URL.

To demonstrate the use of the routing props, I created the src/routing folder and added to it a file called RouteInfo.js with the component shown in Listing 22-3, which displays the values of the match prop's properties.

Listing 22-3. The Contents of the RouteInfo.js File in the src/routing Folder

```
import React, { Component } from "react";

export class RouteInfo extends Component {

    renderTable(title, prop, propertyNames) {
        return <React.Fragment>
            <tr><th colSpan="2" className="text-center">{ title }</th></tr>
            { propertyNames.map(p =>
                <tr key={p }>
                    <td>{ p }</td>
                    <td>{ JSON.stringify(prop[p]) }</td>
                </tr>)
            }
        </React.Fragment>
    }

    render() {
        return <div className="bg-info m-2 p-2">
            <h4 className="text-white text-center">Route Info</h4>
            <table className="table table-sm table-striped bg-light">
                <tbody>
                    { this.renderTable("Match", this.props.match,
                        ["url", "path", "params", "isExact"] )}
                </tbody>
            </table>
        </div>
    }
}
```

The RouteInfo component displays the url, path, params, and isExact properties of the match prop in a table and will allow me to easily add additional details from the other routing props later. The properties are serialized because the values are a mix of objects and Booleans that can cause display problems if used literally. In Listing 22-4, I have added a navigation link to the Selector component, along with a Route that displays the RouteInfo component.

Listing 22-4. Adding a Route in the Selector.js File in the src Folder

```
import React, { Component } from "react";
import { BrowserRouter as Router, NavLink, Route, Switch, Redirect }
    from "react-router-dom";
import { ProductDisplay } from "./ProductDisplay";
import { SupplierDisplay } from "./SupplierDisplay";
import { RouteInfo } from "./routing/RouteInfo";

export class Selector extends Component {

    render() {
        return <Router>
            <div className="container-fluid">
                <div className="row">
                    <div className="col-2">
                        <NavLink className="m-2 btn btn-block btn-primary"
                            activeClassName="active"
                            to="/products">Products</NavLink>
                        <NavLink className="m-2 btn btn-block btn-primary"
                            activeClassName="active"
                            to="/suppliers">Suppliers</NavLink>
                        <NavLink className="m-2 btn btn-block btn-primary"
                            activeClassName="active" to="/info">Route Info</NavLink>
                    </div>
                    <div className="col">
                        <Switch>
                            <Route path="/products" component={ ProductDisplay} />
                            <Route path="/suppliers" component={ SupplierDisplay } />
                            <Route path="/info" component={ RouteInfo } />
                            <Redirect to="/products" />
                        </Switch>
                    </div>
                </div>
            </div>
        </Router>
    }
}
```

Save the changes and click on the Route Info link and you will see the details of the match prop, as shown in Figure 22-2. The values displayed indicate that the path prop of the Route component is /info and it matches the /info URL which the new Link component targets. The information provided by the match prop will become more useful as I introduce more advanced routing features, especially when I introduce URL parameters in the "Using URL Parameters" section.

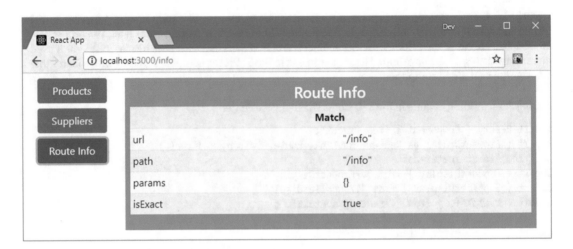

Figure 22-2. *Details provided by the match routing prop*

Understanding the Location Prop

The location object is used to describe a navigation location. The location object provided as props describes the current location and has the properties described in Table 22-5.

Table 22-5. *The Location Properties*

Name	Description
key	This property returns a key that identifies the location.
pathname	This property returns the path of the location.
search	This property returns the search term of the location URL (the part of the URL that follows the ? character).
hash	This property returns the URL fragment of the location URL (the part that follows the # character).
state	This property is used to associated arbitrary data with a location.

The location properties provide some overlap with the match prop, but the idea is that a component can retain a location object and use it to refer to a location instead of using strings as the value for the to prop of the Link, NavLink, and Redirect components. In Listing 22-5, I have added the location prop to the data displayed by the RouteInfo, along with a Link element that uses the location object for its navigation target.

Listing 22-5. Using the Location Prop in the RouteInfo.js File in the src/routing Folder

```
import React, { Component } from "react";
import { Link } from "react-router-dom";

export class RouteInfo extends Component {

    renderTable(title, prop, propertyNames) {
        return <React.Fragment>
            <tr><th colSpan="2" className="text-center">{ title }</th></tr>
            { propertyNames.map(p =>
                <tr key={p }>
                    <td>{ p }</td>
                    <td>{ JSON.stringify(prop[p]) }</td>
                </tr>)
            }
        </React.Fragment>
    }

    render() {
        return <div className="bg-info m-2 p-2">
            <h4 className="text-white text-center">Route Info</h4>
            <table className="table table-sm table-striped bg-light">
                <tbody>
                    { this.renderTable("Match", this.props.match,
                        ["url", "path", "params", "isExact"] )}
                    { this.renderTable("Location", this.props.location,
                        ["key", "pathname", "search", "hash", "state"] )}
                </tbody>
            </table>
            <div className="text-center m-2 bg-light">
                <Link className="btn btn-primary m-2"
                    to={ this.props.location }>Location</Link>
            </div>
        </div>
    }
}
```

Figure 22-3 shows the details of the location prop and the new Link component.

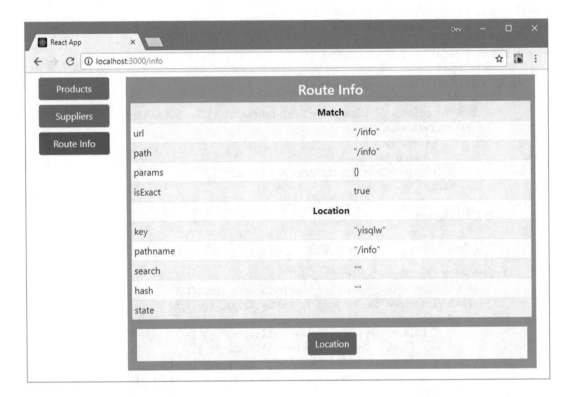

Figure 22-3. *Displaying details of the location routing prop*

Using the location prop as the value for a Link component's to prop isn't especially useful at the moment because it is only able to navigate to the current location. As you will see, components can be used to respond to multiple routes and may receive a series of locations over time, which makes using a location object both useful and more convenient than working with URLs expressed as strings.

Using URL Parameters

When a component is aware of the URL routing system, it will often need to adapt its behavior to the current URL. The React-Router package supports URL parameters, which assign the contents of a URL segment to a variable that can be read by components, allowing them to respond to the current location without having to parse the URL or understand its structure. Listing 22-6 shows the addition of a Route whose path includes a URL parameter and Link components that target it.

Listing 22-6. Defining a URL Parameter in the Selector.js File in the src Folder

```
import React, { Component } from "react";
import { BrowserRouter as Router, NavLink, Route, Switch, Redirect }
    from "react-router-dom";
import { ProductDisplay } from "./ProductDisplay";
import { SupplierDisplay } from "./SupplierDisplay";
```

```
import { RouteInfo } from "./routing/RouteInfo";

export class Selector extends Component {

    render() {
        return <Router>
            <div className="container-fluid">
                <div className="row">
                    <div className="col-2">
                        <NavLink className="m-2 btn btn-block btn-primary"
                            activeClassName="active"
                            to="/products">Products</NavLink>
                        <NavLink className="m-2 btn btn-block btn-primary"
                            activeClassName="active"
                            to="/suppliers">Suppliers</NavLink>
                        <NavLink className="m-2 btn btn-block btn-primary"
                            activeClassName="active"
                            to="/info/match">Match</NavLink>
                        <NavLink className="m-2 btn btn-block btn-primary"
                            activeClassName="active"
                            to="/info/location">Location</NavLink>
                    </div>
                    <div className="col">
                        <Switch>
                            <Route path="/products" component={ ProductDisplay} />
                            <Route path="/suppliers" component={ SupplierDisplay } />
                            <Route path="/info/:datatype" component={ RouteInfo } />
                            <Redirect to="/products" />
                        </Switch>
                    </div>
                </div>
            </div>
        </Router>
    }
}
```

URL parameters are specified as path prop segments that start with a colon (the : character). In the example, the Route for the RouteInfo component has a path prop with a URL parameter named datatype.

```
...
<Route path="/info/:datatype" component={ RouteInfo } />
...
```

When the Route matches a URL, it will assign the value of the second segment to a URL parameter called datatype, which will be passed on to the RouteInfo component through the match prop's params property. If you click the navigation links added to the example in Listing 22-6, you will see different values displayed for the params property, as shown in Figure 22-4.

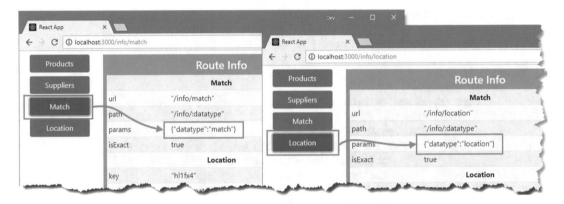

Figure 22-4. *Receiving URL parameters through the match prop*

When the URL is /info/match, the value of the datatype parameter is match. When the URL is /info/location, the value of the datatype parameter is location. In Listing 22-7, I have updated the RouteInfo component to use the datatype prop to select the context data to present to the user.

Listing 22-7. Using a URL Parameter Prop in the RouteInfo.js File in the src/routing Folder

```
import React, { Component } from "react";
import { Link } from "react-router-dom";

export class RouteInfo extends Component {

    renderTable(title, prop, propertyNames) {
        return <React.Fragment>
            <tr><th colSpan="2" className="text-center">{ title }</th></tr>
            { propertyNames.map(p =>
                <tr key={p }>
                    <td>{ p }</td>
                    <td>{ JSON.stringify(prop[p]) }</td>
                </tr>)
            }
        </React.Fragment>
    }

    render() {
        return <div className="bg-info m-2 p-2">
            <h4 className="text-white text-center">Route Info</h4>
            <table className="table table-sm table-striped bg-light">
                <tbody>
                    { this.props.match.params.datatype ==="match"
                        && this.renderTable("Match", this.props.match,
                            ["url", "path", "params", "isExact"] )}
                    { this.props.match.params.datatype === "location"
                        && this.renderTable("Location", this.props.location,
                            ["key", "pathname", "search", "hash", "state"] )}
                </tbody>
            </table>
```

```
            <div className="text-center m-2 bg-light">
                <Link className="btn btn-primary m-2"
                    to={ this.props.location }>Location</Link>
            </div>
        </div>
    }
}
```

The component receives URL parameters as part of the routing props and uses them just like any other prop. In the listing, the value of the datatype URL parameter is used for inline expressions that display the match or location object, as shown in Figure 22-5.

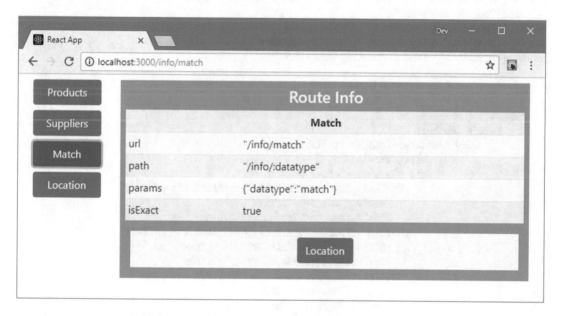

Figure 22-5. *Responding to a URL parameter by selecting content*

UNDERSTANDING OPAQUE URL STRUCTURE

URL parameters are not just a convenient way for a component to receive the contents of a URL segment. They also decouple the structure of the URL from the components that are targeted by it, allowing the structure of the URL to be altered or multiple URLs to target the same content without modifying the component. The component in Listing 22-7, for example, depends on the datatype URL parameter but doesn't have any dependency on the part of the URL from which it is obtained. This means that the component will work with a path such as /info/:datatype but will can also be matched by a path such as /diagnostics/routing/:datatype without requiring changes to the component's code.

The advantage of URL parameters is that the component just needs to know the names of the URL parameters it requires and not the details of where they appear in the URL.

Using Optional URL Parameters

The addition of the URL parameter means that the /info URL will no longer be matched by the Route component. I could solve this by adding another Route, but a more elegant approach is to use an optional parameter, which will allow the URL to match the path even if there is no corresponding segment. In Listing 22-8, I have added a NavLink that navigates to the /info URL and changed the path of the Route component so that the datatype parameter is optional.

Listing 22-8. Using an Optional URL Parameter in the Selector.js File in the src Folder

```
import React, { Component } from "react";
import { BrowserRouter as Router, NavLink, Route, Switch, Redirect }
    from "react-router-dom";
import { ProductDisplay } from "./ProductDisplay";
import { SupplierDisplay } from "./SupplierDisplay";
import { RouteInfo } from "./routing/RouteInfo";

export class Selector extends Component {

    render() {
        return <Router>
            <div className="container-fluid">
                <div className="row">
                    <div className="col-2">
                        <NavLink className="m-2 btn btn-block btn-primary"
                            activeClassName="active"
                            to="/products">Products</NavLink>
                        <NavLink className="m-2 btn btn-block btn-primary"
                            activeClassName="active"
                            to="/suppliers">Suppliers</NavLink>
                        <NavLink className="m-2 btn btn-block btn-primary"
                            activeClassName="active"
                            to="/info/match">Match</NavLink>
                        <NavLink className="m-2 btn btn-block btn-primary"
                            activeClassName="active"
                            to="/info/location">Location</NavLink>
                        <NavLink className="m-2 btn btn-block btn-primary"
                            activeClassName="active" to="/info">All Info</NavLink>
                    </div>
                    <div className="col">
                        <Switch>
                            <Route path="/products" component={ ProductDisplay} />
                            <Route path="/suppliers" component={ SupplierDisplay } />
                            <Route path="/info/:datatype?" component={ RouteInfo } />
                            <Redirect to="/products" />
                        </Switch>
                    </div>
                </div>
            </div>
        </Router>
    }
}
```

Optional URL parameters are denoted with a question mark (the ? character) after the parameter name, so datatype? indicates an optional parameter that will be given the name datatype if there is a corresponding segment in the URL. If there is no segment, the path will still match, but there will be no datatype value. In Listing 22-9, I have updated the RouteInfo component so that it displays details of both the match and location objects if there is no datatype value.

■ **Tip** For a complete list of the different ways that URL parameters can be specified, see https://github. com/pillarjs/path-to-regexp, which is the GitHub repository for the package that processes URLs.

Listing 22-9. Handling an Optional URL Parameter in the RouteInfo.js File in the src Folder

```
import React, { Component } from "react";
import { Link } from "react-router-dom";

export class RouteInfo extends Component {

    renderTable(title, prop, propertyNames) {
        return <React.Fragment>
            <tr><th colSpan="2" className="text-center">{ title }</th></tr>
            { propertyNames.map(p =>
                <tr key={p }>
                    <td>{ p }</td>
                    <td>{ JSON.stringify(prop[p]) }</td>
                </tr>)
            }
        </React.Fragment>
    }

    render() {
        return <div className="bg-info m-2 p-2">
            <h4 className="text-white text-center">Route Info</h4>
            <table className="table table-sm table-striped bg-light">
                <tbody>
                    { (this.props.match.params.datatype === undefined ||
                        this.props.match.params.datatype ==="match")
                    && this.renderTable("Match", this.props.match,
                        ["url", "path", "params", "isExact"] )}
                    { (this.props.match.params.datatype === undefined ||
                        this.props.match.params.datatype === "location")
                    && this.renderTable("Location", this.props.location,
                        ["key", "pathname", "search", "hash", "state"] )}
                </tbody>
            </table>
            <div className="text-center m-2 bg-light">
                <Link className="btn btn-primary m-2"
                    to={ this.props.location }>Location</Link>
            </div>
        </div>
    }
}
```

The value of the datatype parameter will be undefined if no segment in the URL has been matched. The changes in the listing and the addition of the optional URL parameter allow the component to respond to a wider range of URLs without requiring additional Route components to be used.

Accessing Routing Data in Other Components

A Route will add props to the components it displays but can't provide them directly to other components, including the descendants of the components it displays. To avoid prop threading, the React-Router package provides two different approaches for providing access to routing data in descendant components, as described in the following sections.

Accessing Routing Data Directly in a Component

The most direct way to get access to routing data is to use a Route in the render method. To demonstrate, I added a file called ToggleLink.js to the src/routing folder and used it to define the component shown in Listing 22-10.

■ **Tip** This is the same component I used to highlight the active route in the SportsStore application in Part 1.

Listing 22-10. The Contents of the ToggleLink.js File in the src/routing Folder

```
import React, { Component } from "react";
import { Route, Link } from "react-router-dom";

export class ToggleLink extends Component {

    render() {
        return <Route path={ this.props.to } exact={ this.props.exact }
                children={ routeProps => {

            const baseClasses = this.props.className || "m-2 btn btn-block";
            const activeClass = this.props.activeClass || "btn-primary";
            const inActiveClass = this.props.inActiveClass || "btn-secondary"

            const combinedClasses =
                `${baseClasses} ${routeProps.match ? activeClass : inActiveClass}`

            return <Link to={ this.props.to } className={ combinedClasses }>
                    { this.props.children }
                </Link>
        }} />
    }
}
```

The Route component's children prop is used to render content regardless of the current URL and is assigned a function that receives the routing context data. The path prop is used to indicate interest in a URL, and when the current URL matches the path, the routeProps object passed to the children function includes a match object that defines the properties described in Table 22-4.

The ToggleLink component allows me to solve a minor niggle that arises between the NavLink component and the Bootstrap CSS framework. The NavLink works by adding a class to the anchor element it renders when a path is matched and removing it the rest of the time. This causes a problem for some combinations of Bootstrap classes because the order in which they are defined in the CSS stylesheet means that some classes, such as btn-primary, won't take effect until a related class, such as btn-secondary, are removed.

The ToggleLink component fixes this problem by adding an active class when there is a match object and adding an inactive class when there is no match.

```
...
const combinedClasses =
    `${baseClasses} ${routeProps.match ? activeClass : inActiveClass}`
...
```

A Link is still used to generate the navigation element and respond to clicks but is styled by the ToggleLink component such that I make free use of the Bootstrap CSS classes. In Listing 22-11, I have replaced each NavLink with a ToggleLink.

Listing 22-11. Replacing Navigation Components in the Selector.js File in the src Folder

```
import React, { Component } from "react";
import { BrowserRouter as Router, Route, Switch, Redirect }
    from "react-router-dom";
import { ProductDisplay } from "./ProductDisplay";
import { SupplierDisplay } from "./SupplierDisplay";
import { RouteInfo } from "./routing/RouteInfo";
import { ToggleLink } from "./routing/ToggleLink";

export class Selector extends Component {

    render() {
        return <Router>
            <div className="container-fluid">
                <div className="row">
                    <div className="col-2">
                        <ToggleLink to="/products">Products</ToggleLink>
                        <ToggleLink to="/suppliers">Suppliers</ToggleLink>
                        <ToggleLink to="/info/match">Match</ToggleLink>
                        <ToggleLink to="/info/location">Location</ToggleLink>
                        <ToggleLink to="/info" exact={ true }>All Info</ToggleLink>
                    </div>
                    <div className="col">
                        <Switch>
                            <Route path="/products" component={ ProductDisplay} />
                            <Route path="/suppliers" component={ SupplierDisplay } />
                            <Route path="/info/:datatype?" component={ RouteInfo } />
                            <Redirect to="/products" />
                        </Switch>
                    </div>
                </div>
            </div>
        </Router>
    }
}
```

I have relied on the default classes specified in Listing 22-10, with the result that the navigation buttons are added to the Bootstrap btn-primary class when they are active and to the btn-secondary class when they are inactive, as shown in Figure 22-6.

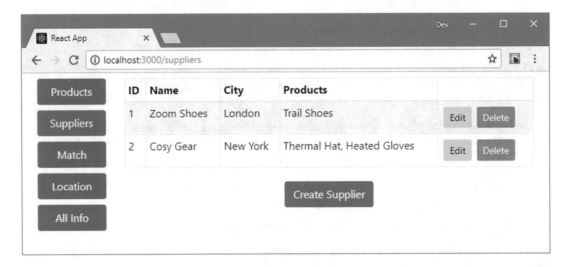

Figure 22-6. *Accessing routing data directly in a component*

Accessing Routing Data Using a Higher-Order Component

The withRouter function is a higher-order component that provides access to the routing system without directly using a Route (although that is the technique used inside the withRouter function). When a component is passed to withRouter, it receives the match, location, and history objects as props, just as though it had been rendered directly by a Route using the component prop. This can be a convenient alternative to writing components that render a Route. In Listing 22-12, I have used the withRouter function to allow the RouteInfo component to be used outside of a Route.

Listing 22-12. Creating a Routing HOC in the Selector.js File in the src Folder

```
import React, { Component } from "react";
import { BrowserRouter as Router, Route, Switch, Redirect, withRouter }
    from "react-router-dom";
import { ProductDisplay } from "./ProductDisplay";
import { SupplierDisplay } from "./SupplierDisplay";
import { RouteInfo } from "./routing/RouteInfo";
import { ToggleLink } from "./routing/ToggleLink";

const RouteInfoHOC = withRouter(RouteInfo)

export class Selector extends Component {

    render() {
        return <Router>
            <div className="container-fluid">
```

```
            <div className="row">
                <div className="col-2">
                    <ToggleLink to="/products">Products</ToggleLink>
                    <ToggleLink to="/suppliers">Suppliers</ToggleLink>
                    <ToggleLink to="/info/match">Match</ToggleLink>
                    <ToggleLink to="/info/location">Location</ToggleLink>
                    <ToggleLink to="/info" exact={ true }>All Info</ToggleLink>
                </div>
                <div className="col">
                    <RouteInfoHOC />
                    <Switch>
                        <Route path="/products" component={ ProductDisplay} />
                        <Route path="/suppliers" component={ SupplierDisplay } />
                        <Route path="/info/:datatype?" component={ RouteInfo } />
                        <Redirect to="/products" />
                    </Switch>
                </div>
            </div>
        </div>
    </Router>
  }
}
```

The withRouter function is used to provide the RouteInfo component with the data it requires even when it is not displayed by a Route. The result is that details of the match and location objects are always displayed, as shown in Figure 22-7.

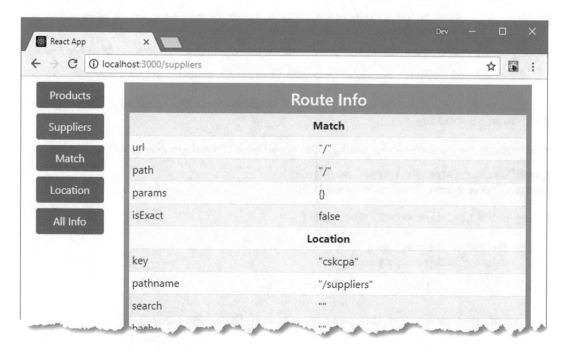

Figure 22-7. *Using the withrouter HOC*

631

The withRouter function doesn't provide support for matching paths, which means that the match object is of little use. The location object, however, provide details of the application's current location, and the history object can be used for programmatic navigation, as described in the next section.

Navigating Programmatically

Not all navigation can be handled using Link or NavLink components, especially where the application needs to perform some internal action in response to an event and only then perform navigation. The history object that is provided to components provides an API that allows programmatic access to the routing system, using the methods described in Table 22-6. The history object provides a consistent interface for navigation regardless of whether the application uses the HTML5 History API or URL fragments.

Table 22-6. *The history Methods*

Name	Description
push(path)	This method navigates to the specified path and adds a new entry in the browser's history. An optional state property can be provided that is available through the location.state property.
replace(path)	This method navigates to the specified path and replaces the current location in the browser's history. An optional state property can be provided that is available through the location.state property.
goBack()	This method navigates to the previous location in the browser's history.
goForward()	This method navigates to the next location in the browser's history.
go(n)	This method navigates to the history location n places from the current location. Use positive values to move forward and negative values to move backward.
block(prompt)	This method blocks navigation until the user responds to a prompt, as described in the "Prompting the User Before Navigation" section.

In Listing 22-13, I replaced the Link in the ToggleLink component with a button whose event handler navigates programmatically.

Listing 22-13. Navigating Programmatically in the ToggleLink.js File in the src/router Folder

```
import React, { Component } from "react";
import { Route } from "react-router-dom";

export class ToggleLink extends Component {

    handleClick = (history) => {
        history.push(this.props.to);
    }

    render() {
        return <Route path={ this.props.to } exact={ this.props.exact }
                children={ routeProps => {
```

```
            const baseClasses = this.props.className || "m-2 btn btn-block";
            const activeClass = this.props.activeClass || "btn-primary";
            const inActiveClass = this.props.inActiveClass || "btn-secondary"

            const combinedClasses =
                `${baseClasses} ${routeProps.match ? activeClass : inActiveClass}`

        return  <button className={ combinedClasses }
                    onClick={ () => this.handleClick(routeProps.history) }>
                    {this.props.children}
                </button>
        }} />
    }
}
```

The onClick handler passes the history object received from the Route component to the handleClick method, which uses the push method to navigate to the location specified by the to prop. There is no visible difference because the anchor elements rendered by the Link components were already styled to appear as buttons, but the ToggleLink component now handles its navigation directly.

Navigating Programmatically Using Components

An alternative to using the history object is to render components that perform navigation. In Listing 22-14, I have changed the ToggleLink component so that clicking the button element updates state data that causes a Redirect to be rendered instead.

Listing 22-14. Navigating Using Components in the ToggleLink.js File in the src/router Folder

```
import React, { Component } from "react";
import { Route, Redirect } from "react-router-dom";

export class ToggleLink extends Component {

    constructor(props) {
        super(props);
        this.state = {
            doRedirect: false
        }
    }

    handleClick = () => {
        this.setState({ doRedirect: true},
            () => this.setState({ doRedirect: false }));
    }

    render() {
        return <Route path={ this.props.to } exact={ this.props.exact }
                children={ routeProps => {

            const baseClasses = this.props.className || "m-2 btn btn-block";
            const activeClass = this.props.activeClass || "btn-primary";
```

```
              const inActiveClass = this.props.inActiveClass || "btn-secondary"

              const combinedClasses =
                  `${baseClasses} ${routeProps.match ? activeClass : inActiveClass}`

          return  <React.Fragment>
                    { this.state.doRedirect && <Redirect to={ this.props.to } /> }
                    <button className={ combinedClasses } onClick={ this.handleClick }>
                        {this.props.children}
                    </button>
                  </React.Fragment>
            }} />
        }
    }
```

Clicking the button sets the doRedirect property to true, which triggers an update that renders the Redirect component. The doRedirect property is set back to false automatically so that the component's normal content is rendered again. The result is the same as Listing 22-13, and choosing an approach is a matter of preference and personal style.

Prompting the User Before Navigation

Navigation can be delayed by rendering a Prompt, which allows the user to confirm or cancel navigation and which is often used to avoid accidentally abandoning form data. The Prompt component supports the props described in Table 22-7.

Table 22-7. *The Prompt Component Props*

Name	Description
message	This prop defines the message displayed to the user. It can be expressed as a string or as a function that accepts a location object and returns a string.
when	This prop will prompt the user only when its value evaluates to true and can be used to conditionally block navigation.

Only a single Prompt is used, but it doesn't matter where it is rendered because it doesn't perform any action until the application changes to a new location, at which point the user will be asked to confirm navigation. In Listing 22-15, I added a Prompt to the Selector component.

■ **Tip**   Only one Prompt is needed, and you should not render additional Prompt instances in the components that perform navigation, such as the ToggleLink component in the example application. You will receive a warning in the JavaScript console if you render multiple Prompt components.

Listing 22-15. Prompting the User in the Selector.js File in the src Folder

```
import React, { Component } from "react";
import { BrowserRouter as Router, Route, Switch, Redirect, withRouter, Prompt }
    from "react-router-dom";
import { ProductDisplay } from "./ProductDisplay";
import { SupplierDisplay } from "./SupplierDisplay";
import { RouteInfo } from "./routing/RouteInfo";
import { ToggleLink } from "./routing/ToggleLink";

const RouteInfoHOC = withRouter(RouteInfo)

export class Selector extends Component {

    render() {
        return <Router>
            <div className="container-fluid">
                <div className="row">
                    <div className="col-2">
                        <ToggleLink to="/products">Products</ToggleLink>
                        <ToggleLink to="/suppliers">Suppliers</ToggleLink>
                        <ToggleLink to="/info/match">Match</ToggleLink>
                        <ToggleLink to="/info/location">Location</ToggleLink>
                        <ToggleLink to="/info" exact={ true }>All Info</ToggleLink>
                    </div>
                    <div className="col">
                        <Prompt message={ loc =>
                            `Do you want to navigate to ${loc.pathname}`} />
                        <RouteInfoHOC />
                        <Switch>
                            <Route path="/products" component={ ProductDisplay} />
                            <Route path="/suppliers" component={ SupplierDisplay } />
                            <Route path="/info/:datatype?" component={ RouteInfo } />
                            <Redirect to="/products" />
                        </Switch>
                    </div>
                </div>
            </div>
        </Router>
    }
}
```

To see the effect of the Prompt, click one of the button elements rendered by the ToggleLink components. You will be asked to confirm navigation, as shown in Figure 22-8.

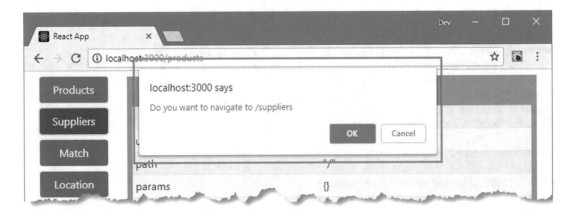

Figure 22-8. *Prompting the user before navigating*

■ **Tip** If you prefer using the `history` object for navigation, the `block` method can be used to set up a prompt that will be presented to the user, as demonstrated in the next section.

Presenting a Custom Navigation Prompt

The `BrowserRouter` and `HashRouter` components provide a `getUserConfirmation` prop that is used to replace the default prompt with a custom function. To present a prompt to the user that is inline with the rest of the application's content, I added a file called `CustomPrompt.js` to the `src/routing` folder and used it to define the component shown in Listing 22-16.

Listing 22-16. The Contents of the CustomPrompt.js File in the src/routing Folder

```
import React, { Component } from "react";

export class CustomPrompt extends Component {

    render() {
        if (this.props.show) {
            return <div className="alert alert-warning m-2 text-center">
                <h4 className="alert-heading">Navigation Warning</h4>
                    { this.props.message }
                <div className="p-1">
                    <button className="btn btn-primary m-1"
                        onClick={ () => this.props.callback(true) }>
                            Yes
                    </button>
                    <button className="btn btn-secondary m-1"
                        onClick={ () => this.props.callback(false )}>
                            No
                    </button>
```

```
            </div>
         </div>
      }
      return null;
   }
}
```

The CustomPrompt component is responsible for displaying a message to the user and presenting Yes and No buttons that invoke a callback function that will confirm or block navigation. In Listing 22-17, I have applied the CustomPrompt in the Selector component, along with the state data required to manage the prompting process.

Listing 22-17. Appling a Custom Prompt in the Selector.js File in the src Folder

```
import React, { Component } from "react";
import { BrowserRouter as Router, Route, Switch, Redirect, withRouter, Prompt }
    from "react-router-dom";
import { ProductDisplay } from "./ProductDisplay";
import { SupplierDisplay } from "./SupplierDisplay";
import { RouteInfo } from "./routing/RouteInfo";
import { ToggleLink } from "./routing/ToggleLink";
import { CustomPrompt } from "./routing/CustomPrompt";

const RouteInfoHOC = withRouter(RouteInfo)

export class Selector extends Component {

    constructor(props) {
        super(props);
        this.state = {
            showPrompt: false,
            message: "",
            callback: () => {}
        }
    }

    customGetUserConfirmation = (message, navCallback) => {
        this.setState({
            showPrompt: true, message: message,
            callback: (allow) => { navCallback(allow);
                this.setState({ showPrompt: false}) }
        });
    }

    render() {
        return <Router getUserConfirmation={ this.customGetUserConfirmation }>
            <div className="container-fluid">
                <div className="row">
                    <div className="col-2">
                        <ToggleLink to="/products">Products</ToggleLink>
                        <ToggleLink to="/suppliers">Suppliers</ToggleLink>
                        <ToggleLink to="/info/match">Match</ToggleLink>
```

```
                    <ToggleLink to="/info/location">Location</ToggleLink>
                    <ToggleLink to="/info" exact={ true }>All Info</ToggleLink>
                </div>
                <div className="col">
                    <CustomPrompt show={ this.state.showPrompt }
                        message={ this.state.message }
                        callback={ this.state.callback } />
                    <Prompt message={ loc =>
                        `Do you want to navigate to ${loc.pathname}?`} />
                    <RouteInfoHOC />
                    <Switch>
                        <Route path="/products" component={ ProductDisplay} />
                        <Route path="/suppliers" component={ SupplierDisplay } />
                        <Route path="/info/:datatype?" component={ RouteInfo } />
                        <Redirect to="/products" />
                    </Switch>
                </div>
            </div>
        </div>
    </Router>
    }
}
```

The getUserConfirmation prop supported by BrowserRouter and HashRouter is assigned a function that receives a message to display to the user and a callback that is invoked by the user's decision: true to processed with navigation and false to block it. In the listing, the getUserConfirmation prop will invoke the customGetUserConfirmation method, which updates the state data used for the CustomPrompt props, with the result that the user is prompted, as shown in Figure 22-9.

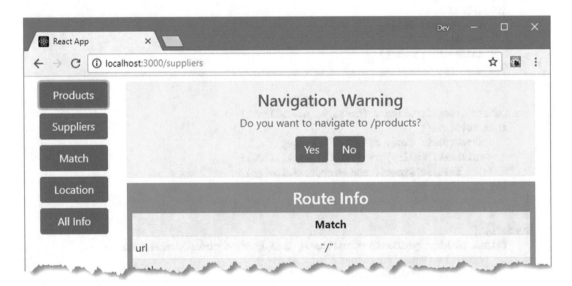

Figure 22-9. *Using a custom prompt*

■ **Tip**   Notice that I still need to use a Prompt, which is responsible for triggering the process that displays the CustomPrompt.

Generating Routes Programmatically

The Selector component uses the ToggleLink and Route components to set up the mappings between the URLs that the application supports and the content they relate to, but this wasn't the way that the application worked before I added support for URL routing. Instead, the App component treated the Selector as a container and provided it with children to display, like this:

```
import React, { Component } from "react";
import { Provider } from "react-redux";
import dataStore from "./store";
import { Selector } from "./Selector";
import { ProductDisplay } from "./ProductDisplay";
import { SupplierDisplay } from "./SupplierDisplay";

export default class App extends Component {

    render() {
        return   <Provider store={ dataStore }>
                    <Selector>
                        <ProductDisplay name="Products" />
                        <SupplierDisplay name="Suppliers" />
                    </Selector>
                 </Provider>
    }
}
```

The use of container components that provide services without hard-coded knowledge of their children is important in React development and can be easily applied when using React-Router because routes are defined and handled using components. In Listing 22-18, I have revised the Selector component to remove the locally defined routes and generate them from the children props instead.

Listing 22-18. Generating Routes from Children in the Selector.js File in the src Folder

```
import React, { Component } from "react";
import { BrowserRouter as Router, Route, Switch, Redirect, Prompt }
    from "react-router-dom";
// import { ProductDisplay } from "./ProductDisplay";
// import { SupplierDisplay } from "./SupplierDisplay";
//import { RouteInfo } from "./routing/RouteInfo";
import { ToggleLink } from "./routing/ToggleLink";
import { CustomPrompt } from "./routing/CustomPrompt";

//const RouteInfoHOC = withRouter(RouteInfo)

export class Selector extends Component {
```

```
    constructor(props) {
        super(props);
        this.state = {
            showPrompt: false,
            message: "",
            callback: () => {}
        }
    }

    customGetUserConfirmation = (message, navCallback) => {
        this.setState({
            showPrompt: true, message: message,
            callback: (allow) => { navCallback(allow);
                this.setState({ showPrompt: false}) }
        });
    }

    render() {

        const routes = React.Children.map(this.props.children, child => ({
            component: child,
            name: child.props.name,
            url: `/${child.props.name.toLowerCase()}`
        }));

        return <Router getUserConfirmation={ this.customGetUserConfirmation }>
            <div className="container-fluid">
                <div className="row">
                    <div className="col-2">
                        { routes.map(r => <ToggleLink key={ r.url } to={ r.url }>
                                            { r.name }
                                          </ToggleLink>)}
                    </div>
                    <div className="col">
                        <CustomPrompt show={ this.state.showPrompt }
                            message={ this.state.message }
                            callback={ this.state.callback } />
                        <Prompt message={ loc =>
                            `Do you want to navigate to ${loc.pathname}?`} />
                        <Switch>
                            { routes.map( r => <Route key={ r.url } path={ r.url }
                                    render={ () => r.component } />)}
                            <Redirect to={ routes[0].url } />
                        </Switch>
                    </div>
                </div>
            </div>
        </Router>
    }
}
```

The Selector processes its children to build up the mappings between URLs and components and generates the required ToggleLink and Route components, which I have supplemented with a Redirect component, producing the result shown in Figure 22-10.

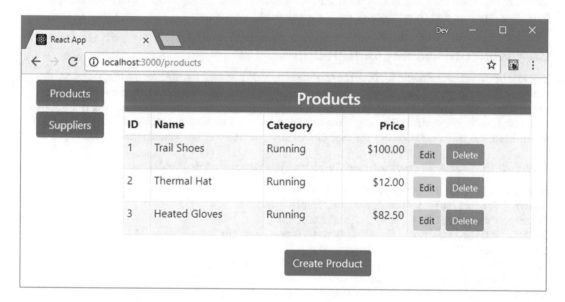

Figure 22-10. *Generating routes programmatically*

Using Routing with Connected Data Store Components

To complete the adoption of routing in the example application, I am going to move the remaining state data that coordinates components out of the data store and manage it with the set of URLs described in Table 22-8.

Table 22-8. *The URLs for the Example Application*

Name	Description
/products/table	This URL will display the table of products.
/products/create	This URL will display the editor to allow a new product to be created.
/products/edit/4	This URL will display the editor to allow an existing product to be edited, where the last URL segment identifies the product to change.
/suppliers/table	This URL will display the table of suppliers.
/suppliers/create	This URL will display the editor to allow a new supplier to be created.
/suppliers/edit/4	This URL will display the editor to allow an existing supplier to be edited, where the last URL segment identifies the supplier to change.

The URLs that the application requires can be handled with a single path with URL parameters, as follows:

```
...
/:datatype/:mode?/:id?
...
```

In the sections that follow, I will update the components in the application so that the data store is used only for the model data, while the details of which content should be displayed to the user is represented in the URL. (This kind of hard separation is only one approach, and you can take a softer line if it suits your project so that some state data is handled in the data store and some through URLs. As with so much in React development, there is no absolute correct approach.)

Replacing the Display Components

The ProductDisplay and SupplierDisplay components have been responsible for deciding whether the table or editor is displayed for a specific data type. The differences between these components have been reduced as features have been added to the example application, and the introduction of URL routing means that a single component can easily handle the content selection for both types of data. I added a file called RoutedDisplay.js to the src/routing folder and used it to define the component shown in Listing 22-19.

Listing 22-19. The Contents of the RoutedDisplay.js File in the src/routing Folder

```
import React, { Component } from "react";
import { ProductTable } from "../ProductTable"
import { ProductEditor } from "../ProductEditor";
import { EditorConnector } from "../store/EditorConnector";
import { PRODUCTS } from "../store/dataTypes";
import { TableConnector } from "../store/TableConnector";
import { Link } from "react-router-dom";
import { SupplierEditor } from "../SupplierEditor";
import { SupplierTable } from "../SupplierTable";

export const RoutedDisplay = (dataType) => {

    const ConnectedEditor = EditorConnector(dataType, dataType === PRODUCTS
        ? ProductEditor: SupplierEditor);
    const ConnectedTable = TableConnector(dataType, dataType === PRODUCTS
        ? ProductTable : SupplierTable);

    return class extends Component {
        render() {
            const modeParam = this.props.match.params.mode;
            if (modeParam === "edit" || modeParam === "create") {
                return <ConnectedEditor key={ this.props.match.params.id || -1 } />
            } else {
                return <div className="m-2">
                    <ConnectedTable />
                    <div className="text-center">
                        <Link to={`/${dataType}/create`}
                                className="btn btn-primary m-1">
                            Create
                        </Link>
                    </div>
                </div>
            }
        }
    }
}
```

This component performs the same task as the ProductDisplay and SupplierDisplay components but receives the data type it is responsible for as an argument, which allows the EditorConnector and TableConnector components to be created.

Updating the Connected Editor Component

The EditorConnector component is responsible for creating a ProductEditor or SupplierEditor that is connected to the Redux data store. In Listing 22-20, I have used the withRouter function to create a component that is provided with routing data but also remains connected to the data store.

Listing 22-20. Using Routing in the EditorConnector.js File in the src/store Folder

```
import { connect } from "react-redux";
//import { endEditing } from "./stateActions";
import { PRODUCTS, SUPPLIERS  } from "./dataTypes";
import { saveAndEndEditing } from "./multiActionCreators";
import { withRouter } from "react-router-dom";

export const EditorConnector = (dataType, presentationComponent) => {

    const mapStateToProps = (storeData, ownProps) => {
        const mode = ownProps.match.params.mode;
        const id = Number(ownProps.match.params.id);
        return {
            editing: mode === "edit" || mode === "create",
            product: (storeData.modelData[PRODUCTS].find(p => p.id === id)) || {},
            supplier:(storeData.modelData[SUPPLIERS].find(s => s.id === id)) || {}
        }
    }

    const mapDispatchToProps = {
        //cancelCallback: endEditing,
        saveCallback: (data) => saveAndEndEditing(data, dataType)
    }

    const mergeProps = (dataProps, functionProps, ownProps) => {
        let routedDispatchers = {
            cancelCallback: () => ownProps.history.push(`/${dataType}`),
            saveCallback: (data) => {
                functionProps.saveCallback(data);
                ownProps.history.push(`/${dataType}`);
            }
        }
        return Object.assign({}, dataProps, routedDispatchers, ownProps);
    }

    return withRouter(connect(mapStateToProps,
        mapDispatchToProps, mergeProps)(presentationComponent));
}
```

The component no longer uses the data store to work out whether the user is editing or creating an object and gets this information from the URL, along with the id value when an object is being edited.

■ **Tip**   Notice that I use Number to parse the id URL parameter, which is presented as a string. I need the id value to be a number in order to locate objects.

I have used the ability to merge props, described in Chapter 20, to create wrappers around the data store action creator so that data is saved to the store and then the history object is used for navigation. The cancel action is no longer required and can be handled directly by navigating away from the current location.

AVOIDING BLOCKED UPDATES

The withRouter and connect functions both produce components that try to minimize updates using the shouldComponentUpdate method, which is described in Chapter 13. When the withRouter and connect functions are used together, the result can be a component that doesn't always update because the React-Router and React-Redux packages perform simple comparisons on props and don't realize that a change has occurred. To avoid this problem, simplify the props structure to allow changes to be more easily detected.

Updating the Connected Table Component

The same process must be performed on the component that connects the tables that display objects to the data store, as shown in Listing 22-21.

Listing 22-21.   Using Routing in the TableConnector.js File in the src/store Folder

```
import { connect } from "react-redux";
//import { startEditingProduct, startEditingSupplier } from "./stateActions";
import { deleteProduct, deleteSupplier } from "./modelActionCreators";
import { PRODUCTS, SUPPLIERS } from "./dataTypes";
import { withRouter } from "react-router-dom";

export const TableConnector = (dataType, presentationComponent) => {

    const mapStateToProps = (storeData, ownProps) => {
        if (dataType === PRODUCTS) {
            return { products: storeData.modelData[PRODUCTS] };
        } else {
            return {
                suppliers: storeData.modelData[SUPPLIERS].map(supp => ({
                    ...supp,
                    products: supp.products.map(id =>
                        storeData.modelData[PRODUCTS]
                            .find(p => p.id === Number(id)) || id)
                            .map(val => val.name || val)
                }))
```

```
                }
            }
        }

        const mapDispatchToProps = (dispatch, ownProps) => {
            if (dataType === PRODUCTS) {
                return {
                    //editCallback: (...args) => dispatch(startEditingProduct(...args)),
                    deleteCallback: (...args) => dispatch(deleteProduct(...args))
                }
            } else {
                return {
                    //editCallback: (...args) => dispatch(startEditingSupplier(...args)),
                    deleteCallback: (...args) => dispatch(deleteSupplier(...args))
                }
            }
        }

        const mergeProps = (dataProps, functionProps, ownProps) => {
            let routedDispatchers = {
                editCallback: (target) => {
                    ownProps.history.push(`/${dataType}/edit/${target.id}`);
                },
                deleteCallback: functionProps.deleteCallback
            }
            return Object.assign({}, dataProps, routedDispatchers, ownProps);
        }

        return withRouter(connect(mapStateToProps,
            mapDispatchToProps, mergeProps)(presentationComponent));
}
```

Once again, I have used the withRouter and connect functions to produce a component that has access to the routing data and the data store. The editing function is handled by navigating to a URL that indicates the data type and id value. Deleting data is a task handled entirely by the data store and requires no navigation.

Completing the Routing Configuration

The final step is to update the routing configuration to support the URLs defined in Table 22-8. In Listing 22-22, I updated the Selector component so that it applies the RoutedDisplay component in its render function. (I also removed the navigation prompt components and code for brevity.)

Listing 22-22. Changing the Routing Configuration in the Selector.js File in the src Folder

```
import React, { Component } from "react";
import { BrowserRouter as Router, Route, Switch, Redirect }
    from "react-router-dom";
import { ToggleLink } from "./routing/ToggleLink";
//import { CustomPrompt } from "./routing/CustomPrompt";
import { RoutedDisplay } from "./routing/RoutedDisplay";
```

```
export class Selector extends Component {

    render() {

        const routes = React.Children.map(this.props.children, child => ({
            component: child,
            name: child.props.name,
            url: `/${child.props.name.toLowerCase()}`,
            datatype: child.props.datatype
        }));

        return <Router getUserConfirmation={ this.customGetUserConfirmation }>
            <div className="container-fluid">
                <div className="row">
                    <div className="col-2">
                        { routes.map(r => <ToggleLink key={ r.url } to={ r.url }>
                                            { r.name }
                                        </ToggleLink>)}
                    </div>
                    <div className="col">
                        <Switch>
                            { routes.map(r =>
                                <Route key={ r.url }
                                    path={ `/:datatype(${r.datatype})/:mode?/:id?` }
                                    component={ RoutedDisplay(r.datatype)} />
                            )}
                            <Redirect to={ routes[0].url } />
                        </Switch>
                    </div>
                </div>
            </div>
        </Router>
    }
}
```

The children provided by the parent component are no longer components and exist only to provide prop values to the Selector so that it can set up the Route components. In Listing 22-23, I have reflected this change in the App component, which now uses a custom HTML element to configure the Selector rather than using the data-specific components directly.

Listing 22-23. Completing the Routing Configuration in the App.js File in the src Folder

```
import React, { Component } from "react";
import { Provider } from "react-redux";
import dataStore from "./store";
import { Selector } from "./Selector";
// import { ProductDisplay } from "./ProductDisplay";
// import { SupplierDisplay } from "./SupplierDisplay";
import { PRODUCTS, SUPPLIERS } from "./store/dataTypes";

export default class App extends Component {
```

```
render() {
    return   <Provider store={ dataStore }>
                <Selector>
                    <data name="Products" datatype={ PRODUCTS } />
                    <data name="Suppliers" datatype ={ SUPPLIERS } />
                </Selector>
            </Provider>
    }
}
```

The result is that the data store is no longer used for coordination between components, which is now handled entirely through the URL, as shown in Figure 22-11.

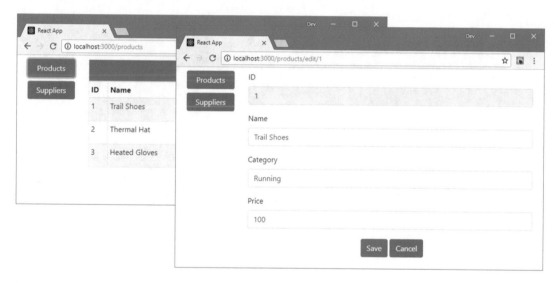

Figure 22-11. *Using URL routing to coordinate components*

Summary

In this chapter, I showed you how to use the advanced features provided by the React-Router package. I demonstrated how to create components that are aware of the routing system, how to use URL parameters to provide components with easy access to data from the current route, and how to use the routing features programmatically. I also demonstrated how components can participate in the routing system while also being connected to Redux, allowing state data to be handled via URLs while the application's model data is managed by a data store. In the next chapter, I show you how to consume a RESTful web service.

CHAPTER 23

■ ■ ■

Consuming a RESTful Web Service

In this chapter, I address the example application's lack of permanent data storage by creating a web service and using it to manage the application's data. The application will send HTTP requests to the web service to retrieve data and to submit changes. I start this chapter by showing you how to consume a web service directly in a component and then demonstrate how a web service can be used with a data store. In Chapter 24, I explain how to use GraphQL, which is an alternative approach to dealing with web services. Table 23-1 puts this chapter in context.

Table 23-1. *Putting Consuming Web Services in Context*

Question	Answer
What is it?	Web services act as the data repository for an application, allowing data to be read, stored, modified, and deleted using HTTP requests.
Why is it useful?	Web services fit neatly into the features available in browsers and avoid having to deal with local storage issues.
How is it used?	Web services are not all implemented the same way, but the general approach is to send HTTP requests where the request method identifies the operation to be performed and the request URL identifies the data to be operated on.
Are there any pitfalls or limitations?	The inconsistent nature of web service implementations means that each web service can require a slightly different set of requests. Care must be taken when consuming the web service in a component to ensure that requests are not sent each time there is an update.
Are there any alternatives?	Modern web browsers support local storage options, which can be a good alternative for some projects. The main drawback, however, is that each client has its own data, which misses out on some of the advantages of a single central repository.

© Adam Freeman 2019
A. Freeman, *Pro React 16*, https://doi.org/10.1007/978-1-4842-4451-7_23

Table 23-2 summarizes the chapter.

Table 23-2. *Chapter Summary*

Problem	Solution	Listing
Get data from a web service	Create a data source that makes HTTP requests and feed the data back into the application using a callback that invokes the `setState` method.	1–11
Perform additional data operations	Extend the data source to send different combinations of HTTP methods and URLs to indicate the required operation. Trigger the requests by responding to component events	12–15
Handle request errors	Use a `try`/`catch` block to catch the error and pass it to a component so that a warning can be displayed to the user.	16–19
Consume a web service with a data store	Use middleware to intercept the data store actions and send the required requests to the web service. Once a request has completed, forward the action to the data store so that it can be updated.	20–24

Preparing for This Chapter

In this chapter, I continue using the `productapp` project from Chapter 22 that was modified in the chapters since. Some preparation is required to install additional packages to the project and create the web service that the application will rely on.

■ **Tip** You can download the example project for this chapter—and for all the other chapters in this book—from `https://github.com/Apress/pro-react-16`.

Adding Packages to the Project

Run the commands shown in Listing 23-1 in the `productapp` folder to add the required packages to the project.

Listing 23-1. Installing Additional Packages to the Project

```
npm install json-server@0.14.0 --save-dev
npm install npm-run-all@4.1.3 --save-dev
npm install axios@0.18.0
```

For quick reference, the packages by the commands in Listing 23-1 are described in Table 23-3.

Table 23-3. *The Packages Added to the Project*

Name	Description
json-server	This package provides a web service that the application will query for data. This command is installed with the save-dev command because it is required for development and is not part of the application.
npm-run-all	This package allows multiple commands to be run in parallel so that the web service and the development server can be started at the same time. This command is installed with the save-dev command because it is required for development and is not part of the application.
axios	This package will be used by the application to make HTTP requests to the web service.

Preparing the Web Service

To provide the json-server package with data to work with, add a file called restData.js to the productapp folder and add the code shown in Listing 23-2.

Listing 23-2. The Contents of the restData.js File in the productapp Folder

```
module.exports = function () {
    var data = {
        products: [
            { id: 1, name: "Kayak", category: "Watersports", price: 275 },
            { id: 2, name: "Lifejacket", category: "Watersports", price: 48.95 },
            { id: 3, name: "Soccer Ball", category: "Soccer", price: 19.50 },
            { id: 4, name: "Corner Flags", category: "Soccer", price: 34.95 },
            { id: 5, name: "Stadium", category: "Soccer", price: 79500 },
            { id: 6, name: "Thinking Cap", category: "Chess", price: 16 },
            { id: 7, name: "Unsteady Chair", category: "Chess", price: 29.95 },
            { id: 8, name: "Human Chess Board", category: "Chess", price: 75 },
            { id: 9, name: "Bling Bling King", category: "Chess", price: 1200 }
        ],
        suppliers: [
            { id: 1, name: "Surf Dudes", city: "San Jose", products: [1, 2] },
            { id: 2, name: "Goal Oriented", city: "Seattle", products: [3, 4, 5] },
            { id: 3, name: "Bored Games", city: "New York", products: [6, 7, 8, 9] },
        ]
    }
    return data
}
```

The json-server package can work with JSON or JavaScript files. If a JSON file is used, its contents will be modified to reflect changes requests made by clients. Instead, I have chosen the JavaScript option, which allows data to be generated programmatically and means that restarting the process will return to the original data. This isn't something that you would do in a real project, but it is useful for the example because it makes it easy to return to a known state, while still allowing the application access to persistent data.

To configure the json-server package so that it responds to requests for URLs that start with /api, create a file called api.routes.json in the productapp folder with the contents shown in Listing 23-3.

Listing 23-3. The Contents of the api.routes.json File in the productapp Folder

```
{ "/api/*": "/$1" }
```

To configure the development tools so that the web service is started at the same time as the development web server, make the changes shown in Listing 23-4 to the package.json file in the productapp folder.

Listing 23-4. Configuring Tools in the package.json File in the productapp Folder

```
...
"scripts": {
    "start": "npm-run-all --parallel reactstart json",
    "build": "react-scripts build",
    "test": "react-scripts test",
    "eject": "react-scripts eject",
    "reactstart": "react-scripts start",
    "json": "json-server --p 3500 -r api.routes.json restData.js"
},
...
```

The changes to the scripts section of the package.json file use the npm-run-all package so that the HTTP development server and json-server are started by npm start.

Adding a Component and a Route

I am going to demonstrate how to consume a web service in isolation and then show you how to use the data in a data store. The existing components in the application are already connected to the data store, and so to show how unconnected components can be used, I created a file called IsolatedTable.js in the src folder and used it to create the component shown in Listing 23-5.

Listing 23-5. The Contents of the IsolatedTable.js File in the src Folder

```
import React, { Component } from "react";

export class IsolatedTable extends Component {

    render() {
        return <table className="table table-sm table-striped table-bordered">
            <thead>
                <tr><th colSpan="5"
                        className="bg-info text-white text-center h4 p-2">
                    (Isolated) Products
                </th></tr>
                <tr>
                    <th>ID</th><th>Name</th><th>Category</th>
                    <th className="text-right">Price</th>
                    <th></th>
                </tr>
            </thead>
```

```
        <tbody>
            <tr><td colSpan="5" className="text-center p-2">No Data</td></tr>
        </tbody>
    </table>
  }
}
```

The component renders an empty table as a placeholder for the moment. To incorporate the component into the application, I updated the routing configuration in the Selector component to add a new Route and a corresponding navigation link, as shown in Listing 23-6.

Listing 23-6. Adding a Route in the Selector.js File in the src Folder

```
import React, { Component } from "react";
import { BrowserRouter as Router, Route, Switch, Redirect }
    from "react-router-dom";
import { ToggleLink } from "./routing/ToggleLink";
import { RoutedDisplay } from "./routing/RoutedDisplay";
import { IsolatedTable } from "./IsolatedTable";

export class Selector extends Component {

    render() {

        const routes = React.Children.map(this.props.children, child => ({
            component: child,
            name: child.props.name,
            url: `/${child.props.name.toLowerCase()}`,
            datatype: child.props.datatype
        }));

        return <Router getUserConfirmation={ this.customGetUserConfirmation }>
            <div className="container-fluid">
                <div className="row">
                    <div className="col-2">
                        <ToggleLink to="/isolated">Isolated Data</ToggleLink>
                        { routes.map(r => <ToggleLink key={ r.url } to={ r.url }>
                                    { r.name }
                                </ToggleLink>)}
                    </div>
                    <div className="col">
                        <Switch>
                            <Route path="/isolated" component={ IsolatedTable } />
                            { routes.map(r =>
                                <Route key={ r.url }
                                    path={ `/:datatype(${r.datatype})/:mode?/:id?` }
                                    component={ RoutedDisplay(r.datatype)} />
                            )}
                            <Redirect to={ routes[0].url } />
                        </Switch>
                    </div>
```

```
                </div>
            </div>
        </Router>
    }
}
```

Running the Web Service and the Example Application

Using the command prompt, run the command shown in Listing 23-7 in the productapp folder to start the development tools and the web service.

Listing 23-7. Starting the Development Tools

```
npm start
```

Once the initial preparation for the project is complete, a new browser window will open and display the URL http://localhost:3000, as shown in Figure 23-1.

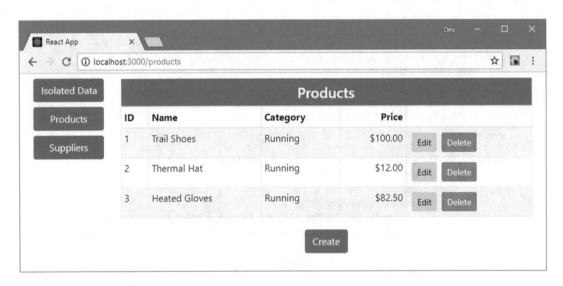

Figure 23-1. *Running the example application*

Open a new browser window and navigate to http://localhost:3500/api/products/2. The server will respond with the following data, which is also shown in Figure 23-2:

```
...
{ "id": 2, "name": "Lifejacket", "category": "Watersports", "price": 48.95 }
...
```

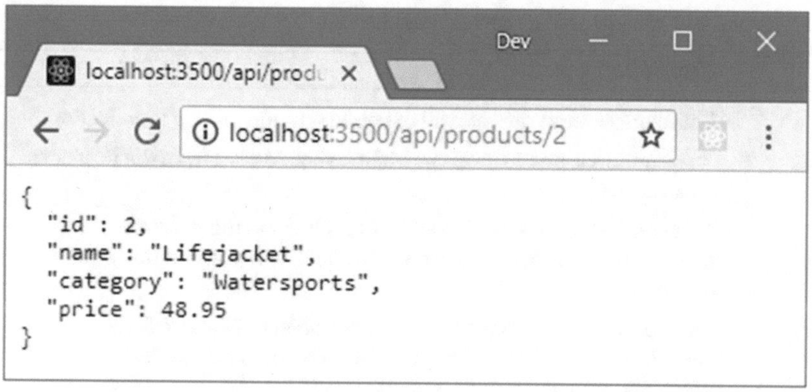

Figure 23-2. *Testing the web service*

The configuration I have chosen for this chapter means that there are two HTTP servers running. The React development server is listening for requests on port 3000 and provides the HTML document that bootstraps the application, along with the JavaScript and CSS files required to present the application to the user. The RESTful web service is listening for requests on port 3500 and responds with data. This data is expressed in the JSON format, which means it is easily processed by a JavaScript application but should not be presented directly to most users.

Understanding RESTful Web Services

The most common approach for delivering and storing application data is applying the *Representational State Transfer* pattern, known as REST, to create a data web service. There is no detailed specification for REST, which leads to a lot of different approaches that fall under the RESTful banner. There are, however, some unifying ideas that are useful in web application development.

The core premise of a RESTful web service is to embrace the characteristics of HTTP so that request methods—also known as *verbs*—specify an operation for the server to perform, and the request URL specifies one or more data objects to which the operation will be applied.

As an example, here is a URL that might refer to a specific product in the example application:

```
http://localhost:3500/api/products/2
```

The first segment of the URL—api—conventionally indicates that the request is for data. The next segment—products—is used to indicate the collection of objects that will be operated on and allows a single server to provide multiple services, each of which with its own data. The final segment—2—selects an individual object within the products collection. In the example, it is the value of the id property that uniquely identifies an object and that would be used in the URL, in this case, specifying the Lifejacket object.

The HTTP verb or method used to make the request tells the RESTful server what operation should be performed on the specified object. When you tested the RESTful server in the previous section, the browser sent an HTTP GET request, which the server interprets as an instruction to retrieve the specified object and send it to the client.

Table 23-4 shows the most common combination of HTTP methods and URLs and explains what each of them does when sent to a RESTful server.

Table 23-4. *Common HTTP Verbs and Their Effect in a RESTful Web Service*

Verb	URL	Description
GET	/api/products	This combination retrieves all the objects in the products collection.
GET	/api/products/2	This combination retrieves the object whose id is 2 from the products collection.
POST	/api/products	This combination is used to add a new object to the products collection. The request body contains a JSON representation of the new object.
PUT	/api/products/2	This combination is used to replace the object in the products collection whose id is 2. The request body contains a JSON representation of the replacement object.
PATCH	/api/products/2	This combination is used to update a subset of the properties of the object in the products collection whose id is 2. The request body contains a JSON representation of the properties to update and the new values.
DELETE	/api/products/2	This combination is used to delete the product whose id is 2 from the products collection.

There are considerable differences in the way that web services are implemented, caused by differences in the frameworks used to create them and the preferences of the development team. It is important to confirm how a web service uses verbs and what is required in the URL and request body to perform operations.

Common variations include web services that won't accept any request bodies that contain id values (to ensure they are generated uniquely by the server's data store) and web services that don't support all of the verbs (it is common to ignore PATCH requests and only accept updates using the PUT verb).

■ **Tip** You may have noticed that the editor components don't allow the user to provide a value for the id property. This is because the web service that I create in this chapter generates id values automatically to ensure uniqueness.

CHOOSING AN HTTP REQUEST LIBRARY

Throughout this chapter, I use the Axios library to send HTTP requests to the web service because it is easy to use, deals with common data types automatically, and doesn't require convoluted code to deal with features like CORS (see the "Making Cross-Origin Requests" sidebar). Axios is widely used in web application development, although it is not specific to React.

Axios isn't the only way to send HTTP requests to web services. The most basic option to use the XMLlHttpRequest object that provided the original API for making requests using JavaScript (and which is capable of handling a range of data types, despite the XML in the name). The XMLHttpRequest object is awkward to use but has wide browser support, and you can get further details at `https://developer.mozilla.org/en-US/docs/Web/API/XMLHttpRequest`. (Axios uses `XMLHttpRequest` to make HTTP requests but simplifies how they are created and processed.)

The Fetch API is a recent API provided by modern browsers that is intended to replace `XMLHttpRequest` and is described at `https://developer.mozilla.org/en-US/docs/Web/API/Fetch_API`. The Fetch API is supported by recent releases of the mainstream browsers but not by older browsers, which can be a problem for some applications.

If you are using GraphQL, then you should consider using the Apollo client, as described in Chapter 25.

Consuming a Web Service

I go through the steps required to consume a web service in the sections that follow, beginning with requesting the initial data that the application will display to the user and then adding support for storing and updating objects.

Creating the Data Source Component

It is a good idea to keep the code that uses Axios to consume the web service separate from the component that uses it so that it can be more easily tested and used elsewhere in the application. I created the src/webservice folder and added to it a file called RestDataSource.js with the code shown in Listing 23-8.

Listing 23-8. The Contents of the RestDataSource.js File in the src/webservice Folder

```
import Axios from "axios";

export class RestDataSource {

    constructor(base_url) {
        this.BASE_URL = base_url;
    }

    GetData(callback) {
        this.SendRequest("get", this.BASE_URL, callback);
    }

    SendRequest(method, url, callback) {
        Axios.request({
            method: method,
            url: url
        }).then(response => callback(response.data));
    }
}
```

The RestDataSource class defines a constructor that receives the base URL for the web service and defines a GetData method that calls the SendRequest.

I imported the HTTP functionality from the axios package and assigned it the name Axios. The SendRequest method uses Axios to send an HTTP request through the request method, where the details of the request are specified using a configuration object that has method and url properties.

Axios provides methods for sending different types of HTTP request—the get, post, and put methods, for example, but using the approach in the listing makes it easier to apply features that affect all request types, as you will see when I add error handling later in the chapter.

HTTP requests made using JavaScript are asynchronous. The request method returns a Promise object that represents the eventual outcome of the request (see Chapter 4 for details of how Promise objects are used). In Listing 23-8, I use the then method to supply Axios with a callback function to use when the request is complete. The callback function is passed an object that describes the response using the properties described in Table 23-5.

Table 23-5. *The Axios Response Properties*

Name	Description
status	This property returns the status code for the response, such as 200 or 404.
statusText	This property returns the explanatory text that accompanies the status code, such as OK or Not Found.
headers	This property returns an object whose properties represent the response headers.
data	This property returns the payload from the response.
config	This property returns an object that contains the configuration options used to make the request.
request	This property returns the underlying XMLHttpRequest object that was used to make the request, which can be useful if you require direct access to the API provided by the browser.

Axios automatically converts the JSON data format into a JavaScript object and presents it through the response data property. As explained in Chapter 4, code that uses promises can be simplified using the async and await keywords, as shown in Listing 23-9.

Listing 23-9. Using async and await in the RestDataSource.js File in the src/webservice Folder

```
import Axios from "axios";

export class RestDataSource {

    constructor(base_url) {
        this.BASE_URL = base_url;
    }

    GetData(callback) {
        this.SendRequest("get", this.BASE_URL, callback);
    }

    async SendRequest(method, url, callback) {
        let response = await Axios.request({
            method: method,
            url: url
        });
        callback(response.data);
    }
}
```

I can further simplify the code by combining the statements in the GetData method, as shown in Listing 23-10.

Listing 23-10. Combining Statements in the RestDataSource.js File in the src/webservice Folder

```
import Axios from "axios";

export class RestDataSource {

    constructor(base_url) {
        this.BASE_URL = base_url;
    }

    GetData(callback) {
        this.SendRequest("get", this.BASE_URL, callback);
    }

    async SendRequest(method, url, callback) {
        callback((await Axios.request({
            method: method,
            url: url
        })).data);
    }
}
```

This approach is more concise, but it is important to make sure you put the parentheses in the right places, such that the await keyword is applied to the object returned by the SendRequest method and the data property is read from the object that it produces. Without care, you can easily create a situation where the HTTP request is sent but the response is ignored if you don't follow this pattern.

Getting Data in the Component

The next step is to get the data into the component so that it can be displayed to the user. In Listing 23-11, I have updated the IsolatedTable component so that it creates a data source and uses it to request data from the web service.

■ **Note** The term *isolated* in the name of the component indicates that the component doesn't share data with any other components and deals directly with the web service. In the "Consuming a Web Service with a Data Store" section, I show you an alternative approach where components share data via the data store.

Listing 23-11. Getting Data in the IsolatedTable.js File in the src Folder

```jsx
import React, { Component } from "react";
import { RestDataSource } from "./webservice/RestDataSource";

export class IsolatedTable extends Component {

    constructor(props) {
        super(props);
        this.state = {
            products: []
        }
        this.dataSource = new RestDataSource("http://localhost:3500/api/products")
    }

    render() {
        return <table className="table table-sm table-striped table-bordered">
            <thead>
                <tr><th colSpan="5"
                        className="bg-info text-white text-center h4 p-2">
                    (Isolated) Products
                </th></tr>
                <tr>
                    <th>ID</th><th>Name</th><th>Category</th>
                    <th className="text-right">Price</th>
                    <th></th>
                </tr>
            </thead>
            <tbody>
                {
                    this.state.products.map(p => <tr key={ p.id }>
                        <td>{ p.id }</td><td>{ p.name }</td><td>{p.category}</td>
                        <td className="text-right">
                            ${ Number(p.price).toFixed(2)}
                        </td><td/>
                    </tr>)
                }
            </tbody>
        </table>
    }

    componentDidMount() {
        this.dataSource.GetData(data => this.setState({products: data}));
    }
}
```

The data is requested in the componentDidMount method, which ensures that the HTTP request won't be sent until after the component has rendered its content. The callback functions provided to the GetData method update the component's state data, which will trigger an update and ensure that the data is presented to the user.

AVOIDING EXTRANEOUS DATA REQUESTS

Do not request data in the `render` method. As I explained in Chapter 13, a component's `render` method can be called often, and starting tasks in the `render` method can generate large numbers of unnecessary HTTP requests and increase the number of updates that React has to perform as it processes the response data.

Even when using the `componentDidMount` method, care should be taken when making requests from components that may be unmounted and remounted, which is the case for the `IsolatedTable` component in the example, which will be mounted by the routing system for the `/isolated` URL and unmounted when the user navigates to another location. Each time the component is mounted, it will request fresh data from the web service, which may not be what the application requires. To avoid unnecessary data requests, the data can be lifted up to a component that won't be unmounted, stored in a context (as described in Chapter 14), or incorporated into a data store, as described in the "Consuming a Web Service with a Data Store" section.

The result is that the data is obtained from the web service and displayed to the user when the Isolated Data button is clicked, as shown in Figure 23-3.

Figure 23-3. Getting data from the web service

Saving, Updating, and Deleting Data

To implement the operations required for saving, updating, and deleting data, I added the methods shown in Listing 23-12 to the data source class, using Axios to send requests to the web service with different HTTP methods.

Listing 23-12. Adding Methods in the RestDataSource.js File in the src/webservice Folder

```
import Axios from "axios";

export class RestDataSource {

    constructor(base_url) {
        this.BASE_URL = base_url;
    }

    GetData(callback) {
        this.SendRequest("get", this.BASE_URL, callback);
    }

    async GetOne(id, callback) {
        this.SendRequest("get", `${this.BASE_URL}/${id}`, callback);
    }

    async Store(data, callback) {
        this.SendRequest("post", this.BASE_URL, callback, data)
    }

    async Update(data, callback) {
        this.SendRequest("put", `${this.BASE_URL}/${data.id}`, callback, data);
    }

    async Delete(data, callback) {
        this.SendRequest("delete", `${this.BASE_URL}/${data.id}`, callback, data);
    }

    async SendRequest(method, url, callback, data) {
        callback((await Axios.request({
            method: method,
            url: url,
            data: data
        })).data);
    }
}
```

The request configuration object passed to the Axios.request method uses a data property to specify the payload for the request, which allows the application to provide JavaScript objects and leave Axios to serialize them automatically.

When you implement data source methods, you will find that some adjustment is required to accommodate the range of ways that web services can be implemented. For example, the example web service will automatically assign a unique id property value to objects that are received in POST requests and include the complete object in the response. The Store method in Listing 23-12 uses the data property to get the complete object from the HTTP response and uses it to invoke the callback, which ensures that the application receives the object as it has been stored by the web service. Not all web services operate this way—some may require the application to include a unique identifier or will return only the identifier in the response instead of sending the complete object.

When modifying an object, a PUT request is sent with the URL identifying the object to be modified, like this:

```
...
this.SendRequest("put", `${this.BASE_URL}/${data.id}`, callback, data);
...
```

The web service returns the complete updated object, which is used to invoke the callback function. Once again, not all web services will return the complete object, but it is a common approach because it ensures that any additional transformations that are applied by the web service are reflected in the client.

Adding Application Support for Creating, Editing, and Deleting Data

To provide support for creating and editing data, I added a file called IsolatedEditor.js to the src folder and used it to define the component shown in Listing 23-13.

Listing 23-13. The Contents of the IsolatedEditor.js File in the src Folder

```
import React, { Component } from "react";
import { RestDataSource } from "./webservice/RestDataSource";
import { ProductEditor } from "./ProductEditor";

export class IsolatedEditor extends Component {

    constructor(props) {
        super(props);
        this.state = {
            dataItem: {}
        };
        this.dataSource = this.props.dataSource
            || new RestDataSource("http://localhost:3500/api/products");
    }

    save = (data) => {
        const callback = () => this.props.history.push("/isolated");
        if (data.id === "") {
            this.dataSource.Store(data, callback);
        } else {
            this.dataSource.Update(data, callback);
        }
    }

    cancel = () => this.props.history.push("/isolated");

    render() {
        return <ProductEditor key={ this.state.dataItem.id }
            product={ this.state.dataItem } saveCallback={ this.save }
            cancelCallback={ this.cancel } />
    }
```

```
    componentDidMount() {
        if (this.props.match.params.mode === "edit") {
            this.dataSource.GetOne(this.props.match.params.id,
                data => this.setState({ dataItem: data}));
        }
    }
}
```

React makes it easy to use existing components in new ways, and the IsolatedEditor component uses the existing ProductEditor and its props to provide it with data and callbacks from the web service data source. Details of the current route are used to request details of a single object using the GetOne method when the user has selected an object for editing, and changes are sent back to the web service using the Store or Update methods. In Listing 23-14, I have added support to the IsolatedTable component for creating and editing objects by navigating to new URLs. I have also added a Delete button whose event handler invokes the data source's Delete method, which sends a DELETE request to the web service.

Listing 23-14. Adding Data Operations in the IsolatedTable.js File in the src Folder

```
import React, { Component } from "react";
import { RestDataSource } from "./webservice/RestDataSource";
import { Link } from "react-router-dom";

export class IsolatedTable extends Component {

    constructor(props) {
        super(props);
        this.state = {
            products: []
        }
        this.dataSource = new RestDataSource("http://localhost:3500/api/products")
    }

    deleteProduct(product) {
        this.dataSource.Delete(product,
            () => this.setState({products: this.state.products.filter(p =>
                p.id !== product.id)}));
    }

    render() {
        return <table className="table table-sm table-striped table-bordered">
            <thead>
                <tr><th colSpan="5"
                        className="bg-info text-white text-center h4 p-2">
                    (Isolated) Products
                </th></tr>
                <tr>
                    <th>ID</th><th>Name</th><th>Category</th>
                    <th className="text-right">Price</th>
                    <th></th>
                </tr>
            </thead>
```

```
            <tbody>
                {
                    this.state.products.map(p => <tr key={ p.id }>
                        <td>{ p.id }</td><td>{ p.name }</td><td>{p.category}</td>
                        <td className="text-right">
                            ${ Number(p.price).toFixed(2)}
                        </td>
                        <td>
                            <Link className="btn btn-sm btn-warning mx-2"
                                    to={`/isolated/edit/${p.id}`}>
                                Edit
                            </Link>
                            <button className="btn btn-sm btn-danger mx-2"
                                onClick={ () => this.deleteProduct(p)}>
                                    Delete
                            </button>
                        </td>
                    </tr>)
                }
            </tbody>
            <tfoot>
                <tr className="text-center">
                    <td colSpan="5">
                        <Link to="/isolated/create"
                            className="btn btn-info">Create</Link>
                    </td>
                </tr>
            </tfoot>
        </table>
    }

    componentDidMount() {
        this.dataSource.GetData(data => this.setState({products: data}));
    }
}
```

The final step is to update the routing configuration in the Selector component so that the /isolated/ edit and /isolated/create URLs select the IsolatedEditor component. I have also set the route for the / isolated URL to match exactly to ensure that the Route for the IsolatedTable component doesn't match the other URLs, as shown in Listing 23-15.

Listing 23-15. Adding a Route in the Selector.js File in the src Folder

```
import React, { Component } from "react";
import { BrowserRouter as Router, Route, Switch, Redirect }
    from "react-router-dom";
import { ToggleLink } from "./routing/ToggleLink";
import { RoutedDisplay } from "./routing/RoutedDisplay";
import { IsolatedTable } from "./IsolatedTable";
import { IsolatedEditor } from "./IsolatedEditor";
```

```
export class Selector extends Component {

    render() {

        const routes = React.Children.map(this.props.children, child => ({
            component: child,
            name: child.props.name,
            url: `/${child.props.name.toLowerCase()}`,
            datatype: child.props.datatype
        }));

        return <Router getUserConfirmation={ this.customGetUserConfirmation }>
            <div className="container-fluid">
                <div className="row">
                    <div className="col-2">
                        <ToggleLink to="/isolated">Isolated Data</ToggleLink>
                        { routes.map(r => <ToggleLink key={ r.url } to={ r.url }>
                                            { r.name }
                                        </ToggleLink>)}
                    </div>
                    <div className="col">
                        <Switch>
                            <Route path="/isolated" component={ IsolatedTable }
                                exact={ true } />
                            <Route path="/isolated/:mode/:id?"
                                component={ IsolatedEditor } />
                            { routes.map(r =>
                                <Route key={ r.url }
                                    path={ `/:datatype(${r.datatype})/:mode?/:id?` }
                                    component={ RoutedDisplay(r.datatype) } />
                            )}
                            <Redirect to={ routes[0].url } />
                        </Switch>
                    </div>
                </div>
            </div>
        </Router>
    }
}
```

The IsolatedTable component displays Create, Edit, and Delete buttons, as shown in Figure 23-4. The Create and Edit buttons present the editor component to the user, which then updates the web service with the changes that the user makes by sending POST or PUT requests. The Delete buttons remove the object with which they are associated by sending a DELETE request to the web service.

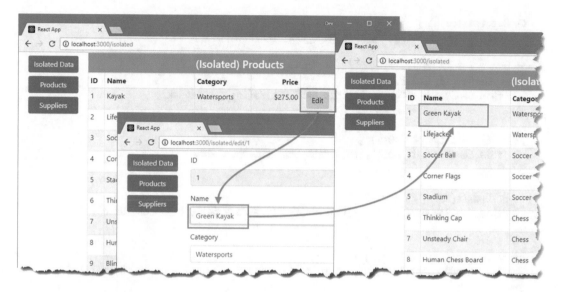

Figure 23-4. *Consuming a web service*

■ **Note** The changes made by the application are stored in the web service, which means you can reload the browser and the changes will still be visible. The configuration of the json-server package at the start of the chapter means that restarting the development tools will reset the data presented to by the web service. See the SportsStore application in Chapter 8 for an example of using json-server for truly persistent data that does not reset when the tools are restarted.

Dealing with Errors

The application assumes that all the HTTP requests will succeed, which is an unrealistically optimistic approach. There are lots of reasons why an HTTP request may fail, such as connectivity issues or server failure. Error boundaries, which I described in Chapter 14, can't deal with problems that arise in asynchronous operations such as HTTP requests, so a different approach is required. In Listing 23-16, I have changed the data source so that it receives a function that it will invoke when there is a problem and use the try/catch keywords to invoke the function when a request fails.

Listing 23-16. Handling Errors in the RestDataSource.js File in the src/webservice Folder

```
import Axios from "axios";

export class RestDataSource {

    constructor(base_url, errorCallback) {
        this.BASE_URL = base_url;
        this.handleError = errorCallback;
    }
```

```
GetData(callback) {
    this.SendRequest("get", this.BASE_URL, callback);
}

async GetOne(id, callback) {
    this.SendRequest("get", `${this.BASE_URL}/${id}`, callback);
}

async Store(data, callback) {
    this.SendRequest("post", this.BASE_URL, callback, data)
}

async Update(data, callback) {
    this.SendRequest("put", `${this.BASE_URL}/${data.id}`, callback, data);
}

async Delete(data, callback) {
    this.SendRequest("delete", `${this.BASE_URL}/${data.id}`, callback, data);
}

async SendRequest(method, url, callback, data) {
    try {
        callback((await Axios.request({
            method: method,
            url: url,
            data: data
        })).data);
    } catch(err) {
        this.handleError("Operation Failed: Network Error");
    }
}
}
```

The advantage of consolidating all the requests through the SendRequest method is that I can use a single try/catch block to handle errors for all request types. The catch block handles errors that arise from requests and invokes the callback function that is received as a constructor argument.

PRESENTING ERROR MESSAGES TO THE USER

The Axios package presents detailed errors when something goes wrong and includes the status code from the response and any descriptive text the web service supplies. For most applications, however, it doesn't make sense to present this information to the user, who won't understand what has happened or know how to fix it. Instead, I recommend presenting a general error message to the user and logging details of the problem at the server so that common issues can be identified.

To receive errors and display them to the user, I added a file called RequestError.js to the src/ webservice folder and used it to define the component shown in Listing 23-17.

Listing 23-17. The Contents of the RequestError.js File in the src/webservice Folder

```
import React, { Component } from "react";
import { Link } from "react-router-dom";

export class RequestError extends Component {

    render() {
        return <div>
            <h5 className="bg-danger text-center text-white m-2 p-3">
                { this.props.match.params.message }
            </h5>
            <div className="text-center">
                <Link to="/" className="btn btn-secondary">OK</Link>
            </div>
        </div>
    }
}
```

This component displays a message obtained from a URL parameter. Listing 23-18 adds a new Route to the Selector component that will display this component for the /error URL.

Listing 23-18. Adding a Route in the Selector.js File in the src Folder

```
import React, { Component } from "react";
import { BrowserRouter as Router, Route, Switch, Redirect }
    from "react-router-dom";
import { ToggleLink } from "./routing/ToggleLink";
import { RoutedDisplay } from "./routing/RoutedDisplay";
import { IsolatedTable } from "./IsolatedTable";
import { IsolatedEditor } from "./IsolatedEditor";
import { RequestError } from "./webservice/RequestError";

export class Selector extends Component {

    render() {

        const routes = React.Children.map(this.props.children, child => ({
            component: child,
            name: child.props.name,
            url: `/${child.props.name.toLowerCase()}`,
            datatype: child.props.datatype
        }));

        return <Router getUserConfirmation={ this.customGetUserConfirmation }>
            <div className="container-fluid">
                <div className="row">
                    <div className="col-2">
                        <ToggleLink to="/isolated">Isolated Data</ToggleLink>
                        { routes.map(r => <ToggleLink key={ r.url } to={ r.url }>
                                { r.name }
                            </ToggleLink>)}
```

```
                        </div>
                        <div className="col">
                            <Switch>
                                <Route path="/isolated" component={ IsolatedTable }
                                    exact={ true } />
                                <Route path="/isolated/:mode/:id?"
                                    component={ IsolatedEditor } />
                                <Route path="/error/:message"
                                    component={ RequestError } />
                                { routes.map(r =>
                                    <Route key={ r.url }
                                        path={ `/:datatype(${r.datatype})/:mode?/:id?` }
                                        component={ RoutedDisplay(r.datatype)} />
                                )}
                                <Redirect to={ routes[0].url } />
                            </Switch>
                        </div>
                    </div>
                </div>
            </Router>
        }
}
```

Listing 23-19 provides the data source with a callback that navigates to the /error URL when a problem arises and adds a button that creates an error by requesting a URL that will always produce a 404 – Not Found error.

Listing 23-19. Handling Errors in the IsolatedTable.js File in the src Folder

```
import React, { Component } from "react";
import { RestDataSource } from "./webservice/RestDataSource";
import { Link } from "react-router-dom";

export class IsolatedTable extends Component {

    constructor(props) {
        super(props);
        this.state = {
            products: []
        }
        this.dataSource = new RestDataSource("http://localhost:3500/api/products",
            (err) => this.props.history.push(`/error/${err}`));
    }

    deleteProduct(product) {
        this.dataSource.Delete(product,
            () => this.setState({products: this.state.products.filter(p =>
                p.id !== product.id)}));
    }
```

```
    render() {
        return <table className="table table-sm table-striped table-bordered">
            <thead>
                <tr><th colSpan="5"
                        className="bg-info text-white text-center h4 p-2">
                    (Isolated) Products
                </th></tr>
                <tr>
                    <th>ID</th><th>Name</th><th>Category</th>
                    <th className="text-right">Price</th>
                    <th></th>
                </tr>
            </thead>
            <tbody>
                {
                    this.state.products.map(p => <tr key={ p.id }>
                        <td>{ p.id }</td><td>{ p.name }</td><td>{p.category}</td>
                        <td className="text-right">
                            ${ Number(p.price).toFixed(2)}
                        </td>
                        <td>
                            <Link className="btn btn-sm btn-warning mx-2"
                                    to={`/isolated/edit/${p.id}`}>
                                Edit
                            </Link>
                            <button className="btn btn-sm btn-danger mx-2"
                                onClick={ () => this.deleteProduct(p)}>
                                    Delete
                            </button>
                        </td>
                    </tr>)
                }
            </tbody>
            <tfoot>
                <tr className="text-center">
                    <td colSpan="5">
                        <Link to="/isolated/create"
                            className="btn btn-info">Create</Link>
                        <button className="btn btn-danger mx-2"
                            onClick={ () => this.dataSource.GetOne("err")}>
                            Error
                        </button>
                    </td>
                </tr>
            </tfoot>
        </table>
    }

    componentDidMount() {
        this.dataSource.GetData(data => this.setState({products: data}));
    }
}
```

Clicking the Error button rendered by IsolatedTable will send a request that receives an error response from the web service, which triggers navigation to the URL that displays the error message, as shown in Figure 23-5.

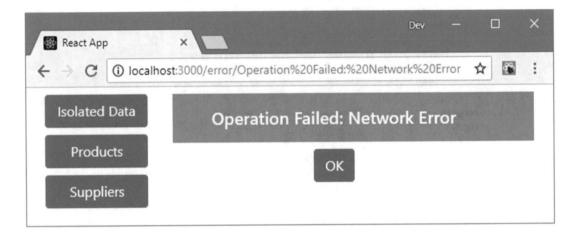

Figure 23-5. *Displaying an error message*

MAKING CROSS-ORIGIN REQUESTS

By default, browsers enforce a security policy that only allows JavaScript code to make asynchronous HTTP requests within the same origin as the document that contains them. This policy is intended to reduce the risk of cross-site scripting (CSS) attacks, where the browser is tricked into executing malicious code, which is described at http://en.wikipedia.org/wiki/Cross-site_scripting. For web application developers, the same-origin policy can be a problem when using web services because they are often outside of the origin that contains the application's JavaScript code. Two URLs are considered to be in the same origin if they have the same protocol, host, and port, and they have different origins if this is not the case. The URL that I use for the RESTful web service in this chapter has a different origin to the URL used by the main application because they use different TCP ports.

The Cross-Origin Resource Sharing (CORS) protocol is used to send requests to different origins. With CORS, the browser includes headers in the asynchronous HTTP request that provide the server with the origin of the JavaScript code. The response from the server includes headers that tell the browser whether it is willing to accept the request. The details of CORS are outside the scope of this book, but there is an introduction to the topic at https://en.wikipedia.org/wiki/Cross-origin_resource_sharing, and the CORS specification is available at www.w3.org/TR/cors.

CORS is something that happens automatically in this chapter. The json-server package that provides the RESTful web service supports CORS and will accept requests from any origin, while the Axios package that I use to make HTTP requests automatically applies CORS. When you select software for your own projects, you must either select a platform that will allow all requests to be handled through a single origin or configure CORS so that the server will accept the application's requests for data.

Consuming a Web Service with a Data Store

The components I defined in the previous section are isolated from one another and are coordinated only through the URL routing system. The advantage of this approach is simplicity, but it can lead to repeatedly requesting the same data from the web service as the user navigates around the application and each component sends its HTTP requests when it is mounted. If the application uses a data store, then the data can be shared between components.

Creating the New Middleware

The store already has actions that receive objects and update the data it contains, so the approach I am going to take is to create new Redux middleware that will intercept the existing actions and send the corresponding HTTP requests to the web service. I added a file called RestMiddleware.js to the src/webservice folder, with the contents shown in Listing 23-20.

Listing 23-20. The Contents of the RestMiddleware.js File in the src/webservice Folder

```
import { STORE, UPDATE, DELETE} from "../store/modelActionTypes";
import { RestDataSource } from "./RestDataSource";
import { PRODUCTS, SUPPLIERS } from "../store/dataTypes";

export const GET_DATA = "rest_get_data";

export const getData = (dataType) => {
    return {
        type: GET_DATA,
        dataType: dataType
    }
}

export const createRestMiddleware = (productsURL, suppliersURL) => {

    const dataSources = {
        [PRODUCTS]: new RestDataSource(productsURL, () => {}),
        [SUPPLIERS]: new RestDataSource(suppliersURL, () => {})
    }

    return ({dispatch, getState}) => next => action => {
        switch (action.type) {
            case GET_DATA:
                if (getState().modelData[action.dataType].length === 0) {
                    dataSources[action.dataType].GetData((data) =>
                        data.forEach(item => next({ type: STORE,
                            dataType: action.dataType, payload: item})));
                }
                break;
            case STORE:
                action.payload.id = null;
                dataSources[action.dataType].Store(action.payload, data =>
                    next({ ...action, payload: data }))
                break;
```

```
            case UPDATE:
                dataSources[action.dataType].Update(action.payload, data =>
                    next({ ...action, payload: data }))
                break;
            case DELETE:
                dataSources[action.dataType].Delete({id: action.payload },
                    () => next(action));
                break;
            default:
                next(action);
        }
    }
}
```

One new action is required, which is to request the data from the web service. This hasn't been required previously because the data store has been automatically initialized with data. The action type is GET_DATA, and Listing 23-20 defines a getData action creator.

The createRestMiddleware function accepts data sources for the product and supplier data and returns middleware that deals with the new GET_DATA action and the existing STORE, UPDATE, and DELETE actions by sending a request to the web service and then dispatching additional actions when the result is received, using the existing features of the data store.

Adding the Middleware to the Data Store

In Listing 23-21, I have added the new middleware to the data store. As noted in Chapter 20, middleware components are applied in the order in which they are added to the store.

Listing 23-21. Applying Middleware in the index.js File in the src/store Folder

```
import { createStore, combineReducers, applyMiddleware, compose } from "redux";
import modelReducer from "./modelReducer";
import stateReducer from "./stateReducer";
import { customReducerEnhancer } from "./customReducerEnhancer";
import { multiActions } from "./multiActionMiddleware";
import { asyncEnhancer } from "./asyncEnhancer";
import { createRestMiddleware } from "../webservice/RestMiddleware";

const enhancedReducer = customReducerEnhancer(
    combineReducers(
        {
            modelData: modelReducer,
            stateData: stateReducer
        })
);

const restMiddleware = createRestMiddleware(
    "http://localhost:3500/api/products",
    "http://localhost:3500/api/suppliers");
```

```
export default createStore(enhancedReducer,
    compose(applyMiddleware(multiActions),
        applyMiddleware(restMiddleware),
        asyncEnhancer(2000)));

export { saveProduct, saveSupplier, deleteProduct, deleteSupplier }
    from "./modelActionCreators";
```

The order is important when considering how the data store is used by the existing components in the application. The `multiActions` middleware created in Chapter 20 allows arrays of actions to be dispatched, and this must come first; otherwise, the new middleware won't properly process actions.

Completing the Application Changes

To automatically request the data on demand, I added a file called `DataGetter.js` to the `src` folder and used it to define the higher-order component shown in Listing 23-22.

Listing 23-22. The Contents of the DataGetter.js File in the src Folder

```
import React, { Component } from "react";
import { PRODUCTS, SUPPLIERS } from "./store/dataTypes";

export const DataGetter = (dataType, WrappedComponent) => {

    return class extends Component {
        render() {
            return <WrappedComponent { ...this.props } />
        }

        componentDidMount() {
            this.props.getData(PRODUCTS);
            if (dataType === SUPPLIERS) {
                this.props.getData(SUPPLIERS);
            }
        }
    }
}
```

The component requests the data after it mounts and knows that the supplier data must be complemented by the product data in order to display the data correctly to the user so that product names can be shown. In Listing 23-23, I have added support for the new HOC in the `TableConnector` component, which ensures that the data required by the application is requested when the application starts.

Listing 23-23. Dispatching Actions in the TableConnector.js File in the src/store Folder

```
import { connect } from "react-redux";
//import { startEditingProduct, startEditingSupplier } from "./stateActions";
import { deleteProduct, deleteSupplier } from "./modelActionCreators";
import { PRODUCTS, SUPPLIERS } from "./dataTypes";
import { withRouter } from "react-router-dom";
import { getData } from "../webservice/RestMiddleware";
```

```
import { DataGetter } from "../DataGetter";

export const TableConnector = (dataType, presentationComponent) => {

    const mapStateToProps = (storeData, ownProps) => {
        if (dataType === PRODUCTS) {
            return { products: storeData.modelData[PRODUCTS] };
        } else {
            return {
                suppliers: storeData.modelData[SUPPLIERS].map(supp => ({
                    ...supp,
                    products: supp.products.map(id =>
                        storeData.modelData[PRODUCTS]
                            .find(p => p.id === Number(id)) || id)
                            .map(val => val.name || val)
                }))
            }
        }
    }

    const mapDispatchToProps = (dispatch, ownProps) => {
        return {
            getData: (type) => dispatch(getData(type)),
            deleteCallback: dataType === PRODUCTS
                ? (...args) => dispatch(deleteProduct(...args))
                : (...args) => dispatch(deleteSupplier(...args))
        }
    }

    const mergeProps = (dataProps, functionProps, ownProps) => {
        let routedDispatchers = {
            editCallback: (target) => {
                ownProps.history.push(`/${dataType}/edit/${target.id}`);
            },
            deleteCallback: functionProps.deleteCallback,
            getData: functionProps.getData

        }
        return Object.assign({}, dataProps, routedDispatchers, ownProps);
    }

    return withRouter(connect(mapStateToProps,
        mapDispatchToProps, mergeProps)(DataGetter(dataType,
            presentationComponent)));
}
```

The final change is to remove the static content that was used to seed the data store, as shown in Listing 23-24.

Listing 23-24. Removing the Static Data in the initialData.js File in the src/store Folder

```
import { PRODUCTS, SUPPLIERS } from "./dataTypes";

export const initialData = {
    modelData: {
        [PRODUCTS]: [],
        [SUPPLIERS]: []
    },
    stateData: {
        editing: false,
        selectedId: -1,
        selectedType: PRODUCTS
    }
}
```

The result is that the initial product and supplier data are obtained from the web service and that any changes will trigger updates to the web service, as shown in Figure 23-6.

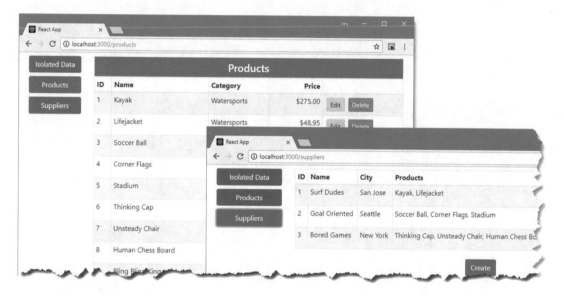

Figure 23-6. *Using the web service with the data store*

Summary

In this chapter, I introduced a web service and used it to obtain the data displayed by the user, store new data, make changes, and delete data. I used the Axios library in this chapter, but there are many other options available, and consuming a web service in a React application is a relatively simple process. In the next chapter, I introduce GraphQL, which is a more flexible alternative to REST for web services.

CHAPTER 24

■ ■ ■

Understanding GraphQL

GraphQL is an end-to-end system for creating and consuming APIs, providing a more flexible alternative to using traditional RESTful web services, such as the one created in Chapter 23. In this chapter, I explain how GraphQL services are defined and how queries are performed. In Chapter 25, I demonstrate the different ways that a GraphQL API can be consumed by a React application. Table 24-1 puts GraphQL in context.

Table 24-1. *Putting GraphQL in Context*

Question	Answer
What is it?	GraphQL is a query language that produces APIs.
Why is it useful?	GraphQL provides the client with flexible access to data, ensuring that the client receives only the data it requires and allowing new queries to be formulated without requiring server-side changes.
How is it used?	At the server, a schema is defined and implemented using resolver functions. The client uses the GraphQL language to send queries and request changes.
Are there any pitfalls or limitations?	GraphQL is complex and writing a useful schema can require skill.
Are there any alternatives?	Clients can use RESTful web services, as described in Chapter 23.

■ **Note** I describe the features of GraphQL that are most useful for React development. For a complete description of GraphQL, see the GraphQL specification at `https://facebook.github.io/graphql/June2018`.

© Adam Freeman 2019
A. Freeman, *Pro React 16*, https://doi.org/10.1007/978-1-4842-4451-7_24

Table 24-2 summarizes the chapter.

Table 24-2. *Chapter Summary*

Problem	Solution	Listing
Define a GraphQL service	Describe the queries and mutations that will be supported and implement the resolvers that provide them	3, 4, 8–10, 20–21
Query a GraphQL service	Specify the query name and the fields that are required in the result	7, 11, 27, 28
Filter results	Specify query arguments	12–19
Make changes using a GraphQL service	Specify the mutation and the fields for the update	22–24
Parameterize queries	Use query variables	25, 26
Request the same set of fields from multiple queries	use a query fragment	29

Preparing for This Chapter

In this chapter, I continue to use the example application from Chapter 23. To prepare for this chapter, open a command prompt, navigate to the productapp folder, and run the commands shown in Listing 24-1 to add packages to the project.

■ **Tip**   You can download the example project for this chapter—and for all the other chapters in this book—from https://github.com/Apress/pro-react-16.

Listing 24-1. Adding Packages

```
npm install --save-dev graphql@14.0.2
npm install --save-dev express@4.16.4
npm install --save-dev express-graphql@0.7.1
npm install --save-dev graphql-import@0.7.1
npm install --save-dev cors@2.8.5
```

For quick reference, the packages by the commands in Listing 24-1 are described in Table 24-3.

Table 24-3. *The Packages Added to the Project*

Name	Description
graphql	This package contains the reference implementation of GraphQL.
express	This package provides an extensible HTTP server and will be the foundation of the GraphQL server used in this chapter.
express-graphql	This package provides GraphQL services over HTTP through the express package.
graphql-import	This package allows GraphQL schemas to be defined in multiple files and imports schemas more easily than reading a file directly.
cors	This package enables Cross-Origin Resource Sharing (CORS) for the Express HTTP server.

Once the packages are installed, use the command prompt to run the command shown in Listing 24-2 in the productapp folder to start the development tools. The RESTful web service defined in Chapter 23 is also started and is still used by the application.

Listing 24-2. Starting the Development Tools

```
npm start
```

Once the initial preparation for the project is complete, a new browser window will open and display the URL http://localhost:3000, as shown in Figure 24-1.

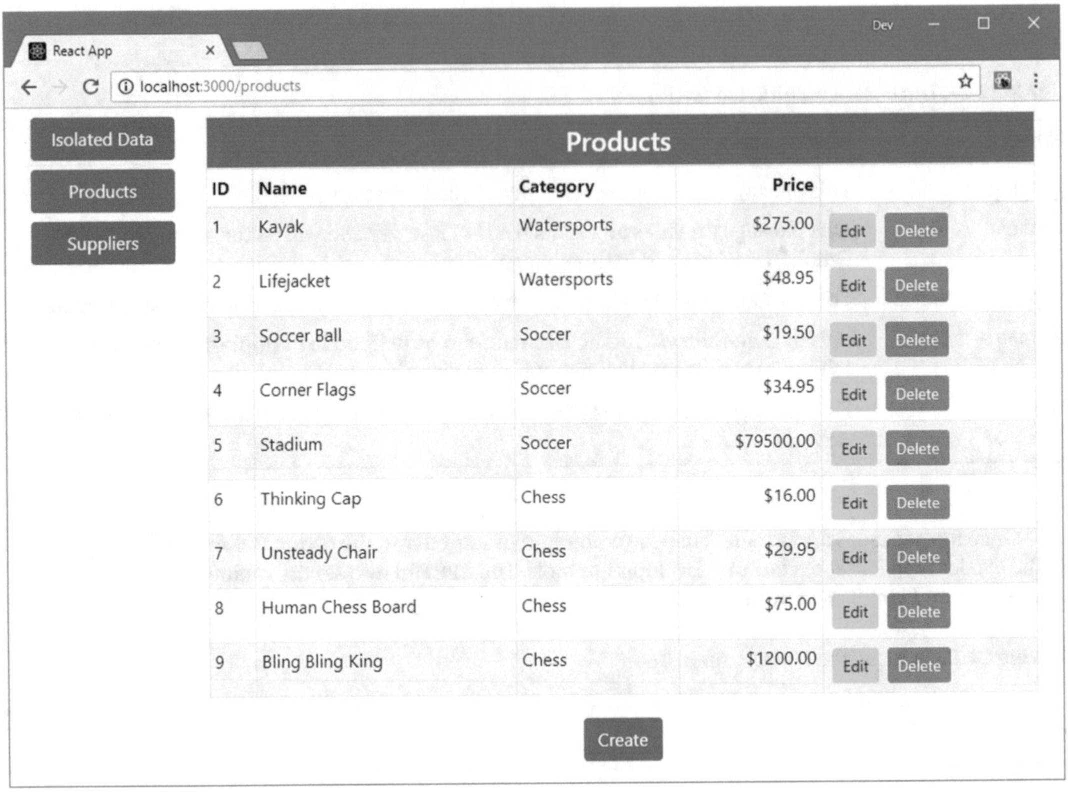

Figure 24-1. *Running the example application*

Understanding GraphQL

RESTful web services are easy to get started with, but they can become inflexible as the needs of the client evolve and the number of client applications using the service increases.

Changes that suit one application can't be made because they cause problems in another application, work backs up so that changes are not made in time for client-application release dates, and infrastructure development teams struggle to balance competing demands for features. You may not have any avenue for requesting changes when you rely on a third-party web service because you are one of dozens or hundreds of development teams all asking for new features.

The result is a poor fit between the application and the web service it relies on. Clients often have to make multiple requests to the web service to get the data they require; this is then merged into a useful format. The client has to understand how the objects returned from different REST requests relate to one another and often has to request data that is then discarded because only a subset of the data fields is required.

The underlying problem with REST web services is that the data they provide and the way they provide it are fixed, and that becomes an issue as the needs of the client application change. GraphQL addresses this problem by allowing the client more control over what data is requested and how it is expressed, with the result that client-side applications can add features that use data in new ways with fewer server-side changes required.

UNDERSTANDING THE DRAWBACKS OF GRAPHQL

GraphQL isn't suitable for every situation. GraphQL is complex and not as widely understood as REST, which can make it difficult to find experienced developers and robust and well-tested tools and libraries. And GraphQL can shift work that would have been performed by the client application into the server, which can increase costs in the data center and require licenses for back-end servers that support GraphQL.

It is important to consider GraphQL as an option, especially if your application is likely to require ongoing development after deployment or you intend to develop or support multiple client applications. But my advice is not to rush into using GraphQL until you are sure that a REST web service won't give you the flexibility you need.

Creating the GraphQL Server

I am going to create a custom GraphQL server that presents the same data as the web service from Chapter 23 The process of creating the GraphQL service isn't required by all projects, especially when consuming a third-party API, but understanding what is happening at the server provides useful insights into how GraphQL works. In the sections that follow, I'll go through the process of describing the types of requests that the client will be able to make and write the code required to deal with those requests.

CHOOSING AN ALTERNATIVE GRAPHQL SERVER

I use the GraphQL reference implementations to create a simple GraphQL server for this chapter. It makes it easy to demonstrate how GraphQL works but doesn't make any provision for working with real data.

For small and simple projects, adding persistent data support with a package such as Lowdb (https://github.com/typicode/lowdb) or MongoDB (https://www.mongodb.com) may be suitable.

For more complex projects, the Apollo server (https://github.com/apollographql/apollo-server) is the most common choice. There are open-source and paid-for plans available, and there is a wide range of data integration options available, such as using GraphQL as a front end to existing REST web services.

Creating the Schema

GraphQL describes the requests that can be performed using a schema, which is written in the GraphQL schema language. I created the src/graphql folder and added to it a file called schema.graphql with the contents shown in Listing 24-3.

Listing 24-3. The Contents of the schema.graphql File in the src/graphql Folder

```
type product {
    id: ID!,
    name: String!,
    category: String!
    price: Float!
}

type supplier {
    id: ID!,
    name: String!,
    city: String!,
    products: [ID]
}

type Query {
    products: [product],
    suppliers: [supplier]
}
```

The schema defined in Listing 24-3 defines two custom types: product and supplier. These types will be used as the results of the queries supported by the GraphQL server. Each result type is defined with a set of fields, each of which is typed like this:

```
...
category: String!
...
```

The name of this field is category, and its type is String. GraphQL provides a set of built-in types, which are described in Table 24-4. The exclamation mark (the ! character) after the field type indicates that values for this field are mandatory. Fields can also return arrays of values, like this:

```
...
products: [ID]
...
```

Table 24-4. The Built-in GraphQL Types

Name	Description
ID	This type represents a unique identifier.
String	This type represents a string.
Int	This type represents a signed integer
Float	This type represents a floating-point value
Boolean	This type represents a true or false value.

The square brackets indicate that the products field of the supplier type will be an array of ID values.

■ **Tip**   Don't worry about the GraphQL type system too much at the moment. It will start to make more sense as you see how the different parts of the server fit together and are used by the client.

In addition to the built-in types, GraphQL supports the Query type, which is used to define the queries that the server will support. There are two queries defined in the schema in Listing 24-3.

```
...
type Query {
    products: [product],
    suppliers: [supplier]
}
...
```

The first statement defines a query called products that will return an array of product objects. The second statement defines a query called suppliers that will return an array of supplier objects.

Creating the Resolvers

The next step is to write the functions that implement the products and suppliers queries defined in Listing 24-3. I added a file called resolvers.js to the src/graphql folder, with the code shown in Listing 24-4.

Listing 24-4. The Contents of the resolvers.js File in the src/graphql Folder

```
var data = require("../../restData")();

module.exports = {

    products: () => data.products,
    suppliers: () => data.suppliers
}
```

Each resolver is a function whose name corresponds to one of the queries and that returns data in the format declared by the schema. The data used by the products and suppliers resolvers uses data loaded from the restData.js file.

■ **Note**   The GraphQL server will be run by Node.js, which does not support JavaScript modules at the time of writing, which means that the import and export keywords cannot be used. Instead, the require function is used to declare a dependency on a file, and module.exports is used to make code or data available outside of a JavaScript file.

Creating the Server

The final step is to create the code that will process the schema and the resolvers and create the GraphQL server. I added a file called graphqlServer.js in the productapp folder and added the code shown in Listing 24-5.

Listing 24-5. The Contents of the graphqlServer.js File in the productapp Folder

```
var { buildSchema } = require("graphql");
var { importSchema } = require("graphql-import");
var express = require("express");
var graphqlHTTP = require("express-graphql")
var cors = require("cors")
var schema = importSchema("./src/graphql/schema.graphql");
var resolvers = require("./src/graphql/resolvers");

var app = express();

app.use(cors());
app.use("/graphql", graphqlHTTP({
  schema: buildSchema(schema),
  rootValue: resolvers,
  graphiql: true,
}));
app.listen(3600, () => console.log("GraphQL Server Running on Port 3600"));
```

The graphql package provides the buildSchema function, which takes a schema string and prepares it for use. The contents of the schema file are imported using the graphql-import package and passed to the buildSchema function. The express-graphql package integrates GraphQL support into the popular express server, which I have configured to listen on port 3600.

To start the GraphQL server, open a new command prompt, navigate to the productapp folder, and run the command shown in Listing 24-6. (The GraphQL server won't automatically reload when there are schema or resolver changes and will have to be restarted for some of the examples in this chapter, which is why I have not integrated it into the npm start command, as I did for the RESTful web service.)

Listing 24-6. Starting the GraphQL Server

```
node graphqlServer.js
```

The GraphQL server includes support for GraphiQL (pronounced *graphical*), which is a browser-based GraphQL tool. To make sure that the GraphQL server is working, open a new browser tab and navigate to http://localhost:3600/graphql, which should show the tool in Figure 24-2.

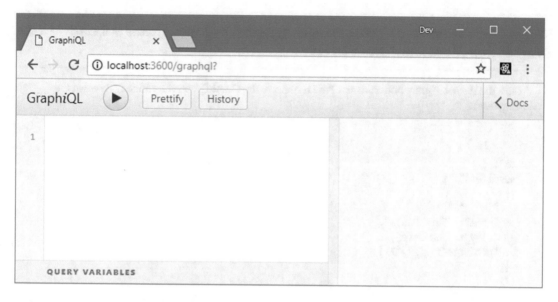

Figure 24-2. *The GraphiQL browser*

Making GraphQL Queries

The GraphiQL tool makes it easy to perform queries before integrating GraphQL into the example application. To query for all the supplier objects, for example, enter the query shown in Listing 24-7 into the left pane of the GraphiQL window.

Listing 24-7. A Query for Supplier Data

```
query {
  suppliers {
    id,
    name,
    city,
    products
  }
}
```

The query is basic, but it reveals a lot about how GraphQL queries work. The query keyword is used to differentiate between requests to retrieve data and *mutations*, which are used to make changes (and which are described in the "Making GraphQL Mutations" section). The query itself is enclosed in curly brackets, also known as *braces*. Inside the braces, the query name is specified, which is suppliers in this case.

When you query a GraphQL service, you must specify the data fields that you want to receive. Unlike a REST web service, which always presents the same data structures, GraphQL allows the client to specify the results it wants to receive, enclosed in another set of braces. The query in Listing 24-7 selects the id, name, city, and products fields.

■ **Note**   There is no wildcard that allows all fields to be selected. If you want to receive all the fields for a data type, then you must include all of them in the query.

Click the Execute Query button to send the request to the GraphQL server, which will return the following result:

```
...
{
  "data": {
    "suppliers": [
      {
        "id": "1",
        "name": "Surf Dudes",
        "city": "San Jose",
        "products": ["1","2"]
      },
      {
        "id": "2",
        "name": "Goal Oriented",
        "city": "Seattle",
        "products": ["3","4","5"]
      },
      {
        "id": "3",
        "name": "Bored Games",
        "city": "New York",
        "products": ["6","7","8","9"]
      }
    ]
  }
}
...
```

This may not seem like a huge departure from a REST web service, but even with this basic query, the client is able to select the fields it requires and the order in which they will be expressed.

Querying for Related Data

The GraphQL service is working, and it can be used to get product and supplier data, which meets the basic needs of the data tables in the example application. However, one of the most powerful features of GraphQL is the ease with which it supports related data in queries, allowing a single query to return results that contain multiple types. In Listing 24-8, I have changed the products field to the schema for the supplier data type.

GETTING SCHEMA DETAILS FOR GRAPHQL SERVICES

Writing the schema gives the best insight into the queries that a GraphQL service supports, but that isn't always possible. If you are not writing your own schema, the first thing to do is look for developer documentation; many public GraphQL services publish comprehensive schema documentation, such as the GitHub API, described at `https://developer.github.com/v4`.

Many services also support GraphiQL or similar tools, most of which support schema navigation. GraphiQL, for example, makes it easy to explore the schema through its `Docs` link, which lets you navigate through the queries and mutations that a service supports.

If there is no documentation and no support for GraphiQL, you can the GraphQL introspection features to send queries about the schema. For example, the following schema query will list the regular queries that a service supports:

```
...
{
    __schema {
    queryType {
      fields {
        name
      }
    }
  }
}
...
```

The special `__schema` query data type is used to request information about the schema. You can find more details of the GraphQL introspection features at `https://graphql.org/learn/introspection`.

Listing 24-8. Changing a Data Field in the schema.graphql File in the src/graphql Folder

```
type product {
    id: ID!,
    name: String!,
    category: String!
    price: Float!
}

type supplier {
    id: ID!,
    name: String!,
    city: String!,
    products: [product]
}

type Query {
    products: [product],
    suppliers: [supplier]
}
```

Instead of returning an array of ID values, the products field now returns an array of supplier objects. To support this change, I need to process the data used by the resolvers to resolve the relationship between each supplier and its related product objects, as shown in Listing 24-9.

Listing 24-9. Resolving Related Data in the resolvers.js File in the src/graphql Folder

```
var data = require("../../restData")();
module.exports = {

    products: () => data.products,

    suppliers: () => data.suppliers.map(s => ({
        ...s, products: () => s.products.map(id =>
            data.products.find(p => p.id === Number(id)))
    }))
}
```

The data is processed so that each supplier object has a products property. The products property is a function that will resolve the related data and that will be invoked only if the client has requested this data field, which ensures that the server doesn't do work to get data that has not been asked for.

Stop the GraphQL server using Control+C and run the command shown in Listing 24-10 in the productapp folder to start it again.

Listing 24-10. Starting the GraphQL Server

```
node graphqlServer.js
```

Navigate to http://localhost:3600/graphql and enter the query shown in Listing 24-11 into the left pane of the GraphiQL window. This query takes advantage of the change to the GraphQL schema to request suppliers and their related product data in a single query.

Listing 24-11. Querying for Related Data

```
query {
  suppliers {
    id,
    name,
    city,
    products {
      name
    }
  }
}
```

When a field returns a complex type, such as `product`, the query must select the fields that are required. The addition to the query in Listing 24-11 asks the server to provide the `id`, `name`, and `city` fields of each `supplier` object and the `name` field from each of its related `product` objects. Click the Execute Query button, and you will receive the following results:

```
...
{
  "data": {
    "suppliers": [
      {
        "id": "1", "name": "Surf Dudes", "city": "San Jose",
        "products": [{ "name": "Kayak" }, { "name": "Lifejacket" }]
      },
      {
        "id": "2", "name": "Goal Oriented", "city": "Seattle",
        "products": [{ "name": "Soccer Ball" },{ "name": "Corner Flags" },
          { "name": "Stadium" }]
      },
      {
        "id": "3", "name": "Bored Games", "city": "New York",
        "products": [{ "name": "Thinking Cap" },{ "name": "Unsteady Chair" },
          { "name": "Human Chess Board" }, { "name": "Bling Bling King" }]
      }
    ]
  }
}
...
```

Notice that the client specifies the fields required for both the `supplier` objects and the related `product` data, which ensures that only the data required by the application is retrieved.

■ **Note** In addition to regular queries, the GraphQL specification includes support for *subscriptions*, which provide ongoing updates for data that is changing on the server. Subscriptions are not widely or consistently supported, and I don't describe them in this book.

Creating Queries with Arguments

The queries that are currently offered by the GraphQL server allow the user to select the fields that are required but not select the objects in the result, which is a requirement for the requests for individual objects. To give the client the ability to customize requests, GraphQL supports arguments, as shown in Listing 24-12.

Listing 24-12. Using Arguments in the schema.graphql File in the src/graphql Folder

```
type product {
    id: ID!,
    name: String!,
    category: String!
    price: Float!
}

type supplier {
    id: ID!,
    name: String!,
    city: String!,
    products: [product]
}

type Query {
    products: [product],
    product(id: ID!): product,
    suppliers: [supplier]
    supplier(id: ID!): supplier
}
```

Arguments are defined in parentheses after the query name, and each argument is assigned a name and a type. In Listing 24-12, I added queries called product and supplier, each of which defines an id argument whose type is ID and which has been denoted as mandatory with an exclamation mark. In Listing 24-13, I have added resolvers for the queries that use the id value to select a data object.

Listing 24-13. Defining Resolvers in the resolvers.js File in the src/graphql Folder

```
var data = require("../../restData")();

module.exports = {

    products: () => data.products,

    product: (args) => data.products.find(p => p.id === parseInt(args.id)),

    suppliers: () => data.suppliers.map(s => ({
        ...s, products: () => s.products.map(id =>
            data.products.find(p => p.id === Number(id)))
    })),

    supplier: (args) => {
        const result = data.suppliers.find(s => s.id === parseInt(args.id));
        if (result) {
            return {
```

```
            ...result,
            products: () => result.products.map(id =>
                data.products.find(p => p.id === Number(id)))
        }
    }
  }
}
```

The resolver function receives an object whose properties correspond to the query arguments. To get the id value specified in the query, the resolver functions read the `args.id` property. I can simplify this code by destructing the argument object, as shown in Listing 24-14.

■ **Tip** Notice I used the `parseInt` function to convert the id argument for comparison. A direct comparison using `===` between an ID value and a JavaScript Number value will return `false`.

Listing 24-14. Destructing Arguments in the resolvers.js File in the src/graphql Folder

```
var data = require("../../restData")();

module.exports = {

    products: () => data.products,

    product: ({id}) => data.products.find(p => p.id === parseInt(id)),

    suppliers: () => data.suppliers.map(s => ({
        ...s, products: () => s.products.map(id =>
            data.products.find(p => p.id === Number(id)))
    })),

    supplier: ({id}) => {
        const result = data.suppliers.find(s => s.id === parseInt(id));
        if (result) {
            return {
                ...result,
                products: () => result.products.map(id =>
                    data.products.find(p => p.id === Number(id)))
            }
        }
    }
}
```

Restart the GraphQL server and enter the query shown in Listing 24-15 into the GraphiQL window.

Listing 24-15. Querying with an Argument

```
query {
  supplier(id: 1) {
    id,
    name,
    city,
    products {
      name
    }
  }
}
```

This query requests the supplier object whose id value is 1 and asks for the id, name, and city fields, along with the name field of the related products, producing the following result:

```
...
{
  "data": {
    "supplier": {
      "id": "1",
      "name": "Surf Dudes",
      "city": "San Jose",
      "products": [{ "name": "Kayak" },{ "name": "Lifejacket" }]
    }
  }
}
...
```

Adding Arguments to Fields

Arguments can be defined for individual fields, which allows the client to be more specific about the data it requires. In Listing 24-16, I have added an argument to the schema definition for the supplier type, which will allow the client to filter the related product objects by name.

Listing 24-16. Adding a Field Argument in the schema.graphql File in the src/graphql Folder

```
type product {
    id: ID!,
    name: String!,
    category: String!
    price: Float!
}

type supplier {
    id: ID!,
    name: String!,
    city: String!,
    products(nameFilter: String = ""): [product]
}
```

```
type Query {
    products: [product],
    product(id: ID!): product,
    suppliers: [supplier]
    supplier(id: ID!): supplier
}
```

The products field has been redefined to receive a string nameFilter argument. No exclamation point has been used, which means that the argument is optional. If no value is used, the default value of an empty string will be used instead. The implementation of the argument is shown in Listing 24-17.

Listing 24-17. Implementing a Field Argument in the resolvers.js File in the src/graphql Folder

```
var data = require("../../restData")();

const mapIdsToProducts = (supplier, nameFilter) =>
    supplier.products.map(id => data.products.find(p => p.id === Number(id)))
        .filter(p => p.name.toLowerCase().includes(nameFilter.toLowerCase()));

module.exports = {

    products: () => data.products,

    product: ({id}) => data.products
        .find(p => p.id === parseInt(id)),

    suppliers: () => data.suppliers.map(s => ({
        ...s, products: ({nameFilter}) => mapIdsToProducts(s, nameFilter)
    })),

    supplier: ({id}) => {
        const result = data.suppliers.find(s => s.id === parseInt(id));
        if (result) {
            return {
                ...result,
                products: ({ nameFilter }) => mapIdsToProducts(result, nameFilter)
            }
        }
    }
}
```

To support the field argument, the function that resolves the products property on the supplier objects accepts a parameter, which is deconstructed to get the nameFilter value and used to filter the related product objects by name. Restart the GraphQL server and enter the query shown in Listing 24-18 into GraphiQL to see how a field argument is used in a query.

695

Listing 24-18. Querying with a Field Argument

```
query {
  supplier(id: 1) {
    id,
    name,
    city,
    products(nameFilter: "ak") {
      name
    }
  }
}
```

Click the Execute Query button, and you will see the following results, which show that the related product objects have been filtered so that only those whose name field contains ak are included.

```
...
{
  "data": {
    "supplier": {
      "id": "1",
      "name": "Surf Dudes",
      "city": "San Jose",
      "products": [{ "name": "Kayak" }]
    }
  }
}
...
```

■ **Caution**   The methods used to receive field arguments are invoked for every request, which can create a substantial amount of work for the server. Consider using a memoization package for complex results, such as fast-memoize (https://github.com/caiogondim/fast-memoize.js).

Because the field argument is applied to the type and not a specific query, the filter can be used in any query for supplier data that includes related product data. Enter the query shown in Listing 24-19 into GraphiQL for a demonstration.

Listing 24-19. Using a Field Argument in Another Query

```
query {
  suppliers {
    id,
    name,
    city,
    products(nameFilter: "g") {
      name
    }
  }
}
```

Click the Execute Query button, and you will see that the related product data for each supplier object in the results has been filtered.

```
...
{
  "data": {
    "suppliers": [
      {
        "id": "1",
        "name": "Surf Dudes",
        "city": "San Jose",
        "products": []
      },
      {
        "id": "2",
        "name": "Goal Oriented",
        "city": "Seattle",
        "products": [{ "name": "Corner Flags" }]
      },
      {
        "id": "3",
        "name": "Bored Games",
        "city": "New York",
        "products": [{ "name": "Thinking Cap" }, { "name": "Bling Bling King"}]
      }
    ]
  }
}
...
```

Making GraphQL Mutations

Mutations are used to ask the GraphQL server to make changes to its data. Mutations are added to the schema using the special Mutation type, and there are two broad approaches available, as shown in Listing 24-20.

Listing 24-20. Defining Mutations in the schema.graphql File in the src/graphql Folder

```
type product {
    id: ID!,
    name: String!,
    category: String!
    price: Float!
}

type supplier {
    id: ID!,
    name: String!,
    city: String!,
    products(nameFilter: String = ""): [product]
}
```

```
type Query {
    products: [product],
    product(id: ID!): product,
    suppliers: [supplier]
    supplier(id: ID!): supplier
}

input productInput {
    id: ID, name: String!, category: String!, price: Int!
}

type Mutation {
    storeProduct(product: productInput): product
    storeSupplier(id: ID, name: String!, city: String!, products: [Int]): supplier
}
```

The first mutation, called storeProduct, uses a dedicated *input type*, which allows the client to provide values to describe the changes that are required. Input types are defined using the input keyword and support the same features as regular types. In the listing, I have defined an input type called productInput that has an optional id field and mandatory name, category, and price fields. This is broadly duplicative of the product type already defined in the schema, which is a common approach because you can't use regular types as the arguments to mutations.

The storeSupplier mutation takes a simple approach, which is to define multiple arguments that allow the client to express the details of a data object without requiring an input type. This is an effective approach for basic mutations, but it can become unwieldy for complex mutations. Both mutations produce a result, which provides the client with an authoritative view of the object that has been created or updated as a result of the mutation, expressed using a regular query type. In Listing 24-21, I have added resolvers for the mutations.

Listing 24-21. Implementing Mutations in the resolvers.js File in the src Folder

```
var data = require("../../restData")();

const mapIdsToProducts = (supplier, nameFilter) =>
    supplier.products.map(id => data.products.find(p => p.id === Number(id)))
        .filter(p => p.name.toLowerCase().includes(nameFilter.toLowerCase()));

let nextId = 100;

module.exports = {

    products: () => data.products,

    product: ({id}) => data.products
        .find(p => p.id === parseInt(id)),

    suppliers: () => data.suppliers.map(s => ({
        ...s, products: ({nameFilter}) => mapIdsToProducts(s, nameFilter)
    })),

    supplier: ({id}) => {
        const result = data.suppliers.find(s => s.id === parseInt(id));
```

```
            if (result) {
                return {
                    ...result,
                    products: ({ nameFilter }) => mapIdsToProducts(result, nameFilter)
                }
            }
        },

    storeProduct({product}) {
        if (product.id == null) {
            product.id = nextId++;
            data.products.push(product);
        } else {
            product = { ...product, id: Number(product.id)};
            data.products = data.products
                .map(p => p.id === product.id ? product : p);
        }
        return product;
    },

    storeSupplier(args) {
        const supp = { ...args, id: Number(args.id)};
        if (args.id == null) {
            supp.id = nextId++;
            data.suppliers.push(supp)
        } else {
            data.suppliers = data.suppliers.map(s => s.id === supp.id ? supp : s);
        }
        let result = data.suppliers.find(s => s.id === supp.id);
        if (result) {
            return {
                ...result,
                products: ({ nameFilter }) => mapIdsToProducts(result, nameFilter)
            }
        }
    }
  }
}
```

The mutations are implemented as functions that receive arguments, just like queries. These mutations use the ID field to determine whether the client is updating an existing object or storing a new one, and they update the presentation data used by the queries to reflect changes. To update a product with the storeProduct mutation, restart the server and enter the GraphQL shown in Listing 24-22 into GraphiQL.

Listing 24-22. Using the storeProduct Mutation

```
mutation {
  storeProduct(product: {
    id: 1,
    name: "Green Kayak",
    category: "Watersports",
    price: 290
  }) {
```

```
    id, name, category, price
  }
}
```

Mutations are performed using the `mutation` keyword, which is the counterpart to the `query` keyword used in the previous example. The name of the mutation is specified, along with a `product` argument that provides `id`, `name`, `category`, and `price`. The fields required from the result are then specified, and, in this case, all of the fields defined by a product are selected.

Click the Execute Query button, and you will see the following results:

```
...
{
  "data": {
    "storeProduct": {
      "id": "1",
      "name": "Green Kayak",
      "category": "Watersports",
      "price": 290
    }
  }
}
...
```

To confirm that the mutation has taken effect, execute the query in Listing 24-23 using GraphiQL.

Listing 24-23. Querying Product Data

```
query {
  product(id: 1) {
    id, name, category, price
  }
}
```

When you execute the query, you will see the following results, reflecting the changes made by the mutation:

```
...
{
  "data": {
    "product": {
      "id": "1",
      "name": "Green Kayak",
      "category": "Watersports",
      "price": 290
    }
  }
}
...
```

The process for using a mutation that doesn't rely on an input type is similar, as shown in Listing 24-24.

Listing 24-24. Using a Mutation Without an Input Type

```
mutation {
  storeSupplier(
    name: "AcmeCo",
    city: "Chicago",
    products: [1, 3]
  ){ id, name, city, products {
      name
    }
  }
}
```

When the query is executed, a new supplier will be created, and the following results will be displayed:

```
...
{
  "data": {
    "storeSupplier": {
      "id": "100",
      "name": "AcmeCo",
      "city": "Chicago",
      "products": [{ "name": "Green Kayak" }, { "name": "Soccer Ball" }]
    }
  }
}
...
```

Notice that the mutation uses `id` values in the `product` field to express the relationship between supplier and product objects, but the result includes the product names. The mutation gets its result from the updated presentation data, showing that the result of a mutation need not be directly related to the data it receives.

Other GraphQL Features

To complete this chapter, I am going to describe some useful features that build on those described earlier. These are all optional, but they can be used to make the GraphQL service easier to work with.

Using Request Variables

GraphQL variables are intended to allow a request to be defined once and then customized with arguments each time it is used, without forcing the client to dynamically generate and serialize the complete request data for every operation. The query shown in Listing 24-25 defines a variable that is used as the argument for the product query.

Listing 24-25. A Query with a Variable

```
query ($id: ID!) {
  product(id: $id) {
    id, name, category, price
  }
}
```

Variables are applied to the query or mutation and are defined using a name that starts with a dollar sign (the $ character) and assigned a type. In this case, the query defines a variable called id whose type is a mandatory ID. Inside the query, the variable is used as $id and is passed to the product query argument.

To use the variable, enter the query into GraphiQL; expand the Query Variables section, which is at the bottom-left side of the window; and enter the code shown in Listing 24-26.

Listing 24-26. Defining a Value for a Variable

```
{
  "id": 2
}
```

This provides a value of 2 for the id variable. Click the Execute Query button, and the query and the variable will be sent to the GraphQL server, with the effect that the product object whose id is 2 is selected, as shown in Figure 24-3.

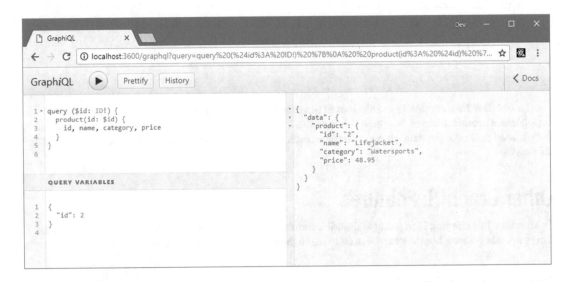

Figure 24-3. Using a query variable

Variables may not appear useful when using GraphiQL, but they can simplify client development, as demonstrated in Chapter 24.

Making Multiple Requests

A single operation can contain multiple requests or mutations. Enter the queries shown in Listing 24-27 into the GraphiQL window.

Listing 24-27. Making Multiple Queries

```
query {
  product(id: 1) {
    id, name, category, price
  },
  supplier(id: 1) {
    id, name, city
  }
}
```

Queries are separated by commas and are contained within the outer set of braces, following the query keyword. Click the Execute Query button, and you will see the following output, which combines the results of both queries into a single response:

```
...
{
  "data": {
    "product": {
      "id": "1",
      "name": "Kayak",
      "category": "Watersports",
      "price": 275
    },
    "supplier": {
      "id": "1",
      "name": "Surf Dudes",
      "city": "San Jose"
    }
  }
}
...
```

Notice that the name of each query is used to denote its section of the response, making it easy to differentiate between the result from the product and supplier queries. This can present a problem when you want to use the same query multiple times and so GraphQL supports aliases, which assign a name that is applied to the results. Enter the queries, shown in Listing 24-28, into GraphiQL.

Listing 24-28. Using a Query Alias

```
query {
  first: product(id: 1) {
    id, name, category, price
  },
  second: product(id: 2) {
    id, name, category, price
  }
}
```

The alias comes before the query and is followed by a colon (the : character). In the listing, there are two product queries that have been given the aliases first and second. Click the Execute Query button, and you will see how these names are used in the query results.

```
...
{
  "data": {
    "first": {
      "id": "1",
      "name": "Kayak",
      "category": "Watersports",
      "price": 275
    },
    "second": {
      "id": "2",
      "name": "Lifejacket",
      "category": "Watersports",
      "price": 48.95
    }
  }
}

...
```

Using Query Fragments for Field Selection

The requirement to select result fields from every query can lead to duplication in the client, such as in Listing 24-28, where both the first and second queries select the id, name, category, and price fields. Selections of fields can be defined once using the GraphQL fragments feature and then applied to multiple requests. In Listing 24-29, I have defined a fragment and used it in the queries.

Listing 24-29. Using a Query Fragment

```
fragment coreFields on product {
  id, name, category
}

query {
  first: product(id: 1) {
    ...coreFields,
    price
  },
  second: product(id: 2) {
    ...coreFields
  }
}
```

Fragments are defined using the `fragment` and on keywords and are specific to a single type. In Listing 24-29, the fragment is assigned the name `coreFields` and is defined for `product` objects. The spread operator is used to apply a fragment, which can be mixed with regular fields selections. Click the Execute Query button, and you will see the following results:

```
...
{
  "data": {
    "first": {
      "id": "1",
      "name": "Kayak",
      "category": "Watersports",
      "price": 275
    },
    "second": {
      "id": "2",
      "name": "Lifejacket",
      "category": "Watersports"
    }
  }
}
...
```

Summary

In this chapter, I introduced GraphQL. I explained the role of the schema and its resolvers, and I demonstrated the process for creating a simple GraphQL service for static data. I showed you how to define queries to get data from a GraphQL service and how to use mutations to make changes. All of the example in this chapter were performed using the GraphiQL tool, and in the next chapter, I show you how to consume GraphQL in a React application.

CHAPTER 25

Consuming GraphQL

In this chapter—the last in this book—I show you the different ways that a GraphQL service can be consumed by a React application. I show you how to work directly with HTTP requests, how to integrate GraphQL with a data store, and how to use a dedicated GraphQL client.

Preparing for This Chapter

In this chapter, I continue using the productapp project from Chapter 24 and the GraphQL service it contains. To prepare for this chapter, the changes described in the following sections are required.

Adding Packages to the Project

Later in the chapter, I create components that receive GraphQL data directly, which requires additional packages. Open a new command prompt, navigate to the productapp folder, and run the commands shown in Listing 25-1.

■ **Tip**   You can download the example project for this chapter—and for all the other chapters in this book—from https://github.com/Apress/pro-react-16.

Listing 25-1. Adding Packages to the Example Project

```
npm install apollo-boost@0.1.22
npm install react-apollo@2.3.2
```

Table 25-1 describes the purpose of the new packages.

Table 25-1. The Packages Added to the Project

Name	Description
apollo-boost	This package contains the Apollo GraphQL client with a configuration that is suitable for most projects.
react-apollo	This package contains the React integration for the Apollo client.

Changing the Data for the GraphQL Server

In Chapter 24, I used the same data as I had previously for the web service to highlight the different ways that REST and GraphQL approach the same problems. For this chapter, I want to make it obvious when the example application stops obtaining data using REST and starts using GraphQL. I created a file called graphqlData.js in the productapp folder with the contents shown in Listing 25-2.

Listing 25-2. The Contents of the graphqlData.js File in the productapp Folder

```
module.exports = function () {
    var data = {
        products: [
            { id: 1, name: "Trail Shoes", category: "Running", price: 120 },
            { id: 2, name: "Heated Gloves", category: "Running", price: 20.95 },
            { id: 3, name: "Padded Shorts", category: "Cycling", price: 19.50 },
            { id: 4, name: "Puncture Kit", category: "Cycling", price: 34.95 },
            { id: 5, name: "Mirror Goggles", category: "Swimming", price: 79500 },

        ],
        suppliers: [
            { id: 1, name: "Just Running", city: "Houston", products: [1, 2] },
            { id: 2, name: "Miles and Smiles", city: "Paris", products: [3, 4] },
            { id: 3, name: "Deep Dive", city: "New York", products: [5] },
        ]
    }
    return data
}
```

Updating the Schema and Resolvers

To prepare for this chapter, I need to extend the GraphQL schema to define mutations for deleting data, as shown in Listing 25-3. I have also removed the input type so that the storeProduct and storeSupplier mutations are consistent.

Listing 25-3. Defining and Updating Mutations in the schema.graphql File in the src/graphql Folder

```
type product {
    id: ID!,
    name: String!,
    category: String!
    price: Float!
}

type supplier {
    id: ID!,
    name: String!,
    city: String!,
    products(nameFilter: String = ""): [product]
}
```

```
type Query {
    products: [product],
    product(id: ID!): product,
    suppliers: [supplier]
    supplier(id: ID!): supplier
}

type Mutation {
    storeProduct(id: ID, name: String!, category: String!, price: Float!): product
    storeSupplier(id: ID, name: String!, city: String!, products: [Int]): supplier
    deleteProduct(id: ID!): ID
    deleteSupplier(id: ID!): ID
}
```

In Listing 25-4, I have defined new resolvers for the deleteProduct and deleteSupplier mutations and updated the storeProduct resolver to reflect the removal of the input type. I also changed the statement that loads the data to use the file created in Listing 25-2.

Listing 25-4. Adding and Updating Resolvers in the resolvers.js File in the src/graphql Folder

```
var data = require("../../graphqlData")();

const mapIdsToProducts = (supplier, nameFilter) =>
    supplier.products.map(id => data.products.find(p => p.id === Number(id)))
        .filter(p => p.name.toLowerCase().includes(nameFilter.toLowerCase()));

let nextId = 100;

module.exports = {

    products: () => data.products,

    product: ({id}) => data.products
        .find(p => p.id === parseInt(id)),

    suppliers: () => data.suppliers.map(s => ({
        ...s, products: ({nameFilter}) => mapIdsToProducts(s, nameFilter)
    })),

    supplier: ({id}) => {
        const result = data.suppliers.find(s => s.id === parseInt(id));
        if (result) {
            return {
                ...result,
                products: ({ nameFilter }) => mapIdsToProducts(result, nameFilter)
            }
        }
    },

    storeProduct(args) {
        const product = { ...args, id: Number(args.id)};
        if (args.id == null || product.id === 0) {
```

```
            product.id = nextId++;
            data.products.push(product);
        } else {
            data.products = data.products
                .map(p => p.id === product.id ? product : p);
        }
        return product;
    },

    storeSupplier(args) {
        const supp = { ...args, id: Number(args.id)};
        if (args.id == null) {
            supp.id = nextId++;
            data.suppliers.push(supp)
        } else {
            data.suppliers = data.suppliers.map(s => s.id === supp.id ? supp: s);
        }
        let result = data.suppliers.find(s => s.id === supp.id);
        if (result) {
            return {
                ...result,
                products: ({ nameFilter }) => mapIdsToProducts(result, nameFilter)
            }
        }
    },

    deleteProduct({id}) {
        id = Number(id);
        data.products = data.products.filter(p => p.id !== id);
        data.suppliers = data.suppliers.map(s => {
            s.products = s.products.filter(p => p !== id);
            return s;
        })
        return id;
    },

    deleteSupplier({id}) {
        data.suppliers = data.suppliers.filter(s => s.id !== Number(id));
        return id;
    }
}
```

The new resolvers remove an item from the data arrays and return the value of their id parameters, corresponding to the ID type used in the schema. When a product is removed, any reference to it from a supplier is also removed to avoid errors when subsequently querying for supplier data.

■ **Tip** I have also changed the `storeProduct` and `storeSupplier` functions so they will treat a request whose object has an `id` value of zero the same as if it contained no `id` value at all. This is a useful technique when dealing with form data because it means that all the form values can be sent to the server without needing to remove the `id` property to differentiate between new and modified objects.

Integrating the GraphQL Server with the Development Tools

In Chapter 24, I started the GraphQL tool directly, without using any of the React development tools. For this chapter, I am going to start the GraphQL server automatically, alongside the development HTTP server and the RESTful web service, which the example application is still configured to use. In Listing 25-5, I changed the `scripts` section of the `package.json` file so that the GraphQL server is started as part of the `npm start` command.

Listing 25-5. Configuring the Project Startup in the package.json File in the productapp Folder

```
...
"scripts": {
  "start": "npm-run-all --parallel reactstart json graphql",
  "build": "react-scripts build",
  "test": "react-scripts test",
  "eject": "react-scripts eject",
  "reactstart": "react-scripts start",
  "json": "json-server --p 3500 -r api.routes.json restData.js",
  "graphql": "node graphqlServer.js"
},
...
```

To start the example application, open a new command prompt, navigate to the `productapp` folder, and run the command shown in Listing 25-6.

Listing 25-6. Running the Example Application

```
npm start
```

The development server, the RESTful web service, and the GraphQL server will all start. A new browser tab will open and display the content shown in Figure 25-1.

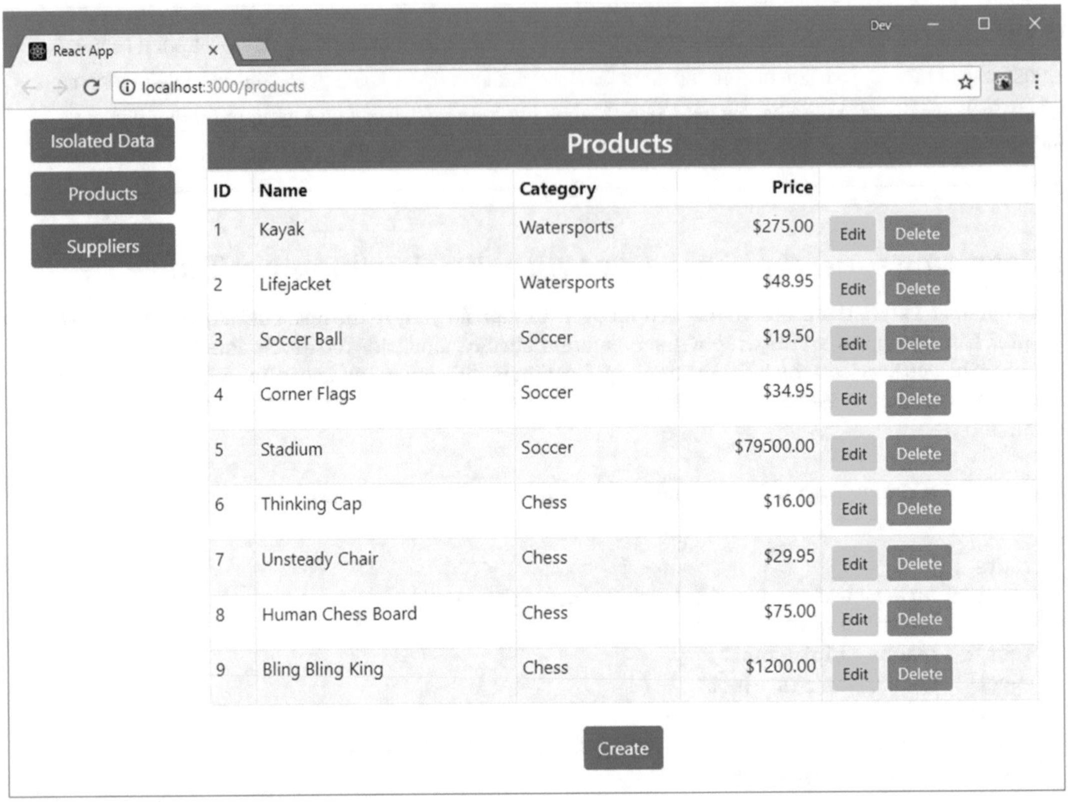

Figure 25-1. *Running the example application*

To ensure that the GraphQL server is running correctly, navigate to `http://localhost:3600/graphql` and enter the query shown in Listing 25-7 into GraphiQL.

Listing 25-7. Querying the GraphQL Server

```
query {
  product(id: 1) {
    id, name, category, price
  }
}
```

Click the Execute Query button, and you should see the following result:

```
...
{
  "data": {
    "product": {
      "id": "1",
      "name": "Trail Shoes",
      "category": "Running",
```

```
      "price": 120
    }
  }
}
...
```

Consuming a GraphQL Service

GraphQL queries are sent to the server using HTTP POST requests, with a JSON request body, like this:

```
...
{"query":"query { product(id: 1) { id, name, category, price }", "variables": null }
...
```

The response is a JSON string containing the results, like this:

```
...
{"data":{"product":{"id":"1","name":"Trail Shoes","category":"Running","price":120}}}
...
```

The use of HTTP and the structure of the request and response make it easy to integrate GraphQL into a React application, following the same pattern I used in Chapter 23 for working with a RESTful web service.

Defining the Queries and Mutations

The starting point when consuming GraphQL is to define the queries and mutations that will be sent to the server. I added a file called queries.js to the src/graphql folder and added the code shown in Listing 25-8.

Listing 25-8. The Contents of the queries.js File in the src/graphql Folder

```
export const products = {
    getAll: {
        name: "products",
        graphql: `query {
                products { id, name, category, price}
            }`
    },
    getOne: {
        name: "product",
        graphql: `query ($id: ID!) {
                product(id: $id) {
                    id, name, category, price
                }
            }`
    }
}

export const suppliers = {
    getAll: {
        name: "suppliers",
```

```
    graphql:`query {
        suppliers { id, name, city, products { id, name }}
    }`
},
getOne: {
    name: "supplier",
    graphql: `query($id: ID!) {
        supplier(id: $id) {
            id, name, city, products { id, name }
        }
    }`
}
}
}
```

Each query is defined with a GraphQL expression and a name, which the application will use to retrieve the data from the response. The queries rely on the variable feature described in Chapter 24. Next, I added a file called `mutations.js` in the `src/graphql` folder and defined the mutations that the application will need, as shown in Listing 25-9.

■ **Tip**   Separating the queries from the mutations isn't required since they are all just strings, but I find it helpful, especially for applications that make heavy use of GraphQL.

Listing 25-9. The Contents of the mutations.js File in the src/graphql Folder

```
export const products = {
    store: {
        name: "storeProduct",
        graphql: `mutation ($id: ID, $name: String!,
                    $category: String!, $price: Float!) {

                    storeProduct(id : $id, name: $name,
                        category: $category, price: $price) {
                            id, name, category, price
                        }
                }`
    },
    delete: {
        name: "deleteProduct",
        graphql: `mutation ($id: ID!) { deleteProduct(id: $id) }`
    }
}

export const suppliers = {
    store: {
        name: "storeSupplier",
        graphql: `mutation ($id: ID, $name: String!,
                    $city: String!, $products: [Int]) {

                    storeSupplier(id : $id, name: $name,
```

```
                    city: $city, products: $products) {
                        id, name, city, products { name }
                }
            }`
    },
    delete: {
        name: "deleteSupplier",
        graphql: `mutation ($id: ID!) { deleteSupplier(id: $id) }`
    }
}
```

There are mutations for storing and deleting product and supplier objects, and the name of each mutation is used in the name property, following the same pattern established for the queries.

Defining the Data Source

I am going to use the same queries and mutations in different ways in this chapter, and I want to hide the details of how data is handled from the rest of the application while following the same broad pattern I used for working with a RESTful web service. To provide a data source that will use GraphQL to perform data operations, I added a file called GraphQLDataSource.js to the src/graphql folder and used it to define the class shown in Listing 25-10.

Listing 25-10. The Contents of the GraphQLDataSource.js File in the src/graphql Folder

```
import Axios from "axios";
import * as allQueries from "./queries";
import * as allMutations from "./mutations";

export class GraphQLDataSource {

    constructor(dataType, errorCallback) {
        this.GRAPHQL_URL = "http://localhost:3600/graphql";
        this.queries = allQueries[dataType];
        this.mutations = allMutations[dataType];
        this.handleError = errorCallback;
    }

    GetData(callback) {
        this.SendRequest(callback, this.queries.getAll);
    }

    GetOne(id, callback) {
        this.SendRequest(callback, this.queries.getOne, { id });
    }

    Store(data, callback) {
        this.SendRequest(callback, this.mutations.store, { ...data });
    }
```

```
Update(data, callback) {
    this.Store(data, callback);
}

Delete(data, callback) {
    this.SendRequest(callback, this.mutations.delete, { id: data.id });
}

async SendRequest(callback, query, data) {
    try {
        let payload = {
            query: query.graphql,
            variables: data == null ? null : { ...data }
        }
        callback((await Axios.post(this.GRAPHQL_URL,
            payload)).data.data[query.name]);
    } catch(err) {
        this.handleError("Operation Failed: Network Error");
    }
}
}
}
```

The class defines the same methods as the REST data source created in Chapter 23, which isn't a requirement but helps show how the different types of service differ. To configure the data source for a specific type of data, the constructor receives a data type string, which is used to select the queries and mutations. When making a request, the GraphQL is sent to the user, along with a `variables` object. The result includes the name of the query of mutation that was performed, which is retrieved from the response using the value of the name property.

```
...
callback((await Axios.post(this.GRAPHQL_URL, payload)).data.data[query.name]);
...
```

Configuring the Isolated Components

Using the same API as the REST data source from Chapter 23 has simplified the process of integrating the GraphQL data into the application by changing the data source in the components that consume data. In Listing 25-11, I have changed the data source used by the IsolatedTable component.

Listing 25-11. Changing the Data Source in the IsolatedTable.js File in the src Folder

```
import React, { Component } from "react";
//import { RestDataSource } from "./webservice/RestDataSource";
import { Link } from "react-router-dom";
import { GraphQLDataSource } from "./graphql/GraphQLDataSource";
import { PRODUCTS } from "./store/dataTypes";

export class IsolatedTable extends Component {

    constructor(props) {
        super(props);
        this.state = {
```

```
        products: []
    }
    this.dataSource = new GraphQLDataSource(PRODUCTS,
        (err) => this.props.history.push(`/error/${err}`));
}

// ...methods omitted for brevity...
}
```

Listing 25-12 makes the corresponding change to the IsolatedEditor component.

Listing 25-12. Changing the Data Source in the IsolatedEditor.js File in the src Folder

```
import React, { Component } from "react";
//import { RestDataSource } from "./webservice/RestDataSource";
import { ProductEditor } from "./ProductEditor";
import { GraphQLDataSource } from "./graphql/GraphQLDataSource";
import { PRODUCTS } from "./store/dataTypes";

export class IsolatedEditor extends Component {

    constructor(props) {
        super(props);
        this.state = {
            dataItem: {}
        };
        this.dataSource = new GraphQLDataSource(PRODUCTS,
            (err) => this.props.history.push(`/error/${err}`));
    }

    save = (data) => {
        data = { ...data, price: Number(data.price)}
        const callback = () => this.props.history.push("/isolated");
        if (data.id === "") {
            this.dataSource.Store(data, callback);
        } else {
            this.dataSource.Update(data, callback);
        }
    }

    cancel = () => this.props.history.push("/isolated");

    render() {
        return <ProductEditor key={ this.state.dataItem.id }
            product={ this.state.dataItem } saveCallback={ this.save }
            cancelCallback={ this.cancel } />
    }

    componentDidMount() {
        if (this.props.match.params.mode === "edit") {
            this.dataSource.GetOne(this.props.match.params.id,
```

```
            data => this.setState({ dataItem: data}));
    }
  }
}
```

Notice that I parse the value of the price property into a Number before the data is sent to the server. The GraphQL server checks the data it receives against the types defined in the schema and will reject string values, which are what form elements typically produce, if another type, such as Float, is required.

When you save the changes to the IsolatedTable and IsolatedEditor components, the application will update, and clicking the Isolated Data button will show the data obtained from the GraphQL server, as shown in Figure 25-2.

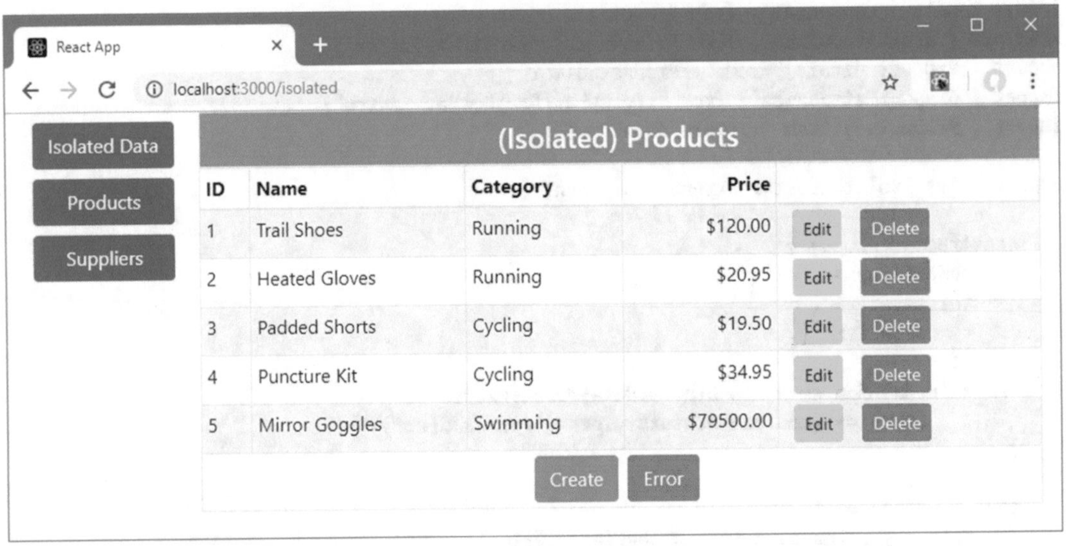

Figure 25-2. *Using GraphQL data*

Using GraphQL with a Data Store

The process for using the GraphQL with a data store is similar to the process I followed in Chapter 23 for RESTful data, using middleware to intercept actions and trigger requests to the server. I added a file called GraphQLMiddleware.js to the src/graphql folder and used it to define the Redux middleware shown in Listing 25-13.

Listing 25-13. The Contents of the GraphQLMiddleware.js File in the src/graphql Folder

```
import { STORE, UPDATE, DELETE} from "../store/modelActionTypes";
import { PRODUCTS, SUPPLIERS } from "../store/dataTypes";
import { GraphQLDataSource } from "./GraphQLDataSource";

export const GET_DATA = "qraphql_get_data";
```

```
export const getData = (dataType) => {
    return {
        type: GET_DATA,
        dataType: dataType
    }
}


export const createGraphQLMiddleware = () => {

    const dataSources = {
        [PRODUCTS]: new GraphQLDataSource(PRODUCTS, () => {}),
        [SUPPLIERS]: new GraphQLDataSource(SUPPLIERS, () => {})
    }

    return ({dispatch, getState}) => next => action => {
        switch (action.type) {
            case GET_DATA:
                if (getState().modelData[action.dataType].length === 0) {
                    dataSources[action.dataType].GetData((data) =>
                        data.forEach(item => next({ type: STORE,
                            dataType: action.dataType, payload: item})));
                }
                break;
            case STORE:
                action.payload.id = null;
                dataSources[action.dataType].Store(action.payload, data =>
                    next({ ...action, payload: data }))
                break;
            case UPDATE:
                dataSources[action.dataType].Update(action.payload, data =>
                    next({ ...action, payload: data }))
                break;
            case DELETE:
                dataSources[action.dataType].Delete({id: action.payload },
                    () => next(action));
                break;
            default:
                next(action);
        }
    }
}
```

This middleware intercepts the actions that are dispatched by the rest of the application and uses the data source class to send a query or mutation to the GraphQL server. In Listing 25-14, I have replaced the REST middleware with the GraphQL code.

Listing 25-14. Enabling the GraphQL Middleware in the index.js File in the src/store Folder

```
import { createStore, combineReducers, applyMiddleware, compose } from "redux";
import modelReducer from "./modelReducer";
import stateReducer from "./stateReducer";
```

```
import { customReducerEnhancer } from "./customReducerEnhancer";
import { multiActions } from "./multiActionMiddleware";
import { asyncEnhancer } from "./asyncEnhancer";
//import { createRestMiddleware } from "../webservice/RestMiddleware";
import { createGraphQLMiddleware } from "../graphql/GraphQLMiddleware";

const enhancedReducer = customReducerEnhancer(
    combineReducers(
        {
            modelData: modelReducer,
            stateData: stateReducer
        })
);

// const restMiddleware = createRestMiddleware(
//      "http://localhost:3500/api/products",
//      "http://localhost:3500/api/suppliers");

export default createStore(enhancedReducer,
    compose(applyMiddleware(multiActions),
        applyMiddleware(createGraphQLMiddleware()),
        asyncEnhancer(2000)));

export { saveProduct, saveSupplier, deleteProduct, deleteSupplier }
    from "./modelActionCreators";
```

Adjusting to the GraphQL Data Format

The data format returned by the GraphQL queries for the supplier data includes the related product data, which means that a separate request for the product data is no longer required and that the components that display the related data must be adapted to the new format. In Listing 25-15, I disabled the automatic query for product data when the application requires supplier data.

Listing 25-15. Disabling the Related Data Query in the DataGetter.js File in the src Folder

```
import React, { Component } from "react";
//import { PRODUCTS, SUPPLIERS } from "./store/dataTypes";

export const DataGetter = (dataType, WrappedComponent) => {

    return class extends Component {
        render() {
            return <WrappedComponent { ...this.props } />
        }

        componentDidMount() {
            // this.props.getData(PRODUCTS);
            // if (dataType === SUPPLIERS) {
            //      this.props.getData(SUPPLIERS);
            // }
```

```
            this.props.getData(dataType);
        }
    }
}
```

In Listing 25-16, I have commented out the code in the TableConnector component that processed the supplier data to incorporate the names of the related products. This information will be directly available to the components now that the data is coming from the GraphQL server. TableConnector also triggers the data request.

Listing 25-16. Disabling Data Processing in the TableConnector.js File in the src/store Folder

```
import { connect } from "react-redux";
//import { startEditingProduct, startEditingSupplier } from "./stateActions";
import { deleteProduct, deleteSupplier } from "./modelActionCreators";
import { PRODUCTS, SUPPLIERS } from "./dataTypes";
import { withRouter } from "react-router-dom";
//import { getData } from "../webservice/RestMiddleware";
import { getData } from "../graphql/GraphQLMiddleware";
import { DataGetter } from "../DataGetter";

export const TableConnector = (dataType, presentationComponent) => {

    const mapStateToProps = (storeData, ownProps) => {
        if (dataType === PRODUCTS) {
            return { products: storeData.modelData[PRODUCTS] };
        } else {
            return { suppliers: storeData.modelData[SUPPLIERS] };
                // suppliers: storeData.modelData[SUPPLIERS].map(supp => ({
                //     ...supp,
                //     products: supp.products.map(id =>
                //         storeData.modelData[PRODUCTS]
                //             .find(p => p.id === Number(id)) || id)
                //             .map(val => val.name || val)
                //     }))
        }
    }

    const mapDispatchToProps = (dispatch, ownProps) => {
        return {
            getData: (type) => dispatch(getData(type)),
            deleteCallback: dataType === PRODUCTS
                ? (...args) => dispatch(deleteProduct(...args))
                : (...args) => dispatch(deleteSupplier(...args))
        }
    }

    const mergeProps = (dataProps, functionProps, ownProps) => {
        let routedDispatchers = {
            editCallback: (target) => {
                ownProps.history.push(`/${dataType}/edit/${target.id}`);
            },
```

```
                deleteCallback: functionProps.deleteCallback,
                getData: functionProps.getData

        }
        return Object.assign({}, dataProps, routedDispatchers, ownProps);
    }

    return withRouter(connect(mapStateToProps,
        mapDispatchToProps, mergeProps)(DataGetter(dataType,
            presentationComponent)));
}
```

To locate objects by ID, I changed the EditorConnector so that it doesn't parse the URL parameter to a Number, as shown in Listing 25-17.

Listing 25-17. Changing ID Matching in the EditorConnector.js File in the src/store Folder

```
import { connect } from "react-redux";
//import { endEditing } from "./stateActions";
import { PRODUCTS, SUPPLIERS  } from "./dataTypes";
import { saveAndEndEditing } from "./multiActionCreators";
import { withRouter } from "react-router-dom";

export const EditorConnector = (dataType, presentationComponent) => {

    const mapStateToProps = (storeData, ownProps) => {
        const mode = ownProps.match.params.mode;
        const id = ownProps.match.params.id;
        return {
            editing: mode === "edit" || mode === "create",
            product: (storeData.modelData[PRODUCTS].find(p => p.id === id)) || {},
            supplier:(storeData.modelData[SUPPLIERS].find(s => s.id === id)) || {}
        }
    }

    const mapDispatchToProps = {
        //cancelCallback: endEditing,
        saveCallback: (data) => saveAndEndEditing(data, dataType)
    }

    const mergeProps = (dataProps, functionProps, ownProps) => {
        let routedDispatchers = {
            cancelCallback: () => ownProps.history.push(`/${dataType}`),
            saveCallback: (data) => {
                functionProps.saveCallback(data);
                ownProps.history.push(`/${dataType}`);
            }
        }
        return Object.assign({}, dataProps, routedDispatchers, ownProps);
    }
```

```
    return withRouter(connect(mapStateToProps,
        mapDispatchToProps, mergeProps)(presentationComponent));
}
```

To display the names of the products, I made the change shown in Listing 25-18 to the
SupplierTableRow component.

Listing 25-18. Selecting Product Names in the SupplierTableRow.js File in the src Folder

```
import React, { Component } from "react";

export class SupplierTableRow extends Component {

    render() {
        let s = this.props.supplier;
        return <tr>
            <td>{ s.id }</td>
            <td>{ s.name }</td>
            <td>{ s.city}</td>
            <td>{ s.products != null ?
                    s.products.map(p => p.name).join(", ") : "" }</td>
            <td>
                <button className="btn btn-sm btn-warning m-1"
                    onClick={ () => this.props.editCallback(s) }>
                        Edit
                </button>
                <button className="btn btn-sm btn-danger m-1"
                    onClick={ () => this.props.deleteCallback(s) }>
                        Delete
                </button>
            </td>
        </tr>
    }
}
```

The next change is to accommodate the new data format when editing supplier data, ensuring that the
id values of the related products area displayed to the user, as shown in Listing 25-19.

Listing 25-19. Selecting Product IDs in the SupplierEditor.js File in the src Folder

```
import React, { Component } from "react";

export class SupplierEditor extends Component {

    constructor(props) {
        super(props);
        this.state = {
            formData: {
                id: props.supplier.id || "",
                name: props.supplier.name || "",
                city: props.supplier.city || "",
                products: props.supplier.products != null
```

```
                    ? props.supplier.products.map(p => p.id) : [],
        }
    }
}

// ...methods omitted for brevity...
}
```

The final change is to parse the string value obtained from the form element for the product price property into a number, which ensures that the data sent to the server matches the Float type specified in the schema, as shown in Listing 25-20.

Listing 25-20. Parsing the Price Value in the ProductEditor.js File in the src Folder

```
...
handleClick = () => {
    this.props.saveCallback(
        {
            ...this.state.formData,
            price: Number(this.state.formData.price)
        });
}
...
```

Save all the changes, and the application will work entirely with data obtained from the GraphQL server and placed in the Redux data store, as shown in Figure 25-3.

Figure 25-3. *Using GraphQL data in the data store*

■ **Tip** If you encounter errors, stop the development tools and start them again using npm start. This will reset the data used by the GraphQL server and undo the effects of changes made in previous sections.

Using a GraphQL Client Framework

I demonstrated how GraphQL can be used with a Redux data store in the previous section because it shows how easily the data can be used and provides a comparison against working with a RESTful web service.

There is a different approach, which is to use a package that replaces the data store and provides GraphQL data directly to the components that need it while caching data to avoid the kind of repeated HTTP requests that navigation between isolated components can lead to.

The package that I use in this section is called Apollo Client, which is the client-side package from the same developers as the Apollo GraphQL server that I mentioned in Chapter 24 (but that works with any GraphQL server). Full documentation for the Apollo Client is available at `https://www.apollographql.com/docs/react`).

■ **Note** The examples in this chapter rely on the packages installed at the start of the chapter.

Configuring the Client

The first step is to configure the client so that it knows where to send the GraphQL requests and mutations. Listing 25-21 shows the configuration statements I added to the App component.

Listing 25-21. Configuring Apollo Client in the App.js File in the src Folder

```
import React, { Component } from "react";
// import { Provider } from "react-redux";
// import dataStore from "./store";
import { Selector } from "./Selector";
//import { PRODUCTS, SUPPLIERS } from "./store/dataTypes";
import ApolloClient from "apollo-boost";
import { ApolloProvider } from "react-apollo";

const client = new ApolloClient({
    uri: "http://localhost:3600/graphql"
});

export default class App extends Component {

    render() {
        return   <ApolloProvider client={ client }>
                     <Selector />
                 </ApolloProvider>
    }
}
```

A new `ApolloClient` object is created to manage the relationship to the GraphQL server, and its constructor accepts a configuration object. The `uri` property of the configuration object specifies the URL for GraphQL requests. There are other configuration options, but the defaults are suitable for most projects (see `www.apollographql.com` for details).

The `ApolloProvider` component is used to integrate GraphQL features with React, and the `client` prop is assigned the `ApolloClient` object.

To simplify the example, I have removed the content contained within the Selector component and the data store. I will define the components displayed by the selector directly shortly.

■ **Tip** I have removed the Redux data store from the application only to simplify the example application. Apollo Client and Redux can be used in the same application, although you should be careful not to store data in Redux that is being managed by Apollo Client because the two will easily get out of sync.

Creating a GraphQL Component

The next step is to create components that will act as a bridge between GraphQL and the content displayed to the user. This is the same basic approach that I have been using throughout this part of the book, and it means that the content rendered to the user is produced by components that do not depend directly on a specific mechanism for data, whether it be the Redux data store, a RESTful web service, or a GraphQL client. I added a file called GraphQLTable.js to the src/graphql folder and added the code shown in Listing 25-22.

CHOOSING AN ALTERNATIVE GRAPHQL CLIENT

I picked Apollo Client because it is flexible and easy to get on with. The main alternative is Relay (https://facebook.github.io/relay), which is developed by Facebook. Relay is more difficult to get started with and only works with GraphQL schemas that follow a particular structure.

There are also packages that offer a subset of the features provided by Apollo Client or Relay, such as Adrenaline (https://github.com/gyzerok/adrenaline).

Listing 25-22. The Contents of the GraphQLTable.js File in the src/graphql Folder

```
import React, { Component } from "react";
import { Query } from "react-apollo";
import gql from "graphql-tag";
import * as queries from "./queries";
import { ProductTable } from "../ProductTable";

export const GraphQLTable = () => {

    const getAll = gql(queries.products.getAll.graphql);

    return class extends Component {

        constructor(props) {
            super(props);
            this.editCallback = (item) => this.props.history
                .push(`/products/edit/${item.id}`);
        }
```

```
render() {
    return <Query query={ getAll }>
        {(({loading, data, refetch }) => {
            if (loading) {
                return <h5
                    className="bg-info text-white text-center m-2 p-2">
                        Loading...
                </h5>
            } else {
                return <React.Fragment>
                    <ProductTable products={data.products}
                        editCallback= { this.editCallback }
                        deleteCallback={ () => {} } />
                    <div className="text-center">
                        <button className="btn btn-primary"
                                onClick={ () => refetch() }>
                            Reload Data
                        </button>
                    </div>
                </React.Fragment>
            }
        }}
    </Query>
    }
    }
}
```

There is a lot going on in Listing 25-22, and it is worth breaking down the component in detail to understand each part. Like the other packages used in this part of the book, Apollo Client relies on higher-order components to provide features. In this case, the GraphQLTable provides features to the example application's ProductTable component. I start by setting up the GraphQL query that will obtain the data, like this:

```
...
const getAll = gql(queries.products.getAll.graphql);
...
```

The gql function accepts a query expressed as a string and processes it so that it can be used by Apollo Client. I already defined the queries required by the application and organized them by data type. The gql function can also be used directly with template strings, which allows queries to be defined like this:

```
...
const getAll = gql`query { products {
    id, name, category, price
}}`
...
```

The Query component provides a component with access to the data returned by a query, which is specified by the query prop, like this:

```
...
return <Query query={ getAll }>
...
```

The query is sent to the server as soon as the Query component is rendered, and it uses a render prop function to provide its features through an object that defines properties describing the outcome of the query, the most useful of which are described in Table 25-2.

Table 25-2. *Useful Apollo Client Render Prop Object Properties*

Name	Description
data	This property returns the data produced by the query.
loading	This property returns true when the query is being processed.
error	This property returns details of any query errors.
variables	This property returns the variables used for the query.
refetch	This property returns a function that can be used to resend the query, optionally with new variables.

For the query in Listing 25-22, I use the loading, data, and refetch properties.

```
...
{(({loading, error, refetch}) => {
...
```

When the component is first rendered and the request is sent to the GraphQL server, the loading value is true. When the request has completed, the component updates, with the loading value as false, and provides the result through the data property.

The query is executed when the Query component is rendered, but the results are cached, which means that no query is sent to the server the next time the data is required. The refetch property provides a function that sends the query again when it is invoked, refreshes the data in case, and updates the component. The function assigned to the refresh property accepts an object that can be used to provide new variables for the query. This is a useful feature, but it means that you must make sure not to invoke the function directly when using an event handler, like this:

```
...
<button className="btn btn-primary" onClick={ () => refetch() }>
...
```

If you don't specify an inline function, as shown, then the event object will be passed to the refetch function, which will attempt to use it as the source of variables for the query and encounter an error.

Applying the GraphQL Component

In Listing 25-23, I have replaced the routing components used by the Selector component so that the GraphQLTable component is used to respond to the /product URL.

Listing 25-23. Changing the Routing Configuration in the Selector.js File in the src Folder

```
import React, { Component } from "react";
import { BrowserRouter as Router, Route, Switch, Redirect }
    from "react-router-dom";
import { ToggleLink } from "./routing/ToggleLink";
// import { RoutedDisplay } from "./routing/RoutedDisplay";
// import { IsolatedTable } from "./IsolatedTable";
// import { IsolatedEditor } from "./IsolatedEditor";
// import { RequestError } from "./webservice/RequestError";
import { GraphQLTable } from "./graphql/GraphQLTable";

export class Selector extends Component {

    render() {
        return <Router>
            <div className="container-fluid">
                <div className="row">
                    <div className="col-2">
                        <ToggleLink to="/products">Products</ToggleLink>
                    </div>
                    <div className="col">
                        <Switch>
                            <Route path="/products" exact={true}
                                component={ GraphQLTable()}  />
                            <Redirect to="/products" />
                        </Switch>
                    </div>
                </div>
            </div>
        </Router>
    }
}
```

Save the changes, and you will see the GraphQL product and suppliers displayed, as shown in Figure 25-4.

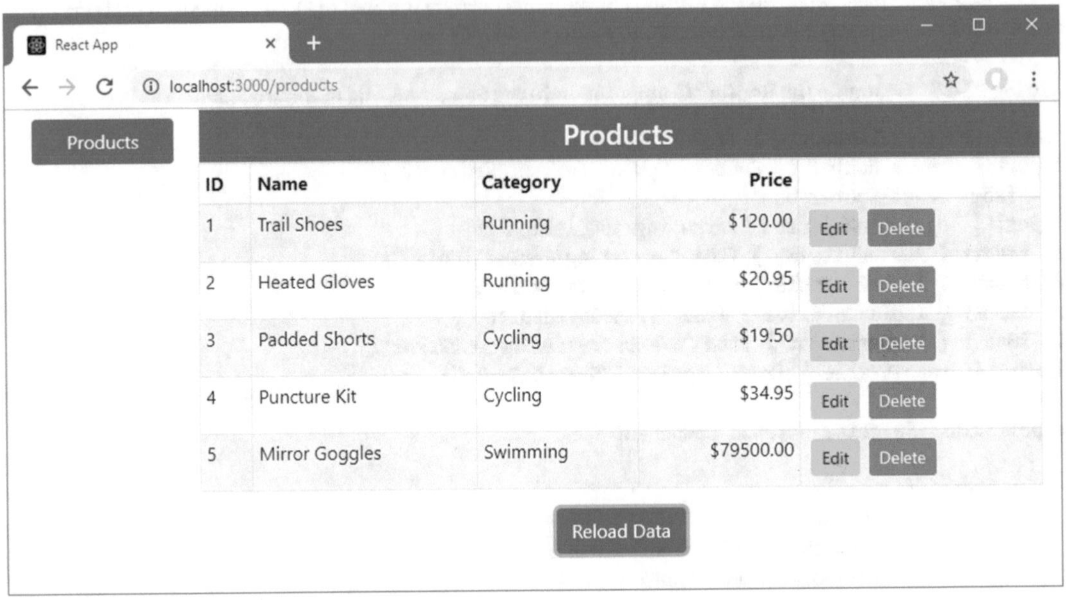

Figure 25-4. *Using a GraphQL client package*

■ **Tip** If you encounter errors, stop the development tools and start them again using npm start. This will reset the data used by the GraphQL server and undo the effects of changes made in previous sections.

If you use the F12 Developer Tools to see the network requests that the browser makes, you will see that queries for data are sent the first time that the routing buttons are clicked but not when the same table is selected again. Click the Reload Data button to invoke the query's refresh function and trigger a new query.

Using Mutations

The Mutation component is used to provide access to GraphQL mutations. In Listing 25-24, I have used Mutation to provide access to the mutations that will delete product or supplier objects.

Listing 25-24. Using a Mutation in the GraphQLTable.js File in the src/graphql Folder

```
import React, { Component } from "react";
import { Query, Mutation } from "react-apollo";
import gql from "graphql-tag";
import * as queries from "./queries";
import { ProductTable } from "../ProductTable";
import * as mutations from "./mutations";
```

```
export const GraphQLTable = () => {

    const getAll = gql(queries.products.getAll.graphql);
    const deleteItem = gql(mutations.products.delete.graphql);

    return class extends Component {

        constructor(props) {
            super(props);
            this.editCallback = (item) => this.props.history
                .push(`/products/edit/${item.id}`);
        }

        render() {
            return <Query query={ getAll }>
                {(({loading, data, refetch }) => {
                    if (loading) {
                        return <h5
                            className="bg-info text-white text-center m-2 p-2">
                                Loading...
                        </h5>
                    } else {
                        return <Mutation mutation={ deleteItem }
                                refetchQueries={ () => [{query: getAll}]  }>
                            { doDelete =>
                                <React.Fragment>
                                    <ProductTable products={data.products}
                                        editCallback= { this.editCallback }
                                        deleteCallback={ (p) =>
                                            doDelete({variables: {id: p.id} }) }  />
                                    <div className="text-center">
                                        <button className="btn btn-primary"
                                            onClick={ () => refetch() }>
                                            Reload Data
                                        </button>
                                    </div>
                                </React.Fragment>
                            }
                        </Mutation>
                    }
                }}
            </Query>
        }
    }
}
```

The Mutation component follows a similar pattern to the Query component and relies on a render prop function to provide access to a mutation. The Mutation component is configured using props, the most useful of which are described in Table 25-3.

Table 25-3. *Useful Mutation Props*

Name	Description
mutation	This prop specifies the mutation that will be sent to the server.
variables	This prop specifies the variables for the mutation. Variables can also be provided when the mutation is performed.
refetchQueries	This prop specifies one or more queries to be performed when the mutation has been completed.
update	This prop specifies a function that is used to update the cache when the mutation has been completed.
onCompleted	This prop specifies a callback function that is invoked when the mutation has completed.

I started by passing the mutation to the gql function so that it can be used as the value for the mutation prop on the Mutation component, like this:

```
...
return <Mutation mutation={ deleteMutation }
    refetchQueries={ () => [{ query: getAll}]}>
...
```

The cached data at the client will often become out-of-date once a mutation is performed, and the Mutation component provides two props that can be used to keep the cache in sync. The refetchQueries prop is assigned a function that receives the mutation result and returns an array of objects, each of which has query and, optionally, variables properties. When the mutation has completed, the queries are sent to the server, and the results are used to update the cache. This is the approach I have taken in Listing 25-24, where I have configured the Mutation to update the cache with the results of the getAll query:

```
...
return <Mutation mutation={ deleteMutation }
    refetchQueries={ () => [{ query: getAll}]}>
...
```

The mutation is provided as an argument to the render prop function.

```
...
return <Mutation mutation={ deleteItem }
    refetchQueries={ () => [{query: getAll}]  }>
        { doDelete => {
...
```

Variables for the mutation can be supplied as a prop on the Mutation component or as an argument to the function. I used a function in Listing 25-24 because I receive the object that is to be deleted through a callback.

```
...
deleteCallback={ (p) => doDelete({variables: {id: p.id} }) }
...
```

The effect is that clicking a Delete button invokes the mutation and then sends queries the server for the updated data, which is displayed to the user, as shown in Figure 25-5.

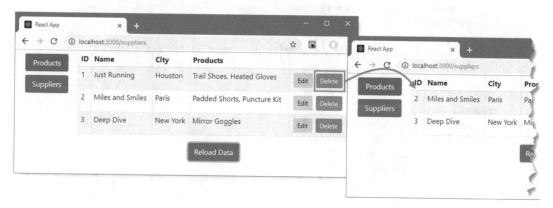

Figure 25-5. *Using a mutation*

Updating Cached Data Without a Query

Re-querying the server after a mutation is useful when the application doesn't know what the impact of the changes will be. For simpler operations, querying for new data is excessive because the application knows exactly what the effect of the mutation will be and can apply this change directly to the cached data. In Listing 25-25, I have changed the configuration of the Mutation so that it no longer performs a query once an item has been deleted and uses a function to update the data cache instead.

Listing 25-25. Updating Cached Data in the GraphQLTable.js File in the src/graphql Folder

```
import React, { Component } from "react";
import { Query, Mutation } from "react-apollo";
import gql from "graphql-tag";
import * as queries from "./queries";
import { ProductTable } from "../ProductTable";
import * as mutations from "./mutations";

export const GraphQLTable = () => {

    const getAll = gql(queries.products.getAll.graphql);
    const deleteItem = gql(mutations.products.delete.graphql);

    return class extends Component {

        constructor(props) {
            super(props);
            this.editCallback = (item) => this.props.history
                .push(`/products/edit/${item.id}`);
        }
```

```
removeItemFromCache(cache, mutationResult) {
    const deletedId = mutationResult.data[mutations.products.delete.name];
    const data =
        cache.readQuery({ query: getAll })[queries.products.getAll.name];
    cache.writeQuery({
        query: getAll,
        data: { products: data.filter(item => item.id !== deletedId) }
    });
}

render() {
    return <Query query={ getAll }>
        {({loading, data, refetch }) => {
            if (loading) {
                return <h5
                    className="bg-info text-white text-center m-2 p-2">
                        Loading...
                </h5>
            } else {
                return <Mutation mutation={ deleteItem }
                        update={ this.removeItemFromCache }>
                    { doDelete =>
                        <React.Fragment>
                            <ProductTable products={data.products}
                                editCallback= { this.editCallback }
                                deleteCallback={ (p) =>
                                    doDelete({variables: {id: p.id} }) } />
                            <div className="text-center">
                                <button className="btn btn-primary"
                                        onClick={ () => refetch() }>
                                    Reload Data
                                </button>
                            </div>
                        </React.Fragment>
                    }
                </Mutation>
            }
        }}
    </Query>
}
}
```

The update prop on a Mutation is used to specify a method that will be invoked when a mutation has completed. The method receives the Apollo Client cache and the results from the mutation and is responsible for updating the cached data using the methods described in Table 25-4.

Table 25-4. *The Apollo Client Cache Methods*

Name	Description
readQuery	This method is used to read data from the cache associated with a specific query. An error will be thrown if you try to read data that is not in the cache, which typically occurs if a query has not yet been executed.
writeQuery	This method is used to update the data in the cache associated with a specific query.

The removeItemFromCache method in Listing 25-25 uses the readQuery method to retrieve the cached data associated with the products query, filters out the deleted item, and writes the remaining items back to the cache using the writeQuery method. The readQuery method accepts an object with query and an optional variables property, and the write query method accepts an object with query, data, and an optional variables property. The result is that when you click the Delete button for a product, the object is deleted from the local cache after the mutation has been completed without the need for an additional query.

Adding Support for Supplier Data and Editing

Now that the basic GraphQL client features are in place, I am going to adapt the GraphQLTable so that it supports product and supplier data and introduce support for editing data. In Listing 25-26, I have changed GrpahQLTable so that it receives the type of data it is working with as a parameter and selects the queries, mutations, and component to display to the user dynamically.

Listing 25-26. Supporting Multiple Data Types in the GraphQLTable.js File in the src/graphql Folder

```
import React, { Component } from "react";
import { Query, Mutation } from "react-apollo";
import gql from "graphql-tag";
import * as queries from "./queries";
import { ProductTable } from "../ProductTable";
import * as mutations from "./mutations";
import { PRODUCTS, SUPPLIERS } from "../store/dataTypes";
import { SupplierTable } from "../SupplierTable";

export const GraphQLTable = (dataType) => {

    const getAll = gql(queries[dataType].getAll.graphql);
    const deleteItem = gql(mutations[dataType].delete.graphql);

    return class extends Component {

        constructor(props) {
            super(props);
            this.editCallback = (item) => this.props.history
                .push(`/${dataType}/edit/${item.id}`);
        }
```

```
removeItemFromCache = (cache, mutationResult) => {

    const deletedId = mutationResult.data[mutations[dataType].delete.name];
    const data =
        cache.readQuery({ query: getAll })[queries[dataType].getAll.name];
    cache.writeQuery({
        query: getAll,
        data: { [dataType]: data.filter(item => item.id !== deletedId) }
    });
}

getRefetchQueries() {
    return dataType === PRODUCTS
        ? [{query: gql(queries[SUPPLIERS].getAll.graphql)}] : []
}

render() {
    return <Query query={ getAll }>
        {(({loading, data, refetch }) => {
            if (loading) {
                return <h5
                    className="bg-info text-white text-center m-2 p-2">
                        Loading...
                </h5>
            } else {
                return <Mutation mutation={ deleteItem }
                        update={ this.removeItemFromCache }
                        refetchQueries={ this.getRefetchQueries }>
                    { doDelete =>
                        <React.Fragment>
                            { dataType === PRODUCTS &&
                                <ProductTable products={data.products}
                                    editCallback= { this.editCallback }
                                    deleteCallback={ (p) =>
                                        doDelete({variables: {id: p.id} }) }
                                />
                            }
                            { dataType === SUPPLIERS &&
                                <SupplierTable suppliers={data.suppliers}
                                    editCallback= { this.editCallback }
                                    deleteCallback={ (p) =>
                                        doDelete({variables: {id: p.id} }) }
                                />
                            }
                            <div className="text-center">
                                <button className="btn btn-primary"
                                        onClick={ () => refetch() }>
                                    Reload Data
                                </button>
                            </div>
                        </React.Fragment>
                }
```

```
                    </Mutation>
                }
            }}
        </Query>
    }
  }
}
```

Notice that this example combines the update and refetchQueries props on the Mutation. I need to keep the supplier data consistent when a product is deleted, but using the readQuery method for data not in the cache produces an error. To keep the example simple—and not to duplicate too much logic from the GraphQL server's resolvers—I use the update prop to perform a simple excision from the cache and the refetchQueries prop to get fresh suppliers data.

Creating the Editor Component

To allow the user to edit objects, I added a file called GraphQLEditor.js in the src/graphql folder and used it to define the component shown in Listing 25-27.

Listing 25-27. The Contents of the GraphQLEditor.js File in the src/graphql Folder

```
import React, { Component } from "react";
import gql from "graphql-tag";
import * as queries from "./queries";
import * as mutations from "./mutations";
import { Query, Mutation } from "react-apollo";
import { PRODUCTS } from "../store/dataTypes";
import { ProductEditor } from "../ProductEditor";
import { SupplierEditor } from "../SupplierEditor";

export const GraphQLEditor = () => {

    return class extends Component {

        constructor(props) {
            super(props);
            this.dataType = this.props.match.params.dataType;
            this.id = this.props.match.params.id;
            this.query = gql(queries[this.dataType].getOne.graphql);
            this.variables = { id: this.id };
            this.mutation = gql(mutations[this.dataType].store.graphql);
            this.navigation = () => props.history.push(`/${this.dataType}`);
        }

        render() {
            return <Query query={ this.query} variables={ this.variables }>
                {
                    ({loading, data}) => {
                        if (!loading) {
                            return <Mutation mutation={ this.mutation }
                                onCompleted={ this.navigation }>
```

```
                            { (store) => {
                                if (this.dataType === PRODUCTS) {
                                    return <ProductEditor key={ this.id }
                                        product={ data.product }
                                        saveCallback={ (formData) =>
                                            store({variables: formData})}
                                        cancelCallback={ this.navigation } />
                                } else {
                                    return <SupplierEditor key={ this.id }
                                        supplier={ data.supplier }
                                        saveCallback={ (formData =>
                                            store({ variables: formData }))}
                                        cancelCallback={ this.navigation } />
                                }
                            }
                        }
                    </Mutation>
                } else {
                    return null;
                }
            }
        }
        </Query>
    }
  }
}
```

This component builds on the same features used for the table. A Query is used to request the data from the GraphQL server, with the variables prop being used to provide the variables required by the query. A Mutation is used to store the data, with the onCompleted prop used to navigate away from the editor once the mutation has completed.

Notice that I have not updated the cached data. Apollo Client has a clever feature where mutations that alter a single object and have responses with an id property and properties that have been changed are automatically pushed into the cache and used by other Query objects. In the case of the editor component, this means that changes to a product or supplier are automatically shown in the data table, without the need to update the cache or re-query for the data.

Updating the Routing Configuration

To complete the example, Listing 25-28 updates the routing configuration for the example application to add support for supplier data and for the new editor components.

Listing 25-28. Updating the Routing Configuration in the Selector.js File in the src Folder

```
import React, { Component } from "react";
import { BrowserRouter as Router, Route, Switch, Redirect }
    from "react-router-dom";
import { ToggleLink } from "./routing/ToggleLink";
import { GraphQLTable } from "./graphql/GraphQLTable";
import { PRODUCTS, SUPPLIERS } from "./store/dataTypes";
import { GraphQLEditor } from "./graphql/GraphQLEditor";
```

```
export class Selector extends Component {

    render() {
        return <Router>
            <div className="container-fluid">
                <div className="row">
                    <div className="col-2">
                        <ToggleLink to="/products">Products</ToggleLink>
                        <ToggleLink to="/suppliers">Suppliers</ToggleLink>
                    </div>
                    <div className="col">
                        <Switch>
                            <Route path="/products" exact={true}
                                component={ GraphQLTable(PRODUCTS) }  />
                            <Route path="/suppliers" exact={true}
                                component={ GraphQLTable(SUPPLIERS) }  />
                            <Route path="/:dataType/edit/:id"
                                component= { GraphQLEditor() } />
                            <Redirect to="/products" />
                        </Switch>
                    </div>
                </div>
            </div>
        </Router>
    }
}
```

When you save the changes, the application will be updated to support supplier data and editing, as shown in Figure 25-6.

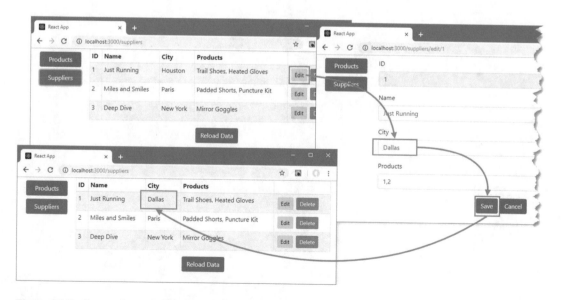

Figure 25-6. *Supporting supplier data and editing*

■ **Tip** If you encounter errors, stop the development tools and start them again using `npm start`. This will reset the data used by the GraphQL server and undo the effects of changes made in previous sections.

Summary

In this chapter, I showed you the different ways that a React application can consume a GraphQL service. I showed you how to use GraphQL in isolated components, how to intercept data store actions and service them using GraphQL, and how to adopt a GraphQL client that manages the data on behalf of the application.

And that is all I have to teach you about React. I started by creating a simple application and then took you on a comprehensive tour of the different building blocks in the framework, showing you how they can be created, configured, and applied to create web applications.

I wish you every success in your React projects, and I can only hope that you have enjoyed reading this book as much as I enjoyed writing it.

Index

© Adam Freeman 2019
A. Freeman, *Pro React 16*, https://doi.org/10.1007/978-1-4842-4451-7

■ L, M

■ N, O

■ P, Q

■ R